Frommer's®

CHINA

THE 50 MOST MEMORABLE TRIPS

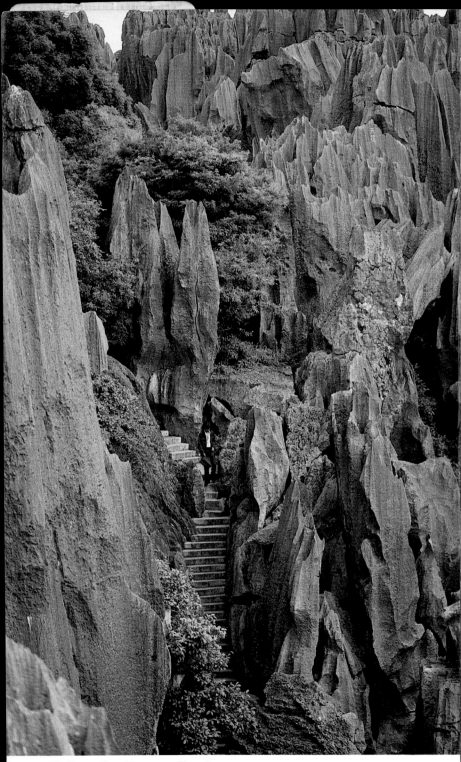

The Lunan Stone Forest near Kunming

The First Emperor's terra-cotta warriors in Xi'an

Aerial view of Hong Kong

Kowloon night market

View of the Great Wall

Palace and moat in Beijing's Forbidden City

The Li River at Guilin

Sunset in the Li River Valley at Yangshuo

Statues in the Longmen Buddhist Caves in Luoyang

Workers leaving the rice paddy fields in the evening in Guizhou

Winter palace in Xi'an

The Pamir Mountains on the Silk Road

CHINA

THE 50 MOST MEMORABLE TRIPS

by J. D. Brown

中国

Macmillan • USA

About the Author

J.D. Brown has lived and worked in China and has written about China as a literary traveler, a travel writer, and a guidebook author. His work has appeared in such diverse publications as the *New York Times*, the *Washington Post*, the *Michigan Quarterly Review, Islands*, and *Newsday*. When he is not traveling in the Far East, he lives in Eugene, Oregon.

MACMILLAN TRAVEL
A Simon & Schuster Macmillan Company
1633 Broadway
New York, NY 10019

Find us online at **www.frommers.com**

ISBN 0-02861636-7

Editor: Alice Fellows
Production Editor: Michael Thomas
Production Team: Eric Brinkman, David Faust, Heather Pope, and Karen Teo
Photo Editor: Richard Fox
Design by designLab, Seattle
Digital Cartography by XNR Productions, Inc. and John Decamillis

Front cover photo: Terraced rice fields in Longsheng
Back cover photo: The Li River near Yangshuo

SPECIAL SALES

Bulk purchases (10+ copies) of Frommer's and selected Macmillan travel guides are available to corporations, organizations, mail-order catalogs, institutions, and charities at special discounts, and can be customized to suit individual needs. For more information write to Special Sales, Macmillan General Reference, 1633 Broadway, New York, NY 10019.

CONTENTS

Monuments of the Middle Kingdom

Journeys by Rivers and Seas

Silk Road Caravan

Sacred Mountains: Pinnacles and Peaks

LIST OF MAPS

Historic China

An Invitation to the Reader

In researching this book, we discovered many wonderful places—hotels, restaurants, shops, and more. We're sure you'll find others. Please tell us about them, so we can share the information with your fellow travelers in upcoming editions. If you were disappointed with a recommendation, we'd love to know that, too. Please write to:

Frommer's China: The 50 Most Memorable Trips
Macmillan Travel
1633 Broadway
New York, NY 10019

An Additional Note

Please be advised that travel information is subject to change at any time—and this is especially true of prices. We therefore suggest that you write or call ahead for confirmation when making your travel plans. The author, editors, and publisher cannot be held responsible for the experiences of readers while traveling. Your safety is important to us, however, so we encourage you to stay alert and be aware of your surroundings. Keep a close eye on cameras, purses, and wallets, all favorite targets of thieves and pickpockets.

What the Symbols Mean

The following abbreviations are used for credit cards:

AE	American Express
DC	Diners Club
EC	EuroCard
JCB	Japan Credit Bank
MC	MasterCard
V	Visa

WHY GO TO CHINA?

C HINA HAS BEEN MY DESTINATION OF choice for two decades. The reasons are various. No other place on Earth quite possesses such an intensity of beauty and strangeness, no other nation has a longer or richer historical legacy, and no other nation is likely to be as important in the 21st century. When I try to explain my own continuing fascination with the China of the past, present, and future, I remember what one scholar, Marcel Granet, wrote more than 60 years ago: "By its extent, its duration, its mass, Chinese civilization is one of the most powerful creations of mankind; none other is richer in human experience." Yet we know little of it. "Why should China remain alien to us if nothing human should remain alien?" Granet asked. "Man will know himself only if he knows all the ways of being human. To achieve that, he must leave home in order to find himself."

Over the last two decades I have left home often and traveled through China's ancient capitals, fabled cities, and countryside villages and towns; crossed its rivers, lakes, and seas; admired its ancient stone monuments, from the Great Wall to the Great Buddha; followed the Silk Road across the deserts to the West; and stood on the summits of its nine sacred mountains. Along the way I have traveled by every available conveyance, from jet to train, from bicycle to camel; stayed in 5-star international hotels and no-star mountain inns; eaten the most delightful creations of one of the world's great cuisines and gulped downed some of the most dismal, too. Travel has been hard at times, but it is growing increasingly easy. Each time I return to the Middle Kingdom, I find large-scale changes and I discover more about China's culture, which remains exotic despite rapid modernization and growing Western influences. At some rare junctures, I even discover something about myself.

What first fascinates me about China is its past, so unlike and so often at odds with the heritage of the West. These contrasts, visible in temples and museums, city walls and pagodas, and in enduring social customs, provide a means to see my own culture from a larger perspective. Chinese art and history are a continual delight, and to see China's past made visible, whether in the vaults where the First Emperor died among his terra-cotta armies or in the Forbidden City where the last emperor was born, brings the dreamy Middle Kingdom to life.

Present-day China also has enormous appeal, although the sheer beauty of the past seldom shines through. Modern China, particularly its urban centers, is shockingly gray and dismal, unexpectedly so for most first-time visitors who arrive with a vision of old China. But the cities of China, as ugly and monotonous as they often are, are undergoing their own metamorphoses, and this has its own fascination. No large country has ever boomed so rapidly and decisively since the Industrial Revolution began in the West two centuries ago. Much of China looks like a construction zone today, but this raw reconstruction lends a vibrancy to cityscapes. China has its sights locked on the coming century. If you want to visit the next superpower as a work in progress, China is your ticket—the new Pacific Century begins in Shanghai, Beijing, Chongqing, and a dozen other boomtowns of the new China.

Nor is this new China simply an overpopulated carbon copy of the Western world. China is charting its own course, holding tenaciously to the tattered strands of its own cultural identity. The new and old China are in collision, and the fireworks illuminate a vast and various stage. Present changes as well as the ancient monuments make China one of the most dynamic destinations on any traveler's map—an open gallery of treasures and traditions in vivid transition, beautiful but ugly, new but old, an imperial dragon but a modern phoenix.

It is now possible to travel to most of the interesting places in China in a style not dreamed of ten years ago, barely possible even five years ago. Major cities have enough Western amenities and foreign tourism facilities in place to make travel on one's own a viable option even for the less adventurous traveler. It's no longer necessarily a choice between hitting the road via ramshackle local buses with backpack and water purification system firmly in hand or spending a small fortune for a grueling 7-day, eight-city, nine-banquet luxury tour. These options still exist—they are still sometimes the best means to see a place—but China has finally begun to make touring on one's own a more amenable and comprehensible process, even if one doesn't speak the language.

In this guide I've recorded in as frank detail as possible 50 of my most memorable travels in China. You should be able to follow in my footsteps if you choose to do so, or make your own detours. I try to point out your options at each destination, listing the best hotels as well as more economical choices when possible; explaining how and where to hire local tour guides, if needed; and pointing out the most interesting sights and how to reach them. In all cases, I've sampled what I list myself, although I can't guarantee they'll all be there in the same condition they were for me. China is changing so rapidly. Not only are prices rising but hotels and cafes are constantly opening, closing, and reinventing themselves,

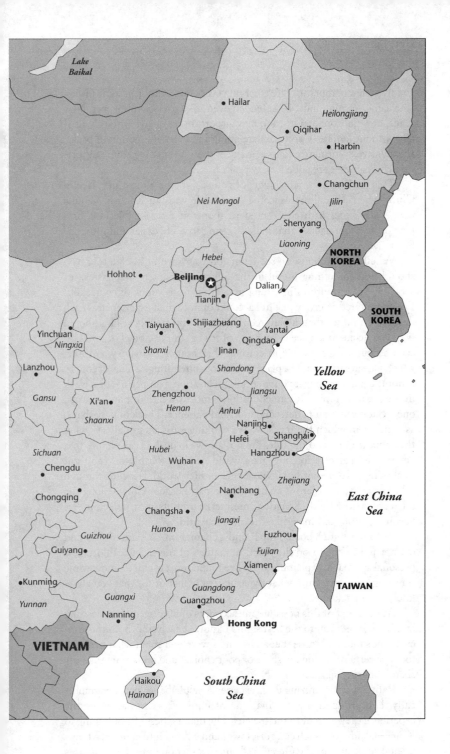

and fresh new competitors are emerging every few months in some places. The same warning must be extended even to matters of transport. New roads, new rail connections, and new airport routes open constantly, usually without fanfare. Cable cars are going in at remote mountain peaks. Inexpensive, informative tours—many of them emanating from new private companies—are added every year.

This is all to your advantage, of course. There's almost no place in China where I wouldn't welcome a new cafe with an English menu, a new 3-star hotel with clean, modern rooms at a reasonable rate, or a new private tour agency that makes getting to a site easier and more informative.

Whether you choose to see China on your own or book a tour, you should find something useful in the following chapters. My tastes, responses, and adventures in China may differ from yours, of course, but I've endeavored to give you a full account of my actual experience at each destination rather than a bare recital of facts and statistics. This should help you decide if a place is your cup of tea or simply a bowl of gruel. In each account, I also weave in considerable strands of history and lore, which I always find makes a place much more interesting. China, of course, is not the place to tour if you're seeking relaxation, pampering, or a week in the mellow tropics. It's an education—mostly a pleasant and unusual one—but it can require determination and patience. Think of it, perhaps, as a puzzle in which the pieces you're working with are not always what they appear to be and the rules are not always logical. If the picture that emerges is that of a looking-glass world, you're probably on the right track. China is different, but it's no longer an alien world. Traveling through it has never been easier for an outsider, in part because China—long the self-contained Middle Kingdom mesmerized by its own reflection—is becoming more and more like the outside world.

As in most guidebooks, you'll find a chapter on Chinese history and culture and a chapter on the practical matters of travel. In both, I take a personal approach, explaining what I've found most useful to know while traveling in China, from what dynasties really matter to what you absolutely must pack.

At the heart of this book are my accounts of 50 places worth visiting in China. I steer you to the best sights I know at each stop, both those on everyone's tour and those that aren't, and I warn you about what to avoid, too. I've certainly made my share of poor choices and seen more than my share of boring sights.

Rather than organizing these experiences alphabetically or geographically, I've grouped my destinations of choice by the nature of the experience they present to the traveler. The major cities—from Beijing to Xi'an—fall into one such category, towns and villages into another. Monumental sites, such as the Great Wall, are in a section unto themselves, as are the oases and great ruins along the Silk Road. Cruises on China's rivers, lakes, and seas are placed together, as are hikes to the tops of China's most beautiful and sacred mountains. Sites that are nearby or in the same region, regardless of what section they appear in, are cross-referenced. When you read the chapter on Xi'an, for example, I alert you to chapters on the holy mountain of Hua Shan and the terra-cotta warriors of Emperor Qin, superb sites located an hour or two away.

China is one of the world's largest countries, as well as the most populous. Ethnically and culturally, it is not as diverse as North America or Europe, but its sights, its landscapes, and its history are quite various. Beijing is a city quite unlike Kunming. The Great Wall bears little resemblance to the Grand Canal. The southern Chinese act and speak differently than the northern Chinese and eat some foods no one else in the world would touch. In fact, each region of China has its own identity, so experiencing Chinese culture, seeing its treasures, and viewing its natural wonders require considerable travel.

China travel is a movable feast of sights and sensations, new and old. The following pages are a taste of what to expect, culled from one traveler's long, memorable banquet in the Middle Kingdom.

FABLED CITIES OF THE NORTH

都市

The most populous nation on earth, China has many of the most populated cities as well. Although barely a third of the Chinese live in its 640 cities, its urban population already numbers 350 million, and by the year 2000 another 100 million city dwellers will be added. Why visit such enormous, noisy, often ugly and polluted centers, crammed with sheer humanity? In part, because the cities are the most vital places to see, in part because they contain China's most celebrated treasures. To experience the Middle Kingdom past and present, one must start in the cities, particularly those with rich and fabled legacies.

For history, the two most important cities to visit are the modern capital of **Beijing** and the ancient capital of **Xi'an.** Xi'an is home to the terra-cotta armies of the first emperor, the royal tombs of 10 successive dynasties, and two pagodas from the golden age of the Tang. Beijing houses the Forbidden City, the Temple of Heaven, and the Great Wall. Xi'an spans the first 17 centuries of China's dynastic history; Beijing, the last 6.

Other cities of considerable historic interest are **Chengde,** located near Beijing, where the Manchu emperors established a countryside Summer Palace that is still surrounded by eight splendid Buddhist temples, and **Kaifeng,** the forgotten capital of the Song Dynasty, located near Xi'an, where (strangely enough) ancient Jewish traditions persist.

Four of China's cities are celebrated primarily for their beauty, and they cannot be passed up easily. **Hangzhou,** on the shores of exquisite West Lake, is justly hailed as the "number one city under heaven," and it is a delightful place to stroll or bike. **Suzhou,** the "Venice of China," still crisscrossed by old canals, possesses the finest array of private classical gardens in China, as worthy of savoring as finely brewed tea. **Xiamen,** a treaty port once known as Amoy on the South China Sea, has a green island in its harbor where cars are banned, warm beaches, and winding lanes lined with European mansions. **Guilin**—the place that launched a million travel posters—is in the heart of China's most haunting landscape. Its limestone pinnacles and pillars inspired centuries of scroll painters. Guilin possesses the most beautiful landscape of any city in China.

Three cities display the raw power of China's economic revolution. **Shanghai** is perhaps the most vital city on the planet, if vitality can be measured by new construction sites, high-lift cranes, and rapid modernization. Shanghai also has plenty of history and mystique. Not lagging far behind Shanghai in the current economic revolution is China's largest municipality, **Chongqing,** with a regional population of over 30 million. This powerhouse on the western Yangzi River, formerly known as Chungking, is also the gateway to the Yangzi River and the Song Dynasty sculptures at Dazu. In the south of China, **Canton (Guangzhou)** took an early lead in modernization and remains one of China's wealthiest, most progressive cities, as well as the historic capital of Cantonese cuisine. In the north, there's **Datong,** capital of coal and steam locomotives. Datong has several superb temples, including the unique Temple Suspended over the Void, as well as magnificent Buddhist cave sculptures dating from its days as the capital of the Northern Wei 15 centuries ago.

Other cities also leave a distinctive imprint on the traveler. **Chengdu,** capital of the western province of Sichuan, known for its teahouses, hot foods, and panda preserve, is one of China's most colorful cities—an interesting contrast to Beijing or Shanghai. **Kunming,** the delightful "city of eternal spring" in exotic Yunnan, is home to more of China's minorities than any other city. **Qingdao,** producer of China's best beer and mineral water, has not only fine sandy beaches but a legacy of German architecture unrivaled in China. **Harbin,** in the far northeastern reaches, renowned for its winter ice sculptures, has its own intriguing old town of Russian architecture, as well as a new tiger-breeding preserve.

Lastly, there's **Hong Kong,** China's most modern, elegant, and wealthy city—the only truly cosmopolitan city in the Middle Kingdom. Long schooled in the ways of the West, Hong Kong's destiny now lies in the East. This is the ideal place to begin and end one's travels in China. Its hotels and restaurants are the best in the Chinese world and its harbor has no equal for spectacle.

Although Beijing, Shanghai, Xi'an, Guilin, and Hong Kong constitute a modern Grand Tour of China—by all means, don't miss them—exploring other cities along the way will broaden the China experience and whet one's appetite for more far-flung adventures.

BEIJING: CHINA'S TREASURE HOUSE

北京

BEIJING HAS MORE ATTRACTIONS THAN any other city in China. At one time, these cultural highlights were the only thing that might have lured a traveler here. Otherwise, China's capital was a sprawling metropolis of long, flat, monotonous avenues inhabited by uninspired socialist architecture, snarled traffic, and frightful levels of pollution. Beijing was also subject to shattering dust storms from the Gobi Desert. It was devoid of nightlife and lacking in pleasant neighborhoods for strolling. This inimical atmosphere has begun to change in the last few years. Beijing has blossomed into a city that an international traveler can enjoy. New shopping and eating venues have spread across the city. The 13,661 restaurants counted in 1990 had nearly tripled to 39,196 by 1995 and may now have tripled once again. Beijing has become China's trendiest city. Pubs and coffeehouses are displacing discos. Teahouses are opening by the score. Bowling, billiards, and swimming are increasingly popular. All-girl rock bands have appeared. Since July 1, 1997, only unleaded fuel has been sold in Beijing, the first Chinese city to mandate such a cleanup. And on a recent annual Tree-Planting Day, over 2 million Beijingers pitched in to help the capital build its much-needed greenway.

Beijing is by no means a paradise, but it is becoming a more vibrant and interesting international city. Social realism and dreariness no longer control the cityscape. The first task of visitors, however, is unchanged: to partake of those places for which the Middle Kingdom, and Beijing, are celebrated. The Forbidden City, the Summer Palace, the Temple of Heaven, Tiananmen Square, and the Great Wall should not be missed. Nor should some of the lesser historical and cultural draws, of which there are dozens. At the same time, exploring Beijing's modern delights and side streets is now also a pleasure.

I have been to Beijing many times under many circumstances, as teacher, tourist, vagabond, and business writer. Rather than cover all the attractions like a scanner, turning out a list of must-sees and must-dos

Beijing

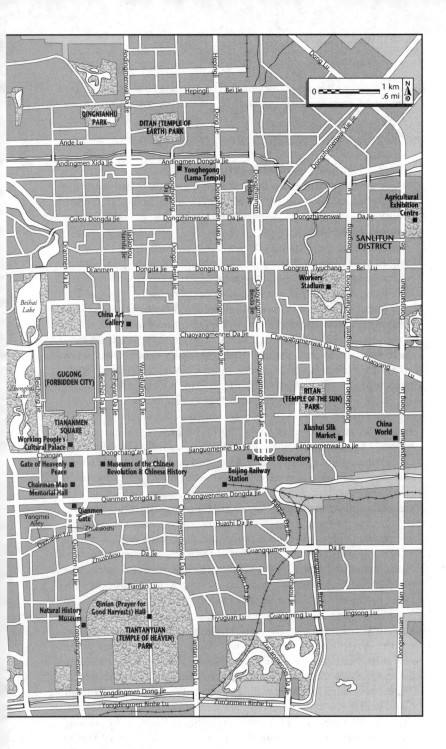

QINGNIANHU PARK

DITAN (TEMPLE OF EARTH) PARK

Hepingli Bei Jie

Hepingli

Dong Lu

1 km
0 .6 mi
N

Ande Lu

Andingmen Xida Jie   Andingmen Dongda Jie

Yonghegong (Lama Temple)

Dongzhimenwai Xue Jie

Agricultural Exhibition Centre

Gulou Dongda Jie   Dongzhimennei   Da Jie   Dongzhimenwai   Da Jie

Jiadaokou Nanda Jie

SANLITUN DISTRICT

Dongzhimen Xiao Jie

Dongzhimen Beida Jie

Dongxing Lu

Di'anmen   Dongda Jie   Dongsi 10-Tiao   Gongren Tiyuchang   Bei Lu

Beihai Lake

China Art Gallery

Chaoyangmen Beida Jie

Workers' Stadium

Gongren Tiyuchang Dong Lu

Dongsanhuan Lu

Chaoyangmennei Da Jie   Chaoyahgmenwai Da Jie

Zhonghai Lake

GUGONG (FORBIDDEN CITY)

Beichang Jie   Beiheyan Da Jie   Beichizi Da Jie   Wangfujing Da Jie

Chaoyangmen Xiao Jie

Chaoyangmen Nanda Jie

Chaoyang   Lu

Zhongnanhai Lu

RITAN (TEMPLE OF THE SUN) PARK

TIANANMEN SQUARE

Working People's Cultural Palace

Gate of Heavenly Peace

Chairman Mao Memorial Hall

Changan

Dongchang'an Jie   Jianguomennei Da Jie   Jianguomenwai Da Jie

Guanghua Lu

Xiushui Silk Market

China World

Ancient Observatory

Museums of the Chinese Revolution & Chinese History

Beijing Railway Station

Jianguomen Binhe Lu

Qianmen Dongda Jie   Chongwenmen Dongda Jie

Yangmei Alley

Qianmen Gate

Zhubaoshi Jie

Huashi Da Jie

Beijing Da Jie

Dazhalan Lu

Zhushikou   Da Jie   Guangqumen   Da Jie

Qianmen Da Jie

Chongwenmenwai Da Jie

Xingfu Da Jie

Xizhaosi Jie

Guangqumen Binhe Lu

Tiantan Lu

Natural History Museum

Qinian (Prayer for Good Harvests) Hall

Tiyuguan Lu

Guangming Lu

Jingsong Lu

Dongsanhuan Nan Lu

TIANTANYUAN (TEMPLE OF HEAVEN) PARK

Yongdingmennei Da Jie

Tiantan Dong Lu

Zuo'anmen Da Jie

Yongdingmen Dong Jie

Yongdingmen Binhe Lu   Zuo'anmen Binhe Lu

7

that reads like a telephone directory, I'll concentrate on those places I've found most worth experiencing, and I'll try to tell you not just what to see but how to see it as deeply as possible. I won't skip the highlights of Beijing, but I do want to take you on some unexpected detours.

Tiananmen Square

This is the Eye of China, the focus of the nation. In the 20th century, it has truly become the middle of the Middle Kingdom. In the 21st century many believe it will become the symbolic center of the Asia Pacific, perhaps even of the world.

Most foreigners recognize it instantly as the setting for the democratic movement that culminated in the events of June 4, 1989. Tiananmen Square had been the focal point of earlier movements as well, and officials are no doubt hopeful that its image worldwide has been softened by such recent events as the national celebration for the return of Hong Kong to Chinese sovereignty on July 1, 1997. It is the largest public square in the world, as befits the most populous nation in the world. Every paving block of the square is numbered, partly so that a standing spot can be assigned to each person who attends one of China's great public forums, such as the annual celebration of National Day on October 10.

Striking out across this wide expanse gives visitors the chance to orient themselves to monuments on every horizon, allowing the immensity of the place to become a microcosm for the immensity of China and its historical and cultural compass. On the north side is the **Gate of Heavenly Peace,** a viewing stand where Mao proclaimed in 1949 that China had stood up on the world stage. His portrait is on the gate, easily visible from the square. Under it is the entrance to the Forbidden City, the palaces of the former emperors. A member of the diplomatic corps in Beijing recounted to me a joke going around among veteran expatriates concerning the Gate of Heavenly Peace. In the past, the famous portrait of Mao on the gate was accompanied by that of three other Communist icons: Marx, Lenin, and Stalin. Marx was pictured in a full beard, Lenin in a goatee, Stalin in a mustache, and Mao clean-shaven. Devilish wags referred to this solemn display as "The History of Shaving."

The avenue between Tiananmen Square and the Gate of Heavenly Peace is Changan, the capital's main thoroughfare. It was widened, as was the square itself, in a massive public works program initiated by the new ruler, Mao Zedong, beginning in 1950. The city walls also came down. Opposite Changan Avenue and the Gate, on the south side of Tiananmen Square, is a monumental remnant of the city walls, **Qianmen Gate,** built in the 15th century as the southern entrance to the imperial city within Beijing, its two massive stone arches easily visible from inside the square. Straight south from the gate along the old Imperial Way is the **Temple of Heaven,** where the Ming and Qing emperors made annual sacrifices to Heaven.

On the east side, Tiananmen Square is bordered by the **Museum of Chinese History** and the **Museum of the Revolution.** On the west side is the **Great Hall of the People,** China's national hall of Congress, where the world's envoys meet China's leaders. Both these architectural giants are open to visitors, and both are a bit dull, particularly if you have little interest in modern Chinese politics.

The **Monument to the People's Heroes** is in the center of the square, a granite obelisk erected in 1958 to commemorate soldiers, farmers, and other patriots who became martyrs to the Communist Revolution. Ironically, it became the focal point of the martyrs to the democratic student movement in 1989. Bullet holes and other blemishes from that night have been removed, surveillance cameras remain on surrounding poles, and the marble platform can seem a haunted place even now.

From Tiananmen Square all roads radiate out, north to the Forbidden City, south to the Temple of Heaven, northeast to downtown shopping and the diplomatic missions, and northwest to the summer palaces. Tiananmen Square is open dawn to dusk daily and admission is free.

Chairman Mao's Mausoleum

In the center of Tiananmen Square, aligned with the north–south axis that runs through Tiananmen Square and links the Forbidden City to the Temple of Heaven, is the Chairman Mao Memorial Hall. It was completed in 1977, the year after Mao's death. You can join the long line outside, facing south, for a 60-second look at Mao lying in state in a crystal sarcophagus. He rests on a black granite slab from Mount Tai, recalling one of Mao's favorite quotations from China's Grand Historian: "Although death befalls all men alike, in significance it may be weightier than Mount Tai or lighter than a swan's down." Every evening Mao is lowered into the floor, to be refrigerated underground. At dawn, he rises with the sun in the east.

This is the quietest, cleanest, and most revered room in China. Cameras and handbags must be checked in booths outside. The mausoleum, situated at the center of Tiananmen Square, reopened in 1998 after a six-month cleanup. In its first 20 years, it chocked up 110 million visitors. The Chairman Mao Mausoleum is open 8:30 to 11:30am daily and admission is free.

The Forbidden City

Site of the palaces of the Ming and Qing dynasties from 1421 to 1924, the Forbidden City (Gugong) is the work of 1 million laborers. The wall that encompasses its 9,000 rooms consists of 12 million bricks. Another

20 million bricks ended up in the walls of pavilions and the surfaces of courtyards. Such is the scale of the Forbidden City with its gorgeous glazed rooftops, red wooden columns, and uplifted eaves. It is a bewildering complex that defines the very word *imperial*. Deep, treeless courtyards are strung between the successive pavilions, with mazes of halls and walls inserted on either side. This is the largest palace enclosure in China, home to 24 emperors, closed off to all but members of the royal court and official delegations for 500 years.

Vastness, beauty, and pleasant confusion are the usual responses once you're inside the compound, and these might be all you take away, too, on the first visit. The best way to navigate and make some sense of this collection is by renting a tape machine as your guide at the entrance. This recorded walk-through hits the high points, identifies the major halls, mentions the important museum pieces on display inside, and helps you bring some sense to the welter of sights within the once-forbidden walls and within the grand pavilions—the thrones, the furniture, the porcelains, the costumes.

It's important to hit the stop button often, however, and explore some of the side streets of the palace city. New exhibits open in different halls year-round, offering a chance to actually go inside one of the original buildings (since entrances to the main interiors are now blocked off). There are exquisite gardens and lovely courtyards all along the main track, and special exhibits culled from the millions of artifacts owned by the Palace Museum are often placed on temporary display. Making your own detours is also a good way to get away from the newest entrepreneurs to be loosed upon the common visitor: the roving bands of vendors interrupting you, even grabbing your arm, in the hopes you'll buy postcards, souvenir albums, and other bounty.

The basic layout unfolds along a north–south axis (conceived of as beginning and ending at the center of the world, here where the second Ming emperor, Yongle, set to work on the Forbidden City in A.D. 1407). Enter under the **Gate of Heavenly Peace** on Changan Avenue, doff your worker's cap to Mao, and proceed straight ahead over the moats to **Meridian Gate (Wumen),** where emperors once reviewed the empire's armies. It now houses the ticket booths for entrance into the Forbidden City. Five marble bridges cross the expanse of the first great courtyard, which leads to the final great entryway, the **Gate of Supreme Harmony,** guarded by stone lions. The immense space beyond is where the entire imperial court, 100,000 strong, was once convened, prostrate before the Son of Heaven who lived within. It's not difficult to imagine a crowd that immense these days, as the Forbidden City is one of the most popular attractions in the world, save early in the morning before the crush begins.

The first ceremonial hall, **Taihedian (Hall of Supreme Harmony),** raised upon a triple-tiered terrace and entered via a marble ramp with

The Forbidden City

Turret

Shenwu Gate

Turret

Hall of Imperial Peace

IMPERIAL GARDEN

Hall of Arts & Crafts (Ming and Qing)

Pleasure and Longevity Hall

Kunning Gate

Palace of Earthly Tranquility

Union Hall

Palace of Heavenly Purity

Hall of Paintings

Qianqing Gate

Clock Museum

Palace Moat

Palace of Earthly Tranquility

Nine-Dragon Screen

Preserving Harmony Hall

Palace Moat

Middle Harmony Hall

Supreme Harmony Hall

Imperial Kitchen

Hongyi Pavilion

Tiren Pavilion

Imperial Library

Zhendu Gate

Zhaode Gate

Xihua Gate

Supreme Harmony Gate

Donghua Gate

Meridian Gate (Wumen)

Turret

Turret

Palace Moat

Palace Moat

carved dragons, was the route followed by the emperor's sedan chair. Inside you can glimpse his golden dragon throne. The massive red columns are covered in a formula of tung oil, clay, hemp, and pig's blood. The **Hall of Middle Harmony (Zhonghedian)** is next in line, a lesser throne room. The third great hall, **Baohedian (Preserving Harmony)** was the venue for the state civil service examinations and royal banquets. Inside is a 250-ton marble block carved with dragons and clouds from the Ming Dynasty.

Beyond these three ceremonial halls are the three main living quarters of the rulers, retainers, and thousands of eunuchs. The first, the **Palace of Heavenly Purity (Qiangingong),** once contained the emperor's bedroom; the second, the **Hall of Union (Jiaotaidian),** the throne of the empress; and the third, the **Palace of Earthly Tranquility**

(Kunningong), the red wedding chamber where the last emperor, Pu Yi, was wedded as child groom in 1922.

The emperors spent most of their time in the palaces along the west side of the Forbidden City. On the east side are palaces now serving as galleries to display the museum treasures of the Ming and Qing dynasties. One (Juxiandong) now houses the **Clock Museum,** probably the most fascinating small gallery in the Forbidden City, filled with old time-pieces from the West collected by a Qing emperor.

Near the rear of the complex, the Kunning Gate opens onto the **Imperial Garden**'s ponds, halls, and rockeries. This is the place to rest, buy a drink or snack, and decide if you want to work your way back south into the heart of the palaces for a second look. You can always tag along with one of the dozens of tour groups that continually throng the courtyards and pavilions, their guides chanting facts and recounting lore in every major language. If you're overwhelmed or exhausted by your initial march, the exit is just north of here, by the **Hall of Imperial Peace (Qinandian),** a shrine to Xuanwu, Daoist god of fire.

The Forbidden City is China's Grand Canyon, the nation's grandest spectacle, but so vast it numbs the mind, often leaving it blank. Of course, this particular spectacle is all the more amazing, being that it is hand-made. The Forbidden City is open 8:30am to 3:30pm daily. Admission is RMB 55 ($6.62); audio rental of "acoustiguide" is RMB 25 ($3).

Summer Palace

In the summer, the emperors pulled up stakes, left the Forbidden City behind, and encamped in the pavilions on the lakeshores of Yiheyuan to the northwest. Summer palaces have existed here for at least eight centuries, but Emperor Qianlong created the present Summer Palace in the 18th century. The Summer Palace is the loveliest imperial park in China, landscaped with gardens and graceful pavilions along the shores of Kunming Lake. It became the pleasure grounds of Empress Dowager Ci Xi (1835–1908), who ruled China during the decline of the Manchus. She rebuilt and restored the Summer Palace at a time when China needed the funds for its own defense, culminating in the construction of the infamous Marble Boat on the northern shore of the Summer Palace grounds. Local guides have dozens of stories blaming Ci Xi for her ruinous extravagances and her Machiavellian political maneuvers, even though it is doubtful that the Empress Dowager was such a witch.

The main entrance is at the East Gate. The important palaces line **Longevity Hill (Wanshou Shan).** The Empress Dowager's throne is in the **Hall of Benevolence and Longevity (Renshoudian),** now something of a 19th-century furniture museum. Nearby is the **Palace of Virtue and Harmony (Deheyuan),** containing a three-level theater where the

Empress Dowager sometimes played the role of Guanyin, Goddess of Mercy. **Jade Waves Palace (Yulantang)** was the residence of young Emperor Guangxu, in whose name Ci Xi was said to rule for 10 years. In the **Cloud-Dispelling Hall (Pianyundian),** Ci Xi received birthday greetings from her advisors, and if you're curious about what she looked like, her famous portrait in oil is here, as rendered by the Dutch painter Hubert Voss in 1903.

The most delightful construction of the Summer Palace, the **Long Corridor (Changlang),** links these palaces to the Marble Boat. Running about a half mile along the lake, this undulating covered walkway is a gallery of scenes that forms an outdoor encyclopedia of Chinese geography, zoology, botany, and myth. Emperor Qianlong saw to its creation in 1750, the British and French burned it down in 1860, and the Empress Dowager resurrected it in 1888. The paintings that decorate the ceiling, beams, columns, and the four intersecting pavilions are crude but bright, like century-old cartoons that map the treasures of the Middle Kingdom. Group tours herd visitors the length of the Long Corridor without a break, but if there is anywhere to pause in Beijing, it is here. The lake scenery is fetching and the painted arcade is a naive and fascinating window on classic Chinese culture. Unfortunately, the crowds usually spill out of the Long Corridor, making peaceful contemplation impossible. Early mornings and evenings bring the only respites. Beijingers say that the Long Corridor is so long that couples who fall in love after they enter set the wedding date by the time they exit.

Beyond the **Marble Boat (Shifang),** looking like a sad cement pavilion in an old amusement park, is a dock where a large ornate ferry takes visitors back to the main gate (RMB 10/$1.20). The view of the hills and pavilions from the lake is almost as magical as the views from West Lake in Hangzhou, after which the Empress Dowager modeled many of the bridges, causeways, and pagodas of the New Summer Palace. The Summer Palace is open 9am to 5pm daily. Admission is RMB 35 ($4.20).

Old Summer Palace

Far less crowded is the Old Summer Palace (Yuanmingyuan), perhaps because it was leveled by British and French troops in 1860 to punish the Chinese during the Opium Wars. The ruins, however, are haunting. Emperor Kangxi built this original summer palace on an even grander scale than his grandson, Emperor Qianlong, did the present Summer Palace. Kangxi's original contained over 200 pavilions, halls, gazebos, miradors, and manmade lakes stocked with goldfish and lotus. Deer and ducks inhabited the ground. Curiously, some of the architecture was not Chinese but European. Jesuit missionaries in the Qing court were pressed into providing blueprints. Foreigners called the Old Summer Palace the

Versailles of China, an apt comparison. In its day, it was the largest imperial garden in the world.

Time is running out on these ruins. Every year there's a new proposal to restore the Old Summer Palace, a tremendous mistake in my opinion, as these bare ruined choirs give voice to the splendors of the past far more eloquently than any modern copy could.

The Old Summer Palace is just over a mile east of the New Summer Palace, but they are worlds apart. The ruins of the European gardens and Grand Fountains are in the easternmost sector, known as the **Garden of Eternal Spring (Changchunyuan).** Built between 1747 and 1759, these European buildings included a concert chamber, an aviary, a maze, and several kiosks, in addition to the fountains from which water spouted from 12 stone animals that once constituted an ingenious water clock. The looting of the Old Summer Palace augmented the collections of the British Museum, as well as the private collections of Queen Victoria and Napoléon. The New Summer Palace was also looted, but the Empress Dowager rehabilitated it in 1888. Yet for all its beauty, it evokes little of the dark romance so palpable in the ruins of the Old Summer Palace.

My own visit there remains vivid, particularly because of one superb ruin, the **Hall of Tranquility**—the most perfect spot in all of Beijing for a picnic. The tumbled-down remains of the stone-and-marble arches and Greek columns that once graced the Grand Fountains, decorated in rococo and Qing patterns, elicit like no other ruins I've seen—even those in Ireland and Greece—the impermanence of man's grandest achievements. The Old Summer Palace is open from 7am to 7pm daily. Admission is RMB 10 ($1.20).

Temple of Heaven

Beijing's grand collection of Ming Dynasty architecture is in the **Temple of Heaven Park (Tiantanyuan),** about a mile due south of the old Qianmen Gate on Tiananmen Square. This was conceived of as the exact meeting point of Heaven and Earth by Emperor Yongle and his geomancers when they completed the round tower on its high square base in 1420. Here the Son of Heaven was obliged to perform sacrifices after praying for the year's good harvest. The annual procession to the Temple of Heaven was so sacred that the people of Beijing could not cast their eyes upon it, and the Temple of Heaven complex was itself a forbidden city until China became a republic in 1912.

The main entrance was traditionally from the south. The **Round Altar (Huanqiutan),** three marble tiers representing Earth, Man, and Heaven, was the Center of the World. It is said that an orator's voice originating from these tiers was magnified and could be heard for miles. Today, the acoustically inclined hasten to the next monument, **Echo Wall**

(Huiyinbi), another round-walled platform where even a whisper directed into the wall is broadcast around the whole circle. I tested this several times, and there did seem to be a carrying echo. It was possible to hear the words someone whispered from the opposite side of the wall. Of course, this phenomenon is transformed into babbling once Echo Wall is engulfed by visitors, all intent on using the wall phone at once.

The primary temple in this heavenly park is the **Hall for Prayer for Good Harvests (Qiniandian),** located to the north. It is one of the most remarkable buildings in China, a round tower capped by a magnificent three-tiered blue-tiled dome, paneled in the most ornate carvings ever produced in China. The vault, 120 feet high, is so perfectly fitted together that not a single nail was used. Fifty thousand glazed tiles coat the conical roof. Four inner columns (the Dragon Well Pillars), representing the four seasons, and two concentric sets of 12 outer pillars, for the months and the 2-hour units of the day, provide the support. The ceiling is a bright, dazzling dragon design. In 1889, a bolt of lightning destroyed the tower, but it has been faithfully reconstructed. These days, visitors can only peer into the grand interior. A decade ago, it was possible to walk inside and feel the full pull of the ancient cosmos.

The park is most heavenly these days in the early morning, before the tour buses pull up. Locals gather for morning exercises: *tai ji quan* (shadow boxing), sword practice, strange forms of *chi gong* (a channeling of internal energies). The retired men stake out benches and display their caged songbirds and crickets. College students, seeking solitude and space for study, pore over their books on benches under an old cypress grove inside the western gate. There the main road (Qianmen Lu) leads straight back the 3 miles to Tiananmen Square. The Temple of Heaven is open Tuesday through Sunday from 9am to 4pm. Admission is RMB 10 ($1.20).

Lama Temple

Beijing's premier temple, locals agree, is the Lama Temple (Yonghegong), northeast of Tiananmen Square, just inside the Second Ring Road. It first served as Emperor Yongzheng's mansion. Emperor Qianlong, his successor, consecrated it as a lamasery in 1744 and hired 500 lamas from Mongolia to run it. In the early 20th century it served as the Bureau of Mongolian and Tibetan Affairs, reverting in recent times to its original functions.

Part of its attraction is its grand scale. The **Hall of the Heavenly Kings** contains Maitreya, the Buddha of the Future, smiling broadly on all visitors. Four celestial guardians, one for each cardinal direction, each accompanied by eight of their top generals, protect the Buddha from a horde of demons. Next in line is the **Hall of Harmony (Yonghedian),** with Buddhas of the past, present, and future. The layout is a lengthy one.

In the fourth hall, **Falundian,** the eastern wing contains statuary locked in amorous embraces. They are usually covered in scarves that serve as fig leaves. These and other draped statues in the Lama Temple are regarded as China's Kama Sutra, reputedly serving as an illustrated sex manual for the sons of emperors. As late as the 1930s, the Lama Temple still had an aura of the forbidden about it. "Devil dances," which included rituals imitating human sacrifice, were regularly performed.

The final great hall is the tallest: the **Tower of the Great Buddha (Wangfuge).** Inside is a second rendition of the Buddha of the Future, standing in at 55 feet. This sandalwood colossus is considered the largest sculpture ever carved from a single piece of wood, a gift to Emperor Qianlong from the seventh Dali Lama. It was here that the Dali Lama's followers once held sway.

The Lama Temple is open from 8:30am to 5pm daily (admission RMB 10/$1.20), and is always busy not only with local visitors and Chinese worshippers but with at least 70 monks in brown robes, heads shaven. If this complex doesn't leave you "templed out," nothing will. My favorite retreat from the crowds is a side tower, the **Pavilion of Perpetual Peace,** which contains a large prayer wheel suspended from its ceiling. The Lama Temple has enough diversions and pavilions scattered through its five courtyards to provide hours of quiet diversion, if you can search them out. Sometimes you can still hear bronze bells suspended from the yellow-tiled eaves singing in the breeze that rocks the swaying bamboo.

Star Gazing

In 1422, just after the Forbidden City was finished, a celestial observatory was built on a corner of the city wall. The Chinese were excellent astronomers, keen observers of the heavens (of whom the emperor was the son). The observatory in Beijing became the most important in the Middle Kingdom. In the early 1600s, Jesuit missionaries in the capital introduced Western methods, hoping to attract converts to Christianity through their ability to predict eclipses. Several of the instruments designed by the Jesuits remain on the roof of the **Ancient Observatory (Guguanxiangtai)** today. The observatory is located on the south side of Jianguomenwai Dajie—the eastern portion of Changan Avenue—where it seems like a stranded piece of history, a Ming Dynasty terrace clinging to the last surviving block of the old city wall.

The Ancient Observatory is an incongruity, located as it is in the heart of Beijing's heaviest traffic and newest office complexes, but it is also a graceful reminder of the imperial past. The eight bronze astronomical instruments on the open roof are visible for better than a mile up and down the busy avenue. Displays inside the two-story museum are usually replicas rather than originals, but the gold foil atlas of the stars, based on Tang Dynasty observations, shows how the Chinese mapped the sky, creating constellations unknown to the West.

This is the ideal place to take a break, both in time and space, if you're walking the seemingly endless street east from Tiananmen Square. The dragon quadrant, celestial globe, ecliptic armilla, theodolite, sextant, zodiac, and other instruments date from the early Qing Dynasty. Whether they are originals or copies isn't clear—not that it matters. The effect is of an antique world, its eyes fixed on the cosmos and its instruments, mounted on a garden terrace, as beautiful as a starry, unpolluted night. The Ancient Observatory is open Wednesday through Sunday from 9am to 4:30pm. Admission is RMB 10 ($1.20).

Streets & Alleys

Once you gorge yourself on the highlights of old Beijing, you're ready to wander its streets. There are dozens of other museums, temples, and parks to visit, but time quickly runs out. Not to experience the streets is not to experience China's modern capital.

The essential architecture of Beijing is not that of the temple or palace but of the courtyard homes and the narrow alleyways, called hutongs. The most interesting group to join in Beijing is the **Hutong Tour,** first organized by a local photographer devoted to urban preservation. Bicycle rickshaws do the heavy work, slicing through the impossible traffic snarls from the back entrance of Beihai Park, along Shisha Lake, down to the old Drum Tower. The Drum Tower contains an exhibit of hutong photographs. The tour group finishes up with tea in an elaborate courtyard mansion.

The backstreets of old Beijing are fast disappearing, but the **Qianmen District** on the south end of Tiananmen Square is a fine place to wander in search of traditional shops, lanes, and hutongs. Start on the southwest side of the traffic circle, walk southeast through the sidewalk vendors, and turn straight down Jewelry Street (Zhubaoshi Jie). The entrance to Jewelry Street is marked by a large bicycle billboard. This street runs north and south parallel to Qianmen Dajie—the old Imperial Way—and it constitutes one of the more crowded outdoor markets in Beijing. After about four blocks, take a right west on Dazhalan Lu (Dahalar Street). Behind the Qing Dynasty facades lining this old theater street are traditional pharmacies and silk shops. At No. 18 Dazhalan Lu is Beijing's **Underground City,** the remains of the elaborate air-raid shelter system, built by hand, that Chairman Mao initiated during the Cold War standoff with the Soviet Union more than 30 years ago. There's not only shopping down there these days but an underground hotel.

Meanwhile, back on Earth, past tea shops and herbal medicine stores, about a quarter mile west on Dazhalan Lu, take a turn north and then west along Yangmei Alley, a hutong of crowded courtyards. The alley soon joins **Liulichang Lu,** Beijing's most famous avenue of antiques. Most of the buildings along here were rebuilt in recent times to resemble an old shopping district. The curio shops, bookstores, musical instrument showrooms, and art galleries are among the best in China. **Rongbaozhai,** at 64 Liulichang, is the most highly regarded art store in China.

While the shops are fascinating in the Liulichang District, the prices are far better east of Tiananmen Square at the **Xiushui Silk Market** and the **Friendship Store.** Changan Avenue turns into Jianguomenwei Dajie as it heads east toward the Ancient Observatory. Keep on the north side for the Friendship Store, the largest in China, with its floors of gifts, crafts, foods, and sundries. The Silk Market is located between the Friendship Store and the Jianguo Hotel. Get there early to avoid the rush. Prices on clothing of all sorts, including designer labels, can be very low, but offer no more than half the vendor's asking price.

My favorite shopping ramble is into the heart of the city on **Wangfujing Street,** which runs north off Changan Avenue a few blocks east of Tiananmen Square. Begin this jaunt by cutting through the **Beijing Hotel.** If you walk through its main corridor from west to east, you'll be walking through an innkeeper's time capsule of grand accommodations in Beijing. The oldest section, in the middle of the long edifice, dates from 1917, its rooms in the French style with brocade wallpapers. The west wing, conjoined in 1954, has a magnificent dining hall up the north stairs. The east wing, added in 1974 and remodeled in 1990, contains 600 modern luxury rooms (but not with service to match). The cathedral ceilings and sweeping staircases run the length of this landmark. On its east corner is Wangfujing Street.

Before Liberation in 1949, Wangfujing Lu (Goldfish Lane) was known as Morrison Street. It catered to China's richest Westerners. Nowadays, Wangfujing caters to China's richest Chinese. The brand new **Sun Dong An Plaza,** China's largest shopping and office complex, 11 stories of steel and glass and underground parking, intended as a "reconstruction" of the century-old Dong An Market, epitomizes the upscale shopping along Wangfujing. Actually, the street contains a wide range of shops and restaurants, from McDonald's to hole-in-the-wall steamed-dumpling shops, from Louis Vuitton to a local specialty shop selling nothing but stuffed animals. The farther you push up Wangfujing, the more traditional and varied the stores. The **Chinese department stores** are particularly worth browsing. They feature an increasingly large range of imported commodities, always have an immense uniformed sales staff on the floor, and frequently put on good old-fashioned demonstrations of their goods right in the aisles. I've seen salespeople try out the latest electronic acupressure devices on shoppers, and I've seen both men and women sitting beside counters receiving demonstration hair dyes, their friends and everyone else crowding in for a closer look.

Beijing's most international neighborhood these days is the **Sanlitun District,** northeast of Tiananmen Square, on the west side of the Third Ring Road, not far from the congregation of foreign-based hotels and businesses (Sheraton Great Wall, Kempinski Hotel, Lufthansa Centre, Hard Rock Cafe). To reach the outdoor cafes, bars, and small shops that cater to foreigners and hip Beijingers, walk west from the Kunlun Hotel to the Huadu Hotel, turn south (left) on Sanlitun Bei Lu, and follow this tree-lined boulevard past Embassy Row a good six blocks. Just north of Gongrentiyuchang Bei Lu, Sanlitun is occupied by dozens of cafes with outdoor seating. Clothing stalls, cheese shops, and other private businesses are booming along here, too. This is Beijing's best (and perhaps only) real place to hang out. When the weather is good, hundreds of expatriates and foreign travelers drop by, unwind in one of the cafes, and enjoy life as it passes. The German-style **Kebab Cafe,** with plenty of outdoor seating, a full international menu, and imported beers (all at imported prices), is my favorite. Stacks of pirated music tapes and CDs are hawked from table to table all along Sanlitun, priced at about $2 (with no guarantee of quality, of course). New eating and drinking outlets spring up every few weeks, as the demand for international venues continues to outrun supply. Ten years ago, finding an English-language menu, let alone a German beer, outside of the big hotels in Beijing was something of a fool's errand. Today it's a hot business.

Equally trendy in this surprisingly trendy city are the teahouses, which are more in keeping with the legacies of the capital. Teahouses once drew in Beijing's literate and wealthy residents, its mandarins, for an evening devoted to the arts and spirited conversation. **Tian Hai Tea House** (located in a hutong just north of Gongrentiyuchang Bei Lu, off Sanlitun; ☎ 010/6416-5676) is among the newest attempts to return to that tradition. The interiors of the teahouse, designed by Beijing artist Son Xiao Hong and his daughter, Song Hui Bin, evoke Qing Dynasty days with their dark woods, bamboos, and wall paintings. Waiters and waitresses dress up in royal costumes. Weekends, musicians take up traditional instruments, such as the erhu and pippa, and Peking opera stars drop in to conduct sing-alongs. The teas of the teahouse are green and jasmine, but fruit flavors have been added, and the menu of northern Chinese steamed snacks and noodles is augmented by salads and ice-cream treats.

Curiously, it's the new teahouses, based on old traditions, that embody the rising spirit of modern Beijing. East seems more comfortable with West than ever before, the past keeps finding new ways into the present, and Beijing seems confident of playing a leading role in the future not just of China but of the world.

PRACTICAL INFORMATION

ORIENTATION

Beijing is China's capital and its most popular tourist destination. Located in northeast China, it is its own municipality, not part of a province. Summers are quite hot, winters quite cold. Visit in late April, May, October, or November for warm, dry weather. Early spring brings dust storms from the Gobi Desert. The most popular day trip from Beijing is the **Great Wall** (see separate chapter in "Monuments of the Middle Kingdom"), 2 hours by bus or car to the north. **Chengde** (see next chapter), an imperial city 4 hours to the northeast, is usually included as an overnight tour. Arrangements to visit these sites are provided by hotel tour desks and China International Travel Service (CITS).

GETTING THERE

By Plane   Beijing's **Capital Airport** (☎ 010/6456-3604) has connections to major destinations inside and outside of China. Many international airlines serve Beijing, including United Airlines (☎ 010/6463-8563), Japan Airlines (☎ 010/6513-0888), Northwest Airlines (☎ 010/6505-3505), and Canadian Airlines (☎ 010/6463-7901). The city's hotels have service desks at the main airport exit. Upstairs, there's a branch of the Bank of China that exchanges foreign currencies for renminbi (RMB). The airport is only 18 miles northeast of the city, but allow at least an hour for the transfer. Airport buses directly outside the main entrance serve several downtown hotels and the central train station. They cost RMB 12 ($1.50). Inquire about their routes, as these can change. Taxis cost RMB 100 ($12) or more. Red cabs charge more than yellow cabs. Many hotels provide free airport shuttles, especially if you fax ahead your arrival times and transfer request.
By Train   From Beijing's **Main Railway Station (Beijing Zhan)** or West **Station (Xi Zhan)**, the largest train station in the world, there are trains to virtually every city and town in China. The newest rail service is the train service launched to celebrate Hong Kong's return to sovereignty in 1997, connecting Beijing and Hong Kong via China's most deluxe train. Train 97 leaves Beijing West Station at 7:30am every other day, taking 29 hours 40 minutes to reach Kowloon Station in Hong Kong. Stops are made at Shijiazhuang, Zhengzhou, Xinyang, Wuchang, Changsha, Hengyang, Shaoguan, and Guangzhou (Canton). Train 98 returns to Beijing from Hong Kong the following day at 3:30pm. The train uses the newest passenger cars made in China. "First-class performance" is promised. Sleeping berths come in three classes: hard sleepers (no compartment, $92 one-way per person), soft sleepers (four-bed compartments, $121 one-way per person), and "Luxurious Soft Sleeper Compartments" (two-bed compartments, $155 one-way per person).

GETTING AROUND

Equipped with a map, you can see most of the attractions yourself by foot, by taxi, or by subway. The **subway system** is modern, clean, easy to navigate, and impervious to traffic jams. Hours of operation are 5:30am to 11pm daily. Tickets

Beijing Subway

Loop Line

Jishuitan, Gulou, Andingmen, Yonghegong

Xizhimen — Dongzhimen
Chegongzhuang — Dongsi Shitiao
Fuchengmen — Chaoyangmen
Jianguomen

Pinggouyuan

East–West Line

Fuxingmen, Xidan

Line Under Construction

Gucheng Lu, Bajiaocun, Babaoshan, Yuquan Lu, Wukesong, Wanshou Lu, Gongzhufen, Junshi Bowuguan, Muxidi, Nanlishi Lu

Changchun Jie, Xuanwumen, Hepingmen, Qianmen, Chongwenmen, Beijing Zhan

are RMB 2 (25¢) per trip. Station arrivals are announced in English and Chinese. If you use a **taxi** instead, make sure it has its meter running (say "da biao"). Many hotels rent **bicycles** (about $3 per hour). Beijing has millions of bikes on the streets at any one time, and there is safety in numbers. If you stay off the big streets and follow the bike flow, you'll be surprised how easy bike riding is in Beijing.

TOURS & STRATAGEMS

Tours China International Travel Service (CITS), with headquarters at 28 Jianguomenwai Dajie (☎ 010/6515-8566; fax 010/6515-8602), arranges guided tours (available in 12 languages) to all major sites. CITS maintains convenient branches in most hotels. Hotel tour desks can book airline and train tickets. American Express, with offices in the China World Trade Center, L115D Shopping Arcade, 1 Jianguomenwei Dajie, can be contacted at ☎ 010/6505-2888. The 24-hour tourist hot line number is ☎ 010/6513-0828.

WHERE TO STAY

Beijing has a fuller range of hotels than any other city in China except Hong Kong, featuring such international chains as Shangri-La, Holiday Inn, Sheraton, Hilton, Otani, Kempinski, Mövenpik, and Radisson. Top choices are listed here.
China World Hotel (Zhongguo Da Fandian). 1 Jianguomenwai Dajie (inside the China World Trade Centre). ☎ 800/942-5050 or 010/6505-2266. Fax 010/6505-3167. 687 rms, 56 suites. A/C MINIBAR TV TEL. $295 double. AE, DC, JCB, MC, V. Shangri-La provides the management. The service is world-class, the amenities considerable. This is where CEOs and world leaders stay. There are four executive floors (Horizon Club) with their own business center and lounge.

Services: Concierge, room service (24-hour), dry cleaning and laundry (24-hour, same day), newspaper delivery, nightly turndown, twice-daily maid service, express checkout, free airport shuttle, foreign exchange counter.

Facilities: In-house movies, pool (indoor, heated), health club (exercise machines, classes), golf simulators (the only two in Beijing), Jacuzzi, sauna, tennis courts (three indoors), squash courts (two indoors), bowling alley (12 lanes), business center (24-hour, conference rooms), tour desk, beauty salon, shopping arcade, newsstand, florist.

Holiday Inn Lido (Lidu Jiari Fandian). *Jichang Lu, Jiangtai Lu (on the road to the airport, northeast of city center).* ☎ *800/465-4329 or 010/6437-6688. Fax 010/6437-6237. 953 rms, 76 suites. A/C TV TEL. $190 double. AE, DC, JCB, MC, V.* This is the world's largest Holiday Inn. With bowling lanes, swimming pools, a supermarket, a drugstore, office and apartment towers, foreign schools, and nearly everything else you can think of located within its compounds—plus attentive service—the Holiday Inn Lido is China's most "complete" hotel, a virtual city-state. At 4 stars, it trails the Shangri-La Hotel only because of its less luxurious appointments and much greater distance from downtown. The superior rooms are worth the extra $20, as they are more spacious and include desks and marble bathrooms.

Services: Concierge, room service (24-hour), dry cleaning and laundry (next day), nightly turndown, express checkout, free downtown and airport shuttle, bicycle rental, foreign exchange counter, Bank of China branch.

Facilities: In-house movies, two pools (indoor, heated), health club, Jacuzzi, sauna, four indoor tennis courts, two bowling centers, business center (24-hour, conference rooms), tour desk, beauty salon, shopping arcade, newsstand, florist, Watson's Drugstore, supermarket.

Shangri-La Hotel Beijing (Xiangge Lila Fandian). *29 Zizhuyuan Lu (west of downtown near Beijing Zoo).* ☎ *800/* 942-5050 *or* 010/6841-2211. *Fax* 010/ 6841-8002. 638 *rms,* 19 *suites. A/C MINIBAR TV TEL. $190 double. AE, DC, JCB, MC, V.* Older sister to the China World Hotel, the Shangri-La Beijing is quieter, farther from the city center, but exceptionally elegant without being pretentious. All rooms contain wall safes, hair dryers, and coffeemakers. There are two executive floors (Horizon Club) with their own business center and lounge.

Services: Concierge, room service (24-hour), dry cleaning and laundry (8am–4pm), newspaper delivery, nightly turndown, express checkout, free downtown and airport shuttle, foreign exchange counter.

Facilities: In-house movies, pool (indoor, heated), health club (exercise machines, classes), sauna, two indoor tennis and one indoor squash court, business center (24-hour, conference rooms), tour desk, beauty salon, shopping arcade, newsstand, florist.

Traders Hotel Beijing (Gumao Fandian). *1 Jianguomenwai Dajie (north and behind the China World Hotel).* ☎ *800/942-5050 or 010/6505-2277. Fax 010/6505-0818. 547 rms, 20 suites. A/C MINIBAR TV TEL. $220 double. AE, DC, JCB, MC, V.* This is Shangri-La's "stripped-down" 4-star business hotel, but not much is stripped down. Guests have plenty of comforts and access to China World's facilities. Traders Hotel Beijing has proven so popular that it recently doubled in size (adding an east wing).

Services: Concierge, room service (24-hour), dry cleaning and laundry (next day), nightly turndown, express checkout, free airport shuttle, foreign exchange counter.

Facilities: In-house movies, fitness club (exercise machines), business center (24-hour, conference rooms), tour desk, newsstand.

WHERE TO DINE

There are scores of good restaurants and bars in Beijing. I can only list a dozen tried-and-true favorites. For up-to-date information on dining and a larger current listing, check the free local newspapers: *Welcome to China: Beijing, Beijing This Month,* and *Beijing Scene.*

Borom Piman. *Jichang Lu, Jiangtai Lu, in the Holiday Inn Lido.* ☎ *010/6437-6688, ext. 2899. Reservations recommended. Main courses $12–$25. AE, DC, JCB, MC, V. Daily 11:30am–2pm and 6–10pm. THAI.* Unfailingly flavorful, this Thai food is Beijing's best. Choose from Western-style seating or mat-covered platforms with leg wells hidden underneath the low tables. The tom yam goong (prawn in hot-and-sour soup) is justly renowned, and the khow ob subparod (fried rice with pork and shrimp in fresh pineapple) is unforgettable. The chefs hail from Bangkok.

Fangshan. *1 Wenjin Jie (on island in Beihai Park).* ☎ *010/6401-1184. Reservations required. Fixed-price dinners $35–$45. Daily 11am–1:30pm and 5–7:30pm. No credit cards. IMPERIAL.* Another special treat associated with Beijing is Imperial cuisine, meals based on the banquet menus of the Qing Dynasty and once served only inside the walls of the Forbidden City. The park setting, replete with elaborate dynastic decorations and costumed waitresses, is worth experiencing. Fangshan's menu comes courtesy of Empress Dowager Ci Xi.

Frank's Place. *On Gongrentiyuchang Dong Lu near the Worker's Stadium and Sanlitun Lu.* ☎ *010/6507-2617. Hamburgers and sandwiches $5. MC, V. Daily noon–2pm and 5pm–12:30am. BURGERS.* Frank's is the original American bar in Beijing, a short walk these days from the trendier Sanlitun strip. Prices are reasonable ($2 for Beijing beers), the license plates on the wall are the right touch, and Frank, an American, is often on hand

behind the bar. The burgers are the tastiest in China. The 20 tables often fill up with expatriates in for a casual dinner, and the dart board is popular.

Henry J. Bean's Bar & Grill. *1 Jianguomenwai Dajie (in the West Wing of the China World Trade Centre).* ☎ *010/6505-2266, ext 6334. Main courses $9–$18. AE, DC, JCB, MC, V. Daily 11:30am–1am. AMERICAN.* One of many flashy new spots for beer, sandwiches, grilled steaks, and live music, this place is particularly comfortable.

Holiday Inn Lido Sunday Brunch. *Patio Coffee Shop, Holiday Inn Lido, Jichang Lu, Jiangtai Lu.* ☎ *010/6437-6688, ext. 1971. Reservations recommended. Buffet RMB 150 ($18). AE, DC, JCB, MC, V. Sunday 11:30am–3pm. INTERNATIONAL.* On Sunday, the most extensive and lively buffet, complete with lucky draws, live entertainment, and unlimited sparkling wine, is in the Holiday Inn Lido's lobby. Children under 10 are free. Plenty of dishes, including Italian pastas, excellent Peking duck, German breads, and cakes and ice cream.

Justine's. *5 Jianguomenwai Dajie (in the Jianguo Hotel lobby).* ☎ *010/6500-2233, ext 8039. Reservations recommended. Jacket and tie recommended. Main courses $12–$35. AE, JCB, MC, V. Daily 6:30am–9:30am, 11:30am–2pm, and 6–10:30pm. CONTINENTAL.* A longtime favorite of expats, this is as close to dining in Europe as you can come in Beijing. Low lights, glass lamps, faultless waiters—and exceptional steaks, imported from Australia and the United States.

Nadaman Restaurant. *1 Jianguomenwai Dajie (Level 3, China World Hotel).* ☎ *010/6505-2266, ext 6127. Main courses $20–$60. AE, DC, JCB, MC, V. Daily 11:30am–2pm and 5:30–9:30pm. JAPANESE.* Debuting in 1997, this Osaka-based restaurant maintains separate sushi and teppanyaki counters. There are four tatami rooms and Western-style seating for 166. The head chefs are from Japan. Everything is contemporary, Japanese, and absolutely spotless.

Shang Palace. *29 Zizhuyuan Lu (Level 1, Shangri-La Beijing Hotel).* ☎ *010/ 6841-2211, ext 2732. Reservations recommended. Main courses $10–$50. AE, DC, JCB, MC, V. Daily 11:30am–2pm and 5:30–10pm. CANTONESE/BEIJING.* Long famous for its dim sum (steamed pastries) and Cantonese-style seafood dishes, Shang Palace is also the best place in town for Beijing's specialty, Peking duck, which is less greasy here than in the duck restaurants downtown. This large, open dining area with red columns is decorated tastefully in Qing Dynasty dragons and clouds.

Summer Palace. *1 Jianguomenwai Dajie (in the lobby of China World Hotel).* ☎ *010/6505-2266. Reservations recommended. Main courses $10–$30. AE, DC, JCB, MC, V. Daily 11:30am–2pm and 5:30–10pm. CANTONESE.* Newly reopened in 1997, China World Hotel's signature restaurant offers superb southern Chinese dishes in a bright, airy dining hall, surrounded by eight private dining rooms. Chefs are from Hong Kong. The dim sum (steamed pastries) are the best in Beijing. Seafood dishes are particularly tasty. The Club Bar just outside the grand entrance is an elegant venue for cocktails before or after a meal.

Windows on the World. *CITIC Building, 28–29/F, 19 Jianguomenwai Dajie.* ☎ *010/6500-3335, ext 2255. Main courses $10–$25. AE, DC, JCB, MC, V. Daily 11:30am–2:30pm, 5:30–10pm. WESTERN/CHINESE.* East meets West with a capital view toward Tiananmen Square at this bustling restaurant favored by businessmen and politicians. The 28th floor serves Beijing duck, fresh seafood Cantonese style, and dim sum, prepared by Hong Kong chefs. The 29th floor serves a lunch buffet with Western and Chinese choices and for dinner a hot pot

buffet where you select the ingredients. There's an extensive wine list.

Yuen Tai. *Great Wall Sheraton Hotel, 21/ F, Dongsanhuan Bei Lu.* ☎ *010/6500-5566, ext 2162. Reservations recommended. Main courses $5–$40. AE, DC, JCB, MC, V. Daily 11:30am–2pm and 6–10pm. SICHUAN.* This place serves excellent peppery Sichuan dishes. The Sichuan scallops with dried red peppers and peanuts are scrumptious and hot. A tea master fills tiny cups from long distance using a teapot spout a yard long. Hanging painted lanterns, carved lattices, and a garden view make this a luxurious dinner choice.

Peking Duck Restaurants Probably the most popular dish with foreigners, at least until they try it, is Peking duck. It's a brash dish, and certainly worth trying. The two most popular places to do so are Bianyifang and Qianmen, but the Wangfujing outlet is the best. Expect slices of duck skin and meat, the crunchier the better—and the less fat the better—with a generous assortment of Shandong Province vegetable side dishes. Peking duck is served banquet style around a table, and you have to get a group together to enjoy it (4 to 12 people is best).

Beijing Wangfujing Quanjude Roast Duck Restaurant. *13 Shuaifuyuan, Wangfujing Lu.* ☎ *010/ 6525-3310. Reservations recommended. Main course $15. No credit cards. Daily 10:30am–1:30pm and 4:30–9:30pm. PEKING DUCK.*

Bianyifang Roast Duck Restaurant. *2 Chongwenmenwai Dajie.* ☎ *010/6712-0505. Reservations recommended. Main course $15. No credit cards. Daily 11am–2pm and 5–8:30pm. PEKING DUCK.*

Qianmen Quanjude Roast Duck Restaurant. *32 Qianmen Dajie.* ☎ *010/ 6511-2418. Reservations recommended. Main course $15. No credit cards. Daily 11am–1:30pm and 4:30–8:30pm. PEKING DUCK.*

CHENGDE: SUMMER HOME OF THE EMPERORS

承德

O<small>N</small> S<small>EPTEMBER</small> 14, 1793, E<small>MPEROR</small> Qianlong received the first delegation from a Western government ever to set foot in China, a British legation headed by Lord Macartney. Matters did not get off to a promising start. The British lord refused to kowtow to the emperor, a ceremony that all visitors to the Middle Kingdom had performed for centuries, bowing deeply and banging their heads upon the ground. The emperor granted no treaties to England that day and declared that requests to open up trade were pointless. "We possess all things," Emperor Qianlong declared. "I set no value on objects strange or ingenious, and have no use for your country's manufactures."

The site of this historic meeting of East and West took place not in the Forbidden City in Beijing but 155 miles northeast in a remote imperial retreat built by Qianlong's grandfather, Emperor Kangxi. This summer palace in the wilderness, located in the country town of Chengde (formerly called Jehol in the West), was by no means a primitive outpost. Befitting the station of the Qing rulers, it was a grand summer palace, larger than Beijing's summer palace and Forbidden City combined, with numerous halls, pavilions, lakes, and hunting grounds. The retreat has survived, largely intact, and today Chengde is a summer resort open to all the people of China as well as sightseers from abroad, as anxious as the royal courts of two centuries past to escape the heat of Beijing and partake of the splendors of the countryside.

Mountain Villa for Escaping the Summer Heat

The road from Beijing is in excellent condition and the scenery is often spectacular, with sharp wooded peaks and valleys. Chengde is surrounded by the same green mountains—no doubt one reason the emperors favored this place. The town of Chengde, which grew up around the parklands, has become a resort center, but it is still no more than a village by Chinese standards, with a population of only 150,000. Tourism has brought some prosperity, although in the nearby fields I did see farmers

The Summer Palace
at Chengde

pulling rounded stones on ropes, used to level the strips between furrows, and I also saw furrows being dug with wooden plows harnessed to the bent backs of peasants, no other beasts of burden being available.

Before the era of automobiles and trains, the journey from the capital to Chengde would have been a formidable undertaking. In 1703, Emperor Kangxi ordered the construction of the "Mountain Villa for Escaping the Summer Heat" (Bishushanzhuang). From the first, it was China's court away from court. Even the throne was transported from Beijing so that the emperor could wield full power while he enjoyed the sports of the privileged. Kangxi was intensely dedicated to the horsemanship and hunting of his Manchu ancestors, and Chengde became his passion. For the next 117 years, this summer retreat was expanded and enriched, the Qing emperors holding court here six months of the year. In 1820, however, Emperor Jiaqing died at Chengde, reportedly the victim of a lightning bolt, a bad omen. It was decades before the court again began its annual decampment of Beijing in favor of the lush, cool valley to the north.

What's most striking today is the vast scale of the imperial retreat, which fills much of the great valley of Chengde, and its rustic setting. In comparison with the ornate and elaborate pavilions and courtyards of the Forbidden City and summer palaces in Beijing, Chengde's compound is raw and wild. Twice the size of Beijing's royal park, most of Chengde's retreat is given over to water, rock, and grasslands—the grasslands that the once-nomadic Manchus, who had grown civilized as the masters of the Chinese empire, called their spiritual home. One of the first foreigners to see the retreat, a Jesuit missionary living in Beijing, wrote that the enclosure was so extensive it required an hour to survey on horseback.

Imperial Palace

Today, Bishushanzhuang is surrounded by a wall 6 miles in circumference. The **east entrance gate (Dehuimen)** is at the Wulie River, on the northwest edge of town, near an intriguing footbridge where locals congregate with long bamboo fishing poles and vendors stock towers of glass aquariums with the fresh catch. No matter that the water under the bridge is turgid and clogged with debris, or that the resort town is noisy and uninviting. The park the emperors built is beautiful, and it is spacious, consisting of enormous fields, lakes, pavilions, and pagodas, the largest imperial garden in China.

West of the entrance gate, atop a small rise, is the old palace (Zhenggong), now the **Bishushanzhuang Museum**. The **Front Palace** complex is where diplomatic business was conducted. For several centuries, China in the summertime was ruled from nine courtyard halls, each fashioned from unpainted wood. These are plain, linear buildings, more like imperial lodges than palaces, landscaped in mighty pines, graveled walkways, and convoluted rockeries. The interiors are sparsely decorated with the furniture and armaments of the time, as well as life-sized waxen figures representing emperors, concubines, court advisors, and foreign diplomats. Envoys were once received in the Hall of No Worldly Lust But True Faith, constructed of fragrant nanmu wood from southwestern China. The royal bedroom is located in the Refreshing Mist Veiled Waters Pavilion. In the Landscape Amid Clouds and Mountains Hall, visitors can reach the second floor by climbing the rockery in front.

The Imperial Summer Villa is open from 5:30am to 6pm daily. Admission is RMB 30 ($3.75).

Royal Garden

Outside the main palace grounds is a set of interlinked lakes, woven with paths, arched bridges, and viewing pavilions, where the Chinese enjoy themselves, rowing boats and splashing each other as they pass. Family picnics are popular here. So are games, if not the hunting sports of kings. Across the flat grasslands today, adults and children together play what looks like blind man's bluff and rover-red-rover. Teens circle up for versions of hacky-sack. The last great private preserve of emperors has become a genuine people's park. Courtyards are commandeered by martial arts demonstrations featuring retired citizens in white uniforms and red sashes. In another courtyard in front of the emperor's palace, preschool children flash swords in formation, some of them barely old enough to walk.

The circular tents known as **yurts,** which the nomadic tribes of the north erected and dismantled as they traveled the grasslands, and which the Manchu emperors also employed during their long summer vacations, have returned to Chengde, albeit in strictly modern fashion. In one large grassy field, several dozen of these Manchurian tents are rented out as overnight accommodations at the Yurt Holiday Inn. The modern models are fitted out with air conditioners, private baths, and color televisions, but not with braziers for roasting venison and other royal game. It was on this lawn, in the emperor's yurt, that England's first envoy to China refused to bow.

Many pavilions from the days of the emperors have survived. The **Literary Nourishment Pavilion (Wenjinge),** once one of China's four great imperial libraries, is northwest of the lakes on a secluded wooded hill. It resembles the classic gardens of Suzhou and Ningbo, with an immense rockery facing a graceful wooden pavilion across a goldfish pool. The rockery has its own caves, paths, and overlooks, and one of its rocks has been shaped and stationed so that from the pavilion those who linger can see the silver image of the moon continuously reflected on the waters.

Along the lakeshores are several dazzling towers and halls, including the **Temple of Eternal Blessing,** a golden birthday gift from Emperor Qianlong to his mother. On **Changlang Isle,** Emperor Qianlong constructed a copy of Suzhou's Changlang Garden. Even prettier is the **Tower of Mist and Rain (Yanyulou),** perched on a hill and reached by a bridge, favored by emperors for its views of the lake in the fog. On the northeast shore is a stunning three-story pavilion, **Gold Mountain Temple (Jinshan Si),** bordered by lower halls, which Emperor Kangxi in a poem likened to a mountain rising from the lake. "To ascend it," he sang, "is like climbing a magical peak."

Lord Macartney rode through the park during his diplomatic mission in 1793 and was charmed by the lake scenes: "The shores of the lake have all the varieties of shape which the fancy of a painter can delineate . . . one marked by a pagoda, or other building, one quite destitute of ornament, some smooth and level, some steep and uneven and others frowning with wood or smiling with culture."

North of the lakes, the grasslands and hills fan out and the walkways become secluded hiking trails stretching beyond the **Garden of Ten Thousand Trees (Wanshun Wan)** and the **Horse Testing Ground**

(Shima Da) where emperors once reviewed archers and horsemen. The Imperial Summer Villa at Chengde essentially re-creates the wild grass-lands of the Manchus north of the Great Wall but softens them with the garden arts and sweeping pavilions of south China.

Little Tibet

Emperor Kangxi had a political motive in moving his summer court to Chengde. He hoped to impress, to beguile, and to subdue the unruly legions to the north, and to placate restive religious and ethnic factions throughout China. This ploy produced a legacy visible today in the hillsides north and east of the Imperial Summer Villa, a string of Eight Outer Temples built in honor of Tibetans, Kazaks, and other peoples. As fascinating as this Summer Palace of the Wild West is, the array of distant hillside temples is even more striking.

A dozen were built from 1713 to 1779. Eight remain open. Two of the neighboring northern temples, Tibetan in style, are the grandest and most unusual. Built 10 years apart, they are the work of Kangxi's grand-son, Emperor Qianlong.

The **Mount Sumera Longevity and Happiness Temple (Xumifushou Miao)** was built in 1779 in honor of the sixth Panchen Lama's visit to Chengde. The design is based on the lama's residence in Shigatse, Tibet. At the rear of this lavish uphill enclosure is a yellow-and-green pagoda erected to celebrate Emperor Qianlong's 70th birthday. At the entrance are two white stone elephants kneeling on bent legs. In the center is the high red wall of the main temple, decorated with Tibetan windows. The walls enclose a massive squarish four-story hall with a copper-tiled roof gilded in a ton of gold, decorated with eight ridge-running dragons, each weighing one ton. The inside of the red walls is lined with tiers of galleries, affording inward views of the square hall and outward views of the valley of Chengde. This was the last copy temple built at Chengde.

The **Small Potala Temple (Putuozongsheng Miao)** a mile to the east was built by Emperor Qianlong 10 years earlier, partly to celebrate his 60th birthday and his mother's 80th. It is the largest temple at Chengde, its 60 halls and terraces covering 54 acres.

To reach the main hall requires a long, steep climb up the hillside. Prayer flags and banners drape its golden beams. The great red wall at its rear evokes the wall of the Dali Lamas' Potala Palace in Lhasa. A massive four-sided stone tablet inscribed, respectively, in Tibetan, Manchurian, Mongolian, and Chinese in the front courtyard proclaims the temple's links to the Potala. Whitewashed outer buildings, capped with dagobas, are empty shells, built for show rather than worship or the repository of saintly remains. Even the richly decorated Tibetan windows on the red wall are blank, serving as pure decorative flourishes to impress the visiting Mongol dignitaries who practiced Lama Buddhism. The stairs up to the red wall are so steep that sedan chair carriers now do a steady business ferrying visitors to the top.

Within the mammoth red walls is a large square pavilion, now empty of its Buddha statue, but capped with an extraordinary tiled roof gilded bright gold. Many of the buildings, such as the Hall of All Laws Falling into One, are gradually being filled with religious artifacts and Chinese porcelains. The arcades in the red wall contain hundreds of images of the Buddha. But perhaps the strangest of the displays is in the **East Hall (Donggang Zi Dian),** situated beneath the red facade, where images of the Red Hat sect perform "esoteric" rituals under cover of their yellow gowns. Such expressions of sexuality, more common in certain holy places in India, are rarely manifested in the temples of China, although at Chengde there are other examples.

All the temples are open daily from 8am to 5pm. Admission is RMB 20 ($2.40).

A Strange Rock

Standing above the wealth of imperial and religious ruins in Chengde's outdoor museum to the glories of the last dynasty is one of the most peculiar natural monuments in China, **Hammer Rock (Bangchui Shan).** It can be seen atop the distant eastern hills from nearly anywhere in Chengde, a forlorn stone pinnacle jutting straight up from a flat ridge, its base narrower than its rounded top. Its shape was suggestive of another object altogether—one the modest tourism authorities would never suggest—and I was sure it had a more provocative local nickname.

Hammer Rock is connected to a parking lot on the east side of Chengde by hiking trails and a ski lift. I decided to take the ski lift up (RMB 31/$3.90) and walk back down. The lift was a 20-minute ride over quiet hills and valleys where farmers and horsemen tended the fields. At Hammer Rock, the view down into the valley was wide and peaceful, the arc of the eight temples neatly outlined on the lower hills.

Hammer Rock was at the far end of a terrifyingly narrow ledge with sheer dropoffs on either side. Moreover, it was teeming with visitors and no railings or path had been provided. One misstep or shove could be fatal. The 60-foot monolith was barely 10 feet wide at its base, and at its base everyone gathered for a moment and touched the rock. I inched my way across the flat ledge and touched the rock myself, discovering later that to do so ensured I would live to the age of 130.

The trail back to the valley runs south past another formation, **Toad Rock,** then down through desolate country to the **Temple of Universal**

Joy (Pule Si), built by Emperor Qianlong in 1766 as a place for yet more Mongol envoys to worship while paying their respects to China's ruler. At the rear of this west-facing temple, more active with monks than the Tibetan-style northern complexes, is a round tower, the **Pavilion of the Rising Sun (Xuguang Ge)**, reminiscent of Beijing's Temple of Heaven. The altar holds a Tantric mandala in the form of a cross and a copper Buddha of Happiness. What's being portrayed in this theater is cosmic sexual union, a theme typical of Tantric Buddhism. The Temple of Joy is aligned perfectly with Hammer Rock to the east, and there is something more pagan than divine afoot on these fringes of Chengde.

The stunning temples and the palaces of the Imperial Summer Villa in the valley below are the last grand expression of the power and wealth wielded by China's final imperial dynasty at its height. The Qing Dynasty was little over a century away from complete collapse. Largely emptied of monks and worshippers, the pavilions of Chengde serve delegations of tourists now. The distant China of emperors and envoys has all but vanished.

PRACTICAL INFORMATION

ORIENTATION

Chengde, in northern Hebei Province, is 155 miles northeast of Beijing. Most visitors include the sights of Chengde on an overnight trip from Beijing, often booking a tour from there. April to November, the weather is warm. Winters are too cold for comfortable sightseeing.

GETTING THERE

By Train Chengde is 5 hours by train from Beijing. There are frequent trains connecting Beijing and Chengde, but no commercial airline service.

By Car, Taxi, or Tour Bus The trip takes 3 1/2 hours over an excellent paved highway.

TOURS & STRATAGEMS

China International Tourist Service (CITS) in Chengde has its offices at 6 Nanyuan Dong Lu, next door to the Yunshan Hotel (☎ 0314/202-6827). They arrange day tours, with English-speaking guides, of the Summer Palace grounds and the surrounding temples. CITS in Beijing also offers 2-day bus tours of Chengde with English-speaking guides (☎ 010/6515-8566 in Beijing or check with your Beijing hotel tour desk).

Accompanied by two German students studying Chinese, I hired a taxi from Beijing at a total cost of RMB 1,600 ($195), including all excursions in Chengde and return to Beijing. Lodging, meals, and admissions (RMB 10 to 30/ $1.20 to $3.60 per site) were extra.

WHERE TO STAY

The **Yunshan Hotel,** 6 Nanyuan Dong Lu (☎ 0314/202-6171; fax 0314/202-4551), and the **Chengde Guesthouse for Diplomatic Missions (Waijiao Renyuan Binguan),** Wulie Lu (☎ 0314/202-1970; fax 0314/202-2269), are the two best hotels in town, both 3-star, both modern, and neither fully up to international standards of service and maintenance. Doubles are RMB 420 ($50) at both hotels.

I stayed at the Chengde Guesthouse for Diplomatic Missions on the river, within walking distance of the Summer Palace entrance, and I was reasonably comfortable. The hotel has a business center, beauty parlor, three dining rooms, and a bar, and the rooms are modern, with televisions and clean bathrooms. They were unable to accept credit cards (JCB, MC, V) on weekends, as the bank processing center was closed.

The 2-star **Yurt Holiday Inn (Menggu Bao Fandian),** Wanshu Yuan (☎ 0314/202-3094), is on the Summer Palace grounds, open April to November. It consists of 50 tents (yurts) with televisions, carpets, and private baths. It has a superb location, but the management and facilities need improvement. The cost is RMB 350 ($43) for a yurt.

WHERE TO DINE

The Yunshan Hotel and the Chengde Guesthouse for Diplomatic Missions both have adequate Chinese restaurants with wide-ranging menus in English. Both are inexpensive (RMB 34 to 75/$4 to $9). An American breakfast in the Diplomatic Missions is minimal (instant coffee, thick toast with jam, an oily fried egg), but it is cheap (RMB 12/$1.45).

Local specialties, which include exotic wild game dishes (rabbit, camel, venison, boar), are served at the **Fangyuan Restaurant** (☎ 0314/202-3429), located inside the Imperial Summer Villa, north of the main palace on the west shore of the lake.

I had a cheap, tasty lunch of jiaozi (steamed dumplings) at one of the **cafes** located under the large canvas awning at the entrance to the Small Potala Temple (Putuozongsheng Miao) north of Chengde, where I watched our taxi driver shell and consume a large goose egg with chopsticks without spilling a single morsel.

DATONG: TEMPLE
OF THE "BIG SAME"

大同

D ATONG IS THE COAL FIELD OF
China, a northern outpost on the Mongolian frontier that stood for centuries as the Middle Kingdom's barrier against the barbarians. It is still something of a frontier town, rough-edged and lagging behind China's cities to the south and east, modern cities that Datong still fuels with its coal. Datong's name comes from the phrase in a Tang Dynasty poem that means the "Big Same," and first impressions are of a vast sameness, a desert plateau scorched with coal pits and riddled with slow-moving coal trucks, the air a black sackcloth of dust.

The great tourist attraction is the Yungang Buddhist Caves, carved into the nearby cliffs in the 5th century A.D., but Datong has other historic treasures. The gray streets yield some of the largest temples in China, and the Temple Suspended over the Void makes the forbidding countryside south of Datong worth crossing. At times, Datong was the supreme city in northern China, capital to dynasties that have all but turned to dust, save for a few spectacular monuments.

Temple of the Liao

The remains of Datong's imperial past can be discovered on foot. The streets are those of a city a decade behind the rest of urban China, not notably punctuated by glass-and-steel department stores and international hotel towers, or filled with imported automobiles and motorcycles. The wide avenues carry bicycles and donkey carts. No lawns, few fountains, no sumptuous greenery under blue skies—this is a hard city of a million workers toiling in the basin of a sea of coal. It's hard to believe that Datong once housed the royal palaces of the Northern Wei Dynasty, from A.D. 398 to 493. The Northern Wei were barbarians, Toba people from the northern plains beyond the nearby Great Wall, thought to be of Turkic origin. The Northern Wei abandoned Datong and moved their capital south to Louyang, but Datong would become China's capital again. The Kingdom of the Liao (A.D. 907–1125), consisting of nomadic Khitan people, ruled China until they were overrun here by yet another band of northern invaders, the Jin, ancestors of the Manchu who would one day create China's last imperial dynasty. Out of this chaos of invading northern kingdoms, one great temple has survived in Datong: the Huayan Monastery, ancestral temple of the Liao kings.

Huayan Monastery is west of the old drum tower along Da Xijie in downtown Datong. Several of its halls date from before A.D. 1100, but the complex was finished under the Jin Dynasty 40 years later. Every hall and pavilion faces east, not south as in traditional Chinese constructions— a reflection of the sun-worshipping traditions of the Khitan conquerors.

I walk my way through the heart of Huayan's halls to the main building, one of the two largest Buddhist temples standing in China. Set on a platform of stone 14 feet high, it shatters the horizon. Nine bays wide, its walls are 3 feet thick. The courtyard contains strange altars on pedestals in the shape of dollhouses. These are used to hold scriptures. Inside, it is dark, cool, and spacious. Known as the **Powerful Treasure Hall (Da Xiong Bao Dian),** its centerpiece consists of the Five Buddhas of the Five Directions, some fashioned from wood, some from clay, and all occupying high thrones. They were made during the Ming Dynasty. The ceilings of the great temple are embellished with dragons, flowers, and the Sanskrit alphabet.

Outside, shaven monks in yellow leggings, brown pants, and gray gowns pace the courtyards and cross through the moon gates. Some are old, some very young. A group of senior citizens gathers on the temple steps, a Chinese peasant tour group. They are dressed head to toe in blue Mao uniforms and caps. They carry the cheap black vinyl handbags of the people and mount the stairs using black wooden canes.

It is a remarkable temple, quiet and unassuming, but surviving on a scale rare in modern China. During the Liao and Jin dynasties, Huayan was the central temple of its own school of Buddhism (later known as Kegon Buddhism in Japan). Huayan Buddhism, based on the Garland Sutra, upholds the essential sameness of all things. In keeping with this doctrine, the temple in Datong takes austerity to a high level.

Back in the streets of Datong I overtake handcarts of coal pucks on their way to makeshift sidewalk ovens consisting of loose bricks. At the **Hongqi Market,** I buy soda pop and strawberries from a bicycle cart. Lucky toddlers race around Post Office Square on electric-powered miniature army jeeps and jet fighters, their grandparents running behind them to catch up. The dust is whipping up, and although the sun is shining hot and hard, I feel as if I'm moving through a dirty snowstorm.

I pass by the wooden gate to the **Nine Dragon Screen (Jiu Long Bi),** the city's most famous sight—a ceramic mural 150 feet long portraying nine dragons rising from the sea in pursuit of the sun. It was created in A.D. 1392 as the spirit wall for the mansion of the provincial viceroy,

Zhu Gui, 13th son of the first Ming emperor, but its setting doesn't suit it (a vacant unkempt lot). The Nine Dragon Screen in Beijing is smaller, but its surroundings are far more brilliant.

I turn east down an odorous back street and come out at the entrance to the old city wall. The **Datong city wall** is as old as the famous city wall of Xi'an. A general of the early Ming empire oversaw its construction, of stamped yellow earth, in A.D. 1372. Much of the 4-mile circumference remains, most of it neglected, exposed and subject to erosion. Here, renovation is under way. New stairs lead to the top of a section of the wall that has been freshly bricked in. Sections that haven't are often used by locals as storage cellars, earthen caves dug into the walls of the city.

On the wall is a newly restored eight-sided seven-story brown-brick pagoda, **Yan Tower.** Suspended from its eaves are golden bells with velvety clappers. I inadvertently flush out a pair of Chinese lovers in a secret embrace. All of us are embarrassed. We smile and go in different directions.

The brick soon runs out. The wall reverts to packed earth. I stand on the southeast corner of old Datong. Broken ramparts of a guard tower survive, its archways collapsing. South of the city wall is a uniform housing development a half-mile wide and 15 blocks deep. Each gray-tiled rooftop is punctuated by a half-dozen regularly spaced smokestacks. Touches of life slop over the edges. The rooftops are littered with laundry, logs, sticks of firewood, rolls of sheet metal, tool handles, oil drums, baskets, and a few cats patrolling for rats or scraps.

Back in the hotel, I meet a young clerk who speaks excellent English. She's just graduated from Beijing's top university with a degree in international business, but rather than follow her classmates to the money-cities on the eastern seaboard she has obeyed her parents. They want her close to home, in Datong. This is still the traditional way, although to me it seemed like finishing Harvard, heading home, and landing a job at McDonald's.

She doesn't seem to mind. When she speaks of Datong and its future in China, she beams. She points out that uptown there's some new development now: big modern department stores, a Crocodile boutique, a California Beef Noodle outlet. She laughs when I ask her what locals call the tiny, gleaming red, two-cylinder taxis with long snouts that dart hither and yon through the streets. Rats, she answers. What do people like to eat in Datong? I ask. Dog meat is extremely popular, she says, but quite expensive at RMB 20 ($2.50) per kilogram in the street stalls. She's looking forward to a special graduation dinner of the same at a friend's house. She reveals the secret to cooking dog: Boil it in a pot, she says, but don't forget to throw in one new brick.

She also suggests that I book a tour to the Temple Suspended Over the Void and see something of how the people live in the countryside. Many of them, she says, still live in caves.

Temple Suspended Over the Void

The next morning, I meet our group: taxi driver, guide, and two Austrian geologists who have been working in Xi'an. We travel for 2 hours over the barren rolling hills south of Datong, a plateau of sandstone, coal, and soda ash, a desert shaved down to a stubble. Villages sprout like oases, built of the same dried earth on which they squat. The two vacationing geologists are not impressed with the "Big Sameness" of the landscape.

Forty twisting, bumpy miles later we reach the town of Hunyuan, where concrete and brick replace mud and straw. Ahead is Heng Shan Bei, a high ridge of limestone, parted by the Mouth of the Dragon, the opening in the **Magnet Gorge.** This gorge was bored out in A.D. 397 by a Wei Dynasty emperor and his 10,000 troops to ease passage through the mountains. On its west wall is **Xuan Kong Si,** the Temple Suspended Over the Void. It was constructed in the 6th century by a team of Daoist monks known as the Feathered Scholars, because to reach the heights of the temple fastened to the immense cliff face the builders must have had wings.

The suspended temple is spectacular from a distance. It consists of 40 cave rooms carved into limestone, fronted with wooden facades, columns, and tiled roofs, all connected by a series of catwalks and bridges perched on jutting beams and posts socketed into solid rock. A mountain gazetteer describes the Temple Suspended Over the Void this way: "The Air-Temple is very steep to come up to, without steps. The Temple Tied Up in Emptiness hangs alone in the Gorge of Porcelain and gets scarcely any sunlight. It contains many shrines and is the abode of ox-riding, sword-bearing immortals. Looking over the side, the scene is like a great ocean; only birds can fly over or monkeys climb out."

These days, of course, visitors come to climb up onto the temple. There are concrete steps to its entrance, a toll booth, and the way along the river in the gorge is lined with souvenir stands selling polished rocks and charms. The temple retains much the same form it possessed for centuries. The wooden catwalks and stairways still appear dilapidated and dangerous. Each small cave hall is festooned with a sacred figure or two, most of them fashioned from plaster and brightly painted. The central altar features a shrine to three religions, with statues of Buddha, Lao Zi, and Confucius in a black beard. The temple has been rebuilt many times over 14 centuries. I saw work going on when I first visited in 1991, but the triple-storied main sections of the temple are still pinioned to the rock with simple timbers. A new parking lot and suspension bridge have been completed in the last few years, but the catwalks of the temple still creak as you walk from shrine to shrine. Above me I can make out evidence of earlier cave altars and footholds. In earlier times, I suspect, the Temple Suspended Over the Void sprawled elsewhere, or perhaps hermits pulled up their ladders there as they entered their own cliff-side nests.

Today there's only one monk in attendance, but I do spot the same vendor I saw years ago wearing a green Mao cap and pacing at the entrance, an eagle perched on his shoulder. The eagle is for hire (RMB 5/60¢) if you want a snapshot.

The Temple Suspended Over the Void is dwarfed by a modern shrine of sorts, a dam and reservoir suspended higher yet at the end of the gorge and hidden from view. The temple remains as startling as ever, a fairy castle of yellow tiles and red wooden columns pinned impossibly to a face of rock.

Cave Houses & Coal

We head back on the long winding road to Datong, stopping on the shoulder to visit one of the cave houses dug out of the steep earthen bluffs. The whole family comes out to greet us: grandpa, mom and pop, a toddler dressed in a red embroidered suit and plastic orange thongs. The patriarch is burnt black by the sun. His few remaining teeth are sharp and yellowed. He's occupied the house "only 50 years," he says. The inside of the cave consists of two large curving earthen chambers tamped smooth. The entry room is used for storage. The second room is living quarters for the family. Lighted by a single bare electric bulb and a six-paned glass window, the living room contains a small coal-burning stove in one corner and no running water. Niches have been scraped out of the walls to shelve shoes and clothing and sturdy wicker baskets of empty green bottles awaiting refunds. The walls are decorated with garish posters of pop stars and teen idols, with scrolls, calendars, liquor bottles, and packages of cookies, with bags of rice and bowls of fruit set on a wooden altar under a mirror. The two Austrians snap pictures. The old man rolls a cigarette and lights up. Under the window is a kang, a wide communal bed built of mud and brick, covered by a rattan mat and heated underneath by coal fire.

The cave house is a neat, homey, warm, cheerful abode. Many are two centuries old. Outside, even the family dog has a matching mud dog house, its own semidetached cave. The earthen walls are smooth but flake at my touch. The toddler is selling tiny cloth horses his mother has stuffed and stitched together. I buy two ornaments for a Christmas tree in a land rather far from this place.

The fields are mean here, their plowed furrows dry. The villages are clusters of hand-shaped earth. Ancient earthen signal towers, left over from the Western Wei Dynasty, tower like massive shanks. The camel caravans that might have passed this way have been replaced by ranks of 60-ton double-trailered coal trucks, some of them produced by Steyr, an Austrian joint-venture corporation. All these trucks are as slow as dinosaurs after a feast, limping up the hills at no more than 5 miles per hour. The drivers wear leafy branches around their necks. Whenever they have to stop on the road—breakdowns are frequent—they hang branches from the back and front of their trucks as a warning. Our guide tells us that recently a truck accident caused a traffic logjam that went on for miles and took two days to free up. We are stalled ourselves for 30 minutes when a coal truck up ahead smashes into two tiny coal carts driven by rototillers.

The black trucks stretch across the long escarpments, coated in grease and bent down with chunks of coal. Local road crews, men with bicycles, shovel dirt into the potholes. A woman with two children guards a pile of coal chunks she's gathered along the road. Nearer Datong, there are coal stations, fields with brick shacks where the trucks stop and unload. The coal is sized by hand and restacked. Oxen and donkeys hitched to wooden plows clear rocks from the fields. Nomads on horseback sweep across the valleys between sandstone buttes. The north is a hard region and Datong is a hard city, racked by wind, the air scratchy with coal dust and desert silt, which makes the survival of its imperial temples all the more precious and its future on the frontier all the more indomitable.

PRACTICAL INFORMATION

ORIENTATION

Datong is located between two sections of the Great Wall on a 4,000-foot plain in northern Shanxi Province, 200 miles west of Beijing. The city can be toured on foot if you stay on the southern side, far from the railroad station. To see the Temple Suspended over the Void, however, a guided tour is recommended.

For many visitors, the sole reason to visit Datong is to see the the ancient Buddhist caves carved at **Yungang**, located a few miles north of the city. For a description of the caves, see the separate chapter on Yungang.

Datong is also the gateway to one of the Five Sacred Mountains of China, the northern Daoist peak of **Heng Shan Bei,** a 2-hour drive south of the city. For a description of the mountain, see the separate chapter on Heng Shan Bei.

GETTING THERE

By Train   There is no airport. The express train to Beijing is a pleasant 7-hour journey. Xi'an is 19 hours by rail to the southwest.

TOURS & STRATAGEMS

China International Travel Service (CITS) has efficient offices in the Yungang Hotel and at the train station (☎ 0352/502-2265; fax 0352/502-2046). I used the train station office, managed by Gao Jin Wu, where day tours were easily arranged, train tickets booked, and hotel reservations secured. If you are not intercepted by a CITS employee at the train station, go into the main entrance on the eastern side and turn left; the office is labeled in English.

For RMB 100 ($12) CITS offers a guided tour (with car and driver) to the Temple Suspended over the Void and the Yungang Buddhist Caves, an excellent value. (Lunch and two admissions, a total of RMB 85/$10, are not included.) "Panda Bus Tours" for groups are also available from CITS to the Great Wall and the Steam Train factory for the same price. All tours leave the Yungang Hotel at 8:30am, the train station at 9am.

WHERE TO STAY

The energetic CITS guides are quite likely to pick you up as you come out of the Datong train station and book you a hotel on the spot. Their economy choice is the new 11-story **Fei Tian Hotel** next door, with doubles at RMB 190 ($23). It is already rundown, however, and the location is too far from downtown. Rooms have a view of a large beer factory and two huge brick smokestacks about an arm's length away. The rooms are new and modern, but everything else, from the elevator on up to the 11th floor, dates from the Stalinist era. Strongly insist instead on the Yungang Hotel.

Yungang Hotel (Yungang Binguan). *21 Yingbin Dong Lu.* ☎ *0352/502-1601. Fax 0352/209-0006). 240 rms. TV TEL. RMB 420 ($51) double. JCB, MC, V.* This 2-star monstrosity has a good location, modest but modern facilities, and a few extra services (a business center, two restaurants, a small lobby bar). The Yungang is not a luxury hotel—so there's no pool or turndown service—but the rooms and bathrooms are Western style (although not well maintained) and the television receives some satellite stations. The good news is that this is Datong's best hotel. The bad news is the same.

WHERE TO DINE

The best restaurant in town has no name, but it is on the south side of **Yingbin Xi Lu,** across from the Yungang Hotel (one door west of the glitzy Hongqi Restaurant). You'll recognize it by the Christmas tree lights on the outside and the sparkling clean chairs and tables inside. It's a comfy little cafe with an English menu, run by a helpful young staff. Main courses cost RMB 25 to 42 ($3 to $5). The big **Hongqi Restaurant** next door is more formal and twice as expensive. The Chinese dishes in both restaurants are good.

The **Yungang Hotel** (☎ 0352/502-1601) has its main restaurant off the lobby, the best place to go for a Western fixed-price breakfast. They also serve fairly inexpensive (RMB 34 to 85/$4 to $10) and quite average Chinese lunches and dinners, featuring hot pots and mutton stews.

HARBIN: TIGERS AND ICE
哈尔滨

Harbin, capital of Heilongjiang (Black Dragon River), China's most northerly province, is best known these days for its **Ice Lantern Festival,** a world-famous ice sculpture display held annually each winter. I visited Harbin in late March, however, after the ice had melted, primarily to see Harbin's newest attraction, its Siberia Tiger Park, where 30 of these endangered animals were freely roaming and being trained for eventual release into the wild.

Harbin is a fascinating city even without its tigers and ice. It is located on the endless Manchurian plains, known for its vast stands of forests, among the largest left in the Far East. The province borders the former Soviet Union, with the Black Dragon River (better known by its Russian name, the Amur) serving as the northeastern dividing line between China and Siberia. Harbin was occupied by Japanese forces in 1931, when the region was known as Manchuria, seized by Russian armies in 1945, and retaken by the Chinese with the establishment of the People's Republic of China in 1949.

Daoli Old Town

The Russian influence is still strong in Harbin, especially in the city's unusual architecture. Onion domes outnumber upturned tile-roofed eaves along Harbin's main street even these days, giving Harbin a cityscape unique among China's major cities. Walking down Zhongyang Dajie to the **Songhua River** in the old town, **Daoli District,** a mile's stroll from the Holiday Inn, I passed dozens of these old buildings with their spires and cupolas, now converted to offices, restaurants, and department stores. The street is composed of cobblestones. Several of the side streets are devoted to pedestrian-only outdoor markets. The largest market is on the street labeled **Xi-11-Dao Jie,** unmistakable because of its crowds and the large Russian-style turrets at its entrance. Clothes, food, pine-nut stands, and beggars line both sides of this alleyway.

A number of the Russian facades on Zhongyang Street are being removed, but their modern replacements are tasteful European-style buildings, much in keeping with the old-town atmosphere. One old building worth taking a peek inside is the ironically named **Modern Hotel,** at 89 Zhongyang Dajie, a Russian-style building opened in 1903 whose lobby has been colorfully, if a little shabbily, restored.

On my slow walk down this street in the Chinese city once called "Little Moscow," I also came across a more modern trend: Western commercialization. Amid onion towers, cupolas, and painted plaster columns are a Kentucky Fried Chicken outlet, complete with a white statue of the Colonel, a TCBY cafe, a Playboy logo store, and Bossini and Crocodile boutiques. These signs of Western encroachment are eating into the heart of most Chinese cities, so I was not entirely surprised to find them even in this northern outpost. The leading foreign presence in Harbin remains Russian, however, as it has since Russians began building a train line linking Harbin to Vladivostok in 1896. Later, in 1917, White Russians fleeing the Communist Revolution arrived in Harbin by the thousands, settling in and erecting scores of Russian-style buildings and churches. During the 1930s, half the 200,000 residents of Harbin were Russian. Although most of them left after China's own Communist Revolution in 1949, Harbin is still a major trading post for consumer goods bound to the north. Most of the Russians come to Harbin on business, not for sightseeing, hoping to pick up items that are scarce enough in Siberia to command high prices. Some Russians trade Siberian goods, such as furs, straight across, with no cash exchanged. Harbin is a center of the fur trade, and there are plenty of coat, hat, and stole outlets along the main street, although these are outnumbered by Western wedding salons featuring photo studios and wedding-gown rentals.

Parks & Temples

Harbin has attractions apart from its old town. **Zhaolin Park** is just a long block east of the main street, on Shangzhi Dajie, and even though the ice sculptures had melted into giant ice cubes by late March, it was worth trooping through the spacious grounds with their gardens and rock formations.

The red-brick **Santa Sophia Church** (on Dong Da Zhi Jie) is a splendid edifice, although usually closed to visitors. It is jammed into an area of new construction, most notably several karaoke entertainment complexes with monumental Roman statuary mounted on their garish facades.

Harbin's Confucian Temple, **Wen Miao,** also on Dong Da Zhi Jie in the Nangang District, is worth browsing through (admission RMB 30/ $3.75). The grounds are large, with a dozen pavilions. Golden dragons emblazon the roofs. Although this complex was not built until 1926, the Confucian grounds contain steles (stone tablets), dated A.D. 551 and A.D. 587, as well as three ornate triple-footed gates and one yurt (its purpose I could not determine).

A more interesting complex, the **Temple of Bliss (Jile Si,** admission RMB 6/75¢), is situated at 9 Dong Da Zhi Jie. It contains a small statue of the god Puxian on an elephant, along with the familiar likenesses of Maitreya, Buddha, and Guanyin. A fair number of monks and nuns inhabit this temple, which is in the shadow of the Qiji Futu pagoda. Although built recently, in 1924, this is the largest temple in the entire province. The street outside is one of the livelier I saw, filled with stalls selling golden Buddhas and glass shrines to the faithful.

War Crimes

One afternoon I got up my courage, hired a taxi, and paid a call on the **Exhibition Hall for the Ruins of the Japanese Troops Invading China,** a war crimes exhibit opened in 1982 at the site of a secret germ warfare research center 12 miles south of Harbin. Here, starting in 1939, the Japanese performed unimaginably horrible experiments on citizens (employing frostbite, bomb explosions, biological agents, and surgical procedures), comparable to those conducted in Nazi Germany's concentration camps. Its existence was covered up until the 1980s.

The exhibit, mercifully, is not so horrifying as the crimes. It consists mainly of a few artifacts from the Manchurian occupation, telltale documents, an incinerator smokestack, and a re-creation of a gruesome operation using life-sized wax figures.

Songhua River

It was a relief after a detour through the horrors of the past to return to the cobblestone main street of Harbin and resume my pleasant stroll down to the swift-flowing Songhua River. A 26-mile embankment was constructed along the river after the floods of 1933, and a spacious promenade, now lined with trees and statuary, was developed on the shore. Despite severing relations with Russia in the late 1950s, the promenade retains its original name: **Stalin Park (Jiangpan Gongyuan).**

The most prominent statue is the **Flood Control Monument,** built the year after one of Harbin's most notable floods, which covered the downtown streets in up to 9 feet of water. The monument is now Harbin's popular gathering point for visitors and locals. Vendors circle the monument, selling hot pine nuts and kites in the shapes of birds.

Like Zhongyang Dajie, the Stalin Park promenade is a prime location for a leisurely stroll, fronting the river for miles. In the summer, scores of tour boats of every possible description (including an all-metal enclosed vessel in the shape of a fish with fins) take passengers out on the river or across to **Sun Island (Taiyang Dao).** Fishermen also beach their open boats on the sandy banks and ice-cream vendors ply their trade along the walkway—quite a festive spot when the sun is shining and sailboats are for rent. (In the deep of winter, the river freezes solid—often remaining so for half the year—and ice-skating becomes the rage.)

Tigers of Siberia

The new **Siberia Tiger Park,** opened in 1996, is located across the Songhua River on Sun Island, where a large recreational district is under development, featuring gardens, swimming lakes, cafes, and a hunting range. I hired a car at the Holiday Inn to reach Sun Island via a bridge south of town. Siberia Tiger Park (admission RMB 30/$3.75) has plans to expand into a large preserve with areas for deer, bears, and swans, as well as shops, a fishing pond, a restaurant, and a fairy-tale theme village. At present, only a museum and large fenced tiger reserve are finished. The museum is a dark, uninspiring cavern of a building with photographic displays (captions in Chinese), a motley stuffed tiger with its kittens, and an informational film about the tigers projected on a screen through a very dirty projector lens. While I was trying to make heads-or-tails of the film, a worker was busily sweeping across the wooden floor where the small audience sat, wielding a huge straw broom.

Visitors board a variety of vehicles for an extended drive through the tiger reserve. I was placed on an old bus with sliding windows, filled with Russian teenagers on spring vacation. There was no guide on the bus and no effort was made to keep us from sliding open the unbarred windows during the tour, but there were numerous tigers stalking the grounds. We had plenty of close encounters. At one point, a caged jeep appeared and the gamekeeper placed a live chicken on the roof. One tiger promptly leaped on top and pounced on its prey. The tigers, including some cubs, looked healthy and seemed at ease on the sandy reserve. The Siberia Tiger Park's mission is to save, study, and breed these great cats in captivity and eventually release them into their native habitat. In order to complete this mission, the tigers must be trained to hunt live prey. I should not have been surprised, therefore, when I learned that a few weeks earlier Holiday Inn had donated a live cow to the park. Hotel employees were invited out that day and bused into the reserve to watch the tigers tackle and devour the poor creature, a procedure not likely to be shown to visitors to Western zoos or drive-through safari parks.

But then, Harbin is not like most places in the West—indeed, not much like most places in China.

The Far North

Having reached the northern edge of the Middle Kingdom at Harbin, I was struck by the variety of life, culture, and landscape that China encompasses. Returning to the airport, I passed a dozen magazine-cover photo opportunities: a plethora of donkey and horse carts driven by dark-faced peasants in floppy-eared hats, crude vegetable markets on roadsides, piles of straw heaped high by hand in the flat fields, cold rivers running swiftly through avenues of wiry trees, and, incongruously, clusters of Chinese theme parks awaiting summer visitors with their Castle-Disneyesque, Sino-Rococo, Magic Middle-Kingdom turrets and spires.

These were amusements seemingly at odds with the harsh climate and country life of the Black Dragon province—this once distant Manchuria of tigers and ice.

PRACTICAL INFORMATION

ORIENTATION

Harbin (population 2.5 million) is 860 miles northwest of Beijing in one of the coldest and least urbanized regions of China. Its province, Heilongjiang, shares a border with Siberia. Many visitors come for the ice-carving festival in January, when temperatures are far below freezing, but spring is often a pleasant, sunny season, and in summer the Songhua River comes alive with boat tours and swimmers.

GETTING THERE

By Plane The flight from Beijing to **Yanjiagang International Airport** requires just 90 minutes. A taxi into town is another 40 minutes, but Holiday Inn will provide a transfer in its van if you fax ahead your arrival time—a wise tactic, since taxi drivers often charge foreigners triple the going rate after claiming their meter is "broken." For airport information, call ☎ 0451/364-3475.

By Train The train ride from Beijing is an 18-hour overnight affair through mountains and into the virtual desert lands of Heilongjiang Province.

TOURS & STRATAGEMS

Tours Two tourist offices organize tours, including extended trips through the province: Heilongjiang China International Travel Service (CITS), 95-1 Zhongshan Lu (☎ 0451/230-2601; fax 0451/230-2476), and Harbin Overseas Tourism Company, located in the Harbin Modern Hotel, 89 Zhongyang Dajie (☎ 0451/461-5846; fax 0451/461-4997). Guided tours, as well as air and rail tickets, can also be booked at hotel desks.

Sightseeing on Foot You can walk through the Daoli District and along the Songhua River promenade. The river is a 20-minute walk from the Holiday Inn.

Special Events Two events worth taking in are the celebrated Ice Lantern Festival, officially conducted from January 5 through February (and into early March if the weather stays cold), and the 12-day Harbin Music Festival in July (exact dates vary from year to year).

WHERE TO STAY

Holiday Inn City Centre Harbin (Wanda Jiari Jiudian). *90 Jingwei Lu (downtown).* ☎ *800/465-4329 or 0451/422-6666. Fax 0451/422-1661. 135 rms, 9 suites. A/C MINIBAR TV TEL. $110 double. AE, DC, JCB, MC, V.* Harbin's only 4-star hotel is conveniently located at the downtown end of Zhongyang Dajie, the main street to the river in the old Daoli District. There's an English-speaking staff, a chef from France, and a new general manager who is dedicated to keeping this the best international hotel in Harbin. A local quintet plays light classical music in the lobby each evening.

Services: Room service (6am–midnight), dry cleaning and laundry (next day), nightly turndown, daily maid service, free airport shuttle, foreign exchange counter.

Facilities: In-house movies, health club (exercise machines), sauna, business center, beauty salon, shopping arcade.

Modern Hotel (Madie'er Binguan). *129 Zhongyang Dajie (downtown).* ☎ *0451/661-5846. Fax 0451/461-4997. 160 rms. A/C MINIBAR TV TEL. $80 double. JCB, MC, V.* Superbly located in the heart of Daoli old town, a few blocks from the river, this turn-of-the-century monument to Harbin's Russian past has a lobby right out of *Casablanca.* It was renovated in 1990, achieved 3-star ranking, and raised its prices but not its service level. The rooms are not as well maintained as at the Holiday Inn. The staff speaks some English and is cheerful. Plenty of Russian businesspeople stay here.

WHERE TO DINE

The Holiday Inn's **Phoenix Restaurant** serves the best dim sum and Cantonese dishes in town, and its **Le Petit Coffee Shop** (☎ 0451/422-6666) has an excellent buffet with Western and French dishes. Reservations aren't necessary. Main courses cost $5 to $14; the buffet is $12. Ice-cream desserts at Le Petit are quite good.

The **Gloria Inn Hotel**, 257 Zhongyang Dajie (☎ 0451/463-8855), just a block from the Songhua River, has an elegant street-level dining room with an international buffet and one of the largest hamburgers I've ever been served (although I wondered halfway through if it were really beef).

Across the street from the Gloria Inn is a new locally run **Hanns Burger** joint, and across the street from the Modern Hotel is the **Huamei Western Restaurant** (142 Zhongyang Dajie), which serves the best Russian dishes in town, with main courses running about RMB 100 ($12).

Local restaurants often specialize in Muslim dishes or wild game, and their quality and price are usually announced by the number of red lanterns suspended from the rafters outside (I've counted up to 10 of these at one site).

For American fast food with peppery seasoning, try the big **Kentucky Fried Chicken** on Zhongyang Dajie at Xi-7-Dao Jie, which is better than the similar **Brownie's Chicken** (a Canadian chain) on Shangzhi Dajie, opposite Zhaolin Park. Expect to pay the same prices you pay outside of China.

QINGDAO: GREEN ISLAND ON THE YELLOW SEA

青岛

QINGDAO, A PORT CITY ON THE Yellow Sea in southeast Shandong Province, is internationally famous for the beer brewed there (spelled *Tsingtao;* it's one of China's leading exports). This is ironic, since the great brewery for some reason is not open for public tours. Instead, Qingdao lures its visitors to its summertime beaches, some of the best in China. For foreign travelers, however, the beaches are hardly a special treat. Rather, it is Qingdao's legacy as a German concession that makes the city worth seeing. Large sections of Qingdao retain whole neighborhoods of turn-of-the-century Western architecture, adjacent to traditional and modern Chinese development— a mixture that makes this hilly and green city on the coast an invigorating refuge from the noisy, polluted, often ugly modern metropolises. The presence of old Western residences and tree-lined avenues in Qingdao are startling and surprising and there's no equivalent in the West: no large boroughs of Chinese temples and tile-roofed shop houses in downtown London or Vienna.

German Town

I headed immediately for the greatest concentration of Qingdao's German legacy, the **Badaguan District** on Taiping Bay near Beach Number 2. A sign in English on Zhengyangguan Lu (the same street called Zhanshan Da Lu as it continues east) directs visitors south into lovely, quiet lanes, each planted with a different tree or flower. There's a maple lane, peach lane, and snow-pine lane, each fronted by Western mansions and landscaped lawns—so westernized, in fact, that it closely resembles an upper-class neighborhood on Lake Geneva. The grand houses with their spacious yards and gardens also reminded me of those at Pebble Beach. A number of these old estates have become exclusive summer beach resorts for workers and party bosses of the government agencies and companies that now own them. Many of the houses are rented out as vacation villas. The Badaguan Hotel, at 19 Shanhaiguan, began as a

German hotel in 1903, was expanded by the Spanish and Japanese in the 1920s, and became a Chinese hotel in 1953. Its main building dates from 1988.

The largest structure in Badaguan is right on the coastline. This **palace** was once the German governor's lodge, an immense castlelike fortress of stone, now open to visitors. Beneath its wall is a rugged beach.

Qingdao's German influence began in 1897, when Kaiser Wilhelm annexed portions of the city and developed it as a railway terminus, deepwater port, and naval station. The brewery went up in 1903. The Germans controlled Qingdao until 1914, when it fell to the Japanese, and the Japanese occupied Qingdao until 1922, when the Chinese regained it.

The Pier

From Badaguan it's easy enough to walk down to the **Number 1 Beach**, Qingdao's longest, and its strip of wooden beach houses and changing rooms. From there, I continued west along the white sands through Lu Xun Park toward **Beach Number 6** (the beaches are not numbered in geographical order). This is the location of Qingdao's harbor landmark, **Qianhai Zhangqiao Pier,** which extends 1,300 feet into the bay to **Huilan Ge,** an eight-sided pavilion. Dating from 1891 and expanded in 1931, it remains the prime gathering point for locals, visitors, and a tidal wave of vendors hawking ice cream, shells, pearls, and photographs. The beachfront by the Pier is rocky, and plenty of people comb those rocks for edible seafood and plants. Overlooking this beach is an esplanade that after dark becomes a lively strolling area for locals. Even here, the pace of life is far more relaxed than in most Chinese cities.

Two Churches

Directly north from the Pier is Zhongshan Lu, Qingdao's main street that now rips through a rapidly modernizing downtown of new department stores, small boutiques, and a mixture of old and new shops, some selling designer-name fashions and Swiss watches. I stopped for lunch at one of many hole-in-the-wall cafes and ordered the local hot pot, as well as clams, bite-sized octopuses, and a 6-inch-wide crab. (The price tab was a bit steep; the crab alone was RMB 35/$4.20.)

Back on the big avenue, I followed Zhongshan Lu north until I could see the **Catholic church (Tianzhu Jiaotong),** located up a steep cobblestone lane to the east. This large stone edifice with its two towering spires was built by the Germans. Still quite active with Chinese worshippers, it is closed to visitors except on Sunday during services. The surrounding streets are lined with German concession buildings, their black iron balconies draped in drying laundry.

East of city center, at the entrance to Xinhao Park, is the **Protestant Church (Jidu Jiaotong),** easy to identify from its high clock tower, which still keeps time. Both of the big churches come into splendid view, along with the red-roofed Western neighborhoods and white-sand harbor beaches, from the top of **Xinhao (Marker) Hill,** a steep trek up from the Protestant church. On the peak are three domes in the shape of mushrooms, stuffed with vendors and panoramic viewpoints.

Mao Slept Here

The most curious treasure in **Xinhao Park,** however, is down toward the harbor on its grassy flanks—a magnificent residence built for the German governor in 1903. This mansion has been converted into a hotel, the **Qingdao Welcome Guest House,** located at 26 Longshan Lu (☎ 0532/286-1985)—also called the Safety Hotel—and its interiors are a museum of the high life enjoyed by colonials during the days of the Qingdao Concession. The stained glass, dark woods, and plush furnishings have survived, perhaps because Chairman Mao and Premier Zhou En-Lai met here in 1957, and Chairman Mao and his wife occupied one of the suites for a month. You can rent the Chairman Mao suite today for RMB 1,600 ($192) a night (although it is a little musty and the bathroom facilities are old). A Chinese family occupying the suite invited me in for a look. They proudly showed off Chairman Mao's green felt-top desk and revealed that it contained a hidden compartment in the right-hand drawer. The hotel's lobby and dining rooms are the original living rooms and dining halls of the mansion, with carved woods, massive chandeliers, and velvet curtains still intact. A German grand piano, built in 1876, occupies one corner of this immense chamber.

A favorite park among locals is **Little Fish Hill (Xiaoyushan),** a short walk south of the mansion. The three-story pagoda (Lanchao Ge) on its peak is stocked with souvenir salesmen and offers an unfettered view of Badaguan to the east and the Pier to the west. This pavilion was once used as a marine observation post. It's a quiet place to survey a quiet seaside city, although beyond its Western neighborhoods, hilly parks, and broad beaches Qingdao is a modern industrial city, China's fourth busiest shipping port, and site of many foreign joint-ventures, especially the factories financed by German and Korean corporations.

Sea Mountain

Next to Qingdao's beaches, which swell with upward of 100,000 vacationers in the summer, the most popular outdoor attraction is **Mt. Lao (Lao Shan),** about 25 miles directly east along the rocky coastline of the Yellow Sea. The highway to Lao Shan runs by one of Qingdao's newest attractions, its **International Beer City,** which is seldom open except for Qingdao's International Beer Festival. The festival begins its 2-week run on August 12, and the grounds host one of the biggest beer gardens outside of Bavaria, supplemented by fireworks, beach volleyball, motorcycle races, sailing and swimming competitions, beer-drinking contests, and whatever else the local promoters can dream up.

The coastal highway is charming any time of year. Stone cutting is a large industry here, where granite dominates the landscape. The Lao mountains rise abruptly to 3,000 feet from the white-boulder shoreline. A trail of stone stairs leads to the peaks (or you can hitch a ride on the chairlift). The path is steep but quite scenic, with increasingly dazzling views down empty abysses to the tiny fishing villages below. The vendors specialize in strings of pearls, the product of those fishing villages, with prices under $5. (The price drops further the higher you hike.) Another popular trailside commodity is a package of three sea treasures: a dried turtle, a tiny "sea-dragon" eel, and a seahorse. Lao Shan mineral water, the most famous in China and the basic ingredient in Tsingtao beer, originates in springs of the Lao mountains, where there were once 72 Daoist temples.

There are still a few temples in these mountains. In Daoist legends, this is the home of the Eight Immortals, who could fly with the clouds. Qin Shi Huang, the first emperor of unified China, is reputed to have visited here more than two thousand years ago in search of the elusive potion of immortality. His visit is commemorated in the sprawling Taiqing Temple, a Song Dynasty complex spread across the cliffs on the eastern shore of the mountain range.

A Temple by the Sea

Lacking time to make a comprehensive trek of this vast sea mountain park, I contented myself with a climb up to **Peach Peak** (along the chairlift line) and then a descent to the **Xiaqinggong Temple,** located on the southern beachfront. This complex, consisting of three temples and courtyards, was established in 14 B.C. and rebuilt during the Song Dynasty 900 years ago. The western temple, **Sanhuang Hall,** contains a copy inscribed in stone of Genghis Khan's edict of A.D. 1271 calling for the protection of Daoist culture. The courtyards are home to ancient cypress trees. There's also a **statue** of the ever-popular Guanyin, Goddess of Mercy, who the locals tell me has the face of a woman but the body of a man. When I asked why, I was told that the goddess was really a man but took on the face of a woman to show a compassionate face to petitioners.

The seaside temple is surrounded by ancient specimens of elms and cypress, a bamboo field, cafes, shops with sea turtle shells, and a parking lot. A few monks wander about, but I doubt this is a vigorous Daoist temple these days. Certainly it is overrun with Chinese visitors in the summer, and money-making has become a major religion.

I returned to the city and to the Badaguan District for a farewell stroll one afternoon in the late spring, finding it the quietest neighborhood I'd ever encountered in China, a green island of parks, beaches, and architecture—if not an elixir of immortality, certainly an ingredient.

PRACTICAL INFORMATION

ORIENTATION

Qingdao, located in southeast Shandong Province on the Yellow Sea, is one of China's best-known seaside resorts. It was occupied by the Germans in 1897, and its architecture still bears a remarkably foreign stamp. In the summer, Qingdao is crowded with Chinese visitors. The rest of the year, it is a quiet retreat, with mild days and plenty of sunshine.

GETTING THERE

By Plane   The airport is 21 miles north of the city. Airport taxis charge up to RMB 150 ($19) for the trip. Dragonair, with an office in the Grand Regency Hotel, 1 Taiwan Lu (☎ 0532/589-6809), has service between Hong Kong and Qingdao. Air tickets on regional airlines can be booked from hotel service desks; there is service between Qingdao and many Chinese cities, including Beijing and Shanghai.

By Train There is a direct but slow overnight train from Shanghai and an express train from Beijing (which nonetheless consumes 18 hours), but the most reasonable way to reach Qingdao is by plane.

By Ship Overnight ferries connect Qingdao to Dalian and Shanghai, at prices comparable to train travel (about $40), but this service usually operates only from May to October.

GETTING AROUND

The city can be toured on foot, but taking a taxi to and from hotels is a good idea. Taxis within Qingdao should charge about RMB 10 ($1.20) per ride. Inexpensive minibuses link the Qingdao train station (on Tai'an Lu, north of Beach Number 6) with Lao Shan scenic spots. Show the driver where you want to go on a map if you don't speak Chinese.

TOURS & STRATAGEMS

Tours Qingdao Overseas Tourist Corporation, located at the Huiquan Dynasty Hotel, 9 Nanhai Lu (☎ 0532/286-1513; fax 0532/287-0983), can sometimes be persuaded to put together special tours for independent travelers, particularly if you have three or four people. This is about the only way to get inside the Tsingtao Brewery and do some beer tasting. Hotel tour desks can offer more convenient tour options. The tourist hot line number is ☎ 0532/387-5345.

Special Events Among annual events, there's the Qingdao International Beer Festival, August 12 to 26, which coincides with a "Love of the Sea" carnival and a city arts fair. During the summer, several hundred thousand Chinese tourists head for the Qingdao beaches daily, considerably altering this island of tranquility.

WHERE TO STAY

Gloria Inn. *21 Donghai Lu.* ☎ *0532/387-8855. Fax 0532/386-4640. 238 rms. A/C MINIBAR TV TEL. $125 double. AE, DC, JCB, MC, V.* This sparkling 3-star hotel opened in 1995. It is a block closer to the sea than the Shangri-La, but its view is blocked by seaside apartments. The rooms are spacious, bright, and well maintained. The business center in the lobby is efficient. While it lacks the swimming pool and other features of 4- and 5-star hotels, it is far better managed and maintained than most 3-star hotels in China.

Haitian Hotel. *39 Zhanshan Da Lu.* ☎ *0532/387-1888. Fax 0532/387-1777. 641 rms. A/C MINIBAR TV TEL.* $175 double. AE, DC, JCB, MC, V. Renovated in 1994, this massive 4-star, 15-story, two-building edifice east of the Badaguan District is a favorite of expatriates. Service is good, as is maintenance. In terms of facilities, it ranks between the Shangri-La and the Gloria Inn, and it is closer to downtown Qingdao and the beaches.

Services: Concierge, room service (24-hour), dry cleaning and laundry (next day), nightly turndown, daily maid service, foreign exchange counter.

Facilities: In-house movies, pool (outdoor, heated), health club (exercise machines, classes), sauna, tennis courts (two), bowling, business center

(24-hour), tour desk, beauty salon, shopping arcade, newsstand.

Shangri-La Hotel Qingdao. *9 Zhanliugan Lu.* ☎ *800/942-5050 or 0532/ 388-3838. Fax 0532/388-6868. 477 rms, 25 suites. A/C MINIBAR TV TEL. $160 double. AE, DC, JCB, MC, V.* Qingdao's newest hotel, opened last summer, is its best. There are 101 executive-floor rooms and two handicapped rooms, all luxuriously appointed with desks and electronic safes. The location is east of downtown and the German quarter, about a 40-minute walk along the sea. There's also a German pub off the lobby.

Services: Concierge, room service (24-hour), dry cleaning and laundry (24-hour, same day) nightly tourndown, daily maid service, express checkout, foreign exchange counter.

Facilities: In-house movies, pool (indoor, heated), health club (exercise machines, classes), Jacuzzi, sauna, tennis courts (two), business center (24-hour, conference rooms), tour desk, beauty salon, shopping arcade, newsstand.

WHERE TO DINE

Qingdao, being a beach town, is renowned for its seafood. To sample the catch, prepared in Cantonese style, one of the best spots is the Hsin Kuang, 19 Zhanshan Da Lu, on the eastern edge of the Badaguan District. There's an extensive menu in English, the dining room has a touch of elegance (linen tablecloths), and the prices are moderate to fairly expensive (RMB 100–200/$12.50– $25 per person, depending on what's ordered).

Probably the best meal I sampled in Qingdao was lunch at the new **Korea Town** restaurant, located a mile east of the Shangri-La Hotel on Zhanshan Da Lu. Again, the prices are fairly expensive (RMB 85 to 250/$10 to $30), but the Korean and Chinese dishes, cooked on grills at the table, are superb.

The **House of Sichuan,** on the sixth floor of the Gloria Inn Hotel, is a cheery setting for a fine chile-laced dinner buffet ($12).

Chinese specialties and local dishes are exquisite at the very expensive Shang Palace restaurant in the Shangri-La Hotel.

The best venue for cocktails is the lounge bar at the Haitian Hotel (in the western building) with a breathtaking view of the sea.

GREAT CITIES
OF THE SOUTHEAST

都市

Hong Kong: The Dragon That Never Sleeps

香港

On July 1, 1997, China resumed sovereignty over its richest, most cosmopolitan city, the former Crown Colony of Hong Kong. Britain had claimed the island of Hong Kong in 1841 after defeating China in the First Opium War and later extended its claim to the Kowloon peninsula, but China never recognized Britain's rule. The return of Hong Kong set off massive celebrations on the mainland.

Now known officially as the **Hong Kong Special Administrative Region (SAR),** Hong Kong was assured a high degree of autonomy for 50 years after the handover. Indeed, few changes will be obvious to visitors. Hong Kong is still an international city, vibrant and brash. It is by far the richest, most sophisticated city in China, the one place where East and West meet on confident, familiar footings.

For Westerners Hong Kong has long been the gateway to China, to its culture as well as to its mainland cities, and it is still the best arrival point for China travelers—a dramatic, fascinating decompression chamber for the journey from the West to the East.

Hong Kong is one of the most beautiful big cities in Asia. The harbor, pinched between Hong Kong Island (officially called Victoria) and the southern peninsula (Kowloon), is the focal point of the city. Day or night, the harbor view is dramatic. As soon as I arrive in Hong Kong, I set out for the Waterfront Promenade that skirts the Kowloon shore (immediately east of the Star Ferry concourse). The skyline of Hong Kong Island, scaling the heights of steep hillsides, is among the most magnificent in the world, rivaled only by that of New York City—and at night, no urban center in the world can match the skyscraping lights of Hong Kong Island for sheer breathtaking beauty.

The green-and-white **Star Ferry fleet** has been crossing the harbor since 1898, and it constitutes one of the cheapest sightseeing thrills in the world. For HK 2.20 (30¢) you can ride on the upper deck in either direction (daily 6:30am to 11:30pm). Take a seat on a hardwood bench as

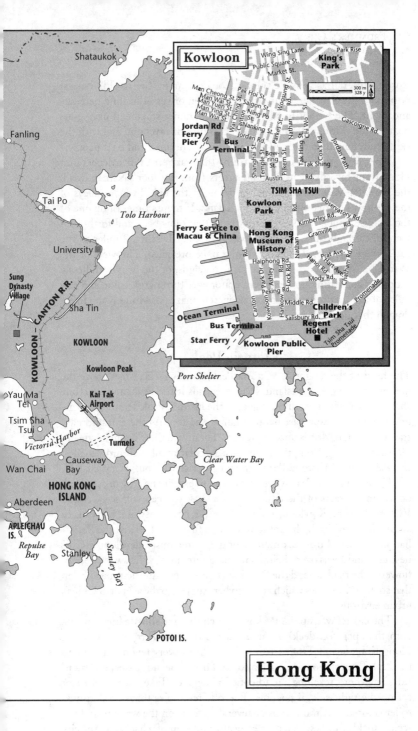

Kowloon

Wing Sing Lane
Park Rise
King's Park
Public Square St.
Market St.
Woosung Rd.
Man Cheong St.
Pak Hoi St.
Saigon St.
Man Wai St.
Nanking St.
Man Yuen St.
Ning Po St.
Man Ying St.
Nanking St.
Man Wui St.
Pilkem St.
Nathan
Tak Hing St.
Chi Wo St.
Gascoigne Rd.
Jordan Rd.
Ferry Pier
Bus Terminal
Jordan Rd.
Jordan Path
Bow-ring St.
Tak Shing
Cox's Rd.
Shanghai St.
Temple St.
Austin Rd.
TSIM SHA TSUI
Kowloon Park
Observatory Rd.
Kimberley Rd.
Hong Kong Museum of History
Granville Rd.
Ferry Service to Macau & China
Nathan
Prat Ave.
Hart Ave.
Haiphong Rd.
Hanoi Rd.
Park Dr.
Ashley Rd.
Lock Rd.
Mody Rd.
Chatham Rd. S.
Peking Rd.
Promenade
Canton Rd.
Kowloon
Hankow Rd.
Middle Rd.
Ocean Terminal
Salisbury Rd.
Children's Park
Bus Terminal
Regent Hotel
Star Ferry
Kowloon Public Pier
Tsim Sha Tsui Promenade

300 m
328 y

Shataukok

Fanling

Tai Po

Tolo Harbour

University

CANTON R.R.

Sung Dynasty Village

Sha Tin

KOWLOON

Kowloon Peak

Port Shelter

Yau Ma Tei

Kai Tak Airport

Tsim Sha Tsui

Victoria Harbor

Tunnels

Clear Water Bay

Wan Chai

Causeway Bay

HONG KONG ISLAND

Aberdeen

APLEICHAU IS.

Repulse Bay

Stanley

Stanley Bay

POTOI IS.

Hong Kong

close to the rail as possible. Hong Kong is among the world's busiest ports, and the Star Ferry cuts across a thicket of vessels calling here day and night. The harbor bristles with the container ships and navy gunboats of the world, with the luxury yachts of Asia's tycoons, and with the skiffs and unpainted junks of Hong Kong's fishermen and boat people.

After walking the harbor and riding the Star Ferry, I dive deeper into Hong Kong by walking its 24-hour streets, from Kowloon's Nathan Road, the "Golden Mile" of duty-free shopping, to the uphill vendor alleys of the Central District on Hong Kong Island. If there's time, I hop one of the historic double-decker electric trams that plow back and forth from Central through the once-notorious Wan Chai District, 2 miles to the east, where the world of Suzie Wong once prevailed. The view of the Wan Chai shop houses and massive neon signs, of the people endlessly shopping and eating in the streets, epitomizes the energy, color, and raw pulse of life that rolls through the concrete mazes of Hong Kong like a dragon that never sleeps.

Victoria Peak

The head of the dragon is Victoria Peak, looming 1,817 feet above the harbor on Hong Kong Island. Everyone calls it the Peak, and everyone should take a trip to its summit aboard the historic **Peak Tram**. The panorama unfolds like a vast painted fan at the top. As the extraordinary travel writer Jan Morris once confessed, "For myself there is still no greater pleasure of Hong Kong than the most familiar of all such promenades: the walk around Victoria Peak, crowning massif of Hong Kong Island."

I head up to the Peak whenever I need to escape the crowded, humid, odoriferous streets of the city. From the Peak you can still see Central, Victoria Harbor, Kowloon, and the New Territories beyond, but you see all this from the high, distant remove. The first time I visited the Peak, I had just returned from six months of living in a dusty, developing Chinese city, and I was overwhelmed first and foremost by the sweet scent of flowers. The road around the Peak is a botanical paradise, a tropical Eden that soothes the senses which are elsewhere subject to the assault of China's urban environs.

The easiest way up the Peak is to catch the **free shuttle bus** (the one with the open top deck), located outside the Star Ferry concourse on Hong Kong Island. From 10am to 8pm it runs every few minutes up to the Peak Tram station on Garden Road. This is one of the steepest "train" rides anywhere, reaching a gradient of 55 degrees. Take a seat in the rear car on the right side, if possible. The ride resembles that of a dignified roller coaster. The tram stops at several stations on the way up, and the scene quickly opens wider, the perspective tilts out of whack, and the city and the harbor fall back downhill as if kidnapped by a landslide. The tram covers the quarter-mile ascent in 8 minutes, but the ride seems to take longer and the rise appears to be nearly straight up. The Tram operates 7am to midnight daily. Tickets are HK 15 ($2) one-way, HK 23 ($3) round-trip.

The lovely polished wooden cars on today's tram are new versions of the cars that began making this curious, neck-breaking climb in 1888 when two gentlemen named Kyrie and Hughes launched the steampowered High Level Tramway, Asia's first cable railway. The Peak was home to the wealthy and off-limits to others in earlier days. There are still mansions on the top of Victoria Peak, but there's also shopping. You can go nowhere in Hong Kong without the specter of shopping. The tram loads and unloads inside the new **Peak Tower** (1997), which is stuffed with shops and with cafes, delis, and even a Ripley's Believe It or Not! "Odditorium." On the noncommercial side, there are also viewing terraces facing Central, the harbor, and Kowloon to the north. When the fog rolls over the edge of the ridge spines, this classic view of Hong Kong, the favorite of a million postcards, takes on a brooding, primordial face.

The path running clockwise around the Peak begins across the street from here, at Harlech Road on the left. Harlech Road, closed to motor traffic, flows into Lugard Road partway around the Peak. The walkway is wide, paved, and flat. I usually walk it in under an hour, even with a dozen stops to admire the views. The vegetation is lush. The broad-leafed woodland that coats the hills and ridges in deep greens, however, is a result of deliberate planting. The Peak, like the whole island, was largely barren rock when the British first arrived.

Now the Peak is a garden of blooms, hillside waterfalls, butterflies, and black-eared kites streaking from the heights of nature into the creases of the city canyons below. Circling the Peak yields long views over the other side of Hong Kong Island, down the deep jungle valleys that plunge into the blue-water harbors of Aberdeen, Stanley, and Repulse Bay on the south side of the island.

One day I decided to walk down to **Aberdeen** from the Peak. I could see the town—famous for its seafood, its massive floating restaurants, and the boat people who lived on junks sheltered in its harbor—and I had a map showing a walking trail to Aberdeen. I located a signpost on the road by Peak Tower. A hiker's guide suggested that I could reach Aberdeen in 45 minutes. I headed down the path, disappearing into the high bamboo grasses. The walk ended up taking me better than 2 hours, but I did manage to keep from getting lost, always heading southward and downward when the dirt trail split.

The views were lovely, of course, but the human settlements interested me more. I passed through several squatters' villages with their shacks pulled together from construction site discards. I also came across one of the largest Chinese cemeteries I'd ever seen, not far above Aberdeen. The stone chairside graves, to which pictures of the deceased are often attached in bronze frames, were swept clean of leaves here, their urns decorated with fresh flowers. I felt ready for the grave myself, as the humidity was nearing the 100% mark that afternoon, but I managed to walk through the last clearing into Aberdeen. It could have been much more challenging, of course, as I realized when I glanced over my shoulder. A true hill walker would have reversed my course, climbing from Aberdeen back up to the Peak, which from below looked as remote as the summit of a lost world.

Shop-Walking in Kowloon

The Kowloon side of Hong Kong on the north side of the harbor is where millions go to shop and eat. They all seem to be here at once. **Nathan Road,** four blocks east of the Star Ferry concourse, is the main thoroughfare on the peninsula, a Golden Mile of shops that stretches far more than a mile these days. The streets and alleys parallel to and intersecting Nathan Road house still more tiny duty-free outlets. They all hawk the merchandise Hong Kong is famous for: cameras and jade, clothing and computers, luggage and furs, toys and watches. Even if you're not a shopper in the least, you can't escape the bug here. It starts out as a twitch in the throat, pretty soon there's a coughing fit, and the next day you've caught a full-fledged case of shopping fever. Window-shopping spreads to price-comparing and ends in a purchase you didn't know you were going to make. My own weakness is luggage. If I could travel to Hong Kong without a suitcase or pack, I would do so, because I could pick up three useful pieces here for the price of one overseas.

An absolute delight in **Tsimshatsui** (pronounced "chim-shaw-choy"), the district that covers the southwest Kowloon shopping district, is the landmark **Peninsula Hotel,** one of the grand old dames of Asian accommodations, and after seven decades still one of the top 10 hotels in the world. The lobby, recently refurbished, defines the word *elegance* in the East. I never pass up a quick walk through the Peninsula. The columns are trimmed in gold, high tea looks quite grand, and the stringed orchestra seems to play from the mezzanine day and night. If you're in shorts or sandals, don't linger. You'll be politely booted out.

The shopping arcade in the basement of the Peninsula isn't as fussy about dress codes, but its outlets are equally elegant—and the prices soar even higher than high tea upstairs. This is the arcade to seek out if your tastes are for the designer names—Gucci, Tiffany, or Armani.

Kowloon also contains the top location for a celebratory drink—not in the stately Peninsula but down on the harbor promenade in its modern competitor, the Regent Hotel. The lobby lounge, with its wall of glass at water level, frames the Hong Kong skyline like an immense, glittering, ever-changing mural of neon, salt water, and steel.

The streets of Kowloon are devoted to little else than shopping. One soon becomes familiar with the street stores, the Chinese arts-and-crafts stores, the huge arcades that burrow into high-rises like caves. The **New World Shopping Centre** on the Waterfront Promenade and the **Ocean Galleries** due north of Star Ferry are the most extensive retail malls, good places to go for air-conditioning, window-shopping, and other pastimes while credit cards heal themselves and revive.

The most sensible way to break this ritual of maniacal "shop-walking" is to make a detour at Kowloon Park.

Kowloon Park

I had been visiting Hong Kong for 10 years before I actually set foot inside this quiet green zone. At 35 acres, Kowloon Park is not on the scale of New York's Central Park, but it is a fine refuge tucked into the heart of a frantic city. You can enter Kowloon Park at its east gate (on Nathan Road, just north of the Mosque), at its northwest gate (via the Canton Road pedestrian overpass), or at its south gate (on Haiphong Road, a block west of the Mosque, across from the Kangaroo Pub). The grounds contain waterfalls, bird ponds, a flock of pink flamingos, an outdoor sculpture garden, a Chinese classical garden (not the best I've seen), several sculpted outdoor swimming pools (and an Olympic-sized indoor facility), a totem pole from Canada, a kiosk from McDonald's, and a history museum that should not be missed.

The **Hong Kong Museum of History** is housed in the British Army's former Whitfield Barracks. Open 10am to 6pm Tuesday through Saturday and 1 to 6pm Sunday and holidays, the museum exacts a mere HK 10 ($1.30) for adults, HK 5 (65¢) for children and seniors, and is free on Wednesday. Its visual history of Hong Kong, arranged chronologically, creates a lasting outline. Hands-on, walk-through displays include a sailing junk, turn-of-the-century downtown street with offices, opium den, and Chinese pharmacy with the original cabinets and instruments in place. Luckily, nothing's for sale in this reconstruction of the past. Otherwise the museum would be as overrun as the streets of Kowloon.

Going Hollywood

Hong Kong Island has its shopping routes, too. The best window-shopping is along **Hollywood Road** and **Cat Street,** where much of China's retail trade in antiques is conducted. From the Star Ferry concourse in Central, walk straight uptown a few blocks and turn right (west) on Queen's Road Central. Keep an eye out on your left (uphill) for **Li Yuen streets** east and west (just past D'Aguilar Street). These are Hong Kong's best-known fabric alleys, narrow lanes that are stuffed on both sides with sheds of bargain silks, cottons, and upholsteries. On one pass through here I noticed that a large number of cats were being kept in the stalls to control the rodents at night. There were many stray cats as well, all of them looking far too thin. I was about to buy some cat food at a corner grocery when I noticed one draper preparing a large communal dinner of fish scraps. She set it down on the sidewalk where the gang of local cats, expecting their daily pay, quickly devoured this pile of leftovers.

If you walk three blocks farther west to **Jubilee Street,** you can hook up with the world's longest outdoor escalator and have a free ride uphill. This escalator is worth its own coffee-table book, as it passes over plenty of chaotically compelling intersections while transporting legions of businesspeople and striking characters.

Dismount at **Hollywood Road** and follow it west. There are junk shops and antique shops along this twisting street, the latter with show windows that look like museum displays of dynastic treasures, with prices to match. The furniture stores, with their blackwood and rosewood pieces, are particularly tempting, although free shipping to your home is not included.

Man Mo Temple

Keep on Hollywood Road until you reach Man Mo Temple, at the corner of **Ladder Street** (a stone staircase where the rich were once escalated up and down in sedan chairs on the shoulders of coolies). Man, the god of literature, and Mo, the god of war, preside over this temple. Quite simply, Man Mo is my favorite temple in China.

Man Mo Temple is rundown inside and out. It's a working temple of the sort that once held sway over China's daily affairs. Inside, the hall is not spacious, but it is packed with monks, local worshippers, and the thickest clouds of incense I've ever struggled to part. The wooden chairs on display on one side of the hall were once used to carry the statues of the Man Mo Temple gods in street processions. These were probably the most important gods in town at one time, since Man Mo Temple was for many years Hong Kong's civic and cultural center for the Chinese community.

Incense spirals hang heavily from the ceiling like coiled chandeliers. These fragrant dragons can burn for a month, their pungent smoke petitioning heaven for health and wealth. I've never been in here but that a steady stream of worshippers isn't crowding inside as well, adding their own burning sticks to the blackening flames. Outside, in the tiny courtyard on Hollywood Road, two old beggar women scurry about, keeping an eye on the sacks containing their worldly possessions. Man Mo Temple has become their street home.

Immediately below Man Mo is Cat Street (Lascar Row), once a notorious strip of brothels, gambling dens, and boardinghouses for seamen. Today it's a flea market, stuffed with fascinating bric-a-brac, from Qing Dynasty coins to opium pipes. It was a few blocks from here, in a small cafe at the top of one of the ladderlike vendors' alleys, that I spotted the actor Jeremy Irons, in town to make a film about Hong Kong's return to China, sitting tall and alone at a simple table, his thoughts far afield.

Temple Street Night Market

Hong Kong's chief night market stretches for better than a mile up **Temple Street** on the Kowloon side. Take the subway to the Jordan Street stop, walk four blocks west from Nathan Road (starting at the Yue Hwa Department Store), and turn right up Temple Street. Every day from dusk to midnight and beyond, Temple Street is an open mall of wall-to-wall vendors offering cut-rate designer jeans and shirts, leather handbags, fake "copy" watches, and whatever's hottest in the toy factories and electronics plants of southern China.

The real action is five or six blocks up Temple Street, where Chinese opera singers come out and perform popular selections in relaxed but highly spirited performances. It's always interesting to watch the men in the audience, sitting on chairs, smoking and eating and gabbing, singing along, clapping fervently, and passing the hat.

A block north of the opera stalls, in the courtyard of a small temple, there are rows of palm readers and fortune-tellers employing birds, cards, turtle shells, old coins, and other props to divine the future of strangers. The tools of their trade are spread out on the sidewalk or placed on card tables under the light of kerosene lamps. Palm readers analyze palms for HK 154 ($20), discuss a client's fate for HK 231 ($30), and lay out a whole life's story for HK 308 ($40). Fortune-tellers use songbirds from Vietnam and mainland China to answer whatever question you pose. They pass your question on telepathically to the bird, and the bird in turn pops out of its cage, selecting a card from a deck. The fortune-teller then interprets what the card says in answer to your question. The performance can cost HK 77 to HK 231 ($10 to $20).

My favorite Temple Street character has long been a streetside dentist who treats toothaches on the spot without benefit of painkillers. I've watched him work for hours hunched down over patients sitting on the dark curbside filling their cavities, attaching stainless steel, ceramic, and gold crowns, and relining false teeth (in 1 hour). He heats his tools over a flame, but he uses no drill to fill cavities. His prices tend to be ten times less than those charged in the West, but then Temple Street is a low overhead operation, small business elevated to the level of performance art.

Stanley

Clear around Hong Kong Island on its southeast side is Stanley, an ancient fishing village once known for its pirates, now known for its designer-clothing market. This is a longstanding tourist stop, so the prices may not be the lowest in Hong Kong, but the selection of name-brand fashions, linens, sports shoes, swimsuits, porcelains, and souvenirs is extensive. Despite its "touristy" reputation, I never fail to enjoy a morning or afternoon in Stanley.

Part of my enjoyment is getting to Stanley. At **Exchange Square bus terminus,** just west of the Star Ferry concourse in Central, I find the 6A or 6X air-conditioned double-decker bus, drop my HK 8 ($1.10) fare in the collection box, grab a seat upstairs, and brace myself. This is one of the most catapulting bus rides in China. Everyone drives on the left side, of course, and everyone drives at the fastest speed possible through the narrowest streets imaginable, and there's no bigger vehicle on the road than this tall bus, which seems to be hurtling up and down the tight switchbacks like a heat-seeking missile. The steep hillsides that are cemented in place all over Hong Kong Island whiz by, clearing the bus windows by inches. After 30 minutes of this amusement ride, you are probably fully accustomed to Hong Kong driving, and as the seaside scenery becomes more and more Mediterranean, you soon arrive at the village of Stanley.

The **Stanley market,** which consists of about 200 covered stalls, is across the street from the bus stop and down the hill toward the beach. At the bottom of the hill, the market splits into two sections, running left and right along the shore. I often explore the left side first, then head back to the end of the western section. Beyond there, a block of trendy bars and grills has recently sprung up, with sidewalk drinking and wonderful continental lunches and dinners with a view of Stanley beach and the sea.

As for shopping, I usually return from Stanley with a few cheap "designer-label" polo shirts (under HK 77/$10), a half-dozen "silk" ties (HK 15 to 23/$2 to $3 each), sometimes some "hand-embroidered" linen tablecloths, and enough "handmade" souvenirs—that are probably handmade in mainland China—to stuff a few dozen Christmas stockings. Occasionally, I pick up the Christmas stockings at Stanley market as well.

Stanley's secret attraction—the squatters' village west of the market, where pigs once were slopped in an ingenious pen fed by a labyrinth of pipes—has been leveled to make way for a massive modern apartment, office, and shopping complex. There are still some brightly painted, hand-built fishing boats on Stanley Beach, but the fishermen have been moved south and east into new low-rise row houses.

The future of Stanley will continue to be shopping, it seems, even after a massive edifice from the past is moved into the village. By the end of 1998, the historic **Murray House,** built in 1844 in downtown Hong Kong and dismantled brick by brick in 1982 to make way for the Bank of China Tower, is slated to open in Stanley—not as a museum, of course, but as a shopping gallery composed of a Chinese department store, souvenir shops, coffeehouses, and delis, and a suitably historic pub.

Aberdeen

Also on the south side of Hong Kong Island is the port of Aberdeen, another old fishing village. Its protected harbor is home to hundreds of people who live on their boats. Catch bus 70 at the Exchange Square bus terminal, a few blocks west of the Star Ferry concourse in Central. The HK 4.50 (60¢) trip takes about 25 minutes. On the piers opposite Aberdeen Centre there are numerous sampan ladies who will practically haul you off the seawall to put you aboard their motorized tour of Aberdeen's waterborne village. If you decide you want a ride with one of the sampan ladies, you'll have to bargain them down to a decent fare (half of what they're asking).

For a no-hassles tour of the flotilla, look for the **Watertours dock,** where the price is set and the driver speaks some English. A tour gives a close-up look at life on the water and inside the junks, most of which have their own color televisions.

The massive floating restaurants in Aberdeen harbor provide free ferries from their docks. You can poke around the culinary barges and head back without a meal, but if you're hungry try a few dim sum (steamed pastries). **Jumbo** is the largest and best of the floating restaurants, open daily from 7:30am to 11:30pm (☎ 852/2553-9111). Its decor is out-and-out, screaming-dynasty, garish red-and-gold carved dragons and cranes (with several thousand painted paper lanterns thrown up to the ceiling for good measure). Jumbo's food is rather high priced and not Hong Kong's best, but it's all good enough for one happy meal.

Before leaving Jumbo, check out the seafood tanks on the lower deck, where hundreds of specimens are enjoying their last swims. The last time I checked, the tanks were posted with a warning in English that rather mysteriously read, PLEASE DON'T DISTURB THE SEAFOOD.

The Walled City

One of the least visited and most fascinating historic sites in Hong Kong is the **Kowloon Walled City Park.** Governed by neither China nor Great Britain, the old Walled City of Kowloon spent most of this century as a lawless no-man's land within walking distance of Hong Kong's Kai Tak International Airport. In 1898, when the Chinese leased the Kowloon peninsula to the British for 99 years, they retained jurisdiction over this tiny 7-acre city-fort, whether by design or through a slip of the mapmaker's brush, no one knows. The next year, British soldiers entered the Walled

City, ostensibly to quell civil unrest, and evicted the 500 Chinese troops stationed there. But the British never established their authority over the Walled City, nor did the Chinese ever relinquish their claim.

The Walled City became a dark sanctuary, sucking in petty criminals, illegal aliens, opium addicts, prostitutes, those on the run, and those too poor to go anywhere else. By the time the Japanese occupied Hong Kong in 1941, the Walled City was a shambles. The Japanese pulled down the walls and used them to extend the airstrip along the harbor (at what became Kai Tak Airport).

At the end of World War II, squatters suddenly poured into the remains of the Walled City. By the 1970s, the Walled City consisted of a supertenement, 12 to 14 stories high. It grew organically. Some 350 buildings went up and each one fused with its neighbor, creating a rabbit warren of interlinked hallways.

Inside this tenement fortress, subject to no building regulations or fire codes, illegal enterprises flourished with impunity. Not all the enterprises were nefarious. Dentists, doctors, and lawyers practiced without licenses, charged rock-bottom rates, and built up a large outside clientele. Well through the 1980s much of the dim sum baked in Hong Kong came from basement ovens inside the Walled City.

I once did a walking tour of the Walled City after it was finally slated for demolition in the early 1990s. Inside was a dark labyrinth. Electricity, water (artesian wells with water pipes connected to rooftop holding tanks), and sewage (trenches) had all been jury-rigged by private developers who charged tenants for their services. The interconnected hallways were a maze for rats and humans alike. Hundreds of rusted crisscrossed pipes and bare copper wires, supporting in their webs an unspeakable mass of wet garbage, paper wrappings, plastic bags, and rotting food scraps, had been strung overhead in the narrow space between buildings.

Hong Kong conducted an unannounced census of the Walled City on January 14, 1987, turning up 33,000 residents in 8,300 premises. There were nearly 1,000 businesses, primarily food processors, plastic fabricators, and carpentry shops. On the outside perimeter, 150 unlicensed doctors and dentists maintained busy shop fronts. Residents were for the most part very poor, and many were engaged in or were the victims of crime. The Walled City was home for 20 years to an extraordinary Englishwoman named Jackie Pullinger, who lived among the residents, seeking to rehabilitate the drug addicts. Later, she launched assistance programs for residents suffering from AIDS.

The walls of this 7-acre tenement started tumbling down on March 23, 1993, when the first bulldozers arrived. The next year construction of a park and classical garden began on the site. Kowloon Walled City Park opened on December 22, 1995, in a ceremony presided over by the last British governor of the colony, the Rt. Hon. Christopher Patten.

This is one of the more interesting, least-visited parks in Hong Kong. Take bus 1 (fare HK 4.40/60¢) from the Star Ferry concourse in Kowloon, a 35-minute ride up Nathan Road and east on Boundary Street. Disembark at the second stop on Tung Street, at the northeast corner of the park. The park is surrounded by a wall in the style of an earlier fortification built by the Qing government in 1843. The eight complimentary landscape sectors inside the walls are also derived from Qing Dynasty models.

The Kowloon Walled City Park should be entered from the old south gate. The foundations of the original south gate and two stone plaques bearing the characters for "South Gate" and "Kowloon Walled City" were discovered here in 1994, in the excavation pit to the right of the entrance. The only historical building still standing is the Yamen, a courtyard complex at the center of the park that served as the military command. Relics, including two old cannons, and photographs of the evolution of the old Walled City from fortress to tenement are exhibited here. In one courtyard there is a stone monument honoring Jackie Pullinger for her decades of charitable work.

Frequented by neighborhood Chinese—mostly grandparents and grandchildren spending time together—the Walled City has been transformed yet again, this time into Hong Kong's loveliest classic garden, with graceful pavilions, long, covered corridors, garden ponds, and goldfish streams that seem to flow out of an antique century.

The Pink Dolphin

Hong Kong's most beautiful marine animal is also its most endangered—the pink dolphin (*Sousa chinensis*). No more than 150 remain in Hong Kong waters, and their delicate habitat is both increasingly polluted and gradually diminishing. You can still see these rare creatures by booking passage on a Dolphinwatch cruise, the best water tour in Hong Kong.

Dolphinwatch sails the waters between massive **Lantau Island** (home of the new Chek Lap Kok Airport) and the New Territories (near the ports of Tuen Mun and Castle Peak), an hour northwest of Hong Kong harbor. The scenery is fascinating enough to justify a day's cruise, but the goal is to spot the elusive, shy pink dolphins at sea, usually in groups of half a dozen, breaking the surface and then diving in search of a meal. The dolphins feed over a wide area, some of it concentrated in the new **Sha Chau and Lung Kwu Chau Marine Park,** a 5-square-mile sector of seawater north of the airport. This "dolphin sanctuary" is subject to the drainage of the Pearl River, which carries much of the sewage and industrial waste of southern China. The new airport has also destroyed portions of the pink dolphin's coastline, and even within the new "sanctuary," gill-netting, dredging, and the off-loading of oil tankers go on unabated.

The number of pink dolphins is in steady decline as a result, and Hong Kong's commitment to wildlife conservation and environmental protection is notably and traditionally unenthusiastic. Nonetheless, the pink dolphin continues to swim freely in these dangerous waters.

On my first cruise, after scanning the waters for more than an hour, we spotted a dozen pink dolphins sporting in the waters in front of the Castle Peak Power Station. We spent 2 hours circling the group. Adult dolphins are 3¹/₂ to 8 feet in length. They are a dazzling comic-strip pink. No one knows quite why they are this fabulous color. The infants, who stick close to their parents, are nearly black, the distinctive blush tones emerging only as they mature.

Pink dolphins were first reported in the waters of southern China in the 7th century during the Tang Dynasty, and they were first sighted by Western travelers in 1637. Without a guide, you'd probably never know that there was a single dolphin pod in these busy waters. This is the most beautiful species of dolphins I've ever seen but also the shiest of the dashing sea animals that Melville called "the lads that always live before the winds."

On selected weekdays (usually Monday, Wednesday, and Friday), **Dolphinwatch cruises** take groups of up to 25 on a chartered cabin cruiser, providing maps, postcards, souvenirs, drinks, and a fine catered lunch along the way. A researcher—often founder Bill Leverett—delivers commentary in English and endeavors to find pods of pink dolphins. The dolphins often surface quite close to the craft, making for spectacular sightings and photos. On Sunday, Dolphinwatch offers a cruise on a much larger two-deck ship. Lunch is taken in a local cafe in the quaint town of Tai O during a stopover on Lantau Island. I prefer the intimacy and longer time at sea aboard the weekday cabin cruiser, but since Sunday is such an impossibly crowded day to sightsee anywhere in Hong Kong, a Dolphinwatch cruise is a weekend adventure hard to match.

To find out the current schedule, ask at the **Hong Kong Tourist Association (HKTA)** office at the Star Ferry terminal in Kowloon or, better yet, contact Dolphinwatch directly (☎ 852/2984-1414; fax 852/2984-7799). Tickets are usually sold in advance at the Splendid Tours desk in the lobby of the Sheraton Hotel, 20 Nathan Road, Kowloon. Tickets for the 7-hour cruise with lunch cost HK 400 ($50).

Cheung Chau Island

Three of Hong Kong's 230 outlying islands—Lantau, Lamma, and Cheung Chau—are served by hourly passenger ferries from piers in the Central District. The 60-minute cruise is a delight, and so are the islands, which offer a restorative escape from the big city. The best getaway is Cheung Chau Island, 7 miles west of Hong Kong, an old fishing village without cars, its harbor teeming with sampans and junks.

Cheung Chau is a chapter out of Old China. Home to seafarers and pirates, occupying just 1 square mile, it has an active waterfront, lively markets, a traditional village, and white-sand beaches where windsurfing is world-class. The ferry from Hong Kong pulls into the western harbor and docks at the **Praya,** the waterfront promenade that is lined with vibrant pink and blue buildings, their ornate balconies suggesting a Mediterranean port. You can walk directly through the old village and across the island to the eastern beaches in just 10 minutes, but the scenic route first leads north (to your left) along the Praya.

The Praya is filled with cafes and food stalls selling hot noodles and shrimp dumpling (wonton) soups. The harbor is packed with rows of junks. These are the homes of Cheung Chau's water people, who live and fish from their floating houses. About 3,000 of the island's 23,000 people live year-round on the water.

If you walk north and west to the end of the beach road, you come to the **dry docks** where large **junks** are still being framed and planked by hand, built in the time-honored manner by craftsmen who keep no blueprints but retain entire designs in their memories. They don't mind if you stop in at their tin-roofed sheds to have a look. Even at its birth, a junk is a gorgeous vessel, its horizontal planks curving in golden stripes from a remarkably high stern to a broad bow, each piece of the puzzle shaped and laid in place perfectly, with room left in the seams for the wood to expand as it cures.

About five blocks from the pier, you'll see the **Pak Tai Temple** on your right, just past the community basketball court. Pak Tai is the god of the sea, the great protector of seafarers, and still highly revered on Cheung Chau. The temple was built in 1786. It welcomes visitors. Inside, Pak Tai is wearing a golden crown. His reign over the sea is symbolized by the snake and turtle pinned under his feet. An iron sword from the Song Dynasty (A.D. 960–1279) is ensconced beside the temple altar. During the Bun Festival (held every spring on dates determined at the last minute by village elders), Tai Pak and the sword are carried into the courtyard in a century-old sedan chair to preside over the celebrations. The side halls of the small temple are worth inspecting, too. Carvings of the Green Dragon and the White Tiger are enshrined here.

From the temple, cut through the village. The lanes are narrow. The shops and cafes frequently contain bedrooms and offices upstairs. This is an old-fashioned Chinese town. Family clans and trade guilds have survived intact. There are several street shrines to the Earth god, incense always burning on their stone shelves. Many of the island's elders, dressed in long vests and leaning on wooden canes, stop every day to pray. One of the shrine inscriptions reads, "If your heart is warm, you will be blessed in old age."

The east side of the island is another world, designed for leisure and water sports. **Coral Beach (Kwun Yum Wan)** and **Morning Beach (Tung Wan)** were the venues for a local islander, Lee Lai Shan, to perfect her windsurfing skills. She went on to become the first and only Hong Kong citizen to win an Olympic gold medal. Heading down the beach, past the six-story Warwick Hotel, the lower beach road leads out to a rock carving from the Bronze Age. These geometric patterns were etched into the sea rocks of Cheung Chau about 3,000 years ago by primitive boat people whose name and fate are lost to history.

If you decide to stay a night or two on Cheung Chau (at either the **Warwick Hotel** (☎ 852/2981-0081; fax 852/2981-9174) or one of the vacation villas the touts on the Praya recommend), you'll have time to explore the more distant temples, cemeteries, and sea rocks on the large southern half of the island. You'll also have time to climb to the viewpoint at the end of the beach road on the northeastern tip of Cheung Chau. HKTA sells a **"Cheung Chau Walking Tour"** booklet keyed to a useful map of the little island (HK 35/$5).

From the Warwick Hotel it's a short walk back across the hourglass waist of the island to the Praya. The village of Cheung Chau is densely clogged with old shop houses, fish counters, Chinese pharmacies, bakeries, herbalist stalls, incense shops, bamboo hat stores, mahjong gambling dens, and plenty of curio shops, pubs, and cafes. The fresh shrimp is absolutely superb here. Any cafe will steam up a plateful—you won't even need a sauce.

After staying out on Cheung Chau a few days once, I found it increasingly difficult to return to Hong Kong. The pace of life on this island of Old China becomes mesmerizing. As night falls, the Praya is ignited by electric lights, lanterns, and candles. The catch of the day sizzles on sidewalk tables. Everyone comes down to the Praya. The old women of Cheung Chau, their bare feet up on benches, exchange the day's gossip. Children race by helter-skelter on their bikes. Grandfathers bring their prized songbirds out to show, hanging the bamboo cages on a tree branch or lantern post. Cats and dogs patrol the streets. Cheung Chau fully becomes a Chinese village—what Hong Kong must have been generations ago before it became a British colony, an international moneymaking machine, and finally China's gateway to the future.

PRACTICAL INFORMATION

ORIENTATION

Hong Kong is now a **Special Administrative Region (SAR)** of the People's Republic of China, but there have been virtually no changes affecting foreign visitors. Most regulations and institutions from the days of British rule remain intact. Visitors from the West will feel more at home in Hong Kong than in any other Chinese city.

The majority of Hong Kong's 6.3 million citizens speak Cantonese (the southern Chinese dialect), many speak English, and many more are learning Mandarin (*putonghua,* the official spoken language of China). Signs are frequently in English, and shopkeepers and waiters often speak some English. Shopping and eating choices are also manifold for foreigners in Hong Kong. The standard of living is roughly 10 times higher in Hong Kong than on the mainland. The city is international and cosmopolitan, the economy capitalistic, the retail sector subject to few duties; at the same time, it is a Chinese community, with the full flavor of that culture.

Most of the urban population is collected along the northern shore of Hong Kong Island and across the harbor on the southern tip of Kowloon peninsula. Hotels and shopping are concentrated in Tsimshatsui (TST) on the Kowloon side and in Central, Admiralty, Wan Chai, and Causeway Bay on the island. The island is connected to Kowloon by the Star Ferry system, the underground subway (MTR), and a highway tunnel. Transportation is highly efficient and inexpensive.

Located at the southeast tip of mainland China, Hong Kong is warm year-round. Summer months (June, July, August) are uncomfortably hot and humid, winters cool and cloudy, making April, May, October, and November prime months to visit.

ENTRY REQUIREMENTS

Travelers are under the same visa requirements as in the past. American visitors, for example, can visit Hong Kong for 30 days without procuring a visa. Travel into mainland China does require the purchase of a visa, as in the past.

MONEY

Hong Kong maintains its own currency system. Rates are pegged to the American dollar, at about HK 7.7 to US $1 (HK $1 = US 13¢). When you arrive, it is useful to convert a few dollars (or RMB) to Hong Kong dollars at the airport banks. Hong Kong has an exchange counter on nearly every corner, but the better rates are given by major banks in Kowloon and Central.

GETTING THERE

By Plane   The new airport at Chek Lap Kok on the outlying island of Lantau in the South China Sea is connected to Kowloon and Hong Kong Island's Central District by the Mass Transit Railway (MTR), a 25-minute ride. Taxis, airport buses, and hotel shuttles and limousines also make the transfer into downtown Hong Kong via the Tsing Ma Bridge, the world's longest road and rail suspension bridge.

Hong Kong is served by most of the world's major airlines. United Airlines (☎ 800/538-2929) has daily flights from San Francisco (nonstop), Los Angeles (nonstop), New York, Chicago, Atlanta, Boston, Miami, Denver, Houston, Detroit, Philadelphia, Seattle, Washington, D.C., and many other American cities. The main United Airlines office in Hong Kong is on the 29th floor of Gloucester Tower in the Landmark Building, 11

Pedder Street, Central, a few blocks north of the Star Ferry concourse (☎ 852/2810-4888).

Dragonair provides the best service between Hong Kong and mainland Chinese cities, including Beijing (2 hours 45 minutes), Chengdu (2 hours 30 minutes), Chongqing (2 hours 15 minutes), Guilin (1 hour), Hangzhou (2 hours), Kunming (2 hours), Qingdao (3 hours), Shanghai (2 hours), Xiamen (1 hour), and Xi'an (2 hours 30 minutes). Dragonair's ticketing office is at 20 Pedder Street, Room 601–603 in the Wheelock House, Central (☎ 800/233-2742 or 852/2868-6777).

Hotels can book tickets on international and domestic airlines (including Chinese airlines) and provide transfers to the airport.

By Train   There are several direct trains daily to Guangzhou (Canton) leaving from the Hung Hom Railway Station in East Tsimshatsui (Kowloon). The 3-hour trip costs HK 250 ($32) and tickets can be booked at CTS (see below) or the train station. There is a new luxury 29-hour overnight train from Kowloon Station to Beijing (Train 97 departing from Hong Kong to Beijing, Train 98 returning from Beijing to Hong Kong), priced at $92 to $155 (HK 707 to 1,192), depending on the sleeper class. An equivalent 29-hour overnight service to Shanghai (Train 99 departing from Hong Kong, Train 100 returning), is priced at $81 to $135 (HK 623 to 1,038), depending on sleeper class.

By Ship   From the China Hong Kong ferry terminal (six blocks up Canton Road from the Star Ferry concourse in Tsimshatsui, Kowloon), there are many options, including the overnight ship or 3-hour jet boat to Guangzhou (Canton) and multiple-night voyages on clean but basic passenger liners to Xiamen and Shanghai, at about half the ticket price of air flights. Book tickets at the ferry terminal, hotels, or China Travel Service (see "Visitor Information").

GETTING AROUND

By Subway   For transportation in Hong Kong, I rely upon the subway system, the Mass Transit Railway (MTR). It is clean and fast. All stops are announced in English. The MTR operates throughout Kowloon and Hong Kong Island from 6am to 1am. Buy a stored value ticket (in most stations) for convenience in getting through the turnstiles. They are sold in denominations of HK 70 ($9), HK 100 ($12.50), and HK 200 ($25). Fares range from HK 4 (55¢) to HK 12.50 ($1.70) per trip, depending on the distance traveled.

By Taxi   Taxis are inexpensive (HK 77 to 31/$2 to $4), but not all drivers understand English. Tip with leftover change.

By Ferry   The Star Ferries, operating from 6:30am to 11:30pm (HK 2.20/30¢), are a superb way to cross the harbor, and the electric trams, which operate from 6am to 1am (HK 1.60/20¢), are the scenic way to go east or west along the shore of Hong Kong Island.

TOURS & STRATAGEMS

Tours   The Hong Kong Tourist Association (HKTA) makes touring a breeze. Their offices are staffed with helpful English-speaking personnel, a library of sightseeing brochures, and free copies of that indispensable visitors' bible, the monthly *Official Hong Kong Guide,* which covers nearly everything you need to know, from where to shop to where to eat. The HKTA office at the Star Ferry concourse on the Kowloon side is open 8am to 6pm weekdays, 9am to 5pm weekends. The HKTA office in Shop 8, Basement, Jardine House, 1 Connaught Place, Central (two blocks south of the Star Ferry concourse on Hong Kong Island), is open 9am to 6pm weekdays, 9am to 1pm Saturday, and closed Sunday. HKTA maintains a multilingual information hot line 8am to 6pm weekdays, 9am to 5pm weekends (☎ 852/ 2807-6177).

HKTA also operates some of the best specialized tours in Hong Kong, including a horseracing tour, a heritage tour of a walled village, a "family insight tour" focusing on a day in the life of an ordinary Hong Kong resident, and a 6-hour "Land Between Tour" of the New Territories north of Kowloon. Tours cost from HK 308 to HK 385 ($40 to $50) per person; some include lunch. Book all these tours at either the HKTA office or at your hotel tour desk.

HKTA also serves as broker for other tour operators. I recently took the "Cheung Chau and Islands Hopping Tour," organized by Watertours, a 4-hour voyage to Cheung Chau Island with a stop at Silvermine Bay on Lantau Island. HKTA sold the tickets (HK 240/$32), and the tour was fully professional.

Visitor Information   For China travel arrangements, including visa purchase, transportation, hotels, and package tours, I use the state-run China Travel Service (CTS), 27–33 Nathan Road, Kowloon (one floor up in the Alpha House, which is actually a few steps west off Nathan Road, down Peking Road; ☎ 852/2315-7149; fax 852/2721-7757). CTS has always handled my requests efficiently and inexpensively. I've booked air flights, hotel rooms, and visas to China. CTS also provides quick passport/visa photo service.

WHERE TO STAY

Hong Kong has more than a dozen 5-star international hotels, representing many of the world's hotel chains. Several of the hotels have achieved legendary status, including the Peninsula in Kowloon and the Mandarin Oriental in Central. The high property values continue to drive hotel rates sky-high, so the only rooms that remain at the moderate-to-inexpensive level are quite slummy. A double in the YMCA can now cost at least $135 a night, a top hotel room with a harbor view three times that and more. Below are my recommendations.

Island Shangri-La. *Pacific Place, Supreme Court Road, Central (above the Pacific Place Shopping Center at Admiralty MTR stop).* ☎ *800/942-5050 or 852/2877-3838. Fax 852/2521-8742. 531 rms, 34 suites. A/C MINIBAR TV TEL. $360 double. AE, DC, JCB, MC, V.* Tallest hotel in Hong Kong, the Island combines European luxury and design with Oriental touches,

such as the 18-story atrium draped with a 150-foot 250-panel silk mural of China's classic landscapes. The lobby, restaurants, health club, pool, and ballrooms occupy the podium (levels 5 to 8); the guest rooms are on levels 39 to 55; and the Restaurant Petrus is on the top floor (56). The rooms, the largest on Hong Kong Island, have an old- world elegance, not to mention Austrian crystal chandeliers and marble-top writing desks. The Library (on level 39) is a dream room of classic European design with its own concierge, where you can browse through or borrow books, magazines, and periodicals from the two-story shelves or stick around for high tea (3–5:30pm).

Services: Concierge, room service (24-hour), dry cleaning and laundry (24-hour, same day), newspaper delivery, nightly turndown, twice-daily maid service, express checkout, foreign exchange counter.

Facilities: In-house movies, lap pool (indoor, heated), health club (exercise machines, classes), Jacuzzi, sauna, business center (24-hour, conference rooms), tour desk, beauty salon, shopping arcade, newsstand, clinic (24-hour), florist.

Kowloon Shangri-La. *64 Mody Road, Kowloon (on the harbor, 15-minute walk from Star Ferry concourse).* ☎ *800/942-5050 or 852/2721-2111. Fax 852/2723-8686. 689 rms, 34 suites. A/C MINIBAR TV TEL. $310 double. AE, DC, JCB, MC, V.* With one of the best waterfront views in Hong Kong, this luxury hotel has white marble from its lobby to its bathrooms. The restaurants, health club, and business center rate among Hong Kong's very best. On the nonsmoking floor (11) even the room attendants are nonsmokers. All rooms come with safes, coffeemakers, and hair dryers. I like it here because the service is attentive, the view of the harbor uninterrupted, and the location quiet.

Services: Concierge, room service (24-hour), dry cleaning and laundry (24-hour, same day), newspaper delivery, nightly turndown, twice-daily maid service, express checkout, foreign exchange counter.

Facilities: In-house movies, pool (indoor, heated), health club (exercise machines, classes), Jacuzzi, sauna, business center (24-hour, conference rooms), tour desk, beauty salon, shopping arcade, newsstand, clinic (24-hour), florist.

Marco Polo. *Harbour City, Kowloon (in the Harbour City shopping center adjacent to the Star Ferry concourse).* ☎ *800/843-6664 or 852/2113-0888. Fax 852/2113-0022. 384 rms, 56 suites. A/C MINIBAR TV TEL. $235 double. AE, DC, JCB, MC, V.* Convenience and elegance are bywords at the three Marco Polo hotels in Hong Kong, all located in the Harbour City shopping complex (Hong Kong's largest). Formerly known as Omni hotels, the three Marco Polos are Hong Kong–owned 4-star properties—which is to say

5-star hotels in any other city. The 16-story Marco Polo Hotel, Hong Kong, couldn't be closer to the action in Kowloon. Its spacious rooms come with large writing desks, hair dryers, coffeemakers, and safes. The Marco Polo's two sisters stand shoulder to shoulder in Harbour City. The 17-story Prince (☎ 852/2113-1888; fax 852/2113-0066), one block to the north, is the same price, but includes 44 executive-floor rooms (Continental Club), while the 18-story Hongkong Hotel (☎ 852/2113-0088; fax 852/2113-0011), one block to the south, is the upscale sibling (rooms start about $50 higher), with harbor-view rooms ($350 double) and the outdoor heated swimming pool shared with her two sisters. All three Marco Polo "shopping center" hotels look brand spanking new and are superbly run.

Salisbury YMCA. *41 Salisbury Road, Kowloon (next door to the Peninsula Hotel, three blocks east of the Star Ferry).* ☎ *852/2369-2211. Fax 852/2739-9315. 380 rms. A/C MINIBAR TV TEL. $135 double, $24 dorm bed. AE, DC, JCB, MC, V.* Superb location and clean, well-appointed rooms, room safes, and coffeemakers—this is one of the world's most deluxe Y's and the best deal in the midprice range. It is often booked up several months in advance. Guests have access to the Y's two indoor swimming pools, fitness center, squash courts, tour desk, bookshop, and hair salon. There's even a concierge. The Mall Cafe off the lobby is a pleasant bargain cafeteria with fixed-price breakfasts, lunches, and dinners (under $10), but guests can also order room service from 7am to 11pm. While the service, food, and amenities aren't the equal of those at the Shangri-La or Marco Polo, the price is a half or a third. The dorm rooms (two bunk beds, separate storage closets) are same-sex, four to a compartment, and far cleaner than hostels and dorms elsewhere in Hong Kong.

Bargain Choices   There are no cheap lodgings that are decent in Hong Kong. I recently stayed at **Chungking House,** Block A, fourth and fifth floors (☎ 852/ 2366-5362; fax 852/2721-3570), in the notorious Chungking Mansion, 40 Nathan Road, Kowloon, the most "deluxe" of the dozens of hostels and guesthouses wedged into this 16-story tenement. The room was spacious but rundown, rife with cockroaches, for whose company I paid nearly $50 a night. The elevator, the back stairs, and the tout-ridden lobby of Chungking Mansion must be negotiated to be believed.

Cleaner rooms are available a block up Nathan Road in Mirador Mansion (56–58 Nathan Road) at the **Man Hing Lung Guesthouse** in Flat F2 on the 14th floor (☎ 852/2311-8807; fax 852/ 2311-6669). The price is about the same. The drawback is room size: These are the smallest doubles imaginable, with narrow bathrooms that become instant stand-up showers. There's no closet. Two friends of mine actually succeeded in doing their laundry in the room's wastebasket. They liked the place, by the way, finding it clean and economical. There are those who like Chungking Mansion, too. Unfortunately, Hong Kong is the last place to visit if you want to save money on accommodations. There are far better cheap places to stay in Tokyo or Vienna.

WHERE TO DINE

In Hong Kong, eating is nearly as important as breathing. Hong Kong people routinely spend far more of their income on dining than do people in other cities. The competition this spawns results in some of the best restaurants in the world, ranging from elegant and expensive Chinese seafood emporiums with views of the harbor to single-table street stalls frequented by connoisseurs of regional cuisines. Hong Kong's choice of Western and Asian restaurants is also considerable. You could stay a month in Hong Kong without chewing a single bite of Chinese chow. This listing indicates a few of my reliable favorites in various categories.

East Ocean Seafood Restaurant. *25 Harbour Road, Wan Chai (3rd floor, Harbour Centre Building).* ☎ *852/2827-8887. Reservations recommended. Fixed-price meals HK 77–192 ($10–$25). AE, DC, JCB, MC, V. Mon–Sat 11am–midnight, Sun 10am–midnight. CANTONESE.* Try the fixed-price meals for some extraordinary mergings of old Cantonese and new California cooking. The entrees are light and fresh, the service stylish, the earth-tone decor upbeat. This is Cantonese with tasty Western twists.

Green View Noodle Shop. *Basement 1, New World Shopping Centre, Tsimshatsui (east of Star Ferry concourse, between the Waterfront Promenade and Salisbury Road).* ☎ *852/2369-0470. No reservations. Main courses HK 35–92 ($4.50–$12). No credit cards. Daily 7:30am–11pm. CHINESE FAST FOOD.* This is the ultimate Hong Kong fast-food cafe, my favorite for almost 10 years now. The service is quick and precise. You are seated with a glass of hot tea, a saucer of fried peanuts, and a clean set of chopsticks. The decor is McDonald's East: columns tiled in green bamboo, toadstool benches, marble tables. A laughing Buddha of a chef throws together noodle plates behind a wall of glass. The English–Chinese noodle menu is a mile long. The braised e-fu noodles are good, the Singapore-style vermicelli even better. The food at the Green View Noodle Shop is fast, filling, cheap, absolutely delicious, the way fast food should be everywhere.

Luk Yu Tea House. *26 Stanley Street, Central.* ☎ *852/2523-5464. No reservations.*

HK 15–46 ($2–$6) per plate. No credit cards. Daily 7am–6pm. CANTONESE (DIM SUM). More for its history and character than for its food (which is merely above average), this is the place that's the most fun to sample Hong Kong's legendary dim sum (steamed pastries). Flag down the metal cases wheeled down the packed rows of diners and point to what you want. The only menus are in Chinese. The setting replicates the original 1925 four-story British teahouse. The ceiling fans, dark wooden booths, stained glass, marble-backed chairs, kettle warmers, and brass spittoons underfoot don't seem terribly Chinese, but the chefs, workers, and tasty pastries are pure Cantonese. Sit back and enjoy the atmosphere, the din, and the delicacies.

Peak Cafe. *121 Peak Road, The Peak, Hong Kong Island (across the road from the Peak Tram Tower).* ☎ *852/2849-7868. Reservations recommended. Main courses $18–$30. AE, DC, JCB, MC, V. Daily 10:30am–11:30pm. INTERNATIONAL.* With a serene view down the south side of Hong Kong Island to the South China Sea, this 1947-vintage garden restaurant offers California, Chinese, and Indian dishes. Best seating is in the glass annex or, weather permitting, in the back garden where barbecue dinners are served. If you're at the Peak, this is the best place to eat.

Shang Palace. *64 Mody Road, Tsimshatsui East (Basement 1, Kowloon Shangri-La Hotel).* ☎ *852/2721-2111, ext 8401. Main courses HK 154–385 ($20–$50). AE, DC, JCB, MC, V. Mon–Sat noon–3pm and 6:30–11pm, Sun 11am–3pm and 6:30–11pm. CANTONESE.* A theatrical setting in imperial red and gilt decor, Shang Palace is grand, gorgeous, and a favorite of gourmets. The entrees cover the entire spectrum of Cantonese classics, from shark's fin to bird's nest to suckling pig and fried rice (which is astonishingly good). The dim sum are light and tasty, too (available noon to 3pm Monday through Saturday and 11am to 3pm Sunday).

Spaghetti House. *57 Peking Road, Tsimshatsui, Kowloon (one block off Nathan Road, one floor up).* ☎ *852/2367-1683. No reservations. Main courses HK 54–115 ($7–$15). AE, DC, JCB, MC, V. Daily 11:30am–midnight. AMERICAN/ITALIAN.* When you need home food like solid pasta and decent pizza, this group of restaurants is utterly dependable. Always crowded for dinner (there's often a wait) and popular with young Hong Kongers, the Spaghetti House pasta and pizzas are the best bets. The decor is strictly American contemporary; it will remind you of a hundred other middle-class restaurants. There are Spaghetti Houses all over Central and Kowloon, including at 10 Stanley Street in Central, 68 Hennessy Road in Wan Chai, and 38 Haiphong Road in Kowloon (across from Kowloon Park).

Western Fast Food   The world's busiest **McDonald's** (outside of Moscow) is in the Star Building facing the Star Ferry concourse in Kowloon, and there are literally dozens of McDonald's nearly everywhere you wander. Given the high price of eating in Hong Kong, McDonald's can be tempting. A good quick lunch chain is **Oliver's Super Sandwiches,** with excellent deli sandwiches assembled to your specifications, as well as a fine selection of baked potatoes. Super Sandwiches has six outlets in Central, four in Tsimshatsui, and many more throughout Hong Kong (☎ 852/2866-8926 for customer services hot line). An excellent taco shop is **Taquería La Placita,** Shop D, Houng Sun Building, 45–47 Carnarvon Road (corner of Hau Fook Street), Tsimshatsui (☎ 852/2366-9466). This is a step up from Taco Bell. The nine taco types ($2–$4) are stuffed with everything from beans to seafood. Seating is a stool at the counter.

GUANGZHOU (CANTON): CHINA'S SOUTHERN GATE

广州

GUANGZHOU, BETTER KNOWN BY its old Western name, Canton, is the center of all things Cantonese—that is to say, south China's people, language, and cuisine. It is also among my least favorite Chinese cities. Hardly a stone's throw from Hong Kong, Guangzhou is all business and industry these days, all freeways and sky-scrapers and factories—hardly a major tourist stop like Beijing and Shang-hai, eastern seaboard metropolises comparable in size and wealth to noisy Guangzhou. All the same, I've discovered after repeated visits that old Canton has its pleasurable treasures, too, several of them unique.

First impressions of Guangzhou are seldom promising, unless one is driven into raptures by construction noise and modern expressways. Guangzhou has some of the most advanced elements anywhere in urban China, some of the highest salaries and most efficient corporations, and its network of new roads and elevated freeways is the most impressive in China. Its traffic is the swiftest and best regulated—or so I thought until I noticed that the on-ramps to these towering expressways are frequented by cars using them as off-ramps as well. The pace in Guangzhou is feverish, and its drivers have learned to swerve with the flow, even when that flow instantaneously reverses itself, heedless of head-on collisions, unannounced U-turns, illegal stops in busy traffic lanes, and other unpredictable detours. This is Cantonese life in the fast lane, without the impediments imposed by common sense, courtesy, or police on most other city streets in the world. The sheer energy, of course, is contagious, and it defines the Cantonese way as it drives full-throttle into the 21st century. Already, the Pearl River Delta region accounts for more than half of China's commerce.

Canton's Central Park

At the heart of the city are older, quieter islands of repose and cul-ture. The city's largest park, **Yuexiu Yuan,** is its best. Built on a grand scale, the green, hilly 247-acre grounds possess a number of boring features, such as three artificial lakes and a 40,000-seat stadium. For most foreign visitors, the **Sun Yat-sen Memorial Hall (Zhongshan Jiniantang),** at the southern foot of the mountain that gives the park its name, isn't that exciting, either. Finished in 1931, 6 years after Dr. Sun Yat-sen's death, the hall and its blue-tiled tower host lectures, plays, and other cultural offerings. It's a grand edifice but simple, engineered so that

Canton/Guangzhou

no interior pillars are required for support. Sun Yat-sen is the province's most beloved native son, credited with leading the overthrow of China's last imperial dynasty and the establishment of China's first republic. He founded the Guomindang (Nationalist Party) in 1923 in Canton, the political party that later tried to unite China under Chiang Kai-shek but fell to the victorious Communist revolutionaries under Mao Zedong.

Still, Sun Yat-sen is claimed by both Nationalists (who fled to Taiwan in 1949) and Communists as the founder of modern China, and almost invariably the main street in China's cities today bears Sun Yat-sen's Chinese name (Zhongshan).

Guangzhou's reputation as a hotbed of revolutionary activity was enhanced not only by Sun Yat-sen's Republican Revolution but by Mao's early Communist movement. From 1924 to 1927, Mao, Zhou En-lai, and other Communist Party founders trained future firebrands at Canton's Peasant Movement Institute, located in the Former Temple of Confucius. Chairman Mao's spartan bedroom is still on view there, in yet another of Guangzhou's politically correct but touristically dull attractions.

What's interesting in Yuexiu Park is, of all things, its museum. By the time I actually came to look inside, I'd visited Guangzhou enough times to expect yet another display of photographs and letters tracing the history of the Communist Party or recording one of several massacres of martyrs to China's revolution. Instead, within the graceful **Pavilion Overlooking the Sea (Zhen Hai Luo),** which European traders called the Five-Story Pagoda, there are fine, well-displayed historical exhibits, arranged chronologically by floor, with signs in English and Chinese. First built during the Ming Dynasty in 1380 and rebuilt as a Pearl River lookout in 1686, this pavilion (Guangzhou's oldest building) is an ideal venue for a historical museum, capped by an elegant teahouse on the fifth floor. My favorite item is a Ming Dynasty water clock, dated A.D. 1316, consisting of three large barrels arranged like stairs that employed a large dipstick to measure the correct time. It's open Tuesday to Sunday from 9am to 4pm (admission RMB 5 /75¢).

The centerpiece of Yuexiu Park is its almost legendary **Statue of Five Rams.** The five rams recall the story of Guangzhou's founding, when five fairies from the Celestial Realm rode their goats into town to present the Cantonese with their first grains of rice. I expected this oft-photographed emblem of the city—a modern sculpture always dismissed as of little artistic merit—to be hopelessly overrun and tacky to boot, but again I was surprised. Perched on a raised platform, this statue, made of granite chunks fitted together to form the five impish rams with their coiling horns, is actually an intriguing piece from many angles, and the honeycomb of flowery paths that surround it are haunted as much by fascinating locals and retirees as by visitors.

Temple of the Six Banyan Trees

One of the most bizarre halls in any Buddhist temple I ever visited in China was at another of Guangzhou's tourist stops, the Temple of the Six Banyan Trees (Liurongsi). Its main attraction is its nine-story **Flower**

Pagoda (Hua Ta), first erected in A.D. 537 and situated squarely in the central courtyard. Behind it is a hall with three statues of the Buddha and one of Guanyin, the Goddess of Mercy, who remains throughout China, as in Canton, the most popular of deities. Several locals bowed low, with incense sticks extended in prayer to the brass goddess. The strange sight, however, is not pagoda or prayer but the death hall. When I entered this hall, immediately to the left of the pagoda, it took me a while to figure out its function. It's a spare chamber, with one monk in attendance. The walls are coated with strips of paper and pictures of the dead. The cost to be posted in this prayer hall, where your image and spirit are constantly administered to by a government-approved religious worker, is by no means strictly charitable: a stiff RMB 6,000 ($720) per posting.

Qingping Market

A better-known oddity of Guangzhou is fully in keeping with its culinary reputation. **Cantonese cuisine** is China's most complex and varied, and Chinese cooking equals or exceeds any other tradition in the world. The Cantonese tastes are perhaps similar in range and daring to those of the French. The popular saying in China is that the Cantonese will eat anything on four legs except a chair. To see that this is no exaggeration, merely browse through Guangzhou's most famous street market, Qingping—which is probably China's most notorious open-air market. The notoriety comes largely from lurid reports about the exotic and domestic skinned animals that are nonchalantly hung from hooks at vendors' stands: from tigers to kitty cats, from pandas to dogs.

Qingping Market today is still a large warren of covered stalls, and animals are one of its offerings. I did walk past cages of dogs and cats and even small deer, all still alive and for sale. Monkeys, snakes, and bats, too, all highly prized and high-priced fare. But this sideshow of animals fresh and slaughtered is a tiny, tiny segment of Qingping Market, as it always has been. Today you can roam from herb lane to antique lane to goldfish lane to mushroom lane to fresh flower lane to songbird lane without coming across a gruesome sight. Of course, the lanes are narrow, crowded, and pungent, and the walkways are not the world's cleanest—heaps of atmosphere, in other words.

Island of Sand

Across from the market is Canton's best reason to linger, **Shamian Island,** a quarter-mile-wide, half-mile-long sandbar that became the chief outpost of British, French, and other foreign traders who forced the port to open its doors in 1843. Britain took the lead, backing its merchants in southern Cathay who hungered to unload opium in Canton and return to England with tea. Britain opened the door to China with the barrels of its cannons, winning concessions from China in what became known as the Opium Wars. In 1859, Britain and France were granted territory on Shamian Island. The foreigners moved right in, shored up the embankments with stone, and maintained two bridges to the quays of Canton, shutting the iron gates at 10pm every night to keep the Chinese out. Shamian was soon populated with Western colonial-style administrative headquarters, banks, Christian churches, a Masonic temple, tennis courts, and a yacht club on the Pearl River.

By 1911, the population of Shamian had reached 300, including Americans, Dutch, Germans, and Japanese, as well as the original English and French residents. On June 23, 1925, Chinese demonstrators, fed up with these enterprising invaders, massed on the city shore to attack, and 52 were shot to death by Western armies. Shamian continued as a foreign post until the Communist Revolution in 1949.

The colonial architecture, the lawns and flower gardens, and the great arching banyan trees have endured, and Guangzhou has seized upon this rare legacy, sprucing up the broad avenues, planting garden plots, and slapping on bright coats of paint wherever a Western facade bobs up. Meanwhile, a raft of cafes, craft shops, galleries, and teahouses have moved in. This strange colonial revival has made Shamian into the most pleasant place in Canton and its chief international gathering place. The old Catholic church, Our Lady of Lourdes, has been reconverted from a printing plant back into a place of worship. The island is a perfectly shaped oval course for jogging or strolling, with a view of colonial architecture and modern enterprise within and the surging **Pearl River** beyond—a river shorter than the Yangzi River or the Yellow River but all the more intense, dumping eight times more water into the ocean than the Yellow River.

I was strolling the riverbanks, watching the women wash their clothes in the rancid waters on a staircase dipping into the quay, when I was approached by an artist who offered to sell me antique painted scrolls that he kept rolled up in his Shamian apartment. Whether these were antiques or not, I couldn't tell, but I was intrigued by the scrolls he unrolled on his living room floor and I parted on happy terms with an ink-wash drawing in hand.

The blossoming of Western-style cafes and foreign boutiques in the old buildings on the island is a recent phenomenon. When I first visited Shamian, the architecture was in languid decay and the main new addition was the stunning **White Swan Hotel** (see "Where to Stay," below), which was very nearly the first modern international hotel to spring up in China, appearing in 1982, and among the first three to receive China's official 5-star rating. The White Swan is hail and hearty as it approaches its 20th birthday in addition to being well maintained, its garden waterfall in the high atrium still cascading like a specimen of captured scenery. The hotel is a modern monument of China's opening to the West, still a grand place to poke around among the lavish antique shops in the basement. Dozens of tour groups throng its lobby and hundreds of overseas businesspeople retire to the Riverside Apartment complex in its spacious banyan garden on the eastern tip of Shamian, where the traffic of Pearl River is always in full swing. Iced tea and a sandwich in the Riverside Garden Coffee Shop with a view of the waterfall within and the river floating by outside at eye level is still a pleasure, a haven from the commerce of the streets to which the White Swan has been the beacon for two decades.

Cantonese Cuisine

In addition to these scattered islands of repose—a park, a museum, a temple, and Shamian itself—Guangzhou has a final appeal: its food. The great cuisine of China was born here, and great Cantonese dining experiences still occur at the birthplace, although superb Cantonese restaurants now populate the world. It is often said, not without justice, that the best Cantonese food is served in Hong Kong, Singapore, Taiwan, New York, San Francisco—in nearly any great capital except Guangzhou. Fortunately, there are some brilliant exceptions. Since I am not a true follower of exotic Cantonese dishes, I leave it for others to try the live snake and monkey brain restaurants for which Guangzhou is notorious. My own choices are far more delicate, depending on fresh seafood and the traditional pungent sauces.

My favorite dining in Canton is at **Bei Yuan** (see "Where to Dine," below), the city's most beautiful garden restaurant. Built in the 1930s, Bei Yuan is segmented into over 40 halls, its tearooms and dining pavilions decorated with carved latticework, covered corridors, and etched window glass. Flowers are the decorative motif. Dim sum, the southern Chinese collection of bite-sized steamed pastries and small delicacies, is served all day, and I could eat them all day, too, although dim sum is usually taken on weekends at elaborate brunches. The best dinner dishes are the winter melon with green pepper and the mushrooms stuffed with shrimp; the signature dish is a stew of mixed delights, ranging from abalone and pork to chicken and trout.

A second garden restaurant with an outdoor setting is **Ban Xi** (see "Where to Dine," below) along the shores of **Li Wan Lake**. It, too, is a dragon of dining halls and classic decorations, with black lacquer furniture, gold leaf ceilings, and etched glass from the Qing Dynasty. Dinners run until midnight, the menu is in English, the Peony shrimp plate is divine, and a lake stroll after dark, after a fine dinner, puts one in the mood to dream of a China that has long passed yet is still accessible in the midst of this supercharged metropolis. The dim sum—or as Cantonese call Chinese brunch, *yum cha*—is superb here, too, but extremely crowded all weekend.

The Cantonese meal that comes first to mind, however, occurred not in lake or garden or in some fine hotel but in the restaurant of a third-rate suburban hotel, **Sha He** (see "Where to Dine," below), a half-hour taxi ride northeast of Guangzhou. The Sha He kitchen has been southern China's most famous noodle emporium for 40 years, and nothing would do until I tried it myself. The dining area, on the second floor of the hotel, is dirty on the edges, and the marble tables and stone chairs are a bit cold, but the flat rice noodles *(ho fan)* are hot and succulent. It hardly matters what sauce, vegetable, meat, or sea creature is added. I asked the general manager, Li Yue Cheang, if I could take a peek at the famous kitchen, where 15 chefs and 30 assistants flail away in utter chaos—or rather, in accordance with a 600-year-old recipe. I was allowed to witness the whole hard process, from sink to wok, in the confines of the hotel's grease-washed dungeons.

The two chief activities of the Cantonese, it seems to me, are business and eating. Excelling at both, they are making Guangzhou the most progressive business city in China and at the same time the tastiest. I know of nothing more divine to do in old Canton than sit down to a Sunday yum cha in a decorated hall with the energy cranked high on all sides and the air crackling with conversation like a thousand lightning rods in a thunderstorm. That's when I drift away like an emperor half asleep, my eyes following the rounds of a dumpling cart loaded with its delicate tidbits: prawns sealed in transparent rice envelopes *(har gau)*, shrimp trussed up in pastry shell bags *(shao mai)*, and barbecued pork stuffed inside plump steamed buns *(hum bao)*. Red tea arcs into my cup, falling from the long neck of a copper pot, snapping me awake. It seems like morning has just begun in distant China.

PRACTICAL INFORMATION

ORIENTATION

Guangzhou is north of the Pearl River Delta, a close cousin of neighboring Macau and Hong Kong, a distant son of Beijing, 1,150 miles to the north. With a population of over 2 million in the city and another 3 million in the suburbs, Guangzhou is the economic capital of southeastern China, dominating its region in the way that Shanghai and Beijing dominate the central and northern segments of the eastern seaboard. Guangzhou has been trading with the West for 400 years, has close ties with modern Hong Kong, and ranks among China's most cosmopolitan and affluent cities.

GETTING THERE

By Plane   Baiyun Airport has flights to cities throughout China, including nearby Hong Kong (35 minutes). Several international airlines also serve Guangzhou, including Thai, Singapore, and Malaysia airlines. For airline information, call ☎ 020/8659-6123.

The ride into Guangzhou from the airport requires about 30 minutes. If possible, fax details of your flight arrival to your hotel so that you can be picked up at the airport. Otherwise, you may face a protracted battle with the taxi drivers and touts who will waylay you outside. You should insist on a functioning taxi meter and pay no more than RMB 50 ($6.25) for the ride, but you could be hustled into paying three times that much. If you arrive by train, bus, or boat, you could also face some bargaining challenges.

By Train & Bus   Trains and buses arrive at more distant stations, east and north of downtown. Departures by express buses and trains serving Hong Kong are available all day. Hotels can book air, train, bus, and boat tickets easily. For train information, call ☎ 020/8668-2043.

By Ship   Boats to and from Macau, Hong Kong, and Hainan Island arrive at Zhoutouzui Wharf on the south side of the Pearl River (for do-it-yourselfers, a 40-minute walk to Shamian Island). A jet-boat catamaran to Hong Kong down the Pearl River takes under 4 hours. For ship information, call ☎ 020/8383-3691.

GETTING AROUND

Guangzhou is not a joy to walk in, nor are bicycles ideal because of the heavy traffic. So be prepared to hail taxis as you go, which is easy downtown. There are plenty of taxis in Guangzhou, and they charge by the size of the vehicle. Every taxi should have a meter. The long-awaited subway is still unfinished.

TOURS & STRATAGEMS

Tours   The main office of China International Travel Service (CITS) at 179 Huanshi Lu (☎ 020/8666-6279) won't set up tours for individuals, but the hotels have branches and tour desks that do an efficient job. The tour desks at the Garden Hotel, the China Hotel, and the Holiday Inn City Centre are the best places to arrange tours.

I recently used the ticketing office near the cinema box office in the basement of the Holiday Inn to purchase an air ticket and a city tour. Both requests were handled by an English-speaking clerk in record-setting time. A half-day city tour (RMB 385/$47 for one person; RMB 245/$29 each for two people) gives a cursory but helpful overview of the city and scenic highlights. You can then return to these sights or discover new ones on your own.

American Express maintains an office at 339 Huanshi Donglu, in the lobby of the Guangdong International Hotel (☎ 020/8331-1771), and can arrange tours through the Guangdong Star International Travel Company, a branch of CITS, Dong Fang Hotel, 120 Liuhua Lu (☎ 020/8666-2427).

WHERE TO STAY

Guangzhou has a dozen international hotels of good quality. All hotels are subject to a 15% room tax and a 5% subway tax.

China Hotel (Zhongguo Dajiudian). *Liuhua Lu (south, across from the Canton Trade Fairgrounds).* ☎ *020/8666-6888. Fax 020/8667-7014. 889 rms, 128 suites. A/C MINIBAR TV TEL. $250 double. AE, DC, JCB, MC, V.* This 18-story, 5-star hotel is the most deluxe in Canton, and would be my second choice after the Holiday Inn. It was the first hotel I stayed at in China. Its rooms were completely renovated in 1997. Every conceivable service is at hand here. Tennis, bowling, a 25-meter outdoor pool, a 24-hour business center—even a coffee bar featuring Starbucks coffee. It has the prime location for the Canton Trade Fair and is favored by business travelers. Many consulates have offices here. It is the kind of hotel you never have to leave, unless you want to see China.

Garden Hotel (Huayuan Jiudian). *368 Huanshi Dong Lu.* ☎ *020/8333-8989. Fax 020/8332-4534. 1,038 rms. A/C MINIBAR TV TEL. $260 double. AE, DC, JCB, MC, V.* Another monster hotel with everything, including China's largest bowling alley, this 30-story tower has been well maintained since opening in 1984. It's a spectacular uptown version of the White Swan, with a business center, pizzeria, tennis, Jacuzzi, sauna, and outdoor pool.

Holiday Inn City Centre Guangzhou (Wenhua Jiari Jiudian). *Huanshi Dong, 28 Guangming Lu.* ☎ *800/465-4329 or 020/8776-6999. Fax 020/8775-3126. 400 rms. A/C MINIBAR TV TEL. $130 double. AE, DC, JCB, MC, V.* The 4-star, 24-story Holiday Inn is considerably cheaper than its 5-star stepsisters, but it delivers Cinderellan features: large standard rooms, a business center, 24-hour clinic, swimming pool, ticketing office, handicapped-accessible rooms, no-smoking rooms, and more. It's my first-choice hotel in Guangzhou. The service is as good as or better than that of the costlier hotel towers. Holiday Inn even has a large movie theater and is a short walk from the Friendship Store.

White Swan Hotel (Baitiane Binguan). *1 Shamian Nanjie (on Shamian Island).* ☎ *020/8188-6968. Fax 020/8186-1188. 834 rms. A/C MINIBAR TV TEL. $240 double. AE, DC, JCB, MC, V.* This was the first of the grand hotels in Canton, its location on Shamian Island is pretty, and its facilities are dazzling, but it is crowded with tour groups and the service is not as good as in some of the other deluxe hotels. Yet it is a beauty and it offers all the 5-star features: not only tennis and squash but a golf driving range and two outdoor pools, one a 20-meter lap pool.

A Budget Choice Now called the **Shengli Binguan** but known locally by its former name, the **Victory**, this old hotel has a newer branch at 53 Shamian Lu (☎ 020/8186-2622; fax 020/8186-2413). Victory is a budget choice favored by backpacking visitors who want a clean bed, modest hotel services, and a great location on Shamian Island. Double rooms, which are modern but not well maintained, cost RMB 665 ($80), far less than the upmarket hotels charge. Facilities and services are on par with Chinese-managed 3-star hotels, meaning there's no swimming pool and few business services. It's a place to sleep, and it is on the north side of the island opposite the White Swan Hotel, where better meals and travel services are available.

WHERE TO DINE

Guangzhou's two most celebrated garden restaurants are **Bei Yuan Restaurant,** 202 Xiaobei Lu (☎ 020/8333-0087), and **Ban Xi Restaurant,**

151 Longjin Xi Lu (☎ 020/8181-5955). I've tried them both, and they offer superb settings, good Cantonese dishes, and delightful yum cha (dim sum buffets).

The best flat noodles in southern China are prepared and served at **Sha He Hotel,** 2/F, 318 Xianlie Dong Lu (☎ 020/8770-5998). It's a 30-minute taxi ride from downtown Guangzhou but worth the experience. Have the hotel desk arrange reservations.

Hotels present some of the best meals in Guangzhou. My favorites for Cantonese dinners are the **Peach Blossom Restaurant** in the Garden Hotel (☎ 020/8333-8989)—decorated in a Three Kingdoms motif, offering a delightful roasted chicken—and **Yuet Fung** in the Holiday Inn (☎ 020/8776-6999)—a bright, rosy place with dim sum, hot pot

(pick your own fish from the tank), and "Monk Jumps Over the Wall," a seafood gumbo double boiled for 6 hours. I can also recommend **Chaozhou Garden** in the China Hotel (☎ 020/8666-6888), where hearty dishes in the Chiu Chow style (a regional cuisine of southern China) are beautifully presented. It was here that I sat down to my first restaurant meal inside China, and my first dish was frog's legs. These hotel dinners are all among the most expensive Guangzhou offers; expect to pay big-city, big-hotel prices.

For economical eats, the city is bristling with KFCs, Pizza Huts, and its first McDonald's. Shamian Island is beginning to offer a number of midpriced sidewalk cafes and small cafes featuring Western and Cantonese dishes—worth taking a chance on.

XIAMEN:
AMOY MON AMOUR
厦门

B ETTER KNOWN TO THE WEST AS Amoy, its name in the local Fujian dialect, Xiamen is among the most charming cities in China, and it was recently voted the cleanest as well. An ordinance forbids the honking of horns, mitigating yet another aspect of pollution common to developing cities in China—and Xiamen is every bit a boomtown. Owing to its location on the East China Sea, directly across from Taiwan, Xiamen has benefited for years from its connections with overseas Chinese. When I first visited in 1987, Xiamen showed signs of being the single most developed place in China, if crates of imported appliances, throngs of motorbikes, and jungles of television antennas were any indication. Every other resident of Xiamen seemed to have relatives abroad and thus a ready conduit to the foreign luxury goods, which until quite recently few in China had the means to procure.

Xiamen is still prosperous, but it has had the good sense not to turn its downtown and harbor into a microcosm of Manhattan or Hong Kong. Rather, the old town is still old and the island in its harbor, Gulangyu—once the stronghold of foreigners—remains a resort of mansions, parks, and pedestrian-only streets that is simply China's most charming reliquary of its colorful colonial past.

Old Town Xiamen

The key intersection in Xiamen is on the inner harbor at the crossroads of **Lujiang Lu** and **Zhongshan Lu,** near the stately Lujiang Hotel with its sea-view balconies. This is where the local buses congregate, the conductors leaning out the windows, shouting their destinations, and banging the side of the bus with a wrench. The ferries to Gulangyu, the gorgeous island of red-roofed mansions and green hills just west across the waterfront, depart from here. The square is the liveliest place in Xiamen, the congregating point for visitors, vendors, shoppers, and fishermen working the docks and wharves.

To explore the **old downtown,** just walk east past the curving facade of the Lujiang Hotel on Zhongshan Lu. This is main street, filled these days with shops large and small, old and new. Many of the side streets are as they have been for decades, consisting of row upon row of shop houses, their columns and colonnades covering the sidewalks.

One of the first treks I ever made in Xiamen was southward from the **main ferry dock** along Minzu Road. The quays are a feverish sprawl of fishing boats unloading their catches, warehouses shuffling palates of imported electronics, and factory yards piled with coal and dried fish. One morning I came across two little children frolicking in one factory yard, running and leaping on the other side of the gate, both of them stark naked and laughing.

Temple, School & Dangerous Strait

If you're up for a long walk, it is possible to stroll all the way down the east shore of Xiamen (which is itself an island, not joined to the mainland until a causeway was constructed after Liberation in 1949). Eventually, Siming Nan Lu leads to **Nan Putuo Temple,** Xiamen's greatest place of worship. Nan Putuo, built into a rocky hillside, is an active Buddhist complex of grand halls, bell towers, inscribed rocks, and pavilions, striking for its white marble and upswept tiled roofs. The temple dates from the Tang Dynasty, but it has been extensively rebuilt in the thousand years since. This is a fine place to watch locals pray for riches and burn incense (which is collected for reuse by numerous monks). At the highest hall there is a magnificent red character, meaning Buddha, carved into a massive boulder. The outcroppings beyond this point, the Peaks of the Five Old Men (Wulao Shan), make for excellent day hikes.

When I visited Xiamen 10 years ago, much of the Nan Putuo halls and courtyards were undergoing another renovation. A small city of stonecutters was encamped at the temple gates. Today, Nan Putuo has been put back together. It teems with visitors, drawn to this southern "home" of China's most popular divinity, Guanyin, Goddess of Mercy.

Just south of the temple is one of China's best schools, **Xiamen University,** founded in 1921 by Tan Kah-kee (Chen Jiageng), a native of the area who moved to Singapore and made his fortune in rubber plantations. If you've never strolled a campus in China before, this might be your chance. Ask at the gate if you may enter or wait for helpful students to approach you to practice their English. Lu Xun (1881–1936), China's most famous modern essayist, taught here for a term in 1926 to 1927, and there's a small exhibit in his memory just inside the main gate. One of Xiamen's students befriended me when I visited here. He gave me a tour of the campus, told me about the inner workings of student dorm life, and took me to lunch at a nearby student cafe.

South of the temple and university is the **Huli Mountain Cannon Platform,** the remnants of German artillery placed here in 1891. Looking across the Formosa Strait, it's just a few miles to two islands, Jinmen and Mazu, that were once much in dispute between China and Taiwan. For years they taunted each other across this strait with loudspeakers, propaganda balloons, and live explosives. The islands figured in the Kennedy–Nixon presidential debates in 1960, when Jinmen and Mazu (now being opened to tourism by Taiwan) were better known to Cold Warriors as Quemoy and Matsu.

Garden Island

Xiamen's most engrossing attraction is **Gulangyu,** the small island in its harbor that is served by innumerable ferries. The main ferry to Gulangyu is across from the Lijiang Hotel. Look for the two big entryways to the pier. There's no charge on the way out to Gulangyu. It's just RMB 2 (25¢) to return. The voyage requires just 10 minutes. These old two-deck ferries have almost nowhere to sit down. They're stand-up ferries with sliding screen doors, rather like cattle cars.

Gulangyu is free of cars, an island for walking. Even bicycles are banned. A few electric carts are permitted, some giving tours. The island is quite hilly but also quite compact. Straight up from the dock is the town, packed with shops and seafood cafes. The streets are cobbled or paved, and they twist and turn like pretzels. You'll get lost, but it's easy to find the way back to the town and ferry dock.

South of the ferry dock a number of the grand buildings and villas occupy the hillside, survivors of Gulangyu's days as a foreign quarter. Western traders moved onto Gulangyu in 1842. The foreigners built the villas, sanitation system, consulates, schools, churches, hospitals, and roads that remain today. In 1903, Gulangyu became Xiamen's official foreign concession. The British and Germans had their consulates on the east side of the little island, as did the Amoy Telephone Company. The **old British Embassy building** still stands atop the first hill on your left as you leave the ferry. It burned a few years ago and is being restored. The towering whitewashed **Roman Catholic church,** on a quiet lane rising above the southeastern shore, is over a century old now (1882) and still used on Sunday, as is the **Sanyi Protestant church,** which the English built in 1904.

Gulangyu seems to be blanketed in hundreds, even thousands, of old villas, many of them now the residences of locals. The original coats of arms in enamel have been removed from the stucco doorways, but the Corinthian columns, two-story porches, plaster curlicues, and immense verandas recall many foreign architectural styles, especially the Portuguese types still prevalent in Macau. Mature banyans, bougainvillea, and bauhinia overhang the winding, walled lanes that enclose luxuriant gardens. Gulangyu seems like a tropical slice out of Southwest Asia with only a few Chinese intrusions.

Placed on the southeast cusp of Gulangyu like a beacon is a mesmerizing statue of the robed warrior **Koxinga (Zheng Chenggong),** who commanded Xiamen with his pirate armada said to consist of 8,000 war junks and 250,000 fighting men. Koxinga expelled the Dutch from Taiwan in 1661. He died there the next year, but he has been remembered ever since as a hero rather than a villain. His statue surveys the sea from atop a sea pillar, which visitors reach via a bridge from a lovely seaside garden. In far less dramatic fashion, this rounded image of Koxinga is as memorable as New York's Statue of Liberty. Its form also mirrors that of the summit of Gulangyu itself, Sunlight Rock.

Nearby the Koxinga statue, up Tian Wei Lu, is the **Gulangyu Guesthouse compound,** with its 1920s billiard room and seaside terraces, where U.S. President Nixon stayed in 1972 when opening up relations with the People's Republic.

The island's best **beach** is due west of Koxinga, on the southern shores. The sands are inviting and a new graceful portico has been built on the shore, but the most interesting areas to explore are along the fringes of the beach, where pathways wind through stone pinnacles that rise from the shore.

Overlooking the beach is one of the island's best-known gardens, **Shuzhuang,** built in 1913 by Lin Er-jia, a wealthy merchant who fled his home in Taiwan when the Japanese occupied it in 1895. It is a small seaside garden that has recently been refurbished with a zigzag bridge, a large goldfish pond, and a massive honeycombed wall of lake rock. Locals seem to like lingering here, and they make a great deal of the pond in a garden on the sea ("A garden in the sea, a sea in the garden," they say). For me it has an artificial, sterile look—an amusement park garden. It's open daily from 7am to 6pm (admission RMB 5 /60¢).

Gulangyu's finest overlook is **Sunlight Rock (Riguangyan),** nearly 300 feet above the harbor, the highest of the island's peaks. Surrounding its base is Yanping Park (admission RMB 20/$2.40). The summit of Sunlight Rock is a short, steep climb along rock paths dotted with flower gardens, old cannons, small cafes, and quite recently a number of amusement arcades, yurts, and contemporary metal sculptures. Sunlight Rock has taken on a carnival atmosphere, but at its higher levels it is simply a beautiful landform of granite boulders and outcroppings rising to a rounded summit of smooth, bare rock. From the top the outlines of Gulangyu, the harbor, and downtown Xiamen to the east are in full view. Gulangyu is particularly fetching from this height, an island garden of villas in red brick and tile.

Gulangyu's most prominent building is the **Xiamen Museum,** a spacious, colonnaded edifice crowned with a large red dome (admission RMB 2/25¢). I was determined to see its interior on my most recent visit, so I retraced my steps back into Gulangyu town and at the ferry dock followed the shore northward up Yanping Lu. I turned up a nearby street and after a few blocks and a few false turns found the museum's gate. It is a curiously hollow, unadorned old hall inside, its four floors divided in the center by a circular atrium. The exhibits are not splashy. The first floor is decorated with photographs of Gulangyu's colonial architecture. Various rooms have different exhibits: relics of recent wars, printing presses, a set of handcuffs. The second floor contains a collection of painted porcelains dating back to the Tang Dynasty, a room devoted to gifts sent by Xiamen's sister cities from around the world (including Baltimore and Sutter Creek, California), tributes from a number of foreign countries, a hall displaying Iron Age weapons, scrolls, wooden rifles, and pieces from a cart, and a Trophy Room festooned with the prizes of local sports heroes. The top two floors were closed, the staff was drinking tea in the staff rooms, and the doors were swung wide open to the tropical sea breezes.

Gulangyu is, in short, a strange and delightful place in China, clearly enchanted. Xiamen is widely known as China's "Garden on the Sea," a name it is actually living up to, even in this age of intense modernization and industrial revolution. Gulangyu has no parallel in China. It is an Eden from a century-long past. The island fathers have wisely ordered all new buildings to conform in spirit and style to its graceful colonial legacy. Evenings, walking the twisting lanes, I've passed more than one garden villa emitting the soothing sounds of a pianist in rehearsal or a private concert. Many of China's best musicians come from here, and the locals, who number barely 12,000, sometimes call Gulangyu by another name, not on the maps: Piano Island.

PRACTICAL INFORMATION

ORIENTATION

Xiamen, population about 600,000, is an island port city in southern Fujian Province located on the Formosa Strait, opposite Taiwan. It became one of China's five Special Economic Zones (SEZ) on December 18, 1981, attracting considerable foreign investment (especially from neighboring Taiwan).

GETTING THERE

By Plane The international airport is 11 miles from downtown. Airport taxis cost about RMB 50 ($6). Dragonair (☎ 0592/202-5389) has regular flights to Hong Kong. Xiamen Airlines (☎ 0592/508-4376) has service to most cities in China. Philippine Airlines (☎ 0592/509-4451) serves Manila.

By Train There are direct trains to Shanghai, but Xiamen is not located on the main Guangzhou–Shanghai–Beijing rail line. For northern destinations, such as Beijing, air transport is much more efficient.

By Ship Passenger ships connect Hong Kong and Xiamen, docking at the Passenger Station of Amoy Port Administration, Heping Pier, Tongwen Lu (a 15-minute walk south from the Lujiang Hotel/Ferry Station). Call ☎ 0592/202-2517 for information. I've returned to Hong Kong several times by ship. It is a pleasant excursion, leaving Xiamen in the afternoon (usually at 3pm) for the 19-hour voyage. The terminal is notable for its luggage escalator, a belt of wooden bars and catches, where you set down your carry-ons; they roll along with you to the second-floor customs desk. My ship, rechristened the *Min Nan,* was formerly a member of the Brittany Ferries fleet. My first-class cabin cost RMB 452 ($54). Facilities were adequate: a private bath and shower, cinema, buffet restaurant, duty-free shop, disco lounge— but no towels in the cabins. Passengers are Chinese, loaded down with luggage and shopping bags.

GETTING AROUND

You can tour Xiamen on your own by foot. Buy a map from the hotel or a street vendor and set out from the ferry terminal south to Nan Putuo Temple, east to old town Xiamen, or west on the ferry to Gulangyu.

TOURS & STRATAGEMS

China International Travel Service (CITS) (☎ 0592/505-1822) has many branches in Xiamen. None are useful for setting up a tour. Rely upon the tour desks in the Marco Polo Hotel or the Holiday Inn for air, rail, and boat tickets and for city tours. American Express has an office in the Holiday Inn (☎ 0592/212-0268).

WHERE TO STAY

Holiday Inn Crowne Plaza Harbourview (Haijin Jiari Dajiudian). *12–8 Zhenhai Lu (downtown).* ☎ *800/ 465-4329 or 0592/202-3333. Fax 0592/ 203-6666. 367 rms. A/C MINIBAR TV TEL. $160 double. AE, DC, JCB, MC, V.* This 22-story tower has been Xiamen's top downtown hotel since 1992. The rooms, each with a safe, are spacious and clean. No-smoking rooms are available. There are two executive floors and an American Express office. Service is highly efficient.

Services: Concierge, room service (24-hour), dry cleaning and laundry (same day), nightly turndown, daily maid service, free airport shuttle, foreign exchange counter.

Facilities: In-house movies, pool (outdoor, heated), health club (exercise machines), sauna, business center (24-hour), tour desk, medical clinic, beauty salon, shopping arcade, newsstand.

Marco Polo Xiamen. *8 Jianye, Hubin Bei Lu (north of city center on Yuandong Lake).* ☎ *800/524-0500 or 0592/509-1888. Fax 0592/509-2888. 312 rms, 38 suites. A/C MINIBAR TV TEL. $160 double. AE, DC, JCB, MC, V.* The newest luxury hotel in town, the Marco Polo's guest rooms are arranged on tiers looking down on its eight-story atrium lobby. The top floor, its Continental Club, caters to business executives. Services are first-rate. Taxis downtown cost RMB 12 ($1.50). All rooms come with a large desk, sofa, and safe. No-smoking rooms are available, as are a medical clinic and delicatessen.

Services: Concierge, room service (24-hour), dry cleaning and laundry (same day), nightly turndown, daily maid service, free airport shuttle, foreign exchange counter.

Facilities: In-house movies, pool (outdoor, heated), health club (exercise machines), sauna, business center (24-hour), tour desk, beauty salon, shopping arcade, newsstand.

WHERE TO DINE

The Marco Polo Hotel's **Lotus Court** (☎ 0592/509-1888) on the second floor has the best Chinese food I've eaten in Xiamen, with impeccable service. The Marco Polo's lobby restaurant, **Cafe Marco,** provides good breakfast and lunch buffets (Western and Asian fare).

Downtown, the Holiday Inn has excellent Sichuan, Cantonese, and Western dining in its restaurants, including the best dim sum breakfasts in town (☎ 0592/202-3333).

The **Lujiang Hotel's rooftop restaurant** overlooking the ferry to Gulangyu has an English menu, hot local Fujian and Cantonese dishes, live seafood, and the city's best evening view (☎ 0592/202-2922).

For fast food, there's a **Pizza Hut** on the harbor one block north of the ferry dock in Haibin Park.

On Gulangyu, I tried several hole-in-the-wall **seafood cafes.** All of them were pleasant, bright, moderately expensive, and marginally clean. Most had no English menus or posted prices, but all had plenty of helpful proprietors used to foreign visitors. Just point at the live seafood of your choice in the plastic pans on the sidewalk and settle on a price before ordering. Xiamen is celebrated for its delicacies from the sea, some of them quite expensive, many of them dried and for sale at stands.

HANGZHOU: NUMBER ONE CITY UNDER HEAVEN

苏州

Arriving in Hangzhou seven centuries ago, Marco Polo pronounced it "the finest, most splendid city in the world . . . where so many pleasures may be found that one fancies oneself to be in Paradise." This impression is in full accord with the familiar Chinese proverb: "In Heaven there is Paradise; on Earth, Suzhou and Hangzhou." Today, Hangzhou's claim to paradise does not lie in its streets, which are ordinary, but in its shoreline and the surrounding countryside, where strolling and biking are the best you'll find in the Middle Kingdom.

The focus of Hangzhou's exceptional beauty is **West Lake (Xi Hu).** It's a small lake, about 3 miles across and 9 miles around. You can walk the circumference in under 4 hours—longer if you linger at a temple, pavilion, cafe, or park. Two causeways—one running on the north shore, the other on the west shore—vary and shorten the journey. The islets and temples, pavilions and gardens, causeways and arched bridges of this jadelike lake have constituted the supreme example of lakeside beauty in China ever since Hangzhou served as China's capital during the Southern Song Dynasty (A.D. 1127–1279). The shallow waters of West Lake are sufficient to fill and beguile the eye's compass but not to overwhelm it. Hangzhou's West Lake remains to this day what one 12th-century visitor proclaimed it: "a landscape composed by a painter."

I've visited Hangzhou's West Lake often, finding each time a serenity that I associate with the Middle Kingdom days of mandarins and moonlit courtyards. Strolling the promenades and crisscrossing the causeways of West Lake, I've entered Old China as in a dream.

Solitary Island

I like to begin my early morning rambles at the aptly named Hangzhou Shangri-La Hotel, situated on the lake's northwest shore, where at dawn the mists often wrap the willow-draped shoreline that resembles an old Chinese landscape. Crossing **Xiling Bridge,** dedicated to poet Su Xiaoxiao, who was entombed here in A.D. 501, I am quickly transfixed by the lush scenery and old architecture of Solitary Island (Gushan), the largest of the four main islands in West Lake. A roadway sweeps eastward across Solitary Island toward the city skyline, past monumental tile-roofed halls built in the style of Qing Dynasty palaces.

As a matter of fact, it was on this very island that the two most traveled emperors of the last dynasty, Kangxi (1662–1723) and Qianlong (1736–95), stayed during their own vacations on West Lake. Sailing down the Grand Canal to its terminus at Hangzhou, these emperors hastened to Solitary Island, staying at pavilions erected solely for their royal excursions. These 18th-century emperors, grandfather and grandson in the Manchu line, came strictly as sightseers. They established a viewing platform on the southeastern tip of the island for a connoisseur's view of sunrise and moonlight. Qianlong named the viewing pavilion "Autumn Moon on a Calm Lake," and today there's a fine teahouse in its place, perfect for sipping green tea. The view is the same today as that which enthralled generations of emperors.

It's worth returning to Solitary Island later to tour the **Zhejiang Provincial Museum** not only to see the oldest grains of cultivated rice in the world(discovered 7,000 years ago in a nearby Hemudu village) but also to survey the skeleton of a whale beached at Hangzhou centuries ago when it, like West Lake, was connected more spaciously to the East China Sea. West Lake was once a river lagoon, until sedimentation removed it from its source and a series of scholar-administrators designed the causeways and islands that have made West Lake a work of art. The museum is open Tuesday to Saturday from 8:30am to 4pm (admission RMB 10/$1.25).

Shadow-Boxing & Ballroom Dancing

Solitary Island is connected to downtown Hangzhou by Baidi, one of the two great man-made causeways that divide West Lake into three parts. These two causeways are the finest stretches to walk on West Lake. Both are scenic and serene. The **Bai Causeway** is named after a Tang Dynasty poet, Bai Juyi, who served as prefectural governor here in A.D. 822–824 and saw to its construction. Composed of silt dredged from the lake, this causeway runs east for half a mile, rejoining the north shore road, **Beishan Lu,** at **Broken Bridge (Duan Qiao),** so-named because when winter snows first melt the bridge appears from a distance to be broken.

The **lakeshore promenade** that encircles West Lake widens at Broken Bridge where it joins the Bai Causeway and runs parallel to the western edge of downtown Hangzhou. Along the way, I always find the pavilions, with their octagonal tiled roofs and upturned eaves, jammed at dawn with devotees of the latest recreational craze, Western ballroom dancing. At the same time the walkway teems with a more Eastern, more

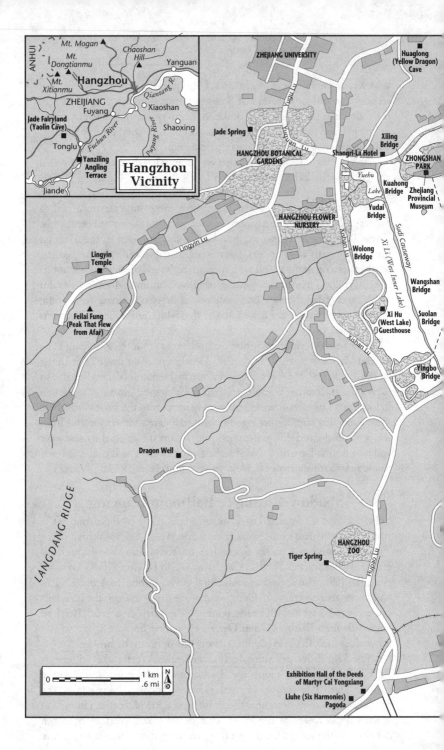

Hangzhou Vicinity

ANHUI
ZHEIJIANG

Mt. Mogan
Mt. Dontianmu
Mt. Xitianmu
Hangzhou
Chaoshan Hill
Yanguan

Qiantang R.

Fuyang
Xiaoshan
Shaoxing

Jade Fairyland (Yaolin Cave)
Tonglu
Fuchun River
Puyang River
Qiantang River

Yanziling Angling Terrace

Jiande

ZHEJIANG UNIVERSITY

Huaglong (Yellow Dragon) Cave

Jade Spring

Lu Lu
Yuyuan Lu

HANGZHOU BOTANICAL GARDENS

Shangri-La Hotel

Xiling Bridge

ZHONGSHAN PARK

Yuehu Lake

Kuahong Bridge

Zhejiang Provincial Museum

HANGZHOU FLOWER NURSERY

Lingyin Lu

Xishan Lu

Yudai Bridge

Wolong Bridge

Xi Li (West Inner Lake)

Sudi Causeway

Lingyin Temple

Wangshan Bridge

Feilai Fung (Peak That Flew from Afar)

Xi Hu (West Lake) Guesthouse

Suolan Bridge

Xishan Lu

Yingbo Bridge

Dragon Well

LANGDANG RIDGE

HANGZHOU ZOO

Tiger Spring

Hupao Lu

Exhibition Hall of the Deeds of Martyr Cai Yongxiang

Liuhe (Six Harmonies) Pagoda

0   1 km
     .6 mi
N

Baochu
Pagoda

Bei Li (North Inner Lake)

Beishan Lu

Hubin Lu

Yan'an Lu

Hangzhou Silk
Weaving Mill

Qingchun Lu

Jianguo Bei Lu

Huancheng Dong Lu

Jindai
Bridge

Causeway

Baidi

HUBIN (LAKESIDE)
PARK

Shengli
Theatre

Zhonghe River

Dongjie River

Jianguo Zhong Lu

Autumn Moon
on Calm Lake

Jiefang Lu

*Xi Hu Lake
(West Lake)*

Hangzhou
People's Hall

Kolyuan Lu

Qingtai Jie

CHILDREN'S
PARK

Yongjin Lu

Nanshan Lu

Laodong Lu

Zhongshan Zhong Lu

Youshengguan Lu

Hangpu Nanlu

Hangzhou
Railway Station

LIULANGWENYING
PARK

Kiaoyingzhou
(Solitary) Isle

Hefang Jie

Three Pools Mirroring
the Moon

WUSHAN
HILL

Zhongshan Nan Lu

Jiangcheng Lu

Wangjiang Lu

Nanshan Lu

Wansongling Lu

Qingao Lu

Xihuangshan Lu

Fengshan Lu

YUHUANG
HILL

Nanxingqiao
Station

JIANGBIN
PARK

Nanxingqiao Passenger
Wharf

Fuxing Lu

Qiantang River

Baita Pagoda
(White Pagoda)

Hangzhou

ancient form of exercise, *tai ji quan* (shadow-boxing). Tai ji is a formal exercise designed to promote health and spirit by directing and enhancing an inner stream of energy called the *chi*. Tai ji has become so popular in China that its basic forms have been systematized by the government, creating an official tai ji form. But just as there are dialects in the Chinese language, so there are regional differences in exercise. Along West Lake, various tai ji schools conduct their prebreakfast classes. Tai ji masters tack up their insignia on trees, and their students (women slicing the crisp air with red-tasseled swords, men outlining the martial arts with bare palm and fist) begin practice, ignoring the pedestrians, bicyclers, baby strollers, street sweepers, and occasional foreign visitors who squeeze through their ranks.

A few paces away ballroom dancers spill out onto the sidewalk in a waltz straight out of Strauss. Partner swings partner until their step-close-step merges with the slow push-and-pull of shadow-boxers. Across the widening avenue, at the Children's Palace square, hundreds of workers toil with mass calisthenics. It's worth getting here early to take in the action. All of China seems to be moving its joints.

The ballroom dancing commences about 6:30am every day, finishing up 2 hours later. If you know a few steps, you'll be warmly welcomed if you join in. I did some tai ji exercises here recently and I found myself the recipient of advice from Hangzhou's masters.

Lakeside Avenue

At Hubin Lu (Lakeside Avenue) the promenade turns south. Along the lake a delightful array of boat launches, souvenir stands, restaurants, Qing-style mansions, and outdoor cafes is encamped. This spacious shore retreat, known as Lakeside Park, is just the spot for tea, snacks, and ice-cream treats. Meanwhile, the city shops across the main street have undergone extensive redevelopment in the last few years. You can edge into the downtown rush for lunch at Hangzhou's new TCBY (The Country's Best Yogurt) or for a pastry at Croissants da France. On the lakefront itself there's a Joe Eagles fast-food restaurant with hamburgers, outdoor seating, and a menu in English. Lakeside Park is also the place for a beer, served at a fashionable new pub in an old mansion, the Casablanca Country Bar.

In some ways Hangzhou's downtown shoreline is coming to resemble a Western shopping mall, but the lake remains as it has for centuries, a gem that is best explored by foot, bicycle, or boat. In fact, the true heart of West Lake must be reached by water. There are no sailboats, canoes, or kayaks to rent on West Lake, but you can hire your own 10-foot, heavy wooden rowboat. There are also small junks propelled by the owner's single oar that will take you out to the islands and ferries—flat-bottomed launches seating 20 under an awning—that pick up passengers along the Lakeside

Park shore. For the small junks, you have to bargain for the fare (usually about RMB 40/$4.80 for 2 hours on the water). The passenger ferries usually sell tickets at roughly twice the price ($10). The touts will find you if you don't get to a ticket booth first, but the easiest place to purchase your ticket for a cruise is back where this morning ramble began, at a dock across the street from the Shangri-La Hotel. Here many a fairly comfortable and sizable motorized launch, its bowsprit the head of a dragon, departs for a 2-hour lake tour, with stops at several of the islands.

Three Pools Mirroring the Moon

The island you should not miss is at the center of West Lake. Known as the **Island of Little Oceans,** it was formed during a silt-dredging operation in 1607. This manmade atoll is, as another Chinese saying goes, "an island within a lake, a lake within an island." Its form is that of a wheel with four spokes, its bridges and dikes creating four enclosed lotus-laden ponds. The main route into the hub of this wheel is the **Bridge of Nine-Turnings,** built in 1727. Occupying the center is the magnificent **Flower and Bird Pavilion,** one of the most graceful structures I have ever visited in China, notable for its intricate wooden railings, lattices, and moon gates. It isn't an ancient work, dating only from 1959, but it's a superb rendition of the best in traditional Chinese architecture. There always seem to be crowds here, although weekday mornings before 10am are the most peaceful times to arrive.

On the southern rim of the Island of Little Oceans is West Lake's defining monument: **Three Pools Mirroring the Moon.** It consists of three water pagodas, each about 6 feet tall. They have "floated" like buoys on the surface of West Lake since 1621. Each pagoda has five openings. On evenings when the full moon shines on the lake, candles are placed inside. The effect is of four moons shimmering on the waters. Even by daylight, the three floating pagodas are a startling touch, the grand flourish of ancient engineers and scholar-administrators who shaped the lake into a work as artful as any classical garden.

The floating pagodas were the creation of Hangzhou's most famous governor, the poet Su Dongpu (A.D. 1036–1101), who placed the original trio of pagodas here, at the deepest point in the lake, to stake out an area where water plants were forbidden to grow. Lily, lotus, and a host of other plants had repeatedly strangled West Lake and still pose a threat. Several times I've seen keepers in skiffs weed the island pools as if they were gardens overrun by weeds. Local legends portray the three pagodas as the feet of an upturned stone tripod plunked into the water to clamp down on a dark monster of the deep.

Boats on West Lake have a venerable history. Emperors were rowed across these waters in elaborate dragon-headed craft. Even Marco Polo took a cruise. "A voyage on this lake," he wrote, "offers more refreshment and pleasure than any other experience on earth. On one side it skirts the city so that your barge commands a distant view of all its grandeur and loveliness. . . . On the lake itself is an endless procession of barges thronged with pleasure seekers." Although the downtown skyline has certainly been transformed over the centuries and the boats for hire today are mere reproductions of the royal barges, West Lake still enthralls pleasure seekers, foreign and Chinese. As many as 20 million visitors throng Hangzhou yearly, a vast number in a city of little more than one million residents. Yet perhaps because the lake is large enough, the walkways wide, and the causeways long, one does not feel as crowded strolling here as when strutting elbow-to-elbow in the streets of Shanghai or upon the Great Wall near Beijing.

Su Causeway

The best view from land of the Three Pools Mirroring the Moon is from the Su Causeway (Sudi), the great dike that connects the north and south shores along the western side of West Lake. This pathway across West Lake has vistas as rewarding as those along the east–west Bai Causeway, but the Su Causeway is three times as long (running nearly 2 miles). Lined with weeping willows, peach trees, and shady nooks, it crosses six arched stone bridges. Locals fish and picnic along its hems. The Su Causeway is named for poet Su Dongpu, who, as the official in charge, set some 200,000 workers to dredging the lake. Su also composed a poem naming West Lake after a stunning young woman, Xi Zi, whose beauty, like that of the lake itself, shone through in laughter or in tears: "Rippling water shimmering on a sunny day / Misty mountains gorgeous in the rain / Plain or gaily decked out like Xi Zi / The West Lake is ever alluring," Su wrote.

The Su Causeway begins on the north shore at a small park, **Lotus Stirred by the Breeze,** at the Distillery, a block west of the Shangri-La Park, across from the patriotic monument to Yue Fei, a 12th-century general. A park favored by Emperor Kangxi, named Lotus Stirred by the Breeze, became the best spot for viewing lotus blossoms. More recently, it has been fronted by a modern shopping center, featuring local crafts and several restaurants specializing in the West Lake carp, considered a great delicacy here. The carp of West Lake are famous in China. Nine hundred years ago, carp in this province (Zhejiang) mutated into the first goldfish and Hangzhou rapidly became the capital of goldfish cultivation, a reputation it enjoys to this day. (It wasn't until 1782 that goldfish were introduced to the West, first reaching London from China.) The two best places to observe the giant ornamental carp and goldfish are at Jade Spring in the **Hangzhou Botanical Garden** (about a mile west of the Shangri-La Hotel, open 8am to 5pm, admission RMB 10/$1.20) and at Huagang (Flower Harbor) Park, which is at the south end of the Su Causeway—its pavilions and fish ponds date back to the Qing Dynasty.

Beside West Lake carp, another celebrated local dish is Beggar's Chicken, discovered by Emperor Qianlong during an 18th-century jaunt along West Lake. The emperor, it is said, chanced upon a Hangzhou peasant who, lacking a proper pan, baked his chicken by coating it in mud and tossing it into a fire. The modern version of Beggar's Chicken is more refined, of course, being carefully seasoned and slowly cooked in clay. The best place to savor this moist invention is in the Shangri-La Hotel's Shang Palace Restaurant.

Baochu Pagoda

Hikes on either of the two great causeways usually consume a morning or an afternoon, depending on one's pace. A boat ride and island walk consume another pleasant half day. A shorter but more strenuous ramble is up the green hillside of the lake's north shore to Hangzhou's most famous landmark, the needlelike Baochu Pagoda, which is visible everywhere from West Lake and adds yet another subtle element to the composition. This pagoda dates from A.D. 968, but has exhibited a tendency to collapse, requiring rebuilding most recently in 1933. Young or old, Baochu Pagoda is an irresistible symbol of West Lake; one morning I set out to see it close up.

Maps didn't give me clear directions, so I simply set out early, walking toward downtown along Beishan Lu from the Shangri-La Hotel. After a 20-minute stroll, I pulled even with the pagoda on the hill and chose a likely looking, rather steep road up. The road petered out into a well-worn trail, which after 10 minutes brought me to the top of the ridge, face-to-face with the solitary 125-foot-high pinnacle. The vista was worth the climb, even though the pagoda, fashioned from solid stone and brick, was devoid of an inner stairway that might have afforded a still more commanding view. The real interest here, as is often the case when one wanders a bit off the tourist track, was the crowd of ordinary people who had gathered that morning. There was a group of housewives, each in her hand-knit sweater, practicing tai ji with a master. Zigzagging through their ranks was a troupe of school kids, dressed like flowers, on a field trip. When they spotted me, they couldn't take their eyes off this unexpected visitor from afar. I rested on a stone wall and watched them play.

An old man emerged from the steep path to the pagoda, cane in hand. His mobility was terribly hampered, but he did not pause to rest. He stamped both feet and strode forward, circling the pagoda courtyard in ever-widening circles, determined to keep moving. Then one little girl broke from her schoolmates, ran up to me, and opened her hand. In her palm lay a single white Chiclet. I thanked her and placed it in my mouth. She ran back, laughing in delight.

Undertaking such rambles in any Chinese city is a sure way to discover the accidentally strange and beautiful, as well as to gain a feeling for the daily life of China. The visitors' sights you've set out to see are quite often secondary.

Laughing Buddha

In Hangzhou, there's another method of transport that's equally instructive: the **bicycle.** China is the land of the bicycle, of course. Everyone seems to own one and to use it constantly. Nowadays, automobiles, particularly taxis, are dominating the streets, but bicycles often have their own wide lanes. For one not in a hurry, particularly for a visitor, the bicycle is a superb form of movement in the city, and in Hangzhou, out of the city as well. The Shangri-La Hotel rents bicycles at reasonable hourly and daily rates, and the equipment (multispeed mountain bikes) is in excellent shape. The gears are useful for mounting the green hillsides surrounding West Lake on three sides. It's west of West Lake that two of Hangzhou's greatest treasures reside—the great Buddhist temple of Lingyin and the tea village of Dragon Well—and both lie within an hour's countryside bike ride. From the hotel, the roads are well marked to both locations and any city map shows the way clearly.

Lingyin Temple, open from dawn to dusk, took me just 20 minutes to reach from the hotel, an easy ride through parklands forested in bamboo and larch, the last 10 minutes on a slight uphill incline. The temple parking lot proved to be extremely crowded, heaped with vendor stalls, buses, visitors, and beggars, but the bicycle parks were clearly marked with pictorial signs. I selected one and paid a small fee, locked up my bike, took my ticket from the vendor, and followed the crowds across a stream to the temple entrance.

Lingyin Temple (Temple of the Soul's Retreat) has been rebuilt a dozen times since its creation in A.D. 326. The present buildings go back decades rather than centuries, but the interiors of the Front Hall and the Great Hall contain some older remnants. This is a typical Buddhist temple in its layout, with the Four Guardians of the Four Directions, two on either side, protecting a rotund image of Maitreya (the Laughing Buddha). Lingyin's Maitreya dates from the 18th century, and behind this image is a statue in camphor wood of Skanda, another protector, which dates from the Southern Song Dynasty when Hangzhou was China's capital. The even larger hall beyond contains an image of Buddha crafted in 1956 from 24 sections of camphor and gilded with 104 ounces of gold—not a bad modern re-creation. Behind this grand Buddha is a fairyland relief of clay figures, with Guanyin, the Goddess of Mercy, at its center. Guanyin, China's most venerated goddess, is still petitioned by those seeking a male child or a miraculous cure. In Lingyin Temple, she is portrayed as standing on a fish with a bottle of merciful waters in her hand (as she is also a protector of mariners). When I was last in this temple I saw two old women and one young man kneeling with lighted incense before the goddess.

The rare attraction at Lingyin is not its crowded, reconstructed temple but the limestone mountain to the south: the **Peak That Flew from Afar (Feilai Feng),** so named because it resembles a holy mountain in India seemingly transported to China. The peak, nearly 500 feet high, contains four caves and about 380 Buddhist rock carvings, most of them created over 600 years ago during the Yuan Dynasty. The caves are a 20-minute walk from the temple. They are always teeming with visitors.

The most famous carving is of another Laughing Buddha, carved in the year A.D. 1000. This Buddha of the Future is laughing with joy at the ultimate glorious fate of the world and he is laughing with amusement at the childish vanities of the unenlightened. His elongated earlobes symbolize his wisdom. His round bulging belly is an outward manifestation of his inner powers.

Scholars consider these carvings the most important of their kind in southern China. They are more animated, realistic, and gaudy than the Buddhist sculptures done earlier on a more extensive scale in northern China and along the Silk Road where Buddhism entered the Middle Kingdom from India. Although you will find much grander Buddhist rock carvings in those more remote regions of China, Lingyin Temple and its flying peak are worth a visit, even if the crowds are of such magnitude that any desire for quiet and contemplation is forever extinguished. Remember that among the Chinese themselves, Hangzhou is near the top of the all-time best-places-to-visit list.

Dragon Well Tea

A less frantic jaunt by bicycle is toward the village of **Dragon Well,** the capital of Hangzhou's famous **Longjing tea,** grown only on these hillsides and revered throughout China as cool and refreshing—a favorite summertime quencher. Longjing tea is said to be a supreme vintage with four special characteristics: its green color, smooth appearance, fragrant aroma, and sweet taste. When Emperor Qianlong came to these hills (perhaps after discovering Beggar's Chicken down by the lake), he picked tea at Dragon Well village and returned to Beijing with leaves for his mother. Thereafter, yearly tributes of Longjing tea were shipped via the Grand Canal to the Forbidden City. The best tea at Dragon Well is still picked and processed by hand. The villagers begin picking in late March or early April. The first of the 30 pickings is by far the best of the 16 grades of Longjing tea now produced. At Dragon Well and in nearby Tiger Spring, where the best spring water for tea brewing was first discovered by a Tang Dynasty monk, you can buy the tea directly from the source.

The bike ride to Dragon Well requires nearly an hour and the road is sometimes steep, but the journey is an exceptional one. This is pure countryside, inundated with large tea plantations, and while three-quarters of China's population lives in the country, few visitors ever get a chance to see their homes. You can at Hangzhou. On the way, you can stop at the **China Tea Museum,** opened in 1990 (open 8:30am to 4:30pm, admission RMB 60/$7.25) and comb through its extensive displays of Chinese teas, ceremonial tea implements, and model teahouses from several regions of China and other countries.

Dragon Well village is, these days, a visitor trap, but not an unpleasant one. Plenty of local grandmas are on hand to kidnap independent travelers, take them into their homes and kitchens, ply them with hand-picked tea, and sell them a few pounds at inflated prices. They can be resisted, but they can also be regarded as a special indulgence.

Ten years ago, when I first visited Hangzhou, I boarded a public bus to Dragon Well village. A peasant woman latched onto me at once and refused to let go. She couldn't speak a word of English and almost none of the official dialect, Mandarin, but she had mastered the jingle, "Longjing tea, Longjing tea," and with this mantra she made many a convert. She promised to guide me to the tea hills. When we arrived, she conducted me on a whirlwind tour of the grounds of the village, where to this day there is a stream of rippling waters and an old pool where tossed coins float on its tense surface.

Of course her true objective was to whisk me through the village amongst clumps of tea bushes and into her house, where she brewed up some Longjing and launched into her hard sell. An old man sitting out front, drawing on a long, narrow pipe, was exhibited as proof of the amazing properties of said tea, one of which is longevity. He was 80, the woman said (and I thought at the time, by god, he looks it). Meanwhile, a neighbor lady dropped in hoping to sell me her tea as well. I managed to escape with a pound of Longjing tea in a plastic bag but not before my host went so far as to point out her children's badly worn shoes and patched clothing. This Dragon Well tea lady was a terrific operator, a harbinger of the entrepreneurial 1990s, certainly not the last of her kind. Today the village still peddles its wares to visitors as aggressively as ever—but there are few places in China where foreigners are so openly and easily invited into a village home. This village is one place where I don't mind the vendors.

Eden of the East

Hangzhou is a rarity in China: a city in a beautiful setting that's made for strolling and biking. You can do the usual things here, too, and they are pleasant enough fillers: Visit the museums (there are new ones devoted to silk, traditional medicines, and pottery, as well as tea); tour the factories (the Hangzhou Silk and Satin Printing and Dyeing Complex is China's largest); and patronize the shops (tea, silk, and painted fans are nationally famous products). But Hangzhou's essence is outside, on the lake, on the walkways, and in the folds of the green tea-laden hills. At the end of the Southern Song Dynasty, in 1279, just 4 years after Marco Polo became the first foreign visitor, Hangzhou was the largest urban center in the world, and probably the most refined. Its Heavenly Avenue was China's main street, lavish and pulsating, a thoroughfare so ripe with splendors it even contained shops for the wealthy featuring fish for pet cats. The imperial glitter has long faded from its more ordinary streets, but the beauty of West Lake endures like a dream, like an Eden of the East.

PRACTICAL INFORMATION

ORIENTATION

Hangzhou is located in northern Zhejiang Province, near the East China Sea, 115 miles southwest of Shanghai. Most visitors arrive by rail from Shanghai, although some come by plane directly from Hong Kong or Beijing. Downtown is concentrated on the east and northeast shores of West Lake. Summers are quite hot and humid, making spring and autumn the times to visit, although winters are mild with only occasional snowfalls.

GETTING THERE

By Plane Dragonair offers direct service from Hong Kong (a 2-hour flight). Dragonair's office in Hangzhou is in the lobby of the Dragon Hotel, Shuguang Road (☎ 0571/799-8833, ext 6061; fax 0571/798-7902). (In the United States, Cathay Pacific handles Dragonair reservations; ☎ 800/233-2742.) Various Chinese airlines connect Hangzhou to most major mainland cities (2 hours to Beijing, 25 minutes to Shanghai). The Hangzhou airport is 9 miles from downtown; taxi fare is about RMB 50 ($6). For airport information, call ☎ 0571/514-1010.

By Train The most common way to reach Hangzhou is via train (3 hours) from Shanghai. Soft-seat train tickets on the Hangzhou–Shanghai run cost about RMB 30 ($3.60) when purchased from hotel tour desks. The No. 7 bus connects the train station to downtown and to the Shangri-La Hotel. For train information, call ☎ 0571/702-3729.

By Ship Hangzhou is also served by overnight passenger boats on the **Grand Canal** from Suzhou (see the chapter on the Grand Canal).

GETTING AROUND

Bicycle Rental If you stay out of downtown, bike riding in Hangzhou can be a pleasure. The multispeed mountain bikes for rent at the **Shangri-La Hotel** (see below) are in top condition (brakes work, tires don't flatten, locks function). Rates are RMB 20 ($2.40) per hour, RMB 50 ($6) per half day, RMB 100 ($12) per day.

TOURS & STRATAGEMS

China International Travel Service (CITS) provides tours only for prearranged groups and has been unable to assist me as an individual traveler. CITS is located on the northeast corner of West Lake at 1 Shihan Lu (☎ 0571/515-2888; fax 0571/515-6667). For local guided tours, you'll have to rely upon the tour desk in your hotel (which is usually a middle-man for CITS or another tour agency that can't seem to deal with foreigners directly).

The business center in the Shangri-La Hotel's West Building offers escorted half-day and full-day tours of Hangzhou,

conducted by local English-speaking guides, with the price based on the number of participants. Half-day tours cost RMB 470 ($57) for a lone individual, RMB 300 ($36) per person for groups of two to five people, RMB 200 ($24) per person for groups of six to nine, and RMB 160 ($19) per person for groups of 10 or more. Full-day tour rates are proportionate, costing RMB 696 ($84) for a lone individual, RMB 420 ($51) per person for groups of two to five people, RMB 320 ($38) per person for groups of six to nine, and RMB 240 ($29) per person for groups of 10 or more.

WHERE TO STAY

Shangri-La Hotel Hangzhou (Hangzhou Xiangge Lila Fandian). *78 Beishan Road (north shore of West Lake).* ☎ *800/942-5050 or 0571/797-7951. Fax 0571/799-6637. 387 rms. A/C MINIBAR TV TEL. $185 double (hillside view), $235 double (lakeside view). AE, DC, JCB, MC, V.* There's no doubt that the Shangri-La Hotel Hangzhou is the number one address in the city, as it has been for the past two decades. Its location is ideal for exploring West Lake. Beginning as a Soviet-style hotel constructed during the 1950s, the Shangri-La has been extensively remodeled and modernized. An elaborate covered walkway connects the hotel's East and West buildings. Rooms in both wings are clean, modern, spacious and well equipped. The lakeside view rooms are worth the extra money for the splendid view. The service is what one expects from a 5-star international hotel: thorough and efficient. The business center handles tours and the luggage counter arranges bicycle rental; both are in the West Building.

Services: Concierge, room service (24-hour), dry cleaning and laundry (24-hour, same day), nightly turndown, daily maid service, express checkout, foreign exchange counter.

Facilities: In-house movies, health club (exercise machines), Jacuzzi, sauna, tennis courts (outdoor), business center (24-hour, conference rooms), tour desk, beauty salon, shopping arcade.

Wang Hu Hotel (Wanghu Binguan). *2 Huancheng Xi Lu (downtown, two blocks from lakeshore).* ☎ *0571/707-1024. Fax 0571/707-3027. 364 rms. A/C MINIBAR TV TEL. $125 double. AE, DC, JCB, MC, V.* Recently renovated and upgraded from 3 to 4 stars, this downtown hotel doesn't offer the service and facilities of the Shangri-La, but it is a less expensive alternative. The staff is not proficient in English. The rooms are large, clean, and feature safes. There's not much of a view and the streets are noisy, but it's only a two-block walk to Lakeside Avenue. If you're on a budget, inquire about cheaper rooms, since some of the floors have not been upgraded yet.

WHERE TO DINE

My two favorite Chinese restaurants in Hangzhou are both expensive, but neither requires reservations or fancy dress.

The **Lou Wai Lou (Pavilion Beyond Pavilion)** restaurant is located at 30 Gushan Lu (☎ 0571/796-9023; fax 0571/702-9023), on Solitary Hill Island, between the Xiling Seal Engraving Society and the Zhejiang Library. Its dining halls are a bit garish, reminiscent of Qing Dynasty decline, and the service is not always tip-top, but the dishes are fine examples of local specialties, such as Beggar's Chicken, West Lake Carp, Shelled Shrimp with Longjing Tea Leaves, Dongpo Pork, and Bamboo Shoots. In past summers, Lou Wai Lou has also offered dinner cruises on West Lake. Expect to pay about RMB 150 ($18) per person for four moderate courses at Lou Wai Lou.

For a full range of Chinese dishes, including some Hangzhou specialties, in a more elegant setting with better service, there's the Shangri-La Hotel's signature restaurant, **Shang Palace** (☎ 0571/797-7951). It's superb. Full dinners cost from $12 to $25 and up, depending on what you order.

Humbler fare is available one-half block west of the Shangri-La Hotel at the **Have-A-Bite Cafe** (the sign is in English), a Chinese fast-food venue that's used to serving up rice and noodle concoctions to Westerners at reasonable prices (RMB 25 to 60/$3 to $5).

For Western-style fast foods, there are (at last count) three **Kentucky Fried Chicken** outlets (including a big one downtown on Renhe Lu, two blocks from West Lake, and a new branch a few blocks west of the Shangri-La Hotel at the intersection of Beishan and Lingyin roads).

For beer, snacks, and late-night entertainment, check out the **Casablanca Country Bar,** 23 Hubin Lu, in Lakeside Park (☎ 0571/702-5934).

The best Western dinners in town are at **Peppino's,** Shangri-La Hotel, East Building, second floor (☎ 0571/797-7951), where the Italian pastas, breads, and brick-oven pizzas are fresh and expertly seasoned, the ice creams and cappuccinos are rich, and the prices are bearable (RMB 80 to 110/$10 to $14 for main courses).

SHANGHAI: CHINA'S BOOMTOWN

上海

To TAKE THE PULSE OF SHANGHAI, the trick is to make a long circuit on foot. I always begin uptown on Nanjing Road, the great shopping street of China, and walk a few miles east to the edge of the Huangpu River, presided over by the green towering roof of the historic Peace Hotel. There I turn south down the spacious promenade that runs between the river and that remarkable architectural museum known as the Bund, where the neoclassical business offices of Shanghai's colonial period form an unforgettable skyline. Then I head back uptown, dropping by the splendid teahouse and garden in the old Chinese Quarter. Continuing west, I pay a visit to the new Shanghai Museum, then swing through the French Concession back to where I started. It's a long walk with plenty of distractions—sometimes I spend two days covering this route—but by the time I finish, Shanghai is under my skin and the crowded, hectic, always surprising streets of congested Shanghai have swallowed me.

Only these days I've added a preamble, adopting a new frame of reference furnished by a new Shanghai that is just now emerging on the other side of the Huangpu River. There, in the Pudong New Development Zone, east of all that used to be Shanghai, a new Shanghai is being born.

East Shanghai

At any given moment, fully one-fifth of the world's high-lift cranes are at work in the city of Shanghai. In one massive convulsion, the urban landscape is being erased and redrawn. When the smoke clears in a decade or two, China's largest city is slated to assume the position now occupied by Hong Kong as the nation's commercial center. The plan is to make Shanghai China's first fully modernized metropolis, its Pearl of the Orient for the 21st century.

Meanwhile, traces of Shanghai's past—its cultural relics, its quaint architectural monuments to Western colonial days, and its legacy of

112

In case you want to be welcomed there.

We're here to see that you're always welcomed at establishments everywhere. That's why millions of people carry the American Express® Card – for peace of mind, confidence, and security, around the world or just around the corner.

do more

AMERICAN
EXPRESS

Cards

In case you're running low.

We're here to help with more than 118,000 Express Cash locations around the world. In order to enroll, just call American Express before you start your vacation.

Express Cash

And just in case.

We're here with American Express® Travelers Cheques and Cheques *for Two*® They're the safest way to carry money on your vacation and the surest way to get a refund, practically anywhere, anytime.

Another way we help you...

do more ®

AMERICAN EXPRESS

Travelers Cheques

poverty and pollution—are seeping into the margins. If Shanghai is where the next century begins, then the future is being nurtured in the craters of 25,000 construction sites.

When you come to Shanghai these days, it is not the notorious Shanghai of old that fascinates so much as the bold Shanghai that's remaking itself. The first thing to do, then, is see for yourself the heart of a new China, which is now located just across the Huangpu River, east of its monuments to the past.

Shanghai's dream of remaking itself already has a monument there, the **Pearl of the Orient TV Tower,** Asia's tallest structure at 1,535 feet. Visible for miles from downtown Shanghai, it stands in the **Pudong New Development Zone,** straight east from the Bund, that familiar museum of moribund European customhouses, banks, and taipan clubs that epitomized Shanghai's business success when foreigners ran the city. To reach that tower and to see the extent of Shanghai's economic boom, I booked a Pudong tour from a hotel travel desk.

The seat of power in Shanghai is shifting east to Pudong, to what will become known as East Shanghai. Pudong is the new city's leading edge, its heart of trade, bordered by the river that feeds the interior of China and the ocean that links it to the Western world. It's not what ordinarily attracts visitors to China, but it's at the essence of what Shanghai is. The TV tower is a genuine tourist attraction, open daily from 8am to 9pm. You buy a ticket outside the gate (RMB 50/$6), check handbags and cameras, and inside enter an elevator that lifts off like a rocket. The uniformed elevator operator recites TV tower statistics from memory in Chinese and English as you ascend a quarter of a mile to the observation deck. There you have a 360-degree view of all of Shanghai, east and west, new and old, and everything that's being squeezed between.

It must be said that Pudong itself is barely off the ground, a drawing board of the future. Much of the work is on an infrastructure that barely shows: transportation, communications, energy. Where Pudong meets the Pacific Ocean at **Waigaoqiao,** a deep-water port is being crafted, capable of servicing ships in excess of 50,000 tons—over three times the size that can navigate the shallow Huangpu River. Pudong's Pacific Ocean facilities could make Shanghai the shipping center of the Far East. In addition, Pudong will be the site of Shanghai's second airport, scheduled to open in 1999, with a passenger capacity of 60 million yearly, substantially more than Hong Kong's new Chek Lap Kok Airport. By the year 2000, Shanghai could become the region's number one aviation hub.

To connect downtown Shanghai to Pudong, the city subway system will add a Number Two Line as early as 1999. The main highway link has already been forged: the Inner Ring Road, a modern freeway that encircles east and west Shanghai. Two more bridges across the Huangpu and a new Pudong railroad station are also planned.

Shanghai

From the observation deck in the Pearl of the Orient TV Tower, I try to measure the extent of these developments. So far, Pudong looks like an empty field of mud compared to downtown Shanghai, but it is here that the most extensive remodeling of Shanghai is taking place, here that blocks of low-rise buildings and farms will be bulldozed and high-tech parks, international offices, and financial complexes will rise. Many of China's provinces will open trade offices in East Shanghai, banks quartered in Beijing will move south, and much of Pudong's rural population will migrate across the river into the vast inland suburbs.

Already the Shanghai Times Square complex in Pudong boasts the largest department store in Asia, Nextage, the second biggest in the world after Macy's. An 88-story office building is now complete. What will be the world's tallest building, the 1,509-foot **Shanghai Financial Centre**, topping the Sears Tower in Chicago and the Petronas Towers in Kuala Lumpur, is in its final stages of construction. This modern tower is a perfect example of the towering city Shanghai is confident of becoming, but the Pearl of the Orient is already East Shanghai's emblem. Its 11 blue-and-green spheres are pearls in the flashy string of Shanghai's sudden wealth, glittering night and day, a bold statement that can't be ignored, even from the downtown streets across the river.

Downtown Shanghai

So far, East Shanghai is only a raw promise, a dream barely scratching the surface of reality. In downtown Shanghai proper, on the west side of the river, modernization is also under way and it has more substance. Altered beyond recognition by torn streets and detours, by demolitions and new building sites, downtown Shanghai resembles a giant erector set dropped from the sky.

I begin my exploration at **Shanghai Centre**, a complex of offices, apartments, and shops that is the most prestigious business address in the city. It is located 2 miles west of the Huangpu River up Nanjing Road, Shanghai's main street. Shanghai Centre is a city within the city, a joint venture opened in 1990 that has become the emblem of the new international Shanghai. Its 472 Western-style apartments house many of the city's high-rolling foreign businesspeople, requiring rents that exceed those in Tokyo, London, and New York. With a shopping mall, supermarket, preschool, health club, theater, exhibition hall, and plenty of pricey restaurants, lounges, and even an espresso bar, some foreign residents scarcely venture out into the city streets. Indeed, why should they? Shanghai, more than ever, is a city of heat and noise, grit and sweat, a factory without walls.

Shanghai Centre also provides 25,000 square meters of office space, each unit let at astronomical rates and augmented by Shanghai's most sophisticated telecommunications system (operated by America's Bell

South). The entire complex is a high-tech version of the Foreign Concessions that once occupied entire neighborhoods in prerevolutionary Shanghai, a fantasy island that would seem unreal were it not that the city around it is taking on the same Westernized appearance.

Susan Schulman, who works for Shanghai Centre, is among the more than 900 foreigners living inside this complex. She shares a one-bedroom apartment with her husband and their cat from America. The monthly rent is approaching $10,000. I asked her if Shanghai is now one of those cities that seems to change overnight. "It's changed every day since I've been here," she answers. "I can barely remember what it looked like when we first came—less than a year ago." She's begun taking a snapshot a week from their apartment window to chronicle what Ian Buruma, writing for the *New York Times,* called "perhaps the greatest urban transformation since Baron Haussmann rebuilt Paris in the 19th century."

To sample this great transformation directly, I walk the length of Nanjing Road east from Shanghai Centre to the **Bund promenade** on the riverfront. There's no more instructive or fascinating walk in Shanghai. I know the road extremely well, having strolled it frequently in the 1980s and early 1990s. Almost nothing along it looks familiar now. Entire blocks are partitioned off to make way for proposed new office and shopping complexes that follow the Western model—mirror images of Shanghai Centre. The construction billboard for Hanson Garden boasts that it will offer "two blocks of 24-story high-class residential flats," a "10,000-square-foot shopping mall," and "underground car parks." Within minutes I pass the massive **Westgate Mall** and a sidewalk arcade featuring fast-food chicken from KK Roasters and pasta and cappuccino from the Gino Cafe. A Burberrys of London is followed by a Nautica outlet store and finally a shop that a decade earlier would have been unthinkable anywhere on Nanjing Road, anywhere in China: a thriving Playboy Store, its bunny logo gracing a variety of upscale merchandise.

I shouldn't be taken aback. This is no longer Mao's fashion show. The younger women in the streets are cavorting in the latest Western fashions: high heels, short skirts, black tights, flashy earrings, and curly, red-tinted coiffures. Shanghai has long been China's capital of fashion, and it always looks outward with intensity. Young couples flock to Western wedding parlors. A Kentucky Fried Chicken occupies the entrance to People's Park.

The trick is to find something you won't find in the great cities of the West. A Hard Rock Cafe has opened at Shanghai Centre. Even the airwaves are aslant with call-in talk shows addressing hitherto taboo subjects. The venerable department stores have undergone glitzy face-lifts. The New World Department Store is the jazziest of them all, with its bubble-glass walls, curving escalators, and camera film kept fresh in a refrigerated case. By the time I come to the end of Nanjing Road on the

Huangpu harbor, the only familiar sight I've passed is here, where the refurbished Peace Hotel still stands. Across the river is Pudong and the TV tower where I started this jaunt, a gargantuan Tinkertoy visible from deep downtown.

Peace Hotel

Before crossing over the river and going down the Bund promenade, I always take a stroll through the lobby of the Peace Hotel on the corner. It is Shanghai's grand monument to art deco, and some of the original design still clings to its walls, columns, furnishings, and carved woodwork.

It was originally the Sassoon House, built by one of Shanghai's legendary immigrant tycoons, Victor Sassoon, a Jew from Baghdad, who ended up owning thousands of city properties. Erected in 1930, it included the redoubtable Cathay Hotel, one of the finest in Asia. Sassoon kept his offices in the pyramid tower. Noel Coward did some writing in one of its suites. And Stephen Spielberg filmed a scene of *Empire of the Sun* here, re-creating the view that a hotel guest would have had of the Japanese bombing of Shanghai during World War II.

In the north wing the hotel jazz band plays swing music every evening. One or two of the members started out in the late 1930s, when this was the number one jazz club in China. Today, it's simply the place for a nostalgic evening of fun.

The Bund

With the exception of the Peace Hotel lobby and roof, old Nanjing Road has all but disappeared. Even the promenade along the Bund has been extended and remodeled, complete with a spiffy new public restroom complex. Only the monumental European architecture of the Bund seems unchanged, and thus more out of place in Shanghai than ever before. These were once the triumphant seats of power of Shanghai's Western masters—the banks, private clubs, and grand offices of the taipans who ran Shanghai for nearly a hundred years, beginning in the 1840s when Shanghai became a treaty port.

Seven of these rock-solid old buildings have new owners and tenants today, and Shanghai plans to sell or lease 10 more to financial institutions from inside and outside China. From north to south, these neoclassical dinosaurs include the former homes of the **British Consulate,** the **Jardine & Matheson trading company,** the stately **Cathay Hotel,** the **Shanghai Customshouse,** the **Hong Kong and Shanghai Bank** (built in 1921), and the **Tung Feng Hotel** (once the site of the Shanghai Club). Other buildings in this lineup include former consulates, brokerage houses, chambers of commerce, and banks from Japan, India, Denmark, France, Belgium, Britain, and Canada.

The Bund's stately skyline still defines Shanghai, setting it apart from any other city in China, but behind this facade higher monuments are rising, and across the river, of course, Pudong is casting its massive shadow.

It would be easy to exaggerate the extent of this transformation. Women still sweep the streets with long straw brooms. China's "floating population" still migrates to Shanghai, homeless in its streets. Few can afford their own motorcycle or automobile, although the local VW plant is turning out 150,000 Santanas yearly for the domestic market. For an increasing number of residents, there is the chance to make money. Shanghai is where most of the stock in China is traded, and the new stock exchange building will be twice as large as Hong Kong's.

At the south end of the Bund promenade there's a curious old brick tower that looks like a nautical pagoda. Spared the relentless march of modernization, it is now the **Bund Museum,** fitted with photographs and artifacts from Shanghai's days as a colonial river port. A cast-iron circular staircase leads to the lookout, where harbormasters once kept an eye on the junks that plied interior China on the Yangzi and clippers that sailed to every great port in the world. The museum is open daily from 8:30am to 4:30pm (admission RMB 5/60¢).

These days, the Bund promenade is filled with far more visitors from inside China than out. Before the working day starts, this is the place to be for morning exercises. Hundreds of residents do their morning *tai ji quan* workouts along the riverside, escaping for an hour into their own slow, quiet worlds before entering the maelstrom of work and commerce. Some of that commerce takes place on the promenade. Tour boats depart for Huangpu River tours, outdoor cafes sell sodas and snacks, ferries cross the river to the Pearl of the Orient TV Tower, and peddlers push their wagons of ice-cream treats up and down the walkway. Artists also wade through the stream of visitors. I was approached by one enterprising artist, armed with scissors, who struck up a conversation as we sauntered along the river. He swiftly captured my likeness, cutting out two paper silhouettes as we walked, mounting both when we paused, and selling them to me on the spot. A moment later, he vanished, a step ahead of the licensing authorities.

The Best Little Old Teahouse in China

From the Bund it's a short walk southwest to Shanghai's **old Chinese Quarter.** Throughout the city, the belief seems widespread that if you build a modern city, wealth will beat a path to your door. Even **Nanshi,** Shanghai's Old Town, harbors this hope. Yu Yuan, the city's classic garden, and Huxintang Teahouse, with its zigzag Bridge of Nine Turnings, remain intact in the heart of old Shanghai. But these two delightful tourist stops are now surrounded by a new shopping mall. Mo's Burgers and Church's Chicken rub shoulders with Lao Fandian restaurant and the

Tong Han Chun Traditional Medicine Store. What's surprising is that the commercial remodeling blends in with the old neighborhood of shop houses, pavilions, and the Temple to the Town God. Shanghai seems aware of the need to preserve the look and essence of its endangered past, even when redeveloping a tourist zone.

Many feel they already know the garden teahouse, **Huxinting Teahouse,** at the heart of Old Town the first time they see it; it could well have served as the model for classic Blue Willow tableware. Yet even this island of tranquility is responding to the construction frenzy currently shaking China's greatest metropolis to its foundations. The alleyways surrounding the teahouse, once lined with small shops and stalls, have fallen to the bulldozer of progress, replaced by a modern shopping mall of department stores and fast-food outlets featuring hamburgers as well as dumplings. The Huxinting Teahouse and adjacent Yu Yuan Garden, Shanghai's premier legacies of Old China, have a fresh setting.

This arena of commercial development, officially known as the **Yu Yuan Shopping Centre,** located in the oldest inhabited section of Shanghai, reflects the classic Chinese low-rise style. The structures that now hug the shores of the pond where the teahouse floats like a lotus flower are faithful to the architecture of a century past. Sweeping tiled rooflines, ornately carved entryways, and massive wooden columns are the rule. The look of the traditional shop house is preserved, even when these antique-style facades house outlets for fast food.

Next door to the teahouse, the remodeled **Lao Fandian,** founded in 1862, is still serving the best local specialties, including spicy hot eel and shrimp dishes. Perhaps the cuisine most often associated with Old Town, however, is snack food. For decades, visitors to the teahouse and garden gorged themselves on a variety of pastries and dumplings, from wheat flour muffins with a variety of fillings to glutinous rice balls with pigeon eggs. This Chinese-style "fast food" (fast to eat but slow to prepare) remains the most popular fare, although hamburgers, milk shakes, fried chicken, and mashed potatoes are catching on.

A few years ago, visitors with a taste for Chinese snacks might have stood in line at the Moslemo Restaurant (run by local minority people), located on the edge of the teahouse lake. Crowded and unkempt, this place afforded a splendid view of the bridge and teahouse, but the food was, at best, hearty. Today, the old cafe has been expanded and cleaned up. Renamed the Nanxiang Snack Bar, it adjoins the Hu Bin restaurant. From a picture window outside you can watch the cooks preparing thousands of little pastries in the kitchen. Lining the western shore of the teahouse lake, this establishment serves traditional steamed snacks that are delicately fashioned and appealing to the palate.

The entire shopping area, which radiates out several blocks from the teahouse, is far more appealing than in the past. Many of the shops continue to offer the small native commodities that made the old bazaar one of China's most famous marketplaces. Chopsticks fill one specialty store, silk cloth another. The newly expanded **Tong Han Chun Medicine Store** dispenses traditional remedies. Other shops stock bamboo products, fans, and incense sticks, and there are larger emporiums that dispense a full range of regional arts and crafts. Two of old Shanghai's best-known products are available at little shops within a block of the teahouse: spiced beans and pear syrup (the latter, Shanghai's answer to the cough drop).

There is up-to-date shopping, too. A new department store a few steps from the zigzag bridge does a brisk business in handbags and luggage, including the latest roll-on suitcases embossed with likenesses of Mickey Mouse. The **World Shopping Centre** on the mall's southwest corner carries plenty of Western imports. The largest new structure is an amusement center teeming with the latest electronic and video games. A vending machine invasion has been launched as well. Coca-Cola machines, automatic teller machines (ATMs), digital height and weight machines, even a brigade of shiny new portable toilets are moving into Old Town Shanghai.

Because of the tasteful remodeling of the teahouse shopping area, the old and the new do coexist neatly. Traditional Chinese dining and shopping mix with the latest from the West. One notable beneficiary of redevelopment has been the **Temple to the Town Gods (Cheng Huang Miao)**. Built on the grounds of a 15th-century temple, its back garden became the southern section of Yu Yuan Garden in 1709. During this century, the Temple of the Town Gods often fell on hard times, once even serving as a warehouse. It is now an active place of worship. In the old days, the temple was the center of seasonal flower shows (plum blossoms in spring, chrysanthemums in autumn), street fairs, and lively markets. Today, that marketplace atmosphere has returned, particularly on Sunday, when Shanghai's largest antique market takes over the temple square.

Weekdays are only slightly less crowded. Visitors number up to 200,000 a day. The teahouse is the sole refuge—a fine place to sip tea at one's leisure while contemplating the frantic pace of life on every side. This five-sided, two-story pavilion, with its dramatic upturned eaves and gray-tiled double roof, dates from 1784. It was built by merchants in the cotton trade as a place to broker their products. No tea was sold on its premises. In fact, Huxinting did not become a teahouse until a century later. Today it is the most visited teahouse in China.

Like the teahouse, **Yu Yuan Garden** is unchanged—a solid, beautiful monument from the past that doesn't require updating. Its undulating dragon walls still shelter its pavilions, pools, rookeries, and winding paths from a changing world outside, making it Shanghai's 16th-century retreat in the center of a city readying itself for the 21st century.

After my most recent visit to Yu Yuan, I am confident in pronouncing it the single most beautiful classical garden in China, surpassing even those of Suzhou. Don't miss it, especially in the morning or late afternoon when the crowds are somewhat less pressing. And don't worry about the name or function of each pavilion. This is a garden to lose yourself in, a maze of delights. It's open daily from 8:30am to 4:30pm (admission RMB 15/ $1.80).

The new Yu Yuan Shopping Centre at the heart of Old Town is old-fashioned in one sense, at least: It is a place for pedestrians only. Taxis and tourist buses line up blocks away on the fringes. The festive atmosphere recalls the era of the temple bazaar, and the style of the remodeled shops enhances one's enjoyment of older pleasures. One enduring pastime—my favorite here—consists of slowly crossing the zigzag bridge and watching the pageant of humanity parade past. The people drawn to the teahouse are as various as the newly refurbished Old Town, as various as today's Shanghai, where residents of two worlds—one passing away, the other unfolding—can meet. The teahouse is a magnet to everyone who comes to Shanghai, a dream of the old ways awakening to the outside world.

French Concession

From 1842 on, Europeans carved up Shanghai into concessions, large neighborhoods where they built villas and residential blocks in the architectural styles of the West. The French Concession, often called **Frenchtown,** with its art deco and Tudor town houses and its neo-Gothic office blocks, survives to this day south of Nanjing Road and west of the Bund.

To reach Frenchtown from the Chinese Old Town, I walk west along Huaihai Road, which runs parallel to Nanjing Road and is also a major shopping street. Locals usually check it out first these days, as new shops often open here before they make their debut (and raise their prices) on the more upscale Nanjing Road.

Frenchtown is over a mile from the Bund, and the walking can be slow owing not only to the plethora of construction sites in the way but to the crush of pedestrians, which can leave your shoulders sore by the end of the day. But Frenchtown's architecture is worth the walk. The cityscape is another page from Shanghai's colonial days. The best-preserved area is along Maoming Nan Lu at the **Jin Jiang Hotel,** a massive complex of dark marble. This is where President Nixon stayed after signing the Shanghai Communiqué, the document that reopened China to the West in 1972, and it's also in the heart of the French District. Across the street is the **Garden Hotel,** a modern tower that contains a unique cultural treasure: the original stained glass, carved ceiling, and staircase of the entrance to the Cercle Sportif Francais, once the exclusive social center of well-to-do foreigners in Shanghai's age of decadence, the 1920s and 1930s.

Fewer traces of notorious Shanghai remain each year. The French Quarter still has some avenues lined with the shops and houses of its heyday (1910–30), and these are being cleaned up and refitted with boutiques for the tourist trade. Several dozen mansions also exist, although few are open to the public. Still, well over 1,400 monumental Western-style buildings have been documented recently in Shanghai, and the major European-built hotels, churches, mansions, private residences, garden villas, and public buildings from the past two centuries will probably be preserved for the next century—with an eye to capturing the growing tourism dollar, if nothing else.

Shanghai Museum

There's a Chinese legacy in Shanghai as well, and it is being preserved, too, although the chief treasures have moved into modern quarters. The new oval-shaped Shanghai Museum, on the south side of People's Square, is China's most up-to-date museum. When I visited it on a Sunday morning, the plaza was teeming with skateboarders, in-line skaters, and children flying paper kites purchased from roving vendors.

Inside, the galleries are as modern as any in the world: the floors carpeted, the explanatory signs in English as well as Chinese, the track lighting precise and illuminating. There are four floors of exhibits, each floor looking down on an immense atrium. Stalls on each floor sell gifts and museum reproductions, and there are two larger gift shops on the ground floor. Galleries devoted to bronzes and stone sculpture are on the first floor. Ceramics dominate the second floor. Paintings, calligraphy, and seals (chops) have separate galleries on the third floor, and coins, jade, furniture, and minority displays are on the top floor. The two most impressive galleries are those of sculpture and of jade, featuring artifacts that span all the major dynasties back to the New Stone Age.

Using the audiophone (included in the admission price) literally throws light on some of the exhibits. The phone is keyed by number to certain exhibits. When you press the number of the selected exhibit, a light beam is activated to highlight that display and an explanatory tape is played on the earphone.

While the museum's 120,000 treasures are not on the scale of those collected in Beijing, Taipei, or even Xi'an, Shanghai shows that it knows how to display its past to a sophisticated international audience. On the second floor there is a fine tearoom for refreshment, with traditional Chinese furniture and a choice of cookies, four different teas, mineral water, and even Brazilian coffee. The museum is open daily from 9am to 5pm (admission RMB 60/$7.25).

The Greening of Shanghai

Shanghai has the look of one of the most polluted cities on Earth, its streets filthy, its rivers glutted with refuse. Its industries are siphoning off so much of the region's underground water that the city is sinking at an accelerated rate, nearly an inch per year now. There are two traffic deaths each and every day on average. Even food can become a pollution problem. Shanghai's mayor recently declared that his number one problem each summer is how to dispose of the one million melon rinds discarded daily.

Shanghai, however, is commited to making its future a livable one. Neighborhoods have formed beautification committees to monitor development with an eye toward aesthetics. Traffic on Nanjing Road and other major arteries has been regulated to avoid the gridlock strangling of such urban centers as Bangkok. A master plan has been developed to clean up Suzhou Creek, which enters the Huangpu at the Bund, and convert it to a recreational greenway for residents and visitors. Lu Shuping, who directs the Municipal Environmental Protection Bureau, says the Suzhou Creek project will proceed in three stages. In the next 2 years, trees and grass will be planted on the banks. By the year 2000, pollution sources will be eliminated. By 2010, Suzhou Creek will be rehabilitated. At the same time, auto exhaust emissions and other sources of pollution will come under municipal regulation.

Urban beautification is already under way. On the Pudong side of the Huangpu River, Riverside Avenue has been widened along a 2-mile stretch. Paralleling the Bund's promenade across the river, East Shanghai's version is being landscaped with terraces, greenbelts, public squares, musical fountains, and cafes.

Two decades from now, Shanghai could indeed become not only one of Asia's most powerful cities but one of its most pleasant. No one can say whether its double-digit economic growth will continue long enough to fuel such a transformation, especially in so short a time. With 13 million residents, Shanghai is China's most populous city, and the United Nations estimates that by the year 2015 Shanghai's population will reach the unimaginable figure of 23.4 million.

One population figure Shanghai relishes is its visitors' census. Seven of every ten visitors to China now pays a visit here. Some 200,000 more visitors arrive each year, which should soon push Shanghai's foreign visitor total to two million yearly.

Meanwhile, Shanghai's golden age has not quite arrived. Despite a relentless block-by-block reconstruction, Shanghai is not yet a modern metropolis, not yet a world financial center, not yet an unpolluted urban paradise. It is a construction site over which a blueprint is spread like a dream. But if any city can link China to the outside world on equal terms, it will be Shanghai. It is a city about to be born. Unshackled by the past, unbound by old traditions, outward-looking, Shanghai seems willing to recast itself whole and take a prominent role on the world stage of a new century. In few other cities in the world can you feel the future pressing so relentlessly.

PRACTICAL INFORMATION

ORIENTATION

Shanghai, which means "Above the Sea," is located near the East China Sea and the Yangzi River Delta, midway between Beijing (700 miles to the northwest) and Hong Kong (750 miles to the southwest). Summers are blisteringly hot, humid, and rainy, and winters are lengthy and cold. Spring brings unsettled weather, making autumn the best time to visit, as days then are generally warm but not humid.

The best day trip from Shanghai is the half-day boat tour of the **Huangpu River** (see "The Huangpu: Shanghai's River of Many Returns"). **Hangzhou** (see above) on West Lake is just $3^1/2$ hours southwest by train. **Suzhou** (see below), city of classical gardens, and **Lake Tai** (see "Tai Hu: China's Great Lake"), both to the north, are even closer by train and make excellent overnight extensions from Shanghai. Tickets to these sites, as well as for the river cruise, can be booked by hotel tour desks and CITS.

GETTING THERE

By Plane   Shanghai's Hongqiao Airport (☎ 021/6253-6530) has connections to major destinations inside and outside of China. Many international airlines serve Shanghai (although not as many as serve Beijing and Hong Kong). United Airlines (offices in Shanghai Centre, Room 204, West Wing) provides daily connections to the United States (☎ 021/6279-8009).

The airport is only 12 miles west of downtown Shanghai, but transfers can take up to an hour because of the traffic and construction detours. Taxi rates should be RMB 60 to RMB 100 ($7.25 to $12), depending on the downtown destination. An airport shuttle bus (RMB 3/35¢), run by China Eastern Airlines, goes as far as an office at 200 Yan'an Xi Lu, not far from Shanghai Centre, 2 miles west of the Huangpu River. Many hotels provide free airport shuttles, especially if you fax ahead your arrival times and transfer request.

By Train   From Shanghai's massive main train station (☎ 021/6317-9234), now fronted by metal detectors, there are trains to most cities and towns in China. Hotel tour desks can book onward tickets. Particularly easy to reach by train from Shanghai are the nearby towns of Hangzhou, Suzhou, and Wuxi (Lake Tai), which are covered in separate chapters.

The newest rail service is that of Train 99, launched to celebrate Hong Kong's return to sovereignty in 1997, connecting Shanghai to Hong Kong via China's most deluxe train. Train 99 leaves Shanghai Railway Station at 8:04am every other day, taking 29 hours 6 minutes to reach Kowloon Station in Hong Kong. Stops are made at Hangzhou, Yingtan, Zhuzhou, and Guangzhou (Canton). Train 100 returns the next day from Hong Kong at 3pm. The train uses the newest passenger cars made in China. "First-class performance" is promised. Sleeping berths are offered in three classes: hard sleepers (no compartments, $81 one-way per person), soft sleepers (four-bed compartments, $107 one-way per person), and "Luxurious Soft Sleeper Compartments" (two-bed compartments, $135 one-way per person).

By Ship Three passenger ships, the Haixin, the Shanghai, and the Jin Jiang, ply the Shanghai–Hong Kong route. It's a 3-night voyage with meals included. Although the facilities are not those of an international cruise ship, these vessels provide an interesting and relaxing experience. There's plenty of time to swap China stories with fellow passengers. A two-berth first-class cabin with private bath and shower costs about $150 per person. The Jin Jiang is the most luxurious vessel. Departures are from the International Passenger Quay, Wai Hong Qiao Harbour, Taipin Lu No. 1 (located a few blocks from Shanghai Mansions, north of the Bund). Book passage from CITS or a hotel tour desk.

GETTING AROUND

To get around Shanghai on your own, use an English-language map and set off on foot or by taxi. Many of the taxis can now print out customer receipts from their meters.

The Shanghai subway is a fairly clean, efficient means to navigate the crowded distances of the city. The main line connects the train station in the north to Jinjiang amusement park in the south, a 10-mile run. The most central stop is at Renmin Park (Renmin Shangchang Station). Tickets cost RMB 2/25¢), no matter what the distance. The subway's hours of operation are 5am to 9pm daily. The system will become more extensive with the opening of the east-west line linking the Hongqiao Airport to the Pudong Area sometime after the year 2000.

TOURS & STRATAGEMS

Tours China International Travel Service (CITS) arranges guided tours in English to all major sites, including Pudong. They were located in new offices at 2 Jinling Dong Lu (☎ 021/6321-7200), near the Bund, but are slated to open a new head office in Shanghai Centre. Hotel tour desks provide the same services. Hotels can also book air, train, and boat tickets.

Fast Facts The **Tourism Hotline** number is ☎ 021/6439-0630. **American Express**, 1376 Nanjing Xi Lu, Room 206, Shanghai Centre (☎ 021/6279-8082), offers traveler's assistance, but does not book tours or transportation, although with an American Express card you can cash personal checks at a number of Bank of China branches in Shanghai. Taxis around town should charge from RMB 15 to RMB 25 ($1.80 to $3).

The best selection of **books** on Shanghai and China is in the bookstore in the shopping arcade just inside the walls of the Jin Jiang Hotel, 59 Maoming Nan Lu, in Frenchtown. For reading up on Shanghai before arrival, try Pan Ling's In Search of Old Shanghai, Nien Cheng's Life and Death in Shanghai, Vicki Baum's Shanghai '37, J. G. Ballard's Empire of the Sun, and Sterling Seagrave's The Soong Dynasty.

Shanghai even has an English-language **radio station**, 105.7 FM, operating daily 9am to 5pm.

WHERE TO STAY

In addition to the hotels reviewed here, Shanghai is served by the **Westin Tai Ping Yang** (☎ 800/223-6800 or 021/6275-8888; fax 021/6275-5420); the **Nikko Longbai** (☎ 021/6268-9111; fax 021/6470-0008); the **Novotel Yuan Lin** (☎ 800/221-4542 or 021/6470-1688; fax 021 6470-0008); the **New Asia Tomson Hotel** in Pudong (☎ 021/5831-8888; fax 021/5831-7777); the **Holiday Inn Crowne Plaza Yinxing** (☎ 800/465-4329 or 021/6280-8888; fax 021/6280-2353); the **Garden Hotel** (☎ 800/223-5652 or 021/6415-1111; fax 021/6415-8866; the **JC Mandarin** (☎ 021/6279-1888; fax 021/6279-2314; and the **Sofitel Hyland Hotel** (☎ 800/221-4542 or 021/6351-5888; fax 021/6351-4088) downtown on **Nanjing Road**. The **Sheraton Hua Ting Hotel** (☎ 021/6439-1000) has reverted to Chinese management. Shangri-La, the largest deluxe hotel chain in China (☎ 800/942-5050), will soon open a hotel in Pudong, and will open the Jingan Nanli Hotel in the year 2000.

Peace Hotel (Heping Fandian). *20 Nanjing Dong Lu (on the Bund).* ☎ *021/6321-6888. Fax 021/6329-0300. 279 rms. A/C TV TEL. $175 double. JCB, MC, V.* This is the classic hotel of Shanghai, with art deco touches still in place. Some of the rooms were modernized in 1996. The rest are spacious and contain original woodwork and furnishings, but they are rundown. There are some grand suites, such as the elaborate India Room, but these are priced at well over $400. The service is slow and inefficient. In general, the hotel is overpriced and cleanliness is not quite up to international standards, but its location is superb and it has the romantic, nostalgic feel of prerevolutionary Shanghai. It carries a 4-star rating, but don't expect to find swimming pools and tennis courts.

Ritz-Carlton Portman Hotel (Boteman Dajiudian). *1376 Nanjing Xi Lu (inside the Shanghai Centre).* ☎ *021/6279-8888. Fax 021/6279-8887. 600 rms. A/C MINIBAR TV TEL. $250 double. AE, DC, JCB, MC, V.* Shanghai's tallest hotel at 50 stories, this is the city's number one business hotel, with the largest guest rooms (280–400 square feet). Writing desks, sofas, three phones, hair dryers, and in-room safes are standard. The adjacent Shanghai Centre (☎ 021/6279-8009) includes a Wellcome supermarket and deli (open 8am to 10:30pm), a Watson's drugstore, and an Espresso Americano coffee bar (☎ 021/6279-8518).

Services: Concierge, room service (24-hour), dry cleaning and laundry (same day), newspaper delivery, nightly turndown, twice-daily maid service, express checkout, free airport shuttle, foreign exchange counter.

Facilities: In-house movies, swimming (heated indoor-outdoor lap pool), health club (exercise machine, classes), Jacuzzi, sauna, tennis court, squash court, business center (24-hour, conference rooms), tour desk, beauty salon, shopping arcade, newsstand.

Shanghai Hilton International (Jinan Dajiudian). *250 Huashan Lu.* ☎ *800/445-8667 or 021/6248-0000. Fax 021/6248-3848. 767 rms, 8 suites. A/C MINIBAR TV TEL. $180 double. AE, DC, JCB, MC, V.* This 43-story tower has service and features second only to the Portman. The lobby is spacious and busy. Rooms have writing desks and settees. Executive floors (36 to 38) have their own lounge.

Services: Concierge, room service (24-hour), dry cleaning and laundry

(24-hour, same day), nightly turndown, daily maid service, express checkout, free airport shuttle, foreign exchange counter.

Facilities: In-house movies, pool (indoor, heated), health club (exercise machines, classes), sauna, tennis court, squash court, business center (24-hour, conference rooms), tour desk, beauty salon, shopping arcade, newsstand.

YMCA Hotel (Qian Nian Hui Binguan). *123 Xizang Nan Lu (two blocks south of Nanjing Road, 1 mile west of the Bund). ☎ 021/6326-1040. Fax 021/6320-1957. 165 rms. A/C TV TEL. $70–$82 double, $118–$178 suite. AE, JCB, MC, V.* This 11-story hotel, fronted by columns and topped by a traditional tiled roof, really was Shanghai's YMCA when it was built in 1929. Over the years, it has dropped its Christian affiliation. I first stayed here 10 years ago, when the condition of the rooms was miserable, but a local management group, Jin Jiang, has upgraded the interiors to the 3-star level. The service is friendly, the rooms small but modern and fairly clean. There's a 24-hour cafe in the lobby that serves Western dishes, a beauty salon, exercise machines, massage room, karaoke ballroom, and even a free airport shuttle. Most guests are Chinese, but the clerks at the counter can speak some English. For budget accommodations (and for those who don't expect too much), this is the best buy in Shanghai.

WHERE TO DINE

Shanghai has its own distinct cuisine, featuring river eel, crabs, and other seafood in light, sweet sauces, but there is a number of international choices in this most international of Chinese cities.

One local specialty you probably won't want to try is snake, valued for its ability to increase vitality. There's been a recent boom in snake restaurants, which now number 6,000, most illegal. Snakes come in live to cafes from the snake market in West Shanghai. One cafe that charges diners $20 per pound for cobra, $35 per pound for pit viper, and $4 per pound for the more common water snake, is said to be packed every night of the week. Sorry, I don't know its address.

The international hotels have excellent restaurants in Shanghai. The Hilton, the Garden, the Portman, and the Sofitel have fine (and expensive) outlets for Sichuan, Cantonese, Italian, French, and other cuisines. Shanghai Centre has an espresso bar, an Italian restaurant (Tony Roma's—renowned for its ribs), and the Long Bar, packed with expatriates from 11am to 3am daily.

International fast-food chains are proliferating in Shanghai. McDonald's is leading the latest charge. I happened to try one located north of the Jin Jiang Hotel in the French Quarter, finding it to be the best-run outlet of its type I'd ever seen in China. A little English was even spoken. While I ate lunch, a local business executive came in, guiding his frail mother by the arm. She'd clearly heard about these fast-food places from the West, but she'd never ventured into the barbarian's den until that afternoon. Her son dutifully steered here through the maze of tables (the place was packed) to the counter, where he pointed to the pictures of foreigners' food. She didn't order, but she was clearly amazed by every shining detail of this strange wokless, riceless restaurant.

Cafe Bistro. *5 Zunyi Nan Lu (in the Westin Tai Ping Nan Hotel, Level 1, on the way to the airport in the Hongqiao Development Zone). ☎ 021/6275-8888. Sun brunch RMB 148 ($18). AE, JCB, MC, V. Brunch 11:30am–2:30pm. BRUNCH/ INTERNATIONAL.* Shanghai's hotels put up elaborate brunches every Sunday, particularly at the Hilton and Sofitel, but the best deal is here. Children (12 years and under) eat for RMB 117 ($14). The buffets usually feature a cuisine (such as Thai) as their monthly special.

Crane Longevity Hall (He Souding). *20 Nanjing Dong Lu (south wing of the Peace Hotel, ground floor).* ☎ *021/6321-1244. Main courses $5–$12. AE, DC, JCB, MC, V. Daily 11am–midnight. SHANGHAI/WESTERN.* This was once the grand dining hall of the south wing of the Peace Hotel. In fact, the building is much older, dating from 1906, and the dining hall still has a lavish, decadent feel, with lace curtains and velvet drapes on the high windows along Nanjing Road. The menu is in English (some of it hilariously misspelled). The best choice is the steamed river eel.

Dragon and Phoenix Restaurant. *20 Nanjing Dong Lu (8th floor, Peace Hotel).* ☎ *021/6321-6888, ext 5201. Reservations recommended for dinner. Main courses $7–$20. AE, DC, JCB, MC, V. Daily 11:30am–2pm and 5:30–10pm. SHANGHAI.* Dragons and bats are carved into the ceiling, the columns are red and gold, and everything else is painted green: This is a return to the Shanghai of glitz and kitsch, and a perfect place to enjoy Shanghai cuisine. The English menu has plenty of choices, from river eel to whole barbecued duck. There are Cantonese and Sichuan choices, too. Pork chops are a specialty here, as are the basket of steamed dumplings ("Palace Under the Sea") and the seafood hot pot. Above all, be sure to reserve a window table on the river side.

Hard Rock Cafe. *1376 Nanjing Xi Lu (Suite A05, Shanghai Centre Retail Plaza, on the west side of Shanghai Centre, street level).* ☎ *021/6279-8133. Main courses $8–$14. AE, DC, JCB, MC, V. Sun–Thurs 11:30am–2am, Fri–Sat 11:30am–3am. AMERICAN.* Opened in 1996, but without the trademark auto plastered to the facade (disallowed by the neighborhood beautification committee), this Hard Rock looks very much like all the others and serves up hamburgers, fries, sodas, and beers that are indistinguishable from those in the West. Nothing is Chinese here but the workers.

Tandoor. *59 Maoming Nan Lu (in the New South Building of the Jin Jiang Hotel).* ☎ *021/6258-2582, ext 9301. Main courses $12–$15. AE, DC, JCB, MC, V. Daily 11:30am–2:30pm and 5:30–11pm. INDIAN.* The best Indian restaurant in Shanghai to appear in many decades, this new establishment has a fine fixed-price lunch of tandoori specialties. The food is traditional, as is the decor. The spices range from mild to hot—and the hot is very hot. The tandoori breads, baked in a clay oven, are superb.

Suzhou: Canals and Classic Gardens

杭州

THERE IS "HEAVEN ABOVE, SUZHOU and Hangzhou below," according to a popular adage. Hangzhou's beauty occupies a broad, natural canvas with West Lake at its center, while Suzhou's beauty is more intimate and artistic. Suzhou's interlocking canals, which have led it to be called the "Venice of the East," its classic gardens, the creation of highly educated officials, and its embroidery and silk studios are the chief surviving elements of a cultural capital that dominated China's artistic scene for long periods during the Ming and Qing dynasties. Even the women of Suzhou, with their rounded faces and pale skin, became the model of traditional beauty in China.

Members of England's first official mission to China (1792–94) summed up Suzhou as the home of China's "greatest artists, the most well-known scholars, the richest merchants" and as the ruler of "Chinese taste in matters of fashion and speech." To this day, Suzhou retains something of its stylish legacy, although I must warn you that the canals of Suzhou are not quite those of Venice. More than ever, the private gardens of the city are the focus of its lingering beauty. Surrounded by a busy moat and crisscrossed by hundreds of narrow, soupy canals, Suzhou is a gray city, unscrubbed and decaying. But in this decay there is a certain charm and authenticity not found in other old cities that have been remodeled and reconstructed into hygienic picture postcards of their former selves. Even with its darkening patina, Suzhou remains one of the most beautiful cities in China.

I hadn't visited Suzhou in 10 years, so I was surprised and pleased to find it much as it had been. The old city, surrounded by remnants of a moat and canals linked to the Grand Canal, has become a protected historical district, 2 by 3 miles across, in which little tampering and no skyscrapers are allowed. Suzhou, in other words, is one of those rare places in China where the ravishes of modernization have been severely restricted and new industrial development has been shifted to suburban zones. In Suzhou's case, what's preserved is all the more remarkable because the

Suzhou

downtown was spared destruction during World War II and its private classic gardens, as well as its canals, have survived over the centuries.

I arrived in Suzhou by train and hired a taxi to my hotel. There I purchased a map *(ditu)* and hailed a pedicab, pointing to my destination and negotiating a fare (RMB 15/$1.80). The downtown is a pleasant array of tree-lined lanes, many of them running alongside canals. My goal was to visit again Suzhou's magnificent collection of private classic gardens, the finest surviving examples of the tradition. These small, exquisite jewels of landscaping art are often choked with visitors, making a slow, meditative tour impossible, but it is only by taking enough time to lose oneself in the design of these gardens that their power and essence are discovered. The gardens of Suzhou are unlike those we are familiar with in the West—even unlike the Japanese gardens for which they once served as models. When Ch'i Piao-chia, a 17th-century scholar, became obsessed with building a garden, he likened himself to both "a master painter at his work, not allowing a single dead stroke" and "a great writer writing essays, not permitting a single inharmonious sentence." A

Chinese garden fuses landscape painting and literary composition to create an art of its own in which nature is shaped but not tamed.

When I first saw the private gardens of Suzhou, they looked to me like large estates consisting of pavilions and open halls, unpaved and irregular pathways, small labyrinths of walls and screens, and heaps of grotesque rocks. There were few flower beds, no manicured lawns, and an absence of logical order. While I could immediately admire their quiet beauty, any deeper design or affects remained obscure. A quick tour of a celebrated garden can be disappointing to an inexperienced visitor from abroad, but with a little patience a Suzhou garden opens up an entirely new vision of the world.

Forest of Lions Garden

The first Suzhou garden I ever toured was **Shi Zi Lin** (Forest of Lions) at 23 Yulin Lu, founded in 1336 by a Buddhist monk and last owned by relatives of renowned American architect I. M. Pei. I set out to see it first. The Forest of Lions Garden consists of four small lakes, a multitude of buildings, and random swirls of tortured rockeries. Its elements are strange to those unaccustomed to Chinese gardens.

The principles of garden landscape design in China are often the reverse of those applied in the West. A classic Chinese garden expresses man's relation to nature, not his control over it. Thus, the symmetry and regularity we expect in a garden have been replaced by an organic, spontaneous pattern. The Chinese garden is a manifestation of the essential (even mystical) order of nature in all its shiftings of vitality and vista. This is the way of nature itself, expressed by the garden at every turn. For this reason, the cult of the lawn never developed in China because the emphasis was on the spirit of nature, uncultivated and various. As one Chinese critic wrote, the large lawns in an English garden, "while no doubt pleasing to a cow, could hardly engage the intellect of human beings."

Neat flower beds and trimmed hedge borders are likewise eschewed in the traditional Chinese garden, since they are too obviously artificial, too "unnatural." The many human elements in the garden—the halls, verandas, and bridges—are regarded as points of intersection with the natural realm rather than the interventions of a superior human hand. It is ultimately the task of the garden artist to arrange courtyard and screen, lake and path, rock and shadow organically, in obedience to the rhythms and patterns of a purely natural world, heightened in a garden for human contemplation.

The rocks and rockeries of the Forest of Lions Garden, therefore, are meant to evoke one element of pure nature, its mountains. These miniature monoliths also recall the sacred mountains of China's past and the twisted, gouged-out morphology of the quintessential Chinese landscape common to scroll paintings. Mountains are also emblems of the Way (Dao), that process of transformation and transcendence in nature that Daoist monks and hermits achieve in their quests for immortality.

The finest of the expressionistic slabs in Suzhou's Forest of Lions Garden came from nearby Lake Tai (Tai Hu). Since the Tang Dynasty (A.D. 618–907), connoisseurs have been selecting the best Tai Hu rocks for the gardens of emperors, high officials, and rich estate owners. During the Song Dynasty (A.D. 960–1126), rock appreciation reached such extremes that the expense in hauling stones from Lake Tai to the capital is said to have bankrupted the empire.

While Tai Hu rocks and honeycombed rockeries seem more bizarre than evocative at first, the Chinese landscape artist regards them as an essential component of nature, compressed to fit into a garden setting. The Forest of Lions Garden was designed to emphasize the role of mountains in nature. It contains the largest rocks and most elaborate rockeries of any garden in Suzhou. It took repeated visits to Chinese gardens before I developed a feel for these rocks, which I can now contemplate with interest. The Qing Dynasty emperors Kangxi and his grandson Qianlong were far more knowledgeable in such matters: They valued the rockeries of the Forest of Lions so highly that they used them as a model for those in the Old Summer Palace in Beijing.

Lingering Garden

The single finest specimen of Tai Hu rock is located in **Liu Yuan,** the Lingering Garden at 80 Liuyuan Lu, a spacious Ming Dynasty estate. Its centerpiece is a 20-foot-high, 5-ton contorted castle of rock called Crown of Clouds Peak. Lingering Garden is also notable for its viewing pavilions, particularly the **Mandarin Duck Hall,** which is divided into two sides: an ornate southern chamber for men and a plain northern chamber for women. Suzhou's contemporary painters maintain a sales gallery in this garden, which is planted in Osmanthus and willow, varieties that are not known for their brilliant flowerings, in keeping with a traditional prejudice for plain, unshowy vegetation. Lingering Garden's name is derived from the original owner's family name, which sounds like the character for the word *lingering.* When it came into the hands of new owners, they substituted the character for "lingering" as the garden's name when they found that their own family name for the garden did not catch on with the people of Suzhou.

Humble Administrators & Stupid Officials

While the first two gardens I visited are celebrated for their rockeries, other Suzhou gardens emphasize different elements. **Zhou Zheng**

The Garden of the
Humble Administrator

Entrance

Garden, at 178 Dong Bei Jie, one of Suzhou's largest and most popular gardens, makes complex use of waters. Zhou Zheng Garden is usually translated as "Humble Administrator's Garden," but garden scholar Maggie Keswick points out that the characters in the name have an ambiguous meaning that can be translated either as "Garden of the Unsuccessful Politician" or "Garden of the Stupid Officials." This garden is located off Dong Bei Jie, just a few blocks northeast of the Lingering Garden.

In this garden, which dates from the 16th century, the Tai Hu rocks are not as prominent as the maze of connected pools and islands. This watery maze is in fact an illusion, since there is only a single, long, meandering lake. It's impossible to tell where the water begins or ends. It even seems to flow under waterside pavilions. The creation of multiple vistas and the dividing of spaces into distinct segments are the artist's means to expand the compressed spaces of the garden. As visitors stroll through a small garden, new spaces and vistas open up at every turn. Such constant change can be confusing, producing what Maggie Keswick calls "that magical confusion which is the essence of garden architecture." Ideally, one walks through a garden not simply to contemplate nature and learn about its underlying patterns but to feel its disorienting power—to break down logical, social, and human definitions of order and enter a state of direct communion with the natural order.

Master of the Nets Garden

While many rich officials and merchants built garden estates simply to entertain, the more scholarly and poetic among the rich wanted to create contemplative retreats. They conceived of the garden as an enclosed series of spaces within spaces, each parcel inviting heightened contact with nature. The human world outside the garden walls was deliberately held at bay. The most perfect of these retreats is **Wang Shi Yuan,** the

Master of the Nets Garden, a masterpiece of landscape compression. Hidden at the end of a blind alley (11 Kuotao Xiang) off Shiquan Jie, a busy street of scroll and handicraft shops, the tiny grounds of the Master of the Nets Garden have been cleverly expanded by the placement of innumerable walls, screens, and pavilion halls, producing a maze that seems endless. The eastern sector of the garden is a cluster of three interlinked buildings, the residence of the former owner and his family. At the center of the garden is a pond, just one mu square (about 2,700 square feet), encircled by verandas, pavilions, and covered corridors, crossed by two arched stone bridges. Set back from this watery "mirror of heaven" with its proportionate rockeries and bamboo is a complex of halls and inner courtyards: a garden within a garden. The halls invite rest and meditation. The most lavish hall, **Dianchun Cottage,** furnished in palace lanterns, dark chairs and tables, and hanging scrolls, served as the model for Mingxuan Garden, the Astor Chinese Garden Court and Ming Furniture Room constructed in 1980 in the Metropolitan Museum of Art in New York City. The original, owing to its setting, has a much more open feel than its museum version.

No longer in the hands of a privileged family or restricted to a few upper-class Confucian scholars, officials, and poets, the Master of the Nets Garden has become a favorite retreat of Suzhou's own citizenry. Grandparents bring their grandkids here on inaugural outings to pose for ceremonial snapshots. Workers snack on seeds and fresh fruits. Lovers dangle their feet in the motionless pond waters. Children chase each other around the rockeries. Rimmed by galleries of carved stone tablets and poetic inscriptions on wooden plaques, the garden is a relic of Old China. Paths meander like wild geese, pavilions unfold like lotus leaves, rocks rise as sharply as mountain peaks, and the gates open in the shape of a full moon. Nature becomes a living poem.

The Three Thousand Swords of Tiger Hill

Even Suzhou's best park, **Tiger Hill (Hu Qiu Shan),** 2 miles northwest of the city, contains classic gardens, although I was stunned on my recent visit to find that large, bright plots of flowers, planted and potted, had become a major feature, as had dozens of robotic figures of the sort one normally sees at theme parks or in department store windows at Christmas. These modern additions have jazzed up the park and appeal to young children and their parents, it seems, but they are really so much garish frosting.

Tiger Hill still contains its remarkable leaning pagoda **Yunyan Ta (Cloud Rock Pagoda),** a seven-story work dating from A.D. 961, now safely shorn up by modern engineering, although it still leans. Under the pagoda is the legendary grave of Suzhou's founder, He Lu, a 6th-century B.C.

leader whose arsenal of 3,000 swords is also said to be buried in the park and protected by a white tiger. The artificial hill on which the pagoda stands was once an island. Below it is a remarkable ledge, the 10,000 Rocks, where according to legend a rebel delivered an oratory so fiery that the rocks lined up to listen. A deep stone cleavage, the **Pool of Swords (Jianchi)**, runs along one side of Tiger Hill, reputedly the remnants of a pit dug by order of the First Emperor (Qin Shi Huang) 2,000 years ago in a search for the 3,000 swords. A natural spring in another of Tiger Hill's clefts is claimed to have cured a monk of blindness, and visitors still seek it out.

All these legends of Tiger Hill are simply colorful stories, of course; the historic sites of China are decked in many such legends. In fact, in the 1950s, excavations of pits at Tiger Hill revealed a three-door passageway with tunnels 30 feet into the hill, heading directly under the leaning pagoda. Although unexplored, the tunnels are thought to lead to a major tomb, a hollow creating unstable foundations that might explain why the pagoda tilts.

Water Gates & Canals

Another leading historical site in old Suzhou is **Panmen Gate,** at 2 Dong Da Lu, which once operated as a water gate and fortress when the Grand Canal was the most important route linking Suzhou to the rest of China. Panmen, built in A.D. 1351, is the only major piece of the Suzhou city wall to survive. Nearby is a large arched bridge, **Wumen Qiao,** over the Grand Canal—the finest place to view the ever-changing traffic—and a small arched bridge over a feeder canal that connects to Panmen. Panmen also has excellent vistas of the old city, including a view of Ruiguang Ta, a 122-foot pagoda built in A.D. 1119.

When I visited Panmen this time, it was teeming with visitors and with an aggressive army of vendors, fortune-tellers, and painters. At the top of the bridge, a local street musician was stroking out the refrains of "Oh! Susanna" on his erhu, a traditional two-stringed instrument. When he spotted me, he grabbed my arm, attempting to shake a few coins into his basket, and he was quite outraged that I, an American presumably enthralled by his choice of an American melody, refused to cough up a donation.

Panmen and the southern streets of old Suzhou are excellent places to walk at one's leisure. Traditional shop houses predominate, the streets are narrow and shaded by trees, the shops include galleries, and there are bridges and lanes where one can watch the canal traffic, an endless stream of barges propelled by hand-held poles as well as motors. Near Panmen, the old city moat widens and the water traffic thickens.

Uptown, the canals narrow. The backs of the white houses still open to the water and quite a bit of commerce is conducted on the water. The canal scenes are unsanitized. The arched bridges are pocked and mud splattered. The canal houses are coated in a stubble of moss and dirt. Scores of cement barges move from outhouse to outhouse to exact the night soil for use in suburban farms. The gondoliers of Suzhou evoke little of the romance of vanished dynasties, but they do reveal the rough-edged world of handwork that hundreds of millions of Chinese do each day. And there is something beautiful still in the canal scene of Suzhou when the arched bridges and simple stucco houses and floating barges line up just right.

The Art of Silk

Suzhou is known for more than its garden arts. Its silk fabrics have been among the most prized in China for centuries, and the art of silk embroidery is still practiced at the highest levels. The **Museum of Suzhou Embroidery** on Jingde Lu (open 9am to 5pm daily, admission free) is both a factory and sales outlet. It contains the most accomplished silk embroideries I have seen in China. The best work on display there, some of it for sale, are canvases of traditional scenes (landscapes, birds, flowers, bamboos) stitched by one artist over the course of 3 years. A few of the embroidery masters have international reputations, and the price on their works soars once they retire. The artists working upstairs in this factory stitch with bare hands, depending only on natural light, without magnifying lenses or other aids. Thinning the filaments of silk thread down to almost invisible lines, they work 2-hour stretches and take 10-minute tea breaks. The embroidery factory also produces the double-sided embroideries on a canvas of thin silk gauze, a technique developed here in which two different figures, front and reverse, are stitched using two needles simultaneously—what the factory guide calls "a secret technique." The finished embroidery is mounted in a mahogany frame carved in Ming or Qing Dynasty style.

A less commercial display of Suzhou's silk industry is offered by the **Suzhou Silk Museum**, at 661 Renmin Lu (open 9am to 6pm daily, admission RMB 5/60¢). The complete history of silk, starting from 4,000 B.C., is presented in pleasant surroundings, complete with signs in English. Perhaps more than any other product, silk made Suzhou a city of importance in China. When the Song Dynasty rulers moved the political capital to nearby Hangzhou, Suzhou became China's cultural capital.

Temple of Mystery

One of Suzhou's least visited monuments is the Temple of Mystery (Xuan Miao Guan). Located in the heart of the old city on Guanqian Jie (open daily 9am to 6pm, admission RMB 10/$1.25), it is engulfed in Suzhou's largest street market, a series of stalls and stands that occupies several city blocks. Constructed in the 3rd century A.D., its 31 halls are reduced today to the singular, massive three-eaved **Hall of the Three Pure Ones (San Qing),** which dates from A.D. 1179. This is the largest early Daoist temple in China, almost 50 yards wide. Its courtyard, bordered by a carved stone Song Dynasty railing, is a favorite hangout for older citizens. Inside is a golden statue of Guanyin, Goddess of Mercy, and some 60 Daoist figures in glass cases. South of this is another large building that clearly belonged at one time to the Temple of Mystery. Unchanged on the outside, this runaway hall is now devoted to souvenirs, musical instruments, and other commodities, all displayed in glass-and-metal counters. Meanwhile, the east and west walls of this emporium are still festooned with the massive statues of warriors and gods of the original Daoist hall.

Suzhou's Temple of Mystery is emblematic of the state of China's legacies. Hanging on by a thread in the center of a rapidly modernizing city, the temple has been altered, divided, and gutted by time, politics, and economics. Yet something visible remains. The old bazaar has been reincarnated. Small, simple stalls still hug the temple grounds, but the newest sort of shopping bazaar is shouldering its way nearer the Temple of Mystery. A spick-and-span pedestrian mall has sprung up within a block of the old temple, with deluxe department stores, cinemas showing the latest action films from America, two Kentucky Fried Chicken emporiums, and boutiques hawking the logos of Crocodile and Playboy.

It is the ancient city that draws visitors today, of course, and the original lines of Suzhou are still clearly imprinted on its chessboard of canals and bridges. More than 170 bridges arch over the 20 miles of slim waterways within the moated city. The poetic private gardens number about 70, with a dozen of the finest open to public view. No other Chinese city contains such a concentration of canals and classic gardens.

The enchantment of the old gardens of Suzhou is both philosophical and sensuous. Nature is supreme and transcendent within the garden walls. The closest equivalent in the Western tradition might be Walden Pond, where Henry David Thoreau escaped the confines of city and civilization in order to confront his essential self. For Western romantics, the natural retreat opens ever outward in a widening circle of grass and field—the cosmos of an untamed New World. For the Chinese mystic, the natural retreat closed ever more inwardly upon itself within the perfect garden— a microcosm of the unchanging ancient Way.

PRACTICAL INFORMATION

ORIENTATION

Suzhou is 18 miles east of Lake Tai in Jiangsu Province. Surrounded by suburbs and new industrial development zones, the old city of Suzhou has a population of 700,000. Within its confines, the gardens, canals, and houses are well preserved. Most travelers stay several days in Suzhou, reaching the city from Shanghai. Suzhou is one of China's busiest tourist destinations, receiving several million visitors a year.

GETTING THERE

By Train   Suzhou is 52 miles by rail northwest of Shanghai. Suzhou has no airport, but it is served by many trains each day from Shanghai. The train trip takes less than 90 minutes. The Suzou Train Station is at the begiining of Renmin Lu, on the north side of the canal, one block east of the bridge.

By Boat   Suzhou is also linked to Hangzhou to the south by overnight passenger boats on the Grand Canal and to Wuxi and Lake Tai to the north. Overnight passage to Hangzhou on the Grand Canal costs RMB 60 to 125 ($7.25 to $14.75), depending on the cabin class. The top cabin class is a compartment consisting of bunkbeds and little else. Tickets may be purchased at your hotel desk.

TOURS & STRATAGEMS

Tours   China International Travel Service (CITS), with headquarters in the Suzhou Hotel, 115 Shiquan Jie (☎ 0512/ 522-3175; fax 0512/523-3593), can arrange tours of the city with English-speaking guides. I used their helpful branch in the lobby of the Gloria Plaza Hotel to book a daylong "Panda Car Tour" of the city (RMB 260/$31) with an English-speaking guide, lunch included. The tour visited two classic gardens, Tiger Hill, Panmen Gate, and the Silk Embroidery Factory.

With this tour as introduction, first-time visitors to Suzhou can then use the map that CITS hands out and tour other sites on their own. Transportation in Suzhou by taxi or pedicab is an easy way to get around, and is also cheap (RMB 10 to 20/$1.20 to $2.40 per trip).

Visitor Information   CITS also books rail tickets, boat tickets on the Grand Canal, and in the summer tickets to evening performances of classical Chinese music in the Master of the Nets Garden.

WHERE TO STAY

Bamboo Grove Hotel (Zhu Hui Fandian). *Zhu Hui Lu (in the south of the city, near Master of the Nets Garden).* ☎ *0512/520-5601. Fax 0512/520-8778. 405 rms. A/C MINIBAR TV TEL. $160 double. AE, DC, JCB, MC, V.* The rooms in this five-story, 4-star, three-unit hotel were renovated in 1994 and are showing some wear. The international management is efficient. Foreign tour groups often stay here. Bicycle rental is available. This place is popular with expatriates as a place to dine and drink.

The hotel's attached garden is a peaceful retreat.

Services: Room service (24-hour), dry cleaning and laundry (next day), nightly turndown, daily maid service, foreign exchange counter.

Facilities: In-house movies, health club (exercise machines), sauna, tennis courts, medical clinic, tour desk, beauty salon, shopping arcade, newsstand.

Gloria Plaza Hotel Suzhou (Kailai Dajiudian). *535 Ganjiang Dong Lu (east of city center).* ☎ *0512/521-8855. Fax*

*0512/521-8533. 300 rms. A/C MINIBAR
TV TEL. $150 double. AE, DC, JCB, MC, V.*
The city's newest luxury hotel is its best.
All the spacious rooms come with a desk,
sofa, and safe. It is within easy walking
distance of the downtown Temple of
Mystery and the Twin Pagodas, built in
A.D. 982, one of the few examples of
identical pagodas still standing in China.
From the south side of the hotel I had a
splendid view of an old neighborhood

of courtyard houses and a glimpse into
the daily life they contain, including
backyard fish ponds.

Services: Room service (24-hour),
dry cleaning and laundry (next day),
nightly turndown, daily maid service, foreign exchange counter.

Facilities: In-house movies, health
club (exercise machines), sauna, business
center (24-hour), tour desk, beauty salon, shopping arcade.

WHERE TO DINE

Hotels offer the best fare in town and
are the only outlets that accept credit
cards.

The fresh, new **Atrium Cafe** in the
Gloria Plaza Hotel has excellent breakfast, lunch, and dinner buffets with a
choice of Western, Chinese, and Asian
dishes (☎ 0512/521-8855). Four Hong
Kong chefs work in the Gloria, which
operates two excellent dinner restaurants
as well, the **Suzhou Express** with a
1920s decor and the **Sampan Seafood
Restaurant.**

The **Bamboo Grove Hotel** has
good Western and Cantonese food in its
restaurants (☎ 0512/520-5601). Efficient service, English-language menus,
and reasonable prices ($10 to $25 per
person) characterize the hotel fare.

The best local food is at the
**Songhelou (Pine and Crane Restau-
rant),** 141 Guanqian Jie (☎ 0512/727-
7006), a downtown establishment that

claims to have been in business since Emperor Qianlong visited Suzhou in the
18th century. The claim is dubious, but
the menu is strictly Suzhou, with braised
eel, sea cucumber, and duck and pork
dishes. Foreigners are seated in a special
room and given menus in English, with
prices of RMB 30 to RMB 120 ($3.60 to
$14.45) per dish. I found the food rather
oily and undistinguished.

East of this restaurant along
Guanqian Jie and south on Taijian
Long, an alley, is the vegetarian cafe
Gongdelin, which is cheaper and
tastier.

There are plenty of other cafes, as
well as a **Kentucky Fried Chicken** outlet on Guanqian Jie, the pedestrians-only
street east of Renmin Lu near the Temple
of Mystery, where Suzhou's newest and
some of its oldest establishments
comingle.

ANCIENT CAPITALS AND CITIES OF THE INTERIOR

都市

Xi'an:
The Old Capital
西安

X<small>I'AN IS CHINA'S CITY OF THE DEAD—</small>
which is to say, China's city of imperial treasures. The first emperor, Qin
Shi Huang (259–210 B.C.), unified China here. Twenty-two centuries
later, in 1979, the 7,000 life-sized terra-cotta soldiers buried with him
were accidentally unearthed, opening an underground city of the dead
that put Xi'an on the world map of tourism. But Xi'an was always China's
leading historical site, serving as China's capital over the course of 11
dynasties, reaching its height in the golden age of the Tang Dynasty
(A.D. 618–907).

For this reason, Beijing and Xi'an are neatly counterpointed as showcases of China's imperial splendors. Beijing was the capital of the last two
great dynasties, the Ming (A.D. 1368–1644) and the Qing (A.D. 1644–
1911); Xi'an was the capital of the first two great dynasties, the Han (206
B.C. to A.D. 220) and the Tang (A.D. 618–907). Beijing reins in tourists
with the Great Wall and the Forbidden City; Xi'an strikes earlier, with
the terra-cotta armies of Emperor Qin and the Big Wild Goose Pagoda
of the Tang emperors.

Xi'an's historical monuments and sites are even more extensive, stretching from the Banpo Neolithic Village, occupied 6,000 years ago, to the
sole surviving city wall of any major city in China, built during the Ming
Dynasty. If ancient Chinese history has no attraction, best skip Xi'an
altogether. As for me, its allure runs deep. I have been revisiting Xi'an
ever since I first lived and worked there in 1984, gauging the changes that
China has gone through during the last two decades, always in relation to
the broader and deeper history that is preserved in its streets and walls
and courtyards of dust.

The Walls of the City

My first impression of Xi'an was formed by a glimpse of its massive city
wall. It transfixed me. Forty feet high, 8 miles round, fashioned from
rammed earth and brick, its old archers' towers intact, this was once the

Xi'an Railway Station

CITY WALL

Xi 8 Lu

7 Lu

Dong 7 Lu

Geming (Revolutionary) Park

5 Lu

Dong 5 Lu

Changle Xi Lu

Jiefang Lu

Huancheng Donglu Beiduan

Hongqin Lu

Xi'an Jade Carving Factory

Renmin Lu

Yangxin Jie

Baxian Guan

Changle Fang

Dongxin Jie

Dong 1 Lu

Dongyue Miao (Daoist Temple)

Subluo Xiang

1 Lu

Nanxun Jie

Protestant Church

Dong Da Jie

Dorgmen Gate (East Gate)

Dongguan Zheng Jie

Huzhu Lu

Heping Lu

Tongjian

Huancheng Donlu Nanduan

Dongguan Nanda Jie

Dongguan Zhengjie Lu

Wolong Si (Buddist Temple)

Sanxue Jie (Suyuanmen)

Provincial Museum (Forest of Steles)

Dongduan

Xingqinggong Park

Xianning Lu

Changcheng Jie

Jianxi Jie

Jiandong Jie

Yanta Lu

Andong Lu

Taiyi Lu

Youyi Donglu

Jianshe Lu

Flood Control Canal

0   1 km
     .6 mi

N

Shaanxi History Museum

To Big Wild Goose Pagoda (Da Yan ta)

Xiaozhi Dong Lu

Xiying   Lu

Xi'an

city wall of the old capital, a fortress of temples and palaces erected on an endless plain of yellow dust. The palaces of the early emperors, the temples of the first Buddhists and Daoists, have disintegrated, but the last incarnation of the wall remains to mark their birthplace.

After more than 10 years of labor, most of it by hand, Xi'an's city wall has been bricked anew and restored to grandeur. The moat along the south side is filled with water. A greenbelt of parks, trails, and outdoor amusements is gradually wrapping its way around the outside of the city. The top of the wall is paved in new stepping stones. Upon arrival, this is the ideal place to survey Xi'an, from atop its 500-year-old ramparts. There's an admission fee (RMB 10/$1.20) collected at entrances inside the wall. The best place to begin is on the southeast, across from the old Provincial Museum. There are entry signs in English.

For the last year, it has been possible to make an uninterrupted circuit of Xi'an atop the city wall by foot. The path is wide and the views over the walls, inside and outside, are always fascinating. From late spring to early fall, the wall is lively with souvenir vendors, tourists, and locals out for a stroll. I've never walked the entire 13K (8-mile) circuit, but it would make a unique annual footrace. There are 18 gates through the wall, the four largest at the north, south, east, and west midpoints, where the traffic now flows in and out. A dozen years ago, much of that traffic was horse and donkey carts, and there wasn't a single taxi. What you see from the wall is a modern city and an old city being shuffled together like two mismatched decks of cards. Solar panels cap the new apartments that rise as high as the wall. At the same time, turn-of-the-century shop houses and old temples hug the foot of the wall for blocks, their roof tiles broken but not destroyed.

From the top of the city wall, the main streets of Xi'an are laid out like a cosmic chessboard. **Nan Dajie** runs straight north, past the big Kentucky Fried Chicken outlet on the left, to the Bell Tower, built in 1384. The **Bell Tower** stands at the center of the city. To its west is the **Muslim quarter,** containing the Grand Mosque and the Ming Dynasty Drum Tower; to its east is the city's main shopping street, **Dong Dajie.** These areas must be explored on foot, as must the quaint arts-and-crafts lane that stretches from the south gate east along the wall to the museum and its celebrated Forest of Steles, the greatest collection of engraved stone tablets in the world.

Looking south from the south gate down Changan Lu, it's possible to see the tips of the chief Tang Dynasty structures still standing in Xi'an's immediate suburbs: the Big Wild Goose Pagoda, built it A.D. 652, and nearer to the wall, the Little Wild Goose Pagoda, built in A.D. 707–709. For more than 12 centuries these were the tallest structures in Xi'an. Today, as skyscrapers begin to surround the old walled city, spotting pagodas becomes increasingly difficult. Just south of the wall there are new hotels, new offices, and right on the moat a miniature golf course.

I prefer the old world, even in its restored version, and the restoration of the Xi'an city wall is not so perfect as to destroy the spell of ruin, decay, and faded grandeur that evokes a royal past. Looking down and into the city, I'm always eager to discover what has changed, what remains, and what is no more.

In a Forest of Steles

The changed and unchanged, the treasures and the losses, are all to be found in the shadow of the southern city wall. Just east of the big south gate, which has become a flowery, landscaped traffic circle, the sleepy curving lane of **Shuyuanmen Dajie (Sanxue Jie)** has been transformed into a street out of Old Xi'an. A brand-new dragon-carved gate arches over its entrance. (The exquisite little pagoda to one side, Baoqing, dates from A.D. 706, but it is barely noticed now.) Lined with electrified lanterns, bordered by painted banners, festooned with red-and-yellow paper globes, **Shuyuanmen Street** has been remade for tourists. Even the wooden-railed balconies are strung with lights. The wooden shop fronts with their elaborately carved doorways sell every conceivable souvenir. There are several shops with fine artwork (paintings and scrolls) and the crafts for which Xi'an and this province are famous: simple folk paintings from the peasant painters of Huxian county, paper cuts, bright folk-art clothing and cloth ornaments, teapots, chopsticks, porcelain, books, and posters. Several of these Qing Dynasty–style shops sell rubbings made from the priceless stone tablets collected in the city's Forest of Steles nearby, worth picking up later here or outside the Shaanxi Provincial Museum if you spot a tablet you like inside.

The cobblestoned street wanders along the wall for half a mile east to the entrance of the **Shaanxi Provincial Museum** (open daily 8:30am to 5:30pm, admission RMB 40/$5). It is located on the spacious garden grounds of the Temple of Confucius, built in A.D. 1374. A number of classical pavilions dot the garden pathways to the heart of the exhibit at the back, the hall of the **Forest of Steles (Bei Lin)**. This is my favorite Chinese museum. It has not changed since it became the repository of China's engraved stone in 1952, and its collections reach deep into the world's oldest continuous civilization.

The dullest hall of stone tablets is the first. This large grove consists of a complete edition of the Confucian Classics transcribed on 114 stone slabs, front and back, in the year A.D. 837, becoming the centerpiece of the Forest of Steles collection established in A.D. 1090 under the Song Dynasty. The oldest such surviving transcription, the stone classics constitute the literal bedrock of Chinese ethics and social philosophy.

Other carved tablets in the remaining halls are probably more interesting today. There are pictorial stones of Old China, poems written with
characters resembling leaves on a bamboo stem, ancient maps, and the
Nestorian Stele (on the left, in building 2), carved in A.D. 781 to record
the arrival of Christianity in China in A.D. 635. Nestorian Christianity,
traveling over the Silk Road from Persia, found roots in the Tang
Dynasty capital and flourished for two centuries in Xi'an before its complete eradication. The Nestorian Stele typifies the dimensions of many of
these tablets: 9 feet tall, a yard wide, a foot thick—solid limestone weighing in at 2 tons, anchored upright by a turtle-shaped base.

In 1984, I saw several workers making ink rubbings directly from
these 1,000 stones, some of them more than 2,000 years old. Each rubbing blackens the stone and takes its toll. A Chinese scholar whom I met
on my most recent visit was appalled to see them still making such rubbings in the late 1990s. Metallic models of all the steles have been cast for
the creation of commercial rubbings, but as this scholar said, "Money
talks," and there are many who will pay for a real rubbing. What I notice
is the damage inflicted by more than ink, cloth, and mallet. Almost all
these stones have been broken in half or defaced by vandals, possibly by
organized vandals at work as recently as the Red Guard movement. I
know from talking to many monks who returned to the remains of the
temples in Xi'an after 1976 that the destruction of religious and historical
pieces was carried out on an unimaginable scale, and much of the damage
will never be undone.

Within the halls along both sides of the museum grounds are a number of China's greatest treasures that do survive, few of them protected
now from the viewer's touch: unparalleled bronzes and jades from the
Zhou Dynasty (1100–212 B.C.), the world's first seismograph (looking
rather like a punch bowl set) from the Han Dynasty, tricolored horses
and scraps of silk from the days of the Tang, and massive stone animals
fashioned 20 centuries ago. I come back to this place often: It defines
what a Chinese museum should be—quiet, old, courteous, Confucian,
infinitely rich within.

Bell Tower & Drum Tower

In the center of Xi'an, visible everywhere from the surrounding walls, are
the city's two Ming Dynasty treasures. Bell and drum towers were at one
time as much an ordinary fixture of city life in China as city walls. The
bell tower included a massive bronze bell which was sounded each morning to mark the beginning of the day, and the drum tower housed a large
drum which was struck to mark the end of the working day. Every place
had these towers, and some still do. None are as famous or grand as Xi'an's
towers.

The Bell Tower is older (1384) and larger than the Drum Tower, and located in the central traffic circle of the inner city. Until 1582, it stood two blocks west at the center of the old Tang Dynasty capital, near where the Drum Tower is now. The Bell Tower is a stately edifice, its three tiers of green-glazed roof tiles soaring on eaves flaked in gold. Engulfed in Xi'an's most congested modern traffic circle, the Bell Tower long ago clanged its last wake-up ding-dong in downtown Xi'an. The wooden interior feels centuries old, but once inside there's not much to see for the RMB 15 ($1.80) admission beyond sets of chimes and the city traffic and latest construction sites from the balcony. The Bell Tower's great bell has disappeared, as has the Drum Tower's great drum.

The Bell Tower and Drum Tower are tied together now by a sparkling new ultramodern city square looking like some minimalistic expression of public art transported from the West: a wide, flat, open courtyard with benches and Plexiglas lanterns where smoking is not permitted (perhaps a first in outdoor urban China). Along the north side of Xi'an city square are three tiers of new shopping arcades built in the neo-traditional Chinese style with bricks and roof tiles. At the west end, on the north side of Xi Dajie (Big West Street), stands the venerable Drum Tower, built in 1370.

The Drum Tower also requires a RMB 15 ($1.80) admission, and there is probably even less reason to go in. The entrance is a stairway on the northwest corner. The upper floor contains Qing Dynasty furniture and a drum collection. The original drum is gone, and the drum tower no longer beats out the end of the day for Xi'an's residents. Both are open daily from 9am to 5pm.

Both towers are gorgeous from outside, superb imperial monuments worth viewing and preserving in an increasingly modern city. The Bell Tower is a beacon to all travelers wandering the downtown streets, while the Drum Tower has become the gateway to Xi'an's old Muslim quarter and its historic mosque.

The Great Mosque

The Great Mosque (Qingzhen Si) of Xi'an dates back to A.D. 742, barely a century after the founding of Islam. Although it is often claimed that this is the largest and the oldest mosque in China, I'm skeptical about both claims. What I can say is that this is the most active and serene mosque in China. It used to be even more peaceful and idyllic. Over the last 10 years, it has been renovated extensively (without disturbing its architectural beauties) and it has been added to virtually every guided tour itinerary. The result is that the narrow alleyway connecting the Great Mosque to Beiyuanmen Lu and the Drum Tower has become clogged with vendors. (They do sell some great walking canes.)

The Great Mosque is easier to find these days. Pass under the Drum Tower and walk north a few blocks. Turn left at the sign to the mosque. Follow the alley of vendors and shop houses as it curves to the right and look for the entrance on the left. It's open from 8am to noon and 2 to 6pm daily (admission RMB 15/$1.80).

Although the Great Mosque was founded in the Tang Dynasty, its present design is Ming, dating from the same period as the present city wall. In the 1990s, most of the timbers were replaced, fitted and recarved to mimic exactly the Ming Dynasty model. Some carving and tile work are still going on. The grounds are long and spacious, giving the sense more of a garden than of a temple. Laid out east to west in the Islamic tradition (Chinese temples face south), the four courtyards lead deeper and farther inward to the main prayer hall at the end.

In the first courtyard there's a 360-year-old carved wooden archway. Side halls off the arch display Ming and Qing dynasty furniture. The second courtyard contains the wide Five-Room Hall, and through it, carved stone fences and gates, also created during the Ming Dynasty. In the third courtyard is the mosque's most famous and beautiful structure, the triple-eaved **Introspection Tower (Shengxin),** the minaret from which Muslims are called to prayer. On either side are halls containing a Ming Dynasty copy of the Koran and a Qing Dynasty map of Mecca. The One God Pavilion, also called the Phoenix Pavilion, is the final passage to the prayer hall.

The prayer hall is eight bays wide, with a glazed blue tile roof supported by large brackets in the Chinese style. There are stone stairs up to the entrance. Inside, the ceiling is carved in flowery Arabic letters, recounting the scriptures. Pages of the Koran are carved into wooden tablets, half of them in Chinese, half in Arabic. The mihrab (prayer niche) faces Mecca. The floor is covered with prayer rugs. A thousand worshippers can fit inside for a single service. Visitors, after removing their shoes, are often permitted to enter the prayer hall, although when I visited most recently entrance was barred to non-Muslims.

This is an exceptionally active mosque, as the Muslim quarter of Xi'an has at least 100,000 resident believers and an Islamic presence that goes back at least 1,200 years. The Muslims who came from the West put down roots, married, and after centuries of assimilation ceased to resemble Arabs, except in their Islamic practices. They became known as a minority people, the Hui. The Hui of Xi'an live largely in their own quarter, wear white turbans, and practice circumcision. They reject usury, divination, theater, and pork. They maintain their own schools, slaughterhouses, cemeteries, and mosques (at least a dozen in Xi'an). Their neighborhoods are now the oldest, their streets the narrowest and most fragrant with cooking in Xi'an. Their houses are low and conjoined. Some still have packed earth floors and sidewalk water pumps. Vendors tend coal-heated pots in the street, selling lamb on skewers, fried breads, and fresh yo-gurt—the best yogurt I've ever eaten.

One reason I like to come here is to watch the Muslim Chinese go about their business in the mosque. The other reason is the peace I feel here. Xi'an, like all Chinese cities, is constantly making noise. But in here, there is almost a silence. The courtyards are like carved wooden screens. Dozens of Hui men shift quietly from station to station toward the prayer hall, bathed and barefooted, their heads covered in thin white turbans, prostrating themselves before Allah, facing Mecca in prayer. Among the treasures of the Great Mosque is a map of the world with a black cube at its center, an Islamic map of the world. Displaced, China lies outside, beyond the western frontier.

Temples

During its zenith under the Tang Dynasty, Xi'an was the home of China's leading Buddhist temples and Daoist shrines. In the 1980s, I explored a number of these sacred sites inside and outside the city walls. Many were just putting themselves back together after coming under destructive at-tacks during the Red Guard campaigns of the Cultural Revolution (1966–76). Some were destroyed so completely they never reopened.

Today at Xi'an there is a **Lama Temple (Guangren Si)** with a library of sutras in the northwest corner of the city, founded in 1705; a **Daoist temple (Dongyue Miao)** to the mountain god of Tai Shan near the east-ern gate, founded in 1116; a **Buddhist temple (Wolong Si)** where the Chen (Zen) sect was said to have been founded in China in A.D. 520, located just inside the southern city wall; and several others with long histories and a recent return to worship.

The temple that has fared the best in this era of reconstruction, how-ever, is the ancient **Daoist Temple of the Eight Immortals (Baxian Guan)**. Located a mile east of the city wall from Zhongshan Gate (in a poor, crowded, working-class lane on Yongxin Jie), Baxian Guan is the city's most active Daoist sanctuary. Scores of monks and nuns in dark robes, heads shaven, circulate through the small restored temples and court-yards, where there are four sites designated for burning incense and several stone tablets engraved with diagrams of a multilayered divine yin-and-yang cosmos. The chief statue is a large image of a many-armed deity remark-ably similar to the Buddhist Guanyin (Goddess of Mercy) reaching out to comfort her petitioners.

On the steps to the main worship hall, I notice a young woman alone on her knees. She has spread out a piece of paper and placed a set of keys, a hank of hair, and a small bone upon it. When I ask her the purpose of this, she tells me that she is praying for the recovery of her father from poor health.

The best time to come to the Temple of the Eight Immortals is on the first and fifteenth days of each lunar month, at dusk, when a popular festival is held. I first attended a full moon rite here in 1984, when the halls were in ruins. It was a noisy affair. Worshippers were sending burnt offerings to their ancestors and one monk stood at the top of the stairs casting down firecrackers to chase away the demons. The rite had no order I could discern. There was singing, the clanging of wooden sticks, the shouting of prayers, and the chanting of rosaries. It was the din of divine chaos, Daoism as it has been in China for more than 20 centuries.

This was the largest Daoist monastery in Xi'an for a thousand years. New apartments and a machine factory have reduced it to a few blocks of recently restored temples. Across the street, a few other surviving halls have been converted to the city's most interesting flea market, where you can rummage through an odd assortment of old coins, chipped ceramics, and the personal possessions of local families. On Wednesday and Sunday mornings, this temple market expands into a twice-weekly antique market of even more odds and ends worth bargaining for: Cultural Revolution posters, Qing Dynasty ceramics, snuff bottles, and opium pipes.

Churches

Christianity was first established in China in A.D. 652, according to the stone tablet in Xi'an's Forest of Steles. The Nestorian version, which traveled out of Persia to the gates of Xi'an in the 7th century, was not quite that of Rome, but the Chinese emperor was satisfied as to the correctness of the "Luminous Religion" (Da Qin) and encouraged its spread. Two hundred nineteen years later, in A.D. 845, the edict was reversed, "foreign religions" were banned, and Christianity did not reappear in China until Western missionaries started to arrive almost 700 years later. More recently, Christianity in China suffered persecution throughout the Cultural Revolution. Almost all churches were closed, but in the 1980s they began, like the temples and mosques, to reopen their doors.

As is common in Chinese cities, Xi'an has two official "patriotic" Christian churches—one Protestant, one Catholic. Although not publicized, foreigners are welcome to attend Sunday services.

The **Protestant Church,** reopened since 1980, is located north off the main shopping street, Dong Dajie. Go one block north up Nanxin Jie (the Friendship store in on the right) and turn left on the first lane. The church is on the north side of the lane, tucked within an unmarked gate, smothered by walls and offices. What is visible from the street is the church's curious tower, part traditional Chinese, part northern European. On Sunday mornings, the worshippers overflow the gate yard, pushing back into the street. If they see you, they'll probably let you through.

The services I've attended at the Protestant church have been ordinary enough. The chapel is unadorned, save for a few scrolls and a gold foil crucifix. A trio of ministers addresses the congregation.

A 30-member robed choir leads in the singing of the hymns, whose melodies may sound familiar to a Western ear. Collection plates are passed. The Lord's Prayer is recited. On your way out, you'll probably be stopped by curious churchgoers, as I have been. Once I was stopped by two old sisters dressed in black, strolling hand in hand. They remembered the Englishmen who had run the church before Liberation (1949). One sister, scrutinizing me matter-of-factly, wondered at last if we were finally coming back.

Xi'an's **Catholic church** is even harder to find the first time. Walk due west on Xi Dajie from the Bell Tower, past the Drum Tower, on for almost 2 miles to Hongguang Jie on your left. Turn south, walk two long blocks, first passing Yandian Jie, then turning left on Wuxing Jie. The cathedral is tucked back on your left as you turn east. Again, if you go here on Sunday morning, you can follow the crowds. Christianity is quite popular in Chinese cities these days, among the young as well as the old. After it was closed down in 1966, the Xi'an cathedral was swallowed up by a candy factory in 1973, which was still running when I first visited in 1984. The priest in those days told me the cathedral was built about 100 years ago by an Italian mission. The style is Romanesque, the material white marble. Inside, there's room for only a few dozen rows of wooden pews. The stained glass is long gone, as is the original furniture, but there are surviving paintings of the stations of the cross hung in gold frames and of St. Francis, a skull at his feet.

The mass is still said in Latin, the confession conducted without benefit of curtain or door. It is Catholicism much as it most recently came to China a century ago, its rituals, its very language, almost forgotten in the West.

Banpo

Xi'an also has an entire chapter from an era of Chinese history that's missing at tourist stops elsewhere: the Stone Age. I don't recommend that you visit the **Banpo Museum (Banpo Bowuguan),** 5 miles east of the city, if you don't have extra time (open daily 9am to 5:30pm; admission RMB 20/$2.40). It's a strange, ugly exhibit, hardly electrifying, yet oddly unforgettable.

In 1953, a village of what became known as the Yangshao culture (4500–3700 B.C.) was excavated on the bank of the Chan River. Much of it is preserved under a large auditorium roof. Inside, visitors snake around the edges of the excavation, peering over the rails at the remains of 46 huts (half underground), fire pits, storage cellars, pottery kilns, and 174 grave sites. The ground has been left here in the middle of the auditorium as it was found.

Hunting, fishing, and farming, these ancestors of the Chinese not only fashioned stone weapons, which are on display, but created striking pottery painted with sharp geometric shapes and the forms of fish and deer. This pottery, much of it displayed in the museum, has a primitive power as potent as that produced by the early dynasties.

The Yangshao society is believed to have been matrilineal. The skeletons and graves are most haunting. Half a dozen of the skeletons can be seen in a corner of the museum under dusty glass in cement cribs. You can almost make out faces on the skulls. Adults were usually buried alone. Children were buried in jars, 73 of them found on this site. At one excavation near the exit, there are eight burial jars standing next to the foundation of a hut. The pattern of the fish on Stone Age pottery, the funeral urns for children, and the gray of this compressed dust—the gray of brain matter, the color of soil after it has utterly died—can stay with you for years. At the very least, Banpo taught me how old the human race really is, and how strange and resilient, surviving so long in places like this Stone Age village or even the streets of Xi'an.

A **Stone Age Theme Park** has opened next door to Banpo, and I haven't found one person who likes it. Even the local tour guides vote thumbs down on this fiberglass village with displays and dancers straight out of a Chinese *Flintstones*.

The New Museum

Xi'an's new museum, the **Shaanxi History Museum** (open daily 9am to 5:30pm, admission RMB 48/$5.75) is a state-of-the-art facility on a par with the most modern museums of Beijing and Shanghai. Located 2 miles south of the city wall (on Xiaozhi Dong Lu at Cuihua Lu), it opened in 1992 and has formed an excellent complement to the old Provincial Museum and Forest of Steles inside the wall. Signs are in English and Chinese, the lighting is good for a change, and the historical relics are among the best in the Chinese world.

The major exhibit is on the first floor at the rear: 39 Tang Dynasty frescoes removed from the walls of underground tombs. These murals provide lifelike snapshots of China's golden past when traders from the West called upon a capital of camel caravans, hunting dogs, and polo tournaments. These scenes of court musicians, dancers, and eunuchs are rendered in pale oranges, reds, and blues, bringing a distant imperial age to life. Although the museum contains an enormous collection of gold, stone, paper, cloth, and jade relics from all the dynasties, the remains of the Tang naturally stand out here. Xi'an was the capital of China when the Silk Road routes to the West were at their richest under 18 successive

Tang rulers, and the museum is stuffed with silks, tricolored ceramics, and ladies' fashions of the time.

Upstairs, the Qin Dynasty (770–206 B.C.) contributes five of its famous terra-cotta soldiers. While there are thousands of these clay warriors at the vaults of Emperor Qin's terra-cotta army (see chapter in "Monuments of the Middle Kingdom") less than 20 miles away, at this museum you can take a close-up, unhurried look. Separated by an inch of glass, you make out the bows on a soldier's square-toed shoes. And you can appreciate the art that went into these figures of royal death. The emperor's men look like flesh and blood buried alive inside skins of clay. Two of their steeds are also on display, neither of them protected by glass. I reach out to stroke their manes, the cold, hard dust from the first Chinese empire.

Pagodas

Xi'an's most monumental relics of the Tang Dynasty are its two pagodas south of the city wall. The **Small Wild Goose Pagoda (Xiaoyanta)** is the smaller and younger of the sisters but also the prettier. It is missing its upper two stories, and its jagged top looks as if an earthquake rattled it. At least one big one did, reducing the Small Wild Goose Pagoda to a 13-story, gracefully tapered blue-brick tower. In fact, it's said that in 1487 an earth tremor split the pagoda in half, head to toe, but in 1556 a second jolt zipped it back together.

Few Tang Dynasty relics remain in the halls of **Jianfu (Commending Happiness) Temple** surrounding the pagoda, but the pagoda's dark, winding stairs are worth climbing for the view. The temple, its gardens and courtyards, and the old pagoda were built by order of the Tang emperor—the temple in A.D. 684 and the pagoda in A.D. 707—as a safe place to store sutras (holy Buddhist manuscripts). At this time there was need for such storage. Increasingly, monks were setting out from Xi'an and walking west to India, returning after many years with Buddhist texts from the source. The monk Yi Jing was the first to make the journey to India by sea. He left in A.D. 671, returning 24 years later (after some time in Sumatra) with 400 holy works. He translated these sutras up until his death in A.D. 713 at the new Small Wild Goose Pagoda.

The **Big Wild Goose Pagoda (Dayanta)**, 2 miles farther south of the city wall, is Xi'an's most famous Tang Dynasty landmark. This seven-story tower, strong and squarish, with large windows from which devotees toss coins for luck, was erected in A.D. 652, again as a fireproof storage silo for Buddhist sutras. It was the first Chinese pagoda I ever saw and the first I studied at length.

This pagoda was built at the behest of China's most famous Buddhist monk, Xuan Zang, who returned to Xi'an in A.D. 652 after 15 years of wandering across the Gobi Desert over the Silk Road to India and Pakistan. Xuan Zang returned with the requisite sutras, carrying all of them in his enormous backpack. His way was lighted by oil lamps affixed to his pack frame. The Forest of Steles contains a famous pictorial stone tablet of this monk on the road, my favorite rubbing. Xuan Zang's journey to the West required 22 years, and the monk's exploits were transcribed into China's most popular epic, usually translated as *The Monkey* or *Journey to the West*. There, Xuan Zang appears as a clever, heroic, mystically empowered monkey who undergoes a series of fantastic adventures on the distant road.

When Xuan Zang returned with his 1,500 manuscripts, he set up a bureau at the Dacien (Great Goodwill) Temple in the southern precincts to translate them from Sanskrit. The Big Wild Goose Pagoda—its name, I suspect, taken from the geese that once landed on its massive eaves— was built on the temple grounds. The whole complex was immense in those days, with 1,000 rooms and 300 monks. Something of a revival is under way in the 1990s. The courtyards have been restored, all the surviving halls cleaned up, and the Big Wild Goose Pagoda is doing big box-office business, second only to the vaults of the terra-cotta warriors. There are vendors galore, a silk carpet factory, a new temple built by local farmers, and a shooting range with machine guns for hire just south of the pagoda entrance.

As for the Big Wild Goose Pagoda, it still manages to look magnificent, perhaps because it can stretch a full, broad, powerful seven stories (200 feet) above the tourist frenzy at its feet. One hundred monks service the grounds, along with hundreds of ticket takers, vendors, tour guides, and hustlers. Open daily from 8am to 5pm, with an entrance fee of RMB 13 ($1.55), the temple grounds are worth a visit, and the pagoda itself in the center, which requires another ticket (RMB 25/$3) just for the privilege to climb, is worth entering as well.

What's remarkable about the view from the top of the Big Wild Goose Pagoda is not simply that this was the highest building in central China for over 1,200 years or that emperors from the Tang Dynasty stood at the same brick portals admiring the capital view; rather, it is the scale of the ancient capital that it reveals. This pagoda and its temples were then a mile inside the walls of the old city, not 3 miles outside of it. For 1,000 years, from the fall of Rome to the Renaissance, this was the greatest city in the East, but it was as remote from the West as Atlantis and as unreal. The golden age of the Tang Dynasty elevated the city to poetic heights. Xi'an was seven times larger then, the supreme metropolis of the medieval world.

The **Tomb of the First Emperor** lies to the east, where his clay soldiers have at last marched back out of the earth. The burial mounds of 11 Han Dynasty emperors and 18 Tang Dynasty rulers radiate out from

Xi'an in concentric bands. The mounds are so large you will mistake them for huge hills, but look carefully: They rise abruptly from the flat fields and they are too regular in shape. The landscape is of royal mausoleums. Most have never been opened. They make up the thousand hills of the old capital and the fallen constellations of vanished dynasties. And the city walls are like a box containing all the mementos of the old capital, open to the elements, natural and human, subject to breakage, theft, deterioration, loss, and rescue from the ages of dust that descend and smother like sleep.

WHAT TO READ

Digging to China: Down and Out in the Middle Kingdom (Soho Books, 1991, 1994), my own account of living and working in Xi'an, gives a detailed picture of the ancient capital in 1984 and a means to measure how much the city and China have changed since then.

PRACTICAL INFORMATION

ORIENTATION

Xi'an is 550 miles west of Beijing in the north–central province of Shaanxi. Xi'an's weather is best in autumn (not as hot and humid as in summer, as cold as in winter, or as dusty as in spring).

Xi'an's most important site is the **Museum of Emperor Qin's Terra-Cotta Warriors** (see separate chapter in "Monuments of the Middle Kingdom"). This ranks as China's most important archeological discovery of the century; nearly all visitors to Xi'an book a half-day tour to see it.

Xi'an is 2 hours west of the most beautiful of China's Five Sacred Mountains, **Hua Shan** (see separate chapter, "Hua Shan: Sacred Mountain of the West"). Recent improvements in transportation to the mountain and the opening of a cable car mean that Hua Shan can be done as a long day trip from Xi'an.

Xi'an, situated at the terminus of an ancient trade route to the West, now serves as gateway to the **Silk Road** (see the section, "Silk Road Caravan") and the oases of the Gobi Desert.

GETTING THERE

By Plane The new airport is quite far from the city, 31 miles to the northwest (at the town of Xianyang). The road is also new and the landscape is interesting because of the number of imperial burial mounds along the way, the unopened tombs of Han and Tang dynasty emperors.

Xi'an is served from Hong Kong daily by Dragonair, Sheraton Hotel lobby, 12 Fenggao Lu (☎ 029/426-2988), a

2^1/$_2$-hour flight. Chinese regional airlines connect Xi'an to most major cities in China, including Beijing (1^1/$_2$ hours), Chengdu (1 hour 15 minutes), Guilin (2 hours), Hangzhou (1 hour), Kunming (2 hours 15 minutes), and Shanghai (1 hour 40 minutes).

Transfer by taxi from the airport takes an hour and costs at least RMB 160 ($20).

By Train   The train station is located at the north end of Jiefang Lu at the city wall. There are ticket windows on the second floor serving foreigners (open 9am to noon and 2 to 5pm), but it is much easier to buy tickets through hotel tour desks.

Direct overnight trains serve Beijing (17 hours), Chengdu (19 hours), Datong (22 hours), Guangzhou (22 hours), and Shanghai (24 hours). Luoyang, site of the Buddhist caves, is 6 hours east by train, and Kaifeng, another ancient capital, is 12 hours east by train.

TOURS & STRATAGEMS

Tours   China International Travel Service (CITS), 32 Chang'an Lu (☎ 029/526-2066), has its two most effective branches across from the Bell Tower in the Holiday Inn (☎ 029/727-9200, ext. 2842) and across from the railway station in the Jiefang Hotel (☎ 029/743-1023). CITS can book all plane and train tickets and arrange tours of Xi'an's many sights.

Hotel tour desks offer their own day tours. The Shangri-La Hotel, for example, offers a 4-hour tour to Banpo and the Terra-Cotta Warriors for RMB 340 ($41) and a 3-hour tour to the Great Mosque, the Bell Tour, the Drum Tower, and the Big Wild Goose Pagoda for RMB 240 ($29).

City Layout   Since the days of the Tang Dynasty, Xi'an streets have been laid out on a north–south, east–west grid. Bei Dajie, Nan Dajie, Dong Dajie, and Xi Dajie—Big North Street, Big South Street, Big East Street, and Big West Street—all converge at the Bell Tower traffic circle in the heart of the city. The walled city is 2 miles north to south, 1¹/₂ miles east to west. Popular walking areas are the city wall, the Old Town street in front of the Provincial Museum, the Muslim quarter (north of the Drum Tower), and Dong Dajie, the main shopping street. Dong Dajie has recently undergone modernization and now features a covered food mall (Tanshi Jie), a Western fast-food outlet (Bob and Bettey's), an enclosed shopping mall (Xi'an Kai Yuan), and Western-label boutiques (Playboy and Crocodile). It's possible to tour the sights inside the city walls, and the city walls themselves, on foot on your own. Taxis are easy to hail and cost RMB 10 to 20 ($1.20 to $2.50) per trip.

WHERE TO STAY

Bell Tower (Zhonglou Fandian). *Southwest corner of Bell Tower.* ☎ *800/465-4329 or 029/727-9200. Fax 029/727-1217. 321 rms. A/C MINIBAR TV TEL. $80 double. AE, DC, JCB, MC, V.* Holiday Inn provides only the management for this hotel, which is not one of their best in China, but the service is adequate for a 3-star property. The location of this seven-story hotel right in the very heart of the city helps make it the best midpriced choice. The view of the Bell Tower is good from the large rooms, which were last renovated in 1994 and

1995 and are showing some wear. There's a disco in the building and bicycle rental in the lobby.

Services: Room service, dry cleaning and laundry (next day), daily maid service, foreign exchange counter.

Facilities: In-house movies, health club (exercise machines), tour desk, beauty salon, shopping arcade.

Hyatt Regency (Kaiyue Fandian). *158 Dong Dajie (four blocks east of Bell Tower).* ☎ *800/233-1234 or 029/723-1234. Fax 029/721-6799. 404 rms. A/C MINIBAR TV TEL. $150 double. AE, DC,*

JCB, MC, V. This 12-story, 5-star hotel, opened in 1990, has all the international luxuries. If you are walking to sights in the city, its location tops that of the Golden Flower. If you are taking taxis or tour buses, the downtown traffic congestion becomes a drawback. The rooms are small but comfortable, and the service is nearly as high as that at the Shangri-La Golden Flower.

Services: Concierge, room service (24-hour), dry cleaning and laundry (24-hour), nightly turndown, daily maid service, free airport shuttle, foreign exchange counter.

Facilities: In-house movies, pool (indoor, heated), health club (exercise machines), sauna, tennis courts, business center (24-hour), tour desk, beauty salon, shopping arcade.

Shangri-La Golden Flower (Jinghua Fandian). 8 Changle Xi Lu (2 miles east of the city wall). ☎ 800/942-5050 or 029/323-2981. Fax 029/323-5477. 453 rms. A/C MINIBAR TV TEL. $120 double. AE, DC, JCB, MC, V. Since its appearance in 1985, the 11-story recently renovated Golden Flower has been Xi'an's most luxurious and efficient international hotel. Rooms are large and the executive-floor rooms (Horizon Club, floors 9 and 10) are particularly plush with in-room safes, robes, hair dryers, and free breakfast. There are good street markets and an active night market in front of the hotel, but a cab ride is required to reach the city wall (about 10 minutes, $2).

Services: Concierge, room service (24-hour), dry cleaning and laundry (24-hour, same day), nightly turndown, daily maid service, free airport shuttle, foreign exchange counter.

Facilities: In-house movies, pool (indoor, heated), health club (exercise machines, classes), Jacuzzi, sauna, business center (24-hour), tour desk, beauty salon, shopping arcade.

WHERE TO DINE

Ten years ago Xi'an was a culinary wasteland, except for the regional steamed dumpling (*jiaozi*) and shish kebab barbecued by street vendors in the Muslim quarter. Both these items are still available, and dining has improved. The hotels provide some excellent restaurants and there are small cafes with decent fare.

The best of the small cafes catering to budget travelers are **Dad's Home Cooking** and **Mum's Home Cooking,** both located north of the city wall on Fenghe Lu opposite the backpacker's favorite lodging, the Flats of Renmin Hotel. Both these cafes offer low-priced Western entrees, from pancakes to hamburgers, with English-speaking staff and their own tour offices, and they are open from dawn to late in the evening. **Kentucky Fried Chicken** has a large, clean new outlet on Nan Dajie, three blocks north of the city wall's south gate.

Shang Palace. 8 Changle Xi Lu (lobby of Shangri-La Golden Flower Hotel). ☎ 029/323-2981. Fax 029/323-5477. Reservations recommended. Main courses $9–$15. AE, DC, JCB, MC, V. Daily 11:30am–2:30pm and 5–10pm. NORTHERN CHINESE/CANTONESE. Best of the hotel restaurants for Chinese cuisine, Shang Palace is richly decorated in Qing-style furniture and carved wood wall panels. The steamed dumplings (jiaozi) are the best I've ever had in Xi'an, making for an ideal lunch, and the Chinese dinner menu (in English) is extensive.

Tang Dynasty. 39 Chang'an Lu. ☎ 029/526-1633. Fax 029/526-1619. Reservations required. Dinner show $20. AE, DC, JCB, MC, V. Daily 7:30–9:30pm. CHINESE. This new dinner restaurant offers a five-course fixed-price meal of regional and international specialties, prepared and served in efficient fashion. A typical menu consists of seafood pastry, black mushroom consommé, jiaozi, king prawns and walnuts, beef tenderloins and rice, fruit salad with snow fungus, petits fours, and jasmine tea. The 1-hour stage show, starting at 8:30pm, includes performances by an ancient Chinese instrument ensemble, Tang Dynasty dancers, solo singers, and the Emperor's Parade Dance as the finale. Your hotel should be able to book this package.

KAIFENG: FORGOTTEN CAPITAL OF THE NORTHERN SONG

开封

KAIFENG IS PERHAPS THE LEAST visited of China's ancient capitals, a walled city south of the Yellow River that served as capital of the Middle Kingdom during seven dynasties, culminating in a 168-year reign that spanned the magnificent Northern Song Dynasty (A.D. 960–1127). The splendors of Kaifeng under the Song emperors are immortalized in an ancient 15-foot-long painted scroll (Going Up-River for the Festival of Clear Brightness), now located in the Forbidden City (Palace Museum) collection in Beijing. Here we see Kaifeng at its vibrant zenith with its wide Imperial Way, arched stone bridges, gleaming temples, lively merchant districts, and camel caravans entering its gates. Today, although it remains a forgotten city, Kaifeng is reconstructing itself for visitors as the 12th-century Song Dynasty capital it once was.

I had long dreamed of seeing what treasures remained inside its city walls. One other attraction, an oddity in China, also appealed to me. Kaifeng had nourished a Jewish community for many centuries, and remnants, even descendants of that congregation, were said to still exist there.

It was not difficult to book an overnight train from Shanghai along the Yellow River to Kaifeng, but once there I could find no tour desk or roaming tout to guide me through the city's highlights. I grabbed a taxi into the city, settled into a Chinese hotel, procured a map, and set out to explore Kaifeng on foot. The distances within the crumbling earthen city walls proved to be reasonably short. In a matter of hours I was able to circumambulate the entire city as I searched for two vaunted treasure troves: those of the Song Dynasty capital and those of a Jewish presence in China.

Imperial Way

Striking out from the Dongjing Hotel near the southwest corner of the Kaifeng city walls and walking north along Yingbing Lu, I quickly came to **Lord Bao Lake (Baogong Hu)** and crossed the bridge that bisects it. I was immediately impressed by the lack of motorized traffic on the wide thoroughfare. I could easily cross the street almost at will, a feat impossible these days in most Chinese cities. Forty minutes later I was standing before the massive gates to the Imperial Way, Kaifeng's recent reconstruction of the Song Dynasty's main avenue. Eight centuries ago the central passage of the Imperial Way was reserved for China's emperors, and to either side were covered arcades where the leading merchants of the kingdom carried on their trades. Those sidewalks for the common folk were once lined with narrow canals planted in flowering lotuses. Today, the tile-roofed shops hawk local snacks, river fish, antiques, calligraphy, and souvenirs. It's a charming, rather sleepy shopping district running three blocks north to the entrance of **Dragon Pavilion (Longting) Park,** once the site of Song Dynasty palaces and imperial gardens. A spacious pleasure park with a central causeway dividing Yangjia and Panjia lakes survives today (admission RMB 15/$1.80). The park's centerpiece is a remarkable raised pavilion constructed atop a tall pyramid base. Dating from 1378, this pavilion was rebuilt during Emperor Kangxi's rule (1662–1723). Joining its massive main hall are eight hallways, one of which contains 63 life-sized imperial figures in wax. In the Dragon Pavilion's courtyard, dozens of sedan chairs, lavishly covered in red silks, are in the hire of Chinese tourists reenacting royal marriage processions. The park is a pleasant place to stroll, teeming with local families, many of whom rent rowboats for the afternoon. There are several floating restaurants in the form of large dragon boats on the two lakes, and the shore is lined with fishermen, many half asleep, their bamboo poles carefully wedged between rocks.

Up the River

Returning to the park entrance, I walked west along the lakeshore about 30 minutes to the **Stele Forest of the Imperial Academy,** an outdoor collection, recently opened, of 3,500 steles (carved stone tablets), many of which date from the Song Dynasty. The grounds were unfinished and uninviting, however, and the number of steles on display was disappointingly few.

Kaifeng's newest grand tourist attraction, adjacent to the stele collection, was not yet complete either. Called **Qingming Park Up the River,** this theme park is designed according to the famous 12th-century scroll of Kaifeng and hugs the Huanghe River, a tributary of the Yellow River to the north. Its streets, shops, wharves, ships, gardens, teahouses, and pawn shops are supposed to evoke the ancient capital in all its splendor, and the brochures promise lively entertainment, from fortune-telling to acrobatics. My guess is that it will prove far too artificial for those foreign tourists preferring the tatters of old Kaifeng to an amusement park, but such dynastic Disneylands are currently all the rage throughout Asia. Perhaps Kaifeng's attempt to cash in will be successful; the city is certainly constructing its Song Dynasty amusement park on a grand scale. At present, it's scheduled to open as early as the summer of 1998.

Iron Pagoda

Having walked the western side of the walled city, I headed northeastward in the afternoon, walking for over an hour before reaching Kaifeng's landmark, the **Iron Tower (Tie Ta).** Erected in 1049, this slender 13-story octagon, 175 feet tall, is actually constructed of brick and covered in glazed tiles that give it a dark metallic sheen. From its top-story portals, I had a wide view of the walled city, which is almost devoid of high-rises and from afar appears as a Chinese city yet to be modernized, a decade out of date or more. There were no towering skyscrapers, no Western fast-food pavilions, no palaces housing 5-star hotels or deluxe department stores.

South of the Iron Pagoda I discovered a section of the Song Dynasty earthen wall that I could mount, but there was little left in the way of archers' towers and watch stations. Weary of walking the dusty backstreets,

I returned via taxi, dreaming of the Song Dynasty wonders barely hinted at today.

The Lost Tribe

Kaifeng is a city of many legacies, the most visible ones from the Song Dynasty, but its strangest legacy is that of its **Jewish community,** which written evidence traces back to the late 10th century A.D. The Jews of Kaifeng, thought to have emigrated from Persia over the Silk Road trade routes, have lived in Kaifeng continuously for 1,000 years, establishing their own synagogue in Kaifeng in A.D. 1163. Two pieces of evidence of the Kaifeng Jewish presence can still be seen in Kaifeng: the stone tablets recording early Jewish history in China and the grounds of the great synagogue (destroyed for good in the last century). I set out to see both.

The stone tablets are still kept on the third floor of the **Kaifeng Museum,** located on the south bank of Lord Bao Lake (although a new facility is rumored to be opening soon). The museum is a large building graced by upturned eaves but is now falling apart, neglected, its staff openly praying for better days (and more funds). Among its 20,000 relics are some Qing Dynasty writings by Kaifeng Jews and two stone tablets, inscribed in Chinese, to commemorate the rebuilding of the Kaifeng synagogue. These tablets are dated 1489 (with the reverse side composed in 1512) and 1679. Each assigns a different date to the arrival of Jews in China, but they are consistent concerning the Kaifeng synagogue, which has been restored on at least 10 occasions since the 12th century. The 1679 stele at Kaifeng records the rebuilding of the temple after the Great Flood of 1642, when the Yellow River inundated and destroyed much of Kaifeng.

Rumors of a Jewish community in China had been circulating since Marco Polo's time but were only confirmed by Westerners after 1605 when Ai Tan, a Kaifeng Jew, met the preeminent Catholic missionary of China, Matteo Ricci. Ai Tan had come to Beijing after reading of the European missionaries and their strange new religion. He suspected that the missionaries were Jews. Ricci, for his part, was thrilled at the chance to meet a genuine Chinese Christian, for Ai Tan announced that he was a fellow believer. Ricci soon realized his mistake, but Ai Tan returned to Kaifeng convinced that Ricci was a fellow Jew from Europe but a bit eccentric in his views. Kaifeng's rabbi later wrote to Ricci, begging him to become his successor and pointing out that odd beliefs were less important than the way a man conducted his life. The good Jesuit's reply to the offer of a rabbinical post in Kaifeng is not known.

The Jewish community continued to worship in Kaifeng until the flood of 1852, which again destroyed the synagogue. The temple was never rebuilt and the Jews remaining in Kaifeng gradually ceased to practice the rituals associated with Judaism. Their place of worship, the

Hebrew language, and all ethnic and racial distinctions that set them apart disappeared. As several scholars later pointed out, never before had Jews been so thoroughly assimilated as in China.

According to a Chinese scholar's census, there were 166 descendants of Jews in Kaifeng as of 1980. A number of these people continue to regard themselves as Jewish today. In 1985, Rabbi Joshua Stampfer of Portland, Oregon, hosted one of these descendants, Qu Yi-nan, a 25-year-old reporter for the *People's Daily* in Beijing. She recalled that her family did not eat pork and that her grandfather always wore a blue skullcap. Under the rabbi's tutelage, Ms. Qu quickly became the only Chinese Jew in the world able to read Hebrew and participate in basic Jewish rituals. (She has since married and settled in Los Angeles.)

Curious to see the grounds of Kaifeng's celebrated synagogue, the **Purity and Truth Synagogue (Qing Zhen Si),** I set out for the intersection of Beixing and Pingdeng streets. I knew that the site was near the Number 4 People's Hospital, north of both the Catholic church and the Great Eastern Mosque. (In no other city in China can one find a Catholic church, an Islamic mosque, a Daoist temple, and the site of a Jewish synagogue within a four-block walk.) I had determined the synagogue's exact location, at 21 Jiao Jing Lu (west of Cao Shi Jie, east of Bei Tu Jie, north of Nan Jiao Jing Hutong, south of Cai Zhen Dong Jie, to be precise), but I could not find it in the maze of streets and alleys, shops and shanties. Twice I asked for directions. Ultimately, I stumbled onto a cluttered, nearly vacant, overgrown lot that fit the description. I knew the synagogue had vanished, that pieces of it had been used to build the Great Eastern Daoist Temple; I knew that the Trinity Church had eventually bought the land and rescued some of the relics (including the carved tablets, which until 1912 still stood, in total abandon, in this same yard); and I knew that a medical clinic had taken over the area occupied for eight centuries by the solitary synagogue (for centuries the only one in China). From the outside, the Kaifeng synagogue would have appeared as a typical Chinese temple of gates, pavilions, courtyards, and ancestral halls, except that its entrance faced east and its worshippers faced west, toward Jerusalem, whereas Chinese temples face south. Here, in Kaifeng, I could not even imagine its existence. Nothing was left but a yard. No trace of gate or foundation. Even the stone of the place of worship had been assimilated into the earth of China.

Kaifeng was missing out on a vital, if small, niche in foreign tourism. Clean up the synagogue grounds, build a small memorial and a museum, employ Jewish descendants as guides, and presto: a unique, exotic travel experience, unlike any other on Earth. Perhaps such a project would make things too easy and misleading. Trying to find traces of the Jewish presence in Kaifeng today certainly gives one a more accurate feel for the ravages of history and the sheer force of cultural absorption.

Temple Market

My last morning in Kaifeng, a Sunday, I set out north again. At the bridge over Lord Bao Lake, a local market was in full swing, its vendors taking over the sidewalks with rather paltry goods. New bras and panties were displayed on clotheslines strung between trees. Belts were custom cut on the spot from wide sheets of leather.

At the north end of the bridge, I turned east into the heart of the city where the old streets were crowded with Sunday shoppers drawn to the open markets near the **Grand Xiangguo Monastery.** Founded in A.D. 555, Xiangguo became one of China's most important Buddhist monasteries under the Tang rulers. When Kaifeng became the Song capital, Xiangguo became the number one temple of the empire, as well as the commercial center of the city. The great floods of 1642 completely erased this monastery, but it was rebuilt under Emperor Qianlong in the 18th century. Within the temple, replete with monks hawking trinkets and worshippers burning incense and stroking prayer beads, are assorted small treasures: a 12-foot-tall bronze Frost Bell (cast during the Qing Dynasty), a Buddhist figure from Song days, Ming Dynasty porcelains, an umbrella once owned by the Manchu Empress Dowager, Ci Xi, and in its own pavilion, a 1000-armed statue of Guanyin, Goddess of Mercy, carved from a single tree. Today, the Xiangguo Monastery area is also Kaifeng's leading open-air market, rife with streetside vendors, creating a pungent, gritty, colorful scene. One enterprising vendor was attracting a large throng with his team of three dancing monkeys.

The market today recalls the temple market of Xiangguo Monastery in the days of the Song Dynasty, which one eyewitness, in A.D. 1147, described in glowing terms:

> From the broad grounds inside the Front Gate rose a ca-
> cophonous chorus of rare birds in cages, cats in baskets, dogs
> straining at the leash, and other animals chained for sale. . . .
> In the courtyard inside the Second and Third Gates were
> tents and sheds and awning covered stalls where traders sold
> rush-cushions, bamboo mats, screens, curtains, basins, spit-
> toons, saddles, bows, swords, fruits, and salted meats. In the
> Square next to the Hall of Buddhas, Taoist priest Meng sold
> his special recipe honey-preserved fruits. . . . Along the cor-
> ridor on either side, nuns, standing behind stalls, sold em-
> broideries, stockings, collars, embroidery patterns, bridal
> headgear, hats, false haircoils, silk threads, in every color and
> shade. . . . Superstitious folk in the backyard of the monas-
> tery sought charms, incantations and talismans, or waited to
> have their fortunes told.

There are still living traces of that old capital as described by Song Dynasty visitors and painted so grandly on scrolls.

Modern Kaifeng is a city asleep, a city of possibilities, waiting for its past to awaken. There are hints in its temples, parks, and ruins of an imperial grandeur largely lost elsewhere in China, where modernization has erased much of the earthy grime and street life that came to dominate urban areas when the last of the great dynasties was extinguished early in this century. Kaifeng is a forgotten capital, its old treasures and communities reduced to a few glittering, tantalizing tatters. It still awaits the magic wand of China's economic reforms to spiff up its ancient treasures, but with 42 relics under government protection and 167 places designated as historical sites one senses that Kaifeng will one day recast the rich past within its aging walls and be among China's most visited cities, once it completes its return journey upriver to a festival of clear new brightness.

THE JEWS OF CHINA

Information about Kaifeng's Jewish heritage, sometimes including special-interest tours, is available through the **Sino-Judaic Institute,** 232 Lexington Drive, Menlo Park, CA 94205 (☎ 415/725-3436).

In Kaifeng, the best contact is Wang Tisha, President, **Judaic Study Society of Kaifeng,** 404 Gongyuan Lu, Building 63, Unit 4, Kaifeng, Henan Province (☎ 0378/595-2374; fax 0378/595-2320).

For background on the Jewish community in Kaifeng, read *East Gate of Kaifeng: A Jewish World Inside China,* edited by M. Patricia Needle (University of Minnesota China Center, 1992). For a portrait of Song Dynasty Kaifeng, see Jacques Gernet, *Daily Life in China on the Eve of the Mongol Invasion 1250–1276* (Stanford University Press, 1970).

PRACTICAL INFORMATION

ORIENTATION

Kaifeng, population about 700,000, lies 6 miles south of the Yellow River in Henan Province on the main railway line between Shanghai and Xi'an. It is served by **overnight train** west from Shanghai or east from Xi'an, a 13-hour journey in either direction. There is no airport. **Taxis** are as cheap as you'll find in China, under RMB 10 ($1.20) to most points.

The **tourist bureau** located in the Dongjing Hotel can book train tickets, but it does not seem able to help individual tourists with local tours or provide English-speaking guides.

Kaifeng has developed little in the way of hotels or restaurants to appeal to individual foreign travelers. The sights are interesting, but staying long here is difficult.

WHERE TO STAY

Only two hotels serve foreign visitors. Neither is worth writing home about.

The **Dongyuan Hotel (Dongyuan Dajiudian),** 1 Xinsong Lu (☎ 0378/ 595-8888; fax 0378/595-6816), the newer of the two top-rated hotels, is inconveniently located in east Kaifeng, outside the city walls. It appears to be cleaner than its chief rival, the Dongjing Hotel.

The **Dongjing Hotel (Dongjing Dafandian),** 14 Yingbin Lu (☎ 0378/ 595-8936; fax 0378/595-7705), is owned by the tourism bureau, contains spacious gardens, and is located in south Kaifeng, inside the city walls, on the main road to the museum, Lord Bao Lake, and the Dragon Pavilion. I stayed at this hotel, which has a 3-star rating. One clerk spoke a little bit of English. The tourism bureau consisted of a locked office and service window, closed most of the time. The business center, located behind the reception desk in a labyrinth of hallways, was also closed most hours, although I did manage to send an international fax from there. The rooms are huge but quite rundown, and everything needs a thorough scrubbing. I rented a deluxe room, the size of a junior suite, for RMB 388 ($46) a night, with adequate private bath and clean sheets. Standard rooms are RMB 288 ($35). The Dongjing contains large dining halls, karaoke rooms, a gift shop, and a courtyard bonsai garden. Chinese buffet breakfast is included (7:30 to 8:30am only). You must fetch a taxi yourself on the street.

WHERE TO DINE

Finding a decent restaurant in Kaifeng is a miserable task. If you stay at the Dongjin Hotel, a breakfast coupon is provided, but the offerings are basic Chinese fare (rice, steamed breads, vegetables, fried pastries, perhaps a boiled egg, tea).

Western breakfast and afternoon snacks are available in the lobby of the Dongyuan Hotel, east of the city walls.

I did try the noodles at **California Beef Noodles,** located at the corner of Ziyou Lu and Zhongshan Lu, downtown, southwest of the Xiangguo Monastery, and they were hearty fare but not worth trying twice. There was no English menu.

Meanwhile, back at the **Dongjing Hotel** there are fixed-price Chinese dinners in the large dining room behind the main desk, largely Sichuan-style fare, for RMB 40 ($4.80).

The **Drum Tower Night Market,** at the corner of Sihou Lu and Shudian Lu in the heart of the city, offers a variety of street fare for the daring, including various shish kebabs prepared on the spot over open fires. This is the best dish I found in Kaifeng.

In general, I found Kaifeng to be a good city for Westerners on diets.

CHENGDU: TEMPLES AND PANDAS

成都

A MASSIVE STATUE OF CHAIRMAN Mao Zedong still presides over downtown Chengdu, the capital of the southwest province of Sichuan. Such monuments were a fixture in all the cities of China up until the Great Helmsman's death in 1976. With the rise of Deng Xiaoping and the economic reforms that transformed China from egalitarian communism into a kind of capitalistic socialism, Mao's image came down, statue by statue—but not in Chengdu. In Chengdu, Mao still gazes southward to the Jin River from his stairway pedestal at Exhibition Hall where Renmin (People's) streets North, South, East, and West converge. He has become a traffic landmark, a city center beacon for anyone who navigates the big streets and small lanes of the city, a monument to mapmaking rather than politics.

Renmin Nan Lu (South People's Street) runs half a mile from Mao's feet to the **Jin (Brocade) River,** a boulevard of shiny modern hotels, shops, and billboards (one of them, at the bridge, a massive electronic TV screen). South of the river on the road to the airport there's an American-style subdivision of villas where there were dusty fields 5 years ago, a mirage that has become a reality, decorated with its own billboards promoting a middle-class paradise.

Yet Chengdu is still crisscrossed by winding streets of century-old shop houses where the merchandise hasn't changed since the age of emperors. Nor has the fiery Sichuan cuisine, preserved in Chengdu as nowhere else. Chengdu is one of China's most colorful big cities, always a delight to explore.

Teahouses & Temples

I begin my explorations at 8am, stopping at one of the outdoor teahouses on the north bank of the Jin River. Many of China's last great teahouses still operate here, recalling the Three Kingdoms' era (A.D. 221–263) when Chengdu was the capital of the Kingdom of Chu and the scholar-officials gathered for conversation, entertainment, and drink at cafes along

Ximen Bus Station

Xicheng (West City) Stadium

Shihui Jie

Xinhua Xi Lu

Tomb of Wang Jian

Xi Dajie

Wangjiatang Jie

Babao Jie

Qinglong Jie

Renmin Zhong

Mosi River

Qingjiang Lu

Shi'erqiao Jie

Xi'an

Huimen Jie

Shiye Jie

Changshun Jie

Shangye Jie

Dongchenggen Jie

Yangshi Jie

Xiyulong Jie

Renmin (People's) Stadium

Chengdu-Wenjiang Hwy

Nanhe River

Qingyang Zhengjie

CULTURAL PARK (QINGYANG PALACE)

Xisheng Jie

Jinhe Jie

Sichuan Exhibition Centre

Mao Statue

Du Fu's Thatched Cottage

RENMIN (PEOPLE'S) PARK

Citang Jie

Renmin Xi Lu

Baihua Bridge

BAIHUATAN PARK

Yangpi Ba

Xiyu Jie

Dongyu Jie

Wenmiao Houjie

Shaanxi Jie

Sichuan Theatre

Wenmiao Qianjie

Yihuan Lu Xiduan

Daciangshu Jie

NANJIAO (SOUTH SUBURB) PARK

Temple of Marquis Wu

Wuhoucl Dajie

Jiangxi Jie

Dianxin Lu

Renmin Nanlu

Ximianqiao Jie

Yongfeng Lu

Yihuan Lu Nanduan

0 — 500 m
546 y

N

Sichuan Provincial Museum

Chengdu

the river. Perhaps the most famous figure to frequent these cafes of leisure was the Tang poet Du Fu, who composed several hundred poems to the "Brocade City" where he lived in exile.

Du Fu's cottage, his home in Chengdu, has survived as a park and tourist attraction, but unless you are a scholar of Chinese poetry desiring to pay homage to its greatest poet, there's no reason to visit. I did so some years ago and the visit was not memorable. The park did not come into existence until three centuries after Du Fu arrived in Chengdu (A.D. 759) and there is nothing belonging to him here, particularly not the rather recent thatched hut. The cottage is open daily from 9am to 5pm (admission RMB 20/$2.40).

A visit to the **memorial hall of Zhuge Liang,** China's greatest military strategist and gentleman-scholar, who lived in Chengdu during the time of the Chu rulers 17 centuries ago, is likewise not worth pursuing, unless you happen to be imbued with the literature of the Three Kingdoms and the heroic deeds of Zhuge Liang; if so, a pilgrimage would be fascinating. Otherwise, keep to the streets of Chengdu, its teahouses and temples. The hall is open daily from 9am to 5pm (admission RMB 15/$1.80).

Seating myself in a bamboo armchair at one of the **river teahouses** chosen at random, I am quickly served a cup of flower tea. The cup includes a cover to keep the brew hot and an upturned saucer for lifting. To sip tea properly, grip the saucer in thumb and fingers while slipping the lid slightly back with the raised index finger. It takes practice to become a skilled Chengdu tea drinker. For an investment of 50¢, customers can linger for hours.

Vendors drift through, hawking trinkets and sticks to clean the ears. Ear cleaning is a passion in Chengdu. Downriver, *tai ji quan* masters and other early risers are finishing up their exercises on the mist-laden promenade. Tobacco salesmen are also at work on the sidewalks, selling strong, thick sheaves that are meant to be trimmed and stuffed in the tiny bowls of bamboo-stemmed pipes.

I stop for breakfast at the Long Chao Shou Special Restaurant a few blocks north of the river, partaking of the "little eats" (*xiao chi*—dim sum pastries and dumplings) that make up the traditional morning snacks of Sichuan.

Then I wave down a cab on the street and pay a call on **Wenshu Temple,** a mile north of the Mao statue. Wenshu, the center of Chan (Zen) Buddhism in Chengdu, was founded 13 centuries ago. Today, it is the city's most popular Buddhist retreat, nearly always crammed with families burning incense and bowing to Wenshu (God of Wisdom), Maitreya (Laughing Buddha of the Future), and Guanyin (Goddess of Mercy). The five great halls are drenched in incense. The carved eaves, doors, columns, and wooden figures are particularly fine work. In fact, the monastery maintains an outdoor courtyard where craftsmen work all day under an awning carving religious statuary for use at the temple and for sale to the public. The wood-carvers don't mind if you watch. Many are young apprentices, happy to practice their English.

Wenshu's oldest hall contains images of 17 generations of abbots, duly worshipped by a large number of monks. This is an extremely active temple. Here I meet and, with his permission, photograph an 86-year-old monk named Nansheng. He became a Buddhist monk at age 16 in Shaanxi Province (the next province north). Wenshu had been his residence since 1966. Now extremely frail, Nansheng spends much of his time sitting on benches, counseling the younger monks, and napping. A number of temple volunteers, mostly older women, tend to his daily needs, fetching his rice bowl and washing his clothing.

Wenshu maintains its own outdoor teahouse in a garden court shaded by ginkgo trees and its own vegetarian restaurant located inside a hall that is always jammed for lunch. The street at the entrance, Wenshu Yuan Jie, is a **temple market** with a medieval look, clotted with stalls selling prayer beads, holy medallions, incense, and firecrackers, not to mention shoe soles, underwear, and bottled water. After looking through the stalls, I cross town by taxi, stopping a mile west of the Mao statue at Chengdu's most popular Daoist temple.

Qingyang Gong (Green Goat Temple) is as lively a place of worship as the Buddhist shrine. Most Chinese who worship at one of these temples will in fact call on the other, thereby doubling their chances that some god will grant their wish. Qingyang's main temple, the Hall of the Three Purities, is decorated in brightly painted dragons. The bronze statues of the two "good luck" goats at the altar have been showered in coins and rubbed smooth by the hands of hopeful worshippers. Golden statues of the Three Purities—the Jade Emperor of Heaven, the god of the North Pole, and Lao Zi, founder of Daoism—are the focus of continuous bowing and chanting. I walk inside while a formal service is being conducted by seven monks and three nuns. They are chanting to the sounds of drums and bells. Four very poor peasants in front of me, their clothes turning to rags, are completely prostrate, almost speaking in tongues, echoing every note of the rites fervidly.

Eating Fire

Across the street from Qingyang Gong I decide to try the Sichuan specialties of the **Chen Ma Po Dou Fu Restaurant,** named for the quintessential spicy dish of the region. Fiery *doufu* (bean curd) is at the heart of Sichuan cookery. Mapo doufu consists of spicy bean curd, shredded pork, chopped spring onions, and an intense chile sauce pushed to the limits by aromatic vinegar. This particular restaurant claims to occupy the site where mapo doufu was invented during the Qing Dynasty reign of Emperor

Tung Chi (1862–75). The story goes that a certain Chengdu chef named Chen Ling Fu was married to a talented mapo, which is a woman with a pock-marked face. Her talent was in the kitchen, where she devised a bean curd dish sprinkled with red "pocks" of chile pepper.

The mapo doufu that immortalized this 19th-century "kitchen granny" must be numbingly hot to qualify as authentic; at this namesake restaurant, it could not be more authentic or much hotter. Like many restaurants in Chengdu, this one has a ground floor that caters to working-class communal dining, while the floor above is reserved for banqueting and more leisurely dining. I savor my dinner on the second floor in a room of darkly stained wood and carved columns, its window shutters thrown wide open to the noisy temple street life across the way.

Here, as elsewhere in Chengdu, I experience *ma-la* (very hot) dining at its best. I alternate between the hot doufu and a milder fish-flavored doufu, its sauce a deft mixture of vinegar, garlic, ginger, spring onions, and a modicum of hot bean paste. I order a third bean curd entry, too, known as drunken doufu, a sweet dish of shredded bean curd in an intoxicating sauce. The hot-and-sour soup *(suanla tang)* subtly complements all three strongly flavored, hotly spiced dishes.

"All Sichuan cooking exists as an excuse to consume hot peppers," a Chengdu local once told me. Perhaps so, but the chile peppers that now seem to define many Sichuan dishes are a relatively late addition—and a foreign one to boot. Chile peppers were introduced to China only in the 16th century, by way of Central America.

Pandas

Eighty percent of the world's 1,000 remaining giant pandas reside in Sichuan Province. In 1978, the **Woolong Nature Preserve** was established 86 miles northwest of Chengdu to protect this animal from extinction and allow scientists to study it in the wild. While there are tours to Woolong from Chengdu, the trip is usually futile if your goal is to see a free-roaming panda. Dedicated researchers often go months without a sighting. The Chengdu Zoo can also be a disappointment. While a half-dozen or more pandas reside here (the most of any zoo in the world), they are displayed only in cages or on one outdoor cement island with a tree and slide, and most afternoons they are asleep.

The best chance to see a giant panda in the near wild, then, is during an early morning tour of the **China Research Base of Giant Panda Breeding,** located 7 miles northeast of city center. Opened in 1990 but closed to the public until 1995, the research base hopes to breed both the greater panda and lesser (or red) panda in captivity. But this is not a zoo, at least not an old-fashioned zoo like the Chengdu Zoo 4 miles down the road. Although the pandas are caged at times in breeding houses at the research base, they are also let out to roam across 80 acres of steep hills, forests, and bamboo groves. Visitors follow along on slate walkways, separated by deep moats from a dozen bearlike giant pandas and an equal number of more catlike red pandas who go their own ways, sometimes sitting up a few feet away, other times disappearing into the forest.

I visit in the early morning, leaving at 7am and arriving just after the visitors' gate opens (8am). By noon, pandas are usually curled up, out of sight, dead asleep, so morning's the best time to visit. The hills are encased in fog as I disembark, but before long I spot a giant panda scratching his back against a stump. He appears to have just been fed, but he lazily rolls onto all fours, ambles over to a patch of bamboo, sits down, and goes to work stripping off shoots. A panda's main occupation is eating bamboo—sometimes up to 18 hours a day are spent this way in the wild. At the research base, however, more time is spent napping than eating.

The little red pandas are more active. I watch several of them running through the trees, scampering down the steep inner embankments of the moats, and fighting like raccoons over bits of territory.

This is as close to an uncaged panda as I'm ever likely to get, so I follow those that I find for about two hours. Only a few other tourists are out this early, and the mist still coats the bamboo, blotting out the hilltops. I can pretend for a moment that I am in the unfenced outdoors, that these pandas are free, that I am seeing a sight few humans have ever been allowed to witness.

The research base contains a hospital that is not open for tours and several outdoor panda sculptures. The base hopes to dramatically expand its facilities, acreage, and panda population in the next century, although that depends on finding sources for increased funding.

The research base's **Panda Museum,** unheated when I visit in December, is loaded with stuffed pandas. This motley collection of taxidermy in poorly lit dioramas belongs in a grim socialist museum of the 1950s, which this 1990s display too closely resembles. Some of the exhibits seem overly clinical as well, like the jars preserving specimens of panda sexual organs (the penis is short, the vagina long) and the week-old panda baby, 8 inches long. Nearby is a photograph labeled "Get Semen by Electrical Inspiring." For the most part, the Panda Museum is pathetic. The understocked, uninspired gift counter probably doesn't bolster the funding, and the butterfly museum upstairs isn't even open when I visit.

The giant panda, which was not known to the Western world until 1869, when French priest Pere David purchased a panda skin in Baoxing County, Sichuan, has become a logo for modern China, particularly its wildlife. Conservation of that wildlife is another matter. With proper management and promotion, the panda base in Chengdu could easily become southwest China's largest draw for Western tourists, a source of revenue for China's underfunded wildlife conservation efforts. For now, the panda research base is a step in the right direction—a small step— and despite its drawbacks the only site in the world where so many tourists can see so many pandas in one pleasant preserve. The research base is open daily from 8am to 5pm (admission RMB 40/$4.80 includes museum).

Backstage at the Opera

I might have gotten to the temples, the teahouses, and even the panda research base on my own, but I would not have gotten backstage at the Sichuan Opera without the guidance of the amazing Mr. Lee. Mr. Tray Lee is a product of the new, more economically liberal China. He is a freelance tour director who works his way through cafes and hotel lobbies where foreigners gather, dishing out his name card, describing his tours, and opening photo albums of the sights to which he can take you. His business card gives his title as "Mr. Lee, Tour Manager" and proclaims **"Lee's Budget Tours Service** (Since 1989). No Risk!!! Use the Service First, Pay Later!!!" He lists his phone, fax, and pager numbers, as well as his home address. Best of all, his tours (to schools, to hospitals, to factories, to kindergartens, to the countryside) are just as Mr. Lee advertises them: fairly priced, efficient, and personal.

Mr. Lee tells me that he'd been trying for years to open up the Sichuan Opera to backstage tours, finally succeeding in 1990. We arrive 2 hours before show time (2pm) at the **Jinjiang Theatre** (on Huaxingzheng Jie, a mile east of Mao's statue). Sichuan Opera originated nearly 300 years ago as an offshoot of performances at local festivals in Shaanxi Province to the north. The local Sichuan dialect, rich in punning possibilities, was soon employed in the opera, which borrowed from traditions in the Peking and Cantonese operas to the east. Sichuan Opera stories often concern the common people of the region. By comparison, Peking Opera is polished, urbane, and lofty.

The **Sichuan Opera Company** of Sichuan Province, with 300 employees, operates from offices and apartments in the Jinjiang Theatre. Performers range in age from 13 to 60. Several singers trace their lineage in local opera back for generations. Regular Saturday and Sunday performances are given for foreign tourists and the public, part of a schedule that numbers 200 performances annually. Many of the best singers must supplement their income by cranking out pop songs and ballads in Chengdu nightclubs, however, since funding for the opera is minimal at best. Older people support traditional singing, but younger generations follow Western-based musical forms. In 1993, this opera company received a boost when it was invited on a performance tour of Taiwan.

(at your service)

To reach the other side of the world the easy way, use **AT&T DIRECT**℠ SERVICE. Simply dial the access number for the country you're in (for a list of AT&T Access Numbers, take the wallet card provided) and you'll be connected to English-speaking operators and get AT&T's quick, clear connections. Plus, you can use your AT&T Calling Card or any of these major credit cards. Now, what could be easier than that?

I t ' s   a l l   w i t h i n   y o u r   r e a c h .

Backstage, I'm able to wander from performer to performer as they apply their makeup at a long table. This laborious process is performed under bare lightbulbs using small hand mirrors and paints extracted from makeup kits. The cosmetics are thick and colorful. In an adjoining room, the costumes, masks, shoes, and props are readied. Hanks of black hair for beards and bangs are greased and attached. In a large back room, actors retrieve their costumes from trunks. Performers drift in and out nervously, warming up their voices.

Twenty actors form an average weekend cast. Mr. Lee introduces me to the story director, Shang Zhen Kun, and to the performance director, Zhang Ji Che, who have chosen excerpts from four operas to perform today. You can attend the weekend performances on your own, but it certainly helps to have an interpreter, such as Mr. Lee, at your side. The auditorium is an aging, intimate chamber with wide tiers where armchairs and wooden tables are arranged in rows. Teacups, tea, thermoses, and packaged snacks are provided. The audience is composed almost entirely of retired local men, who chatter and gossip once the show begins.

Mr. Lee outlines the plot of each operatic excerpt, starting with *Coming to the Palace for the Second Time,* the story of two officials who come to the palace to ask the queen to help a man who is about to become king. This is a fable about modern business, Mr. Lee suggests: Forgive and forget the past; forge ahead to a brighter future.

In the second piece, *A Husband's Nightmare,* a husband goes to the city, makes his fortune, and abandons his wife in the countryside. After she commits suicide, her avenging ghost haunts her husband's dreams. Waking up, he dies of fright. This is a warning, Mr. Lee maintains, about the power of American women and their dominance over men, a situation that Mr. Lee sees as poisoning traditional male-female relationships in China. Mr. Lee confesses that he is seeking a more subservient wife in rural Sichuan, so far without success. Lest you find Mr. Lee's views utterly Neanderthal, consider that his impressions of America are based on his favorite foreign films, two of which include *Home Alone* and *The Bridges of Madison County.* One tells him how children are treated in America, the other how American marriage and adultery are faring.

The third operatic excerpt, *How the Love Letter Came into Being,* concerns a minority woman who writes a letter to a Chinese soldier, and the last story, *Husband and Wife Bridge,* is based on an actual event that took place in northwest Chengdu. A teacher spearheads a bridge project that runs into opposition from officials who are in cahoots with the local mafia's ferryboat business. The teacher is assassinated, but his wife delivers a rousing memorial at his tomb, an episode that is drawn out for 3 hours in the full opera.

We are treated to what amounts to arias from famous Sichuan operas, accompanied by musicians on violin, flute, zither, drums, and cymbals, punctuated with high-pitched singing and acrobatics on the nearly bare stage. The hour's performance is quite sufficient to give foreign viewers the flavor. This is opera without elaborate scenery and grand stagings, more in keeping with the casual teahouse atmosphere in which Sichuan Opera is usually performed. And with the backstage tour included, attending Sichuan Opera becomes a delightful way to spend a Sunday afternoon.

Chairman Mao Museum

Mr. Lee, son of a soccer coach, was born 28 years ago in Shenyang Province, but he grew up in Chengdu and he knows the older streets well. One afternoon we end up at 23 Wu Fu (Five Happinesses) Street in an older neighborhood. The aging wooden shop house at this address has been converted into the **Chairman Mao Badge Museum and Research Facility.** The mastermind of this collection of Mao memorabilia is Wang An Ting. He's sitting back on a bamboo lounge when we enter the front room. Wang, a former factory worker, is about 60 years old and very hard of hearing. He was born in this house, and his grandson and wife live in the back room, where they have a bed, table, and a 27-inch color TV. Wang asks me to sign his large guest book, a register that includes the names of visitors from Germany, France, Japan, Russia, and various cities in China who have come to him to augment their own Mao collections.

The main room and the side room are stuffed—floors, walls, and ceilings—with nothing but Mao: Mao posters, commemorative Mao plates, red flags, ceramic busts, red-and-gold Mao buttons of every size, and Mao's little red book of quotations in its every edition. Corner tables serve as altars to Mao, complete with candles. Coffee tables block the aisles, hundreds of Mao buttons under their sooty glass tops. Red armbands from the Cultural Revolution (1966–76) as well as newspapers from that period of upheaval are pinned to the walls, as are Big Character posters heralding the various social and political movements that tore through the 1950s and 1960s like typhoons.

Chairman Mao is enjoying a nostalgic revival throughout China, which is impelled by a desire for more orderly, if more impoverished, days. Many people feel that an image of Mao, like that of a Buddhist or Daoist god, can bring good fortune. Taxi drivers from Beijing to Chengdu have dangled portraits of Mao from their rearview mirrors ever since a rumor spread a few years ago about a cab driver with such an emblem whose life was spared in a traffic accident. Wang himself tells us that the life of the former governor of Sichuan was recently saved "by the spirit of Mao."

Mao's ghost is certainly visible enough in this cramped pack-rat museum. Wang tells us he has "10 big bags" of Mao items in his collection, and I believe it. His own house has been turned upside down by this passion. Wang is desperately looking for a patron to move his museum to larger, classier quarters. Meanwhile, he spends each day waiting for the next visitor to drop by while he stamps out his own shiny new Mao buttons on a small press. As I depart, Wang An Ting hands me a half-dozen buttons and his bilingual business card on which he is billed as "Head of the Mao Tse-tong's Medals Research Society in China (Preparatory)," "Honorable Member of Shanghai Researchist Coordination Committee," and "Contemporary Cultural Relic of Chief Editor."

Later, outside the Chengdu post office, the enterprising Mr. Lee asks me for one of the newly minted Mao buttons, which he proceeds to pawn off on a not-so-wily street vendor as a "Cultural Revolutionary antique."

Later, at dusk, when the sky turns copper red, I'm walking back to my hotel, past the saluting statue of Mao, clean and white, when I notice a street musician setting up his act. He's playing an erhu, a traditional Chinese cello with two strings—except that his is an electric erhu. He has wired its sound box to an amp. He has strapped a microphone to its neck. As he saws away with his bow, he stomps out a thunderous rhythm with both feet by beating on metal wash pans flipped upside down. He's the Bob Dylan of a new China. This is where the sidewalks of New York start to merge with those of Chengdu, where East and West meet head-on in the intersections of the next century. This is an erhu unlike any ever strummed before in all the centuries of teahouses and temples, of calligraphers and emperors. It's a tune to the future, a song Mao never heard.

PRACTICAL INFORMATION

ORIENTATION

Chengdu, a city of over 9 million, including suburbs, is located in the center of Sichuan Province, China's subtropical "rice basket," nearly a thousand miles southwest of Beijing. Summers are hot and rainy (especially July and August) and should be avoided. Winters are cloudy and foggy but mild. Tourist season begins in April and ends in November, with November probably having the best weather.

Chengdu is a few hours north of one of China's greatest outdoor monuments, the **Great Buddha at Leshan** (see separate chapter under "Monuments of the Middle Kingdom"), which can be visited in one day. Chengdu is also the gateway to **Emei Shan,** the Western Peak of Buddhism (see separate chapter), which requires at least a 2-night stay. Both these sites can be reached from Chengdu by public bus or group tour.

GETTING THERE

By Plane   Shuangliu Airport is 11 miles south of the city. Dragonair, with offices in the Sichuan Hotel, 31 Zongfu Lu (☎ 028/675-5555, ext 6105), has direct flights from Hong Kong (2 hours). Chinese airlines serve Chengdu from most major cities in China (2 hours from Beijing, 2 hours from Guangzhou, 2 hours from Shanghai). Taxis charge at least RMB 65 ($8) for the 30-minute transfer to city center over a four-lane newly paved highway.

By Train The **train station** in located at the northern end of Renmin Bei Lu, about 5 miles north of the Mao statue in city center. Trains from Beijing (36 hours), Guangzhou (48 hours), and Shanghai (48 hours) are tiring. (Air flights make more sense.) The overnight trains from Xi'an (16 hours) and Kunming (25 hours) go through scenic mountain terraces and tunnels, and constitute a reasonable alternative to air travel.

By Bus The bus makes sense for destinations within Sichuan Province and for trips to or from Chongqing on the Yangzi River. Express buses, fairly comfortable, with kung-fu movies playing continuously on TV monitors overhead, connect Chengdu and Chongqing. Via the new 210-mile Chengyu Expressway, this trip takes under 6 hours, half the time of the train and at lower cost ($12).

GETTING AROUND

To see the city on your own, the key is to purchase a map. **Walking** the backstreets is fascinating, as is strolling the promenade on the northeast bank of the Jin River.

Taxis are easily flagged down. The drivers don't speak English, but the map helps. Taxi rides across town cost RMB 10 to RMB 20 ($1.20 to $2.40).

Bicycles can be rented at the Traffic Hotel, 77 Jinjiang Lu, southeast riverbank, for about $2.50 per day.

TOURS & STRATAGEMS

China International Travel Service (CITS), across the street from the Jin Jiang Hotel at 65 Renmin Nan Lu (☎ 028/665-0780; fax 028/667-2970), can book air, train, and bus tickets and set up tours, with English-speaking guides, to all the major sites. Tour desks in the hotels can do the same.

I strongly recommend the services of China's best freelance tour operator while you are in Chengdu. **Mr. Lee, Tour Manager,** speaks excellent English, charges competitive rates for all tours and tickets, and gives personalized,

reliable service. He often finds foreign tourists at the Traffic Hotel. He can be reached by phone, pager, or fax (☎ 028/ 555-4250 from 8 to 11pm daily; fax 028/ 555-4250; pager 028/558-1588, no. 6022; telemessage holder 432-3388, no. 8638 [24 hours]). Mr. Lee offers excellent countryside tours (his favorite), backstage opera tours, and visits to schools, traditional medicine hospitals, factories, the panda base, and anything else you can dream up. Most tours cost $10 to $20 per person.

WHERE TO STAY

Holiday Inn Crowne Plaza Chengdu (Jiari Jiudian). *31 Zongfu Lu (four blocks east of the Mao statue).* ☎ *800/465-4329 or 028/678-6666. Fax 028/678-6599. 433 rms. A/C MINIBAR TV TEL. $170 double. AE, DC, JCB, MC, V.* This 33-floor tower, opened in 1997, is Chengdu's newest and most luxurious

hotel. The lobby, with its Italian marble floors, gold-trimmed columns, and European murals, is opulent and vast. The rooms, all equipped with writing desks, safes, and coffeemakers, are large, too. Each floor contains three suites with separate showers and bathtubs. There are two "executive floors" (21 and 22), no-smoking rooms, and rooms for the handicapped. The hotel's Rainbow Nightclub is a massive disco with elegant private rooms that include their own bathrooms and steam baths—a facility in China that is so luxurious that it is nearly impossible for Old China hands to comprehend, as is this hotel.

Services: Concierge, room service (24-hour), dry cleaning and laundry (24-hour, same day), nightly turndown, daily maid service, free airport shuttle, foreign exchange counter.

Facilities: In-house movies, pool (indoor, heated), health club (exercise machines), sauna, tennis courts, bowling alley (12 lanes), business center (24-hour, conference rooms), tour desk, beauty salon, shopping arcade.

Jin Jiang Hotel (Jin Jiang Binguan). *180 Renmin Nan Lu (one block north of the Jin River).* ☎ *028/558-2222. Fax 028/ 558-1849. 523 rms. A/C MINIBAR TV TEL. $150 double. AE, DC, JCB, MC, V.* For decades, this nine-story landmark was the best (and sometimes the sole) place for foreigners to stay. It is worth strolling through just to see its elegant public areas and massive dining halls, as well as to survey its shops and services. Last renovated in 1993, the Jin Jiang has tried to keep up with the times by creating lavish facilities, including a 5-star section in the rear wing with two floors of suites. The south wing has excellent standard rooms, while the east wing has some older rooms starting at $100 for a double. The facilities are the most extensive in Chengdu: a full-service post office, film developing, bakery, shopping arcade, medical clinic, dentist on call, gymnasium, outdoor pool, tennis courts, bowling alley. It is only in the level of efficient, conscientious services that the Jin Jiang lags behind the new Holiday Inn Crowne Plaza.

Traffic Hotel (Jiaotong Fandian). *77 Jinjiang Lu (next to the Xinnanmen bus station, southeast bank of Jin River).* ☎ *028/555-1017. Fax 082/558-2777. 200 rms. TV TEL. $25 double. No credit cards.* This is among the best-run budget hotels in China, set up with backpacking foreign travelers in mind. It is suitable for any independent traveler. The front desk staff and the elevator operators are friendly. Standard doubles come with heat and private bathrooms that are clean but worn. The best rooms are the deluxe doubles (just $30), with larger, newer bathrooms. The hotel hallways and lobbies are also well worn, but there are two gift shops, a kiosk with drinks and snacks, a notice board, luggage storage, an exchange desk, two tour offices, a bicycle rental shop, and an economy restaurant serving decent Chinese and American dishes at $1 to $3 a plate. Breakfast is included with the room.

WHERE TO DINE

Sichuan is best known around the world for its red-hot cuisine. Its spicy bean curd, aromatic *kung pao* chicken, tangy *dan dan* noodles, sweet-and-sour soup, and many other pungent dishes are fixtures on Chinese menus from Los Angeles to London. Sichuan fare has become synonymous with a delightful form of fire-eating, and there's no more inviting way to tour Chengdu, Sichuan's capital, than dish by dish.

Eating in Chengdu is not strictly a journey through fire. Sichuan cuisine has seven traditional flavors. In addition to hot, there are sweet, sour, bitter, peppery, salty, and fragrant. These seven flavors and the "eight methods" of cooking yield some 4,000 separate dishes, which in a Sichuan banquet are alternated to provide a variety of flavors. The *ma-la* ("very hot") dishes of Sichuan ignite the taste buds, but the yin-yang of contrasting, provocative, and piquant flavors is what satisfies the palate. Sichuan is the cuisine of fire, but the flame has many colors.

In addition to serving up some of the best Sichuan dishes on Earth, Chengdu has good local hot-pot cafes in the streets and Cantonese and Western restaurants in its hotels.

Chen Ma Po Dou Fu Restaurant. *113 Xiyihuan Lu (across from Qingyang Temple, 2 miles west of Mao statue). No telephone. Main courses RMB 16–67 ($2– $8). No credit cards. Daily 8am–11pm. SICHUAN.* Several Chengdu cafes claim the same name and history as the original site where this Sichuan masterpiece, *mapo doufu,* was first served a century ago. This branch certainly serves the best spicy doufu (bead curd) dishes I've ever sampled. The second-floor tables and carved wooden decor have a lot of character, much nicer than the dirty dining hall below. You can look out on the street through an open window, its shutters thrown back, and enjoy the numbingly complex spices of a number of doufu specialties, including a sweetly flavored drunken doufu. The hot-and-sour soup *(suanla tang)* complements every dish.

Long Chao Shou Special Restaurant (Longchaoshou Canting). *Chunxi Lu (at Dong Dajie, north of the Jin River). No phone. Sampler RMB 25 ($3). No credit cards. Daily 8am–9pm. SICHUAN.* This is Chengdu's most famous snack restaurant, serving a spectrum of *xiao chi* ("little eats," dim sum Sichuan style). Dumpling connoisseurs prize these creations for their color, appearance, aroma, and flavor. The dining area is a mess. Order the sampler for RMB 25 ($3) at the window and take a place at one of the crowded tables. You'll be served 14 different snacks, including soup, dumplings, preserved meats, pickled vegetables, cabbage flower cakes, wontons, and sweet tangyuan pastries. I liked about

half of what I sampled. During breakfast (8–10am) and lunch (noon–2pm), it can be difficult to find a seat. The snack flavors are strong and various, underlining an old Sichuan saying, "A hundred dishes, a hundred flavors" *(Bai cai, bai wei).*

Shu Feng Garden (Shufeng Yuan). *153 Dong Dajie (on corner of Hongxing Lu, southeast of Mao statue).* ☎ *028/ 665-7629. Main courses RMB 25–125 ($3–$15). No credit cards. Daily 11:30am– 2:30pm and 5:30–11pm. SICHUAN.* One of Chengdu's newest Sichuan restaurants, it is one of the finest and most elegant. The third floor is a shrine to the hot pot. Buffet tables hold more than 80 ingredients. Weekends are enlivened by musical revues. The decor is Old European, with white plaster walls, gilded moldings, and sculpted cherubs. Chengdu hot pot begins with a broth made by boiling chicken, beef, or cow bones garnished with hot bean paste from nearby Pi County (renowned for its long-lived population). Peppercorn, spices, and noodles are added. Thin slices of eel, beef, chicken, carp, pig's liver, bean curd, and tender vegetables are boiled to taste at the table. Shu Feng's hot pot is excellent and only costs $4 per person.

On the second floor, setting and cuisine change. The decor is Qing Dynasty "southern bridge" style with bright red columns, silken scrolls, and lacquered rosewood furniture. The best dishes are dan dan noodles laced with pimentos, dry-fried diced pork with bamboo shoots, boiled beef in hot sauce, cauliflower with Sichuan-style bacon, chicken ball soup, sizzling crispy rice with pork and gravy, tea-smoked duck *(zhang cha yazi),* kung pao chicken *(gong bao jiding),* and chrysanthemum cake for dessert.

Service is attentive. When our electric lazy Susan came unhooked, the waitress responded immediately, connecting two loose ends of the raw electrical wire by hand.

Sky Lounge. *31 Zong Fu Lu (mezzanine level, Holiday Inn Crowne Plaza).* ☎ *028/ 678-6666. Main courses $5–$20. AE, DC, JCB, MC, V. Daily 6:30am–11:30pm. INTERNATIONAL.* If you tire of Sichuan fire in your food, this elegant coffee shop serves all the American and European foods you may have been missing. The breakfast buffet ($10) is excellent, as are the daily high tea buffets ($6.50 from 11:30am to 2:30pm) and the Sunday champagne brunches ($15 from 7am to 2pm).

Other Choices   The Jin Jiang Hotel serves international dishes in its two-story atrium off the lobby and excellent Sichuan and Cantonese selections in its elegant **Chinese restaurant** on the ninth floor (☎ 028/558-2222). The Holiday Inn Crowne Plaza has the first American barbecue in Chengdu, the **Mississippi Grill,** on the 25th floor; an expensive Japanese restaurant, **Kiyosato,** with four private rooms, on the 25th floor as well; and a large, lively **Cantonese restaurant** off its lobby (☎ 028/678-6666).

CHONGQING: POWERHOUSE OF THE YANGZI RIVER VALLEY

重庆

CHONGQING, BETTER KNOWN TO Westerners under its old name, Chungking, is a city of the future. Located well up the Yangzi River, in the steamy southwestern province of Sichuan, Chongqing has not been a favorite of tourists, who have used it mainly as an overnight stop when boarding or disembarking from Yangzi River cruises. That was how I first saw Chongqing, all in one afternoon after cruising up the Yangzi through the Three Gorges, and I was not impressed. I did not dream of returning. But return I did, partly to sample some genuine Sichuan cuisine, partly to see the Buddhist carvings at nearby Dazu. Yet finding myself in the city for a few days, I discovered that there was much more to Chongqing than a quick glance revealed.

Chongqing is not a romantic city, despite its reputation among Chinese as the "Capital of Mist" and the "City of Mountains." The mist today is liable to be smog; the mountains are simply steep streets winding pell-mell up and down soot-covered hills. Rather, Chongqing is a city of the moment, a city of commerce, industry, and development on a scale seen few other places on the planet. It is in every sense a gargantuan city, brimming with raw power, a thirst with an appetite for the future. Among its many construction sites is one where the world's tallest building is slated to rise, outstripping recent claimants to that title in Malaysia and Shanghai.

Population & Pollution

Chongqing has a population that corresponds to its gigantic ambitions. On March 14, 1997, Chongqing became a municipality, a designation shared by only three other cities in China (Beijing, Shanghai, and Tianjin). No longer part of Sichuan Province, Chongqing is now free to handle its own affairs and finances, answering to no one but Beijing. The new Chongqing municipality extends over 14 districts, most of them downriver, where 1.3 million people face resettlement before the massive Three Gorges Dam is completed in 2013. The bottom line is that Chongqing's municipal population increased rather dramatically on March 14, 1997—to an unimaginable 30.23 million residents.

The downtown population of Chongqing, those residing in its "Manhattan," a narrowing peninsula bounded by the confluence of the Yangzi and Jialing rivers, was unchanged by redistricting. The city of Chongqing, as opposed to the municipality of Chongqing, numbers a mere 3 million residents, with the close suburbs north and south of the rivers contributing another 11 million.

Chongqing is also China's most polluted city, but it has launched a 29-part Green Program designed to reduce acid rain dramatically (meeting state standards by the year 2000). Chongqing is committed to building 300 factories to control water pollution, with half these facilities to be placed along the long reservoir created by the Three Gorges Dam. To become a beautiful city, as well as a powerful one, Chongqing will need to create environmental cleanup programs on a suitably massive scale. For now, it is an industrial city, a workhorse of commerce and shipping. But mere ugliness does not exclude it from being an interesting place.

Chongqing, in fact, is no tourist town, and that's its attraction. If you want to see a real Chinese metropolis, all its raw edges unconcealed and building for the next century, this is the place, 1,500 miles upstream from Shanghai. But as much as Chongqing is China's gritty city of the future, it is also a product of its past.

Chongqing received its present name in A.D. 1190 from Emperor Zhao Dun of the Southern Song Dynasty. He had conquered this city on the Yangzi, formerly known as Yuzhou and later Gongzhou, just before he ascended to the dragon throne. Finding himself twice blessed, he named the city that was his stepping stone to power Chongqing, meaning "double celebration" or "twin fortune." That doubling of good fortune is repeating itself today as this powerhouse of the upper Yangzi fuels the expanding economy of China and at the same time opens a new Gate to the Sky.

Industry

While in Chongqing in 1945, Premier Zhou Enlai wrote a poem beginning, "We are hoping for brightness, ten thousand miles ahead." Half a century later, this new China has begun to arrive in earnest and Chongqing is one of its chief powerhouses. Much of the material that Shanghai converts to wealth at the mouth of the Yangzi River originates upriver at Chongqing. In supplying new China with the basic products of a healthy economy—rice and grain, cotton and silk, coal, iron, and natural gas—Chongqing has become a showcase of modernization and economic development. Opened to direct foreign trade in 1979, Chongqing benefited

Chongqing

Jianxin Dong Lu

Jialing River

Zhou Mansion

Zhongshan 4-Lu

Guiyuan Garden
(Sweet Osmanthus Garden)

Jialingjiang
Bridge

Renmin Lu

Renmin Hotel/
Congress Hall

Renhe Jie

Zhongshan 3-Lu

Zaozianya

Xinshancheng
Chinese
Pharmacy

Chongqing
Stadium

PIPASHAN
PARK

2-Lu

Chongqing
Museum

Pipashan Zheng Jie

Zhongshan

Xiananqu Lu

1-Lu

ELING PARK

Changjiang

Chongqing Railway
Station

Shanhuba Isle

Chongqing Vicinity

Tongliang

Mt.
Jinyun

Beibei

Beishan Stone
Sculptures

Dazu

Jialing R.

Nanshan
Park

Bishan

Chongqing

Youtingpu

Yongchuan

Chongqing
Changjiang
Bridge

Holiday
Inn

HAITANG
PARK

from early programs that gave its factory managers decision-making power and the freedom to invest in expansion. In the more freewheeling economy of the 1990s, Chongqing has cashed in on those experiments. Its integrated iron and steel complexes, oil refineries, paper plants, copper smelters, motor vehicle factories, textile mills, and chemical and cement plants are the stuff of progress. Chongqing is fast becoming the Shanghai of western China, the inland colossus of industry and trade.

Chongqing's role will inevitably expand over the next two decades as the Yangzi River is itself transformed. At present, Chongqing's ability to ship its materials and products downstream is limited by the river channel. While shipping is no longer the treacherous business it was in the days of junks and trackers in harness, the Yangzi still permits no ships greater than about 3,000 tons (the size of many pleasure cruisers) to reach Chongqing. With the completion of the Three Gorges Dam (Sanxia) on the Yangzi early in the next century, however, a reservoir 600 kilometers long (372 miles) will reach west to Chongqing, enabling the passage of cargo ships of more than three times the current tonnage. Along with the anticipated benefits of flood control and increased hydroelectric power in the Yangzi basin, this massive project should propel Chongqing to even greater prominence as the upper Yangzi's chief manufacturer and trader.

Evidence of Chongqing's mounting wealth is visible in its rapidly changing cityscape. Chongqing is still blanketed in river fog much of the year, its rocky hillsides so steep and numerous that the bicycle—that icon of China—is eerily absent from the streets. In fact, I didn't see a single bicycle during my last visit, not even one being pushed uphill. The alleyways caked with coal dust, the twisting avenues, and the cliffside houses with front doors on the top floors are still part of Chongqing's tough-as-nails cityscape, but shining towers of steel and glass—the skyscraper offices and apartments of a new Chongqing—are shouldering their way through the heart of the city, displacing these grim reminders of the past. Locals say that Chongqing is starting to look like Hong Kong, another hilly city built on manufacture and trade. It's no Hong Kong yet, but it's on its way.

Part of what I find interesting about Chongqing is its roughness. The very foundations of its commerce seem exposed to view, like the skeleton of a skyscraper. The curving avenues, the relentless hills, the endless construction sites, the wide rivers bubbling up with boats and ships and piers and cranes, add to its dynamic feel. Chongqing has long been a city of energy, a city of furnacelike heat in the summer, a city of shipping and freight and industrial haze. I felt its energy every time I walked its streets and steep alleys.

The Gate to Heaven

From **Liberation Monument (Jiefang Bei),** the clock tower at city center, I kept losing my bearings in this metropolis of curves, even as I enjoyed peering into its small shops filled with old scrolls, carved seals, umbrellas, and bambooware, with wool from Tibet and silks from Sichuan that once made Chongqing a port prized by European traders. Along **Zhongshan Lu** I passed cafes featuring skewers of meat and vegetables awaiting a dunking in hot oil—the sidewalk version of Chongqing's most celebrated dish, hot pot *(huo guo),* which is given more elaborate treatment in the city's best restaurants and hotels. Down **Shangqing Lu** there are outdoor food markets with tea-smoked duck and bite-sized baozi, and after dark, street fairs with still more food and merchandise.

At the eastern tip of the city, where the Yangzi and Jialing rivers converge, I explored the number one urban sight in Chongqing: the **Gate to** the Sky (Chaotianmen), and its docks, linked to the city by black cliffs that run 300 steps up and down. Here the *ban ban jin*, the porters with cargo strapped to their backs or suspended from bamboo poles across their shoulders, hike the 300 cliffside stairs to and from the mudflats and wharves. During World War II, when Chongqing's population swelled as eastern China fell to the Japanese and China's capital moved here, the American General Joseph Stilwell occupied a house high on these flanks above the miserable cantilevered tenements that still survive. Cable cars are strung across both rivers like tourist banners. The northern terminal is a gray cement tower serviced by a wobbly elevator (with an attendant). I rode the dilapidated contraption back and forth (RMB 1.2/14¢ each way), standing up (there were no seats), a bit terrified but awed by the view. It is like a cable car ride over a half-mile-wide wilderness of iron and steel, barges and freighters, oil and fire. In a gritty way, this is the essence of Chongqing, the beauty in the marrow of a naked city.

Large bridges connect the downtown peninsula of Chongqing with the north and south shores, and rattling steel ferries, without seats or benches, deliver far more workers than the cable cars ever could.

At the turn of this century, Chongqing was still a backwater, a walled city enclosing barely 250,000 inhabitants. Between 1937 and 1946, when it served as China's wartime capital, the population tripled and new agencies, industries, and educational institutions poured in from throughout China. Chongqing never looked back. The Qing Dynasty city walls came down. An industrial capital took root. Today a new superhighway runs along the downtown shore and a subway is nearing completion to serve the next millennium.

Pipashan

The full panorama of this increasingly modern industrial megacity unfolds below **Pipashan Park** on Loquat Hill, at over 1,000 feet the highest point in the city. Weary of more hill walking and dubious that I could find the way, I hired a taxi to deliver me to the park gate. I still had to walk up a long hill to the summit. There, a teahouse pavilion **(Hongxing)** rises from garden terraces, a favorite haunt of retired men intent upon card games. There's also a circular monorail, crude and rusting away; its passengers ride the rail on attached bicycles. But it's the view that consumes one's attention. To the north is the Yangzi; to the south, the Jialing— massive rivers, apparent equals from this perspective, meeting at the Chaotianmen docks, the gate to the sky, where the long peninsula of downtown Chongqing tapers to a forked point poised to strike like the head of a fire-breathing dragon.

As it was nearly dusk, I waited for the sunset, which got lost in the smudgy horizon. But I was glad that I waited. After dark, the view from Pipashan Park is far more dramatic. Ignited by the beacons of office, highway, and factory, Chongqing becomes an island winging through the rivers of heaven, an enchanted foundry floating on the arms of two great rivers.

Chongqing Museum

The next morning I headed back downtown. On the south side of Pipashan is the Chongqing Museum, an antiquated repository of artifacts. Chongqing is supposed to be a city without relics or treasures, without refined Chinese legacies, but the museum has glints of a deeper, richer past. Human history stretches back 3,000 years in Chongqing, to the days of the Ba Kingdom when nobles were buried in large wooden boats suspended from the river cliffs. Two of these maritime coffins are now suspended in the Chongqing Museum, as is a major collection of Han Dynasty tomb-bricks, their carvings depicting the courtyards and chariots of 2,000 years ago. There's also a dull display of dinosaur eggs and skeletons, as well as a modern art gallery where artists push their works for sale. The museum is a clunky warehouse, poorly lighted and dilapidated. By the time I left, kids on school field trips were at least adding some high-spirited laughter and chatter to its dark, staid chambers. The museum is open daily from 9am to 5:30pm (admission RMB 5/65¢).

Luohan Temple

The brightest sight in downtown Chongqing is Luohan Si, a Buddhist temple that dates from A.D. 1000. It is one of the most active temples in China. At the busy intersection outside its entry gate, the sidewalks are filled with Chinese visitors, local Buddhists, and blind fortune-tellers. Inside the gate, a long, narrow entryway is flanked with rock carvings—shrines where dozens of worshippers kneel, burn incense, and pray. Within the pavilions are modern clay statues of the 500 arhats, Buddhist followers who have reached the first state of enlightenment. Behind a large golden likeness of the Buddha is a mural depicting Siddhartha, the living Buddha, cutting his hair to renounce the world. The temple looks far older than it is, having been thoroughly reconstructed after the ravages of World War II, but the sheer activity within gives it an unmistakable air of authenticity. This is no tourist trap; it's an island of Old China, bobbing in an ocean of modern commerce and construction. You can visit the temple every day from dawn to dusk (admission RMB 10/$1.25).

PRACTICAL INFORMATION

ORIENTATION

Chongqing is located in southeastern Sichuan Province, far inland on the upper Yangzi River. The chief attraction for sightseers is **Dazu,** an ancient grotto of Buddhist carvings to the west that makes for an excellent day trip (see separate chapter).

Note: Since March 8, 1997, Chongqing phone numbers have contained eight (rather than seven) digits. Most seven-digit numbers were converted to the new eight-digit numbers by adding a 6 at the beginning, but the old seven-digit numbers starting with 90 have added an 8 in the third position (immediately after the 90). Chongqing's new area code is 023 inside China, 23 outside China. (The old area code was 811.)

GETTING THERE

By Plane The **Jiangbei Airport,** serving many cities in China (including Hong Kong, via Dragonair), is 18 miles from city center, but allow an hour for the RMB 150 ($18) taxi ride.

By Train The railway and bus stations are located on Nanqu Lu in southwestern Chongqing, near the Yangzi River. The train from Shanghai or Beijing can take 50 hours or more; you are better off flying.

By Bus Luxury buses, quite comfortable, now connect Chongqing to Chengdu, Sichuan's capital, via the Chengyu Expressway (4 hours, 200 miles; RMB 90/$11).

By Ship Many visitors arrive at the wharves of Chongqing after a Yangzi River cruise upriver from Wuhan. From there, it's best to take a taxi to a hotel, although you can reach the city by walking upriver to a local ferry and crossing over to the downtown peninsula. Taxis should cost RMB 15 to RMB 25 ($2 to $3.50).

TOURS & STRATAGEMS

If you come by cruise ship, particularly by Victoria Cruises, they can usually arrange a tour of the city. China International Travel Service (CITS) is located inside the Renmin Hotel, 173 Renmin Lu (☎ 023/6385-0806). Your best bet if you travel independently is your hotel tour desk.

WHERE TO STAY

Renmin Hotel (Renmin Binguan). *173 Renmin Lu.* ☎ *023/6385-1421. Fax 023/6385-2076. 250 rms. A/C TV TEL. $75 double. JCB, MC, V.* This landmark hotel, built in the Russian style in 1953, connects directly to the Nationalist Congress Hall, a monumental edifice that resembles the Temple of Heaven in Beijing and is frequently visited by tourists. Its best feature is its downtown location. The rooms are large, but maintenance and service are not up to international levels. The East Wing was renovated in 1994, so its rooms are modern and still fairly clean. The coffee shop serves some Western food and the staff speaks a bit of English.

Yangtze Chongqing Holiday Inn (Yangzi Jiang Jia Ri Jiudian). *15 Nanping Bei Lu.* ☎ *800/465-4329 or 023/6280-3380. Fax 023/6280-0884. 383 rms. A/C MINIBAR TV TEL. $130 double. AE, DC, JCB, MC, V.* Although located well east of downtown, the 4-star, 21-story Holiday Inn is the only international-level hotel in town. It is well managed. The staff speaks English, both the Western and Sichuan restaurants offer excellent food, and the spacious rooms were renovated in 1995. The 16th-floor Executive Club has its own lounge. No-smoking rooms are available. The Heatwave Disco is open daily from 7pm to 2am. There is no downtown shuttle bus. This is the hotel where expatriate businesspeople live and relax in Chongqing.

Services: Concierge, room service (24-hour), dry cleaning and laundry (same day), nightly turndown, daily maid service, foreign exchange counter.

Facilities: In-house movies, pool (outdoor, heated), health club (exercise machines), putting green, sauna, tennis courts (outside), business center (7am–2am), tour desk, beauty salon, shopping arcade.

WHERE TO DINE

Sichuan food, spicy and authentic, should not be missed. In Chongqing, it's impossible not to run into a local streetside **hot-pot restaurant;** on every block, there are two or three, and you can't miss them. Ordering is easy. Just ask for "huo guo" (hwo gwo). You'll be served raw vegetables and meats that you cook in a pot of boiling oil at your table.

Golden Sand. *15 Nanping Bei Lu (lobby of Holiday Inn).* ☎ *023/6280-3380. Reservations recommended. Main courses $5–$12. AE, DC, JCB, MC, V. Daily 11:30am–2:30pm and 5:30–9:30pm. SICHUAN.* This is the best Sichuan restaurant in town. The hot-pot items are simmered in a divided pot—one part containing spicier oil than the other. Seating is in private rooms with round tables or in a larger dining area.

Western Choices The Holiday Inn also has an excellent German bistro, the **Bierstube,** open daily 6:30 to 11:30pm, with authentic German food and drinks in an intimate setting; and Western-style barbecues nightly in the **Sunset Grill,** open daily 6:30pm to midnight.

Inexpensive Choices Inside the Luohan Temple, there's a **vegetarian restaurant** with inexpensive noodles and tofu dishes. And on the streets surrounding the Holiday Inn, there are several Western-style **coffeehouses** with international dishes, such as spaghetti, at reasonable prices.

KUNMING: CITY
OF ETERNAL SPRING
昆明

SITUATED ON A HIGH, LUSH PLATEAU
in extreme southwestern China's Yunnan Province, bordering Vietnam,
Kunming was long regarded by the Chinese as untamed and remote—in
fact, as barely civilized. Officials fallen from favor in the imperial capital
were routinely banished to these backwaters of the Middle Kingdom,
where tribal peoples were constantly in rebellion. Even today, over a quarter
of Yunnan's 35 million people are minorities, members of 24 groups that
have retained their non-Chinese customs and dress.

This preponderance of racial minorities imparts a splash of color and
diversity to Kunming that is missing in most other cities of China, where
the crushingly homogeneous Han Chinese, nearly 99% of the population, hold sway. Kunming even maintains an Institute for Nationalities, a
university of over 20,000 minority students.

This said, I found upon my recent return to Kunming after a 10-year
absence that even here China's rapid modernization is altering the
cityscape. The pace of life in Kunming can no longer be described as that
of a village. General Claire Chennault, who stationed the legendary Flying Tigers and the Fourteenth U.S. Air Force here during World War II,
described Kunming as a "sleepy backwoods Oriental town" where "water
buffalo, cattle, and herds of fat pigs were not uncommon sights." They are
uncommon enough now. The streets are paved and jammed with new
cars, buses, and trucks, like any street in the West, and lined with ever-
taller offices and department-store towers. Ten years ago, Kunming bore
few outward signs of an American presence. Today, the Americans have
returned to Kunming—not in person, for there are few foreign faces in
this city, but as models for Kunming's future. The architecture, the automobiles, the department stores, the clothing—it's all in the American
mode.

The old Kunming is slipping into the backstreets and curling up in a
few parks and temples. That's precisely where one has to go these days to
find the remains of what has long been one of China's most exotic cities.
Fortunately, a search can still turn up strange treasures.

Kunming

← To Bamboo Temple

Mayuan Station

West Bus Station

Hongshan Lu

Jianshe Lu

YUNNAN UNIVERSITY

Huancheng Bei Lu

Fengning Jie

Qingyun Lu

Qianju Jie

Beimen Lu

CUIHU (GREEN LAKE) PARK

Cuihu Dong Lu

Cuihu Nan Lu

Huashan Xi Lu

Kunshi Lu

Yunnan Provincial Agricultural Exhibition Hall

Renmin Xi Lu

Wucheng Lu

Daguan Jie

Dongfeng Xi Lu

Shengli Assembly Hall

Zhuantang Pond

Xinwen Lu

Guofang (National Defence) Stadium

Guanghua Jie

Tongdao (Bird & Flower Market)

River

Daguan Lu

Huancheng Xi Lu

Yunnan Provincial Museum

Daguan River

Jinbi Xi Lu

Jinbi Xi Lu

Fuxing Xincun

← To Daguan Park

Pagoda of West Temple

Huancheng Xi Lu

Kunming Vicinity

Kunming Botanical Institute

Heilong (Black Dragon) Pool

Qiongzhu (Bamboo) Temple

Golden Hall

Daguan Tower

Kunming

River

Anning Hot Spring

Yunnan Nationalities Village

Xishan (Western Hills) Forest Park

Dragon's Gate

Chenggong

Yangzong Lake

Yiliang

Lake Dian

Stone Forest

Lunan

Nanpan

Chengjiang

Haigeng Lu

YUANTONG ZOO

Yuantong (Full & Smooth) Temple

Kunming North Station

Panlong River

Huancheng Bei Lu

Linguangjie

Chuanjin Lu

Yuantong Jie

0 | 600 m
| 656 y

N

Qingnian Lu

Taoyuan Jie

Beijing Lu

Xinghua Jie

Huashan Nan Lu

Changchun Lu

Renmin Dong Lu

Huancheng

Kunming Theatre

Weiyuan Jie

Baita Lu

Tuanjie Lu

Zhengyi Lu

Nanping Lu

Dongfeng Dong Lu

Dong Lu

Nancheng Ancient Mosque

Bank of China

Workers' Cultural Hall

Provincial Stadium

Jinbi Lu

Tuodong Lu

Houxin Jie

Pagoda of East Temple

Wujing Lu

East Bus Station

To the Stone Forest →

Tangshuang Lu

Beijing Lu

Jinbi River

Huancheng Nan Lu

Minhang Lu

Huancheng Nan Lu

Wujing Lu

Panlong River

Kunming Railway Station

Downtown

The streets of Kunming have lost much of their exotic flavor with the economic boom of the 1990s. The main department store at the downtown intersection of Nanping Lu and Zhengyi Lu has been replaced by a glistening **new super store** (open 9am to 9pm daily). Inside, the marble stairs with spittoons on every landing have been superseded by brandnew escalators. The staff is decked out in clean uniforms. The counters are stocked with heaps of cosmetics and electronic appliances from abroad. There are still enough local commodities to make a quick swing through the aisles worthwhile, but the poorly lit, cavernous emporium of the 1980s is gone.

North up Zhengyi Lu a few blocks at the corner of Jingxing Jie is the **Nancheng Ancient Mosque** at 59 Zhengyi Lu, still the small edifice it was a decade ago when I first entered it. The Hui people (Chinese Muslims) have made it into a more formal tourist site, with trinkets and postcards for sale outside. After removing your shoes, you can enter the plain prayer hall and have a quiet look around. The mosque has fared better than a nearby Buddhist temple, which was smashed by the Red Guards during Mao's Great Cultural Revolution (1966–76). Left in a pile of glazed green roof tiles and red bricks, with its stone temple lion that had been toppled onto the sidewalk like a smashed idol, this temple has now been replaced by a high-rise office building, four stories of blank concrete and whitewash.

While the backstreets in downtown Kunming are beginning to lose their rough appeal, I still see plenty of **street markets** northwest of the main downtown traffic circle, their stalls stocked with fresh flowers, tropical fruits, and pork bellies. Itinerant quilt makers thread their looms on the sidewalks. Seamstresses tend their treadle sewing machines. A block west of the mosque on the north side of Jingxing Jie, the **Bird and Flower Market** fills a large alley (Tongdao Jie) selling caged songbirds, lizards, monkeys, and other creatures from Yunnan's southern jungles. Continuing north to the next main boulevard, Guanghua Jie, I cross through an **open-air antique market** as well, full of prayer rugs and ethnic handicrafts.

Some of the street life has shifted east out Nanping Lu to the huge public square at the **Workers' Cultural Hall.** This is about a half mile from downtown, where Nanping Lu turns into Dongfeng Dong Lu, Kunming's prime east–west boulevard and the location of its leading international hotels. This square, which occupies both sides of the street, fills up before 8am with Kunming's exercisers—dancers, *tai ji quan* groups, and badminton players. After 8am it becomes congested with shoppers, idlers, and vendors offering foods I can't identify. One entire row of vendors sits behind small tables with hand-painted signs advertising their services. These are the blind masseurs of Kunming, who for a pittance

($1) will deliver a crushing back massage right on the square or on plat-forms set up in nearby patches of a city park. There are also fortune-tellers, ice-cream hawkers, batik vendors, and a large portion of Kunming's floating population milling around—unemployed peasants from the coun-tryside.

These days, the farther you move from the heart of the city, the more country people you see trying to make their way in from the fringes, sell-ing rural crafts, produce, and their skills on the streets. Many of them are dressed in minority clothing, knowing that for today's Chinese visitors, as well as for foreign tourists, an exotic costume gives them a sales edge. The longer I wander the streets of Kunming, the clearer becomes the split between the rural life of the past and the urban rush of the present. Mend-ing that split will take decades more. In Kunming, the urbanization of China's vast rural population is at its inception—where it stood in America more than a century ago.

Green Lake

Northwest of city center, a 40-minute stroll up Dongfeng Xi Lu, then a right on Cuihu Nan Lu, is Kunming's answer to Central Park, Green Lake (Cuihu). Some of the neighborhoods here are still populated with the two-story wooden-shuttered houses that characterized city life in Kunming a century ago, but most are being torn down.

At the eastern entrance to Green Lake Park vendors are conducting games of ring toss on the sidewalks. The prizes are cheap ceramic figu-rines. Stalls sell intricately sliced curlicues of fresh pineapple on a stick. Lined with willows, the lake is gorgeous, crisscrossed by small arched bridges in imitation of Hangzhou's more famous West Lake. The best time to come is on Sunday, when the pathways are crowded with families on their weekly outings, and the best season is winter, when days are warm and sunny and the large flocks of black-headed "laughing gulls" with their cackling cries arrive from breeding grounds in Siberia, as they have been doing for the last 10 years. The gulls not only enjoy the legend-ary "eternal spring" weather of Kunming but the crumbs of steamed bread, sold in plastic bags by vendors, that visitors toss them.

Green Lake Road, running south of the park entrance, has recently developed into a trendy "international" avenue of small cafes. The French Parasol Restaurant and the Cafe De Jack (see "Where to Dine," below) have bistro atmospheres and serve up inexpensive sandwiches and drinks from their bars. I stopped for lunch at the Cafe De Jack, looked through their collection of jazz records and Western paperbacks, and settled down at a corner table. The decor is rundown Parisian, its wooden walls covered in posters, its wooden floors unpolished. The toilet in the back is a hole in the floor, the door handle a nail. I ordered a ham sandwich for RMB 12 ($1.45), served club style with fries and sliced bananas in yogurt. Kunming is not Paris, but it certainly seems continental in the recesses of Cafe De Jack, and I spent a few hours there talking with an expatriate student from France who frequents the place.

The Best 500 Arhats in China

Most tourists bent on seeing a temple at Kunming head east from Green Lake to **Yuantong Si,** a thousand-year-old Buddhist complex with a new statue of Sakyamuni in white marble, a gift from the king of Thailand. The most interesting religious shrine, however, is the **Bamboo Temple (Qiongzhu Si),** 8 miles northwest of city center. A taxi is the easiest way to get there (RMB 20/$2.40).

The Bamboo Temple dates back to the Tang Dynasty (A.D. 618–907), but the present halls were rebuilt in the 1880s when the amazing sculptor Li Guangxiu arrived on the scene. Molding clay over wooden skeletons, Li composed the most demented congregation in China, perhaps in the world. Had Goya and Dalí collaborated as sculptors, the 500 arhats of the Bamboo Temple would have been their masterpiece.

The 500 arhats (or 500 luohans) are a fixture in major Chinese monasteries. They are the 500 followers of Buddha who achieved their own salvation. Concerned only with personal redemption, they practice deliverance from the mortal world in bizarre, often grotesque ways. In Li's version, the 500 figures perch tier upon tier, filling two halls. Their faces twist and erupt in wild contortions, creating a vivid three-dimensional mural of exaggerated emotions from joy to despair to madness. Devotees ride oceanic crests on the backs of animals, mythic and natural. Eyebrows 2 feet long sprout from perplexed foreheads. An arm streaks 10 feet across the room, its finger shattering a ceiling of clouds like a thunderbolt. This is the ultimate mixture of surrealism and expressionism, Buddhism and dementia. Li Guangxiu is said to have parodied the faces of his contemporaries in Kunming, who criticized his art not for its extreme exoticism and depiction of horrors but for its realism. For sheer inventiveness, these 500 arhats put even modern Western comic book illustrators to shame.

Grand View Park

Also on the outskirts of Kunming are the city's most luxuriant flower gardens. **Daguan Gongyuan (Grand View Park),** 2 miles southwest of city center, is a 150-acre botanical paradise on the shores of expansive Lake Dian (Dianchi). Kunming is known as the "City of Eternal Spring" for its mild year-round climate; it is also known as the "City of Flowers" for its horticultural and herbal riches. The walkways, arched bridges, courtyards, and ponds are interspersed with colorful flower gardens. The Queen of England, on the first visit to China by an English monarch in history, planted rose bushes in this park on the afternoon of October 17, 1986.

I know because I was caught in Kunming's first major traffic jam that day, the result of streets suddenly closed off in anticipation of the Queen's entourage passing by. I visited Daguan Park the next day but couldn't find the Queen's roses.

Returning a decade later, I still find no one to direct me to the royal plantings. Daguan Park has become a playground for Kunming's youth, full of snack stalls and carnival games, but it has its ancient sites. **Daguan Pavilion (Tower of the Magnificent View)** contains poems in fine calligraphy extolling the beauties of the park, including a nostalgic 118-character rhyming couplet, the longest in China, etched upon the gateposts by Sun Ranweng in the early 18th century (and recarved there in 1888 after Moslem rebels destroyed the original).

Daguan Pavilion was built 300 years ago and rebuilt in 1869 after a fire. Emperor Kangxi saw to construction of the original tower in 1690. He used it to enhance his view across Lake Dian to the Western Hills. In profile, these hills outline the figure of a woman reclining, her long hair rippling into the lake. Locals calls the range "Sleeping Beauty Hills," and its steep flanks, connected by ferries from Daguan Park, are honeycombed with carved stone shrines and temples, capped at the peak by Grand Dragon's Gate.

Grand Dragon's Gate

The **Western Hills (Xi Shan)**, a band of sheer cliff faces, rise 2,000 feet above the shore of Lake Dian (elevation 6,200 feet) in the flat farmlands 10 miles southwest of Kunming. A series of paths, stairways, and tunnels—linking a succession of stone temples, seemingly perched in thin air—has been carved into the face of the cliff, spiraling ever upward to Dragon's Gate at the summit. For the fit hiker, the entire 5-mile journey from the bottom, starting at the town of Gaoyao, takes nearly 4 hours, particularly if the way is crowded, as it usually is, with hundreds of fearless Chinese sightseers.

Most of the effect and the best vistas can be had by starting farther up. I hired a taxi from Kunming (RMB 210/$25 for the afternoon) and was driven most of the way up the Western Hills to **Sanqingge (Pavilion of Three Purities),** a Daoist temple complex on nine terraces. Once a 13th-century imperial villa, Sanqingge is nowadays a parking lot and tourist trap of restaurants and souvenir stands, a 2-mile walk below Dragon's Gate. Less than a mile from here the **cliffside grottoes**—originally cut out of the sheer stone walls by Wu Laiqing and his band of daring monks over a 54-year-period starting in 1781—begin in earnest. This is not a walk for those with even a faint touch of vertigo. The caves and niches along the way contain statues trimmed from rock, serving as shrines to Guanyin (Goddess of Mercy) and other Daoist deities.

Grand Dragon's Gate overlooks Lake Dian straight below. In the far distance eastward, the new high-rises of Kunming are also visible. Lake Dian, 30 miles across north to south—the sixth largest lake in China—is divided by a causeway. The waters in the northern section were dammed a few years ago to serve as a massive sewage treatment facility.

In fact, the entire lake is so poisoned by pollutants that few fishermen can make a living anymore. Many families have been given permits to pursue a new profession, becoming vendors along the cliff paths and temples of the Western Hills. Their stalls and tables, selling everything from bottled water to polished rock images of the gods, now line the pathway to Dragon's Gate from bottom to top. A new cable car stretches from the far side of Lake Dian to Dragon's Gate, too. It is the second cable car built in the Western Hills during the 1990s. Another connects Dragon's Gate to **Taihua Temple,** 3 miles lower down on the Western Hills.

The best route remains the 2-mile walk from Sanqingge to Dragon's Gate and back. There are fewer vendors, more overlooks, and plenty of recessed shrines here. The cave walls are scorched black with burning incense. At the top, where you can lean out over the stone railings and glimpse the stone path you've just edged up, is one of the grander views in all of China—the view a Daoist immortal might have taken, perhaps, in which all human perspectives dissolve: Cities, farms, lakes, and roads become mere lines on a cosmic map, and the mind floats free of all its past moorings, buoyant as a cloud.

Yunnan Nationalities Village

In 1992, Kunming opened its version of an ethnic theme park, an attraction that is sweeping China and other Asian countries. The Yunnan Nationalities Village is 7 miles west of downtown on the shores of Lake Dian. It is linked to Kunming by a wide expressway and to the top of the Western hills by that new cable car, and is open from 9am to 5pm daily.

I've visited several of these parks in China and Kunming's is the best, or at least the most extensive, with two dozen exhibits of ethnic village architecture, crafts, costumes, and—if you're there when a big tour group happens through—song and dance performances. A motorized shuttle train links the exhibits. Horses can be rented as well. The park is open daily from 9am to 5pm (admission is RMB 28/$3.40).

Some of the minority people, all in village costume, speak enough English to explain a bit about their cultures, and there are snapshot opportunities, but the experience is not one I find worth repeating. Better to see the minorities in their actual villages in Yunnan (in the Stone Forest, a popular day trip from Kunming, or in the town of Dali, farther to the west).

Stone Forest (Shi Lin)

Kunming's most celebrated attraction is a geological wonder, the lime-stone pillars clustered in the Stone Forest, 50 miles to the east. There's a new highway to the **Sani minority village** of Five-Tree in Lunan County at the park entrance. A decade ago the highway followed a more circuitous route, usually broken by a stop midway at the Nut House, on the shores of Lake Yangzhong where the American Air Force partook of R&R during World War II. It constituted a pleasant stop in the 1980s. Tea in a glass and walnuts in the shell were served up in the lobby of the Nut House, which looked like a stately 1940s inn.

In the 1990s, the highway to the Stone Forest is becoming overrun with roadside attractions, amusement parks, burgeoning towns, and a raft of gift shops. Many of the Stone Forest tour buses that leave from Kunming's hotels every morning stop at the San He Yuan restaurant, a modern "minorities" cafe where one sits on short benches on a straw floor. Behind the restaurant there's a shooting range, where visitors can rent everything from a military rifle to a machine gun. And even placid Lake Yangzhong has received a face-lift. A large resort village has gone up on its shores, along with a golf course and a factory with a tall belching smoke-stack.

Yet the countryside here still ranks among the most beautiful in China. The ride to the Stone Forest is more interesting than the site itself. Road-side factories are busy carving up figures of lions from white stone. Ducks are cooked in small brick furnaces outside cafes, much as lobsters are steamed outdoors in Maine. We pass several horse carts serving as local buses, 10 people standing on each trailer. Trucks haul massive piles of brick and stone. The Yunnan countryside is a vast quarry. The side roads are blocked by herds of goats. The green fields are worked by ponies and water buffalo.

At the end of the road, now just a 90-minute ride from Kunming (it used to take 4 hours), the Stone Forest erupts like a primordial dream. Acres of vertical limestone shafts, exposed 270 million years ago when the ocean receded from southwest China, sprout like an immense grove of bamboo. Wind and rain have drilled creases and fissures into each tall pillar. The Stone Forest is like a cavern raised above the ground, its dome lopped off, open to the blue sky.

Miles of pathways twist through the karst landscape, edging along reflecting pools and rising on stone steps to pavilions perched on the limestone summits. It is a maze of massive stone pickup sticks, dropped by a playful deity. Sani women in full ethnic dress stand at every turn, offering to be guides or directing visitors to kiosks.

In the late 1990s the park painted red signs on the sides of the rocks in English as well as in Chinese. "Better to Rest Here for a While," one

The Stone Forest

Ticket Office

Shilin Lake

Post Office

Parking Lot

Ashima Rock

CITS

LESSER STONE FOREST

Shizi Pavilion

Shizi Pond

Stone Screen

Lotus Pond

XIAOBUSHAO HILLS

DABUSHAO HILLS

Wonderful Scenery of Stone Forest

Wangfeng Pavilion

Lotus Peak

GREATER STONE FOREST

Stone Forest Circling Hwy

Jianfeng Pool

Elephant on a Stone Terrace

Rhinocerous Looking at the Moon

Buddha Stone

Thousand Year Old Tortoise

Mother and Child

reads. Other signs identify the chief formations: "Thousand-Year-Old Tortoise," "Elephant on a Platform." New stones pave the trails and a new section with a broad green lawn has been opened for visitors.

I traipse for several hours through the Stone Forest, ending up at **Sword Peak Pond,** where buildings have been erected selling trinkets and fast food. Photographers for hire dress up tourists in ethnic outfits for vacation portraits. The Stone Forest doesn't fully emit its grandeur until the tourists disappear in the late afternoon. Then you can take a solitary stroll through this microcosmic version of the uncanny peaks of Guilin, reduced to a thick grove of 100-foot-tall stone columns. It resembles a petrified forest left standing in the wake of geologic time, a thicket of gigantic exclamation points, a geologist's field of dreams.

This is why it's best to stay the night at the Stone Forest. There are several guesthouses at the park entrance and in Five-Tree Village across the bridge on the other side of Stone Forest Lake. Just before dusk you can enjoy the sights and the people at a slower pace, perhaps even make a purchase of Sani batiks, which are lovely. The people are friendly once the heat of the sales day wears off. On many nights, there are performances of Sani dances at the inns or in the park, enthusiastic affairs where the audience is encouraged to join in. And **Stone Forest Lake,** between the park entrance and the bridge to the village, is stunning at sunset, the pillars sprouting from its waters like castle turrets in the fading light. The air is fragrant and the sky is choked with stars.

The ride back across the high Yunnan plateau is unforgettable. The villages are built of the red clay. Long red peppers and yellow ears of corn dangle from gray-tiled roof eaves, curing in the sunlight. The Sani farmers till their fields, dressed in embroidered clothing—bright reds and golds. The shoulders of the road are coated with rice spread out to dry. Along the wide riverbanks, the oval kilns of brickmakers are clustered one after the other like the tents of nomadic tribes. This is the Chinese Connemara, possessed solely by the sharpest elemental colors: the red of the soil, the green of the hillsides, the white of the limestone, the blue of the sky—a palette as wild as a comet plunging into the sun.

But the road from Kunming is turning into one long resort strip, and Kunming is losing its remote and exotic flavors. Get here soon, before the past is entirely obliterated.

PRACTICAL INFORMATION

ORIENTATION

Kunming, with a population of 1 million inside its urban boundaries, is the capital of Yunnan Province in southwest China. Its subtropical location and high elevation (6,213 feet) make it a lovely place to visit, even in winter. May and June are peak months for foreign travelers, but the Chinese tourists favor December. October is the most beautiful month of all.

Kunming is the gateway to the fascinating Bai minority village of **Dali** (see separate chapter), an hour's flight or an 8-hour bus ride on the Burma Road, west from Kunming.

GETTING THERE

By Plane   The airport is 5 miles south of city center, a RMB 30 ($4) taxi ride. Kunming is served by **Dragonair,** 575 Beijing Lu, Golden Dragon Hotel lobby (☎ 0871/313-8592), with a daily flight to Hong Kong (3 hours). Several Chinese airlines provide connections to and from cities in China, including Beijing (2¹/2 hours), Chengdu (1 hour), Guilin (1¹/₂ hours), and Shanghai (2¹/₂ hours). Purchase tickets at hotel tour desks.

By Train   There is a long-distance train to Chengdu (overnight, 24 hours) that travels through glorious mountain scenery. Shanghai, Beijing, and Guangzhou are also connected by rail to Kunming, but because of the mountainous geography these trips can require several days and nights (up to 60 hours). Flying is a more efficient, if costlier, option.

GETTING AROUND

With a map, you can tour downtown sites on foot. It takes about 90 minutes to walk from the Holiday Inn to Green Lake. Exploring by taxi costs RMB 15 to RMB 30 ($2 to $4) per trip.

Outlying sites, such as Dragon's Gate, can be reached by taxi or tour bus (or by rented bicycle or public bus, if you are more adventurous).

TOURS & STRATAGEMS

Visiting the Stone Forest   To reach the Stone Forest, ask the hotel to book a taxi or catch an early morning bus at the Western Bus Station on Renmin Xi Lu or a minibus leaving from the King World Hotel on Huancheng Nan Lu. The last buses return to Kunming from the Stone Forest entrance at 3pm.

You can stay overnight at the 2-star **Stone Forest Hotel (Shi Lin Binguan)** in front of the main gate to the Stone Forest Park entrance (☎ 0871/771-1405). The rooms, with private baths, are worn but clean

($55 double), and the hotel has a restaurant.

Tours   China International Tourist Service (CITS), 1 Wuyi Lu (☎ 0871/313-8888), offers day tours of Kunming and the Stone Forest with English-speaking guides, but it is much easier to book tours (and plane tickets) directly from the hotel tour desks.

A day tour of the Stone Forest, including lunch, can be booked in the Holiday Inn and costs RMB 180 ($22); a tour of the Western Hills costs RMB 160 ($19), lunch included.

WHERE TO STAY

Camellia Hotel (Chahua Binguan). *154 Dongfeng Dong Lu (2 miles east of city center).* ☎ *0871/316-3000. Fax 0871/314-7033. 279 rms. TV TEL. $40 double. No credit cards.* Still the favorite of independent budget travelers, this 13-story hotel has three levels of accommodation in its three wings: standard doubles with private bath (renovated in 1989); budget doubles, also with private bath, but smaller and more rundown; and dorms with shared showers that are in high demand. Rated at just 1 star, the hotel offers few luxuries, but for

backpacking travelers it provides a message board, luggage storage, tour desk, foreign exchange counter, and bicycle rental. The staff speaks little English but tries to be helpful when pressed.

Green Lake Hotel (Cuihu Binguan). *6 Cuihu Lu (across from Green Lake Park entrance).* ☎ *0871/515-8888. Fax 0871/515-3286. 448 rms. A/C MINIBAR TV TEL. $125 double. AE, DC, JCB, MC, V.* The new 17-story building, opened in 1993, contains 306 modern rooms rated as 4 stars. The five-story old section, remodeled in 1980, contains 142 rooms that are spacious but rundown and cost $75 for a large double. The facilities in the newer building are quite luxurious. Those in the older building are not. The service is not as attentive as at the Holiday Inn, but the location on Green Lake is convenient and quiet.

Holiday Inn Kunming (Yinghua Jiari Jiudian). *25 Dongfeng Dong Lu (1 mile east of city center).* ☎ *800/465-4329 or 0871/316-5888. Fax 0871/313-5189. 243 rms, 9 suites. A/C MINIBAR TV TEL. $118 double. AE, DC, JCB, MC, V.* Opened in 1993 and renovated in 1997, the 18-story 4-star Holiday Inn offers the best service and facilities in Kunming for international travelers. Rooms are large, clean, and modern. Executive floors 15, 16, and 17 offer more luxury and their own lounge (at $172). There are also no-smoking rooms and rooms with handicapped access. The Babalu Disco is a popular nightspot (open 8pm to midnight) and the full-service tour desk offers a complete range of tours and tickets.

Services: Room service (24-hour), dry cleaning and laundry (24-hour, same day), nightly turndown, daily maid service, free airport shuttle, foreign exchange counter.

Facilities: In-house movies, pool (indoor, heated), health club (exercise machines), sauna, bowling alley (16 lanes), business center (24-hour, conference rooms), tour desk, beauty salon, shopping arcade.

WHERE TO DINE

Yunnan cuisine has a number of distinct dishes. The most famous is Crossing-the-Bridge Noodles, a hot pot consisting of steaming chicken broth to which you add noodles, vegetables, mushrooms, and meats, seasoned with chile peppers. The oil on top keeps the food swimming below warm. The dish was invented a century ago, according to legend, by the wife of a scholar who carried the pot across the bridge to her husband's study, where he enjoyed the dish hot despite the long trip from the kitchen. Fried goat cheese and french fries are also local favorites. Yunnan sweet ham, Yunnan coffee, and Yunnan mushrooms are highly regarded throughout Asia. The mushrooms are considered medicinal by those in the know. Hundreds of Japanese travel to Kunming primarily to consume special varieties of locally gathered fungi, paying small fortunes for a plate of the rarer specimens. The Ji Zong mushrooms, long and stringy, are treasured for their ginseng-like properties. Many Yunnan dishes are laden with an allegedly healthful, fat-reducing pharmacopoeia of herbs and spices. Chicken stewed with medicinal herbs in an earthen dish *(qiguoji)* is another specialty that is quite delicious.

The **Kunming Hotel,** 145 Dongfeng Dong Lu, across from the Holiday Inn (☎ 0871/316-2172), serves the best Yunnan dishes, including Crossing-the-Bridge Noodles, steampot chicken, and as a special order, an entire banquet prepared from a single goat. The dining room is plush and so are the prices, up to $50 a person for the goat banquet.

Cheaper versions of Yunnan dishes, including fried goat cheese patties, french fries, steamed chicken, and Crossing-the-Bridge Noodles, are available just off Dongfeng Dong Lu up Baita Lu (across from the Holiday Inn) at the **Yunnan Typical Local Food Restaurant.** The service is not friendly nor is the decor appealing, but the cafe has an English menu, low prices (RMB 18 to 34/$2 to $4), and well-prepared local fare.

Holiday Inn features the best Western food in town. **Sam's Bar & Grill** on the 18th floor (☎ 0871/316-5888, ext 6576; open daily 3pm to 1:30am) has American favorites from hamburger to pizza for $5 to $10 per entree. The **Marco Polo Restaurant** on the second floor is a coffee shop with breakfast, lunch, and dinner buffets ($9–$23), offering a choice of international dishes, from Chinese to Italian. **Charlie's Bar and Beer Garden** in the lobby is a crowded pub with live music nightly until 1am.

The **French Parasol Restaurant** and **Cafe De Jack,** mentioned earlier, are a few doors apart on Green Lake Road, just south of the Green Lake Park entrance. They open early and close late (hours irregular). Both provide tasty sandwiches, pasta dishes, beer, wine, coffee, and tea at reasonable prices (RMB 18 to 85/$2 to $10).

GUILIN: CITY OF HEAVENLY TERRACES

桂林

THE SCENERY AT GUILIN IS UNLIKE that of any other city on Earth. The peaks "rise as suddenly from the Earth as trees in a forest," writes one Chinese poet, "surrounding the city like mountains floating in an imaginary sea," claims another. These flights of fancy have a literal basis at Guilin. These craggy peaks and pillars of limestone must have been the models for the traditional landscapes painted for centuries on silk scrolls. Until I visited Guilin, I assumed the impossibly contorted, improbably steep, vibrantly swirling mountains of these artists simply did not exist. At Guilin, they do. They exist inside the city as well as in the countryside. Guilin is a city in the heart of an extraordinary karst landscape where it's not always easy to separate the real from the visionary.

When I first visited Guilin in 1986, in October, at the peak of tourist season, every hotel authorized to take foreigners was full. I was kicked out of the cavernous Li River Hotel after a single night, without ceremony or apology. Through sheer determination, luck, and door-to-door begging, I ended up in the older wing of the Ronghu Hotel, where I slept under a torn mosquito net, lulled into dreams by the melodic drip of the toilet.

A decade later, at least the hotel situation has changed. Holiday Inn, Sheraton, and others have moved into a city that ranks among China's top five tourist attractions. In fact, my complaint about Guilin these days is that the tourist business is ruining what was once a quiet little city in a sublime setting, driving up prices, knocking down old neighborhoods, and fanning the fires of capitalism's darker side: greed. Nevertheless, I was happy to find a hotel that would accept a reservation and not expel me should a large tour group suddenly appear on the scene.

Solitary Beauty Peak

Ensconced in a reliable hotel, I made plans to revisit the places that had made the deepest impression on me. I set out first for Solitary Beauty Peak (Du Xiu Feng), one of several limestone pillars in downtown Guilin that can be climbed. Qing Dynasty poet Yuan Mei described this peak eloquently:

> No trace of its origins, no clues to parentage,
> Dropped from the sky, a lonely peak.
> Strange are the hills of Guilin, nine out of ten,
> But Solitary Beauty is the strangest of all.
> Three hundred sixty stairs to the top
> And the whole of Guilin at its foot.

During the Ming Dynasty (A.D. 1368–1644), the city's ruler, a relative of the emperor, built his mansion at the foot of this peak. Later, it became the regional site for the Imperial Examinations, taken by all those in China who competed for positions in the civil service. Today, Solitary Beauty Peak is enclosed within the walls of Guangxi Provincial Teachers' College. In fact, as I walked north up Zhongshan Lu, I was met by an art student from that college, eager to practice his English. We walked together to the college gate, guarded by two stone lions. Inside the walls, I stared up at the 500-foot-high limestone peak that occupied the center of campus.

At the foot of the stairs to the peak there is a chamber, "Book-Reading Cave," which resembles the reading room of a marble library, an apt formation for the site of the old empire's examinations. Like the other famous crags within the city, Solitary Beauty Peak holds the ruins of temples along its flanks and at its summit an unearthly view of the city and the endless chain of peaks. Alone now, I marched up the tall stone-and-concrete steps, a steep and winding trek. The panorama from the top is quite exceptional. To the north, I had a dazzling view of **Whirlpool Hill (Fuboshan)** and **Brocade Hill (Diecaishan),** the two other most famous karst towers in town. To the south, I could trace the Li River as it twisted between **Pierced Hill (Chuanshan)** and **Elephant Trunk Hill (Xiangbishan;** see below), which seemed to be drinking from the river.

The city itself was undergoing an extensive rebuilding, as nearly every city in China is. Guilin's new buildings were not too high. Most seemed to be apartments under eight stories. A campaign of high-rise construction in Guilin would block its stunning topography, ruining its appeal, but fortunately the horizon was still open. The campus spread out below was particularly attractive because it was more traditional, its soaring tiled roofs and courtyards more in keeping with the landscape. Guilin is not

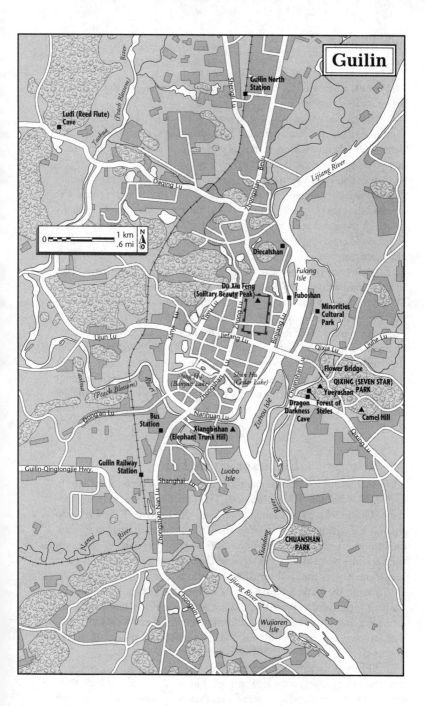

Guilin

Ludi (Reed Flute) Cave

Guilin North Station

Daqing Lu

Diecaishan

Fulong Isle

Lijiang River

Du Xiu Feng (Solitary Beauty Peak)

Fuboshan

Minorities Cultural Park

Lijun Lu

Jiefang Lu

Qixia Lu

Flower Bridge

Rong Hu (Banyan Lake)

Shan Hu (Cedar Lake)

QIXING (SEVEN STAR) PARK

Yueyashan

Dong'an Lu

Nanhuan Lu

Dragon Darkness Cave

Forest of Steles

Camel Hill

Bus Station

Xiangbishan (Elephant Trunk Hill)

Guilin-Qinglongjie Hwy.

Guilin Railway Station

Shanghai

Luobo Isle

Narxi River

CHUANSHAN PARK

Chongxin Lu

Lijiang River

Wujiaren Isle

0   1 km
     .6 mi

N

209

everywhere a beautiful city, but it is enmeshed in a natural setting that is visionary in its intensity.

Perhaps that's why there are so many art students and art galleries in Guilin. On top of Solitary Beauty Peak these days, some of the art students have taken to selling postcards and sodas to tourists. It's certainly a city pushing to make a buck off its visitors.

I spent an hour savoring the view from the summit. Solitary Beauty Peak is the most dramatic of Guilin's vertical hills and its most central. I've climbed the other city hills in the past, but this one was sufficient upon my return. A thousand years ago the poet Chang Ku climbed Solitary Beauty Peak and likened it to a stone pillar holding up the southern sky, "standing aloof between Heaven and Earth." Even earlier, in the 5th century, poet Yan Yanzhi had given this peak its name and noted how, "towering, it floats in the middle of the town" like the mast of a stone ship.

At the foot of Solitary Beauty Peak the student I had met was waiting. We walked down to a local restaurant (named "Local Restaurant") on the east end of Cedar Lake (Shan Hu) near the Li River and feasted on river shrimp. The plates we ordered cost RMB 85 ($10) each—my first indication that Guilin was more than living up to its recent reputation as a tourist rip-off. I had never paid such prices at a street restaurant in China, particularly in a small city where seafood was readily available. At least the seafood was tasty, the owner gregarious, and the lakefront shady.

Elephant Trunk Hill

That afternoon I visited Elephant Trunk Hill on my own (open 9am to 6pm daily; admission RMB 10/$1.20). This park lies on the southeast corner of Guilin where the Taohua River joins the Li River. I climbed onto the "back of the elephant" where a small pagoda is dedicated to Puxian, an immortal servant of the Buddha who is always depicted as riding on the back of a white elephant. From the top of Elephant Trunk Hill there is a serene view of the Li River running south through a deep karst valley.

Leaving the park, I took a wrong turn in the streets and ended up walking for several miles through unpleasant, congested city streets before I regained my bearings. While the motorized traffic is much less than in many comparable interior cities, it's still heavy enough to be annoying to pedestrians.

The city is anticipating more traffic. A new superhighway connects downtown westward to the new airport. The road is lit. Bikes have their own pathway, separated by a wire fence. A new economic zone has been staked out along the freeway, its roads paved, utilities laid, apartments and offices completed, and the foreign-venture factories are starting to hum—just out of sight of old Guilin.

Two Lakes

Guilin's main north–south thoroughfare, Zhongshan Lu, divides its two lakes, **Banyan Lake (Rong Hu)** to the west and **Cedar Lake (Shan Hu)** to the east toward the Li River. These lakes are the remnants of the moat that girded Guilin during the Tang Dynasty (A.D. 618–907). A section of the city's ancient south gate has been restored on the north shore of Banyan Lake, alongside a banyan tree said to be eight centuries old.

Banyan Lake is encircled by pathways, roads, and a bridge. It is landscaped in willow and peach trees, as well as the occasional osmanthus (cassia) for which the city is named. Guilin means "Forest of Osmanthus," a flowering bush whose blossoms exude a sweet aroma each autumn. At dusk Banyan Lake is fringed in colored lights. Its island pavilions and bridges are lit up, too, making this the ideal place for a romantic stroll. One evening I emerged from the Holiday Inn to take a walk around the lake. As soon as I crossed the street, I was intercepted by a pedicab driver claiming to be a moonlighting student. He offered to sell me a trip around the lake. I declined. He then tried to sell me a massage from a young lady, and finally, the young lady herself.

I walked on, remembering a more innocent time, just 10 years earlier, when I met another young man at Banyan Lake. He was nearly penniless, I'm sure. He spoke enough English to tell me that he was a "bum," a bum in the old sense, I think. He had been wandering China on his own for months, something thoroughly uncommon a decade ago—or today, for that matter, when resident permits, difficult to obtain without a job, are required to stay in any city. All he had in his possession was a diary. "I am," he said, "a rolling stone." His dream was to get a job as an English-speaking guide for foreign tourists in Guilin. We rented a rowboat on Banyan Lake and spent the afternoon talking about the world.

Today, the same rowboats with their swan-shaped bows are for rent on Guilin's lakes. They appear just as heavy in the water, just as turgid to row. But speed is not the objective on these pavilioned lakes. One really wants to float away. The wanderer I met 10 years ago floated away that afternoon. I'll never know his fate. He despaired of ever landing a government job, lacking he said the right "connections" *(guanxi)*. He told me he enjoyed his unusual freedom to the fullest. He never asked me for money, not even money for food.

In this Forest of Osmanthus, amidst these towering stone pillars, more than ever today it's money that seems to hold everyone in thrall.

Seven Stars & Cormorants

Seven-Star Park (Qixing Gongyuan) is named for its seven peaks that resemble the stars of the Big Dipper. This constellation fallen to Earth is a lovely park on the west side of the Li River. I walked to it one morning with my acquaintance from the art school. It's an hour-long walk through the heart of Guilin's busy downtown, across the Li River, and onto **Flower Bridge (Huaqiao),** built of wood in 1456 and rebuilt in stone after the Flood of 1540. Flower Bridge is a graceful arching span encased in a tiled roof gallery over the little Xiaodong River that borders Seven-Star Park.

Seven-Star Park is for walking, and we walked several miles of its pathways, first turning north in search of the park's chief natural attraction, **Seven-Star Cave.** With its RMB 50 ($6) admission tag, it's overpriced, but the caves of Guilin are as famous as its limestone hills, so I won't say you shouldn't take an hour's stroll through this brightly lit cavern, one of Guilin's most fascinating and biggest (although Reed Lute Cave, west of the city, is more beautiful). Visitors have left messages carved on the walls of Seven-Star Cave for the last 13 centuries.

On the other side of the cave we had a fine view of **Camel Hill,** which resembles its name. I declined the chance to climb to its summit. The amusement park at its foot was neither inviting nor busy. Its small Ferris wheel, its bumper cars, and even its new water slide seemed to be rusting and cracking into oblivion.

Turning south, we walked downriver along the Xiaodong to Seven-Star Park's primary cultural treasure, its **Forest of Steles,** an overhanging cliff under which calligraphy, poems, and pictures have been carved on thousands of stone tablets over the past 1,600 years. The peak here is called Crescent Moon Hill (Yueyashan), site of **Dragon Darkness Cave (Longyin Dong),** renowned for its crinkled, scaly walls that resemble the imprint of a departed dragon.

We decided to follow the path up the side of the hill for a view of the river. It was from here that, 10 years earlier, I'd had my first view of cormorant fishing in China. Fishing with these birds is an old tradition, particularly in Guilin. A single cormorant, it is said, can catch enough fish to support an entire family. I'd watched an old fisherman below working with five cormorants. He tied each bird's neck with a ribbon to prevent it from swallowing the fish it snatched. To call his cormorants back to the flat bamboo raft where he stood, the fisherman whacked the river surface sharply with his pole while he jumped up and down fiercely in his bare feet. Whenever a bird returned its catch to his hand, he praised it in a voice that carried to the top of Crescent Moon Hill.

It seems that the cormorant fisherman has moved on, too, since then. The only ones I saw in Guilin this time worked on the river's edge in parks where they charged tourists who wanted their pictures taken with them and their birds.

Minorities, Touts & Discos

The commercialization of Guilin has reached its newest form with the opening of the **Minorities Cultural Park (Feng Qing Yuan),** which is located on the east side of the Li River about a 40-minute walk north from Seven-Star Park, one of the ethnic amusement parks so popular in China and throughout Asia. Guilin's version is open daily from 9am to 5pm, and charges RMB 70 ($9) per foreigner, RMB 25 ($3) per Chinese citizen. Its grounds are filled with brand-new models of China's minority architecture. The minority people themselves, who perform at each village stop, are authentic enough.

The province, Guangxi Zhuangzu Autonomous Region, consists of over 3 million members of the Zhuang minority. Many Zhuangs, as well as Miao and Dong people, are thrilled to be spending a summer working in "the big city." While wandering through the village I witnessed performances by gong-and-drum bands, ethnic dancers, and qi gong experts. The *qi gong* demonstration consisted of 10 people in colorful ethnic costume standing on two slabs of marble placed across a young girl's stomach for a period of 1 minute. What this had to do with minority culture in China, I could only wonder, but that's show biz. The one display I did enjoy was a lodge devoted to ancient ethnic musical instruments. I was invited to play several of the gongs, and I obliged, even though as I exited the music hall I was charged RMB 5 (60¢) for the privilege.

Like most minority villages in China, Guilin's version is truly set up only for tour groups. There are no explanatory signs in English for independent foreign travelers, who could better spend their time and money by going to the minority regions directly.

We walked back into town and sat down for lunch in what I took to be a real dive, a seafood cafe that advertised itself with tubs of live delicacies outside—fish, eels, crab—and cages of snakes within. There were tree snakes, water snakes, and five-step snakes available (five steps being the farthest you can get after being bitten by one). I skipped the snakes and went straight to regular Chinese fare. First came a plate of fresh greens, then a plate of hacked-up chicken, its head and claws still in view. The third plate was pork slices in bamboo; the fourth, bamboo shoots in vinegar with rubbery slices of pig stomach. The bill came to slightly more than that of yesterday's lunch. It was time to move back into the international hotel restaurants for my dining.

A word of warning: There are plenty of people in the streets of Guilin preying on independent tourists. Some of these hustlers are students. To avoid rip-offs at local restaurants, tell your local companion you want to spend a specific amount and not a fen (penny) more at the cafe. You can avoid such street guides, of course, and the local cafes, too, but an official city tour will cost you as much anyway. I didn't mind being taken advantage of in this way, so long as I could afford it, and I was in the hands of a student who was a nice fellow all the same.

That evening, I succeeded in prodding the art student to take me uptown to a very local disco for some cheaper entertainment. The venue was an old school gymnasium, so darkened that the waitresses had to locate tables using flashlights. There was no cover charge. I paid only for the sodas. There were flashing lights around the dance floor, where a few young people danced the disco dances of the 1970s, finishing up the evening with what looked like the bunny hop.

Reed Flute Cave

If you've never ridden a bicycle in China, do so in Guilin. The hotels rent bikes by the hour or day. Bike riding appears more dangerous than it is. Once you're in the flow with other bicycles, it's a relaxing way to travel. Just remember to clang your bike bell like a maniac at every intersection. Guilin is compact enough so that you can ride a bicycle into the countryside in a matter of minutes. My favorite destination is Reed Flute (Ludi) Cave, 5 miles west of downtown, about an hour's ride. You can also reach the cave by public bus, taxi, or an organized city tour. The cave is open daily from 8:30am to 11am and 12:30 to 4pm (admission RMB 40/$4.80).

Setting out from Holiday Inn on the southwest tip of Banyan Lake, I cycled north along Xinyi Lu to Lijun Lu, a major intersection. Turning left, I kept on Xinyi Lu for most of the journey, passing Hua Gai An Temple, Yinshan Hill, Xishan Hill, and Baiyan Hill before the road curved north at Lion Crag and hugged the east bank of the Peach Blossom (Taohua) River. At Daqing Lu, the road abruptly ended, crossing the river over Feiluan Bridge and heading northwest another half mile to the entrance of Reed Flute Cave. The countryside was green, the river clear, the scenery increasingly spectacular. At the cave, there were flat rice paddies with some of Guilin's most dramatic limestone peaks looming in the background. This is the scene that appears on countless travel posters, one of the most beautiful spots for photography in China. In person, the scene exceeds all photographic reproductions.

As for Reed Flute Cave, it's worth a half-hour tour. Park your bike in one of the bicycle lots and lock it. This cave once served as an air-raid shelter during World War II when America's Flying Tiger squadron was based in Guilin. Today it is one of China's better-illuminated caves. The quarter-mile-long array of passageways is wet, cool, twisting, and narrow; the stalactites and stalagmites are ornate; and there is one grand chamber, the **Crystal Palace,** where the hero of China's epic novel, *Journey to the West,* is said to have slain the evil Dragon King with a magic needle. The needle, of course, is also in the cave, a garishly lit, harpoon-sized pillar.

I'm not a true spelunker, but it's almost mandatory to take in a cave or two while in Guilin. There are really two Guilins in this karst wonderland. One Guilin is aboveground. The other is below the surface. Poet Yuan Mei compared the two in a graphic verse:

Seeing the blue hills from the outside
Is like touching the exterior of a person.
Seeing the hills from the caves inside
Is like plucking the internal organs.

Reed Flute Cave is probably the single most impressive portion of "underground" Guilin. It's also much too popular. You'll have to shove your way past a hundred vendors and an occasional camel or two towed by aggressive photographers. But for a view of the countryside, its fields and uncanny peaks, it's worth fighting the crowds.

Five Virtues

Guilin possesses "five famous virtues": spectacular **caverns,** exotic **rock promontories,** fragrant **osmanthus, green hills,** and **clear waters.** It is finally the hills that most beguile me. I would return again and again simply for a view of Guilin's remarkable hills. There are grander mountain peaks, snowcapped, immense, and formidable, but none so peculiar and so numerous, planted thick as a forest. "Only at Guilin, in a single sweep of the eye, can you see so many peaks spring from the ground like shoots of jade bamboo, jostling one another, some as near as a stone's throw, others faint in the distance," wrote a Song Dynasty (A.D. 960–1280) traveler, Fan Cheng-ta. "For their astonishing strangeness surely the hills of Guilin rank first in the world."

PRACTICAL INFORMATION

ORIENTATION

Guilin, population 700,000, is located in southwest China's Guangxi Province, 1,000 miles from Beijing, 225 miles west of Guangzhou (Canton) and Hong Kong. The main attraction is cruising the Li River from Guilin south to the village of Yangshou. The **Li River** cruise is covered in a separate chapter. So is the remarkable village of **Yangshuo** (see "Yangshuo: Stone Garden of the Bright Moon"). To see the minority villages of Guangxi Province north of Guilin, **Sanjiang** and **Longsheng,** consult the separate chapter, "Sanjiang, A Bridge of Wind and Rain." Southern Guangxi Province is also the location of a remarkable town on the sea, **Beihai** (see "Beihai: Pearls and Sandworms").

GETTING THERE

By Plane Guilin's new airport is now in operation, 18 miles west of city center. It is served by Dragonair from Hong Kong and by Chinese airlines from most other cities in China. Upon arrival in Guilin, I took the CAAC shuttle bus waiting outside at the curb into downtown (RMB 20/$2.40) and a cab from there to the Holiday Inn (another RMB 20/$2.40). Airport taxis charge at least RMB 120 ($14.45) for the complete transfer.

Air tickets can be booked from hotel tour desks. Flights to Guangzhou (Canton) and Hong Kong take about an hour; to Kunming, 1¹/₂ hours; to Shanghai, 2 hours; and to Beijing, 2¹/₂ hours. For Hong Kong flights, the Dragonair office in Guilin is located on Bingjiang Nan Lu in the Sheraton Hotel on the second floor (☎ 0773/282-5588, ext 8895).

By Train & Bus Mountainous geography has isolated Guilin, making air flights the most practical way to reach the city. There are rail and bus connections, but these methods require overnight rides, often with transfers in between.

GETTING AROUND

After taking an orientation tour, it is easy to find your own way to additional sites by foot or bicycle. Guilin is a compact area, and maps are readily available in hotel gift shops or from street vendors. Bicycles can be rented at Holiday Inn, Sheraton, and from shops on Zhongshan Lu, the major shopping street, at rates of RMB 25 to RMB 50 ($3 to $6) per day. These are useful for reaching Seven-Star Park (a 2-mile ride) and Reed Flute Cave (a 5-mile ride).

Be wary of putting your fate in the hands of locals who make your acquaintance on the streets. They will most likely end up costing you more than official CITS guides charge while delivering less information.

TOURS & STRATAGEMS

Local Tours China International Travel Service (CITS), 14 Ronghu Bei Lu, on the north shore of Banyan Lake (☎ 0773/282-7254; fax 0773/282-2936), arranges city tours with English-speaking guides. Holiday Inn (see "Where to Stay," below) offers a half-day city tour with an English-speaking guide for RMB 250 ($30).

Package Tours Many tour operators in Hong Kong, including CITS, offer complete package tours of Guilin, including a Li River cruise. Hotels, meals, airfare, and a local English-speaking guide are included. This is an expensive but popular option, favored by many people who are visiting Hong Kong but want to sample what the mainland offers. See the Hong Kong chapter for a list and description of tour agents and operators.

WHERE TO STAY

Hotels are heavily booked in the peak tourist months of May, June, September, and October. Book well ahead. The 5-star Guilin Royal Garden Hotel, on the east bank of the Li River, caters almost exclusively to tour groups, mostly to Japanese tour groups, and is not conveniently located for independent travelers. The 4-star Holiday Inn and the 5-star Sheraton have the best locations and facilities. Of 3-star locally managed hotels, the best of the lot is the Fubo Hotel.

Fubo Hotel (Fubo San Zhuang). *121 Binjiang Lu (next to Fubo Hill and the Li River in northeast Guilin).* ☎ *0773/282-9988. Fax 0773/282-2328. 150 rms. A/C MINIBAR TV TEL. $75 double. AE, JCB, MC, V.* This four-story hotel opened in 1992, making it the best of the cheaper inns in Guilin, with fine views. It is, however, locally managed, and services are not as efficient as those at the Holiday Inn and Sheraton. English-language communication is not always clear, either. Don't expect turndown service, a swimming pool, or a newsstand. Still, it has modern rooms that are fairly clean, satellite TV stations, a tour desk, a shopping arcade, laundry service, room service, a rudimentary business center (usually open 8am to 10pm), and a Chinese restaurant, all at a reasonable rate (for Guilin).

Holiday Inn Guilin (Guilin Binguan). *14 Ronghu Nan Lu (southwest corner of Banyan Lake).* ☎ *800/465-4329 or 0773/282-3950. Fax 0773/282-2101. 259 rms. A/C MINIBAR TV TEL. $110 double. AE, DC, JCB, MC, V.* Rooms on all nine floors are nearing completion of a 3-year renovation program. The best rooms are on the ninth floor, each possessing cathedral ceilings and balconies with a view of Banyan Lake. Rooms with king-sized beds cost $120; children under 12 stay free with a parent. Service, rooms, and restaurants are of good international quality. I rate this the best place to stay in Guilin.

Services: Room service (6am–11pm), dry cleaning and laundry (next-day service), daily maid service, foreign exchange counter.

Facilities: In-house movies, pool (outdoor courtyard, heated), health club (exercise machines), Jacuzzi, sauna, tennis courts (on annex roof, $9 per hour), business center (Mon–Thurs 8am–11pm, Fri–Sat 8:30am–11:30pm; fax service 24 hours at front desk), tour desk, beauty salon, shopping arcade.

Sheraton Guilin (Wen Hua Fandian). *Bingjiang Nan Lu (facing Li River).* ☎ *800/325-3535 or 0773/282-5588. Fax 0773/282-5598. 430 rms. A/C MINIBAR TV TEL. $110 double. AE, DC, JCB, MC, V.* The superb atrium lobby and waterfall, the scenic location on the river, and the fine selection of restaurants make this my second choice. The hotel is favored by tour groups. Independent travelers and foreign business people tend to favor the less expensive, more intimate Holiday Inn. On the other hand, Sheraton has some superior features, including its long (20-meter) swimming pool. The superior rooms ($130) and rooms with balconies ($160) are larger than those at the Holiday Inn.

Services: Concierge, room service (24-hour), dry cleaning and laundry (24-hour, same day), nightly turndown, daily maid service, foreign exchange counter.

Facilities: In-house movies, pool (outdoor, heated), health club (exercise machines, classes), Jacuzzi, sauna, billiard room, business center (24-hour), tour desk, beauty salon, shopping arcade.

WHERE TO DINE

Local restaurants, which specialize in seafood, snake, and exotic wild animals, are difficult for foreigners without proficiency in Chinese to approach. There are no menus in English, as well as no hygiene standards in force. Moreover, those few local street cafes that do serve foreign visitors invariably charge three to five times what they should. Stick with hotel restaurants unless you're dining out with a local you trust.

The Holiday Inn restaurants include **Sichuan Garden** (☎ 0773/282-3950), a good place for dinner since the chef is Sichuanese, and the **Patio Cafe** in the lobby, which serves a range of international dishes from grilled quail (RMB 45/$5.50) to beef filet (RMB 95/$12), as well as pastas, *nasi goreng*, cheeseburgers, and pizza. The lobby bar is unusual in that it produces its own microbrews, usually resembling a mild lager, at RMB 18 ($2) per mug or RMB 60 ($7.25) per pitcher—with tastes that are surprisingly comparable to the microbrews you find in Portland and Seattle.

The Sheraton Guilin also has a fine **Sichuan restaurant** (☎ 0773/282-5588), a **fast-food outlet** with excellent hamburgers and wontons, and a **Food Street–theme cafe** that serves the local Guilin specialties you find in night markets—river fish, prawns, pigeon eggs, catfish soup—at higher prices (RMB 18 to 42/$2 to $5 per selection) but also at higher standards of preparation and cleanliness.

NATURAL WONDERS AND COUNTRYSIDE ADVENTURES

乡村

T HE CHANCE TO SEE THE COUNTRYSIDE
of China, to visit a town or village at one remove from the massive cities
and well-trodden tourist sights, should not be slighted. Some say this
is where the real China begins. For the traveler, it can be a taste of the
old ways that long ago disappeared from the cities, even of an idyllic
paradise.

For the most part, towns and farms are difficult to visit. Transportation, accommodations, and food services are not highly developed in the
countryside. But China is changing. As the economy improves, inroads
have been cut for tourists hoping to get off the beaten track, without
becoming dedicated backpackers willing to rough it on an alien frontier.

In fact, if you visit Guilin and the scenic Li River these days, it is not
difficult to stay in the river town of **Yangshuo.** There's a new hotel there,
as well as a dozen cafes that cater to Westerners. The town is small, friendly,
and situated in the heart of the famous karst landscape that exceeds even
Guilin in its beauty.

From **Yangshuo** or **Guilin,** it is also possible to go a bit deeper into the
countryside by booking a fairly rough tour, using local buses and inns, to
the mountain village of **Sanjiang,** where the Dong minority people lead a
traditional way of life that has little in common with urban China. The
everyday sights in such an area are extraordinary.

Also rough to reach is **Wulingyuan,** China's first "Yellowstone-type
national park." Located in a remote minority region of Hunan Province,
south of the Yangzi River, this park contains limestone peaks and pillars
that rival those of Guilin. Guilin is packed with tourists, of course, while
Wulingyuan remains relatively pristine and undiscovered (except by the
Chinese themselves, who crowd in all summer for hiking, spelunking,
and white-water rafting).

A town with a white-sand beach, tropical weather, and exotic seafood
is rare in China, but **Beihai,** on the South China Sea, is China's answer to
the beach resorts of Thailand. Relatively undeveloped and unexplored by

outsiders, Beihai is worth the detour. There's a first-rate hotel there and some unusual excursions, including a ferry to a coral island where nearly all the inhabitants are Catholic.

No doubt the best town for travelers—and my own favorite place to visit in all of China—is **Dali.** If your travels bring you into southwest China, to **Kunming,** then Dali becomes mandatory. Situated in the snowcapped peaks of Yunnan Province, Dali is the home of the Bai people, and they have learned how to make Westerners feel at home. This is as close as one comes these days in China to a true Shangri-la, and if you reach Dali, it may prove difficult to leave.

Dali: The Far Kingdom
大理

At the crossroads to Burma and Tibet, in the western province of Yunnan, Dali is a small town in an exquisite setting, pinched in a narrow band between a long lake and a high mountain range. West of Dali are the shores of Lake Erhai, 3 miles across and stretching 25 miles north; east are the snowcapped Cangshan Mountains, whose highest peak is over 13,500 feet. In the past, Dali was the capital of an indigenous minority kingdom, for centuries independent of Chinese control. Today Dali is an antique village, home to the Bai minority.

Dali's weather is even more pleasant than that of Yunnan's capital, Kunming, the renowned City of Eternal Spring. One of the loveliest places in all of China, Dali is also the friendliest; the Bai people, the warmest. If I could choose only one place to spend my days in the Middle Kingdom, it would be here.

Rough Landing

Nevertheless, my arrival is not auspicious. In Kunming, I couldn't seem to down my breakfast. In the waiting room at the Kunming Airport, I sat in a puddle on a plastic chair, soaking me through. After a 1-hour delay, the plane to Dali flew northwest toward the Tibetan border. I arrived quite ill. I rode into town on the airport bus, rather than hiring a taxi to Dali—a mistake. I was dropped off in a large, busy, uninviting town—more a city than a town. I wandered the streets looking for a hotel and finally realized I'd ended up in the wrong place altogether, in Xiaguan rather than in Dali (a common mistake since Xiaguan is often called Dali, and Dali is called Old Dali).

I flagged down a taxi and it transferred me north, to the magnificent village of Old Dali, but the hotel downtown was full. Taking pity on me, the driver found a hotel south of town, an empty one that had just opened and charged 10 times what I wanted to pay. But I was in no shape to quarrel. Chills and aches seized me, my stomach ballooned, and diarrhea and vomiting had their way with me. I lay in bed for 14 hours, barely able to move, poisoned, it seems, by what I'd eaten in Kunming the day before.

In the morning I check out. The hotel taxi takes me into town and the driver refuses to charge me a cent for the ride, the first free taxi ride I've ever taken anywhere. I find a room at the downtown Dali Hotel. I've seen enough of the streets to know I'll love the place. It is extremely quaint, the closest thing China possesses to a medieval village, and it is filled with cafes and hostels catering to foreign travelers who have made it to the far southwestern edge of China. Already I'm recovered enough to set out and see what the town offers. My cure, however it was exacted, seems miraculous. I comb the streets for breakfast.

It doesn't take me long to find **Cafe de Jack.** There are two main streets catering to travelers: Huguo Lu, running east and west, and Bo'ai Lu, running north and south. Parallel to Bo'ai Lu is Fuxing Lu, which connects the north and south gates of the old city. After a few minutes I master the layout. The guesthouses along Huguo Lu all have painted wall murals advertising their amenities in English. Souvenir shops double as full-service tour agencies. The tiny cafes in wooden buildings, their front walls paneled in glass, provide Western and Chinese foods at economical prices. Three of four connected blocks in the center of town cater to foreigners.

Inside Cafe de Jack, an overhead sign warns NO GRASS SMOKING. This and the other small cafes of Dali have the down-and-out feel of a coffeehouse in Greenwich Village, circa 1967. I pull up a rattan chair at a small table, order eggs, toast, and strong coffee for RMB 10 ($1.20), and watch the world go by on horse-drawn carts. It is Old China outside—a remote China as well. Many of the Bai people heading for work are dressed traditionally, which is to say colorfully, in bright tunics sashed at the waist, dazzling headdresses, and black cotton shoes trimmed in crimson ribbons. The Bai, who are a branch of the Yi minority, differ from the Han Chinese in at least one fundamental way: They place a higher value on friendship than kinship. Certainly they have made Dali as friendly a city to outsiders as one will find anywhere in China.

Erhai Lake

I walk out of Cafe de Jack and turn east down Huguo Lu, stepping into a little shop selling carved rock chops. A signboard outside promises LATE NIGHT MONEY EXCHANGE, tours to village markets, and air tickets. They copy my passport on their fax machine, book my return flight to Kunming, and arrange a taxi to take me to the Dali Airport the day after New Year's. I wish all transactions were so easy in China.

I take a right turn down Fuxing Lu and a left turn on Renmin Lu, the next big street, strolling east toward the shores of Lake Erhai. Renmin Lu dead-ends; I jog to the right half a block, then head toward the lake again on a winding dirt road that starts at a sign in stone reading DA YUANZI.

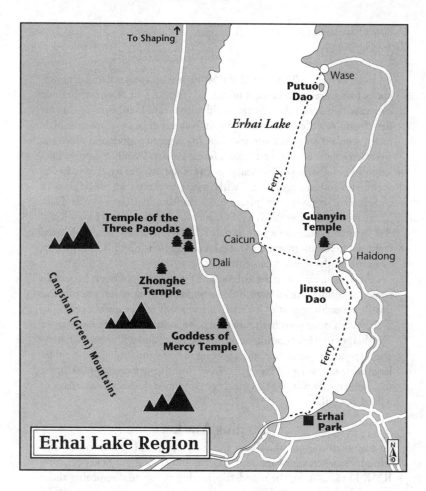

Erhai Lake Region

The dirt road weaves through fields from Dali across to a village named **Caicun** that is strung along the lakeshore. It's an hour's walk. The wall of mountains behind me takes up half the sky. Ahead, Erhai Lake—its name means ear-shaped—is a narrow blue band lined with more fierce mountains. The sun is shining brightly, although it's late December, two days after Christmas. Twice I'm passed by horse carts ferrying people between the villages, and they stop for me each time, but I prefer to walk. It's good to be able to walk at all.

The village on the lakefront is a maze of tiny corridors. It's easy to get lost, and I do. Paths branch off to the lake where fishermen dry their nets and cormorants their outstretched wings. Double-ended junks are tied up to stone jetties, and large black-and-white cows wander the fields. Kids stand in the courtyards of clay and wooden houses setting off firecrackers. Parents are lighting the crackers for the smaller tykes, who are in the throes of exquisite delight.

I hail a horse cart and ride back to Dali. I have a late lunch across the street from Cafe de Jack's in **Leah's Place.** This is a new cafe and it is run by Leah herself, a 22-year-old Bai woman who speaks fluent English, cooks like a dream, and waits on the tables, too. I sit at one of her two sidewalk tables and discuss the world with Leah. Her boyfriend, a student from New Zealand, is studying in Kunming. Leah whips up a plate called *eggplant gonghao*, a stir-fry with ginger, green pepper, and soy sauce, from a recipe she's acquired from a foreign guest. I wash it down with a smoothie, consisting of banana, yogurt, cinnamon, and ice cream. Leah's menu also features raisin buns with honey, an American breakfast with french fries, wonton soup, pizza, and a choice of coffees and teas. Dark Yunnan coffee fetches RMB 6 (75¢), pure Kona coffee from Hawaii RMB 8 ($1), Huangshan tea for sore throats RMB 4 (50¢), and snow tea brewed from white leaves grown on Cangshan Mountain RMB 3 (35¢) a cup. Nothing on the menu is more than $2.

At dusk, Leah's mother arrives. She takes a cup of Green Mountain snow tea inside. She's a beautiful Bai woman, her skin dark, her face in profile resembling that of a Peruvian Indian. It is a peaceful evening in Dali, with almost no other tourists in town, until an Englishman named Eric barges in. He's wearing heavy hiking boots and a Guatemalan poncho, carrying a guitar case, and sporting his straight red hair at shoulder length. He knows Leah. He's just arrived from Hong Kong for the Christmas holidays, back in Dali, I quickly am informed, to propose marriage to a local Bai girl.

Shaping Market

At the north end of Erhai Lake, the village of **Shaping** is famous for its Monday market. Cafes and tour agencies in Dali sell bus tickets, costing RMB 11 ($1.30), for the round-trip, leaving at 9am and returning about noon. The road edge is planted in mature eucalyptus trees, a legacy of the French influences that once penetrated this part of China from the colonial capitals of Vietnam and Indochina.

The Shaping market spreads across a dusty hillside near the highway. When I arrive, the alley into the market is so clogged with vendors on carts and trucks that I have to wait before I can begin to squeeze through. Shaping is a marketplace packed with Bai vendors hawking housewares, batiks, vegetables, spices, paintings, silver jewelry, and cut-and-polished stone. Dali is well known for its marble, and on the road to Shaping we've passed many rock-cutting yards with crude machinery designed to slice the quarried boulders into neat slabs. Dali marble, with its grains suggesting classical landscapes, has ended up decorating the chairbacks and tables of the Summer Palace at Beijing and the walls of the private gardens of Suzhou.

I spend several hours culling the market stalls. Whole sections of the hillside are devoted to woven baskets, the vendors pitching umbrellas and sitting down in the dust next to their goods. Yards of dark blue batiks hang from clotheslines. Posters of smiling girls are pinned to a wall of dried mud bricks. Down in a hollow below a cluster of earthen brick kilns, locals corral dozens of horses, some for trade, most as a means to get home.

The women are dressed to the teeth for the market, many of them topping off their red, white, and blue jackets and long quilted tunics with plumed caps trimmed in bands of sequins. They carry their babies as they do their long fluted baskets, lashed to their backs. Two old women in matching red vests and long blue skirts shop for spices, sampling the wares from open sacks. Farmers rush through the crowded lanes with bright pink piglets squealing in their arms. There's hardly a Han Chinese face in the crowd. The faces of the Bai and other minorities are sunburnt black, their clothing a dazzling rainbow of dyes.

I come across a young man playing one of the oldest confidence games on earth. Adroitly shuffling cups over seeds on a newspaper in the dust, he's raking in loads of cash from gullible onlookers. He seems to be working his shell game with a shill, who often wins, of course, while the innocents lose. The con men scurry from corner to corner, setting down, then folding up their game, always one step ahead of the authorities.

The main road in and out of the Shaping market is still jammed when I try to leave. Vendors and buyers from the countryside still arrive, standing on the open beds of trailers, where they also stack their sacks and baskets. Their smiles are broad. It's market day, the brightest day of the week.

I return in the early afternoon to Dali, meeting Eric in the streets. We walk down Huguo Lu for lunch at the **Yunnan Cafe,** one of the first foreigners' cafes to open in Dali. I try the tortilla chips with salsa and a bean burrito. The cafe maintains a lending library and sells a number of books in English. Upstairs, Dr. Mu Qing Yun performs facial massages, acupuncture, and qigong. Qigong is the application of inner vital energy force to heal and enhance vitality. Qigong can also be used to throw an opponent across the room by the mere press of a fingertip, or so it is said.

Eric is very apprehensive about his marriage plans. He has proposed, but Ling says she must have her parents' approval. Ling's parents live in a Bai village on the other side of Lake Erhai. They are coming to Dali tomorrow to meet Eric. Eric met Ling at a local guesthouse, where she still works. She's barely past 18—he's well past 40. He knows a smidgen of Chinese; she knows almost no English. Eric tells me that he's been kicking about Asia for 20 years, finally settling in as a club musician in Hong Kong. He's worried that Ling may be after his money, but he says he's in love.

Leah says that several of the women in the village have married Westerners. The Bai people seem to accept such arrangements more readily than many Han Chinese do. At least two of the cafes in town are owned by foreigners who have married locals, one by an American, one by a German. But Ling's parents are quite traditional. They know nothing of the West.

We troop uptown to Leah's and drink beer and fruit juice on the sidewalk. Eric decides his boots need repairing before he meets his future in-laws. A shoe man appears as if on command. He talks me into a shine as well. We remove our shoes. The shoe man disappears with them around the corner. Half an hour later he's back. The shine is superb, the price a dollar. He says my shoes are made of excellent leather. They should be, I say; I bought them in America, but they were made in China.

By late afternoon, the sunshine has moved across the street. We follow the sun, basking at an outdoor table at Cafe de Jack. A young American woman joins us. She's just checked in after a 50-hour overland trip from Hong Kong. She hardly seems dazed. Two days from now she must retrace her steps by rail and bus back to her expatriate job in Hong Kong. Dali is a Christmas vacation.

We meet other foreigners and a few locals. After long travels elsewhere in China, I'm content to let the sun rise and set on Dali. Leaning back, conversing, eating and drinking, I let the world do the traveling for a change. This is a kind of leisure almost impossible to find in China, one I'd almost forgotten existed.

Mr. China Son's Cultural Exchange Cafe

The most remarkable person in Dali, one of the most remarkable men in China, is Uncle Li. His full name is He Liyi. He was born in a Bai village in 1930. Eventually, he became the first Bai in history to go abroad. He is home now, proprietor of **Mr. China Son's Cultural Exchange Cafe,** just up the street from Leah's. When I wander in, he immediately makes me feel at home. His English, Uncle Li's third language after Chinese and Bai, is marvelous. He learned English from BBC broadcasts after selling a pig to buy a short-wave radio.

Uncle Li's life story is the stuff of 30 novels. In fact, he has published that story, written in English. *Mr. China's Son: A Villager's Life* appeared in 1993 (Westview Press). His autobiography received excellent reviews in America, but, alas, few copies were sold—a pity, since there are no first-person accounts of 20th-century life in rural China to rival it. Uncle Li has been able to reprint a few copies for sale only in Yunnan, which he keeps on hand at his cafe. He opened the cafe on June 22, 1995, having reached the age of retirement. I buy a copy of his book. Uncle Li writes a long, generous dedication on its title page, puffing away on his long-stemmed pipe.

His story is direct, personal, and extremely frank. In the late 1950s he spent years in a labor camp. After his release, he made his living by fetching night soil from public toilets for use as fertilizer. He divorced and

Old Dali

remarried. He experienced what he calls "years of unspeakable humiliation and suffering," but he is not a bitter man today. After returning from a summer in England in the late 1980s, he settled into village life, opened his cafe, and now hosts foreigners who chance his way.

I sign Uncle Li's guest book. He tells me about his son, He Lujiang, a teacher in the English section of the Dali Medical College in nearby Xiaguan. Then he asks me for a favor. He wants to renew contact with a missionary he met in China before Liberation in 1949 who might live in my home state. He remembers the man's four children by name. I agree to investigate when I return to America.

As for Eric, our love-struck friend, Uncle Li offers to serve as middleman during the crucial meeting with Ling's parents. In exchange, Eric agrees to stage a performance of his music in Mr. China Son's Cultural Exchange Cafe the same night. Uncle Li guarantees that the negotiations will be successful. He shuffles through his supplies, looking for poster material to publicize Eric's performance. He hands me a sign he had been laboring over, announcing in English that patrons of Dali's new "plush toilet" are obliged to pay the attendant 5 mao (about 6¢) per flush.

The message needs no correction. The next day I see it posted on the wall when I pay a visit to the RMB 200,000 ($25,000) public lavatory at the west end of Huguo Lu. It is indeed the only public toilet in all of Dali that could be described as plush, although there isn't a piece of tissue to be had in the place.

The Three Pagodas

I become so embroiled in the daily life of Dali that I almost cease to play tourist, but on New Year's Eve day I make a pilgrimage to the sights I can reach on foot, which are plentiful. A mile north of town on the main highway is Dali's most famous historic landmark, the **Temple of the Three Pagodas (San Ta Si).** These three towers are situated at the very foot of the 10th peak in the massive Cangshan range. Founded in A.D. 825, the temple was later destroyed, but the three pagodas survive, although experts date them back no further than the Tang Dynasty (A.D. 618–907). They are still venerable enough to be the oldest such monuments in the region. The four-sided, 16-story middle pagoda, **Qiantun Ta,** is the tallest, at 226 feet; its two eight-sided, 10-story sisters are shorter, at 138 feet each. They are a graceful trio from a distance, finely tapered in the style of the Little Wild Goose Pagoda in Xi'an. The pagoda builders of Dali, in fact, were said to have come from Xi'an, which was then the Tang Dynasty capital.

The temple on the grounds is for the worship of Guanyin, Goddess of Mercy. Locals tell the tale of how a monk was working on a bronze statue of the goddess at this site when he ran out of bronze. Suddenly, bronze balls rained down from the heavens. The people melted down the bronze raindrops and the statue was finished. There isn't much to do here but admire the beauty of the brick towers and their setting against the snowcapped peaks. The towers are sealed up. The grounds are ringed by hundreds of vendors' stalls, many of them selling slabs of the local marble, their grains resembling mountain peaks. The temples are open daily from 8am to 5pm (admission RMB 10/$1.25).

I return to town and pace the length of Dali from the north gate to the south gate, hardly half an hour's walk. It's a pretty village all the way, still filled with two-story wooden houses, their double-tiered tiled roofs dividing the upper and lower floors. The fronts are planked and faced with folding doors, carved windowpanes, and wooden railings stained a dark red. A typical Bai house has a courtyard, usually decorated in flowers and shrubs, particularly camellia and bougainvillea. In Dali, the Bai women are known as "Golden Flowers."

The **south gate** to the old city is a two-story pavilion with soaring eaves set on top of a remnant of the 30-foot-high battlements that once ringed the city. From the heights of this gate, there's a complete view of

Dali town, the near mountains, and the long lake heading north. On my way back to Leah's, I stop as a large funeral passes in the cobbled street. It's a simple, happy procession. The mourners wield brightly colored banners, and the coffin, carried by hand, is draped in a long, white sheet. As one life ends in Dali, a new year is set to begin.

The New Year

I spend my New Year's Eve at Uncle Li's. Eric rips through a one-hour set of his favorite songs, well received by a dozen backpacking travelers and a small tour group in for dinner. Uncle Li, drawing on his pipe, is beaming. Eric's intended comes late with a friend. She's extremely shy and leaves when Eric finishes up without saying a single word. I fear the session with her parents went poorly, but Uncle Li tells me later that everything is settled. Eric is to finance her college education starting in the spring, and she's to see no one else in the meantime. Things will play out as they will. As for Uncle Li, he will face a new challenge in the coming year. A barbershop is opening next door, one which like many others, it seems, is a front for a brothel. I doubt it lasts very long next to such a formidable foe.

Meanwhile, Eric seems happy with the nuptial arrangements brokered by Uncle Li. I meet up with him on New Year's Day at Leah's Cafe. Leah draws us a hiking map, complete with pagodas. We strike up the foothills of the **Congshan (Green Mountains).** These 19 peaks, each 10,000 to 13,500 feet, form a screen of stone and snow paralleling the shores of mile-high Erhai Lake. We pass through the walls of the stately **Yita Temple.** Its 10th-century pagoda is silent, closed up. The steep road leads us past stonecutters and farmers up toward **Zhonghe Temple,** at the base of 12,000-foot Zhonghe Peak. We don't make it that high. Instead, we stop and rest on the rocks scattered through an alpine meadow and admire the view. The eye sweeps across pagodas down to Dali and across Dali to the lake, and up the lake into the mountains leading to the Tibet plateau. It is a long, deep, high valley of even more remote villages and other tribal peoples, conquered and lost time and again by China's imperial armies. Tomorrow I turn eastward, back into China, resuming harder travels, but Dali refreshes me. Someday I mean to return. Of all the provinces I have visited in China, none has anchored itself more pleasurably in my imagination than Yunnan. This is China's Shangri-La.

WHAT TO READ

Mr. China's Son: A Villager's Life by He Liyi (Boulder, Colorado: Westview Press, 1993) gives a frank and gripping picture of Bai life in China over the past six decades. The author sells copies at his cafe in Dali.

PRACTICAL INFORMATION

ORIENTATION

Dali is 160 miles northwest of **Kunming,** the capital of southwestern Yunnan Province. Kunming (the subject of a separate chapter) is 900 miles west of Hong Kong. Yunnan Province borders Laos, Burma, and Tibet.

Dali is located in a mountain valley at an elevation of 6,496 feet. Its climate is pleasant and sunny year-round, although winter nights can be nippy. Perhaps the most interesting time to visit Dali is during the annual Sanyuejie (Third Moon Festival), which starts on the 15th day of the third lunar month (often falling in April). For six days and nights the Bai people of Dali and minorities from elsewhere in Yunnan gather in the foothills of the Green Mountains to sing, dance, and attend a large market. The problem is that accommodations are extremely scarce then, as they also are in June and July, the months of the high tourist season.

Over 80% of China's Bai minority, numbering 1.1 million, live in Dali and the surrounding villages and countryside, an area known officially as the Bai Autonomous Prefecture.

GETTING THERE

By Plane   The new Dali Airport at Xiaguan (10 miles south of Dali) has daily flights to and from Kunming, the gateway to Dali. On my 35-minute flight, the Yunnan Airlines flight attendants started serving refreshments 9 minutes before landing. There is an airport shuttle bus that meets all incoming flights at the Dali Airport, but don't take it unless you want to go to Xiaguan. Hire a taxi instead, and share it if possible. The transfer takes about an hour and can cost up to RMB 50 ($6) per person.

By Bus   For a full dose of Yunnan scenery, passengers have a choice of a number of buses that travel the **Burma Road** for 257 miles between Kunming and Dali. It is a long, not always comfortable 9-hour trip over a mostly paved, winding road that served as a vital supply link between Rangoon and Kunming during World War II. The bus station at Dali is just inside the South Gate of the city on Fuxing Lu. Bus tickets can be purchased from any of a dozen travel agencies located in downtown Dali on Huguo Lu and Bo'ai Lu.

Work on a rail link connecting Xiaguan and Dali to Kunming is under way, despite the steep terrain.

TOURS & STRATAGEMS

The small storefront **travel agencies** on Huguo Lu, with signboards advertising their prices out front, are all surprisingly efficient and reliable. They provide day tours, taxi rentals, and air and bus tickets, and they can direct you to bicycle rental stands. Many of the Dali cafes provide similar services, and in fact the cafe managers often serve as guides for foreign travelers and tour groups.

Asian Pacific Adventures in Los Angeles has specialized for many years in group tours of southwest China, in particular of Yunnan Province, including Dali (☎ 800/825-1680 or 213/935-3156).

WHERE TO STAY

There are a half-dozen guesthouses in downtown Dali offering basic dormitory-style accommodations. Favored by backpacking independent travelers, they offer beds and shared bathrooms and showers for as low as RMB 10 ($1.25) per night, with some doubles as well. The **No. 2 Guesthouse** (no phone) on the western end of Huguo Lu, off Bo'ai Lu, is the old standby, the first guesthouse to open to foreigners in Dali (1984). The **MCA Guesthouse** (no phone), well south of town on Fuxing Lu, is inconveniently located far from the action on Huguo Lu and Bo'ai Lu, but it does offer a beautiful outdoor swimming pool. The **Old Dali Inn** (☎ 0872/267-0382), also known as the No. 5 Guesthouse, on Bo'ai Lu (south of Renmin Lu), is the best of these guesthouses, with two wings of two-story wooden Bai buildings and a courtyard.

Tour groups and more upscale independent travelers stay at the 2-star **Jinhua Binguan,** at the corner of Huguo Lu and Fuxing Lu (☎ 0872/267-3343; fax 0872/267-3846). It offers

basic double rooms with private baths and showers for RMB 350 ($42). Two miles south of Dali on the main highway, the **Asia Star Hotel** (☎ 0872/267-1699; fax 0872/267-2299), a China–Taiwan joint venture, has just opened. It is a 4-star international-class luxury hotel with clean, well-appointed double rooms starting at RMB 750 ($91). The staff is friendly, but they spoke no English the night I stayed there.

My choice was a compromise. At the **Dali Hotel,** 245 Fuxing Lu, south of Renmin Lu (☎ 0872/267-0387), I took a RMB 100 ($12.50) double with private bath that looked out on a picturesque courtyard garden, hemmed in by the tiled-roof wings of the hotel. Everything was in romantic decay: the bed, the shower, the carpets, the courtyard balconies. The Chinese-speaking staff was efficient, and the mute masseur who had an office in one wing was always in the lobby to help me as I came and went. From the Dali Hotel, it was a pleasant 5-minute stroll north to the cafes on Huguo Lu and Bo'ai Lu.

WHERE TO DINE

The traveler's life revolves around the cafe scene in Dali. The foreigners' cafes are located along Huguo Lu and Bo'ai Lu. The meals are inexpensive but good, the staff—mostly young Bai—unusually friendly and helpful. Cafes come and go each year. They open about 7:30am and close around midnight, if they are doing any business then.

My favorite is **Leah's Cafe** on the west side of Bo'ai Lu (one block south of Huguo Lu), largely because Leah herself is an excellent cook and the friendly confidante of foreign travelers. Directly across the street, **Cafe de Jack** is a

popular hangout, renowned for its pizzas. Both these cafes offer outdoor seating, perfect for sunbathing: Leah's in the morning, Jack's in the late afternoon.

Also popular for food and drink are the **Tibetan Cafe** and the **Sunshine Cafe,** directly opposite each other on Huguo Lu (east of Bo'ai Lu). Farther east down Huguo Lu, past the Fuxing Lu intersection, is the **Yunnan Cafe,** with Mexican and Italian specialties, a lending library, traditional Chinese massage upstairs, and an interesting view across the street of a storefront carpenter at work.

By all means drop in at **Mr. China Son's Cultural Exchange Cafe**, 67-5 Bo'ai Lu (west side, between Huguo Lu and Renmin Lu). Proprietor He Liyi sells autographed copies of his riveting autobiography (in English), cooks up Western and Bai dishes, helps with practical problems that foreign travelers need solved, even makes up early morning (6:30am) breakfasts if you order in advance.

Yangshuo: Stone Garden of the Bright Moon

阳朔

Guilin is reputed to have the best scenery under Heaven, but 50 miles downriver the karst landscape at Yangshuo is even more intriguing. Yangshuo, which means "Bright Moon," is a village laid out in a garden of stone towers, haunting and surreal. Here the swirling, oddly contorted 300-foot limestone pinnacles sprout around every corner and in every empty field. The tour boats that ply the Li River from Guilin end their trips at Yangshuo, and buses transfer passengers back upstream to the Guilin, but there's no reason not to linger. Yangshuo is as close to paradise as a traveler gets in southwest China these days. I'd been wanting to explore Yangshuo for a decade, ever since I first set foot in the village, and this time I simply made Yangshuo, rather than Guilin, my base.

Yangshuo's main street, Xi Jie, connects the Li River docks to the Guilin Highway. It is an anomaly in China, cobblestoned and free enough of traffic to walk in the middle most of the time. Stranger still, it is dotted with small cafes that cater almost exclusively to independent foreign travelers. After checking in at a hotel, I stop in for lunch at **Minnie Mao's,** which is decorated rather like a crash pad from the 1960s with guitars and posters on the wall. A few tables and rattan chairs line the side walls and there's a bar at the back. The menu is in English, and many of the dishes are Western. I order a plate of noodles, a soda, and for dessert a sundae, which consists of ice cream sprinkled with bits of apple, banana, and mandarin oranges. The bill comes to RMB 14.50 ($1.75), about 10 times less than an international hotel charges.

Minnie Mao's is a complete service cafe, as are half a dozen others in Yangshuo, meaning it also runs a travel agency, its tour prices posted in the back of the food menu. Other services include cheap faxing, IDD telephones, and even e-mail. It isn't long before I've spoken to several backpacking travelers who wander in. Some of them are staying for weeks.

Yangshuo reminds me of similar towns in Nepal and Thailand, where foreigners can get what they need with ease. Almost none of China's cities have developed along these lines—China started out strictly controlling tourism, favoring well-managed tour groups housed in increasingly expensive and isolated hotels. In Yangshuo, everything is smooth sailing, particularly for outsiders. Prices are not astronomical for tours, hotels, or restaurants. This isn't quite China, perhaps, but it's how China must become if it is ever going to be truly an international crossroads.

My first night in Yangshuo I end up eating dinner in another Western cafe run by locals. This one happens to be the first foreign cafe set up in Yangshuo, in 1983, even if it has since moved around the corner and changed its name to **Susannah's.** This is the establishment, at any rate, where President Jimmy Carter ate in 1987. The menu is extensive but cheap—nothing over a few bucks. I order a plate of mashed potatoes, something I haven't had for months in China, simple and delicious. The young manager and his "right-hand man" join me at the table and by the end of the evening we cut a few deals to see some sights together. Yangshuo is the kind of town where it doesn't take long to enter into the daily lives of the people who work with foreigners. Before I leave I'll know the people from Susannah's Cafe quite well—again, a rare experience elsewhere in China.

Moon Hill

In the morning, I team up with Harold, the manager at Susannah's. We walk down Xi Jie to a row of bikes for rent on the sidewalk, next to the Paradise Hotel where I'm staying. I pick out a mountain bike, pay RMB 5 (60¢), and we head down the highway, turning south along the Li River at the bridge. The countryside is, of course, gorgeous, those celebrated rock peaks soaring straight up like enormous pick-up sticks dropped by the gods on both banks of the river. The air is nippy and my hands are completely frozen to the handlebars after the 40-minute 6-mile ride to Moon Mountain (Yueliang Shan).

At the entrance there's a shack on a dirt road where I buy tickets (RMB 3/35¢) and the woman in charge watches our bikes. It's another 40-minute hike to the top of **Moon Mountain,** so named because its peak is an enormous stone arch with an opening the shape of the moon. Stone stairways wind through the thick bamboo and brush to the top. Here I can see the Li River at its most spectacular, lazily winding through hundreds of stone towers, squares of vegetables and rice checkerboarding the flat ground. Harold knows the way from Moon Hill to nearby caves—Black Water Caves, New Water Caves, Dragon Caves, all with underground streams, bats, waterfalls, and swimming pools—but I'm content to let the morning run its course from the top of this peak. Why go underground when the most monumental stalagmites on Earth erupt aboveground under a blue sky beside a river? We spend an hour talking about how much money people make in America and how many cars

Map labels:
Yangshuo
Turtle Islet
Xian Qian
Bank
Binjiang Lu
Li River
YANGSHOU PARK
Cafes
Paradise Hotel
Green Lotus Peak
Pantao lu
0 250 m / 273 y
N
To Yueliang Shan (Moon Mountain), Fuli, & Xingping

they own. Harold is frantic to make his fortune in China. He's just turned 24, with no college, but his grasp of English is sharp enough. He's impatient and impulsive.

Later I warm up in the **Mei You Cafe,** next door to Minnie Mao's. Mei You is a play on the Chinese phrase familiar to legions of independent travelers—*mei you* meaning "don't have," the constant refrain sounded by the staff in hotels, restaurants, stores, and offices when a request is made that is too bothersome at the moment to fulfill. The Mei You Cafe in Yangshuo, however, has just about everything one needs—good food, tours, help, advice. The dining room contains eight tables with tablecloths. The walls are decorated in the flags of many nations, the straw hats of local peasants, farming implements, and hollow gourds called *hulis,* representing longevity. The bar at the back serves imported drinks. The local beer, Liquan, is flat but cheap, just RMB 4 (50¢) for a quart bottle.

Breakfast at Mei You is RMB 10 ($1.20) for eggs, toast, coffee, and fresh orange juice. The Mei You also serves a special snake dinner for gourmets. You get to eat the snake, drink its blood, and keep the skin—the whole package only RMB 90 ($11). At the back of the English-language menu is a breakdown of Yangshuo tours, including a demonstration of cormorant fishing after dark for RMB 40 ($4.80). I order the trip, not the snake. The woman on duty adds some coal pucks to the burner under my table, which warms me up nicely, then returns to her knitting, a striped wool sweater.

In the afternoon I wander the cobblestoned street, **Xi Jie (West Street)** northwest to the Li River. The street is lined with old wooden buildings, many of them selling scroll paintings, T-shirts, batiks from nearby Guizhou Province, and carved stones. The stone of this karst region is famous in China, and these trinkets can be expensive.

At the river, where the tour boats from Guilin tie up in the afternoon, there's an extensive outdoor arcade of souvenir and junk dealers, worth combing through. Art students from Guilin display their latest works. Old coins, probably fakes, as well as Mao buttons, Mao's *Little Red Book*, and other recent artifacts of the Cultural Revolution (1966–76) can be picked up here for a dollar or so.

If you spend a week or longer, Yangshuo is the ideal place to take an introductory course in Chinese culture. The **Buckland Foreign Language School** on Xi Jie (which also owns Susannah's Cafe) offers quick instruction in the Chinese language, Yangshuo cooking, classical brush painting, and kung fu and tai ji quan, at about RMB 25 ($3) per session.

Evenings, the cafes rock with Western pop music, set up laser video screens, or simply sell big bottles of beer to foreigners who congregate inside. I decide instead to go fishing by moonlight.

Cormorant Fishing

Fishing with cormorants is an ancient tradition in many parts of China. I first saw it done on the Li River, where to this day it is an honored enterprise. The birds are outfitted with a noose, tied fairly tightly around their long necks. They dive in harness for fish, capturing them in their beaks and returning to the boat, the knotted string preventing them from swallowing the catch. Their master collects the fish. The boats are flat, narrow rafts consisting of five or six large, round bamboo trunks tied together and upturned at the stem. The fisherman stands on the raft, using a pole to propel the boat. His cormorants perch on his outstretched arms, diving on command. It is said that one good cormorant can feed an entire family.

The **cormorant tours** leave after dark from the Yangshuo docks. We board a large motorized skiff and follow the bamboo rafts as they glide into the river. Lamps on poles illuminate the rafts, their glow luring fish up from the depths. It's a fine adventure to watch on a warm summer's eve, although it is cold as we set out and I'm relieved after an hour on the waters to return. In Yangshuo, it is said that the fishermen allow their cormorants to swallow every seventh fish they catch. It keeps everyone content.

Fuli & Xingping

Yangshuo's landscape is stunning enough. The setting of the nearby villages, such as Fuli and Xingping, is even more extraordinary. In the summer, boats take passengers downriver to Fuli or upriver to Xingping. There are even inner tube rentals for those who want to float downriver. The weather is too cool and tour groups too scarce for such ventures when I visit in January, so Harold suggests we take the local bus (RMB 5/65¢), which by fits and starts gets us first to Fuli and then across the Li River, north to Xingping.

Fuli is a tiny town that holds an outdoor food and crafts market for locals every three days. There isn't much for foreigners to buy here, but the peasants who pour in are fascinating to watch. Many are minorities, and they come to market in their most colorful clothing. I traipse back and forth among the rows of produce, pots and pans, hoes and rakes and harnesses, without my wallet or bag, since teams of pickpockets are known to work these country markets and foreigners are an obvious target.

Xingping is a river town that the tour boats pass on the way down from Guilin. It is located in the thickest jungle of spiraling karst pinnacles in the entire region. The streets are paved in rock, the houses are assembled with stone, and the port, where dozens of flat-bottomed tour boats dock in the winter, looks like a "Welcome to China" poster, the sharp peaks layer upon layer across the harbor, like a wall of lotus petals. There's a fine, spacious stroll garden on the far edge of this harbor, where an outdoor banquet is in progress. We almost join in, when Harold realizes it is a wake, the meal following a funeral.

Instead, Harold picks out a cafe on the main street of Xingping, run as most of them are by a family. We order up a hot pot and some beer. Things are not going well for him at Susannah's Cafe. He quarrels with the women he manages, who are irate that he's taken the afternoon off to accompany me. His girlfriend, who also works in the cafe, has just broken up with him and he's crushed, then angry. He says he's been dreaming of saving enough money to open his own restaurant—but it doesn't appear he'll last much longer in this job. Harold makes less than $100 a month, his only skill is his English (peppered with a dictionary of slang he's picked up from backpackers), and if he loses this job he'll have to go back to work with his brother, a local mechanic.

Green Lotus Peak

Everyone who's ever pulled into Yangshuo on a boat down the magnificent Li River has been transfixed by **Green Lotus Peak (Bilian Feng)**, which towers over the harbor. The sheer northern face of its little sister peak is often likened to an ancient bronze mirror, and Green Lotus Peak itself is said to resemble an open bloom reflected in the river. A path leads up from the bank to a two-story pavilion, **Yingjiang Ge.** There's a museum nearby with copies of Li River paintings by Xu Beihong, the town's most famous artist, who lived in Yangshuo in the mid-1930s.

Green Lotus Peak is the finest spot in Yangshuo to enjoy a snack on a sunny afternoon, watching the boats come in off the Li River and snap the harbor market to life. The old fishermen hop down the wharf—pole, baskets, and cormorants in tow—posing for pictures, "10 yuan" a shot (RMB 10/$1.20). The best local snack is the Shatian pomelo, a large grapefruit renowned for its medicinal properties and loaded with vitamin C

(10 times that of an apple). Piled in pyramids on roadside stands, it is sold even at night, the displays lighted by fluorescent bulbs.

The river traffic changes minute by minute, the long tour barges giving way to fishing rafts and family junks. There's a legend told of the river in which two brothers, Son of the East and Son of the West, compete for the same girl. Her name is Jade. She finally sees both her suitors racing toward her and in a split second she draws a line across the sand with her hairpin, hoping to separate herself from both of them. The Son of the West is swifter. He crosses the line in the nick of time, before it becomes a wide river, and he claims Jade. Her line in the sand becomes the jade hairpin to which poets compare the Li River, and the Li River itself carries the meaning of separation.

Yangshuo seems a separate world. Karst castles surround Green Lotus Peak, their names conjuring up a fairy realm of images: Lion Peak and Kitten Hill, Horse Head Ridge and Peach Tower, Dragon Mountain and White Crane Peak. Perhaps this is the lunar landscape the ancients imagined existed elsewhere only on the Moon, a bright garden of limestone parted by a heavenly river with banks of green-waving bamboo. But it is also a place as modern in some ways as the West, a point of international contact as jolting as any in Beijing or Shanghai or Guangzhou.

PRACTICAL INFORMATION

ORIENTATION

Yangshuo is located 50 miles south of **Guilin**, 1,000 miles southwest of Beijing, and 225 miles west of Hong Kong, in Guangxi Zhuang Autonomous Region. The climate is subtropical, with high rains and humidity in the summer. Winters are usually mild, although a bit chilly.

October and April are the prime months to visit.

See the separate chapters on four nearby places to visit in the same province: **Guilin,** the **Li River, Beihai,** and **Sanjiang.**

GETTING THERE

Yangshuo is a village without air or rail connections. Guilin, 50 miles north, is the transportation center and gateway to Yangshuo.

By Plane to Guilin   Guilin is served by Dragonair (800/233-2080 in the U.S.) from Hong Kong (1 hour) and by Chinese airlines from many other cities, including Beijing (2 hours 15 minutes), Shanghai (2 hours), Kunming (1 hour 20 minutes), and Xi'an (1 1/2 hours).

Dragonair's office in Guilin is at the Sheraton Hotel, 2/F, Bing Jiang Nan Lu (☎ 0773/282-5588, ext. 8895; fax 0773/283-2080).

By Train to Guilin   Direct trains connect from Kunming (30 hours) and Guangzhou (20 hours).

Guilin to Yangshuo   A plethora of **buses** make the 90-minute run from the bus station in Guilin and return from the bus station in Yangshuo. Ask for a bus directly to your destination—the buses leave when full and charge approximately RMB 10 ($1.25).

An alternative is to hire a **taxi** at a hotel desk in Guilin; on the new expressway the ride takes 70 minutes, costing about RMB 250 ($30). In Yangshuo, the cafes can book minibuses or taxis back to Guilin or direct to the Guilin airport.

Minnie Mao's Cafe can book taxis to the Guilin Airport (with one day's notice), and also air and rail tickets for many destinations in China (with three days' notice).

CITY LAYOUT

The Guilin Highway (north to Guilin, south down the Li River) takes a jog at Yangshuo, running east and west along the south side of town. The main intersection is at Xi Jie, the cobblestoned street that runs northwest through town to the boat docks on the Li River. The **Yangshuo bus station** is two blocks west of this intersection (on the north side of the Guilin Highway). The cafes and hotels are clustered around the main intersection and up Xi Jie toward the docks. Bike rentals are available along Xi Jie.

Foreign currency exchange is handled only at the Bank of China (located on the harbor, north of the entrance to Xi Jie), open daily 9am to noon and 1 to 5pm.

TOURS & STRATAGEMS

Day tours can be booked easily in any of the cafes on Xi Jie. Minnie Mao's Cafe offers fascinating tours of the area. If you spend time in any of the cafes on this street, you'll meet other travelers and can organize a group for almost any kind of tour in the area, including boat trips up and down the Li River.

WHERE TO STAY

You no longer need to be a backpacker willing to rough it to enjoy Yangshuo. A new 3-star internationally managed hotel, the Paradise Yangshuo Resort, opened in late 1996.

Paradise Yangshuo Resort. *102 Xi Jie (one block north of the Guilin Highway on the west side).* ☎ *0773/882-2109. Fax 0773/882-2106. 112 rms. A/C MINIBAR TV TEL. $100 double. AE, DC, JCB, MC, V.* This two- and three-story courtyard-style resort is situated on its own park grounds with small lakes, arched bridges, and karst pinnacles so close you can almost touch them from your window. The oak floors are as refreshing as they are rare in China. Bathrooms and furnishings in this Malaysian–Chinese joint venture are sparkling clean. Water must be boiled in the electric coffee pot provided. Children under 12 stay free in their parents' room. Larger suites are also available ($150 to $300 per night).

Services: Dry cleaning and laundry (next-day service), daily maid service.

Facilities: In-house movies, health club (exercise machines), games center (billiards, cards, mahjong), business center (open 8am–10pm), shopping arcade.

Inexpensive Choices The **Si Hai Hotel** on Xi Jie (east side of street, across from the Mei You Cafe; no phone) is right in the thick of things, and the noise of the late-night cafes can be annoying. Dorm rooms and rundown basic doubles are available, the doubles (with private bath) renting for $30. The **Golden Leaves Hotel** (☎ 0773/882-2860) across from the bus station has slightly better doubles (for $40) and a helpful staff, as does the **Jinlong** (☎ 0773/882-2674) on Die Cui Lu, which is at an intersection with the Guilin Highway several blocks west of the bus station. None of these hotels offer any amenities.

WHERE TO DINE

The cafes catering to Westerners all offer reasonable prices, Western and local dishes, imported drinks, tour agencies, ticket booking services, plenty of information, and English-speaking staff in a laid-back atmosphere. The best are on the west side of Xi Jie, a block north of the Paradise Hotel. My favorites are **Mei You Cafe** (with its RMB 10/$1.20 Western breakfast and coffee), **Susannah's Cafe** (Yangshuo's original Western restaurant, where Jimmy Carter once ate), **Minnie Mao's** (with its inexpensive noodles and complete travel desk), and **Sunshine Cafe** (with movies in the evenings). All are open from 7:30am to at least midnight daily.

On either side of Xi Jie where it joins the Guilin Highway are the **Green Lotus Restaurant,** with nice outdoor tables and the most elegant Chinese and Western dishes on the street, and **MC Blues Bar,** with plenty of high-energy music, burritos, fried bamboo rats (a type of rat, fried whole and served on a stick), and choose-what-you-dip hot pots. Along the Guilin Highway there are still more choices, including **Planet Yangshuo,** good for a late-night drink, and **Wild Swans,** which has a library of new and used books in many languages.

The Paradise Hotel, 102 Xi Jie (☎ 0773/882-2109), has two international-level restaurants, located in a separate new building across from the lobby. The **Xiang Jiang** is a coffeehouse serving breakfast, lunch, and dinner buffets featuring continental, American, and Asian dishes (RMB 100 to 168/$12 to $20). The **Xiang Shan** offers Cantonese, Sichuan, and local Yangshuo dishes covering a wide range of prices. Neither was functioning on a regular schedule when I visited in January—spring, summer, and fall are the busy seasons—but the setting and the cuisine are the best (and by far the most expensive) available in Yangshuo.

Sanjiang: A Bridge
of Wind and Rain

三江

GUILIN, YANGSHUO, AND THE LI
River encompass China's most famous scenic landscape, but the province—Guangxi Zhuang Autonomous Region—is elsewhere largely unexplored by tourists. I became curious about some of the villages in the northern region of the province, however, and, teaming up with Klaus, a German I met over dinner in a cafe, convinced a cafe manager in Yangshuo to act as a guide, something he had done before for other foreign travelers.

I wanted to see the Dong minority village of Sanjiang and the rice terraces near Longsheng. Neither Sanjiang nor Longsheng are names that come to the top of the list when you talk about places to visit in China, of course—which made them all the more attractive. I wanted to see villages, sights, and peoples that one ordinarily never dreamed existed in the China of Beijing, Shanghai, Xi'an, and Guilin.

Across the Dragon's Spine

We set out from Yangshuo at 9am, taking the local bus up to Guilin, a 90-minute ride. Harold, our guide, was in bad shape. At the Guilin bus station he found a Chinese pharmacy and bought pills for his ailing stomach. He told us he thought something was seriously wrong. The 3-hour trip into northern Guangxi was rough. The buses were uncomfortable to begin with, rickety, the seats crammed in so that one's knees are cramped against the seat in front, and the suspension is nearly nonexistent. We rose and fell with every bump in the potholed road. The bus frequently stopped to take on village passengers, many of them loaded down with sacks of produce destined for market. Most of the passengers were men, and they all smoked furiously.

The scenery became more rugged. The northern region of the province is dominated by spectacular mountain ranges. The passes are marked by nearly endless turns and curves in the road, which the driver negotiated at the highest speeds possible. We had glimpses of remote farms, their old terraces climbing steep peaks step-by-step, each green platform formed by hand. The road was frequently blocked by cows and water buffalo. Slow-moving tractors hauled trailers of logs to town. I had never seen this much logging in China. The forests were thick in the mountains. We passed dozens of roadside mills stacked with lumber, bamboo trunks, and sheets of veneer drying in the sun.

At the village of **Longji** 12 miles south of Longsheng, we got off the bus to see the **Dragon's Spine Rice Terraces.** Over the centuries the Yao minority people have sculpted 2,000 foot peaks here with terraces that are the most astounding in China. Harold was too woozy to make the climb, but Klaus and I were eager to hike, accompanied by several old Yao ladies who tried to sell us their handicrafts on the way to the top.

The Yao people are not the only minority in the region. The Dong, the Miao, and the Zhuang also call northern Guangxi home. The Zhuang people are China's largest minority group, numbering more than 15 million, most of them concentrated here in their aboriginal homeland. Able to assimilate Chinese ways and customs quickly, the Zhuang are largely indistinguishable today from the Han Chinese. Their language, with links to Thai, is distinct, however, and at many of the minority villages spoken Chinese is as obscure as English.

The town of **Longsheng**, where we would spend the night, a busy, ugly urban strip on the Sang River, is the closest thing to a Zhuang capital. Harold found a room with three narrow beds at the Xiantao Hotel, a six-floor walk-up. Klaus and I decided to do some exploring. We walked into the streets. Along a north-running tributary of the Sang River we strolled through the local market, a ripe, odoriferous sidewalk display of bleeding goats freshly slaughtered and dried rats in various sizes ready for frying or boiling.

Mapless, we followed the river west for a mile, crossing a bridge into the terraced farmlands. Cow paths led us through villages of wooden houses and over the boundary walls of dozens of rice plots, fallow in January. Farmers greeted us shyly as we made our trek, not an easy one as paths through the villages were often swallowed up by the fields. Fishermen trolling the river sometimes waved to us. By the time we returned to Longsheng, crossing another cement bridge, we were ready for dinner.

In the Xiantao Hotel's main dining room, we feasted on a variety of local dishes and drank beer and glasses of a sweet wine that was warmed in a hot pot. It was dark when I climbed the outside stairs back up to the sixth floor. On the landing outside the restaurant I collided with a goat. At first I thought he was stuffed, but he was still alive, tethered to the railing and waiting his turn to visit the kitchens. Longsheng was not a town of delicacy and delight. The dark streets were noisy with the sounds of karaoke bars and cinemas, the volume level with that of jackhammers. Our room, a cement shell floor to ceiling, was freezing cold. I slept with all my clothes on under two quilts, and I still shivered. There was a shower

Longsheng

Farms

Sang River

To Sanjiang ←

To Hot Springs →

■ Xiantao Hotel

Riverside ■ Hotel

To Guilin →

Longsheng (inset label)

Chengyang (Dong Village)

11 mi

Sanjiang

20 mi

20 mi — Hot Springs

Longsheng (see inset)

12 mi

Longji (Rice Terraces)

70 mi

Guilin

Yangshuo

Sanjiang Area

N

nozzle on the wall in our bathroom that belched out hot water in the morning. The toilet had no flushing mechanism beyond the pail that stood like a spittoon to one side. Spittoons were stationed at the foot of each bed as well. I began to dream of a Holiday Inn someday reaching even these mountain towns.

The Bridge at Chengyang

We rose early enough to catch the 7am bus to Sanjiang, center of a rural region where the Dong minority still maintained their traditional villages. The bus was a circus. I know it sounds like a third-world cliche, but part of the way I rode with a bag of live chickens in the aisle wedged against my foot. The engine cover next to the bus driver was piled high with sacks of rice, on which several passengers were seated. The strangest cargo we picked up along the way, however, was 10 large sacks of rocks, which with superhuman effort were loaded by one man, bag by bag, until the aisle was chock-full. Somehow the bus continued under its own power, despite the additional tonnage, completing the trip west to Sanjiang in under 3 hours.

At Sanjiang, Harold hired a minivan for the 40-minute drive on un-paved country roads to the Dong village of Chengyang. The driver was a young woman with whom Harold flirted, particularly when one of the tires was punctured and she pulled over to change it. None of us gentle-men offered her a hand, nor did she need one. She changed it in a snap.

Klaus and I meanwhile enjoyed the countryside, particularly when we reached the valley of a small river. The riverbank was lined with a series of wooden waterwheels, several of which were still in operation. They are used now as in the past to scoop water from the river to irrigate the fields.

At Chengyang we had our first look at the most famous sight in the region, the **Bridge of Wind and Rain (Fengyu Qiao),** built by the Dong villagers in 1916. Construction took 12 years. It is considered the finest of the 100 wind-and-rain bridges still standing in China. These are su-perbly crafted covered bridges that not only serve as meeting places where people exchanged village gossip, protected from rain and wind, but as the location of religious shrines. The Wind and Rain Bridge at Chengyang is China's most beautiful. Five stone piers, one on each bank of the Chengjiang and three erected in the shallow riverbed, provide support for the 210-foot-long 11-foot-wide span. Each support is crowned with an elaborate three-tiered pavilion with layers of soaring eaves. The five pavilions are linked by matching white-trimmed roofs. The covered bridge is fashioned from cedar. As with the Temple of Heaven in Beijing, this pavilion bridge was constructed without a single nail, secured solely by wooden pegs. From a distance, it resembles a bridge transformed into a long imperial corridor and temple complex.

The Dong village of **Chengyang** on the other side of the river has occupied the lush green valley for three centuries. Dozens of traditional wooden-plank houses the size and shape of barns, built atop mud-brick basements where pigs are penned, surround the village pond and a placid stream, called the Pingtan. The upper two stories of a typical house are lined with spacious balconies, supported by peeled timber columns that also support the tiled roofs. We were invited inside one house by a local English-speaking villager. The living areas are entered by wooden stairs or ladders. Inside, there are simple, dark, unadorned rooms with bare wooden walls. An open hearth on the floor serves as a stove. We were invited to sample the Dong tea, made from bricks of tea leaves that steep for 20 minutes. It was a deeply flavorful brew.

The village was electrified, but the unpaved streets were traveled by few cars or trucks. Hand-pushed wooden carts and bicycles were the prin-cipal machines. The women, most of them dressed in gray pants and black coats, with white cotton scarves covering their heads, were washing buckets of laundry in the stream. The hillsides and valley floor were ter-raced in plots of vegetables, grains, and rice. Lumber, stone, and straw seemed to be the other principal commodities. There didn't seem to be any power tools about, even in the tiny mills. Everything was done by hand.

A small shop selling snacks and village crafts stood by the entrance to the bridge. I bought several carved wooden decorations and a bottle of spring water. As we headed back across the Wind and Rain Bridge, we were intercepted by a gaggle of local women in black and indigo quilted jackets armed with baskets and knit bags of crafts and trinkets. They accompanied us across. All down the river the waterwheels turned slowly like ancient bamboo Ferris wheels.

Longsheng Hot Springs

The next morning we caught another bus out of Longsheng going the other direction, east down the Sang River. This trip was only an hour, but mostly uphill, past stunning mountain rice terraces and wooden villages. The Yao minorities dominated the countryside in this direction. Higher up, between forested peaks, we arrived at the local hot spring, **Wen Quan.**

The hot spring is currently undergoing a massive hotel and resort development. We walked the road to the pool at the top, about a mile. The road is lined with dozens of restaurants and crude inns. Harold explained that as well as those who came to take the waters, this place was also the haunt of businessmen and officials who came to take pleasures of another order—about 200 prostitutes work the resort. I immediately decided not to indulge in a massage (RMB 50/$6) and headed instead for the outdoor mineral pool (RMB 40/$5), a large, steaming cement basin surrounded by tiled bathhouses, mountain peaks, and the statue of a goddess. Klaus and I enjoyed a 20-minute soak in the moderately hot spa waters.

A clear stream tumbles out of the mountains by the hot springs. If you cross it via a ragtag suspension bridge, you can hike into the forested hills where there are wild monkeys, according to the locals. We chose to take lunch instead at one of the sidewalk cafes specializing in two dishes: sticky rice cooked in bamboo shoots and dried strands of pork.

The road back to Longsheng and then south over the winding mountain that passes down into the karst plateau of Guilin and Yangshuo was like a return from a medieval wilderness to modern Chinese civilization. Harold was able to keep the bus windows shut, although he would find he was without job or girlfriend when he got home. He now seemed unconcerned. He'd made contact with the bus conductress and rode next to her up front on the engine cover.

At the edge of the mountain roads I kept seeing the villagers, men and women, trekking up and down the terraced slopes. They had machetes holstered to their sashes for slashing tree limbs. The limbs were bundled and driven to town where they became charcoal sticks for heating stoves. Occasionally we passed hunters, their rifles essentially handguns equipped with long pipes for barrels. From a distance, they looked like blunderbusses. Klaus fell asleep. He didn't seem to know a word of Chinese, or English either, but he had been on the road in China for 55 days straight, roughing it on buses like this one, alone, visiting villages and waterfalls every bit as remote as the Bridge of Wind and Rain. I began to doze, too, as we came down out of the mountains, descending as if from a lost world where cedar barn houses loom like dinosaurs and bamboo waterwheels spin like ancient banners that the passing centuries forgot to tear down.

PRACTICAL INFORMATION

ORIENTATION

Sanjiang and Longsheng are located on the mountainous northern border of the Guangxi Zhuang Autonomous Region, about 70 miles northwest of Guilin, 1,000 miles southwest of Beijing, and 225 miles west of Hong Kong. This remote region is dominated by minority groups, chiefly the Dong, Yao, Miao, and Zhuang, hill tribes that pursue terrace farming, hunting, and logging. Longsheng is on the main highway to Guilin. Sanjiang is west of Longsheng.

GETTING THERE

Frequent **buses** make the 3¹/₂-hour trip to Longsheng daily from Guilin. The fare is RMB 20 ($2.40). Longsheng is connected by frequent daily buses to Sanjiang (2¹/₂ hours, costing RMB 5/60¢).

The nearest **air and rail** service is in Guilin (see the **Guilin** chapter for details).

TOURS & STRATAGEMS

Tours Formal and informal guided tours can be arranged in **Yangshuo**. The cafes on Xi Jie in Yangshuo abound with tour options to Sanjiang and Longsheng. I arranged my tour with a person who worked at Susannah's Cafe in Yangshuo, although nearby Minnie Mao's Cafe and the Mei You Cafe offer more formal tours of the region.

The two of us paid our Yangshuo guide RMB 350 each ($42), which covered transportation, admissions, and lodging for two nights in Longsheng, with visits to the Wind and Rain Bridge and Dong minority village near Sanjiang and the mountain hot spa east of Longsheng.

Visitor Information In Longsheng, travel information is available at the Riverside Hotel (see below); in Sanjiang, at the Wind and Rain Bridge Travel Service (☎ 0772/861-3369).

WHERE TO STAY

If you hire a guide, he or she can make the decision about where to stay. If you are on your own, the best place to stay and eat is not at Longsheng but at Chengyang Wind and Rain Bridge, 11 miles north of Sanjiang, in the **Chengyang Bridge National Hostel** (☎ 0772/861-1444). This is a new wood building built in the Dong style, with dorm rooms and small doubles (shared bathrooms). The friendly staff speaks some English. As you might expect, this hotel, like all the others in the region, offers no frills whatsoever. Otherwise, at Longsheng, head for the **Riverside Hotel (Kaikai Lushe)** (no phone), downhill toward the bridge from the bus station on Guilong Lu. An English

teacher runs this dormitory/hostel and she's an unbeatable source of information. There are no frills, no private bathrooms, and rates are levied per bed (RMB 40/$4.80). I stayed at the **Xiantao Hotel** (no phone) on Xinglong Zhong Lu, one block south of the bridge into downtown. A room with three beds and a private bath with shower, in rundown condition, cost RMB 90 ($11) total. The power frequently failed and there is no elevator. This seems to be the best hotel in town (there are others like it). It would be difficult to get a room here unless you speak Chinese. Again, there are absolutely no frills, except for a tiny black-and-white TV.

WHERE TO DINE

A guide will make life easier in Longsheng and Sanjiang. None of the hotel or street restaurants cater to foreigners in any way. If you don't speak Chinese, try the **food stalls** (point-and-eat) around the downtown bridge on Xinglong Xi Lu or the **floating barge restaurants** on the

riverbank, which sell hot-pot lunches and dinners for about RMB 60 ($7.25) per person. The best place to eat is at the **Chengyang Bridge National Hostel** (see above); the staff serves dinner on the balcony.

WULINGYUAN: CHINA'S YELLOWSTONE

武陵源

THE CHINA OF VAST, CROWDED cities—and even the China of endless farming communities and terraced fields—occupies but a fraction of the Middle Kingdom's geography. Most of China is rugged and remote, dominated by nearly uninhabitable mountainous terrain. Yet there are few parks devoted strictly to the outdoors, to nature as the supreme destination. The most notable exception I've run across is a park located in western Hunan Province, not near anything at all, known locally as Zhangjiajie but officially as the much easier-to-pronounce Wulingyuan Scenic and Historic Interest Area, a vast nature reserve that UNESCO designated as a World Heritage Site in 1992. Local boosters have proclaimed Wulingyuan "China's first Yellowstone-type national park," but it's just beginning to be developed for visitors from the outside world. I recommend it only to the hearty, although it could become a major attraction if it's made more accessible.

Wuling has always been difficult to reach. For the Chinese, Wuling is synonymous with the remote and the inaccessible. Small mountain villages, some reachable only by ropes, have clung to these slopes since the Ming Dynasty (1368–1644). There are stories of a certain Han Dynasty lord named Zhangliang who lived here as a hermit 2,000 years ago. A Tang Dynasty (A.D. 618–906) writer, Liuzhongyuan, praised its wild scenery. Otherwise, a history of the region is nearly nonexistent.

Getting to Wuling on one's own is pretty daunting. There are a few organized tours leaving from the Hunan capital of Changsha, and CITS there can be convinced to provide an English-speaking guide, if you have the money. I was fortunate. I'd met a local who insisted that Wulingyuan was the most beautiful place in China, and when I challenged him on this point he agreed to take me there.

It can sometimes be tough to travel with a local Chinese in the difficult way that Chinese travel. From Changsha, we took a bouncing overnight bus, equipped with narrow bunk beds and quilts, 250 miles west to Zhangjiajie City (Dayong). The beds weren't long enough, the roads were

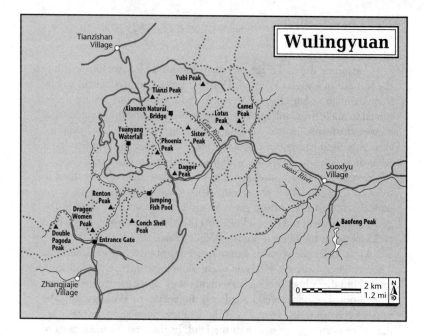

uniformly unrepaired, and when we arrived 8 hours later at dawn I'd hardly slept a wink. We ate breakfast on the street, were besieged by touts, and eventually found a minibus that delivered us to the park entrance at Zhangjiajie Village. To attempt this on your own seems to me insane at best, no matter how gorgeous the scenery, but some hearty travelers do.

Dragon Woman's Peak

Wulingyuan has been divided by the local park administration into a 65,208-acre core area and a 31,320-acre buffer zone. The park core is a deep basin of peaks and pillars, streams and limestone caves, drained by the Suoxi River. A web of hiking trails and steep stone stairways is connected to a rudimentary road system in the buffer zone. There are hillside farms populated by several of China's national minorities. What makes Wulingyuan distinctive, however, is its array of majestic quartz sandstone pillars, erupting from the valley floor and piercing the constant mist. These strange pinnacles resemble those found at better-known tourist sites such as Guilin and Yunnan's Stone Forest, but Wuling's stone columns tower over those in Yunnan and appear more statuesque than those at Guilin.

I first glimpse these pillars a few steps beyond the park entrance, where we are surrounded by stone sentinels on a gargantuan scale, as high and as sheer as any I have ever seen. It is as if a thousand steep peaks have been sliced into narrow, vertical shafts hundreds of feet tall, then turned and shaped on nature's lathe by eons of wind and mist, heat and ice.

Consulting the trail maps engraved on stone tablets, we find a path to the summit of Dragon Woman's Peak. Porters try to persuade us to hire their bamboo sedan chairs, covered in red awnings, but we are determined to make the climb under our own power. Several times we pause at natural platforms on the winding stone stairway where local vendors, emptying their bamboo packs, hawk tea, soft drinks, and handicrafts. It takes us an hour to draw even with the tips of the quartz spires.

Even the sharpest, most inaccessible of these shafts is wreathed in trees and bushes. There are about 3,100 of these strange pillars in the park. Eighty-five have been given fanciful names, such as Double Pagoda, Conch Shell, and Rabbit Watching the Moon (Tuerwangyue), which at 4,149 feet is the highest point in Wulingyuan.

As we enjoy the scenery, a troupe of minority dancers entertains us. Their children overtook us on our ascent, skipping effortlessly uphill, leaving behind the echoes of their "mountain songs" as we gasped for oxygen. The national minorities add a cultural dimension to Wulingyuan. Minorities constitute less than 7% of the Chinese population, but they are the major occupants of over half the land. In the western mountains of Hunan, the Miao people alone constitute 10% of the population. At Wulingyuan the Tujia and Bai minorities predominate, with a scattering of Miao people. The minority farming villages are mostly in the buffer zone. Ten mountain strongholds *(shanzhai),* built in the Ming and Qing dynasties and often reachable only by ropes, remain in the park but are no longer occupied. Today some of the minorities are engaged in performing their songs and dances, selling native crafts, carrying sedan chairs, and running inns and restaurants.

Descending the west face of Dragon Woman's Peak, we encounter lines of porters hauling heavy sacks on shoulder poles—sacks of concrete for the latest construction project. Soon a cable car will whisk sightseers to the top of Dragon Woman's Peak, just one of many improvements now under way.

A Village on the Rim

When we reach the valley floor, **Zhangjiajie Village** is clogged with travelers, many dressed in their finest clothes, as if they've arrived for a wedding reception rather than a backpacking adventure. Wulingyuan receives about 350,000 visitors yearly, nearly all of them from within China. Some come for a casual stroll, some for a serious trek, some even for a honeymoon, as my friend did last year.

Having allotted just two days to cover the high points of Wulingyuan, we cannot tarry. If I ever return here, I'll stay one extra day, to slow the pace if nothing else. We follow the stream running through Zhangjiajie

Village into a valley forest of oak, maple, and Chinese plum, and cross a flat wooden bridge. There we locate another steep stairway rising into the creases of massive stone slivers. Halfway up, a fine mist envelops us. Wulingyuan is often under clouds and rain is a constant feature all summer. Farther up, we break through the clouds.

The trail continues to rise, whipping back and forth a dozen times. Eventually, we head away from the river valley toward the top of a wide, level ridge, stopping at a hillside village of terraced rice paddies for a simple lunch. An unpaved road runs through the village, and we are able to hail a bus grinding its way east along the northern rim of the basin. An hour later, we stop at a roadside inn on the ridge and rent a room for the night.

The **inns inside the park** are new, locally built, and a disaster. Since they're new, they're still somewhat clean, but they are spartan. You get a bed with a quilt and a bathroom that may not have its plumbing in working order. Meals come from one or two cafes down the street—extremely basic fare: noodles, vegetables, and meat in unimaginative variations from bowl to bowl. Not a soul here speaks English; even standard Chinese (*putonghua*) is almost a novelty.

At dusk we enjoy a superb view of the basin below. The canyon walls make a sheer drop. The valley teems with thousands of wrinkled spires that could have served the ink-brush artists of old as the supreme model for their uncanny landscapes. On the horizon are layers of blue-and-gray mountains, softly rounded. I feel as if I am standing atop a roofless cavern where a sea has receded, leaving exposed a chamber of lances and spears, impaled in the earth by a regiment of giants.

The Bridge Across the Sky

The next morning we continue on foot along the northern rim of the park toward **Tianzishan Village,** pausing at several overlooks to view some of the 239 natural scenic spots identified in the core area. At Tianzishan, one vista point has been developed into a wayside commemorating a local military hero. The stone formations below are said to resemble a cavalry division massed for inspection by a general.

At a partially completed visitors' center in the style of a pagoda, we descend a stone stairway into the heart of the basin, weaving among Wulingyuan's largest columns. The trail branches off, enabling us to climb up and down several sharp peaks before rejoining the main path. At a stone archway known as **"The Bridge of the Immortals"(Xianrenqiao),** we come upon a Chinese tour group decked out in yellow baseball caps. They are being entertained by a vendor with a monkey on a chain, the only specimen of the park's wildlife I've seen. Wulingyuan is a preserve for nine rare and three vulnerable species of plants, as well as a number of threatened mammals, including the Asiatic black bear, the Chinese water deer, and the clouded leopard. No clouded leopards have actually been seen in the park, but there are signs that a few inhabit the area.

Perhaps the single most spectacular rock formation appears halfway down the basin trail—**Tianqiaoshengkong (The Bridge Across the Sky)**—an archway joining two massive vertical columns. We ease out to a platform with a metal railing constructed to give a close-up view of the stone bridge, which visitors can also cross if they dare. Under this 130-foot-long stone span, the canyon walls drop straight into an abyss 1,171 feet deep. A survey by UNESCO suggests that it "may be the highest natural bridge in the world." Trees clinging to the arch lend it the appearance of a floating forest spread like a banner between two stone towers.

Yellow Dragon Cave

We reach the valley floor at the vacation town of **Suoxiyu**. Suoxiyu contains several large, modern hotels, opened a few years ago to capture an anticipated increase in overseas travelers, a boom yet to materialize. This would be the place to stay for some luxury and comfort, a good base for day trips whether you come on your own or on a tour. In Suoxiyu we hire a motorized cart and ride 12 miles into the countryside to **Yellow Dragon (Huanglong) Cave.** About a third of Wulingyuan consists of limestone caves and underground streams. Of the 40 caverns, Yellow Dragon is the most spectacular. About 7 miles long, it features a chamber with a 150-foot waterfall and ferryboat rides on its subterranean river. The cavern is fully developed for tourists, complete with English-speaking guides, photographers for hire, and an avenue of vendors lining the lane outside its pavilion entrance—a hint of what Wuling Park will become in the future.

At present, Wuling Park is a wilderness paradise, an unpolished gem. It already possesses a superb system of paved walkways and stone stairs. But Wulingyuan dreams of placing itself at the forefront of Chinese tourism, improving its facilities in order to pamper as well as delight outdoor vacationers. If the local administrative power moves ahead with its ambitious programs of afforestation, conservation, and personnel training, and if the paving of the roads and upgrading of accommodations continue, Wulingyuan could indeed become a Chinese Yellowstone.

Wulingyuan remains difficult to reach and difficult to travel through—still an emblem of the remote and the inaccessible. Whether Wulingyuan is truly the most beautiful place in China, as my friend from the same province insists, is a matter of taste, but its ranks of stone spears brushing the vaults of heaven in a valley of forests, rivers, and caves form a natural tapestry unsurpassed elsewhere in China.

PRACTICAL INFORMATION

ORIENTATION

Wulingyuan (better known to the Chinese as **Zhangjiajie**) is located in a remote northwest section of Hunan Province, about 700 miles west of Shanghai and 500 miles north of Hong Kong. Wulingyuan was first declared a national park in 1983. Since 1988, it has been managed by the **Wulingyuan Administration Bureau,** based in Zhangjiajie City (☎ 07483/61-8010). In 1992, it was listed as a UNESCO World Heritage Site, and ambitious conservation programs, including limits on tourism, were announced. The nearest major city is Changsha, Hunan's capital, 160 miles northwest by air, 250 miles by rail or road.

Spring and fall are mild but rainy, winter is cold, and summer—when hundreds of thousands of Chinese visit the park—is hot and humid.

GETTING THERE

Changsha, capital of Hunan Province, is the transportation hub of the region. Unfortunately, it is 8 to 10 hours' travel by road or rail from Wulingyuan. **Zhangjiajie City** (formerly called Dayong) is about 20 miles south of the park entrance. It contains a rail station and airport. At the park entrance, there is a small town called (to confuse matters) **Zhangjiajie Village.** The bus, rail, and airport terminals are connected to the village and park entrance by roving minibuses that make the 1-hour transfer for RMB 20 ($2.40) per person.

By Plane   **Zhangjiajie Airport** has newly opened air routes to a dozen cities in China, including Beijing (2 hours), Shanghai (3 hours), and Guangzhou (4 hours). It handles 250,000 passengers annually, but flights to individual cities are seldom scheduled on a daily basis except in late summer. **Changsha,** a hard 1-day (or overnight) trip from Zhang-jiajie, has a major airport with connections to many Chinese cities.

By Train   The **Zhangjiajie Train Station** is 6 miles south of town. There are now overnight express trains to and from Beijing and Guangzhou, a daylight express train to Changsha (8 hours), and an overnight express train being planned to connect with Shanghai.

By Bus   Buses to and from Changsha require at least 8 hours to cover the 250-mile route. From Zhangjiajie City, it is another hour by bus to the main park entrance at Zhangjiajie Village.

GETTING AROUND

Transportation inside the park is poorly developed. You can hike the trails or hail local buses that circle the rim as they stop at villages. A local bus connects Suoxiyu Village and Zhangjiajie City, a spectacular 3-hour trip over the mountains on the southern edge of the park.

Suoxiyu Village, located at the southeast entrance to the park, is also a good base for hiking into the park, viewing the nearby Yellow Dragon Cave, and booking a white-water raft trip (summers only) on the Suoxi River.

TOURS & STRATAGEMS

Visitor Information China International Tourism Service (CITS) has a branch in the Zhangjiajie Hotel in Zhangjiajie Village, near the park entrance (☎ 07483/71-2718). In Zhangjiajie City, CITS has an office at 34 Jiefang Lu (☎ 07483/22-7295 or 07483/22-2928). The guided bus tours in both instances cater almost exclusively to Chinese-speaking groups. If the hotels in the area don't have useful tours, one possibility (other than hiking on your own) is to hire an English-speaking guide from the CITS office in Changsha to accompany you. In Changsha, the CITS office is at the Lotus Hotel (Furong Binguan), 8 Wuyi Dong Lu (☎ 0731/443-3355).

WHERE TO STAY

In Zhangjiajie City, the best hotel is the 4-star **Dragon International Hotel (Xianglong Guoji Dajiudian),** 46 Jiefang Lu (☎ 07483/22-6888). Double rooms are $75. The staff might be able to help arrange a guided tour of Wulingyuan. Although rated at 4 stars, the Dragon does not reach international standards in service and its facilities are limited.

In Zhangjiajie Village, at the park entrance, the **Zhangjiajie Binguan** (☎ 07483/71-2718) offers modern double rooms in its new wing (RMB 290/$35) but is otherwise quite basic.

In Suoxiyu, the **Wulingyuan Hotel** has modern rooms and a tour desk (☎ 07483/61-8288) but seems to be open only in the summer months.

Inside the park, hikers must rely on **local inns** (RMB 85 to 168/$10 to $20 per night). I stayed in an inn south of Tianzishan Village on the canyon rim, newly built and run by local minority farmers. The bedroom contained two single beds with quilts (no sheets), a TV set, and a tiny bureau. The bathroom possessed a Chinese-style toilet, a sink that drained directly onto the floor, and a shower nozzle fastened to the wall. The water was steaming hot, once we alerted the staff across the street that we wanted to shower.

WHERE TO DINE

Zhangjiajie (both city and village), **Tianzishan,** and **Suoxiyu** have inexpensive restaurants featuring spicy Hunanese dishes, but the cuisine is not outstanding nor are English-language menus available. The hotels have restaurants that are more accessible to foreign travelers.

BEIHAI: PEARLS
AND SANDWORMS

北海

Until the 1990s, Beihai was an obscure coastal port on Beibu Bay in the South China Sea facing Vietnam. The emperors favored Beihai for its pearls, still a thriving industry in this sunny town 275 miles due south of Guilin. But the pearl city also has Silver Beach, pronounced the best beach in China, and as the big cities on China's eastern seaboard began to boom, so did Beihai, as a tropical resort. The resort boom has already quieted down, leaving Beihai still largely undiscovered. Few Westerners pass through.

Just 340 miles west of Hong Kong, a short hop by air, Beihai sounded like an ideal getaway. My interest was piqued by stories I heard. Beihai had served as a treaty port a century ago, opening to Western traders in 1876, and a European legacy could still be seen in the architecture of its main street. The harbor was crowded with fishing junks, colorful enough to be favored by movie directors filming historical novels about Old China, and the seafood was judged to be exquisite, particularly the shrimp and a local delicacy, the sandworm. And far out in the bay were volcanic islands, virtually untouched by modernization, where Catholic cathedrals were still standing, the islanders predominantly Catholic. I decided I would take a look at this countryside seaport and its silver beaches in tropical China before it was overrun by yet another resort boom.

Old Town

The four-lane 9-mile expressway from the Beihai Airport is flat, straight, new, and nearly empty when I arrive. Green fields in red soil stretch toward rolling hills on either side. Water buffalo graze the median strip, cows cross the highway, and bicycles roll along the inside lanes, often heading against traffic. Barefoot peasants in straw hats march up the off-ramp to the town. They have piled the grain on the pavement to dry. There's plenty of room for country life on the wide expressway.

The entrance to my hotel is lined with massive palm trees. The lobby floors are marble, trimmed in teak. Two-story glass panels frame a picture of the sea. Like most of the resort hotels, this one faces the northern shore of the Beihai peninsula. Silver Beach is across town, on the southern shore. I hire a guide at the hotel to show me around Beihai. She's from Beijing. She says she loves the slow, friendly pace of life in Beihai, so far from that of the capital.

Beihai's fishing industry is concentrated in **Di Jia Town** in a protected inlet on the northwest tip of the peninsula. Every morning, the large fishing junks tie up at the pier on Haijiao Lu and the middlemen meet them. The catch is examined, bartered over, and carted away to markets and cafes in large baskets. The junks and wooden houses along Beihai's north shore have barely changed over the centuries. Many of the hundreds of junks anchored here are owned by the families who live in the houses on the shore, but they have prospered in the 1990s and no longer man the boats themselves, hiring the captains and crews for the dangerous business at sea. Many of the boats docked here house the more than 10,000 boat people in Beihai, ethnic Chinese expelled from Vietnam in the late 1970s.

Much of the day's catch ends up in the fish market on Yunnan Lu, south of the harbor. A new building has been constructed for the vendors there, but the atmosphere is traditional enough. Under a spacious covered concrete concourse, open on all sides and supported by dozens of square columns, the women of the fishing villages squat or sit on the wet pavement beside their plastic pans filled with live seafood. There are no tables or platforms. The women are mostly minorities, including the Zhuang who have occupied the southern reaches of Guangxi Province for several thousand years, and the Jing, Vietnamese who have lived on the islands off Beihai for the past four centuries. They weigh each purchase with the traditional handheld scale, consisting of a bamboo stick gripped at its midpoint, a weight dangling from one end, the purchase from the other. Dried seafood specialties capture the big prices here.

At the heart of Beihai, a mile east of the fishing harbor and market, is **Zhongshan Lu,** the "Old Street" District of European embassies. The British, French, German, and Dutch all set up consulates here as soon as the Qing Dynasty signed the Yantai Trading Agreement of 1876. Foreigners set up their own offices, schools, and churches, and Zhongshan Lu is still lined with these European-designed edifices, most now occupied by grocery stores, pearl shops, Chinese offices, and apartments.

The buildings the Europeans left behind are not as grand as those on Shanghai's Bund, but they are striking. Built of brick, plaster, and concrete, their fronts faced with immense wooden doors, the upper stories of these rather plain buildings extend into the street, covering the sidewalks. The upper floors are supported by columns and arches, giving the sidewalk the cool, shady aspect of an arcade. The facades of the taller buildings, usually just three stories, have some decorative flourishes at their

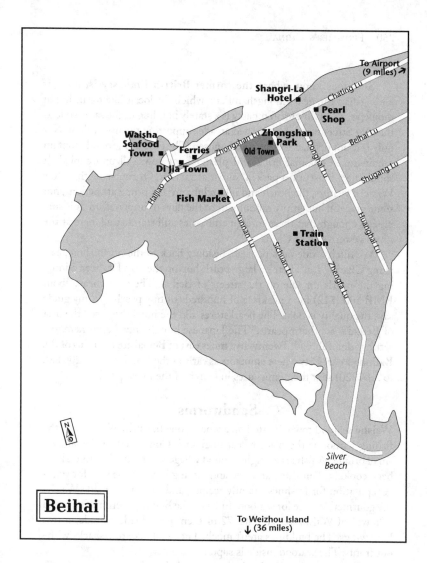

Beihai

To Airport
(9 miles) ↗

Shangri-La
Hotel ■

Chating Lu

■ Pearl
Shop

Beihai Lu

Waisha
Seafood
Town ■

Zhongshan Lu

Zhongshan
■ Park

Old Town

Ferries ■

Dongbai Lu

Shugang Lu

Di Jia Town ■

Hajiao Lu

■ Fish Market

Yunnan Lu

Sichuan Lu

Huanghai Lu

■ Train
Station

Zhengfa Lu

N

Silver
Beach

To Weizhou Island
↓ (36 miles)

peaks, but the overall effect is plain and massive. Pedestrians tunnel through the sidewalk arcades, shopping and running their daily errands. There's a curious absence of motorized traffic along Old Street these days.

Walking in those streets, I happen to look up and spot a cross. Below it is a sign, in English, BEIHAI CHRIST CHURCH. The windows have arched panes of clear glass, but they could easily have been filled with stained glass a century ago. Since it's Sunday, I suggest we drop in. We're directed upstairs. Inside a large, plain room a service is under way. A place for us is cleared at once. We sit on a back pew. A psalm is being sung and the church is full. I stay only a few minutes, feeling like an intruder, no matter how welcome I may be. They say there are many Christians in Beihai, my guide remarks. It is her first look inside a Christian church.

She does know where the **former British Embassy** is, just off Zhongshan Lu, near Zhongshan Park, which the locals like for its hill of monkeys. The two-story embassy is a stately building in the same style as the Old Street facades, an arched arcade supporting the upper floor. Not only is it not open, it is empty and unused. The embassy grounds contain a half-dozen colonial brick-and-plaster bungalows, all unoccupied. It should be a museum, a park, a tourist attraction. Of course, with so few Western visitors, the beach and nightclubs are the prime attractions, not some graceful but empty monument of the days of imperialism. It is surprising enough that these foreign embassies still stand at all, here at the southwestern end of China.

We hitch a ride on a pedicab, heading back to the north shore, east along Chating Lu. There's a large pearl shop on the way. I've been admiring the pearls for sale on the streets of Beihai. They are cheap, about RMB 100 ($12) for a necklace of hundreds of tiny pearls, but my guide says the quality is poor. The pearl stores and the hotel shops sell the best of Beihai's "southern pearls." The Japanese buy the raw pearls here, the settings done abroad. Twenty-five miles east of Beihai are the ruins of the **Bailong Pearl City** where emperors as early as the Han Dynasty (206 B.C. to A.D. 220) sent their emissaries in search of the finest pearls.

Sandworms

Waisha seafood town, located on a woebegone flat strip of sand near the fishing harbor, is the place to eat in Beihai. Connected to Beihai by a small bridge, Waisha is a neighborhood village where the fishermen have been cooking their catch at home and serving it up on the spot for years. A reputation for freshness, family recipes, and low prices made Waisha the gourmet's choice for seafood. In 1996, the Beihai government opened a "town" of Waisha restaurants, 72 of them placed side-by-side in two long wings. The buildings aren't much: They look like row shacks without fronts. The seafood inside is superb.

Selecting a **cafe** from the six dozen nearly identical storefronts seems impossible. They are not numbered or named, but they seem to all have local followings. Customers window-shop the tanks and plastic pails until some display of live seafood hooks them. The cafe I select is superb. It is also the only one with a big fat pussy cat out front. Long-haired, white and reddish yellow, with yellow eyes, she is tethered by a jeweled collar and beaded leash to a folding wooden chair. I know I've found the right place.

Four enormous rectangular tiled tanks the size of bathtubs, each with a pump, are the living menu. The cafe cat's leash can't quite reach the tanks. The restaurant has five round tables, each with a cloth, and a floor of beach sand. We order seven seafood dishes, including a fresh clam soup for two. The RMB 140 ($17) tab includes beer, tea, and a plate of noodles. The clams and the snails are excellent. The shrimp, some enormous in size, are divine. They must be peeled at the table. A small plate of regional celery refreshes the palate. Snails are next on the itinerary. I dig them out with a toothpick. The last dish is the best: two dozen plump, freshly boiled sandworms, which look as hideous as their name suggests. Four to six inches long, segmented, wriggling, and pink, they are dug up from these very sands in which my chair is sitting. They are chopped up and cooked to a divine sweetness.

The cafe cat has her lunch as well. She snaps up fish bones tossed to the sand, takes them under a chair, and shreds them over her rice bowl.

If you come here in the evening, my guide confides, you see quite a spectacle, like no other in China. Every night, a procession of luxury cars pulls in and lines up at their owners' favorite cafes. There are dozens of such exotic cars—we're not talking just the ordinary Cadillac, Lexus, or Mercedes. A Ferrari for starters. A Rolls Royce or two. The more expensive and exotic, the better. The real estate boom made a few overnight millionaires in Beihai, but their motorized toys arrived illegally via Vietnam and other ports, snatched from the streets of Hong Kong, Tokyo, Los Angeles, and New York. Bought for a song in Beihai. The police turn a blind eye here. In the rest of China, however, these racing machines remain contraband. Their owners can drive them around and around, back and forth to their heart's content, but only in Beihai. They are like high-priced adult kiddy cars, and at dusk they all line up so that their owners can feed on the best fresh seafood in Southeast China.

The Dancing Maidens of Silver Beach

Silver Beach is 7 miles south of the fish market and downtown Beihai. Ranked as "the first beach in China" by tourism officials, it is a 14-mile stretch of white sand with gentle waves and a notable absence of sharks. In the summer, the Chinese flock to Silver Beach for sand-castle contests, volleyball, wading, sunbathing, and in the evenings tent camping on the beach. In the winter when I visit the beach is nearly deserted, although the sun is out and the temperature mild. A cleanup crew, lying down in the sand, jumps into action when they see us approach.

One of the oddest things about Silver Beach is the new architecture surrounding it. Dozens of fantasy resorts, white and red villas with turrets and towers, vaguely European, now empty, line the highway to Silver Beach, along with Swiss chalets and garish theme parks. During Beihai's early 1990s boom, developers and overseas investors moved in, erecting scores of seaside palaces for the expected onslaught of free-spending tourists. Tourists do come to Silver Beach—which really does look like one of China's finest beaches—but not in the large numbers once dreamt of by landowners and resort operators.

I walk the long, flat beach in January, trying to imagine how it looks in the summer, filled with vacationers like a beach in Thailand or Miami. The wide brick promenade, planted with palms, runs to a horizon punctuated with red turrets. There is almost nothing anywhere that indicates this beach is in China—certainly no temple roofs or tiled pavilions with golden finials. The centerpiece is a curious modern **sculpture and musical fountain:** an immense hollow globe sheathed in writhing copper panels, a massive southern pearl set on a marble pedestal, its equator encircled with eight beautiful maidens. These maidens of the pearl, linked in a circle by garlands held loosely in their hands, are vibrant sculptures twice life-sized. They are also completely unclothed. Frightfully well endowed, they are classical nudes borrowed from the Western tradition, as are the other fanciful monuments that populate Silver Beach.

When the fountain is operating in the summer, the dancing maidens no doubt appear more chaste. Local boosters hail this musical fountain as the world's largest, its jets spraying more than 220 feet into the air. On festival days, including the Spring Festival (Chinese New Year), the Lantern Festival (in February or March), the China Orchid Fair (in late February), the International Sand Sculpture Contest (in August), and the Beihai International Pearl Festival (in October), the fountain square holds exhibits, performances, and nightly fireworks.

A final incongruity is the camel. Even before the fantasy resorts encompassed Silver Beach, a local entrepreneur had been trying to drum up business by enticing visitors to take a ride and pose for snapshots on the ocean sands aboard his two-humped business partner, who would probably have been more at home in the deserts of the distant Silk Road. The venture has been successful. Not only is the camel a summer fixture in Silver Beach, he has company. Other camels walk the sands these days, too.

An Island of Catholics

Due south of Beihai, 36 miles by sea, 90 miles east of Vietnam, **Weizhou Island** is a tropical Eden of lava and coral. It is also where Christians from Beihai fled persecution and where a century-old Catholic cathedral stands in the center of a Chinese island village.

I arrived Rambo-fashion as the ferry was about to depart. The hotel thought departure from Beihai was at 9am, which it is when the fast boat is running, but Monday is a slow boat day and the departure is at 8:30am. The cab driver knew. When I told him my destination, he began to drive like a maniac, swerving in and out of traffic, nearly driving on the sidewalk. He kept opening the glove compartment to consult his imitation gold Rolex watch, shouting "Ba dian ban" (8:30) and shifting up another gear. I kept looking through the back window, thinking we were in a movie chase scene. I made it to the ferry landing with five minutes to spare, purchased a ticket, and scurried aboard.

The slow boat to Weizhou takes 3 hours on this particular morning. The seating area reminds me of a bus. There are 50 seats. All face the TV monitor, which plays two complete kung-fu action movies. It is a relief to pull into Weizhou harbor. It's a small island, 10 or 12 miles across in any direction, and a low island—no soaring peaks, just a rolling plateau a hundred feet above the water. In the port, several dozen large fishing junks are at anchor. Our ferry ties up at the main wharf. There are low, ugly cement buildings along the shoreline, against the banded sandstone cliffs of the plateau, and to the right, a new town commercial center with white-tiled walls housing village cafes, shops, and fish markets.

I have no idea what to do on this island—no map, no guidebook. A friendly tout motions me off the wharf to a bus. I look inside. There are a few people already seated. I shrug. There isn't much option. The bus fills up and departs. The driver gives a tour in Chinese. He drives down shore, then up to the plateau. Here a dirt road cuts across banana plantations. With the exception of a few buses and a stray taxi, the road is dominated by ox carts. We descend to the beach again, to a much more beautiful stretch, utterly pristine, with dramatic outcroppings of rock.

We take a walk on the beach. What I notice first are the innumerable shells underfoot, unbroken and brightly colored. Next, I'm entranced by the strange sea rocks that rim the shore, draped in trees and ferns. They consist of hundreds of narrow, flat, uniform layers of sand and lava. Several children dressed in red and orange have anticipated our arrival. They are skipping along the sands carrying strings of pearls and baskets of shells for sale. Orange starfish cling to boulders embedded in the beach. There are fishing junks scattered up and down the shore, waiting for the tide to take them out.

Our ultimate destination is the **French cathedral** in a small village in the middle of the island. We follow the red dirt road inward through large sugarcane fields, past a People's Liberation Army outpost, into the village. Many of the houses are built of stone with dark tiled roofs. Cactus grow beside them, low to the ground. Our bus stops at the town square. There, like a tropical mirage, rises a three-story, stone-and-brick, century-old cathedral, dwarfing the tiny village of mud streets, stonecutting yards, and ox carts loaded down with cane, rocks, and tree limbs.

This cathedral was built shortly after the Yantai Trading Agreement of 1876. It seats about 300 under a high arched ceiling. Framed portraits of Christ with Chinese captions are affixed to the walls. To one side of the raised altar there is a forest of candles; to the other, a sculptured rock cave. The missionaries to Beihai seem to have been unusually successful. Hundreds of Christian converts fled to Weizhou Island during times of persecution, finding refuge in this church. Its priest lives in Beihai now, and there are services on the island only on important religious occasions, such as Christmas and Easter, despite the fact that at least 80% of Weizhou's population is Catholic.

From the village cathedral, this Chinese tour heads over to the island lighthouse, a modern construction. There, on a paved path that leads by a series of switchbacks down the cliff face, we reach a volcanic shoreline, all lava, rife with small sea caves and blowholes. The layered cliffs and volcanic outcroppings are covered in small cactus plants—not at all the kind of beach one associates with China. But this is southern China, nearly as far south as the Middle Kingdom stretches, nearer the Equator than Hong Kong or Macao.

The coral island of Weizhou, like the pearl city of Beihai, is a simple seaside paradise with a curious Western legacy. In a nation teeming with Industrial Age cities and tourist-clogged imperial treasures, both Weizhou and Beihai are quiet, unhurried, and undiscovered.

PRACTICAL INFORMATION

ORIENTATION

Beihai is a port on the South China Sea, 340 miles west of Hong Kong, less than 100 miles east of Vietnam, in the southern province of Guangxi. The weather is tropical, warm year-round. High season for Chinese tourists is during the humid months of July and August. In September, rains and an occasional typhoon can strike. March, April, and May are pleasant months to visit, although Silver Beach, rated the best beach in China, really doesn't start operations until June.

Beihai is 275 miles south of **Guilin, Yangshuo,** and the **Li River** (see separate chapters).

GETTING THERE

By Plane The Beihai Airport, 9 miles east of downtown, can be reached from 11 cities in China, including Beijing (3 hours), Shanghai (2 hours), Kunming (1¹/₂ hours), Guilin (45 minutes), and Hong Kong (1 hour). Few of these flights are daily; some, like the flights to and from Hong Kong, are rather expensive charters. The nearest city with extensive and frequent air connections is Nanning.

By Train Since 1996, Beihai has been connected to China's rail network via **Nanning,** a 3-hour trip. From Nanning, a major terminal, the train lines run northwest to Chengdu (26 hours), northeast to Guilin (10 hours), Beijing (41 hours), and Shanghai (46 hours), east to Guangzhou and Hong Kong (36 hours), and southeast to Pingxiang (4 hours) on the Vietnamese border.

By Bus By bus from **Nanning** is a 5-hour trip.

By Ship There is a daily 10-hour ferry from Haikou on China's Hainan Island.

GETTING AROUND

Transportation around town is inexpensive. **Taxis** and **pedicabs** cost about RMB 13 ($1.60). Bicycles can be rented at the hotels for less than $1 per hour.

The slow **ferryboats,** known as Feiyao vessels, leave for Weizhou Island from Beihai's northwest pier on Haijiao Lu at 8:30am daily. Tickets are RMB 50 ($6) each way. The voyage takes 2 to 3 hours. The return trip leaves Weizhou at 2:30pm. The Freida ferry is a faster alternative (75 to 90 minutes), but it doesn't run every day. Freida tickets cost RMB 150 ($18) round-trip. The tour bus meeting passengers on the Weizhou Island dock charges RMB 20 ($2.50) for the 2-hour tour. Seafood lunch at a cafe (no English menus) in the new civic building near the dock costs RMB 30 to RMB 40 per person ($3.60 to $4.80).

TOURS & STRATAGEMS

China International Travel Service (CITS), 6 Beibuwan Lu (☎ 0779/303-3038; fax 0779/305-4477), provides tours of Beihai, plane tickets, and maps. Hotels can also assist with booking tickets and day tours.

WHERE TO STAY

Shangri-La Hotel (Xiangge-Lila Fandian). *33 Chating Lu (on the north shore).* ☎ *800/942-5050 or 0779/206-2288. Fax 0779/205-0085. 338 rms, 26 suites. A/C MINIBAR TV TEL. $90 double. AE, DC, JCB, MC, V.* This 17-story 4-star resort hotel is the only place to be if a typhoon strikes (as one did in September 1996)—its rooms don't flood and it is the only hotel with its own auxiliary power system. Despite being the best hotel in Beihai, the Shangri-La is not expensive. The rooms are large, and they include a writing desk, coffeemaker, and hair dryer. There are two executive floors (Horizon Club, 13th and 14th floors) with concierge services and two handicapped-accessible rooms (one twin, one king). Specify a seaside room for the view. Service and amenities are first-rate.

Services: Room service (6am–midnight), dry cleaning and laundry (24-hour), nightly turndown, daily maid service, free airport shuttle, foreign exchange counter.

Facilities: In-house movies, pool (outdoor, heated; separate children's pool with water slide), health club (exercise machines), Jacuzzi, sauna, tennis courts (two outdoors), business center (7:30am–10:30pm, conference rooms), tour desk, beauty salon, shopping arcade.

WHERE TO DINE

The best seafood (shrimp, snail, sandworm) is at **Waisha,** a fishing town across a bridge from the town harbor (off Haijiao Lu in northwest Beihai). There are 72 "no-name" cafes here, most run by local fishing families. Look for the one with the cat on a leash. Expect to pay RMB 70 to RMB 100 ($8.45 to $12) per person for a six- to eight-course dinner.

Western, Asian, and Chinese breakfast buffets, fixed-price lunches, and weekend dinner buffets are served in the

Shangri-La Hotel's **Coffee Garden,** 33 Chating Lu (☎ 0779/206-2288), open daily 6am to midnight. This is an elegant coffee shop, with rattan furniture, teak-paneled walls, and a picture-window view of the bay and sculptured swimming pool. The set breakfast (pot of coffee, orange juice, rolls, toast, omelet with ham and cheese, potatoes, bacon, sausage, rice crispies, hot and cold milk) costs RMB 44 ($5.40), including tax.

Shang Palace. *33 Chating Lu (second floor, Shangri-La Hotel).* ☎ *0779/206-2288. Dinner reservations recommended. Main courses RMB 30–300 ($3.75–$37.50). AE, DC, JCB, MC, V.*

Daily 7–11am, 11:30am–2pm, and 5:30–10pm. CANTONESE. This elegant sea-view restaurant with nine private dining rooms employs chefs from Beijing and Hong Kong. The dim sum (steamed pastry) menu for breakfast or lunch has 22 choices priced at RMB 6 to RMB 8 (75¢ to 95¢) per plate. Cooks prepare the day's live seafood of your choice in nine ways (steamed, fried, stewed, stir-fried, as sashimi, etc.). The seven vegetarian dishes, such as pan-fried lotus root with pickled olives and black fungus, are the best deal in the house at about RMB 32 ($4).

MONUMENTS
OF THE MIDDLE
KINGDOM

古迹

SEVEN WONDERS OF ANCIENT CHINA, created out of stone and clay, have survived the elements of nature, the wrath of emperors, and the rise and fall of dynasties to become monumental treasures of Chinese art and history. Some are world famous, some define the essence of Old China, and some remain well off the tourist track, but all are splendid creations, worth seeing today.

Most famous is the **Great Wall,** the dragon's spine of Old China, which can be appreciated at three separate locations a few hours north of Beijing, including at a site named Simatai, where the wall has not been restored and polished up for tour groups.

Nearly as well known is the **First Emperor's Terra-Cotta Army** at the ancient capital of Xi'an. Accidentally unearthed by a farmer in 1974, the 8,000 life-sized and lifelike warriors, horses, and chariots have stood guard on Emperor Qin's tomb for 2,174 years. Their excavation has been called the 20th century's most important archeological discovery. It is fitting that China's two most celebrated monuments are linked historically as well, since it was the first emperor who also unified the various fortifications of the kingdoms he conquered, forging what we now call the Great Wall.

Imperial power is represented by these two monuments, but energy of another order—religious and artistic—is embodied at four more remote sites. When Buddhism arrived from India on the fabled Silk Road in the 1st century A.D., China was gradually transformed socially and spiritually. Artists responded by hollowing out holy caves and decorating these shrines with paintings and sculpture, now regarded as imperial masterpieces. Hundreds of Buddhist rock carvings and cave murals survive in China, but four grottoes are supreme.

The **Silk Road Grottoes at Mogao (Dunhuang)** are China's most splendid treasure house of Buddhist cave paintings. The first cave at this site, located in the far northwest of China, was carved out in A.D. 366.

269

The **Stone Sculptures at Yungang (Datong)** were begun slightly later, in A.D. 460. The Buddhist statues carved there, in the shadow of the Great Wall, were the most spectacular sculptures China had yet produced.

The Northern Wei Dynasty (A.D. 386–534) that oversaw the sculptures at Datong moved their capital south to the Yellow River and continued the tradition in the **Buddhist Caves at Longmen (Luoyang).** Here Buddhist rock sculpture reached a new zenith under the master sculptors of the golden Tang Dynasty (A.D. 618–911).

A fourth great site of Buddhist rock sculpture is at **Dazu** in southeast Sichuan Province, where 10,000 brightly painted carved figures—humanized under the Song Dynasty (1127–1279)—are packed into a curved rock cliff called the Great Buddha Crescent.

A seventh monument, preserved in stone, is also located in Sichuan Province: the **Great Buddha at Leshan.** Carved into a sheer cliff, this colossal Buddha towers 233 feet above the swirling Min River. Started in A.D. 713 and completed 90 years later, the Great Buddha at Leshan is the largest stone Buddha in the world.

The artistry and history embodied in each of these monuments is integral to a deeper appreciation of Chinese civilization. Fortunately, we can now see each treasure in the exact location where it was built or cast, painted or carved many centuries ago. With but slight exaggeration, we can call these monuments the Seven Wonders of the Ancient Chinese World.

THE GREAT WALL: THREE VIEWS FROM BEIJING

万里长城

THE GREAT WALL IS CHINA'S MOST renowned monument, frequently heralded as the only man-made object visible from space. That is a dubious, if compelling, claim. I have not orbited the Earth, but I do know that the Great Wall, despite its combined 6,200-mile length, is not only a slim edifice but one that is more broken than whole, not uniform in color or contour, and rife with gaps the size of small countries. More than half of the wall has been demolished over the centuries. Much of it lies in ruins, earthen strips that are barely distinguishable from the hills and valleys out of which it was formed. Still, this dragon's spine of Old China, every inch laid by hand, was a massive project, certainly worthy of heavenly praise.

The Chinese call it Wan Li Chang Cheng, the long wall of 10,000 li. A li is an ancient unit of measure, roughly equivalent to one third of a mile. The wall's origins go back to the 5th century A.D. (and perhaps earlier yet), when the rival kingdoms of the Warring States Period (453–221 B.C.) built walls in central China as defensive ramparts against their enemies, including barbarian tribes. The first emperor of unified China, Qin Shi Huang Di, fortified the barriers in the 3rd century B.C. Over a 10-year period, 300,000 conscripted laborers, many of them slaves, knit the walls into a continuous rampart to protect the northern frontier. New sections extended the wall east 1,700 miles to the Yellow Sea.

The Great Wall was constantly repositioned and extended along new routes as successive dynasties rose and fell. In the year A.D. 607 alone, more than a million workers toiled on this line of defense, but thereafter the Great Wall was largely abandoned. The conquest by the Mongols from the north and their establishment of the Yuan Dynasty (A.D. 1271–1368) rendered the wall obsolete. After China reverted to native rule under the Ming Dynasty (1368–1644), however, the rulers became fearful of another barbarian onslaught and set in motion the last great phase of wall building. This was not enough to keep out the Manchurians, who overran the Ming defenses and created China's last dynasty, the Qing (1644–1911).

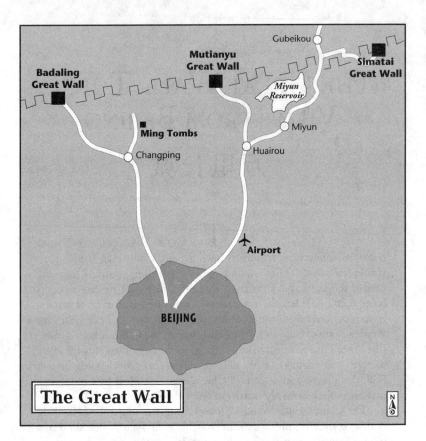

The Great Wall

Today, the Great Wall can be visited where it meets the sea in the east (at Old Dragon Head near the town of Shanhaiguan), where it disappears into the desert on the Silk Road to the west (at Jiayuguan), and at several junctures in between. But by far the most popular approaches are near Beijing, where there is a choice of three dramatic sections. The Great Wall at Badaling, Mutianyu, and Simatai are all within an easy day trip of Beijing, and all three are appealing. Badaling is where most tourists walk on the Great Wall. Mutianyu is a fine alternative, beautifully restored and often less crowded with visitors. Simatai is a wild, nearly unrestored segment, farther from Beijing and thus far less inundated with tour buses. All three sections are 300 to 500 years old, dating from the Ming Dynasty, and all three are beautiful sections of the Great Wall, coiling up and down impossibly steep terrain. They are each a fitting representative of the greatest wall ever built by man—what one 19th-century traveler called a "fantastic serpent of stone."

The Great Wall at Badaling

Almost everyone who tours China, from heads of state to vagabonds crossing Asia with backpacks, pays a call on the Great Wall at Badaling, 42 miles northwest of Beijing. This is a grand section of the wall, set in a steep, forested mountain range. The wall, its stairs, and the magnificent watchtowers were carefully restored beginning in 1957. While many a traveler pooh-poohs Badaling as a deplorable tourist trap, crowded beyond all endurance, I have never been disappointed by it. The Great Wall is China's number one tourist attraction, after all, and China is the world's most populous country. The Great Wall at Badaling, then, is the prime site for immersion into the Chinese world, past and present.

Construction of the Ming Dynasty Great Wall began in 1368 and continued for almost 200 years. Built of stone, it stretched 2,484 miles east to west and averaged 24 feet in height, 21 feet in width at its base, and 18 feet wide on top. The interior was a mixture of tamped earth and rubble. The sides were covered in stone, the top in layers of brick. The brick we associate with the Great Wall wasn't introduced until the Ming builders set to work. Gateway arches and watchtowers run the length of the wall, which served as a highway through the mountains. Five horses could ride abreast, drawing carriages.

The wall at Badaling has been restored to reflect its Ming Dynasty grandeur. The main parking lot and squares, filled with vendors these days, reflect China's modern economic boom. A long stairway runs up to the wall. You can turn left (north) or right (south) and walk a mile or so in either direction. The segment on the left is a bit steeper, but I find it more scenic, and that's the way I usually head.

The incredible steepness of the Great Wall and the high rise of its stair treads always astound visitors. Walking up to the highest watchtower is often enough to exhaust a traveler thoroughly, especially on a hot day. There's no reason to hurry. The scenery is splendid. The two-story watchtowers, consisting of a guardroom below and an observation house above, are fine places to recuperate.

The northern section of the wall rises to the highest watchtower at Badaling, then runs down to the south. If you walk it to the end, about two thirds of a mile from the entrance, you can head north again on an unrenovated spine of the wall that has a much more primitive feel. Few tourists venture out this far. The stairs are crumbling and the sides of the wall are broken, exposing the earthen filling.

If you choose to walk Badaling in the other direction, south atop the wall, the trek is longer, more than a mile. At the far end there's a terminal for the Great Wall cable car. Beyond there, the Great Wall reverts to its former ruins, which one is free to explore. (Liability laws are weak in China, meaning broken bones and other mishaps suffered in public places seldom receive much compensation.)

The Qinglongqiao West train station is near the southern end of Badaling. This is the first railroad to be built entirely with Chinese labor and funds (1909). It tunnels under the Great Wall. Locals tell me that in the winter, when the Great Wall at Badaling is dusted with snow, a train trip from Beijing is a delight. There are almost no tourists on the wall, the sun is bright, and the mountain peaks and guard towers are gorgeous.

Since most of us do not visit Beijing in winter, we must descend the Great Wall in the heat of tourist season—and it is a fiercely steep descent down these high stairs, making some travelers feel like walking down backward. The modern handrails can help. At the bottom of the wall is the "Great Mall" of endless souvenir stands, a movie hall, and cafes. Prices are exceptionally high for trinkets, crafts, and "I Climbed the Great Wall" T-shirts, even when you bargain like mad. I bought a tacky sword at Badaling once, paying half what the vendor asked, which still turned out to be twice the price charged by Beijing and Hong Kong department stores for the identical saber. Oh well, I told myself, it did come from the Great Wall.

The Great Wall at Badaling is open Monday through Friday from 6am to 6:30pm and on weekends from 6am to 10pm. Admission is RMB 30 ($3.75). The cable car is RMB 55 ($6.80) round-trip.

The Great Wall at Mutianyu

The Great Wall at Badaling proved so popular that authorities restored a second section of the wall in 1986, at Mutianyu (55 miles northeast of Beijing). Mutianyu was supposed to relieve the overcrowding at Badaling, particularly on weekends. The ploy has not really succeeded, but I'm glad that Mutianyu is open. Its setting is more rough and rugged than that at Badaling, even if it now has summer traffic jams of its own.

The mile-long segment of the Great Wall of Mutianyu was among the first built during the Ming Dynasty, beginning well over 500 years ago. As at Badaling, a long stairway leads up to the wall. The hike can take up to 30 minutes, so you might want to use the nearby cable car. If you turn right at the top of the entrance, you can walk the ramparts for over a half mile. At the end, there is a barrier. Visitors are not permitted to venture beyond this point. All you can do is contemplate the wall in ruins, which gives one an excellent idea of what most of the Great Wall, even those sections built just a few hundred rather than a few thousand years ago, looks like now.

Returning on the wall in the other direction leads to the cable-car station, which is the kindest way back down (in respect to your knees and thighs). The Great Wall at Mutianyu is open daily 6:30am to 6pm. Admission is RMB 30 ($3.60). The cable car is RMB 80 ($9.65) round-trip.

The Great Wall at Simatai

The Great Wall at Simatai is quiet, remote, and virtually unreconstructed. Fortification aficionados consider Simatai the most beautiful section of the Great Wall. It is beautiful, but its main aesthetic attraction is its state of ruin. This is how the Great Wall really looks 500 years after the Ming constructed it. Simatai is also a paradise for hikers and hill walkers with its dramatic natural scenery, the contours of the sharp peaks heightened by the outline of the Great Wall and its crumbling watchtowers.

I visited Simatai twice recently, first by hiring a car with driver and guide, then by just hiring a car. This put Simatai within 2 hours of downtown Beijing. The cheaper but rougher alternative is the public bus that leaves the Dongzhimen bus station in Beijing at 7am and arrives at Simatai 3 or 4 hours later.

The Chengde Highway to Simatai is smooth, the countryside green. At Miyun Reservoir, the terrain steepens. The roadside is clotted with fishing families selling their catch, enormous reservoir trout, many 3 feet long, sheathed in plastic and suspended on posts like lanterns. At Gubeikou, 70 miles northeast of Beijing, a country lane winds 7 more miles through the foothills to Simatai Village and the entrance to the wall. The town at the base is tiny. The main street leading to the wall has a few beef noodle cafes, souvenir shops, and vendor shelters stocked with T-shirts and Great Wall tablecloths, but this is a mere minnow pond of sellers compared to the ocean of hawkers flooding the gates to Badaling and Mutianyu. Towering high over the village is the formidable outline of the Great Wall at Simatai, slithering like a dragon's back over a series of sharp, clipped peaks.

Beyond the village there is a half-mile walk up to the first stairway and watchtower. The sandy path rises and skirts the small Simatai Reservoir, where in the heat of summer tourists from Beijing board pleasure boats for a sail along the Great Wall. But from the water the wall remains high and remote. The reservoir lies in a deep crease dividing two sections of the wall: Simatai to the east, Jinshanling to the west.

Ascending the stairs to the first watchtower at Simatai is a matter of pounding a few hundred stone steps, the treads of this staircase often just half as deep as an average foot length. The climb is a struggle, but the view from the first of the ascending towers, taken through open cannon archways, is magnificent: endless mountain chains to the deserted north; watchtowers crowning the ridgelines east and west; and the reservoir, village, and farmlands far below, rolling southward toward Beijing.

This first portion of the Great Wall at Simatai has been restored, as have virtually all the walkways and towers that tourists see along Badaling and Mutianyu—but from here on at Simatai, the wall has been left to crumble. A sign at the entrance boasts that Simatai is the most dangerous segment of the Great Wall, and indeed it is. The grand stairways disappear. The pathway becomes a ledge of rock and sand along the outside of the rising wall, narrowing to sheer drop-offs. Sometimes there are no footholds at all. Shedding its stair treads over the centuries, the wall is as treacherous to scale as a water slide of gravel.

The wall bricks, each with its own stamped number, date from the Ming Dynasty. Many of the bricks have fallen away, exposing the original earthen core with which the large work gangs capped the mountain peaks. From the towers on the wall, signals of fire and smoke once alerted those inside the wall to impending invasions from without.

At Simatai one can still see the results of the Ming building program. The toll taken by five centuries of weather and civilization is substantial, but far from complete. Simatai survives as a wild run of ruins, its main outline intact, stretching from peak to chiseled peak on ridges sometimes pitched to 70-degree inclines. Best of all for the traveler, Simatai is as peaceful as it is untouched and as beautiful as the mountains it dances across.

Coming down Simatai is more daunting than going up. Locals recount stories of visitors who have broken into tears during the descent, unnerved by the steepness, the lack of stairs, the unstable footings. Some come down on the stairless top of the wall backward, on all fours. The name *Simatai* shares the same sounds in Chinese as the words *dead horse platform*, a reference to a horse that fell in a famous battle fought beneath the wall here. So far, no tourists have added their names to this venerable tradition.

In fact, there is a safer way to scale Simatai. East of the entrance is a **gondola**. Visitors can hop a ride partway up and climb a new, safer set of steep stairs to the 2,624-foot-high eighth tower on the wall. From here, it is said that on a clear evening you can see the lights of Beijing. You can also get far away from the city. When I first visited Simatai, in the spring, only four other visitors arrived, and it was only a little busier in the early summer when I returned.

There are 14 watchtowers at Simatai, stationed at quarter-mile intervals and strung across the peaks until the wall dissolves into scattered bricks, piles of sand, and fragments of bone from the workers who were buried within the wall. "To think that these walls, built in apparently inaccessible places, as though to balance the Milky Way in the sky, a walled way over the mountaintops, are the work of men," one 19th-century traveler gasped, "makes it seem like a dream." Indeed, Simatai is magical, but beauty transcends ordinary reality wherever one walks today along the Great Wall of China.

The Great Wall at Simatai is open daily 8am to 5pm. Admission is RMB 10 ($1.20). The cable car is RMB 40 ($4.80) round-trip.

PRACTICAL INFORMATION

ORIENTATION

From Beijing, the three main sites to visit the Great Wall are at **Badaling** (42 miles northwest), **Mutianyu** (55 miles north-east), and **Simatai** (77 miles northeast). Badaling, the most popular site, is beautiful but crowded. Mutianyu, fully renovated and opened more recently to tourists, has also become very popular with tour groups. Simatai, most of which is not restored, is less crowded and requires more hiking effort. To avoid the crowds, visit the Great Wall on weekdays rather than weekends, early in the morning if possible. Springtime is the most pleasant time to go to the wall; June through September is high tourist season.

All three sites are day trips from **Beijing** (see separate chapter).

GETTING THERE

To Badaling   A new expressway connects Beijing to the Great Wall at Badaling. Tour buses make the trip in about 90 minutes, unless the expressway is clogged with other buses or there's been an accident (which is not uncommon). Government-sponsored tour buses (the green no. 1 buses) make the run every 20 minutes in the morning, beginning at 6am and leaving from in front of Qianmen Gate (at the south end of Tiananmen Square), costing RMB 9 ($1) each way. For information, contact the Beijing CITS office (see below). The **train** from Beijing to Hohhot stops near the Badaling section of the wall at Qinglongqiao West train station. The rail journey (no. 527 train) takes about 3 hours from Beijing's Yongdingmen train station, departing at 9:40am (one-way fare RMB 20/$2.40). There are many other trains as well.

To Mutianyu   If you are not on a tour, you can catch a **minibus** to Mutianyu in front of the Great Hall of the People. A kiosk sells tickets (RMB 10/$1.20 each way) the day before. Morning departure times vary, so check ahead. There is no train service.

To Simatai   To reach the Great Wall at Simatai, book a **tour** at the hotel or through CITS (see below), hire a **taxi** (about RMB 400/$48), or book a **minibus** (RMB 100/$12 round-trip) at the tourist office in the Jinghua Hotel, Nansanhuan Xi Lu (☎ 010/6722-2211).

TOURS & STRATAGEMS

Tours to Badaling & Mutianyu China International Travel Service (CITS), with headquarters at 28 Jianguomenwai Dajie in Beijing (☎ 010/6515-8566; fax 010/6515-8602), arranges guided tours to the Great Wall. CITS maintains convenient branches in most hotels.

CITS group tours to the Great Wall at Badaling leave from various hotels at 8:30am daily and cost about RMB 400 ($48) per person, including lunch and a tour of the uninspiring Ming Tombs. CITS group tours to the Great Wall at Mutianyu leave at noon on Tuesday, Thursday, and Saturday from various hotels and cost about RMB 300 ($37) per person.

Tours to Simatai   There are no group tours to the Great Wall at Simatai, although private guided tours can be arranged by CITS and hotel tour desks. I booked a tour with a private car and English-speaking guide, for RMB 1,200 ($145), at the tour desk of the Trader's Hotel, 1 Jianguomenwai Dajie (☎ 010/6505-2277). I later returned to Simatai by hiring a taxi for the day on my own, costing RMB 400 ($48).

WHERE TO STAY

As the Great Wall is a day trip from the capital, consult the chapter, "Beijing: China's Treasure House," for lodging choices. Adventurous visitors have been known to take sleeping bags and tents, dodging officials to camp out on the Great Wall.

WHERE TO DINE

All three Great Wall sites have **food stands** (beef noodles for $2 a plate) and **cafes**. If your tour includes lunch, you'll dine at one of the restaurants catering to foreigner groups with fixed-price set Chinese lunches. The Great Wall at Badaling even has a branch of Kentucky Fried Chicken. If you're on your own for food, best pack a lunch in Beijing and enjoy it on the wall.

THE FIRST EMPEROR'S TERRA-COTTA ARMY

兵马俑

THE FIRST EMPEROR TO UNIFY CHINA, Qin Shi Huang (259–210 B.C.), spent more years constructing his tomb than he did building the new Chinese capital where he lived and reigned. Emperor Qin's tomb is capped by a 125-foot-high grassy mound, making it one of the largest *tumuli* in the Xi'an region that is clotted with imperial burial mounds. Beneath the mound is a grave the size of a city, its underground walls stretching for miles. The First Emperor's tomb has not been opened, but 1 mile to the east peasants made an astonishing hit while digging for well water in the drought of 1974: the first of three vaults of life-size terra-cotta soldiers, horses, and chariots that had stood guard inside the outer wall of the First Emperor's mausoleum, undisturbed and unremembered, for 2,174 years.

The clay army was excavated, painfully reassembled shard by shard, and opened to public display on National Day, October 10, 1980. As a professor in Xi'an once remarked to me, only partly in jest, the local people ought to give Qin Shi Huang the Nobel prize in world tourism. The First Emperor's terra-cotta armies were a sensation. Hailed as the century's most important discovery in Chinese archeology, the buried warriors catapulted Xi'an into the forefront of Asian tourism. These excavations rival the Great Wall as China's most visited sight.

Is the buried army worth such hyperbole and promotion? Yes—even though increased tourism is doing its best to blunt the full effect and even though the method of displaying the site has never been satisfactory. Housed under ugly, massive shed roofs, the vaults must be viewed from distant catwalks, while what one really longs for is a close-up look, an intimate stroll among the infantrymen, archers, generals, and steeds. That's not permitted, unless you are a visiting head of state; nor are photographs permitted. Yet the site is China's grandest historical spectacle, the field where its first dynasty was buried and came out of the earth again. Despite the crowds and viewing restrictions, the power and monumental beauty of the site pour through.

One aspect I've come to appreciate over the years is the workaday manner in which the vaults are displayed. This is still a work in progress. Teams are often gathered in the pits, sifting, cataloging, and assembling more and more figures as tourists file by. The site is expanding. A second and third vault opened to public view in the 1990s. More excavations will follow. I may not be able to walk up and down the rows where the terracotta forces of the first emperor stand, but I can look over the shoulders of those who have put them back on their feet and opened the vaults after 22 centuries in darkness.

Vault 1

The **Museum of the Terra-Cotta Warriors and Horses of Qin Shi Huang,** as the site is officially designated, has opened three vaults to view. Altogether, they contain about 1,400 items—the soldiers, charioteers, archers, horsemen, and horses of the First Emperor's death guard. The first vault, the one discovered in 1974, contains 6,000 of the 8,000 horses and soldiers, and this is the place to begin.

At first glimpse, this excavated field (203 feet wide, 755 feet long) can be bewildering. The infantrymen are arranged in columns filling 11 corridors, each furrow 15 feet deep. The 38 ranks face east, toward their emperor's tomb. All the soldiers are life-size, standing five-foot-eight to six-foot-one in height. All are remarkably lifelike, with individual faces modeled on the actual soldiers of the emperor's army. They carry real weapons—crossbows, spears, swords, and arrowheads steeped in lethal levels of lead. Probably the most astonishing statistic is that just 1,000 of the 6,000 clay soldiers have been reassembled and stationed here.

In this vault lay China's oldest crossbow and its first brick wall. The paint, which has been scorched, eroded, and peeled away from the terra-cotta figures, once provided a unifying element. The mineral dyes were bright the day they were applied. The gray soldiers we see now were once resplendent—the generals robed in green, the infantry sheathed in black armor—and the ears and nostrils of their horses were painted red as blood, their teeth and hooves white as limestone.

The rear portions of Vault 1 have barely been disturbed, and this is where you'll often get a good view of what the archeologists are up against: a seemingly hopeless jigsaw puzzle of shattered clay pieces sunken under yet more clay soil, waiting to be put back together. Some workers have been toiling at the pits for 20 years. On a typical day, eight people endeavor to solve the puzzle presented by each figure one piece at a time. Fragments can lay in storage for many years before their place is discovered. Computers are beginning to aid in ending this reassembly nightmare.

As impressive as the restored military forces are, I prefer to look into the pits of the unassembled: the disembodied heads, arms, hooves, and raiments still imprisoned by the dust, floating to the surface like the wreckage of an ancient Atlantis.

Vault 2

The second vault, housed in a more pleasing but still gloomy marble hall, opened on October 10, 1994. It displays an excavation in progress as well, but one that has just begun. Few of its pits are opened. Another 10 years may be required before all the pieces are dug up, and reassembly could take longer.

Vault 2 contains archers, infantrymen, charioteers, and cavalry. Vault 1 is devoted primarily to foot soldiers, while in this vault the cavalry advances to the fore. One hundred sixteen of the horses are saddled, the earliest evidence in China of such a device. Three hundred fifty-six horses pull eighty-nine war chariots. There are 900 soldiers here, as compared to the 6,000 in Vault 1.

Vault 2 was first detected in 1976 upon the suggestion of a local farmer, test drilled, and covered back up until March 1994 when a formal excavation began. The first step, still under way, was to remove the soil concealing a roof of ancient timbers and mats, and then to remove the roof itself. If you look carefully at the exposed dig, you can see the ancient roof beams used by the original builders. This section of the underground city was built by digging furrows into the ground, paving the floor with bricks, casting the statuary and placing it in precise formation, then covering the furrows with a strong roof that supported a new field of dust, soil, and crops, farmed until the generations forgot what was immediately under their feet.

There is strong evidence that these timbers and ceilings suffered a fire shortly after the death of the First Emperor. Historical accounts indicate that General Xiang Yu looted the royal tomb and torched the underground vaults in 206 B.C. in a failed campaign to succeed to power. (The first emperor of the Han Dynasty soon gained the upper hand.)

Several of the figures unearthed in Vault 2 have been put on special display in glass cases on the visitor mezzanine. The kneeling archer is dynamic, the goateed officer is dashing, and the general is commanding, but I prefer the cavalryman and his horse. The stylized steeds of Qin Shi Huang's army, said to be modeled on the desert horses of Gansu Province, are plump, vivacious, and fluid, just the sort of horse I'd choose for battle—and for beauty.

Vault 3

The third vault is the smallest. It apparently served as the command post. Most of its 68 figures appear to be officers, based on their dress and height. Higher-ranking officers stand taller than those of lower rank. Ordinary soldiers are clad in scaly armor so finely sculpted that the head and stem of each nail are distinct. Generals are clad in war robes, double-tailed caps, and massive square shoes turned up at the toes like soaring tiled roofs. Their magnificent wooden chariot and its four horses wait in attendance.

The figures appear to be in consultation, devising strategies of war, an art that the first emperor pursued brilliantly and single-mindedly, as he swiftly and often ruthlessly brought all the warlords and kingdoms of China under his rule and molded them into a single Middle Kingdom.

Bronze Chariots

A **museum** in the entrance courtyard (now located to the left of Vault 1) displays one (and sometimes both) of the two bronze chariots found just 20 yards west of the base of the first emperor's burial mound in a 25-foot-deep pit. Half life-sized, pulled by four bronze horses in gold traces, driven by an intricately rendered driver, each two-wheeled chariot is a decorative piece of extraordinary detail and richness. The windows open, the silver latch on the door of the curved bronze compartment turns, even the driver's fingerprints are etched in.

These are presumed to be models of the royal chariots of the time. The *High Chariot* is the one with the bronze umbrella and short cart. The

Comfortable Chariot was designed to carry concealed passengers. The purpose of these models is no longer known, perhaps merely "to keep a drowsy Emperor awake," as the poet Yeats has written.

Future Digs

The local authorities have always kept their plans for future excavations around Xi'an carefully under wraps. Few of the burial mounds of Han and Tang emperors have been opened for science or tourism, including the most intriguing tumulus of all, the First Emperor's.

Qin Shi Huang's burial mound is a tourist site, but there's nothing to see there except a view of the plain from the top and a closer view of the vendors, antique dealers, and folk artists who line the trail to the top. What's inside the tomb—if Qin's successors or later generations of grave robbers haven't already gotten to it—is an ancient city of treasures. China's Grand Historian, Sima Qian, the Herodotus of the Middle Kingdom, has left a vivid account of what the First Emperor took with him and what his city of endless night looked like. Qin reached the throne at age 13. His buried city consumed the days of 700,000 conscripted laborers over the next 36 years. In life, Qin presided over the unification of China. He regulated the currency, the weights and measures, the span of cart axles, and the writing of the language in his new empire. Qin is also remembered for his pitiless persecution of intellectuals and his burning of ancient books. He is credited with completing the Great Wall. But his greatest surviving artifact is his own tomb and the underground armies that guard it.

The Grand Historian gives this account of the First Emperor's tomb:

> The workers dug through three subterranean streams and poured molten copper for the outer coffin, and the tomb was filled with models of palaces, pavilions, and offices, as well as fine vessels, precious stones, and rarities. Artisans were ordered to fix up crossbows so that any thief breaking in would be shot. All the country's rivers, the Yangzi and the Yellow River, were reproduced in quicksilver, and by mechanical means made to flow into a miniature ocean. The heavenly constellations were shown above and the regions of the Earth below. The candles were made of whale oil to insure their burning for the longest time.

We are also told that the emperor's childless concubines and those who worked on the tomb were buried alive. The mausoleum was planted in trees and grass "to make it seem like a hill," as the burial mound does to this day. There is no mention of the buried city walls, of underground palaces, of a vast terra-cotta army standing a mile to the west.

Yet there are tantalizing hints, thanks to recent digs in the area, of what lies buried between the terra-cotta army and the tomb of the old emperor. We know that the burial mound occupies half the area of Qin's underground inner city. Remains of a palace have been detected within the walls of the inner city. An outer city with its own much longer wall, perhaps 3 miles around, encompasses the royal mausoleum. Its contents are largely unknown, although the skeletons of horses and the two priceless bronze chariots were found in these precincts. Outside these walls, more skeletons of horses have been found, indicating that it may be the site of the royal stables, and seven human skeletons have turned up as well, which some think are those of Emperor Qin's own children murdered in a palace intrigue. Ruins of a zoo containing exotic animals and the grave sites of prisoners forced to build the mausoleum have also turned up.

One can envision the day when the entire buried city of China's first imperial dynasty is revealed, although if mass tourism trends continue, Qin's dead capital could become nothing more than an instant theme park. For me, it has always been a dream city anyway. In dreams, I can strip back all the layers of dust and undress the plains of Xi'an; I can stroll among the palaces of jade, the streets of blue brick, the garden walls of stamped brick; and I can tarry in the corridors with a motionless army of kneeling archers, wooden chariots, and vigorous horses, their heads straining, necks glistening, manes forever flying over the grasslands beyond the Great Wall.

PRACTICAL INFORMATION

ORIENTATION

The Museum of the Terra-Cotta Warriors and Horses of Emperor Qin Shi Huang (usually called "the terra-cotta warriors," for short) is located 18 miles east of Xi'an.

The three vaults under excavation cover about 5 acres and contain 8,000 warriors and horses, as well as 6,000 more artifacts (chariots, bridles, weapons, musical instruments).

Photographs inside the vault buildings are strictly forbidden. You can buy sets of slides, photographs, and picture books at concession stands inside and outside the vaults. Official photographers offer to take a group photo with the terra-cotta warriors in the background for RMB 150 ($21). During my most

recent visit, the catwalks were fairly crowded with tourists, and dozens of them (mostly Chinese) were snapping pictures left and right. Several monitors were rushing around the arena screaming at the offenders, but I saw no cameras seized or fines levied (fines run up to $100), and the picture-taking that day continued with little abatement.

There are shops inside all the vault buildings and on the grounds inside the main gate. Outside the gate, where the buses park, a souvenir city flourishes with everything from postcards to folk-art vests and baby slippers for sale. Bartering is expected outside the gates. The stalls seem calm and well regulated compared to the chaos that used to reign here. Stepping off the bus from Xi'an, visitors used to be rushed by a living terra-cotta army of vendors, all shouting "Yi kuai, yi kuai," which means "One yuan, one yuan" (RMB 1). Today's chant is more likely to be "One dollar, one dollar," a good indication of how inflation has taken off in the more prosperous 1990s.

TOURS & STRATAGEMS

Most visitors make the terra-cotta warriors their number one stop when touring Xi'an (see separate chapter), the focus of a half-day or full-day guided tour by bus or car. Two hours are usually spent at the Museum of the Terra-Cotta Warriors, which is enough time for a first visit.

Admissions & Open Hours The museum is open 8am to 6pm daily, with admission paid at the main gate now set at RMB 80 ($9.65) and rising fast. There is a separate admission charged for the hall containing the bronze chariot display (RMB 25/$3).

Tours Tours with English-speaking guides of the terra-cotta warriors can be booked through China International Travel Service (CITS) branches in Xi'an. These are located across from the railway station in the Jiefang Hotel (☎ 029/743-1023) and across from the Bell Tower in the Holiday Inn (☎ 029/727-9200, ext. 2842). Major hotels in Xi'an also have terra-cotta warrior tours.

I took the 4-hour "Terra-Cotta" tour offered by the Shangri-La Golden Flower Hotel, 8 Changle Xi Lu (☎ 029/323-2981). The local guide spoke excellent English, the minibus was in good condition, and the itinerary included 2 hours at the terra-cotta warriors, 1 hour at Banpo Neolithic Village (see chapter on Xi'an), and 1 hour at Huaqing Hotsprings. The price was RMB 340 ($41) per person.

On Your Own Independent travelers can take bus no. 306 or no. 307 from the Xi'an bus station, located at the northern end of Jiefang Lu (RMB 8/$1). These buses use winding country roads to reach the terra-cotta museum, a slow (1 hour) but absorbing route. The new highway, a toll road opened in 1991, is quicker (30 minutes) and smoother, but you'll see fewer faces of farmers along the way—faces that still closely resemble those of the terra-cotta warriors themselves.

Other Sites Nearby Group tours often include other sites as well, particularly **Huaqing Hotsprings,** located a few miles from the terra-cotta warriors at Li Shan (Li Mountain). This used to be an interesting stop, but the old imperial bathhouses are totally remodeled, the massive Nine-Dragon Pool is new, and the surrounding pavilions have received a recent face-lift. Huaqing no longer possesses the atmosphere it once evoked of an ancient summer retreat for Tang emperors and their favorite concubines. It is open daily 8am to 7pm (admission RMB 30/$3.60).

THE SILK ROAD GROTTOES AT MOGAO (DUNHUANG)

莫高石窟

OF THE TOP FOUR BUDDHIST GROTTOES in China, the Mogao caves at Dunhuang are considered supreme. Nevertheless, visitors are often disappointed. The caves containing the priceless wall paintings and sculptures created at this ancient oasis on the Silk Road, honeycombing a sheer cliff face, are all sealed by locked doors. The guides must constantly search for the person with the door key. In a morning or afternoon, one can see only a tiny portion of these treasures locked in the stone. The effect is cumulative, meaning one must be patient, viewing this display cave by cave, piece by piece. At the other three major grottoes—the Yungang caves at Datong, the Longmen caves at Luoyang, and the Buddha Crescent at Dazu—visitors can freely wander in front of magnificent sculptures, open to wide and dramatic views.

Nevertheless, the treasures at Dunhuang—those not shipped abroad by Western explorers at the turn of the 20th century, that is—are the benchmarks of Buddhist art in China, and I was glad to have seen them for myself. Several days' viewing here is more rewarding than a few quick hours, and it helps to arrange the caves in rough chronological order in one's mind. The styles and themes change over the centuries, and with a little background the history of Buddhism and the Silk Road itself unfolds at Dunhuang like chapters in a stone picture book.

The Cave Builders

China's richest treasure house of Buddhist paintings, statues, and manuscripts was created in the Mogao caves 16 miles southeast of Dunhuang over a thousand-year period stretching from the 4th century to the 14th century A.D. Nine dynasties rose and fell over this long period, and the artists of each period contributed. The first cave was hewn in A.D. 366 by Lie Zun, a Buddhist monk who was inspired by the golden rays of the sun illuminating the cliff face. Lie Zun commissioned a fellow pilgrim to paint the walls with holy images, decorating a shrine where he could pray for his safe passage over the Silk Road.

Thus, the purpose of this desert gallery was set from the first—a divine insurance policy for the caravans of the Silk Road. The grottoes had as much to do with business and politics as religion. The rich merchant families and the rulers of Dunhuang sponsored the carving and painting of many of these grottoes. Such acts, no doubt, cast them in a favorable light to Buddhist believers who ran the rich caravan trade. The grottoes functioned as shrines where traders and pilgrims could pray, but above all as a place where Silk Road travelers and merchants could petition for divine protection of their caravans, which faced daunting obstacles in crossing the deserts that loomed east and west of Dunhuang.

Over the centuries, the repute of Dunhuang increased. New dynasties often sent their best artists there to construct and decorate new grottoes to commemorate their rules and cement their commitment to the religious community. Over 45,000 murals and 2,000 statues, fashioned from stucco rather than the loose sandstone of the cliff, have survived, housed in almost 500 caves. The desert air has preserved the art for 15 centuries.

The chief dynasties represented in the art are the Northern Wei (A.D. 386–534), the Western Wei (A.D. 535–557), the Sui (A.D. 581–618), the Tang (A.D. 618–917), and the Five Dynasties (A.D. 907–960). The styles vary with the dynasties. The themes were all derived from the various schools of Buddhism as they arrived and were adapted in China.

The earlier figures of Buddha and his attendants retain a strong Indian influence, rendered in rigid, geometric poses, but the Chinese gradually added movement and realism to these figures that reached their zenith with the Tang artists, who created 213 of the 492 caves that survive. The backgrounds painted on the cave walls flow with cloud scrolls, floral patterns, fantastic landscapes, and architecture that almost from the first came from Chinese models. The main themes are derived from the life of Sakyamuni as he journeys to enlightenment and from the holy manuscripts (sutras) that preach the cosmic doctrines of karma and reincarnation and portray the mortal world as one of vanity, illusion, and suffering.

To heighten depictions of these themes, the Dunhuang painters plastered the walls and ceilings with mixtures of mud, dung, straw, animal hair, and a smooth coating of clay to which they applied tempura (water-based) pigments of vivid blues, yellows, greens, reds, cinnabar vermilions, fleshy pinks, and powdered gold leaf. The statues are made either with plaster over wooden frames or with plaster over figures cut from cave rock. The caves are squarish, often with a large figure of Buddha on a dais at the back and attendants on both sides. The large chambers measure about 30 feet wide and deep, 16 feet high, while the smallest caves are barely the size of a tiny bedroom with ceilings as low as 54 inches. The ceilings may be sharply pitched, lantern shaped, or domed in a series of tapering, concentric squares.

For the casual observer, the main technical point to observe is the evolution of the art from the rigid, narrow, representational figures in the early caves to the rounded, realistically rendered, more human figures portrayed in the later Sui and Tang Dynasty caves, as the gulf between the divine and the earthly all but disappears.

Guardian Angels & Foreign Devils

The history of Buddhist art in China contained in the museum of caves at Dunhuang is part of the larger political history of the Silk Road. As the Tang Dynasty declined, the Silk Road was subject to invasions from Tibetans and groups spreading a new religion, Islam. The Xi Xia Kingdom (1038–1368) gained the upper hand, chasing Buddhists out of Dunhuang. The Mogao caves were abandoned. Monks sealed their documents and sutras in a single cave and fled the invaders. The Dunhuang grottoes remained unused and undiscovered for at least 800 years. Near the beginning of the 20th century, a Daoist monk named Wang Yuanlu, seeking refuge from the famines in Hubei Province, arrived at Dunhuang, and clearing out a cave, discovered a door leading to a dark inner chamber filled with thousands of manuscripts and paintings. The Chinese government, unable to finance the removal of the treasures, ordered Wang to reseal the inner storehouse, but Wang, intent on raising funds to restore the Mogao grottoes, began to sell the treasures to the highest bidders.

It was Westerners who recognized the worth of the newly discovered manuscripts and who came across the Silk Road to snap them up for the museums they represented. Sir Aurel Stein arrived first, in 1907. He purchased silk painted banners, 7,000 scrolls, 500 paintings, and other relics, which he crated up and transferred to the British Library, where they still reside. Paul Pelliot came the next year, selecting paintings and 5,000 scrolls for the Bibliotheque Nationale in Paris. Japanese, Russians, and more Western collectors quickly followed, including Langdon Warner, who removed sculptures and wall paintings and shipped them from Dunhuang to the Fogg Museum at Harvard in 1924.

In the end, Dunhuang was left with virtually no manuscripts. A sutra copied onto paper and dated A.D. 406, and a paper scroll of the Diamond Sutra dated A.D. 868, considered the world's first printed book, are now in England. Fortunately, most of the wall paintings and much of the statuary remains where it was created, in the desert caves of Dunhuang, beyond the reach of foreign specialists who are seen by some as the heroic preservers of a Chinese history that would have been lost otherwise and by others as modern-day raiders of the Silk Road.

Inside the Grottoes

I visited the Mogao caves, 15 miles southwest of Dunhuang, on a bright spring morning. The Mogao grottoes are open daily from 8:30 to 11:30am and 2 to 5pm. Admission (RMB 80/$9.65) included a local guide, an English-speaking student attending the Dunhuang Research Academy, which is devoted to the study of the caves, Dunhuangology having become a major field of study in Chinese archeology. I rented a flashlight at the ticket booth (RMB 3/35¢ with a deposit of RMB 10/$1.20)—the caves are unlighted—and crossed a wooden bridge over the Da River to the sandstone cliff.

All the caves are numbered, although not in any discernible order. The oldest caves are in the central portion of the mile-long cliff. Four tiers of cement walkways with railings, replacing wooden ladders and catwalks in the 1950s, connect the grottoes.

Roughly 40 of the 492 chambers are usually available to tourists, with the guide deciding which ones to visit. Since these are often locked and there are no signposts, a guide is useful, although one can crisscross the platforms on one's own, dropping in at open doors and latching onto various guided groups. There are many interesting caves that are off-limits to ordinary visitors, including Caves 462 and 465, containing figures engaged in sexual union, a representation of divine enlightenment that is a frequent theme of Tantric Buddhism, which was popular during the Yuan Dynasty (1271–1368) when this cave was painted.

The most dramatic sculpture is behind a nine-story wooden pagoda. Decorated with paintings of the zodiac and erected a century ago, the tower of soaring eaves rises to the summit of the sandstone ridge. Inside **(Cave 96)** is a 113-foot-tall Buddha, carved from the sandstone cliffs during the high Tang Dynasty (A.D. 705–781). Seated, wearing the robes of an emperor, this *Maitreya Buddha (Happy Buddha of the Future)* is the fourth largest in the world and the largest single clay sculpture at Dunhuang. It was repainted in the 19th century and its left hand was repaired a decade ago.

Among the caves I was shown, these are of particular note:

Cave 16 is where Wang Yuanlu stumbled onto the treasures of Dunhuang at the beginning of the 20th century. The nine figures on the platform are a recent addition (Qing Dynasty, 1644–1911), but the tile floor is probably from the late Tang (848–906). The west wall is a Five Dynasties (907–960) mural depicting the holy mountain of Wutai Shan, its temples labeled, and the east wall contains portraits of a ruling family of the region from the same period, who sponsored the cave art. The ceiling is decorated in the *Ten Thousand Buddha* motif, the repeated pattern achieved by the use of block stamps or stencils that were painted in. The lotuses decorating the walls date from the 11th century. It was usual for artists of later dynasties to add to or even paint over existing shrines, as space for new caves was eventually exhausted.

Cave 17, linked to the passageway to Cave 16, is where Wang Yuanlu found the trove of scrolls, sutras, and paintings that Sir Aurel Stein and other Westerners bought and shipped to museums abroad, starting in 1907.

Caves 61, 62, and **63** date from the Yuan Dynasty (1271–1368), when the Mongols seized control of China. The statues, presumably posed in the sexual positions favored by Tantric Buddhism at the time, were demolished by Moslems. The 40-foot-long wall mural of the holy mountain of Wutai Shan, its scores of temples labeled, is splendid and dates from the Northern Song (960–1127) when Dunhuang's ruling family opened a painting academy devoted solely to artwork in the Mogao grottoes.

Cave 98 is from the Five Dynasties (907–960). The ceiling is funnel shaped. The Cao Yi Jin family, high officials of the period at Dunhuang, sponsored this and several other caves, notably Cave 427. The wall portraits are of the ruling family of Khotan, a city on the Silk Road. The king wears a beaded hat. There are also lively scenes of female musicians and a royal hunting party.

Cave 130 contains a magnificent Buddha, 86 feet high, carved during the high Tang period (705–781). The platform and statue are original, except for the Buddha's right hand, which broke and was replaced during the Northern Song (960–1279). The murals on the side walls are also from the Northern Song. This is the second tallest statue at Dunhuang, and it can be appreciated from the ground or from the two upper galleries. The head measures 22 feet high, the ears 6 feet.

Cave 148 contains the 53-foot-long, golden-faced *Sleeping Buddha of Dunhuang*. It was carved in 755 to portray Buddha about to enter Nirvana. Seventy-two disciples are in attendance. The east wall contains a painting of the Western Paradise, the Buddhist "heaven."

Cave 152 features a passageway with tiles and ceiling paintings from the Northern Song (960–1127), with two Daoist figures in the back chamber.

Cave 237 has a statue of Guanyin, Goddess of Mercy, in its center, with Manjusri, God of War, riding a lion, and Pusan, God of Compassion, atop the holy mountain of Emei Shan. These figures were added during the Qing (1644–1911) in a cave whose wall paintings of the Buddha and the Western Paradise were placed here in the middle Tang (781–848).

Cave 257, with a pillar in the center, contains unretouched paintings from the Northern Wei (A.D. 386–534), some of the oldest art at Dunhuang. The figures are dressed in Indian clothing, and the facial features are not Chinese. The mural on the west wall portrays the story of a drowning man rescued by the Deer King, a representation of Buddha.

Cave 259, said to contain the oldest artwork at Dunhuang, holds several statues of Buddha carved during the Northern Wei (A.D. 386–534). The figures are stiff, the heads squarish, the nose hooked, the lips curled (into a smile often compared to that of the *Mona Lisa*)—all characteristics of the Buddhist sculpture in India at the time.

Cave 427 was a gift from the Cao family, high officials at Dunhuang during the Northern Song (960–1279) who controlled the Silk Road routes for 120 years. Husband, wife, and family are portrayed on the front passage walls. A pillar holds up the gabled roof over the chamber at the back, which contains nine stately, long-bodied statues of Buddha, sculpted during the Sui Dynasty (A.D. 581–618). The three figures in the middle are *Buddhas of the Present;* the three on the left, *Buddhas of the Past;* and the three on the right, *Buddhas of the Future.*

Cave 428 has a lotus and peacock ceiling and stamped clay figures of the *Ten Thousand Buddhas* on the walls, but its attraction is the picture of court life given in the Northern Zhou Dynasty (A.D. 557–581), a brief period linking the Wei and Sui dynasties from which little survives. Over 4,000 royal contributors to the cave art are pictured on the east wall, along with the halls and pavilions of the time. There is also a panel depicting the story of three brothers who hunt a tiger. One brother unselfishly gives his life to the tiger so that she can feed her cubs, and he is reborn as Buddha. My guide told me that in 1922 white Russians fleeing the revolution bivouacked in this and other caves, which they blackened with fires, damaged with bullets, and stripped of gold leaf.

Morning or afternoon tours generally take in just a dozen of these and other caves, hardly enough to gain a full appreciation of what exists at Dunhuang. Spend a second day, if possible, and by all means visit the museum at the entrance to the site, a joint venture between China and Japan, opened in 1995. The **Research and Exhibition Center** (open daily 9am to 5pm) contains lighted replicas of seven caves, copies of the missing manuscripts, and relics from the caves. A tour of the center (RMB 20/$2.40) helps put the intricate and complex desert gallery into perspective.

I once covered 17 grottoes in 2 hours with a local guide, but this proved too rapid to enjoy and study the paintings, particularly the details in the murals. At Dunhuang, it is the paintings that dominate. At other grottoes, it is the sculpture, much of it on a grander and more prolific scale than at Dunhuang. But the painted miniatures of Mogao, in hundreds of caves, record thousands of stories and scenes from the days of the Silk Road that are otherwise lost. Inspired by the sutras carried across mountains and desert into China on the backs of early pilgrims, artists for nine centuries painted their best work on the walls of these caves. The holiest shrines of the Silk Road are also its supreme works of art.

PRACTICAL INFORMATION

ORIENTATION

The Mogao caves (Mogao Ku) are located 15 miles southeast of Dunhuang, a desert oasis in northwest Gansu Province on the Silk Road, 1,500 miles west of Beijing. Summers are quite hot, but July and August are high season for tourists, mainly those from China, Japan, and other parts of Asia. May and October are more pleasant and less crowded months to visit.

GETTING THERE

By Plane   There are direct flights to Dunhuang from Xi'an (3 hours), Beijing (4 hours), and other cities in China, particularly during the summer.

By Train   The main train line through Gansu Province stops well north of Dunhuang at **Liuyuan**. Frequent **buses** make the 80-mile transfer to Dunhuang in about 3 hours. From Liuyuan, it is a 36-hour train ride to Xi'an, 57 hours to Beijing, and 16 hours in the other direction (west) to Urumqi.

TOURS & STRATAGEMS

Most Westerners reach Dunhuang and the Mogao caves on group tours of the Silk Road. I booked an independent tour of the Silk Road from China Travel Service (CTS) in Xi'an. See the introduction to the Silk Road chapters for details.

Tours   China International Travel Service (CITS) has a branch in Dunhuang at 1 Dong Dajie (☎ 0937/882-2494).

They can provide local transport and guides to the Mogao caves. The tour desk at the Dunhuang Hotel, 14 Yangguan Dong Lu (☎ 0937/882-2538), is most experienced with Western travelers.

Any minibus or taxi driver hailed in the streets of Dunhuang knows the way to the Mogao caves. They should charge a fare of no more than RMB 20 ($2.50). At the caves, English-speaking guides are assigned to visitors at the main ticket booth.

Visitor Information   Photography is strictly prohibited. Cameras and all bags, including purses, must be checked at the ticket booth. An RMB 2 (25¢) deposit is required.

WHERE TO STAY & DINE

The best accommodations are at the Dunhuang Hotel. See the chapter on Crescent Moon Lake under "Silk Road Caravan" for information.

If you are staying the full day at the Mogao caves, either pack a lunch or try one of the cafes or stands near the ticket booth.

THE STONE SCULPTURES AT YUNGANG (DATONG)

云岗

THE MOST SPECTACULAR ARRAY OF ancient stone carvings in China is at the Yungang caves, 10 miles west of the northern coal city of Datong. There, 40,000 workers and artists set to work on a sandstone cliff, beginning in A.D. 460, chiseling out caves and sculpting huge Buddhist statues from stone on a scale not attempted previously. Datong was then capital of the Northern Wei Dynasty (A.D. 386–534). More than 51,000 statues remain at Yungang, most of them completed by the time the rulers moved their capital south to Luoyang, in A.D. 494, where they set about carving another major Buddhist grotto at Longmen, although the work at Yungang continued until A.D. 525.

The massive figures at Yungang are rounded, lively human images. Many have sharp noses and beards, features of Indian and Persian, rather than Chinese, origin. Many of the craftsmen came to Datong from Central Asia, crossing the Silk Road into northern China over the same route that Buddhism itself traveled. The first caves, however, were finished under the direction of a brilliant local monk, Tan Ho, who is credited with creating the most monumental images of Buddha and with initiating the earliest stone-carved caves in China.

The caves face south. On the bluff above, there are earthen sections of the Great Wall, plowing across the sands like ocean liners stranded in a desert. *Yungang* means "Cloud Hill." Centuries of wind-blown sand and dust have eroded the openings of the caves, once protected by wooden pavilions. The statues inside are open to the elements and to the eyes of visitors. The 53 major caves cover a half mile of the weathered cliff face.

Confucians, who dominated the class of scholars and officials for nearly 1,500 years after the Yungang caves were completed, sneered at the carvings as the height of folly rather than wisdom, dismissing them as if the caves were a big comic book for the superstitious. The carvings were created by a non-Chinese dynasty (the "barbarian" Toba tribe from north of the Great Wall) and based on a foreign religion (Buddhism from India). Thus, the sculptures at Datong were ignored for centuries, not studied seriously until a scholar from Japan, Isoto Chuta, arrived in 1903. Western art dealers followed, crating up several dozen statues and the heads of nearly 700 Buddhas and their religious attendants for shipment to Europe, America, and Japan, where they still remain in various collections. Even so, most of the art is still in place at Yungang.

The Yungang caves were built as an illustration of the Northern Wei Dynasty's power and its dedication to Buddhism as the state religion. Emperor Wen Cheng appointed Tan Hao as China's religious leader, and Tan Hao responded by ordering five statues carved in the cliffs representing the emperor's five predecessors, who had been regarded as living Buddhas. These five monuments are located today in the center of the Yungang grottoes **(Caves 16–20),** barely changed after 15 centuries.

The Eastern Grottoes

I toured the Yungang caves one morning with two Austrian geologists I met on the overnight train up from Xi'an. They had not been impressed by the desolate landscape of Shanxi Province or by the sights of poor Datong. At the caves, however, they were overwhelmed. I was impressed, too. Here at last was a site worthy of Old China, a stone gallery as vibrant today as it was 1,500 years ago.

We began our walk along the cliffs at the eastern end, to the right of the main entrance. Local guides proved unnecessary. There were plenty of signs in English and even a large signpost with a bilingual map of Yungang. The first four caves **(Caves 1–4),** set apart from the rest by a ravine that slashes through the cliff, are not spectacular. **Cave 3,** however, is the largest at the site, 43 feet high inside (the cliff looming to a height of 80 feet at this point). The Monastery of the Enchanted Cliff once stood inside, and Tan Hao himself taught Buddhism here. Three Buddhas remain in **Cave 3.** The central Buddha, seated, one hand raised to his chest, is 30 feet tall. The carving of these statues may have occurred during the Sui Dynasty (A.D. 589–618) as an act of contrition by an emperor who murdered his father.

The Central Grottoes

Caves 5, 6, and **7** are more dramatic than the first four to the east. The Old Monastery of the Stone Buddhas, built in 1652, is located here, and three wooden towers cover the cliffside, protecting the cave entrances. At one time, many temples fronted the cliff, but only this monastery remains. We wandered through its small courtyards, where monks and vendors had pitched their prayer bead and soda stands, and entered **Cave 5,** where a 55-foot-tall Buddha with red eyes, blue hair, and a gold face illuminates the shadows. The image is arresting, even terrifying. Yungang's largest Buddha—with ears 10 feet long—was probably built to honor one of the Northern Wei emperors. The bas-relief sculptures that decorate the walls of the cave are delicately carved, and their abundance is typical of the Yungang style.

Cave 6 is equally impressive. At the entrance, Emperor Kangxi, who visited in 1697, inscribed four characters meaning "the grand unity of all doctrines." Inside, there is a 49-foot-high square tower carved from rock in the center of the square chamber. The wall and the pillar are densely decorated in ornate carvings with stories from the life of Buddha, vividly rendered in deep relief.

Caves 7 and **8** form a pair that fuses Indian and Chinese art. The Indian gods Shiva, with five faces and six arms, and Vishnu, with three faces and eight arms, ride an eagle and a bull, popular figures from Han Dynasty Chinese sculpture. Shiva and Vishnu are posted at the entrance to **Cave 8;** two carved lions lie contentedly at the foot of Buddha in **Cave 7.**

The remaining caves along the eastern wall **(Caves 9–15)** are richly adorned in a sea of fine bas-relief and statuary, all carved from stone and often painted in bright colors applied by a 19th-century donor. Hundreds of *apsareses* (Buddhist angels) swirl up the cave walls and across the ceilings. Buddha's followers ride elephants and meditate atop lotus flowers in a universe of plants, animals, and flowing designs. **Cave 12** contains wall carvings of 5th-century palaces and a splendid mural of musicians accompanying Buddha on ancient flutes, drums, and lutes. The large Buddha sitting cross-legged in **Cave 13** has his right arm supported by a four-armed figure standing on his knee, an innovation in Chinese sculpture found first at Yungang. **Caves 14** and **15** are heavily eroded, their front walls crumbling over the centuries, but both retain thousands of carved figures in their niches.

The Western Grottoes

The caves at the far western end of the cliff are small and far less magnificent than those to the east. Many of them are badly eroded inside. **Cave 21** is the most impressive of the group. A tapered five-story pagoda stands in the center, its peak a lotus flower touching the ceiling. **Cave 50,** a hike up the end of the sandstone ridge, is worth a peek, too. Its walls are carved with acrobats and its ceiling with angels, birds, and flying elephants, making it a kind of stone Big Top.

The most striking caves, however, are on the western side but nearer the center: **Caves 16–20,** the first five caves carved at Yungang, their large Buddhas inside commemorating the first five emperors of the Northern Wei. These caves form a unified cluster. **Cave 16** on the right is filled with a 43-foot-high standing Buddha, one arm flung outward. The figure has a heavy appearance. His face is round, his eyes set deep. The lower portions of his body have suffered severe erosion, making it appear as if he were emerging from the dust. **Cave 17,** finished in A.D. 480 according to its inscription, contains an even more massive Buddha, 50 feet tall, sitting with legs crossed, with a smaller attendant on either side. In **Cave 18,** the most impressive of the five Buddhas stands on a lotus flower, symbol of beauty flowering out of the muck that constitutes the earthly realm. His legs are short and massive, contributing to his powerful being. The folds of his robe are carved with processions of bodhisattvas (followers who have achieved enlightenment but chosen to return to Earth to inspire others). The four bodhisattvas who attend the Buddha are the most fully humanized and lively figures at Yungang. The monstrously divine and the merely human seem to meet in this shrine.

Cave 19 consists of three chambers. A 55-foot-tall Buddha sits in the middle, where surrounding walls, their niches filled with bodhisattvas, resemble the cells of a beehive. The caves to either side are elevated 16 feet off the ground and open like enormous second-story windows to reveal the 26-foot bodhisattvas inside.

The final cave on the west side of this cluster, **Cave 20,** is scarcely a cavern at all. An earthquake removed the front of this cave. The Buddha sits exposed in a huge halo-shaped niche. Seated, hands on legs, this 35-foot image of the Buddha has shoulders 20 feet wide. He seems set in an immobile eternity, his huge drooping ears a symbol of the worldly decorations he has cast off.

A student from Datong, noticing us as we eyed the smiling statue, said this was the Buddha of the Present. On the right, he said, the Buddha of the Past stands against the surviving wall, one hand raised. On the left, there was no figure. The Buddha of the Future, the student said, has been erased.

Perhaps so. It would be fitting. The carved figures of Yungang reflect the glories of the past as resoundingly as any monuments in China. This grandeur is revived in the present for those who visit and see what remains with their own eyes. Nothing like this exists outside, in the uninscribed deserts of the future.

PRACTICAL INFORMATION

ORIENTATION

The Yungang caves are 10 miles west of Datong, which is 200 miles west of Beijing. See the Datong chapter and also see the Heng Shan Bei chapter. The best months to visit are May and October, since winters are quite cold and summers are very hot and dusty.

GETTING THERE

There is no airport at Datong. The express train from Beijing takes 7 hours; the overnight train from Xi'an requires 19 hours. The caves are near Datong. Local tours are inexpensive to arrange (see below). The no. 2 bus, with frequent departures from Datong's northern train station, takes more than 30 minutes to travel the 10 miles but costs just RMB 8 (95¢). Taxis are quicker and cost about RMB 20 ($2.40).

TOURS & STRATAGEMS

Admissions & Hours   Admission to the Yungang caves is RMB 25 ($3) and they are open daily 9am to 5pm.

Tours   At Datong, China International Travel Service (CITS) has efficient offices in the Yungang Hotel, 21 Yingbin Dong Lu (☎ 0352/502-4176), and at the train station (☎ 0352/502-2265; fax 0352/502-2046). I used the CITS office at the train station to arrange transportation to and from the Yungang caves, with good results.

CITS also offers a guided tour with car and driver to the caves and other sights for RMB 100 ($12) per person. The fee does not include lunch or admission. The tour takes about 6 hours, leaving at 8am, returning at 2pm.

WHERE TO STAY & DINE

Visitors to the caves stay in Datong, where the best hotel is the Yungang Hotel. See the chapter, "Datong: Temple of the 'Big Same,'" for complete information. If you are going to be at the caves during lunch, you're best off packing food purchased ahead of time at the Yungang Hotel. There are no cafes at the cave site, although Chinese snacks and drinks are sold at kiosks.

The Buddhist Caves
at Longmen (Luoyang)
龙门

AFTER CREATING ITS MASTERPIECE OF Buddhist cave art in Datong, the Northern Wei Dynasty moved its capital south to Luoyang in A.D. 494 and began construction of a second sculptural gallery, the Longmen caves. The project turned out to be even more ambitious. Today, 1,352 caves survive, and nearly 100,000 statues have been catalogued, twice the repository left at the Yungang caves in Datong. The larger scale is explained by the longevity of the project: More than half the carvings at Longmen date from the much later Tang Dynasty period (A.D. 618–907), when Chinese art and sculpture reached its zenith.

The Northern Wei artists set to work at a limestone cliff running a half mile north to south along the west bank of the Yi River (known as the Dragon's Gate), 9 miles south of Luoyang. As at the other great Buddhist caves, Longmen was raided by Western art collectors in the early 20th century. Thousands of the holy figures were decapitated, their heads sawn off, crated up, and shipped abroad. An entire cave tableau is now on display in New York City at the Metropolitan Museum of Art.

Emperors, generals, rich clans, and devoted Buddhist leaders all took a hand at creating these shrines for political and social purposes. The carvings cover a history of over 500 years. There are no signposts to help foreign visitors, but the caves are laid out in major clusters, reflecting successive periods of construction. The caves are not deep. Centuries of erosion, flooding, and earthquakes have exposed most of the large figures to the sky, the caves receding to large oval niches. Hundreds of small niches pock the cliff face as well. At dawn, when Longmen can be viewed from a distance on the east side of the Dragon's Gate, the rays of the rising sun turn the entire ridge into a golden beehive. The cruder, more rounded figures were carved earliest, in the 5th and 6th centuries. The more complex, ornate, and lively statues date from the 7th and 8th centuries, when Tang art was in flower.

Luoyang

I reach the ancient capital of Luoyang by train, traveling east from another old seat of dynastic power, Xi'an. This is the route that the royal court took in the later days of the Tang Dynasty as its members came to favor Luoyang over the imperial capital of Xi'an as their residence. Luoyang gives almost no impression of its royal past these days. Its landmarks are a tractor factory (China's first), a ball-bearing works, a mining machinery plant. Little is left of the old capital where Daoist founder Lao Zi ran the library 2,500 years ago; where the Han Dynasty Imperial College enrolled 30,000 of the nation's finest scholars in the 1st century A.D.; where the Northern Wei Dynasty opened 1,367 Buddhist temples; where the Sui emperor connected his palace to the Grand Canal so that officials and merchants could sail from the middle of China northeast to Beijing and southeast to Hangzhou in the 6th century; where for 934 years Luoyang was truly the central point of the Chinese imperial compass. Old Luoyang has made way for a thousand factories. A million residents are entering the industrial age. The peonies transported from Xi'an by decree of the Empress Wu in the 7th century are famous here still, but the legendary Seven Sages of the Bamboo Grove, who removed themselves from the political turmoil of the Jin Dynasty (A.D. 265–316) to devote themselves to poetry and music, aren't drinking wine and scribbling in Luoyang anymore. Their bamboo groves have been bulldozed down.

Nevertheless, I come to Luoyang in search of history and beauty, which I hope to find in the unaltered countryside at the Longmen caves. I check into the Youyi Binguan, the Friendship Hotel, and eat breakfast in a hall called the Western Dancing Restaurant (its logo, two square dancers in cowboy boots). The booths, covered in orange vinyl, are too low and too deep to be comfortable. Outside, I cross a public park, filled with trees but not a single blade of grass, and catch the no. 60 bus to the caves.

Bingyang Grottoes

The main entrance to Longmen is at the northern end of the cliff, where the road from Luoyang crosses the river. The bus stops on the east side of the bridge and I walk back to the ticket booth. Spacious cement-and-stone walkways lead southward along the riverbanks. The large caves are protected by railings. Dozens of stone figures tower over the walkway, which has the look of a petrified Macy's Thanksgiving Day parade with the large floats and balloons turned to stone.

The first cave on the right, **Qianqi Si (Qianqi Temple),** was carved in the early Tang in A.D. 641. Buddha sits on a stone platform, draped in graceful folds. His attendants—bodhisattvas who have reached Nirvana

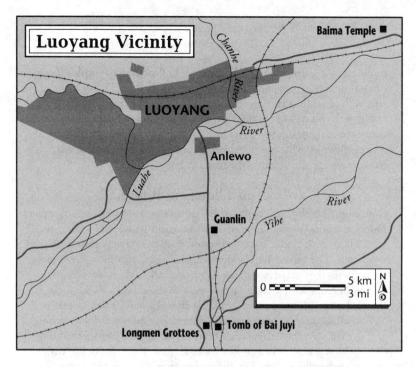

Luoyang Vicinity

Baima Temple ■

Chanhe River

LUOYANG

River

Anlewo

Luahe

River

Guanlin
■

Yihe

0 ▭▭▭▭ 5 km
           3 mi

N

Longmen Grottoes ■ ■ Tomb of Bai Juyi

but returned to Earth to show others the path to enlightenment—are elegantly carved female figures.

The next three works, the **Bingyang caves,** are a massive cluster with many Buddhist figures. *Bingyang* means "Greeting the Sun," as these east-facing monuments do. The first of the three caves is one of the earliest in Longmen, begun around A.D. 500, although many of the figures were not finished until 150 years later. The bare-chested Buddha seated in the middle of the first cave measures 24 feet tall.

The middle Bingyang cave is also among the earliest carved here. An inscription claims that 802,366 craftsmen labored on it for over 20 years. The result is a shrine containing 11 Buddhas. The magnificently robed Buddha seated at the center in the lotus position, one hand raised to Heaven, the other stretched toward the Earth, is 26 feet high. His smiling face is surrounded by a halo. A fiery halo is carved on the cave wall behind, framing Buddha's head. Angelic creatures, the Buddhist angels known as *apsareses,* fly across the half-dome ceiling. In 1935, a large section of this cave with carvings and statues of figures adoring the Buddha was removed and shipped to the United States. Among the missing are the praying figures of the cave's patron, Northern Wei Emperor Xuan Wu and his wife.

The southern Bingyang cave is less richly adorned. It dates from the Northern Wei as well, but the Buddha at its center seems rather tired and sleepy, more weighed down than buoyant. The Bingyang triptych is followed by the **Jingshan Si (Veneration of Goodness Temple) Cave,** carved out in the 7th century at the beginning of the Tang Dynasty. Guardians of the Buddhist faith, swords raised, are carved in relief, but they did not have the power to keep out Western art collectors who have beheaded many of the figures in this cave. It is difficult after viewing Longmen to innocently enjoy what was taken from it and placed on museum pedestals halfway around the world in the name of preservation.

Cave of Ten Thousand Buddhas

Continuing south, I reach one of Longmen's greatest treasures, **Wanfo Dong,** the aptly named Cave of Ten Thousand Buddhas. In fact, there are 15,000 small Buddhas carved into the walls of this profusely decorated cave. The ceiling itself blooms with a single vast lotus flower, inscribed with the date of its carving, A.D. 680. Each of the 54 lotuses on the back wall erupt with a bodhisattva figure in the middle. Buddha sits at the center on a lotus throne, its panels stamped and carved in the *Ten Thousand Buddha* pattern, with seated musicians below and a dancer in swirling silks. At the entrance is a headless statue of Guanyin, the Goddess of Mercy, vibrant in her pose, sweeping away the flies of life with a swatter and sprinkling the life-giving dew from a bottle. Her statue was carved in A.D. 681, as a commission of the Empress Wu Zetian.

Empress Wu ruled China at the end of the 7th century, subjugating her Tang Dynasty consort Gao Zong and pursuing her devotion to Buddhism by overseeing the construction of thousands of temples and shrines. She is known as a ruthless monarch, the leading figure in many palace intrigues and love affairs. Luoyang became her second capital (after Xi'an) and she spent much of China's treasury supporting Buddhism here, initiating many of the splendid caves and sculptures at Longmen.

Next door to the Cave of Ten Thousand Buddhas is the **Lotus Flower Cave,** which also features a flower on the ceiling. The standing Buddha has been decapitated and the forearms are missing. A fiery halo surrounds the entire body, emphasizing its divine purity. This cave is of earlier origin than its next-door neighbor to the north, having been chiseled out in A.D. 527 when the Northern Wei still held sway.

The Big Cave

The next major cave to the south is **Juxian Cave (Honoring Ancestors),** by far the largest at Longmen. The opening is 100 feet wide. The Buddha inside stands 56 feet tall. This is Empress Wu's grandest creation at Longmen, carved in A.D. 675 and paid for out of her allotment for cosmetics. The celestial guardian who defends the faith, located on the north wall, is a splendid and fierce sculpture. He carries a pagoda in his right hand and tramples a demon under his foot, his left hand defiantly planted on his waist. In her day Empress Wu entered this shrine through the back of a wooden temple. Never humble, Empress Wu is said to have ordered the sculptor to use her face as the model for that of the colossal Buddha. Art experts consider these figures the best ever sculpted during the Tang Dynasty. They are indeed realistic figures emanating power, highly decorated, finely detailed, and naturalistically posed. The large Buddha itself is serene and remote by contrast, elevated by the artist to a higher realm.

Caves of Medicine & Fire

The remaining caves to the south are small. The entrance to the **Medicine Cave (Yao Fang Dong)** is engraved with prescriptions for 120 diseases, ranging from diabetes to madness, from the pharmacies of the mid-6th century. The Buddha and his attendants inside date from several dynasties, including the Northern Wei and the Tang.

The **Guyang Cave** is probably the oldest cave open at Longmen, dating from A.D. 495, and also one of the newest. The Buddha at the center lost his head along the way, but during the last dynasty, the Qing (1644–1911), it was restored. The new head is said to resemble that of the ancient founder of Daoism, Lao Zi, and the cave is locally referred to as Lao Zi's den.

The **Fire-Burnt Cave (Huo Shao Dong)** next door was also carved early, about A.D. 522. Blackened, it appears to have been struck by lightning. The **Stone Room Temple Cave (Shi Ku Si Dong)** has a fine adoration theme in which a procession of officials in high hats, ladies in long gowns, and court attendants carry umbrellas, fans, and lotus flowers to honor Buddha. In the last cave, Ludong, which has an inscription from A.D. 539, there are wall carvings of the halls and pavilions of the time, used to illustrate Buddha's mortal journey through life as Sakyamuni. It is also decorated with carvings in the halo flame design, which burns across the walls of the caves of Longmen like the morning sun.

Several hours of cave-viewing whet my appetite. I sit down on a low stool in front of a table where two peasant ladies smile at me as they scoop up a bowl of cold noodles topped with a hot red paste. They are happy to have me, their only customer at noon, and they don't even bother to ask where I'm from, what I do, or how many children I have—the usual questions asked of lone foreigners. Perhaps they know nothing of the West. A vendor joins me. A portrait photographer, he tethers his brown horse to the trunk, which contains the imperial costumes in which he decks out his customers. The sun is high and fierce. The golden ridge of Longmen turns a dismal yellow-gray, the lifeless color of the surrounding sands. I walk north to the bridge over the Dragon's Gate River. The fire that ignites this ancient gallery of gigantic Buddhas and lotus flowers has been swallowed by the throats of a thousand silent caves, and even the voice of the most powerful empress in China is drowned in the whisper of the wind that pulls the sands across the long cliff like a curtain.

PRACTICAL INFORMATION

ORIENTATION

The Longmen caves lie 9 miles south of **Luoyang,** an ancient capital in Henan Province, 200 miles east of Xi'an and 550 miles west of Shanghai. The Yellow River passes about 50 miles to the north. Summers are hot and humid here. Dust storms are common in the spring. Late fall and early winter are the best times to visit.

Song Shan, the Central Mountain of the Five Sacred Mountains of China and home to the celebrated kung-fu temple at Shao Lin, is just 50 miles east of the Longmen caves. If you travel to Luoyang, the Longmen caves and Song Shan (including the Shao Lin Monastery) are musts. See the separate chapter on Song Shan.

GETTING THERE

By Plane   The small airport north of Luoyang receives several flights each week from Beijing (1 hour 40 minutes), Guangzhou (2 hours 45 minutes), and a few other cities in China. In the summer there are charter flights from Hong Kong (2 hours 20 minutes). The nearest major airport is in Zhengzhou, 100 miles west.

By Train   Luoyang is well served by trains. Express trains arrive from Beijing (14 hours), Shanghai (18 hours), Xi'an (6 hours), and Zhengzhou (2 hours). Taxis or minibuses from the train station to hotels cost RMB 20 to RMB 50 ($2.40 to $6).

TOURS & STRATAGEMS

The Longmen caves are a day trip from the city of Luoyang.
Admission & Open Hours   The Longmen caves are open 8am to 6pm daily. The admission is RMB 25 ($3). By far the best time to view the caves, which face east, is in the morning. Arrive by 8am if possible. The rising sun illuminates the fading paint on the intricate carvings.
Tours   China International Travel Service (CITS) has helpful branches in the Friendship Hotel, 6 Xiyuan Xi Lu (☎ 0379/491-3701), and the Peony Hotel, 15 Zhong Zhou Xi Lu (☎ 0379/491-3699). They can provide guided tours to the Longmen caves (RMB 240–480/

$30–$60 per person, depending on the size of the group).
On Your Own   Public buses cover the 9-mile distance from Luoyang to the Longmen caves in 35 to 45 minutes (making many stops on the way). The fare is about RMB 10 ($1.20), depending on the exact departure point. Bus no. 60 stops by the park across from the Friendship Hotel. Bus nos. 53 and 81 also connect Luoyang to Longmen. The return route and bus numbers are the same.

Taxis can also be hired from hotel desks or in the street. The fare is highly negotiable but should be below RMB 250 ($30) for the round-trip.

WHERE TO STAY

Five-star and 4-star hotels of international quality are on the drawing board, but for now you have your pick of two 3-star hotels.

Friendship Hotel (Youyi Binguan).
6 Xiyuan Xi Lu (2 miles west of city center). ☎ *0379/491-2780. Fax 0379/491-3808. 325 rms. A/C TV TEL. $65 double. AE, JCB, MC, V.* This hotel dates back to the 1950s, when hotels for foreigners in China were built with help from the Russians. The four-story West Building dates from that period and it is terribly run-down. Insist on staying in the newer East Building. The rooms are large but still not well maintained. The tub/shower combinations are modern. The hotel has an exercise room, an outdoor pool in the summer, bicycles for rent, and a foreign exchange counter. The uniformed staff will help arrange tours and the hire of private cars.

Peony Hotel (Mudan Dajiudian). *15 Zhong Zhou Xi Lu (1 mile west of city center).* ☎ *0379/401-3699. Fax 0379/401-3668. 196 rms. A/C MINIBAR TV TEL. $100 double. AE, DC, JCB, MC, V.* The 17-story Peony, opened in 1990, is more modern, better located, and a bit more luxurious than the Friendship Hotel. The rooms are smaller. There's a health club with exercise machines, a tour desk, a gift shop, and a foreign exchange counter.

WHERE TO DINE

The Friendship Hotel (☎ 0379/491-2780) and the Peony Hotel (☎ 0379/401-3699) have good **Chinese restaurants** with English-language menus. The Peony Hotel's restaurant is more expensive ($20 to $30 per person for dinner). Western food is served at both hotels as well.

Along the main downtown street, Zhong Zhou Zhong Lu, there are several restaurants that serve foreigners and provide English-language menus. Two friendly places here are the **HM** restaurant, serving Western dishes, and the **Xuangong** restaurant, serving Chinese dishes. Both charge RMB 35 to 67 ($4 to $8) for main courses.

At the Longmen caves, there are **stalls** selling cold noodle dishes (RMB 5/60¢), soft drinks, bottled water, and tea.

DAZU: THE SLEEPING BUDDHA OF PRECIOUS MOUNTAIN
大足

OVER THE CENTURIES BUDDHIST pilgrims who journeyed to the holiest shrines in Western China obeyed a famous dictum: "Go up to Emei Shan, go down to Baoding Shan." Emei Shan is one of Buddhism's four sacred mountains, while Baoding Shan (Precious Mountain) at Dazu is one of China's four great centers of Buddhist sculpture. These sacred carvings are located in Sichuan Province in western China, in Dazu District, about halfway between the cities of Chengdu and Chongqing. Dazu is not a convenient location for the traveler, but its countryside remoteness is part of its attraction, a fine reason to head into the Chinese countryside. Moreover, for anyone fascinated by the monumental remnants of Old China, of which so few survive, Dazu and its Baoding Shan sculptures are a must.

Baoding Shan possesses the best of the sacred carvings in Dazu, containing about 10,000 of the over 50,000 religious sculptures scattered throughout this highland district. Compared with the other major rock carvings at Dunhuang, Louyang, and Longmen, the Dazu specimens are of the most recent composition and are arranged in the most compact arena for viewing. This concentration of thousands of carved images within a natural amphitheater enhances the visual intensity of Dazu. Dazu's carvings are also the most realistic of the great holy sculptures, the least abstract and rigid, the most earthy and human, with the broadest social context.

While rock carving began in Dazu during the Tang Dynasty (in the 7th century A.D.) and continued well into the Qing Dynasty (China's last imperial epoch), the sculptures here reached their artistic zenith during the Southern Song Dynasty (1127–1279), when the sculptors turned their attention to creating the unusually unified, compact, and colorful Buddhist grotto at Baoding Shan.

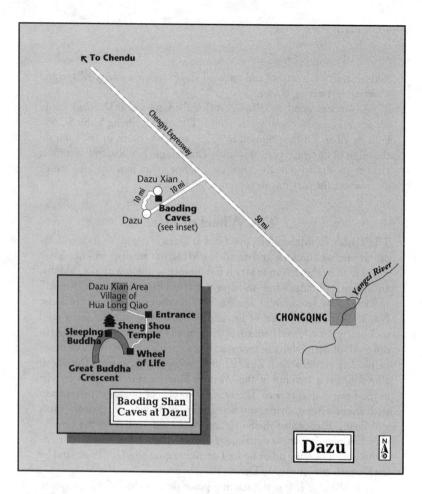

To Chendu

Chengyu Expressway

Dazu Xian

10 mi

10 mi

Baoding
Caves
(see inset)

Dazu

50 mi

Yangzi River

Dazu Xian Area
Village of
Hua Long Qiao

Entrance

Sleeping
Buddha

Sheng Shou
Temple

Wheel
of Life

Great Buddha
Crescent

Baoding Shan
Caves at Dazu

CHONGQING

Dazu

N

Great Buddha Crescent

A friend and I set out for Dazu early one morning from Chongqing. We hired a local taxi for the 70-mile journey, which despite the good roads consumed almost 3 hours in either direction. At Dazu Xian, we parked in the village of Hua Long Qiao (Dragon Flower Bridge) and walked to the grotto entrance. The main gate and temple are set on a ridge above a stream. On the other side of the gate, worshippers were burning incense while kneeling before small images in rock alcoves. Below us the pathway to the Buddhist grottoes wound downward into a lush river valley.

Zhao Zhifeng, a monk well versed in Tantric (Esoteric) Buddhism, launched this last great venture in outdoor religious sculpture more than seven centuries ago. The work required 70 years to complete. The setting Zhao Zhifeng selected is dramatic enough: a horse-shaped gully a third of a mile long with sheer cliffs towering up to 90 feet high. Known as the Great Buddha Crescent (Da Fu Wan), it is a natural grotto, hidden in the folds of misty mountains and terraced slopes below a sleepy village and above a meandering stream.

As we descended into the Great Buddha Crescent at Dazu, we could see several temples towering overhead. The oldest, **Sheng Shou Si,** was built by Zhao Zhifeng himself in 1179 (and last rebuilt in 1684 during the reign of Qing Emperor Kangxi). This temple is still active, but most visitors are drawn directly down steep stone stairs into the crescent of cliffs where the carvings were completed in 1249.

The Wheel of Life

The Tantric Buddhism long practiced at Dazu is noted for its use of incantations, meditations, and mandalas. Mandalas are diagrams of cosmic forces used by the devout to attain instantaneous union with the Buddha, and these mandalas surge through the crescent as a prominent motif, surfacing most strikingly at *The Wheel of Life,* the exquisite figure in **niche No. 3.** This ornate wheel of life and death, carved in relief from solid rock, is supported from beneath by tiny human attendants and gripped in the teeth of a superhuman monster, representative of the forces of death in life. The master artisan Zhao Zhifeng occupies the center of the wheel; above him is a pavilion of the Western Paradise, the Buddhist heaven beyond the mortal sphere. The outer two rings of the great wheel teem with animals living, dying, and being born, portraying the cycles of birth and death. Ribbons of divine figures ripple outward from the turning wheel. Altogether, it is a dynamic phantasmagoria on the theme of reincarnation, unlike any other figure I've ever encountered in China, and by itself worth the journey to Dazu.

The Wheel of Life is the starting point on one side of this sculpture garden, a section dominated by carvings of the leading deities of Buddhism. In **niche No. 8** (the caves are scrupulously numbered), there is a 1,000-arm *Guanyin (Goddess of Mercy),* an all-seeing eye carved into each of her open palms. The many arms represent Guanyin's almost unlimited capacity to reach out and help others; the many eyes, her ability to see every aspect of life with compassion. Encompassing 88 square yards of the recess, this wheel of mercy is the largest representation of its kind in China.

Sleeping Buddha

The keynote sculpture at Dazu, however, and one of the most famous in China, is the *Sleeping Buddha* at the midpoint of the crescent. Here, on a grand yet serene scale, the entrance of the historical Buddha, Sakyamuni, into Nirvana is rendered in a dreamscape. The *Sleeping Buddha* unites the formal devotional aspects that characterize older Buddhist grottoes in China with the more down-to-earth, human elements that set Dazu apart.

Here, in the bow of the Great Buddha Crescent, Prince Sakyamuni reclines on his right side, his back disappearing into stone. The carving measures 96 feet head-to-knees, forming a backdrop for a splendid ensemble of life-sized, lifelike attendants (bodhisattvas and officials in hats) who wade waist-deep through a river of stone in which their prince sleeps the unearthly sleep of the enlightened. The attendants flow gently to and fro before this magnified figure, facing different directions, expressing their individual devotion and dwarfed by a divinity so near he can be touched.

The art at Dazu is dynamic and naturalistic, the figures lively and fluid. The niches alternate between acts of devotion and flourishes of storytelling. Not far from the *Sleeping Buddha* is **niche No. 12,** *Nine Dragons Bathing the Prince,* depicting the baby Buddha being bathed in a fountain. Water drips into the bathing pool from the mouth of the lowest of nine carved dragons. Farther on are the most populous and lifelike galleries, where thousands of figures adorned in bright colors line tiers on the cliff walls. In **niche No. 15,** the common masses are devoted not to worship but to carrying out the mundane principles of parental care and filial piety. These are among the central themes of native Confucianism. Buddhism, transplanted from India, was clearly having to adapt to Chinese ways.

Heaven, Earth & Hell

The scenes of childbirth, nursing, and nurturing carved in relief at Dazu are unlike any of the representations at the other major Buddhist sculpture shrines in China. At Dazu, these carvings resemble three-dimensional comic strips complete with engraved captions. A devoted mother washes her infant's clothes. A father offers a peach to the babe nestled in his arms. Century-old parents watch over their 80-year-old child.

In another colossal comic strip devoted to filial piety in **niche No. 17,** Prince Sakyamuni returns to repay the kindness his parents showed him as a child by now offering his own arm as nourishment. This story is an adaptation of an episode from the Confucian canon's *Twenty-four Examples of Filial Piety* in which a daughter-in-law is celebrated for her extreme devotion when during a famine she cuts off a finger to feed her elderly parents-in-law. At Dazu, in other words, Buddhism and Confucianism are finally fused.

These warm family scenes are succeeded by two vast tiered niches whose theme is decidedly more grim: portrayals of the Final Judgment. One niche promises elevation from the cycles of death and rebirth to a higher consciousness. **Niche No. 21,** however, illustrates the other side, concentrating on the tortures of the damned. Evil-doers are tormented by monsters, hideous machinery, and an unending waterfall of freezing ice in panels reminiscent of the gruesome visions of Hieronymus Bosch or Aw Boon Haw. Numerous transgressions (more Confucian than Buddhist, perhaps) are dramatized. A drunken husband fails to recognize his wife; a drunken father fails to recognize his son; and a drunken elder sister fails to recognize her younger sister. Even a gentle, beatific farm woman, benignly feeding her chickens, is here consigned to the lower depths, presumably because she will violate Buddhist prohibitions against the slaughter of animals and the eating of meat.

A few of these large stone panels are more formal, peopled with religious figures and worshippers. The tiers of **niche No. 22** and the walls of the *Cave of Full Enlightenment*, at **niche No. 29,** are lined with traditional Buddhist figures, some fierce, some benign. The deep influences of Indian art rise to the surface, reflections of the venerable achievements at the Longmen or Mogao sculpture troves. But it is the new style of the Song masters that distinguishes Dazu. In **niche No. 30,** at the tip of the crescent opposite *The Wheel of Life,* the themes are worldly and entirely indigenous: oxen-raising and cattle-herding. Farmers, displayed in 10 continuous groupings, lovingly tend their beasts and share a genuine comradeship. These scenes of rural life are translated by the devout as symbolic representations of religious obedience and the taming of one's own animal nature, but for the secular tourist the outstanding elements in these countryside idylls are earthbound and sensuous. In the Song Dynasty, religious sculpture becomes increasingly natural and worldly, more Confucian and more Chinese—hence, the popular saying that at Dazu's Baoding Shan Buddhism becomes "Chinese pure and simple." And such an art—spiritual yet natural, formal yet human—does reach its most expansive expression at Baoding Shan.

Nirvana in Stone

After a few hours of viewing the cliffside gallery, we hiked back up to the village and asked our taxi driver to join us for lunch. She selected one of the unnamed indoor-outdoor shanty cafes. The family that owned the business and lived in its back rooms set to work chopping up the vegetables and preparing the trout that we would soon be dipping fresh and raw into a boiling pot of oil—a rural Sichuan hot pot that proved to be hearty and nourishing and (because we were presumed to be wealthy foreigners) undoubtedly overpriced at RMB 50 ($6) per person, including all the tea and local beer we could consume. We didn't mind the price. We were interested in watching the family prepare our meal in the kitchen at the back of the house, which lacked plumbing, and in the life on the village streets where the children ran up and down the hills rolling metal wheels with long pokers. The wheels were seldom wholly round, but several of the children were quite deft at keeping them rolling despite the bumps, holes, and assorted obstacles on the streets.

After lunch we walked the village and took another look down on the Great Buddha Crescent, its otherworldly art, painted in vibrant reds and blues, and its dreaming Buddha at odds not only with the modern Western world from which we'd come but with the simple, poor village above. Here indeed is the "precious summit" of a monumental Buddhist sculpture that permeated and enriched China for a thousand years and ended at Baoding Shan, where its receding image now sleeps in a Nirvana of stone.

PRACTICAL INFORMATION

ORIENTATION

The Baoding Shan Rock Carvings are located in Dazu County, Sichuan Province, a 3-hour drive from Chongqing via the new Chengyu Expressway that connects Chengdu and Chongqing. Dazu is a day trip from **Chongqing,** which is located in southwest China 650 miles from Beijing, 1,500 miles upstream on the Yangzi River from Shanghai.

GETTING THERE

There is no air or rail service to Dazu. Traveling by tour bus or hired car, the turnoff to Dazu is at milepost 257. The Expressway, a four-lane toll road in excellent condition, exacts RMB 40 ($5) per car if you're coming from Chongqing.

TOURS & STRATAGEMS

Guided trips to Baoding Shan can be arranged at the travel desk of the Yangtze Chongqing Holiday Inn, 15 Nanping Bei Lu (☎ 023/280-3380), for RMB 700 ($84) per person.

You can hire a taxi for the day for about RMB 650 ($78) total, negotiating the price yourself on the street. The taxi driver will not speak English and will not serve as a guide.

The admission at Dazu is RMB 45 ($6) per person plus RMB 10 ($1.25) to park the car.

Books in English about the Dazu sculptures can be purchased in the village at the grotto entrance. Books can be most helpful because the signs beside the various sculptures are in Chinese only, although the grotto numbers are rendered in English.

WHERE TO STAY

As there is no suitable lodging in the area, Dazu should be regarded as a day trip from **Chongqing.** See the Chongqing chapter for lodging choices.

WHERE TO DINE

If you don't want to risk lunch in a village cafe, be sure to come with your own picnic goodies, purchased the night before in Chongqing. Bottled water, soft drinks, and beer are readily available from street vendors in Dazu.

The Great Buddha at Leshan

乐山大佛

At Leshan, 100 miles south of Chengdu, the capital of southwest China's Sichuan Province, there's a saying: "The mountain is Buddha, Buddha is the mountain." The words may be poetic, but the meaning is quite literal: There is a mountain here, and the mountain is a Buddha.

A gigantic image of the Buddha is carved into the cliff face of Lingyuan Mountain on the east side of the Min River. Rising 233 feet straight up from the shore, it is called the *Great Buddha of Leshan (Leshan Dafo)*. It is one of the few wonders to survive from the Tang Dynasty (A.D. 618–907), and one of the most monumental.

Building Buddha

The handiwork of a devout, indefatigable monk named Haitong, who set to work with hammer and chisel in A.D. 713, this statue of Maitreya, the Buddha of the Future, is frequently hailed as the largest carved Buddha in the world. Its statistical dimensions befit the superhuman realm. Even seated, hands on knees, the *Great Buddha of Leshan* rises to the height of 35 men. Buddha's head is 50 feet high. Each eye is 10 feet wide. Buddha's extenuated ears are 20 feet long, his shoulders 90 feet broad, and his bare feet, which nearly touch the river, 30 feet across, wide enough to seat 100 sightseers at a time.

The good monk Haitong did not live to see the completion of his sculpture, which was 90 years in the making. It is said that he once plucked out his own eye to impress would-be donors to the project. His mission was to create a guardian presence vast enough to subdue the treacherous waters, to protect the passing boatmen and their cargo, to suppress the river's floods. Today, the waters still teem with commerce and boatmen, many of whom earn a living by ferrying tourists to this singular shrine.

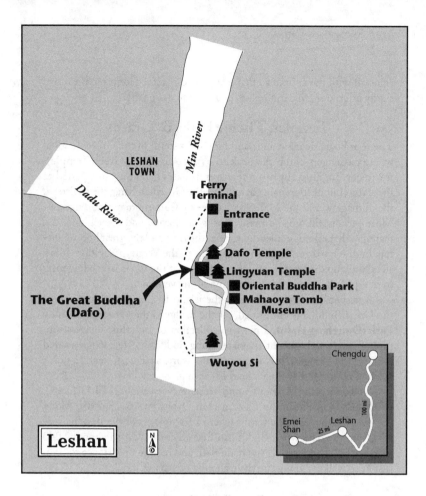

Leshan

Sailing to Buddha

Although gargantuan, the Great Buddha has a graceful form and benevolent expression. The classic view is straight on from the roiling river Min, where the statue has survived the elements, politics, and ravages of wind and erosion for 13 centuries. Unpainted open tour boats, with standing room only, ply the channel for a full frontal view of the Great Buddha. While these boats are not comfortable, they are sturdy and maneuverable. Smaller speedboats and even a few skiffs rowed by hand also look for passengers at the quay near the main entrance to the Great Buddha. The skiffs look rather fragile. The currents are quite severe.

From the river, Buddha appears to be enthroned in a deep recess—sitting in a closet of red sandstone. You can see tourists and pilgrims streaming up and down the stairs carved into the cliff walls on either side of the great image. They dance across Buddha's toes. The riverboats usually swing back and forth in front of Buddha, sometimes slowing to a standoff with the current so that everyone can get a decent picture. On a sunny afternoon, this can make for a spectacular portrait.

Temples, Theme Parks & Graves

The tour boats tie up at an island mountain south of the Great Buddha, where passengers climb the peak to **Wuyou Si (Dark Green Temple),** the major Buddhist shrine on the river. It dates from the same period as the statue, but its four main chambers—the Guardian King, the Maitreya, the Tathagata, and the Mahavira halls—are from more recent dynasties. More recent still are the many kiosks of charms and souvenirs and a teahouse that affords a splendid view of the river and the great holy mountain on the horizon, Emei Shan, gateway to the Western Paradise. It is a steep walk up the temple, and the river view at the top is worth lingering over, especially with a drink from one of the vendors.

A suspension bridge connects the island to Lingyuan Shan, where the Great Buddha is enthroned. At the bridge is the **Oriental Buddha Park (Dongfang Fodu),** a modern collection of Buddhist images from throughout Asia, highlighted by a reclining Buddha 557 feet long—touted as the world's longest. It is also one of the world's tackiest, clearly a quick work in plaster rather than a marble carving.

Next door is the Mahaoya Tomb Museum (admission RMB 15/$1.85), with burial relics from the Eastern Han Dynasty (A.D. 25–220). Along the river are the tiny cave tombs where a few images of the Buddha survive from the days when Buddhism first arrived in China almost 2,000 years earlier. These are off the main path and require persistence to find. Just keep walking along the river, about a quarter of a mile.

Buddha's Feet

Across the bridge, the trail rises again to the heights of Buddha's crown. A labyrinth of steps, the **Stairs of Nine Turnings,** descend to the feet of the statue. These narrow stairs are crowded with onlookers who wind down Buddha's left side.

At the base, children usually make a stone stage of Buddha's colossal feet, acting out songs, dances, and kung-fu routines, while parents and grandparents spread out their picnic lunches on the toenails. Recently, however, park authorities have been putting up signs forbidding people to stand on any part of this "Cultural Relic." I doubt this prohibition lasts.

The Buddha's recess is honeycombed with cutout shrines where a multitude of holy statues once resided. Almost all have disappeared in robbery or rain. On the other side of the Great Buddha, nine more turnings of stairs upward bring climbers level with Buddha's ears. Up close, the forehead in profile is a smooth dome, patched with what looks like concrete. The survival of the statue has had much to do with an ingenious drainage system concealed behind the Great Buddha that empties the rain and hillside runoff into the river below, but a close inspection of Buddha's head makes me think that the rock has been patched and cleaned up over the centuries, too. Otherwise, this statue seems to be in miraculous condition, impervious to the elements and the passage of time.

Buddha's Crown

Buddha's head was once capped by a seven-story pavilion, but this was dismantled during the warfare that erupted at the end of the Yuan Dynasty. Above and behind, there's another temple, **Dafo Si,** the Great Buddha's own. A short road leads down to the north entrance where the buses and river ferries wait. The temple grounds are an ideal spot to linger, to take in the river scenery from the high platforms on Buddha's right side, at one remove from the world of man below.

On Buddha's south side is another temple, **Lingyuan,** dating back to the 7th century but renovated in the 17th century, with yet another laughing Buddha of the Future residing inside. From this side of the carving, there are fine views of Buddha in profile and some statues that most tourists don't get to see, images of the sculptor Haitong and a cave said to have been his monastic retreat.

In Buddha's temple there is the stone likeness of a celebrated Song Dynasty scholar, Su Dongpo, who lived near Leshan. The pond where Su washed his brushes is still at Buddha's crown. In his most famous poem, Su relinquishes the desire to become a great figure on the world's stage, preferring to "journey about like a wine-laden cloud" among the rivers and hills of Leshan.

Through the centuries, through the ebb and flow of empires—even into this age when mass tourism has replaced pilgrimage and ant-sized gawkers climb from knee to noggin—the Great Buddha maintains its serene countenance, eyes nearly closed, lips in a knowing smile.

PRACTICAL INFORMATION

ORIENTATION

The Great Buddha at Leshan is 100 miles south of **Chengdu,** the capital of Sichuan, about 1,000 miles southwest of Beijing. Leshan is a small town. Most visitors to the Great Buddha set out from Chengdu in the early morning, returning in the afternoon. Travelers to the nearby sacred mountain of **Emei Shan** (see separate chapter) often stop at Leshan on their way to or from Chengdu.

GETTING THERE

The nearest train station requires a 1-hour minibus to connect to Leshan, and there is no service by air. The easiest means to get to Leshan is by hiring a driver and guide from CITS, a hotel tour desk, or an independent travel operator such as Mr. Lee in Chengdu (see below). Tour Buses leave from hotels or from the bus stations in Chengdu and the journey takes 3 to 4 hours. Public buses take about 5 hours.

TOURS & STRATEGEMS

Plan to make Leshan a day trip. Even the budget hotels in Chengdu are far superior to what's offered in Leshan.

Admissions & Open Hours Admissions to the main gate, to the various temples, even to the stairways, can add up to $5. The ferryboats can charge almost that much, too. All temples and sites are open from 8am to 6pm.

Tours Day tours to the *Great Buddha at Leshan* can be booked at Chengdu's China International Travel Service (CITS), 65 Renmin Nan Lu (☎ 028/665-0780), or from hotel tour desks. Mr. Lee (☎ and fax 028/555-4250) offers a Leshan tour with a private car and himself as guide (about RMB 250/$30 per person).

WHERE TO DINE

The Great Buddha Temple has a **vegetarian restaurant** and courtyard vendors hawk drinks and snacks, but you would be better off eating an early breakfast and packing your own picnic lunch before leaving Chengdu. Day tours sometimes include lunch at a local restaurant.

Journeys
by Rivers and Seas

江河

CHINA IS USUALLY CROSSED BY ROAD, rail, and air, but its waterways are legendary and today's traveler has an opportunity to float through some of the Middle Kingdom's most interesting and grand terrain. Boat travel offers yet another perspective on China's scenery, history, and culture—one that is often quite pleasurable.

The **Yangzi River,** China's fabled waterway, may be closed to cruise ships early in the next century as the Three Gorges Dam project, the largest in the world, bottles up the third longest river in the world. The Yangzi's most scenic section, the Three Gorges, is destined to be submerged by the new reservoir. Since this is the best river cruise in China, I urge you to take it sooner rather than later. Cruise ships depart all summer from Wuhan in the east and Chongqing in the west.

China's most spectacular river scenery is along the **Li River,** from Guilin to Yangshuo. The limestone pinnacles that line the river on this 4-hour cruise are the stuff of scroll paintings and vacation posters. For visitors to **Guilin** and **Yangshuo,** this is the number one excursion.

River scenery of another kind is featured along the **Huangpu,** the industrial and shipping lane that cuts through Shanghai and flows into the East China Sea at the mouth of the Yangzi River. Mile for mile, this is the most important river in China's economy, and the ship and boat traffic along its 18-mile run is intriguing, as are the views it affords of the biggest boomtown in the modern world, **Shanghai.**

A river built by humans, the **Grand Canal,** the world's longest canal at over 1,000 miles, has been employed for centuries as a major trading and cultural link between north and south China. Although reduced in size, the Grand Canal is still used today, its locks and wharves always busy, particularly along the route connecting the garden cities of **Suzhou** and **Hangzhou,** which travelers can now retrace in flat-bottomed river barges.

Another form of cruising with historical and cultural links to Old China takes place on **Lake Tai,** China's most famous inland body of water. Setting out from the silk city of Wuxi, ferries now cross this vast lake to scenic islands, and the shores of Lake Tai provide other attractions, including caves, the pottery town of Yixing, and the hillside where the world's largest statue of Buddha has just been completed.

Finally, there are the seas that have sealed off China from the West for most of recorded history. The Yellow Sea, the East China Sea, and the South China Sea make for some of the most interesting cruise ship destinations in Asia. It is now possible to book a luxury cruise along the east coast of China that calls upon the great ports, including Hong Kong, Xiamen, Shanghai, and Tianjin (with a shore excursion to Beijing). A cruise ship can provide a taste of China in comfort and style—perhaps the perfect introduction for the traveler who doesn't want to rough it the first time out.

THE YANGZI: UP AND DOWN CHINA'S LONG RIVER

长江

A CRUISE UPON ASIA'S MOST FABLED river, the Yangzi, has been the dream and sometimes the nightmare of millions of merchants and boatmen, farmers and poets, emperors and outlaws, since Chinese civilization began. Unchanged for centuries, the scenery is various, earthy, and spellbinding, particularly at the Three Gorges, where the third longest river on Earth is forcibly contained (as a Song Dynasty poet wrote) like "a thousand seas poured into one cup."

The Yangzi is *The Romance of the Three Kingdoms* made visible, each bend in the river a passage from that classic Chinese novel of history, adventure, and lore that is set in a tumultuous 60-year period starting in A.D. 220. Although most foreigners are not familiar with this book, all Chinese are, and the Yangzi River has mythic, as well as natural, qualities.

Of more pressing concern for all travelers are plans to block the scenic heart of the river—from the **Three Gorges** all the way upstream to Chongqing. This most dramatic section of the Yangzi will eventually be drowned by the Sanxia Dam, the world's largest construction project. Thus, the rush is on to see the Long River (Changjiang, as the Yangzi is known in China) before it disappears.

Upriver from Wuhan (Day 1)

I joined that rush in the spring, traveling slowly upriver from Wuhan, then swiftly back downriver from Chongqing, twice traversing the Three Gorges, entranced in both directions by the river's natural and mythic charms. But I was intrigued as well by glimpses into the ways that life is conducted along its banks, ways old and new, which are destined to recede from view like the edges of a dream crumbling at dawn.

After a walking tour of **Wuhan's waterfront,** where many buildings from the days of British occupation still stand, I boarded the ship in the evening. The 6-day, 5-night cruise upriver to Chongqing would traverse 841 miles of the Yangzi, barely a fifth of its east-to-west 3,906-mile length. The river was dark. All I could see from the railing were lights, some passing, some receding, and over-head the lights of the stars that never seem to move, even over China's longest river.

Yueyang Tower (Day 2)

The next morning, I have my first look at the Yangzi above Wuhan. The placid waters are wide, dotted with small whirlpools but devoid of rapids. Long, rusty barges heaped with coal, rice, and other products of the interior chug downstream toward Shanghai, the sailors call-ing out and whistling as the cruise ships pass. Sheaves of grain are un-loaded along the way and stacked on shore in piles the size and shape of barns. Logs are transferred to towns by hand.

Even here the Yangzi is etched with the history of the Three King-doms period (A.D. 220–280), when the Wei, Shu, and Wu kingdoms contended for control of China along the Yangzi. At **Red Cliff (Chibi)**—scorched that color, it is said, by the flames that engulfed the Wu and Shu armadas in their cel-ebrated battle with the Kingdom of Wei in A.D. 208—pavilions and a museum of weaponry commemo-rate this critical confrontation. Zhuge Liang, China's most re-spected military strategist and po-litical advisor, was present at the battle, in which the Wei army, led by the villainous Duke Cao Cao, met defeat due to his brilliant stratagems.

Our ship made its first port of call at **Dongting,** China's second largest freshwater lake. Massive accumulations of silt have reduced the size of what was China's largest lake, but its beauty and history are unaffected. On the east side is **Yueyang Tower,** where admirals of the Three Kingdoms period once reviewed naval maneuvers. The tower dates from the 8th century. It was most recently rebuilt in Song Dynasty style in 1985, complete with the Thrice Drunken Pavilion where Daoist Immortal Lu Dongbin engaged in revelries.

The Walled City of Jingzhou (Day 2)

From the mouth of Dongting Lake upriver, the land is flat, girded by the 111-mile-long Jingjiang Dike that originated 16 centuries ago. This bulwark against flooding ends at Sashi, 334 miles from Wuhan. **Sashi** is the gateway to the Jingzhou, whose city walls (10 miles long, 30 feet high—last rebuilt in A.D. 1646) were fashioned, according to local legend, by Three Kingdoms' hero Guan Yu, later deified as a Chinese god of war. Jingzhou has a **splendid museum** that contains the remains of a Han Dynasty county governor, Mr. Sui, who died in 167 B.C. at age 60 of a stomachache. Preserved in water and mercury sulfide within a tripartite cedar coffin and buried 10 meters deep, the mummy was unearthed in 1975. After 2,142 years, the corpse proved to be perfectly preserved, with arm and leg joints still flexible.

Damming the Gorges (Day 3)

The upriver gateway to the Three Gorges is at **Yichang,** once a foreign treaty port and the great transshipment point for Yangzi traffic. Here China's largest dam to date, Gezhouba, was completed in 1986. Boats and ships must pass through its hydraulic locks. Gezhouba has raised the level of the Yangzi some 65 feet behind its walls. The ship's crew runs an informal lottery with the passengers here. Whoever comes closest to predicting the time we pass out of the locks is the winner.

Above the Gezhouba, I spot the M.S. *Kunlun* at anchor. Once Chairman Mao's state boat, it later served as a luxury cruiser for wealthy tourists. Neglected now, it seems to be quietly rusting away. A new generation of cruisers has usurped its place on the river, led by the *Victoria I, II,* and *III,* vessels designed solely for navigating the Yangzi safely, with shallow drafts and double-bottom hulls. These cruisers incorporate Western luxuries and services.

Major historic sites and scenic vistas are fully introduced by onboard cruise directors. Our approach to the Three Gorges Dam work site was accompanied by a thorough, sometimes critical, discussion of the project.

The Three Gorges Dam, to be located at Sandouping Village, 27 miles above the Gezhouba Dam, will raise the Yangzi to almost unimaginable heights. More than 20,000 workers and 3,000 engineers are on site, and both shores teem with heavy construction. Situated on a ribbon of granite that crosses the more fragile limestone basin of the Yangzi, the Three Gorges Dam will be 6,600 feet (1.23 miles) wide and 607 feet high, dwarfing all other dams ever built. The projected completion date is the year 2015. The cost could easily exceed $30 billion. This cement barrier will create a reservoir 370 miles long, transforming the wild Yangzi into a calm lake that will submerge 13 cities, 140 towns, 1,352 villages, 657 factories, and 75,000 acres of cultivated land, necessitating the relocation of at least 1.3 million people. The deep, narrow Three Gorges themselves will be reduced to a few floating islands.

First proposed by Sun Yat-sen in 1919 and seconded by Chairman Mao in 1958, this project is slated to provide as much as 15% of China's electricity, reduce the severity of flooding, and facilitate passage of considerably larger ships through the Three Gorges to and from Chongqing in Sichuan, China's rice bowl. Our *Victoria* cruise ship, at 3,000 tons, is currently the heaviest ship able to navigate the Yangzi; after the great dam is completed, ships more than three times its size will link Sichuan to Shanghai.

At present, the channel flow of the Yangzi is being redirected so that the dam itself can be poured. A bypass system is being created to enable cruise ships to continue to pass upriver through the Three Gorges, which should not be submerged for at least another decade.

Into the East Gorge, Xiling (Day 3)

The new dam site is within the bounds of the easternmost of the Three Gorges, **Xiling Gorge,** the scenic highpoint toward which a cruise upstream builds. Here the mountains suddenly rise from the banks of the Yangzi, forming a massive wall on both sides, pinching and speeding the river flow. These gorges were created 70 million years ago as an inland sea withdrew to the east, its waters slicing into the limestone faults and creases where two large mountain systems had been smashed together. This primordial geology is written on the steep cliffsides that threaten to eclipse the sun. Xiling, the longest of the three at 47 miles, actually consists of a number of gorges named for legends of the Three Kingdoms or the resemblance of their formations to other objects. The **Sword and the Book of the Art of War** is the gorge where Zhuge Liang stored grain for his troops and hid his book of military strategy. Other gorges within Xiling include the **Oxen Liver and Horse Lung Gorge** and the **Gorge of Shadowplay.**

Xiling Gorge was once one of the most hazardous regions on the Yangzi, rife with rapids and whirlpools. A pile of human bones once resided on its banks, heaped in the shape of a white pagoda, as a reminder to navigators of the dangers here. Seventy years ago one British naval commander described the Three Gorges as the bottleneck of the Yangzi, "boiling, seething infernos of tumbling, tossing water, whirlpools, eddies, backwaters and sudden vertical 'boils.'" One in ten junks was stranded in the gorges; one in twenty, lost forever.

Xiling Gorge is still not easy to navigate, but more than a hundred shoals and reefs have been dynamited in recent times, and the river is now lined with several thousand navigational buoys with all-weather beacons. These buoys resemble small dinghies and they must be relocated every two weeks, since the channel changes that often as waters rise and fall and silt is carried from bank to bank.

The gorges are in some places cloven with steep ravines where hillside farms produce wheat, rice, maize, legumes, rapeseed, and tangerines. For some of these severely isolated farms, the main link to the outside world is provided by junks and small barges that act as ferries. In the next century, they will be underwater.

Floaters (Day 3)

At **Zigui,** just past the small stream of Xiang Xi, home to Han Dynasty heroine Wang Zhaojun, cruisers pass out of Xiling Gorge. Cruise ships often spend the night here, entertained on the wharf by local peasant singers and dancers. Zigui is the home of poet Qu Yuan, whose Ming Dynasty statue resides at a memorial hall. When his advice went unheeded by the king of Chu, Qu Yuan drowned himself in Dongting Lake. Ever since, he has been commemorated by China's annual dragon boat races (on the fifth day of the fifth lunar month) and by the eating of zongzi, a packet of sweet steamed rice tied in leaves that villagers originally tossed into the sea to lure fish away from Qu Yuan's body.

For centuries, the Yangzi served as the graveyard for those too poor to afford a land burial. Even today, one can spot corpses. Our American tour director counted 23 corpses on her 40 trips last year, including six in a single gruesome day. The river people call them "floaters." The ship's captain reports seeing Yangzi corpses every day. People fall in and can't swim, he says with a smile. I keep my eyes on the river the whole way, but all I see are the rowboat channel markers like caskets in a river still treacherous to navigate.

Through the Middle Gorge, Wu (Day 3)

Upriver from Zigui is the entrance to the middle gorge, **Wuxia (Witches Gorge).** Wu Gorge contains the most dramatic mountain peaks on the Yangzi, crowned by Goddess Peak, which has a likeness in stone of Yao Ji, youngest of the 12 daughters of the queen mother of the East. These 12 sisters stole away to Earth and met Yu the Great, tamer of floods, who was fighting the 12 dragons of the floodwaters. The sisters slayed the dragons and were eventually immortalized as the 12 peaks that assisted mariners in navigating Wu Gorge. In the midst of this gorge is **Gathered Immortals Peak and the Kong Ming Tablet,** supposed to have been inscribed by Zhuge Liang himself when he served as prime minister of the Shu Kingdom. In a Tang Dynasty poem written here, Li Bai (A.D. 701–762) recalled how his boat tried for three days to surmount a single set of rapids. "But for all this time the peak remains beside us," he wrote. "I wonder how many of my hairs turned gray."

Wu Gorge ends at the **Golden Helmet and Shining Armor valley** where the gray walls of enfolded limestone resemble ancient armor and the rounded mountaintop shines like a golden helmet. We dock overnight at the town of Wushan, home to legendary Emperor Yu who created the Three Gorges. Wushan marks the end of the middle gorge and is the gateway to excursions on the Daning River, site of the Three Little Gorges (Xiao Sanxia).

Interlude in the Three Little Gorges (Day 4)

Trips up and down the **Daning River,** first offered to tourists in 1985, are aboard small motorized sampans. The river is so fierce, however, that at one point passengers must disembark and walk along the bank (lined with local vendors) while their boat struggles to overcome the rapids, the boatmen pushing their bamboo poles into the shallow streambed to gain enough leverage. The 20-mile trip upriver through the Three Little Gorges takes several hours, and many visitors find the scenery more impressive than that along the Yangzi, the peaks sharper, the current of the little river swifter and more violent. Sights along the way include bands of monkeys and old coffins suspended from holes carved into the cliff face. Lunch is often provided at Twin Dragons Village, where sampans turn around for a fast, water-splashed return downstream.

The Three Little Gorges pack the excitement of white-water rafting and the scenery of a deep river valley into one compact package, but I found myself preferring the bigger gorges, their massive scale an emblem of the great riverway dividing north and south China.

Out from the West Gorge, Qutang (Day 4)

In the early afternoon we reached the western gorge, **Qutang Gorge,** the shortest of the Three Gorges (just 5 miles long), but also the grandest and wildest. Here the Yangzi narrows to as little as 300 feet, only one ship is allowed to pass at a time, the vertical peaks rise upward of 3,700 feet, the water deepens, glistens, and charges like molten lava, and the wind itself is flattened and funneled through. As an ancient verse puts it, "Peaks pierce the sky as we course through the deep passage beneath." The mountains appear to have been split apart by the blade of a massive ax. Iron pillars, now submerged, were employed in Tang Dynasty times to string up defensive barriers, and later to tax barge traffic. A stone perched on the top of a black rock far overhead is aptly named **Rhinoceros Looking at the Moon.** At the upstream entrance, there's a series of zigzag square holes cut into the cliffs. Known as **Meng Jiang's Ladder** after the exploits of a Song Dynasty soldier, it is actually the remains of a stairway to the top of the peak where a city once resided in the 6th century A.D. Wooden coffins suspended on this same cliff have been dated back to 1000 B.C.

At **Baidi Cheng** and **Fengjie,** cruise ships reach the upriver end of the Three Gorges. It was here that Zhuge Liang trained troops during the Three Kingdoms era and here that China's two greatest poets, Li Bai and Du Fu, both of the Tang Dynasty (A.D. 618–907), resided. Du Fu lived for 2 years in Fengjie, where he composed over 400 poems. At Baidi Cheng, Liu Bei, ruler of the Shu Kingdom, died of despair after failing to avenge his brother, Guan Yu. At Baidi Temple, these and other heroes of the Three Kingdoms are commemorated today.

Altogether, the Three Gorges occupy only a 125-mile section of the Yangzi, a mere fragment, but the central scenic gem of the riverway. On an upriver cruise, the gorges become the culmination of a slow battle against the great inland current that crosses China, its power mounting and reaching a crescendo as it is funneled through the gorges as through an hourglass. Downriver, the gorges appear suddenly, dramatically, and are traversed in a fraction of the time. As Li Bai observed 1,200 years ago: "In the morning leaving Baidi Cheng, it was as if we went on clouds; from there to Jiangling is one thousand li, but in one day the racing waters brought us down." Each way, although the sensation is different, the power of the river underlies the experience, its force so compelling that even a modern traveler can taste something of what the Yangzi was in centuries past. The paths of the trackers, harnessed by quarter-mile-long ropes of twisted bamboo to loaded junks and later steamboats, are still visible where they were carved into the sides of these massive canyons— traces of superhuman labor that will be submerged early in the next century when the river itself is further tamed and modernized.

City of Ghosts, Fengdu (Day 5)

Between the Three Gorges and Chongqing, the most peculiar stop is **Fengdu,** China's "Ghost City," where a temple to the God of the Underworld, Yinwang, commands the summit of **Ming Shan Peak.** This is the place of final judgment in the Yangzi basin. Here I climb long rows of stairs, 600 steps in all, to meet Yinwang. I must pass through all the stages—from a Ming Dynasty bridge to a Ghost Gate—that the soul is said to travel at the moment of death. At each stage I must perform some feat: Cross a bridge in three steps, run up a flight of a hundred stairs in a single breath, balance for three seconds on a round rock. If I fail, hell will claim me and my destination in the afterlife will be dire. Like most visitors, I do survive the long journey to the top, where Daoist, Buddhist, and Confucian temples mingle, amusement-park statues of the Underworld line the courtyards, and Yinwang the King of Hell sits in judgment, assisted by four supreme judges. A Swiss-made chairlift whisks the nonbelievers and those in a hurry straight to the top, too, where the panorama of the Yangzi and the surrounding mountains is splendid.

Back in the park at the base of Ming Shan, I watch the locals gather in the afternoon. Among the many beggars is a blind mother with two children in tow. A group of old people is practicing *tai ji quan* at such a slow pace, they seem to be ghosts themselves. The fog on the river swirls like a weightless cloth, winding and unwinding. The banks of the river grow faint as we resume our cruise upriver. The last walls of the Three Gorges behind us rise like the sides of a stone crib. When we pull out from the muddy banks of Fengdu, even the Mountain of the Underworld is lost in the mists.

Chongqing (Day 6)

At Chongqing, a city so hilly even bicycles are a rarity, a Yangzi cruise can either begin or end. Pulling upriver, one savors the power of the river, as irresistible as the flood of time, silted with the legends and hardships of the past. Speeding downriver, the flow is far swifter; the direction is toward the future, when the river's power will be harnessed not on the backs of the people but by the walls of the world's largest hydroelectric plant.

On my return cruise from Chongqing to Wuhan, a day shorter, we stop at many of the same villages with their old shops, where one can still pay to have a tailor patch an umbrella. There's little time to dwell in the alleyways of the past, however. Along here the famous towns of the Yangzi will be drowned in another generation in order to power a new China.

Sailing downriver, the Three Gorges unroll twice as quickly, rushing by in a dream. Coal factories drape the steep banks. Fishermen on small trawlers crank in their nets by hand. Women pound the day's laundry on the rocks. The Yangzi broadens. The mountains dissolve into fields so level and low I can't see over the border of the river. This river is as brown as the Mississippi, alternately treacherous and placid, beautiful and raw, grand and ordinary, with all the life of China, old and new, gathered on its banks, a scroll unwinding in harmony with the ever flowing river, changing with the seasons and soon to be changed forever.

Downriver, at the end of my second voyage on the Yangzi, I say farewell, saddened as was the Tang Dynasty poet Li Bai when he parted with a friend heading upstream:

> At Yellow Crane Tower I bid farewell to Meng Haran
> And watch his boat's sails go farther, ever farther,
> Until they vanish in blue sky,
> But my heart runs with the Yangzi water flowing, ever
> flowing.

WHAT TO READ

Your Yangzi cruise will be enhanced if you read John Hersey's *A Single Pebble*, a novel about prerevolutionary, pretourism days on the river; and Richard McKenna's *The Sand Pebbles*, a gunboat epic that was made into a popular movie. Paul Theroux's *Sailing Through China* takes a sharp, personal look at cruising the Yangzi in the 1980s.

Probe International has published a collection of essays by Chinese scholars and journalists who oppose the massive hydroelectric dam project, *Damming the Three Gorges*. A general guide, filled with facts and lore, is Judy Bonavia's *The Yangzi River*, an Odyssey Illustrated Guide published in Hong Kong and available in many travel bookstores overseas

PRACTICAL INFORMATION

CRUISES

The best cruising months are September and October, since the rainy season in the Yangzi basin can extend from May through August. I made my cruises in March and April, however, finding the weather delightful.

Chinese Ferries Yangzi River ferries depart from Wuhan (for upriver trips) and from Chongqing (for downriver trips) year-round, but their facilities are crude. They function better as a means of inexpensive transport than as tour boats. They can be booked at wharves along the Yangzi.

Chinese Tour Boats There are numerous Chinese tour boats operating March through November on the Yangzi, some of them with quite luxurious cabins and facilities, but management and staff are not used to foreign

travelers. Chinese tour boats can be booked in Wuhan or Chongqing through China International Travel Service (CITS) outlets (☎ 027/281-6553 in Wuhan; ☎ 023/6385-0806 in Chongqing).

Victoria Cruises One of the few Western-managed Yangzi River cruise lines is Victoria Cruises, based in New York. Victoria meets the comfort and service expectations of Western travelers with well-appointed new ships and American-trained cruise directors. The quality of cruise directors is crucial on the Yangzi, and Victoria hires the best I've seen: two native English speakers per ship who are fluent in Chinese, expert in Yangzi River history and sights, and dedicated to serving passengers. The Victoria fleet *(Victoria I, II,* and *III),* built in the 1990s specially for cruising the Yangzi, accommodates

154 passengers, all in outside staterooms and suites with picture windows, desks, closets, private baths, air-conditioning, and closed-circuit televisions. In many ways, a Victoria Cruise borrows from the luxury ocean cruise experience offered in the Caribbean and Mediterranean, but a closer analogy is to the more adventurous cruises operating in Alaska.

Victoria Cruises offers upriver departures from Wuhan to Chongqing (6 days/5 nights) and downriver departures from Chongqing to Wuhan (5 days/4 nights) from mid-March to early December. Prices, based on double occupancy, run from $560 to $690 for a standard cabin up to $1,400 to $1,720 for the largest suite, depending on the season. The April-to-May and September-to-October bookings are the most expensive. Shore excursions cost a total of $65 extra. Victoria Cruises is able to book air flights as well. One couple I met from Philadelphia had come to the Yangzi strictly for the cruise. They booked the entire package, including round-trip airfare, from Victoria Cruises. For brochures and bookings, contact your local travel agent or Victoria Cruises, 57-08 39th Avenue, Woodside, New York 11377 (☎ 800/348-8084 or 212/818-1680; fax 212/818-9889).

THE LI RIVER: A SILKEN SCROLL IN STONE

漓江

G UILIN'S LI RIVER (LI JIANG) HAS posed for more painters and photographers than any other place in China—and for good reason. This is "the best scenery under heaven," as an old saying goes, the best scenery if you like clear rivers, green bamboos, and sheer, twisting limestone pinnacles. Han Yu (A.D. 768–824), a Tang Dynasty poet, composed the classic description of the Li River: "The river is a blue ribbon of silk, / The hills are hair pins of jade."

Leaving Guilin

Tour boats by the hundreds make the daily 52-mile journey down the Li River to Yangshou. My vessel was typical: a flat-bottomed barge, rounded at each end, with seating and tables inside the long cabin and an open observation deck on top. While waiting to depart, I purchased a *pomelo,* a thick-skinned gigantic relative of the grapefruit, from one of the peasant vendors who sailed alongside on a raft of hollow bamboo shafts lashed together like a rural Chinese surfboard.

The first phase of the passage, from Guilin down to the village of Yangdi, is merely a prelude. **Elephant Trunk Hill (Xiangbi),** on the west shore, is one of Guilin's most popular parks and remarkable natural monuments. It clearly resembles an elephant drinking from the Li River. All the great limestone formations in Guilin and down the Li River are said to resemble something or someone, but Elephant Hill takes little imagination to identify. From the water, I have a perfect view of the hill's trunk, and between that trunk and the elephant's legs, **Moon-in-the-Water Cave,** which is said to resemble a silver moon floating on the Li River. Perhaps if the moon is out, it does. Small boats can enter this cave when the water level permits. Jibei Chushi, a Song Dynasty poet, wrote "In Praise of Moonlit Nights" here, a dreamy paradox that reads:

> The silver moon is deep below the river.
> The silver moon floats upon the river.
> The river flows where the moon cannot go.
> Where the moon goes, the river cannot flow.

Elephant Trunk Hill is succeeded on the east bank by **Pagoda Hill (Baota Shan),** capped by a Ming Dynasty pagoda that is said to imprison a thousand-legged demon. The hill is also renowned for its maple trees and the red leaves that grace it in the fall. **Pierced Hill (Chuan Shan)** stands next to Pagoda Hill; it is noted for the large round opening in its side, aptly named Moon Cave. There follows on the west bank two craggy towers of note: **Fighting Cock Hill (Douji),** said to resemble roosters at a showdown, with coxcombs prone and wings spread, and **Clean Vase Lying in the River,** both back on the west bank. As I say, this is a mere prelude to the bands of fantastic peaks that lie ahead. At the town of Qifeng (Strange Rock), there's the first hint of the majestic scenery ahead. Here the peaks and hills thicken into a forest.

Three hundred million years ago this region was swallowed by the sea. Two hundred million years ago it reemerged, and the exposed limestone was sculpted by acidic rain, mist, and wind-blown dust. These karst peaks were then sliced apart and honed into immense pillars over the last two million years. The result is a forest of stone shafts and crags that seems to have grown straight up from the banks of the Li, topping out at heights of 200 to 300 feet.

There's a mythic counterpoint to this geological tale of bizarre formations. The story goes that long ago, when the South China Sea threatened to engulf Guilin, the gods decided enough was enough: They would move the northern hills south as a floodgate. The gods transformed the hills into goats in order to herd them south, but a fierce, blasting wind scattered the goats willy-nilly down the Li River where they changed back into the unruly peaks we see today.

None of the strange hills and cliffs that rise directly from the riverbanks are named for goats these days, but there are hills and pillars named for oxen, islands, a ferry, a lonely lady, an emperor's crown, and a panel of natural embroidery, intricate as stitched silk. Every hill has a story, but I'm content to drift unguided. The river is hushed, well beyond the city streets of Guilin, and the landforms are commending silence. I feast on each curve of the river, hungering for the next impossible formation. A buffet lunch is served below, a generous one of Chinese dishes, fish, vegetables, and fruits. I've seen the foodstuffs cleaned in the river water, but I decide to eat until I'm full. The Li is one of the clearer rivers in China, cleansed by the reaction of carbonic acids with the limestone rocks.

After lunch, I climb back up on the observation deck and bathe in the scenery. We are passing villages of thatched huts. Fishermen are scooping the river bottom for shrimp with funnel-shaped nets. Children are wading and swimming in the sandy bend of the river. Enormous groves of bamboo reach out from the banks, shooting out like green feathery petals. This is a primeval land of extremes: a tropical valley hemmed in by mountains of cold limestone.

From **Yangdi Village,** the midway point of the cruise, it's nearly another hour's float to **Mural Hill (Hua Shan),** probably the river's most famous cluster of razor-sharp peaks. The shadings and fissures on its many faces are said to resemble a fresco of horses bolting, leaping, neighing, rearing, and running. For centuries hopeful would-be officials, scholars on their way upriver to attend the imperial examinations scoured Mural Hill with desperate eyes: The more horses they discerned, the higher their test scores, it was said. To see nine horses engraved on the flanks of Mural Hill was to secure the highest mark on the exams. I fail to discern a single worthy steed in the hues of this hill, but 800 years ago the poet Chou Hau did better:

> How many thousands of years ago
> Was this screen carved in stone?
> The more it is pelted by rain and winds
> The clearer its image.

South of Mural Hill we pass the village of **Xingping** on the east shore. At this ancient county seat, the scenery is unsurpassed. Xingping is an ink-wash landscape fashioned from water and stone. No artist is required. Scores of myths are stored in the odd karst pillars and peaks that resemble scepters, snails, and carp, as well as the followers and fingers of Buddha. Groves of bamboo and willow wave from the banks, which are now spread 300 feet apart as the river's flow becomes almost limpid.

At the end of the river journey, the tour boats pull in at the village of **Yangshou,** where the scenery according to tradition "excels even that of Guilin." The blue hills stretch forever south, west, and east. We tie up at Nanxu Gate under the implacable **Green Lotus Peak (Bi Lian).** The quay swarms with roving vendors. Fishermen pose with cormorants, the birds they've taught to retrieve fish. The tour buses back to Guilin are parked nearby. Above the dock, south along the river, is the eight-sided River Pavilion (Yingjiang Ke), an ideal place for a final view of the river's exquisite landscape.

The buses pull out from the narrow village streets late in the afternoon. The vendors converge on the buses, rapping on the windows, holding up their wares. I first took this road north back to Guilin 10 years ago. At that time, workers were building a new highway beside the old one. They were building it entirely by hand, hauling rock, splitting it to size with mauls, fitting it stone by stone into the roadbed, and paving it over, shovelful by shovelful. The sole heavy equipment on the site was an old steamroller, like a machine out of a childhood storybook. At night the road-building brigades lay down in the roadbed and slept under the stars.

No words or pictures precisely express the spell cast by the uncanny scenery of the Li River. Fan Cheng-ta, who traveled through China during the Song Dynasty (A.D. 960–1280), once complained, "I have often sent pictures which I painted to friends, but few believed what they saw. There is no point," Fan decided, "in arguing with them." Once you've been down the Li River, you'll know what he meant. The reality of the river surpasses the finest print of the camera, the most fantastic simile of the pen, the most extravagant stroke of the ink brush.

PRACTICAL INFORMATION

CRUISES

Li River scenic boat cruises are all-day trips from Guilin (see separate chapter, "Guilin: City of Heavenly Terraces"), where arrangements can be made at hotel tour desks. River trips depart every morning about 8am and arrive in Yangshou, 52 miles south of Guilin, in the afternoon (after about 6 hours on the river). There's a stop for shopping at the street market in Yangshou; then the tour buses make the 2-hour return trip to Guilin, arriving by 5:30pm.

Tours China International Travel Service (CITS) sells Li River tours from its office at 14 Ronghu Bei Lu (☎ 0773/ 282-7254). I booked my Li River tour at the Holiday Inn Guilin, 14 Ronghu Nan Lu (☎ 0773/282-3950). The RMB 480 ($58) ticket included an English-speaking guide, a Chinese buffet, and the return bus ride to Guilin. The cruise boat was built for the river, with inside seating, picture windows, a Chinese rest room (not sanitary), and an open-air, stand-up viewing deck with railings on the roof. More deluxe cruise boats (with higher ticket prices) can be booked here during high tourist season, May through October.

Timing Your Trip The 270-mile-long Li River flows southward through Guilin. It is always too low in winter to permit boat tours, although it is possible even then to book a short boat tour (2 hours) in Guilin that leaves from Xingping, a village an hour to the south. By April, the water is usually high enough to permit longer boat tours, which often start about 15 miles downriver at Zhujiang (or even farther along, at Yangdi) and end at Yangshou (a 4- to 5-hour trip). The best months for river travel are April and May, and September and October, when the river is usually deep enough for a full Guilin–Yangshou passage. Of course, these months are also the most popular with tourists (up to 3,000 a day), meaning the river can become quite crowded with tour boats. The ideal time to cruise the Li River, then, is early April or late October. In the summer months, the temperature is hot and the humidity high, even on the river. In winter, the temperature and humidity are often at their most pleasant, but the Li River is too low to cruise.

THE HUANGPU: SHANGHAI'S RIVER OF MANY RETURNS

黄浦江

SHANGHAI IS ONE OF CHINA'S greatest seaports, but it is not located on the sea. Rather, the Huangpu River serves as the city's shipping artery both to the East China Sea and the mouth of the Yangzi River, which the Huangpu joins 18 miles north of downtown Shanghai. The Huangpu's 36 miles of wharves are the most fascinating in China. The port handles the cargo coming out of the interior of China, from Nanjing, Wuhan, and other Yangzi River ports, including Chongqing, 1,500 miles deep into Sichuan Province, the rice bowl of China. From Shanghai, which produces plenty of industrial and commercial products in its own right, as much as a third of China's trade with the rest of the world is conducted each year—a substantial part of it flowing up and down the Huangpu River. Mile for mile, this is the most important river in China.

The Huangpu is not a long river, flowing out of Dianshan Lake, about 30 miles west of Shanghai. Nor is it deep—less than 30 feet deep on the average. Constant dredging (once done by hand and winch) is necessary to keep the passage navigable. Mudflats line the shores. In fact, the "bunds" of Shanghai refer to those mudflats, secured by dikes of stone and earth. The Bund and its promenade are landmarks of Shanghai's 19th-century struggle to reclaim a waterfront from the bogs of the Huangpu.

Cruising the Huangpu

Mornings and afternoons tour boats make the 3½-hour voyage up the Huangpu to the Yangzi River delta. From the river, I find that there are unrivaled views of Shanghai's port facilities, the ships of the world that dock there, and the junks and Chinese barges that clot the narrow river avenue. Unrivaled, too, are the postcard views of Shanghai's celebrated European skyline to the west and the booming cityscape of Pudong to the east.

Buying a ticket one Saturday morning on the Bund promenade, I was able to board a tour boat before noon, settling into a soft chair on the

Huangpu River

Jiadiang

Changjiang River

Wusong Mouth

Wusong

Gaoqiao

JIANGSU

Wusong River (Suzhou Creek)

Zhenru Temple

SHANGHAI

SCENIC AREA OF DIANSHAN

Qingpu

Dianshan Lake

Guanwang Temple

SHANGHAI MUNICIPALITY

Songjiang

Huangpu River

ZHEJIANG

Jinshan

0   10 km
     6.2 mi

N

upper deck. Surrounded by picture windows, served hot tea and nuts, I leaned back as we pulled away from the Shanghai waterfront. But I couldn't sit still. I went out on deck as we pulled away. The monumental granite offices, banks, consulates, and hotels of Shanghai's past colonial masters formed a stately panorama to the west, while the Pearl of the Orient TV Tower and the new skyscrapers commanded the east bank, forming the tallest and most expensive building project in the world. I tried to scan both banks at once, as well as keep my eye on the river traffic itself.

We headed north, passing **Huangpu Park** where the Bund begins, across from the **Peace Hotel** and its stunning green pyramid roof, still the loveliest piece of architecture in Shanghai, east or west. The park borders **Suzhou Creek** and is dominated by a new monumental sculpture, soaring ribbons of marble that rise like Shanghai's economic expectations. Huangpu Park was once the British Public Gardens. It is widely reported today that a sign was posted at its entrance reading "Dogs and Chinese Not Allowed." In fact, dogs were not allowed in the garden, and according to a separate ordinance, neither were Chinese except by permission of their foreign employer. This exclusionary insult stung the Shanghainese for a century, until they regained sovereignty over their city in 1949.

Suzhou Creek is spanned by **Waibaidu Bridge,** which once linked the American and British concessions. The Americans staked out the northern shore; the British claimed the downtown waterfront. Waibaidu Bridge was originally a wooden toll bridge built in 1856 by an enterprising Englishman. Steel girders replaced timber in 1906. Sixty feet wide, with two 171-foot-long spans, the bridge was regularly crossed by human-powered rickshaws, introduced to Shanghai from Japan by a Frenchman. Trams were soon routed across the bridge, too, as were motor cars, which had been driving the streets of Shanghai since 1901.

Today, the Suzhou Creek bridge is inundated day and night with taxis, trucks, buses, and a goodly portion of the nearly 500,000 automobiles registered in Shanghai. The mouth of the creek as it empties into the Huangpu is lined with some of the most readily visible and revolting pollution on any river in the world. The shores of the Huangpu are just as unsightly. The Huangpu is muddy. Its dark waters are deluged not just with the sewage of one of the largest cities in the world, not just with the effluent from thousands of cargo ships and motorized barges, but with the floating heaps of a modern commercial city that disgorges its plastic containers, packaging, and foodstuffs into its sewers, streets, rivers, and canals, which all seem to tilt toward the Huangpu. Although ancient poems liken the Huangpu River to a thousand flowers, these days the silted waters must accommodate the discharge of 10,000 factories and the assault of five million tons of untreated sewage annually, a staggering burden. Most frighteningly, the Huangpu is still Shanghai's primary source of drinking water, laden as it is not only with untreated unmentionables but with chemicals such as phenol and mercury as well. But at least the Huangpu is not swarming with corpses as it was in the bad old days before Liberation, when the river served as Shanghai's floating cemetery for paupers.

Less than a mile north of Suzhou Creek is the **International Passenger Terminal** where luxurious cruise ships tie up. The Huangpu River jogs sharply east at this point on its way to the Shanghai shipyards, where cranes and derricks load and unload a logjam of freighters. The freighters are interesting in that they are stamped with the country names of the world's shipping giants: America, Japan, Holland, Russia, Norway. I have seen vessels registered to archenemies unload side-by-side in Shanghai.

Across the river on the eastern shore, vast coal yards crop up, along with petroleum storage facilities. At the **Yangshupu Power Plant,** the stacks are tipped with flames night and day. It was here that I first began to sense fully Shanghai's industrial might. The river seemed endless and its industrial ranks—the dry docks, factories, and power plants—equally unlimited, like an army of millions massed on both shores of a worldwide economic battlefield.

The Bund and the Pearl of the Orient TV Tower rapidly fade from view as the Huangpu slowly begins to curve northward again. We cross under **Yangpu Cable Bridge,** together with **Nanpu Cable Bridge** to the south, two of the largest such structures in the world, both completed just a few years ago to link the east and west banks of the river. Shanghai's modern boom is accelerating on both sides of the Huangpu, which is still its main shipping link to the world and into the rich interior of China.

What overwhelms river passengers even more than the long industrial shoreline is the traffic slinking up and down the waterway. The Huangpu is, on the average, just 600 feet wide. It is like a superhighway without visible lanes, glutted with gigantic freighters, tugs, tiny sampans, and above all the undulating trains of unpainted wooden barges, tied together to save fuel, forming serpentine dragons on a serpentine river. Flotillas of these heavily laden barges, their gunwales just above the waterline, usually number a dozen or more. Their open holds are stuffed with coal, lime, brick, produce, scrap metal, and a thousand other commodities in transit. The rear cabins are homes to families who sleep and cook and work and play on the Huangpu. The family bicycle is often parked on deck. Potted flowers festoon the cabin roofs. Noisy outboard engines, often in teams of four or five, propel the barges from the stern. Laundry lines stretch from cabin roof to prow. Dishes are washed and meals are cooked with water scooped from the brown river. More than 2,000 oceangoing ships compete with the 20,000 barges, fishing junks, and rowboats that stalk the Huangpu every year.

There are also navy gunboats and even an occasional submarine anchored on the shores. A sign in English nailed to the railing of our tour boat deck sternly warns that photographs of military craft and installations are strictly forbidden, but there's no one this morning to enforce the ordinance. Ten years ago I spotted a pre–World War II submarine lounging alongside a pier on the Huangpu River. This time, after passing a dozen gray gunboats, looking less than threatening, I spot the same U-boat as before.

I spend most of the cruise outside on the upper deck, leaning over the rail, absorbed by the continuous parade of barges, ships, and factories. Our northern destination is **Wusong Kuo,** where the harbormasters wait beneath a ghostly pale clock tower, its hands frozen. This marks the Yangzi River delta, where the Huangpu disappears into the convergence of far mightier waterways: the Yangzi River and the Pacific Ocean. The estuary is as vast as an ocean, although it is neither ocean nor river here but a netherworld of water moving in contrary directions on crisscrossing tides, salted and silted, muddied and fresh. The river currents churn against the implacable wall of the East China Sea. An armada of vessels, large and small, waits in the estuary for a sea change, for shipments to be readied, for their turn to come at the Shanghai docks. On this watery tarmac, the population of boats surpasses that of any man-made marina. The vessels wait and bob up and down, moving nowhere on their anchors as if time itself has stopped.

Our tour boat ventures only far enough out into this twilight zone of tides and currents to pivot slowly and turn back into the narrowing passageway of the Huangpu. The boat has come alive. It's lunchtime. Families head downstairs for the buffet. Some of them have not left their sofas the entire voyage, at peace on the water, I suppose. They have been watching the closed-circuit televisions in the upper deck lounges. Some have nodded off, a cup of tea still in their hands. As for me, my eyes have been wide open the whole way, feasting on the crowded river traffic, the thickest I've ever seen on a river. For the return trip I pull up a wicker deck chair, sip my hot tea, nibble on the fruit, nuts, and a chocolate bar I packed, and watch the procession of barges as endless as silk shops and clothing stores on Shanghai's Nanjing Road, where the human traffic is just as thick.

Our boat eventually sails into Shanghai as countless clipper ships and ocean steamers have over the past 150 years, bearing outsiders for their first glimpse of the great colonial skyline of the Bund. The 1920s neo-classic edifices, built by Shanghai's conquering taipans, still dominate the waterfront, but new skyscrapers of the 1990s are crowding in on them from behind now. And across the Huangpu, on the eastern shore, there's an entirely fresh skyline mounting the stage, more imposing, soaring far higher, the product of Shanghai's modern taipans who are enterprising local Chinese rather than carpetbagging Westerners. Nevertheless, the architecture of East Shanghai is also strictly international, a Western import—but now an import rather than an imposition. Our ferry slowly parts this divided architectural curtain of old brick and stone, of new glass and steel, coming to rest at its quay on a river of commerce and industry that has few rivals East or West—a waterway not of China's past but of its future.

PRACTICAL INFORMATION

CRUISES

Huangpu River cruises depart from a wharf on the south Bund promenade in downtown Shanghai. The day-tour tickets can usually be purchased from a hotel tour desk or from offices on the Bund promenade. The north ticket office is in a well-marked kiosk across Zhongshan Road from the Peace Hotel on the Bund. Be sure that the ticket-seller points out the departure wharf (it could change). These days Huangpu tours usually depart from the wharf that is directly in line with the south ticket office, due east of the Jinling Lu–Zhongshan Lu intersection.

I purchased my ticket from the south ticket office at 239 Zhongshan Dong Lu (on the lower-level sidewalk that runs alongside the promenade, south of the pyramidal Diamond Restaurant looming overhead). The booking office (☎ 021/ 6374-4461; fax 021/6374-4882) is well marked in English and the clerks can figure out what you want.

Schedules & Prices   Three cruises are offered daily Monday through Friday with departures at 9am (returning 12:30pm), 2pm (returning 5:30pm), and 7pm (returning 9pm). On Saturday and Sunday, departures are at 11am (returning 2:30pm), 3:30pm (returning 7pm), and 8pm (returning 10pm). The 2-hour evening cruises don't travel all the way north to the Yangzi River delta, but they are spectacular because the cityscape, boat traffic, and factories are lighted up. The weekday cruises are a little cheaper because they do not include buffet meals. Tickets for Special Class A (a soft seat, no-smoking lounge with tea service,

wraparound picture windows, and private deck on the bow) are RMB 100 ($12) on weekdays, RMB 118 ($14) on weekends. Loudspeakers broadcast an informative narrative of the voyage in English, Japanese, and Chinese, but it is difficult to hear over the noise of the ship and the river traffic. These tour boats are wide two-deckers, about 150 feet long, with a kiosk selling snacks; a bar selling tea, coffee, sodas, and beer; and a buffet dining room used for weekend and evening voyages. The buffet consists of Chinese foods, not very tasty, akin to dishes offered in the West at low-cost all-you-can-eat restaurants. Drinks, purchased at the dining room bar, are extra. The staff, some of whom live on the boat, speak little English but keep things running in good order.

THE GRAND CANAL:
A RIVER BUILT BY HAND
大运河

C HINA'S GRAND CANAL, MEASURING
1,112 miles north to south from Beijing to Hangzhou, is the longest canal in the world, and one of the oldest. Its first section was dug in 486 B.C. by the king of Wu in order to dispatch soldiers and grain during a campaign of conquest. In 361 B.C., extensive canals were dug from Kaifeng, and it was said that in this period one could travel by boat from Beijing all the way south to Guangzhou. During the Han Dynasty (206 B.C. to A.D. 220) and the Southern and Northern dynasties (A.D. 420–589) weirs and dams were built on the canals that served as locks. Winch systems were also developed, the earliest employment of ship-lifting mechanisms in the world.

Yangdi, second emperor of the Sui Dynasty (A.D. 589–618), made the longest single contribution to the Grand Canal, conscripting one million workers to construct a shipping channel linking his capital at Luoyang in central China to the Yangzi River basin and to northern China as far up as Beijing. In 611, Emperor Yangdi sailed to Beijing from central China aboard a four-deck, 180-foot-long royal barge with a carved dragon's head as its mast. A thousand vessels attended the emperor. To haul this procession, 80,000 coolies in harness were employed, and 40 new palaces were built along the way. Yangdi died on the Grand Canal during his third excursion, hanged by rebellious members of his own court. In 984 the first double-lock was built on the Grand Canal; the first double-lock built in the West, in Italy, was not completed until 1481. During the Song Dynasty (1127–1279), the new capital of Hangzhou hooked itself up to the Grand Canal as far as the Yangzi River. And finally, under the Yuan Dynasty (1271–1368), when the capital moved up to Beijing, the Grand Canal received a new emphasis, linking Beijing in the north and Hangzhou in the south, as it does to this day.

Like the Great Wall, the Grand Canal has fallen into ruins at many places, although long segments are still in use, particularly in the Shanghai region of eastern China, where many lakes and rivers were realigned and joined over the centuries. The most active segment for modern travelers is now between Suzhou and Hangzhou, the southern terminus of the Grand Canal for over 13 centuries. It was this stage that I wanted to sail, hoping to trace something of China's long history where it is still deeply carved into the Earth.

Emperors on the Canal

The motive to build a grand canal on the scale of the Great Wall was chiefly imperial greed. The capitals of successive dynasties always required a water route to the regions that produced not only necessities such as rice but luxuries such as tea and silk. Since the major rivers of China flow from the west to the east, the emperors built an entirely new river over the centuries, as massive as the Yellow River or the Yangzi River, in order to create a flow of goods on a north–south axis that bisected their palaces and treasure houses. As they cut the various channels, they encountered an engineering problem. Differences in terrain and water flow led to varying water speeds. To harmonize the Grand Canal, water gates were constructed. The Panmen Water Gate still stands in Suzhou. It was just east of this monument on the city moat that I boarded one of the dozens of passenger ferries that sail the Grand Canal to Hangzhou.

For the last six centuries the primary function of the Grand Canal has been to transport grain and other articles as tax and tributes north to the capital of Beijing. There is a saying that it was the Grand Canal that brought the city of Beijing into existence. The moat that once surrounded the Forbidden City connected directly to the Grand Canal. The bricks in the Forbidden City, the Temple of Heaven, and the Ming Tombs all came up the Grand Canal. Two hundred thousand tons of rice were required by the rulers in the north, but owing to waste, traveling expenses, and the tenacious middle men of the Middle Kingdom, twice that much grain had to set out from the south. More than 10,000 rice barges, replaced every 10 years, plied the Grand Canal. Other ships carried cloth, food, salt, porcelain, lacquerware, bricks, bamboo, and timber to Beijing. Scholars used the canal to reach the capital for the imperial examinations. A special bureaucracy evolved to regulate and maintain the canal, repairing the earthen embankments, planting trees, dredging waterways, and arresting pirates. Laborers were stationed every mile, 10 per outpost. In 1902, many of the officials in charge of water management were dismissed and canal transport was officially abandoned. Rail service had come into play.

Smaller boats continued to use segments of the canal for local shipping. In the 1950s, the canal was dredged and enlarged in the south, where it is now open year-round. The section that runs through Suzhou down to Hangzhou contains 20 locks, as well as culverts and water-pumping stations. It is also so thick with ships and barges that I doubt canal travel will ever become a thing of the past in China, the anachronism it has become in America.

Water City of the East

Suzhou is a romantic place to begin a Grand Canal cruise. Known as the "Water City of the East," Suzhou rose to prominence by shipping its silk embroidery up the canal to China's imperial courts, establishing a high reputation in the arts that it never relinquished. Square bricks from Suzhou's kilns paved the Forbidden City. An inner moat encases this city of interlaced canals; a gated outer waterway connected Suzhou to the Grand Canal. Panmen, the old water gate in southwest Suzhou, consists of two sections: an inner brick gate 12 feet wide and an outer granite gate 9 feet wide. The walls between were used to entrap and inspect canal ships that called upon the city. The **Panmen Water Gate** is still in place, as is the nearby **Wumen Bridge,** one of the largest arched stone bridges on the canal and now the entryway to Suzhou's wharves. Suzhou has everywhere the marks of a Grand Canal city. The whitewashed houses of Suzhou still have crimson doors that open on the inner waterways that feed the Grand Canal. You can cross more than a hundred bridges in Suzhou: arched stone bridges, ladder-shaped bridges, even house-spanning bridges *(lian jia qiao)* that connect two parts of a dwelling.

Two miles west of the city, the Grand Canal sweeps by **Cold Mountain Temple,** jogging inland to join Suzhou's city moat to the southeast. This is where poet Zhang Ji, arriving at the temple by canal boat during the Tang Dynasty, wrote this delicate passage, which resounds in Chinese literature:

Moon sets and crows caw in the frosted sky;
River maples and the lights of fishing boats break into my
troubled sleep.
Beyond Suzhou lies Cold Mountain Temple;
At midnight the clang of the bell reaches the traveler's
boat.

I did not hear the clear bell in the frosted sky clanging in Cold Mountain Temple as I embarked on the canal boat at Suzhou. Instead, I heard the horns of two dozen nearly identical canal boats as they backed out from the piers to begin their journeys to Hangzhou. These are not dainty ferries, outfitted to resemble the elegant dragon boats of the emperors who once sailed the Grand Canal. Nor are they modern ferries, comfortably tailored for the international tourist. They are rusty steel double-deckered passenger ferries that have worked hard and long. Their deluxe staterooms are simple, crude, deteriorating closets with a set of narrow bunk beds, a nightstand, an oil heater, and a spittoon on the floor. They have windows to let in the breeze and glass doors that open directly onto the outside deck. Although the knob was missing from my door, I could still lock it from the inside. But alas, the real drawback is that these are overnight cruises upon the Grand Canal. We depart in the late afternoon, with only a few hours on either end for daylight. I try to make the most of the light, clinging to the railing above the bow.

The **city moat** where we push off is exceedingly narrow. The ship must pivot neatly and precisely to begin the journey. I'm surprised but fascinated when three of these bargelike flat-bottomed passenger ships undock together. The vessel on our port side is the only one using its engines. The deck hands, leashing and unleashing the ropes that hold the three ships together, maneuver us into the middle of the canal so that we drift into a staggered line. Then the crew hooks us together, end to end, using an iron pole on a swivel to lash stern to bow. My canal boat is second in line. The lead boat does all the work. We are gently towed forward, the black smoke of the first canal boat streaming back on us.

Night Passage

The Grand Canal is not beautiful, but it is as fascinating as the work-a-day canal boats, themselves just a step up from the barges that surround our small flotilla. These barges, each about 60 feet long, with simple cabins on their sterns and open holds running forward to rounded stems, also like to hold hands. They too are often linked end to end in the tow of small tugs. Those barges that choose to go it on their own are powered by outboard engines with long, straight shafts. Often, a single barge will have four or five of these engines mounted in a row across the stern.

We pass scores of fishing junks tied up at docks, white flags fluttering on their sterns, then turn south, passing under a long, blackened bridge. We're on the Grand Canal. Sunset is already coloring the sludge of the sky. The barges are low in the water, crushed by loads of brick, coal, and sand to feed the factories that line the canal. The passage is narrow at times, although once out of Suzhou it widens to 300 feet or more. The only scenery on the banks is of flat farmlands and grime-coated factories. The chimneys of coal-powered factories ignite with orange flames. Several discharge effluents into the canal, colored a thoroughly unearthly blue. The Grand Canal is an industrial river, made and run by humans, and it is black with discharges. I can smell from the railing a powerful mixture of diesel oil and diarrhea, really an open sewer.

Many waterways cut in and out of the Grand Canal. It's a main artery for farms and factories all across this vast plain of rapeseed and rice that radiates out from Shanghai. The Grand Canal cuts straight and true. Scores of low bridges span it. Thousands of vessels run up and down its length, stopping to load or unload at factories and towns and farms on the embankments, or to head down a side canal to towns and businesses that are still served by waterways. There must be hundreds of villages that depend on canal barges, places no tourist ever sees.

The passing barges are also homes. I see dogs, cats, bicycles, plants, and laundry lines. On deck a woman cooks the family dinner on a small coal stove. Fourteen barges linked together are the most I see, and I see that number often. Perhaps it's the maximum allowed in tow on the Grand Canal.

In the southern outskirts of Suzhou, the Grand Canal embankment is straddled by **Precious Belt Bridge.** Over a half mile long, it consists of 53 stone arches. It is the longest arched bridge on the Grand Canal. It was finished in A.D. 819, after the prefect's governor donated his precious belt to fund its completion. I barely notice it in passing. I am watching the barges coming at us in the darkness. Running lights consist of a son or daughter standing on the bow waving a flashlight.

I lie back on the hard bunk. It's too hot for a quilt. I can't sleep long. The oncoming traffic is continuous. Ships pass within a few feet, like apartment buildings hurtling through the night. The engines rattle and scream, the ship horns blast away, and the larger vessels such as ours sweep the water and canal banks with searchlights. Sometimes I hear shouts.

End of the Grand Canal

After 5am, I don't sleep another wink. A faint sun creeps into overcast skies. I rub my eyes, but the panorama of gray factories, coal yards, smokestacks, and cranes does not brighten. The fishermen are up. They are trolling the waters with baskets for shrimp. I wonder how these people can survive on the Grand Canal. It is a severe world. Even this voyage seems little better than a 13-hour Greyhound bus tour of a sewer.

Yet as we near Hangzhou, last stop on the Grand Canal, the banks become stone, neatly laid by hand, and the promenades are shaded by groves of willow and maple. We dock at Genshan Harbor near the tripled-arched **Gongchen Bridge,** the last ancient stone crossing on the Grand Canal. The lead boat angles in and cuts us loose. We drift into the dock. "Above there is Heaven," goes the popular saying, "Below are Suzhou and Hangzhou." And between these rivers there is still the Grand Canal, reaching across the land like the dark, powerful arm of an ancient warrior, a palpable link with the China of the emperors.

PRACTICAL INFORMATION

CRUISES

June and July are the best months to make this voyage, particularly since sunset is at its latest and viewing the Grand Canal is extended.

Canal boat passage can be booked through China International Travel Service (CITS) in Suzhou. The main office is in the Suzhou Hotel, 115 Shiquan Jie (☎ 0512/522-3175; fax 0512/523-3593). I booked my ticket to Hangzhou at the tour desk (a branch of CITS) in the Gloria Plaza Hotel. The price for the entire two-berth cabin was RMB 256 ($31), which included a RMB 60 ($7.25) service charge. This was a first-class ticket. Second-class tickets (four berths to a room) are considerably cheaper (about RMB 50/$6 per person). Cabins are crude, without sinks or private baths. In fact, these canal ships have no showers or tubs. Toilets are unisex and Chinese style (hole in the floor). Dinner is served aboard, but I avoided it by packing a picnic lunch in Suzhou, including bottled water. All other passengers were Chinese, some from overseas, and all were quite friendly.

Canal boats depart Suzhou at 5:30pm and arrive in Hangzhou the next morning at about 7:30am. The boat is docked in Suzhou at the Nanmen Passenger Boat Terminal, northeast of the bridge that crosses the moat on Renmin Nan Lu.

TAI HU: CHINA'S GREAT LAKE

太湖

Lake Tai (Tai Hu) is the most fabled body of fresh water in China, a vast natural mirror embracing two ancient kingdoms: the Kingdom of Wu and the Kingdom of Yue. Tai Hu is often draped in mists, likened by poets to the clouds between water and mountain. On its shores are the ancient garden city of Wuxi and the pottery town of Yixing, famous for its caves. In the lake itself are scattered temple islands.

The Gardens of the Grand Canal

I based myself in **Wuxi** in a hotel on the Grand Canal, which is still connected by a river to the northeast shore of Lake Tai. Wuxi has a history of 3,000 years, but the city is now a center of industry, lacking the natural and cultural beauty of nearby Suzhou and Hangzhou. Nevertheless, along its western edges Wuxi touches the great lake, affording fine vistas, and several of Wuxi's old garden parks are worth investigating.

Xihui Park, bordered on the east by the Grand Canal, is Wuxi's chief downtown attraction, topped by the seven-story Dragon Light Pagoda (Long Guang), first built during the Ming Dynasty. Within Xihui Park's sprawling, well-manicured grounds is **Jichang Garden,** Wuxi's most famous private garden. Once the site of a Buddhist temple, Jichang became the retirement villa of an official who finished the garden in 1520. Jichang is laid out much like the famous classic gardens of Suzhou, replete with ponds, halls with slim columns and upturned eaves, old steles (carved stone tablets), and rockeries consisting of massive Tai Hu stones whose bizarre shapes and indentations are the result of long dunkings in the great lake. Jichang Garden was a favorite of Emperor Qianlong, who in 1750 ordered the construction of a similar garden in Beijing's Summer Palace. The covered walkways of Jichang Garden lead to higher vantage points in which the terrain of the surrounding Xihui Park becomes the "borrowed scenery" of this small garden, a fundamental "expansion" technique of Chinese garden design.

Jichang Garden contains a display of Wuxi's most famous handicraft, **Huishan clay figures,** which are miniature sculptures of pleasingly plump little children and rotund characters from operas and plays, originated four centuries ago by local peasants and now created at the adjacent **Clay Figurine Research Institute.** Clay for these figurines, which are produced both by hand and by mold, comes from Hui Shan, a mountain connected to Xihui Park by a cable car.

The center of Xihui Park is a large artificial lake fed by a stream. I was visiting in the spring, when the park hosts a tulip festival with fields of bright tulips imported from Holland and even a working windmill. Sitting on a bench at the edge of the stream, admiring the scenery, I noticed in the corner of my eye a large rat darting toward me. As it hopped daintily across the foot of the woman seated on my right, I reacted without thinking, kicked straight out, and punted the racing rat high into the air. It rose and fell into the stream, disappearing with a splash. The whole transaction was a single reflex, so swift my bench-partner was never aware of the intrusion.

Another garden, **Liyuan,** lies in southern Wuxi on Li Lake, a back bay of Lake Tai. Celebrated as the garden of Xi Shi, a legendary beauty of the Spring and Autumn period (403–221 B.C.), it was rebuilt between 1927 and 1930 and expanded by the government in 1952. It actually consists of two older gardens built along the shore. Noted for its peach blossoms in the spring, this complex of watery gardens features a veranda with 89 windows that frame changing views of fish ponds, rockeries, flowering bushes, and the Pavilion of the Four Seasons. A long, covered cement corridor hugs the lakeshore, ending at a floating restaurant modeled and named after Jumbo, Hong Kong's famous culinary barge. Liyuan is not one of the more beautiful gardens in the region, and I was not enthralled. It more or less lives up to its name, translated as the Garden Eaten by the Worms.

Sailing Lake Tai

The best reason to stay in Wuxi is Lake Tai. The finest vistas are at Wuxi's **Turtle Head Isle (Yuantouzhu),** a turtle-shaped peninsula that juts into the lake. Turtle-Head began as a garden in 1918 and grew into a large park of teahouses, halls, walkways, and vistas. Entrance costs RMB 25 ($3). The lake viewpoints along the peninsula's shoreline are equipped with pavilions. The finest view is from a small modern lighthouse.

North of the lighthouse is a large pier with ferries to **Three Hills Island (San Shan Dao),** a 20-minute boat ride west into Tai Hu. I lined up there and boarded the vessel with hundreds of local schoolchildren. The view back to Turtle Head Isle and the Wuxi lakeshore was splendid, a light fog rising from the shallow, glassy surface where fishermen glided past in their boats. Three Hill Island has been developed recently as a walk-through amusement park with an artificial cave, brand-new pavilions, sedan-chair rides, and groups of wild monkeys. Its local name is Fairy Island, which befits its new theme-park atmosphere. Views of the lake, its other islands and distant shores, were once reason enough to cross Lake Tai—reason enough still for me. The center of the island park is a four-story mock temple with the gargantuan, garish plaster statue of an ancient emperor inside its atrium. Again, the views from the top are superb. The return journey on the ferry can be soothing, too. For a moment, skimming the waters, I have a glimpse of the Lake Tai that the old poets celebrated: vast, flat, misty, a contemplative vacuum quietly reflecting the heavens.

The Teapots of Yixing

I experienced another aspect of Tai Hu when I traveled west to Yixing, the most famous center of teapot production in China. Yixing teapots are available in any large souvenir shop worth its salt in China. They are now mass produced in this region, some in factories employing over 10,000 workers. Even the lakeside freeway from Wuxi is lined with ceramic: with ceramic light poles, with retail yards of glazed roof tiles and garden ornaments, with huge ceramic pots.

Pottery production began in Yixing more than 3,000 years ago. For the last 2,000 years, Yixing has turned out the finest glazed china in China, relying on a local clay known as purple sand. Tea sets from Yixing are said to impart a taste to brewed tea that is essential for complete enjoyment.

The road to Yixing is a superhighway through two Chinas: one old, one new. In one respect, the road resembles an old avenue, its median strip decorated in trimmed hedges, its light poles arranged like brown-and-yellow ceramic columns decorated in dragon coils, glass globes suspended on either side like lanterns. Dozens of old canals feed Lake Tai, and slabs of marble and newly raised Tai Hu rocks fill the courtyards of roadside merchants. We pass a market town where canvas big tops have been pitched for an old-fashioned roadside carnival, complete with barkers drawing in their marks. In another respect, however, the road reminds one of China's feverish economic boom. Scores of smokestacks boil over day and night, coughing out black-and-yellow coils of pungent smoke, thick as carpets. It is one of the most visibly polluted areas I have visited in China, sharply at odds with a serene lake and ancient teapots. Officials are aware of environmental problems in the region and they are taking action. Cleaning up Lake Tai is a major priority under the ninth Five-Year Plan (1996–2000). Wuxi residents already pay a monthly RMB 2 to RMB 4 (25¢ to 50¢) sanitation fee for waste treatment. Jiangsu Province has ordered 241 industries to control their discharges and treat pollutants by the year 1998, when 43 new sewage treatment plants should be on-line. By the year 2010, 90% of city and township sewage discharges are to be treated (along with 30% of the rural sewage), meaning that by that date the water of Lake Tai should be drinkable.

At Dingshu, a small town 15 miles south of Yixing, I make a short visit to **Purple Sand Village,** a new model town of two-story villas with patios, sales rooms, and workshops located on the ground level. Some of China's best-known potters, having made enough to give up their factory jobs, live here. In this model teapotters' village, I met members of some of the most celebrated artisan families and watched them at work, molding the clay by hand on small tables, shaping pots, cups, and saucers, and applying decorative touches with their fingertips. The pots are fired for 24 hours in small kilns, then shipped to galleries or patrons or kept at home on sales shelves. Signed, such sets sometimes command prices above $1,000. Photographs on the walls often show a potter in the embrace of an illustrious visitor such as Chinese Premier Li Peng. Less refined, far less expensive Yixing teapots and cups are for sale at the stalls along Dingshu's main street. A visit to the town's **Ceramic Exhibition Hall** is also worth a half hour, as it features exquisite pots from several dynasties, modern creations by today's artists, and such everyday ceramics as bathroom fittings.

Underground Yixing

Yixing's reputation for teapots is international, while its reputation for limestone caverns is still confined to China. I visited two of Yixing's caverns, both in the countryside east of Lake Tai on roads leading out of Dingshu. I'm not a devotee of caves, but the caves of China are unusual, almost always fronted by temples and imbued with ancient stories of hermit monks or Romeo-and-Juliet tragedies from feudal times. The caves are not brilliant affairs. They are rough-edged and poorly lit, but the roads to the caves are interesting. Large tea plantations and hulking rock quarries punctuate the flat fields that encircle much of Lake Tai and the lower Yangzi River basin. Women in straw hats stuff handbaskets with tea leaves. The dusty roads are clogged with small tractor-trailers hauling rock from quarry to crusher.

The first cavern I visited, **Shanjuan Cave,** was named for a legendary ancient poet who refused an offer to become king, preferring utter freedom. He lived as a recluse in the cave. Open to the public since 1935, Shanjuan contains a large chamber called Lion and Elephant Hall after its size, the texture of its ceiling, and two large stalagmites that resemble the creatures. In its deepest recesses, an underground river winds for a quarter mile through the Crystal Palace. There I boarded a small wooden flat-bottomed boat. The oarsman planted his feet on the deck and pushed off using a long pole, propelling us into the dark. The water chamber is lined with 75 tiny caves, most of them unfathomable, even when our pilot attempts to illuminate them with his flashlight.

Outside Shanjuan Cave, a walkway along a stream leads to a temple complex that commemorates China's Romeo and Juliet, two young lovers who met as students 15 centuries ago. Since women were not allowed to attend schools in those days, the girl disguised herself as a lad. At school, she fell in love with another student. By the time this misadventure was disentangled, the boy, learning that the girl was betrothed to another, had taken his life. The girl, about to wed an older man chosen by her parents, threw herself into his grave. They emerged together as butterflies. Their tomb is said to be at this temple, which has dolled itself up with painted wall murals recounting the story. I have heard the same story recounted at two other locations in China, both claiming to be the place of its origin.

The second cavern I visited, **Zhanggong,** fronted by a sprawling Daoist temple rising up a terraced hillside, proved to be larger and more intricate, with 72 interlinked chambers. Entrance required a local guide with a flashlight and purchase of an RMB 19 ($2.30) ticket (with RMB 1/ 12¢ added as a "safety insurance fee"). Zhanggong's bewildering mile of passageways resembles a labyrinth for fairies. The largest room, Hall of the Sea Dragon Kong, opens through a long funnel of twisting rock to the sky, and the sky in turn is reflected in a pool on the rock floor below. I was glad to emerge into the light, failing to find either of these caves conducive to meditation.

World's Largest Buddha

The newest attraction on Lake Tai is the most massive of all—the largest Buddha in Asia. Erected on Ling Shan, a forested hill 11 miles west of Wuxi, and unveiled in October 1997, the **Ling Shan Buddha** presides over two new temples and a large wall mural engraved with a pictorial map of the Western Paradise. This is something of a Chinese Land of the Giants. In the shrine's main courtyard there is an enormous golden hand sprouting from the Earth, Buddha's hand (37 feet tall, 17 feet wide, and weighing in at 13 tons). The Big Buddha is fashioned from bronze— from 1,638 sheets of bronze—each sheet 5 yards square. Standing atop a hefty 28-foot platform, the statue is 240 feet tall and tips the scale at 700 tons. By comparison, the Buddha on Hong Kong's Lantau Island, completed by the same company in 1993 and heralded as the largest in its class (seated, outdoor, bronze), is a mere 81-foot, 250-ton child. Construction of the Big Buddha at Ling Shan was initiated in the fall of 1994. Twenty chanting monks arrived to bless the undertaking. Wuxi and Lake Tai tourism officials are no doubt hoping that a million times that many tourists come to make their own offerings (tickets RMB 20/ $2.40) at the feet of the world's biggest standing Buddha.

Second Spring of the World

Lake Tai has always had its curiosities, first and foremost the limestone boulders that its lathing waters shape and scrape for use in the rockeries of classic gardens. For centuries, massive garden stones have been submerged in this lake. Emperor Huizong, who ruled China from 1101 to 1126, emptied most of the Middle Kingdom's treasury in pursuit of more and more fantastical Tai Hu rocks. A famous Song Dynasty dandy and artist, Mi Fei, would routinely kowtow to his favorite Tai Hu rock, which he addressed affectionately as his older brother. Yet in the vastness and strangeness of Lake Tai, there are small but intense nuggets of ancient beauty. Xihui Park in Wuxi, where I drop-kicked a rat into a stream, also contains **Erquan Pool,** a Tang Dynasty spring that Lu Yu, author of the *Classic of Tea (Cha Jing),* immortalized as the "Second Spring of the World" for its superb sweetness and viscosity for the brewing of the perfect tea. During the Song Dynasty, Yixing clay and Wuxi spring water became the emperor's cup of tea, and both are still found on the shores of Lake Tai. It is also said that the reflection of the moon in Erquan Pool is exquisite beyond all words. Indeed, the blind folk musician Abing was inspired when he heard about the moon mirrored in this pool to compose one of China's most enduring and plaintive songs, another echo, faint as mist on a great lake, of the hidden depths of China's long history.

PRACTICAL INFORMATION

ORIENTATION

Lake Tai (Tai Hu) is China's third largest freshwater lake, bordering Jiangsu and Zhejiang provinces. **Shanghai** lies nearby, directly east. **Yixing,** the pottery region, is on the west shore. **Wuxi,** a Grand Canal port, is on the northwest tip of Tai Hu.

GETTING THERE

Wuxi is the most convenient base for touring the lake and its shoreside attractions. Located on the Beijing–Shanghai train line, Wuxi is 40 minutes from Suzhou, 2 hours from Shanghai, and 3 hours from Nanjing by rail. There is no airport.

Wuxi's taxi drivers are friendly. A **crosstown taxi** should cost less than RMB 20 ($2.40). Hotel tour desks can book your train tickets to Wuxi as well as onward train tickets.

TOURS & STRATAGEMS

China Travel Service (CTS), 59 Chezhan Lu (☎ 0510/230-4906; fax 0510/230-2743), offers custom individual tours. I arranged a 2-day tour for one person with private car and guide, lunches included, that took in the gardens of Wuxi, Lake Tai, and the pottery shops, caves, and monuments of Yixing county for RMB 1,200 ($145). The best contact at CTS is Ms. Chen Yue Fen (English name, Celina), who can also be contacted by the duty manager in the lobby of the Wuxi Holiday Inn.

WHERE TO STAY

Wuxi's two best hotels square off face-to-face across a large traffic circle on the west side of the city. I stayed at the Holiday Inn; across the way is the Pan Pacific.
Holiday Inn Milido Wuxi (Meilidu Dajiudian). 2 Liangxi Lu. ☎ 800/465-4329 or 0510/586-5665. Fax 0510/580-1668. 188 rms, 31 suites. A/C MINIBAR TV TEL. $105 double. AE, DC, JCB, MC, V. Located on the banks of the Grand Canal, 3 miles from Lake Tai, the nine-story Milido maintains excellent service levels. With its recently renovated rooms and extra features, including bicycle rental, it must be one of the best 3-star hotels in China. The Aviary Lobby Lounge is unique: Its curving outside wall of glass opens to an attached outdoor screened aviary of tropical birds and plants. (One

further note: The hallways of the Holiday Inn have piped-in Hawaiian music—but, hey, it is a Holiday Inn.)
  Services: Room service (24-hour), dry cleaning and laundry (next-day service), nightly turndown, daily maid service, foreign exchange counter.
  Facilities: In-house movies, pool (indoor, heated), health club (exercise machines), business center (24-hour), tour desk.
Pan Pacific Wuxi Grand Hotel (Wuxi Dafandian). 1 Liangqing Lu. ☎ 800/327-8585 or 0510/580-6789. Fax 0510/270-0991. 342 rms. A/C MINIBAR TV TEL. $116 double. AE, DC, JCB, MC, V. At 20 stories the tallest building in Wuxi, the Pan Pacific provides plenty of luxury, from its soaring atrium to its Chiense carpets and ceramics. The

rooms (including rooms for disabled travelers) are spacious and clean. At 4 stars, it has more facilities (including a clinic, post office, and four restaurants) than the Holiday Inn, but the service is not always comparable.

Services: Concierge, room service (24-hour), dry cleaning and laundry (next-day service), nightly turndown, daily maid service, foreign exchange counter.

Facilities: In-house movies, pool (indoor, heated), health club (exercise machines), sauna, business center (24-hour), beauty salon, shopping arcade, tour desk.

WHERE TO DINE

The **Jumbo Floating Restaurant** at Li Garden (☎ 0510/670-8888) is owned by the nearby Lakeside Hotel (Hubin Fandian) and features Tai Hu specialties (mainly eels, shrimp, and lake crab) for RMB 20 to 50 ($2.40 to $6).

The Holiday Inn Milido's **Regent Restaurant** (☎ 0510/586-5665) offers similar regional specialties in more hygienic surroundings. The Holiday Inn also has an excellent Cantonese restaurant, **Peng Lai Court** (☎ 0510/676-5665) has similarly reasonable prices (RMB 42 to 100/$5 to $12) and a view of the Grand Canal.

CHINA BY SEA: CRUISING THE EAST COAST

东海岸

AMONG CHINA'S MOST FABLED CITIES are the great ports on the east coast: Tianjin and Yantai on the Yellow Sea, Shanghai and Ningbo on the East China Sea, Xiamen (Amoy) and Hong Kong on the South China Sea. This fortuitous maritime alignment would make an ideal itinerary for tours by ship, except that China has not yet become a major destination for international cruise lines. Nevertheless, several companies, including Royal Caribbean, Princess, Crystal, Seabourn, and Holland America, do conduct luxury cruises that include ports up and down China's east coast between Beijing and Hong Kong—although such cruises may occur as seldom as once every two years.

Curious to experience this approach to China, I booked a Royal Caribbean cruise of China—even knowing that the whole notion of such cruises went against the grain of my previous travels in China, most of which were independent and solitary.

I was not prepared to enjoy myself, but I was immediately enchanted. China can be a particularly daunting country to tour independently, largely because its infrastructure of hotels, transportation, and travel services is still not well developed for foreigners. It can also be wearing on group travelers who—because of the scale of China—must pull up stakes virtually every morning for either a hard day of sightseeing or a jostling transfer by air, rail, or road to another city. Seeing China via cruise ship is, by comparison, an Edenic experience. In short, a luxury cruise provides an easy way to tour a difficult place.

A cruise eliminated my need to pack and repack. I no longer had to negotiate the vagaries of Chinese train stations, bus terminals, or airports every few days. All my food worries dissolved, too: no more searches for decent restaurants in strange cities. I found myself traveling like a member of the imperial court in a private cabin, stopping each day at legendary cities for an escorted tour, topped off by yet another sumptuous banquet. I didn't even have to worry about getting a China visa before the

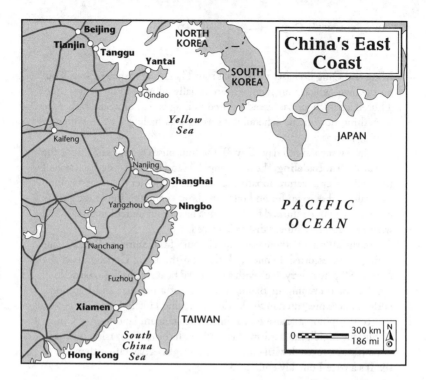

trip. Cruise members can be included in a group visa. Above all, after a dusty day of land touring, the pleasure of returning to the comforts of "home" aboard the cruise ship cannot be overstated. A cruise is a perfect way to get your feet wet in China, providing perhaps the most comfortable introduction of all to the Middle Kingdom.

Quintessential Beijing (Days 1–3)

China's capital is not on the sea, not even on a major river, but it is the first stop on most cruises of China. A century ago, ships were the primary means by which Westerners reached China; today, it's the airplane. Cruise passengers from America, Canada, Europe, Oceania, and Asia now converge on Beijing by air, are met and ushered through immigration in an eye-blink, and then transfer to a deluxe hotel.

Beginning a China cruise in landlocked Beijing is not such a strange idea. This is the first visit to China for most cruise passengers, so to miss the highlights of Beijing is to miss out on some of the supreme sights of China. The cruise line arranges to have all their passengers boarded and banqueted in the same hotel and escorted to the major sights via a phalanx of tour buses staffed by local English-speaking guides.

The first full day (Day 2) of my particular cruise commenced with an American buffet breakfast and lunch followed by an afternoon tour of the **Forbidden City** and **Tiananmen Square.** The Forbidden City tour turned out to be cursory—too brief, yet sufficient to give the flavor of the

Ming and Qing Dynasty treasures. From Tiananmen Square I struck out on my own, which tour members are usually allowed to do at any time. Thus, if a passenger has already visited Beijing before or would rather see something not on the schedule, it's as easy as hailing a cab—which in Beijing is easy.

On the second full day (Day 3), the tour buses set out at 8am for the **Great Wall at Badaling,** the most popular (and most crowded) section of the wall. After a lecture aboard the bus, the guides let the tourists climb the wall on their own for an hour, which was enough time to escape the hordes. Everyone returned for lunch at a restaurant under the Great Wall where a series of Chinese dishes is served.

In the afternoon, there was a quick tour of the **Summer Palace,** consisting of an escorted 1-mile walk through the Long Corridor, past the Marble Ship, to a ferry dock with a chartered boat ride back to the parking lot. The final evening in Beijing consisted of a banquet and traditional performances presented in the landmark Beijing Hotel.

To this point, a cruise tour mimics the standard land tour of China, hitting the highlights hard and fast, although the cruise version is already notably more relaxed, with only two major sights a day rather than five or six. It's a pace I quickly embraced.

Tianjin Departure (Day 4)

On the way to Tianjin to board the cruise ship, we spent 2 hours at Beijing's **Temple of Heaven.** The tour was poorly conducted: We were given too much time to mill around one great temple that is closed inside, and no instructions were issued about how to find the park's other attractions. The guides discouraged such explorations. I set out on my own nonetheless and ended up involved in a badminton-like game that a sidewalk vendor was marketing. Then it was back on the buses for two hours.

From **Tianjin,** 50 miles east of Beijing, we were whisked past downtown 30 more miles east to the modern docks at Tanggu, which are heavily industrialized. Tianjin is China's fourth largest city (population about 9 million) and its most important northeastern port, but this afternoon was to be our first afternoon at sea. No more tour stops. We boarded the ship, checked out our cabins, partook of a fine buffet lunch, mustered on deck for the lifeboat drill, and settled into cruising the Yellow Sea. Leaving the port, we were treated to an extensive view of cargo facilities and the freighters of the world loading and unloading there.

In many ways, we could have been on a luxury cruise ship in the Mediterranean, the Caribbean, Alaska, or almost anywhere else in the world. The facilities (modern), the staff (international, English-speaking), and the cuisine (Western) gave no hint of China. It was like visiting China on a floating hotel, a deluxe resort with casino, pool deck, nightclubs, spa, beauty salon, medical clinic, and duty-free shop, attended by cabin stewards, cruise directors, roving musicians, and a host of waiters and chefs.

At the same time, emphasis was placed on the China experience. A port lecturer from Beijing held daily briefings on the next day's port of call. A China expert delivered background lectures on the Middle Kingdom. A staff member conducted morning *tai ji quan* exercises. The focus was on the shore excursions—the chance to see the sights in China, often in cities that most China visitors never enter. A China cruise, whether on Royal Caribbean or another major cruise line, is always "port intensive," meaning that passengers have plenty of opportunity to see something of China's sights and culture while enjoying the international offerings provided onboard.

Yantai (Day 5)

Our 7-hour bus tour of Yantai, a cheerful city of 1.4 million, located on the northern coast of Shandong Province (300 miles southeast of Beijing), was typical of the shore excursions offered by cruise lines in China: extensive and fascinating. Passengers were handed over for the day to the buses and guides furnished by the local branch of China International Travel Service (CITS).

Yantai is an ice-free northern port, once known as Chefoo to U.S. Navy personnel, Christian missionaries, and other foreigners who settled here in the late 19th and early 20th centuries. From the harbor I could see that Western-style buildings still stood from those colonial days, but in the harbor itself fish-farming had become the main business. China is the world's largest fish producer, accounting for 60% of all aquaculture production. The rafts and nets of shrimp raisers dotted Yantai's protected waters, where fish-farming methods date back to the 7th century. A third of China's prawns come from Yantai's waters.

The shore tour did not linger long in the harbor or downtown, where new high-rise buildings and international boutiques, including Mickey Mouse and Playboy logo stores, were muscling out the older red-stone buildings with their bright orange-tile roofs. We pressed on to **Yuhuang Temple,** touring its 600-year-old grounds on foot. In one courtyard, a vendor had set up a ring toss on the walkway between the old drum and bell towers. I pitched a half-dozen times but left without a single trinket. Heading uphill, I mounted the circular stairs of the Yunhuang Pavilion for a view of the city and harbor. The temple, like the city, was easygoing and friendly. Even the vendors pushing postcards seemed low-key, a delightful change from the aggressive sellers inundating the sights in Beijing.

Our group lunched at the Yantai Hotel and shopped in the hotel hallway for bargain-priced needlepoint pillow covers and Christmas stockings. In the afternoon, we strolled through the **Yantai Museum,** originally an ornately carved guild hall, and the adjacent Temple to the Sea Goddess, which was shipped in 1864 from Fujian Province and assembled here. This was one of the few southern-style temples in northern China, as indicated by its sweeping roofline, glazed ceramics, and ornamental carved dragon. While there are bigger and better temples in China, it was interesting to see what exists in smaller, out-of-the-way districts. Outside the temple walls where the buses waited, I browsed through a local food market, coming across one vendor who kept two small white dogs on leashes. Less than a decade ago, such pets were virtually impossible to find in China, but everywhere, from Beijing to Yantai, change is swift.

Our final stop was not on the sightseers' map: a prosperous suburban village called **Qu Lan.** We first visited the **Bright Pearl Market,** a modern shop house where the proprietor and his family conducted business in the front and lived in the back rooms. We shared tea and soft drinks with the owner himself, toured his house, and tossed him questions about his life and dreams. He took a turn interviewing us, his chief question being how much we paid for the cruise. The answer no doubt astonished him but also gave him something even higher to aim for.

Just down the street from the market, we gathered for a look at the neighborhood kindergarten, one of the best, no doubt, in China. As we entered the playground, the children welcomed us with dances. We were invited into the school to observe two classrooms. The children greeted us by clapping, then went about their classwork, assembling Lego-like pieces spread out on a large table. I noticed that in an attached room there was a communal nursery consisting of 25 cribs stacked chockablock five to a row, with a pillow and quilt neatly piled on each mattress. As we left the kindergarten grounds, a circle of children performing an umbrella dance bid us adieu.

Altogether, it was an extensive day's touring, but another nice thing about a cruise is that there are many options. One can take a half-day rather than a full-day tour—or no tour at all. The ship was always our home.

Shanghai (Days 6–8)

After two nights and a day sailing from the Yellow Sea south into the East China Sea, we entered the Huangpu River and chugged upstream to China's most fabled port, Shanghai. The colonial skyline of the Bund, Shanghai's downtown harbor frontage, was a spectacular sight, especially from the water. This was the same scene Westerners would have witnessed after weeks or months at sea on schooners or steamers in the days before Liberation (1949) when foreigners ran this notorious port.

The ship docked less than a mile north of the Bund. A series of guided bus tours was scheduled for the next two days, but Royal Caribbean also gave us the option of striking out on our own at any port of call. They always furnished a free downtown shuttle to get us started. As I have visited Shanghai many times, I decided to sightsee on my own, although the shore excursions were intriguing: city tours, Shanghai cultural tours, and 11-hour day extensions by bus and train to nearby Suzhou (City of Gardens) or Wuxi, with a boat trip there on the Grand Canal.

The drop-off point for the cruise shuttle bus was the **Friendship Store**, one block north of the Bund and Nanjing Road, China's number one shopping street. The bus ran in both directions every hour up to 10:30pm. Were I to find a restaurant in town, I had the option of skipping the ship's massive supper and returning later for the night's live cabaret (or midnight buffet).

Shanghai is the highlight of a China cruise for many passengers. For first-time visitors, I'd recommend taking a city tour first, then striking out for shopping and nearby sightseeing the next day. As always, the cruise experience can be as relaxing or as hectic as one makes it, but I saw no one who stayed aboard the whole time in Shanghai. Although many of my fellow passengers were retired, their spirit for exploring Shanghai and other ports on foot was exceedingly high.

Ningbo (Day 9)

Our next port of call was not far south of Shanghai. Ningbo ("Peaceful Harbor") is a trading port known throughout Asia for the acumen of its businesspeople. Many Ningbo immigrants to Hong Kong have made their fortunes in shipping and other industries under the laissez-faire regime of the British colonialists. Today, Ningbo is undergoing an immense construction boom of its own. Since 1996, Ningbo has put up dozens of new towering hotels, department stores, and office complexes. While Ningbo is smaller and less high-powered than booming Shanghai, it isn't lagging far behind.

The shore excursion at Ningbo, again aboard buses manned by the local tourism office, took us through a gorgeous mountainous region of tea plantations, bamboo groves, and new hillside graveyards. These cemeteries were the most elaborate and well kept I'd come across in China, built in large measure for overseas Chinese who desire (and can afford) burial near their ancestral homes.

Our main destination in the Ningbo countryside was **Tiantong Temple,** a 3rd-century center of Chan (Zen) Buddhism. It is one of China's larger temple complexes, with many pavilions rising up its terraces. Over a thousand monks used to live here; today the population is said to be 300. There are also scores of retirees residing on the grounds, volunteers whose laundry I saw hanging from the balconies. In the front courtyard there was a large pond where Buddhist monks, sworn to respect all living creatures, still release fish they've rescued from the market.

Fish and fish markets are a staple of Ningbo life. Our bus stopped at the **Gaoting Market** in a covered arcade downtown. This was a wet market, not spiffed up for foreign visitors, and thus quite interesting to browse. I bought litchi nuts there and enjoyed them on the way to lunch, which was held in the elegant new East Seaport Hotel. Only two things threw the charming waitresses there: finding the English word when passengers asked what they were eating and understanding why their guests wanted to take the hotel chopsticks as souvenirs.

Our final stop in Ningbo was at the **Tianyige Library,** China's oldest library. Oddly enough, the last thing we would see there were books. Virtually none of its thousands of rare volumes are on display or open to ordinary readers. Nevertheless, the pavilions and gardens were pretty and the large stone cats in the courtyard were quite unusual statues.

Xiamen (Days 10–11)

Recently voted the cleanest city in China, Xiamen—once known to Westerners as Amoy—is a vibrant port that can be explored on foot during a shore excursion. There's quite a bit of walking involved, chiefly because Xiamen's penultimate attraction is the beautiful green island in its harbor, **Gulangyu,** where no cars, taxis, or buses are allowed. Gulangyu is quite hilly as well, so visitors can put in some strenuous miles. Nevertheless, do not miss it. This is perhaps the most charming little burg in China for strolling. The local guides, often lacking experience with marshaling groups, usually leave passengers pretty much on their own to poke around the old mansions, gardens, and souvenir shops, which was fine with me, although I think so much independence upset some of my fellow cruise passengers.

Our Xiamen all-day port tour also included a swing through **Nan Putuo Temple,** the most beautiful temple we would see on this cruise. Lunch was served at the new Marco Polo Hotel, which provided the best Chinese food and service of any port we visited. Each dish that made its way, banquet style, to our lazy Susan was fully identified in English.

Hong Kong (Days 12–14)

The last stop on the southward version of our cruise was Hong Kong, which reverted to Chinese rule in 1997. China's newest city is also its most modern, most wealthy, and most Westernized. Hong Kong is the ideal port to visit last in China. The shopping, the food, and the transportation are all superb, far beyond what's offered on the mainland. For a full description of what to do and see in Hong Kong, see the chapter "Hong Kong: The Dragon that Never Sleeps."

The ship served as our hotel and restaurant for two nights, docking at the most prestigious slip in Asia, between the Star Ferry concourse and the Ocean Terminal shopping center in Kowloon. Organized tours were available but hardly necessary. The **Hong Kong Tourist Organization (HKTA),** a block away on the Star Ferry pier, provided everything needed to see Hong Kong on one's own.

The Cruise Experience

My Royal Caribbean cruise was in most ways typical of those offered by other major lines calling on Chinese ports: It was a comfortable, insulated experience for the most part, yet instructive and revealing whenever one stepped ashore. Even touring China from a coastal cruise ship, one cannot escape the realities of Chinese life completely. That's what separates a China cruise from all others and what makes it particularly memorable. The level of service and the standard of living at each port have risen dramatically since the 1980s—have risen rapidly even since the mid-1990s—giving China a raw vitality that few other countries in the world possess.

With this sudden release of energy after years of isolation, China's travel industry still has shortcomings in dealing with visitors from the outside world, particularly with visitors stepping off a luxurious cruise ship. Some ports lack enough trained English-speakers, enough first-class restaurants, enough well-kept sights, even enough first-class buses, to handle hundreds of foreign guests simultaneously. But a China cruise passenger should be ready for some adventure, not to mention a few raw edges. Those who want to learn more about the ancient culture and at the same time see what this emerging superpower looks and feels like will not be disappointed if they come by cruise ship.

A cruise is not the way to see China in great depth, of course, since each port call is brief. Shore excursions, while opening some special doors, also must pass by many that time does not permit to open. Still, I was surprised by my own moments of pleasure on my first China cruise. Such moments were frequent, and the comfort and security of sea travel proved seductive. As an introduction to China, a cruise is nothing short of a grand way to travel, affording an ample taste of what lies deeper within.

PRACTICAL INFORMATION

CRUISES

Visiting China aboard a luxury cruise line is a marvelous introduction. Among major cruise lines that include two or more ports of call in China during their 1998–99 sailings are Princess Cruises, Seabourn Cruise Line, Crystal Cruises, and Holland America Line. Royal Caribbean Cruise Lines formerly conducted regular excursions every spring and fall that focused exclusively on the Middle Kingdom, but with the sale of the *Sun Viking* these were discontinued at the end of 1997.

A high level of onboard service for each of these cruise lines is maintained in China. In fact, the amenities, facilities, programs, meals (Western cuisine), and entertainment are the same as these lines provide on their cruises throughout the world. The China cruises, however, usually feature enhancement lectures by recognized China experts, port-of-call briefings by a representative from the Chinese International Tourist Service (CITS), and special onboard activities and classes devoted to Chinese culture. Group shore excursions are conducted by local Chinese tourism organizations; all feature air-conditioned buses (although some buses are aging) and English-speaking Chinese guides (although some are quite new at the business).

Itineraries   Princess Cruises offers two 13-day "Orient/China Cruisetours" in October 1998, with stops at Beijing, Shanghai, and Hong Kong (as well as at Nagasaki and Seoul). Per person fares (including airfare) range from about $4,000 to $9,000, depending on cabin selection. Extensions include extra days in Beijing and an overnight in Xi'an (☎ 800/568-3262).

Holland America Lines offers a 14-day Osaka to Hong Kong cruise, departing October 6, 1998, and April 12, 1999, with stops at Dalian, Beijing, Shanghai, Xiamen, and Hong Kong. This cruise also includes optional tours of Kyoto and Nara in Japan and Suzhou and Wuxi while the ship is in Shanghai. Per person fares range from about $3,000 to $7,000, depending on cabin selection. Airfare is not included. Holland America also offers a Hong Kong to Osaka cruise departing on March 29, 1999, and April 26, 1999. There are stops at Hong Kong, Shanghai, Beijing, and Dalian, with shore excursions to Suzhou and Wuxi. These cruises also make stops in South Korea and Japan. Per person fares (airfare not included) range from about $3,500 to $7,000. Call ☎ 800/426-0327 or 800/626-9900 for brochures.

Seabourn Cruise Line has scheduled a 12-day Hong Kong to Shanghai cruise, departing March 4, 1999, and a 12-day Shanghai to Hong Kong return cruise, departing March 11, 1999, with a shore excursion to Wuxi. Per person fares range from about $10,000 to $20,000 (☎ 800/351-9595).

Crystal Cruises offers a 13-day "Oriental Odyssey" from Yokohama to Beijing, departing September 24, 1998, with stops at Shanghai, Qingdao, and Beijing. Per person fares range from about $8,000 to $11,000 and include a 3-night postcruise hotel package in Beijing. Per person fares for suites range from about $14,000 to $27,000. Crystal Cruises also offers a 12-day "Asian Crossroads" cruise from Beijing to Hong Kong (via Japan and Taiwan), departing October 7, 1998, with stops in Beijing, Shanghai, and Hong Kong. Per person fares range from about $7,000 to $10,000 and include a 3-night precruise hotel package in Beijing. Per person fares for suites range from about $13,000 to $25,000 (☎ 310/785-9300).

Royal Caribbean Cruise Lines offered the most extensive China cruises at reasonable rates, but no China cruises are currently planned. It is worth checking to see if these cruises have resumed, however, as they are well organized and rewarding. For up-to-date brochures, contact Royal Caribbean (☎ 800/526-7225).

Costs   Including airfare, rates per person (based on double occupancy) for a 10- to 14-day cruise that includes China can range from under $3,000 to over $25,000, depending on the particular cruise line and grade of cabin selected. Shore excursions range from $50 to

$150 per person. For tips, add $100 per person (minimum). Drinks, gifts, shore purchases, and gratuities to Chinese shore guides (around RMB 25 to 42/$3 to $5 each) are usually extra.

Many passengers supplement a China cruise with precruise and postcruise tour packages to such destinations as Guilin and Xi'an. These extensions are offered as options when the cruise is booked. These tour packages usually run three to five days, and cost $1,200 to $2,500 per person.

Reservations   The cruise lines prefer that passengers deal with travel agents rather than with the cruise lines directly. Your local travel agent can book a cruise to China, including air transport, shore excursions, and precruise or postcruise extensions. Be sure that your travel agent fills out the **China visa application** for you, which makes you part of the cruise's group visa. It is expensive and time-consuming to procure an individual China visa yourself, and it is not necessary if you book a cruise.

SILK ROAD CARAVAN

丝绸之路

Eᴀꜱᴛ ᴀɴᴅ Wᴇꜱᴛ ꜰɪʀꜱᴛ ᴍᴇᴛ ᴍᴏʀᴇ than 2,000 years ago on the fabled Silk Road, for centuries China's only major connection to the outside world. The Silk Road was a trade route that crossed the Gobi Desert from China into Central Asia where Persian and other merchants transferred fine Chinese silks into the courts of imperial Rome. In return, China received strange new commodities from the West. The most lasting import, however, was cultural, artistic, and religious—the introduction of Buddhism from India.

Buddhism altered the face of China, shaping its temple architecture and religious arts. Buddhist missionaries found a tolerant home in the Chinese capital, Chang'an (now Xi'an) during the Tang Dynasty (ᴀ.ᴅ. 618–907), when the silk trade reached its zenith and long caravans of up to 1,000 camels routinely arrived at the western gates after crossing the desert frontier. This is the way Marco Polo is said to have reached China from Italy in the 13th century, centuries after the fall of Rome and the disintegration of the mighty Han and Tang dynasties.

In the last few years, for the first time in history, a trickle of tourists has entered northwest China, retracing the route of the Silk Road. From Xi'an, 550 miles west of Beijing in north central China, modern travelers are now crossing the remote provinces of Gansu and Xinjiang. They are stopping at the legendary oasis towns and rummaging through the medieval marketplaces of Urumqi and Kashgar. Along the way they pass the ruins of desert cities, the caves of splendid Buddhist sculptures, the last outposts of the Great Wall, and lakes and mountain passes clinging to the fringes of imagined heavens. The Silk Road spaces through which they move are vast and empty, populated by nomads and wild camels. The towns between are remote, marked by mosques rather than temples, occupied by Uighur Muslims rather than Han Chinese. The Silk Road winds through a lost world, an alien landscape of howling sand dunes and silent snowy peaks. It is a China most visitors have yet to see.

The Silk Road

The Explorers

The first official Chinese mission on the Silk Road set out in 138 B.C. from the capital at Xi'an. Emperor Wudi of the Han Dynasty (206 B.C. to A.D. 220) charged General Zhang Qian and his 100-man caravan to make contact with the desert tribes of the west and to forge an alliance against the Huns (the Xiongnu), who were raiding China with impunity. The Chinese general made it all the way to Persia. He didn't return from the Silk Road for 13 years. At his death, Zhang was awarded the imperial title of "Grand Traveler."

Other grand travelers followed, mostly caravans of ordinary traders and monks rather than diplomats and soldiers. By the 1st century A.D., silk garments were such a rage in Rome they were considered a drain on the treasury. Oasis towns sprang up to replenish the Silk Road caravans that sometimes perished in the fierce Taklamakan Desert, whose very name means "enter and do not return."

As trade flourished, Buddhist monks and pilgrims set out from India to China, spreading their art and religion. In the oasis towns of China, wealthy local merchants were soon sponsoring the creation of large shrines in nearby sandstone caves, where Buddhist statues and frescoes were sculpted as divine petitions for the safe passage of the caravans. At Dunhuang, where the main north and south routes from the West merged, the greatest repository of Buddhist manuscripts, paintings, and statuary outside of India was fashioned at the Mogao caves (see "The Silk Road Grottoes at Mogao" under "Monuments of the Middle Kingdom").

Silk Road pilgrimages became a two-way street. The Chinese monk Fa Xi'an (A.D. 337–422) set out from Xi'an in 399, passed through Dunhuang, and crossed over the Himalayas into India. He returned to China by sea 15 years later. China's most renowned religious pilgrim, Xuan Zang (A.D. 600–664), traveling at night on foot and by horseback, set out on the Silk Road in 629, studied in Indian monasteries for 14 years, and returned to Xi'an in 645 with over 500 sutras (Buddhist scriptures) and relics. The Big Wild Goose Pagoda, which still stands in Xi'an, housed his souvenirs, and the 16th-century comic epic, *Journey to the West*, also known as *Monkey*, has immortalized his journey for Chinese readers ever since.

Marco Polo (1254–1324) became the first Western explorer to compose a popular and lasting account of the Silk Road. Many scholars regard his travels as fictional—an account cobbled together from the anecdotes and adventures of many traders—but Marco Polo's observations of the trade route across China often ring true.

In the early 20th century, the Silk Road beckoned to foreign explorers as never before. In a rush to empty the newly rediscovered Buddhist caves and ruined cities of their ancient treasures, Sven Hedin of Sweden, Baron Otani of Japan, Paul Pelliot of France, Von le Coq of Germany, Langdon Warner of America, and above all Sir Marc Aurel Stein of Britain made difficult and dangerous forays on behalf of major museums in the West. Thousands of manuscripts, relics, frescoes, and statues ended up in overseas collections by the time this race was over.

Fortunately, not everything was pilfered in the name of history, scholarship, and nationalism. The Silk Road retains many of its relics and much of its remoteness. Today, for the first time, organized tourism is making inroads, and the Silk Road's exotic treasure house is opening to outsiders.

WHAT TO READ

The most complete guide, tailor-made for the China portion of the Silk Road, is Judy Bonavia's *The Silk Road: From Xi'an to Kashgar* (Passport Books, 1993). Vikram Seth's *From Heaven Lake* (Vintage, 1987) is a fine travel narrative through the region. Peter Hopkirk's *Foreign Devils on the Silk Road* (Oxford University Press, 1986) is a lively history of the gold rush by foreign explorers for the cave treasures of Dunhuang and elsewhere earlier in this century.

PRACTICAL INFORMATION

ORIENTATION

Starting from Xi'an, the Silk Road sweeps northwesterly up through the Hexi Corridor of Gansu Province. Anyone heading to the West would have been squeezed through this 750-mile-long channel, 125 miles at its widest, with the Qilan mountains to the south and a series of bone-dry deserts and mountain ranges to the north. The most impressive sight in the Hexi Corridor is **Jiayuguan Pass,** where the Silk Road narrows to a bottleneck and the western terminus of the Great Wall served as China's frontier outpost. This area is known as Yumen, the Jade Gate, and to most Chinese minds it was truly the end of the civilized world.

Beyond the **Jade Gate,** the Silk Road divides at Dunhuang, site of the magnificent Mogao Buddhist grottoes. The north and south routes through the **Taklamakan Desert (the Tarim Basin)** reunite at **Kashgar.** The desert is the central feature of Xinjiang, a province the size of Alaska, making up one-sixth of China. Kashgar is nearly as far west as you can go in China. The borders of Kyrgyzstan, Tajikistan, Afghanistan, and India are close at hand, and so is Pakistan via the Karakoram Highway. From Kashgar, the Silk Road enters the high mountain passes, reemerging at Samarkand in Central Asia.

The majority of the 23 million people of Gansu are Han Chinese. Mongols, Tibetans, Kazaks, and Huis (Islamic Chinese) make up a considerable minority population as well. In Xinjiang, the distribution changes remarkably. The Turkish-speaking Muslim minority Uighurs make up a majority in many places, such as Kashgar, while the Han

Chinese, bolstered by recent "economic transplants" from eastern China, hold sway in other towns, such as Urumqi. Kazaks, many still leading a nomadic life, often dominate in rural areas. With a population of just 15 million, the gigantic Xinjiang Uighur Autonomous Region still feels uninhabited through most of its stretches. The Silk Road becomes increasingly desolate, increasingly Islamic, and increasingly remote as the traveler moves west. By the time one reaches the present Chinese border near Kashgar, it again seems as if one is about to step off the edge of the modern inhabited world.

TOURS & STRATAGEMS

There are three possible ways to tour the Silk Road.

Group Tours The most popular and comfortable method of touring the Silk Road is by group tour. Groups follow much the same routes and often stay in the same hotels and eat in the same places as independent travelers, but they do so faster and in the hands of guides, local and foreign, who are charged with keeping everything running like clockwork (tickets, tour buses, meal times, nightly entertainment where available, site lectures when needed). The tours I've observed seem well run. Hotel and restaurant conditions are often below international standards (generally worse than is found in other regions of China), and transport by bus or train can sometimes be a hardship, but for anyone in reasonably good health and with the right frame of mind—namely, the Silk Road is an adventure in a remote region of the world, rather than a luxury cruise—Silk Road group tours are not strenuous or stressful.

Many adventure tour operators offer 16- to 30-day group tours (usually 12 to 20 people per group) that include

sectors of the Silk Road both in and out of China, often with such destinations as Islamabad (Pakistan), Lahore (India), and Hunza (Jammu/Kashmir). Tours of Xi'an and Beijing are often included. Cost, including airfare, runs about $6,000 to $12,000 per person—not making it one of the cheaper tours in the world, but transportation in particular is expensive over the great distances covered. These extended trips on the Silk Road usually depart in May and June and in September and October. Some of the best operators include **Geographic Expeditions** (☎ 800/777-8183), **Abercrombie & Kent** (☎ 800/ 323-7308), **Asian Pacific Adventures** (☎ 800/825-1680), **Wilderness Travel** (☎ 800/368-2794), **Overseas Adventure Travel** (☎ 800/221-0814), **Travcoa** (☎ 800/992-2003), and **Mountain Travel/Sobek** (☎ 800/ 227-2384).

Independent Tours Another option is to set up an independent tour through a Chinese tour operator. Traveling alone, I decided to book ahead so that I had a local guide in each place I visited, hotel reservations, meals, and all transportation (plane, train, private car). I negotiated for the best lodgings and methods of transport available at each juncture.

My individual Silk Road tour was put together in two days by China Travel Service (CTS) in Xi'an. Based on my proposed itinerary, Susan Su (Su Yan Hua), the CTS business manager, made the arrangements by phone and fax from Xi'an and procured the air tickets. The cost was higher than I expected, in part because I was traveling alone, in part because I needed all the bookings done quickly, and in part because the only cheaper way to put together a Silk Road tour is on your own. Everything promised for my tour was delivered as advertised (with the exception of a RMB 200/$24 fee levied on me by the local travel officials in Urumqi when their booking of my hotel fell through).

My 8-day Silk Road tour for one began in Xi'an and included Jiayuguan (and the end of the Great Wall), Dunhuang (and the Mogao grottoes), Turpan (and the ancient cities, tombs, and wells), Urumqi, Tianchi (Lake of Heaven), and Kashgar (and the Sunday market), with the return to Xi'an after a second night in Urumqi. The all-inclusive price was $2,650, payable in cash (RMB). CITS in Beijing or Hong Kong can make similar arrangements. In Xi'an, contact Susan Su, **China Travel Service (CTS),** 3rd Floor, 63 Changan Road, Xi'an (☎ 029/523-0257, or mobile phone 029/909-0136; fax 029/526-1821).

On Your Own If you are an intrepid, resourceful, youthful, rugged backpacker or a China hand experienced with backroads travel, you can do the Silk Road on your own. Train tickets, bus tickets, and flights can be purchased, local hotels booked, restaurants patronized, and regional CITS offices, city buses, or taxis hired to get to the historic sites. For the determined who wish to be free of guides, daily deadlines, and other "hindrances," independent travel is rough but ready.

JIAYUGUAN: END OF THE GREAT WALL

嘉峪关

ACCORDING TO A POPULAR MYTH, THE Great Wall ends at the Jade Pass (Yamen) near Jiayuguan, a town far up the Hexi Corridor in the northwestern province of Gansu. When the First Emperor, Qin Shi Huang (259–210 B.C.), unified ancient sections of the wall in 211 B.C., Jiayuguan did mark the end of the Great Wall, but during the subsequent Han Dynasty (206 B.C. to A.D. 220) the wall was extended farther west, with beacon towers stretching deep into the desert. These extensions were eventually swallowed up by the desert sands. When the Great Wall achieved its surviving form under the Ming Dynasty (1368–1644), including those segments visited today near Beijing, Jiayuguan again became the garrison on the final frontier.

In 1372, General Feng Shang drove the Mongols out and built a fort at the end of the Great Wall. It became known as "The Greatest Pass Under Heaven," and it remains standing today in Jiayuguan. West of here, the vast Gobi Desert opens its threatening jaws. Every traveler setting out from Jiayuguan Pass followed the same custom, hurling a stone at the western wall. If the stone bounced back, it meant the traveler would come back to China. If not, there would be no return.

Wei-Jin Tombs

The flight from Xi'an to Jiayuguan, 800 miles, takes nearly 3 hours, and the winds over Gansu Province are bumpy. I'm the only Westerner aboard, but there are 75 Japanese tourists, too. The Japanese are great fans of the Silk Road and its Buddhist treasures. Inside the China Northwest Airlines jet prop plane, it smells like old socks. An hour into the flight, I can see an endless pink-and-cream-colored desert below and a few white oasis towns with small fields and blue reservoirs connected by a thin string of roads. As we set down in Jiayuguan, I spot the snowcapped Qilian mountain range to the south, the unbroken wall of the Hexi Corridor.

I'm met by a local guide, Martin Yuan, who briefs me on the town. Jiayuguan has a population of 120,000, of whom 8% work in a single Russian-built steel factory, the largest in northwest China.

We set out first not for the garrison at the end of the Great Wall but for a site less dramatic although quite ancient: the Wei-Jin tombs. Thirteen tombs were built during the Northern Wei (A.D. 220–265) and Western Jin (A.D. 265–316) dynasties 12 miles northeast of town. This cluster consists of rounded mounds about 6 feet high, heaps of sandy soil scooped up from the desert flatlands—as desolate a graveyard as I have ever seen. Driving the 12 miles out to the Wei-Jin tombs, we pass many fields of such mounds. Some 14,000 tombs of officials have been counted in the area. The 13 Wei-Jin tombs open to visitors (open 8am to 10pm, admission RMB 10/$1.25) were discovered in 1972. The burial chambers are several stories under the ground; the mounds are merely markers.

We stroll down the stairs into **Tomb 6,** which like many others has been looted by grave robbers in the past but still retains its chief treasure: the brick paintings depicting daily life. This tomb consists of three burial chambers, representing the three courtyards of the official and his wife who are buried here.

The walls of this first small underground chamber are constructed of 1,700-year-old bricks laid without mortar. The bricks are brightly painted with scenes of animal husbandry—the herding of goats and the tilling of fields by oxen in this oasis, fed by subterranean rivers originating in the distant mountains. In the second chamber, connected by a low archway, the walls depict the journey this official and his wife made to the Chinese capital, Luoyang, an immense overland trip more than a thousand miles to the east—the trip of a lifetime. There are scenes of rich banquets, processions, and entertainments enjoyed at the capital. In the final burial chamber, the picture bricks record the official's worldly wealth, his boxes of jewels and shelves of silks, the treasures traded on the Silk Road. These brick paintings are simple renditions outlined in black, with red the most enduring color. The coffins are also here, on the floor against the final wall.

The Fort

Jiayuguan Fort, the single most stunning sight along the Silk Road, is 4 miles from town (open 8:30am to 12:30pm and 2:30 to 6pm; admission RMB 20/$2.40). The garrison at Jiayuguan Pass is magnificent. It rises from the desert sands and is composed of the same earth. The walls are 35 feet high, the outer fortifications 3,400 feet around. The outer wall has turrets for the archers and several pavilions at the corners, watchtowers for the troops stationed here during the Ming Dynasty.

It is easy to see why the wall ended here and the fort could control the traffic of the Silk Road. The Hexi Corridor is pinched between the high

Jiayuguan Fort

Gate of Enlightenment

Gate of Conciliation

Guandi Temple

Pathway

Wencheng Pavilion

Open Air Theater

Exhibition Hall

Great Wall

Qilian Mountains and the Black Mountains of the Mazong (Horse Mane) range to the north. Across this pass, earthen walls extend like raised arms east and west, forming a long fence.

Inside the outer wall is an inner wall surrounding the **barracks** where the general and his troops were stationed. The **inner eastern gate,** crowned with a 50-foot-high tower built in 1506, guards a courtyard running to the outer wall where caravans could be held for questioning before continuing into China. The western gate has a similar double-walled courtyard that served as the departure station for those crossing the desert out of China.

Climbing the wall, walking from turret to turret, blockhouse to blockhouse, I look west from the pass into the desert. China's first official mission over the Silk Road, headed by General Zhang Qian, went out through here in 138 B.C. and returned 13 years later with just two survivors. Even earlier, Lao Zi, founder of Daoism, is reputed by believers to have passed through Jiayuguan and the Jade Gate (Yamen) on his way to the Western Paradise.

The fort at Jiayuguan could not be in a more dramatic desert setting, nor could it look at once more imposing and more forlorn. The present fortification is partly reconstructed with brick, with improvements made as recently as 1988, but the original Ming Dynasty earthen walls are fully exposed and the old watchtowers are still in place. Within the inner walls there is an ornate, tiled-roof opera **theater,** built during the Qing Dynasty (1644–1911) for entertaining the Great Wall troops, its empty open stage sheltered by soaring eaves. A single camel and a saddled horse are tethered in the inner courtyard, their master and his portrait camera waiting for customers.

My guide takes me down into the empty yard of the fort and tells me some local stories. According to one, the emperor charged a local man with procuring the bricks necessary to build the fort. If his count was off, even by a single brick, he would pay with his life (the ancient answer to cost overruns). The man predicted that 100,000 bricks would be required for the project, and he confidently placed the order. As it turned out, only 99,999 bricks were needed, but he was able to conceal the leftover brick when the royal inspector arrived by placing it unmortared along the inner wall. The unmortared brick is still somewhere on the wall, according to my local guide.

Entering the western courtyard between the inner and outer walls of the fort, he tells me another story. Once there were two sparrows, very much in love. One became shut inside the fort; the other escaped into the desert. The trapped bird waited and waited, singing out until it pined away. Today, when you hurl a rock at the inner wall, you can still hear its cry. I pick up a stone, and like thousands of travelers who stood here on the Silk Road, I hurl it against the wall, sanded smooth by the desert winds.

PRACTICAL INFORMATION

ORIENTATION

Jiayuguan, a trading post and oasis during the Han Dynasty, served as the fort protecting the western entrance to China from the Silk Road during the Ming Dynasty. Today it is an industrial town deep in Gansu Province, 1,300 miles west of Beijing. At an elevation above 4,000 feet, Jiayuguan is usually not scorching hot in the summer. Early spring and late fall are known for fierce dust storms, however, and winters for extreme cold temperatures.

GETTING THERE

By Plane   China Northwest Airlines has one flight daily to Jiayuguan from Xi'an, a 2¹/₂-hour trip.
By Train   The train station is about 2 miles south of the city center, served by buses (labeled No. 1) and taxis. Jiayuguan is 30 hours from Xi'an, 51 hours from Beijing. There are four trains daily. Tickets can be booked at hotel travel desks.

TOURS & STRATAGEMS

Visitor Information   The Jiayuguan International Travel Service, 2 Shengli Bei Lu (☎ 0937/622-6598; fax 0937/622-6931), can provide English-language guides and tours of Jiayuguan, Dunhuang, and other points along the Silk Road.

Jiayuguan has opened a **Great Wall Museum** (8:30 to 11:30am and 2:30 to 6pm; admission RMB 20/$2.40), but it is not impressive. There are photographs and maps, very few relics (and some of those are copies), and a model showing how the Great Wall was built (pounded earth at the core, sun-dried mud brick or granite exterior). A gift shop and an old war plane are stationed in the courtyard.

WHERE TO STAY

Great Wall Hotel (Chang Cheng Binguan). 9 Jianshe Xi Lu (between train station and downtown). ☎ 0937/622-5200. Fax 0937/622-6016. 160 rms. TV TEL. $65 double. AE, JCB, MC, V. This five-story 3-star modern hotel built in the shape of a fort is the best in town. Rumpled, unmaintained carpets line the long hallways. The rooms are spacious and dusty. The private bathrooms (tub showers) are new and clean (the hotel opened in 1991). Towels, linens, and bathroom amenities are provided daily. Long-distance international calls can be made from the room, but they go through the hotel switchboard. Off the lobby there is a large gift shop with local crafts, and beyond that, in a separate building, a dining hall that serves meals to tour groups. From the hotel's "faux-ramparts" there is a fine view of a local minaret and the Qilian mountain range, towering over 20,000 feet to the south. This is a modern hotel, adequate for cleaning up and sleeping, but there are no luxuries, not even air-conditioning.

WHERE TO DINE

The best meal I ate in Jiayuguan was at the local **outdoor market** downtown. Martin Yuan, the local guide, took me in hand. Skewered mutton is cooked over open coals—20 skewers are braised at a time. You sit on a long bench inches away from the coals. The cook hands you a batch of five or six. You strip the mutton off the metal skewer with your teeth. As you eat, the cook's daughter slices more mutton from the carcass of a sheep hanging from the stall (about 2 feet from where you sit). She dices and spices the mutton strips. Each emptied skewer is tossed into a box to one side. The meat is extremely spicy and delicious. A dozen skewers cost about RMB 10 ($1.20). The town is relatively prosperous, thanks to the big steel mill, and local ironworkers are said to eat 200 mutton shish kebabs at a sitting, washing them down with cheap local beer.

Jiayuguan is too small and remote to provide Western-style restaurants. Neither McDonald's nor Kentucky Fried Chicken has paid a call. I had a Chinese dinner (mutton as the main course) at the clean new restaurant run by the local tourist office, the **CITS Tourism Restaurant** (☎ 0937/622-6470), three blocks from the Great Wall Hotel on Changcheng Xi Lu.

CRESCENT MOON LAKE: THE SINGING SANDS OF DUNHUANG

敦煌

T WO THOUSAND YEARS AGO, Dunhuang (Blazing Beacon) was a vital and flourishing caravan stop, the westernmost oasis under Chinese control. Three major trading routes from the West merged here, making Dunhuang a major supply center.

The history of this outpost reflects the changing political winds that have swept across the Silk Road over the centuries. Tibetans ruled Dunhuang for almost two centuries before a Chinese warlord drove them out in A.D. 851. After the Tang Dynasty fell, the Uighur people swept in and established the Kingdom of Shachow in 911. Mongols took over in 1227, as Genghis Khan stormed in from the Gobi. Muslim forces cleared out the region in the 16th century. The Chinese resettled Dunhuang once again in 1760. History students need a scorecard to tell who was on first in Dunhuang.

The most crucial event in Dunhuang's history unfolded early on, in the 4th century A.D., when work began on the Buddhist sculpture and murals in the Mogao caves. As the importance of the Silk Road diminished at the end of the Tang Dynasty (A.D. 618–907), Dunhuang languished for centuries, but in the 20th century these ancient grottoes made Dunhuang an important desert town once again and a major stopover for travelers.

Of course, modern travelers no longer arrive on sand-dune marching camels. Tourism has replaced trade as the touchstone of Dunhuang's new wealth, and the Mogao caves are the chief attraction for Chinese, Asian, and the few Western travelers retracing the Silk Road route.

My immediate goal at Dunhuang, however, was to get on a camel and cross a few dunes myself. The great Mogao caves would wait for another chapter of travels. I wanted to see a still more ancient phenomenon at Dunhuang, what Marco Polo called the "rumbling sands" of Crescent Moon Lake.

The Road to Dunhuang

The Silk Road across the desert sands from Jiayuguan northwest up the **Hexi Corridor** to Dunhuang used to require three weeks by camel caravan. Today there is a 240-mile blacktop highway connecting the two oases. The **Qilian Mountains** to the south are oil rich. China's first oil field was opened west of Jiayuguan in the Qilian foothills in 1936. The train cars barreling down the Hexi Corridor are loaded with black oil cars. We pass a large nuclear plant as well. Gansu is a very poor province, but it is supplying much of the raw energy for the rest of China, fueling the economic boom in the more populous eastern provinces. After a 2-hour drive, the southern mountains fade into the flat horizon. Sand and sand bluffs dominate the severe landscape. Thorn bushes are the only vegetation, except at rare villages where earthen houses are clustered around a green oasis and the domes of small mosques rise toward the clear skies. Goatherds dressed in tatters move across the sandy fields of the Gobi with their small flocks.

Deep into the desert we reach the ruins of **Qiaowan,** the dream city where Qing Dynasty emperor Kangxi (1654–1722) ordered a palace built. He became obsessed with a dream set on the Silk Road. In the dream he saw a palace located on a river with two enormous trees, one shaped like a crown, the other like a sash. He dispatched two officials to locate the place and finance the dream temple. The officials built a humble walled dwelling instead, pocketing most of the construction funds. When Kangxi discovered their deceit, he had the officials slain, using the skins of the wrongdoers to cover the heads of the palace drums. Only ruins remain at Qiaowan now.

The drive to Dunhuang consumes $4^1/_2$ hours, even on a paved road. Drivers here learn to fight the monotony of interminably straight, flat stretches and the frequent eruption of massive potholes, entire unpaved strips, and barely passable detours that appear unannounced. There are road crews—men and women with nothing but shovels and bicycle carts—patching the roadway every 2 or 3 miles, and traffic must slow to a stop to negotiate what the elements have torn to bits. At noon we reach Dunhuang, a long, green oasis lined by trees for many miles where a river, the Danghe, cuts through the sands, exposing stone bluffs. Here tractors pull carts of crushed stone into town and hardened, sunburnt men, hauling tree limbs to market, nap on their trailers under shade trees.

The Singing Sands

Three miles south of downtown Dunhuang there are enormous white sand dunes, part of the Singing Sand Mountains (Mingsha Shan). The dunes look like a poster of the Sahara. In their deep folds they trap underground springs, creating **Crescent Moon Lake (Yueya Quan),** a celebrated pool where Silk Road travelers, including Marco Polo, paused to drink.

The afternoon sun is blisteringly hot when Martin Yuan, my local guide from Jiayuguan, and I set out to cross the fine sands for Crescent Moon Lake. Donning a straw hat, plastered in sunscreen, I'm already sweating after the first few steps. My feet sink several inches into the crunching sands. It's like crossing a beach, a thousand miles from the nearest sea. Under awnings a hundred camels and their drivers wait for riders. Heated by the sun, slowed by the Gobi sands, I hire us each a camel (RMB 30/$3.60 each) for the 15-minute trek each way—otherwise facing a long, hot walk. Obviously, I would have dropped dead in my tracks if I'd been one of the early traders trying to cross these dunes.

The two-humped Bactrian camel has inhabited the Silk Road for 2,000 years. They roam wild over the Gobi to this day. Single-humped camels could carry as heavy a load, but they lacked the stamina and speed of the two-humped version. They are enormous creatures but fairly docile under their masters' watch. My camel knelt on his front legs, then his back legs, and I climbed aboard between his two humps. The humps, parted by a heavy blanket, proved to be a most comfortable saddle. Tethered to the driver's camel in a caravan of three, we loped across the sands at a steady pace, gently rising and falling with the camels' walk. We skirted a large oval concrete pool on our right, used to store water. On our left was the largest of the sand dunes, towering over a hundred feet above us. The site charges an RMB 20 ($2.40) entrance fee.

Beyond the pool we turned right and headed for a beautiful three-storied pavilion with soaring eaves that had been erected on the edge of Crescent Moon Lake. Martin told me the original pavilion had been savaged by the Red Guards during the Cultural Revolution (1966–76). The restoration was remarkable: The pavilion still had its air of antiquity and its upper balconies proved marvelous observation points for the dunes and the lake. Our driver halted the little caravan, lowering our camels.

Crescent Moon Lake these days is a narrow slash of water situated between the pavilion and a formidable wall of sand rising 600 feet nearly straight up from its northern bank. Dunhuang had been experiencing a drought, and the lake was quite low, but still rather pretty, a reed-studded belt of blue in a bowl of white mounds. We ordered cups of tea and sat on a veranda, the remains of a Buddhist temple where incense is still lighted. The lake received its name from its crescent-moon shape. The local people attach a story to the lake. It is a story like many of the Silk Road, of parting and grief. Here in Dunhuang a young girl parted with her lover, who set out to cross the desert. He never returned; the caravan was lost. She died in mourning, with one eye forever opened in the shape of a crescent, watching the desert for the return of her lover.

Returning by camel, we dismounted and climbed the largest mound, **Mingsha Dune,** 820 feet high, a veritable mountain of sand that seemed an endless task to scale. I removed my shoes, soaked in the fine sands. At its summit, the view of the oasis was superb, a long, green island in the midst of a sea of sand, and to the west, whipped-cream dunes that stretch for 80 miles into the empty horizon. We sat atop the dune until the sun became too fierce, then descended like children, seated, "sand sliding" to the bottom, trying to make the sands sing as they have for eons here, although I could hear only a whisper of their legendary music.

On our way out Martin told me about a party of 70 foreigners who'd visited the singing sands a few years back and formed a long caravan indeed. The group was led by one of my famous American compatriots, he said, a chap named Bill Gates, founder of Microsoft—one of the richest "traders," I pointed out, who'd ever ridden a camel on the Silk Road.

Then the wind came up, stirring the sands to a fine powder. The sound was a low rumble, often likened to a drumroll by Chinese poets. A Dunhuang legend tells of a Chinese army camped here that was surrounded by the enemy once darkness fell. The Chinese army beat its war drums, and its call to arms was answered by the gods, who dispatched a sandstorm across the desert, burying both armies alive at Crescent Lake. To this day, people claim to hear the buried armies wailing and beating on their drums when the winds roll in.

"Man made the Buddhist caves," according to a local adage, "but the gods made Crescent Moon Lake," and these desert gods, it seems, can unmake caves, lakes, and even whole armies in the wink of an eye.

PRACTICAL INFORMATION

ORIENTATION

Dunhuang is a desert oasis in northwest Gansu Province near the border with Xinjiang Province, about 1,500 miles west of Beijing. Summers are very hot, making May and October the mildest months to visit. In July and August, the town fills up with thousands of tourists from China, Japan, and other parts of Asia, with a smattering of Westerners. While the oasis population is over 150,000, the downtown section is small and compact, with about 15,000 urban residents.

The major attraction for visitors to Dunhuang are the ancient Buddhist murals and sculptures at the **Mogao caves** (see "The Silk Road Grottoes at Mogao"). **Crescent Moon Lake (Yueya Shan)** and **Singing Sands Mountain (Mingsha Shan)** have the best sand dunes on the Silk Road.

GETTING THERE

By Plane   With the opening of a new **airport** at Dunhuang, flights from Xi'an (3 hours), Beijing (4 hours), and other cities in China are becoming more frequent.

By Train   The main train line through Gansu Province stops well north of Dunhuang at the small town of Liuyuan. From Liuyuan, frequent buses make the 80-mile connection to Dunhuang (about a 3-hour trip). From Liuyuan, it is a 6-hour train ride east to Jiayuguan, 36 hours to Xi'an, and 57 hours to Beijing. Heading west, the train to Turpan is 13 hours, to Urumqi 16 hours.

By Car & Bus   The paved road from Jiayuguan (240 miles) is served by hired cars (5 hours) and buses (8 hours).

TOURS & STRATAGEMS

This was my second stop on an 8-day independent tour of the Silk Road arranged by China Travel Service (CTS) in Xi'an. The site is located 3 miles south of city center at the end of Dingzi Lu. During high season (July and August), try to come here as early in the morning as possible (by 8am) or near dusk (after 6pm) to avoid the intense heat.

Visitor Information   The Dunhuang China International Tourist Service (CITS) (☎ 0937/882-2494) has a branch at 1 Dong Dajie (two blocks west of the Dunhuang Hotel, downtown). They can provide local guides, but the tour desk at the Dunhuang Hotel, 14 Yangguan Dong Lu (☎ 0937/882-2538), is more experienced with Westerners.

WHERE TO STAY

Dunhuang is prospering as tourism flourishes, spurred by an increase in domestic travelers from inside China. At present, the Dunhuang Hotel provides the best accommodations and services for Westerners.

Dunhuang Hotel (Dunhuang Binguan). *14 Yangguan Dong Lu (four blocks east of city center off Dong Dajie).* ☎ *0937/882-2538 or 0937/882-2415. Fax 0937/882-2195 or 0937/882-2309. 155 rms, 16 suites. A/C MINIBAR TV TEL. $75 double. AE, JCB, MC, V.* This 3-star three-building compound is where China's state leaders stay (including present leader Jiang Zemin and late paramount leader Deng Xiaoping). The VIP Building is not usually open to tourists, so the new North Building—strikingly clean and modern—is the best section to stay in. It has its own lobby (with white plaster statues and colored ceiling lights) and staff, and an attached dining room that serves excellent Western and Chinese fixed-price meals (up to 12 dishes, including spaghetti). The staff speaks little English but tries to be helpful. The South Building (across the street) contains the shopping arcade, gym, and most of the 15 dining halls.

Services: Laundry (24-hour), daily maid service, foreign exchange counter.

Facilities: In-house movies, health club (exercise machines), sauna, business center (open 9am–7pm), tour desk, beauty salon, shopping arcade.

WHERE TO DINE

If you are in Dunhuang on tour, your guide will set up meal times and restaurants. The Dunhuang Hotel, 14 Yangguan Dong Lu (☎ 0937/

882-2415), has excellent Chinese and some Mongolian dishes in its restaurants (RMB 42 to 125/$5 to $15). The **Terrace Cafe** in the lobby has drinks and Western-style snacks (sandwiches, cakes).

South of the bus station on Dingzi Lu there are a number of **small cafes** with cheap Western dishes catering to independent foreign travelers. Their names (Shirley's, Charley Johng's) and menus are in English.

Two blocks from the Dunhuang Hotel (west on Dong Dajie toward the city center traffic circle), there's a large **night market.** Entrance is on the south side of the street through a gate; look for the lights, food stalls, and outdoor billiard tables. Local food, including excellent spicy mutton on skewers, is cooked by sidewalk vendors. Sweet melons, grapes, and other regional fruits are also sold in the streets.

TURPAN: OASIS
OF THE GRAPE
吐鲁番

T HE FIRST THING THAT STRIKES
outsiders traveling west from Gansu Province into Xinjiang Province is
that they are no longer quite in China. This vast northwestern region—
China's Alaska—is divided into northern grasslands and southern deserts
by the Heavenly Mountains (Tian Shan). The dramatic, arid landscape is
a sharp break from what's found in the rest of China, but Xinjiang's
ethnic makeup is an even more striking departure. Kazakh nomads
predominate in the northern pastures; Uighur farmers are a majority in
the southern desert basin; and most of the Han Chinese, a distinct
minority, are recent arrivals.

Xinjiang is foremost the land of the Uighurs, who account for almost
half of the province's 13 million people. They are Turkic-speaking, fiercely
Islamic, and decidedly non–Han Chinese. They look and dress like Central Asian people of Turkish descent. Here the Silk Road passes through
a middle ground of history and race like no other land on earth, an Islamic culture under Chinese rule in a land of irrigated oases and bone-
white heat.

A Uighur empire rose up in the Tarim Basin in the 8th century.
Uighurs controlled the Silk Road routes through Xinjiang. First they
adopted Buddhism, then Islam as their faith. During the Qing Dynasty,
they were swept up in the 1862 Muslim rebellion led by Yakub Beg. The
Chinese did not regain control over Xinjiang, which had become known
as Chinese Turkestan, until 1877. In this century, there has been an un-
easy truce between the Chinese and Uighurs, sometimes broken by protests, even by violence.

At Turpan, in the heart of Xinjiang, the northern route of the Silk
Road steps down into the second deepest continental basin on Earth (next
to the Dead Sea). Turpan is 260 feet below sea level, while nearby Moon
Lake (Aiding Hu) is 505 feet below sea level. This low lake is indeed
lunar, encrusted in salt, freezing in winter, melting in summer. Two-
thousand-year-old beacon towers still guard the lakeshore, where some

Map labels:
To Urumqi
Bezeklik Caves
Flaming Mts.
TURPAN (see inset)
1 mi
Emin Minaret
Jiaohe Ruins
6 mi
Karez Wells & Museum
Astana Tombs
Gaochang Ruins

Inset map labels:
Gaochang Lu
Qingnian Lu
Oasis Hotel
Wenhua Lu
To Karez Wells
Laocheng Lu
John's Information Cafe
Turpan Guesthouse
Jiefang Jie
To Emin Minaret

Turpan

N

of the salt factory workers, sent from coastal cities to labor here during the Cultural Revolution (1966–76), have never returned to their homes.

Turpan, just 34 miles from Moon Lake, is far more hospitable. In fact, it is a model Silk Road oasis, a sleepy desert town shaded by poplar trees and grape arbors, peopled by Uighurs in traditional dress and irrigated by a vast system of hand-dug underground channels that funnel the melting snows of the Heavenly Mountains into Turpan. This 2,000-year-old irrigation system has kept Turpan alive while other desert boomtowns have withered up and died. Two of those ancient cities, empty and returned to the sands with which they were built, still remain on Turpan's doorstep, two of the most impressive imperial ruins anywhere on the Silk Road.

Bezeklik Thousand Buddha Caves

Turpan is China's hottest city, its "Land of Fire," with summer temperatures routinely reaching a roasty 40 degrees Centigrade (104 degrees Fahrenheit). I arrive on the first of May and the temperature is already 2 degrees above that. I have been doing nothing but traveling for hours. The day before I was driven for 3 hours from Dunhuang north to Liuyuan, past the earthen ruins of the Han Dynasty Great Wall, past a group of five wild camels, and over the Horse Mane Hills where the sand disappeared and the exposed rock, shattered into bits the size of fingertips, coated everything in lunar gravel. At Liuyuan I boarded an overnight train stuffed with happy Japanese tourists. I arrived at Turpan at 4am, where my local guide, Christina, and a driver met me in the dark. They suggested I nap a few hours in my room in the Oasis Hotel (a fourth-floor walk-up), but of course I couldn't. I was eager to see the sights of Turpan, its old mosques and graves, its fabulous wells, its ruined cities, the Flaming Mountains, and Bezeklik.

Bezeklik is a major Buddhist site in the heart of the Flaming Mountains 35 miles northeast of Turpan. Beginning in the Southern and Northern dynasties (A.D. 420–589), caves were hewn into the cliffside, and large murals, like those at Dunhuang, were painted on the walls and ceilings. The site is now known as the Bezeklik Thousand Buddha Caves. (In Uighur, *bezeklik* means simply "place of paintings.")

The **Flaming Mountains** line the northern rim of the Turpan Depression. Consisting of barren red limestone, the 60-mile-long bluff resembles a tableau of fiery tongues when ignited by the afternoon sun. It is a sight familiar to Chinese readers of the novel *Journey to the West*, an allegorical version of Buddhist monk Xuan Zang's historic journey by foot from China to India over the Silk Road in the 7th century. The trip from Dunhuang west to Turpan, which took me less than 24 hours by car and train, would have taken Xuan Zang or any other pilgrim or caravan trader at least three weeks—three terrible weeks in the desert. Xuan Zang got lost here. Running out of water, he wanted to turn back but wandered on, half dead. He made it, of course, to Turpan—or rather, to the city of Gaochang, now in ruins near the site of the Bezeklik caves—where he taught for several months.

Bezeklik is situated in absolutely stunning surroundings, high up a cliff in the Murtuk River gorge. From a distance, the caves cut into the ridge and the brick temples, as well as the smooth mosque domes, look like a holy city chiseled out of a vertical mountainside. Close up, Bezeklik is nearly empty—worse, it has been looted and defaced. The painted walls of its 83 grottoes with their arched ceilings have nearly all been erased or stolen. The Buddhist statuary is also missing. It is a superb Buddhist grotto emptied as if by desert winds or stone-eating monsters.

In fact, Bezeklik has been emptied by men. The Uighurs themselves, having converted to Islam in the 10th century, did not look favorably upon the Buddhist images in their midst. They defaced some murals, beheaded statues, sealed up the caves in sand, and built domed mosques in place of the brick temples. Much of this took place in the 1870s, when Turpan and most of Xinjiang Province broke away from Chinese control and became Chinese Turkestan.

Greater destruction came from the West. The German Albert von Le Coq arrived in Turpan in 1902; he departed with 2 tons of treasures and relics. Two years later, he returned for more. Other expeditions from Europe arrived, crating off whatever remained. At Bezeklik, the German experts found Turpan's treasure house: 1,000-year-old murals in perfect condition with bright portraits of Buddha over the centuries, yellow-robed monks from India, and even a red-haired traveler from the West. The best frescoes were removed and shipped to the Museum for Indian Art in Berlin for safekeeping—beyond the reach of Uighur farmers and Islamic fanatics, it was argued at the time. Later, World War II bombing raids destroyed the Bezeklik wall murals in Berlin, where only fragments remain on display.

A man with a key opens the doors to several caves. There are 83 grottoes here; about 40 retain frescoes, all in poor condition. The few defaced murals I see give strong hints of the vibrant reds that dominate the art here and of the glowing greens and blues the painters employed as trim. On one arched ceiling, I can make out a familiar motif, the 1,000 Buddhas in meditation, row after identical row, unrestored and crumbling.

Ancient Cities

South of the Thousand Buddha Caves are the ruins of **Gaochang (Kharakhoja),** an ancient desert capital founded in the 2nd century B.C. as a garrison on the Silk Road. It served as the capital of Xinjiang (the Western Territories) during the Tang Dynasty, starting in A.D. 640. From 840 to 1209, Gaochang became the Uighur capital. It was destroyed in 1275 and has stood unoccupied ever since.

The dry air and lack of rain have preserved the outlines of Gaochang's adobe outer walls (3 miles in circumference) and inner buildings—its Bell Tower and a few of its many Buddhist temples.

At the entrance, we hire a young Uighur driver and hop aboard his flatbed donkey cart for an hour's ride (RMB 15/$2) inside the ancient walls. The pace is slow and the donkey driver relaxed—this is the proper speed at which to drive through a ghost town on the Silk Road. It is a sizable ghost town, nearly a mile across. At the center of this city of sand there is a large temple, its platform and shrine still evident, and close by a two-story circular pavilion surrounded by a square wall where the pilgrim Xuan Zang preached in A.D. 630 on his way to India.

The city is empty of human remains, of course, but the royal graveyard, a few miles away, is now receiving visitors. The **Astana Tombs** have been blessed with centuries of dry weather, meaning the corpses, their silk wrappings, and even the foods buried with them have survived in fine fettle. The earliest of the 500 graves is dated A.D. 273; the latest, A.D. 782. The burial chambers are 16 feet below the earth. Wall murals depict the pleasures of family life and the beauties of nature, particularly of birds. Among the 10,000 relics excavated at Astana is a pair of woven linen shoes and a fossilized jiaozi (steamed dumpling), both specimens from the Tang Dynasty.

Coburial of husband and wife was common. Inside the last of the three chambers open to the public, the mummies of a man and a woman lie next to each other, under glass, on a rough mat. Their hair has grown long in death and so have their fingernails. They have barely begun to disintegrate with the passage of 12 centuries, but they look dry, very dry. If a splash of water stirred them to life now—it looks as if it could—what a strange world would greet their imperial gaze, my foreign face perhaps the most terrifying image of all.

On the opposite side of modern Turpan, 6 miles to the west, is a second ruined city, **Jiaohe (Yarkhoto),** perched on a leaf-shaped 100-foot-high plateau between two rivers. A mile long, a quarter mile wide, it is nearly the size of Gaochang, but it is better preserved. The outlines of many of its buildings are sharper, there are some signposts in English, and UNESCO has contributed to its preservation.

Jiaohe, like so many Silk Road towns, began as a garrison during the Han Dynasty. It reached its peak under Uighur control in the 9th century during the Tang Dynasty. It has been abandoned for more than five centuries, but it has preserved its ancient cityscape in sand and brick. A Buddhist temple stands at city center, with Buddhas (heads now missing) carved into its niches. Streets and the courtyards of houses were dug into the ground. Jiaohe looks like a life-sized model of a Tang Dynasty city, sculpted from a high sandstone column standing between river gorges, or like an oasis stripped by a miraculous wind of every piece and particle that was not composed of sand or brick.

Karez Wells

Turpan is 80% Uighur. Christina, my guide, is a local Han Chinese, meaning she probably went to a Chinese school and was not taught the Uighur language. Uighurs attend their own schools, in which Chinese is studied as a second language. Each side coexists sweetly, it seems. Christina has a dream of visiting America. She wants to see the west—the Wild West of cowboys that she knows from the movies. I tell her that today Turpan is the Wild West. She has another dream she wants to make a reality in America: She wants to listen to jazz in a jazz bar, together with her friends. So pervasive are these media images of America that they penetrate even the remotest oasis on the Silk Road, shaping the images of a generation.

In the morning, we visit **Emin Minaret,** a mile east of the city, the prettiest tower on the Silk Road. Also called Sugong Tower, it was built of blue brick and completed in 1778. The bricks of the circular, smoothly tapered tower are laid in various patterns: waves, pyramids, and flower petals. The architect was a Uighur named Ibrahim. Attached to the 144-foot minaret is a white stone mosque, the largest in the region. Its interior is plain. The roof is of woven mats. The floor is covered in prayer rugs. The Iman's seat is a humble, straw-woven chair.

The Emin Minaret is surrounded by grape arbors. Grape vines came into China on the Silk Road 2,000 years ago and Turpan planted them immediately. At the western base of the Flaming Mountains, there's an entire valley called Grape Gorge (Putao Guo), a park of vineyards and fruit groves with trellised walkways and courtyard picnic tables. The grapes are dried in hundreds of ingenious outbuildings ventilated by the open brickwork of their walls, creating the sweet raisins for which Turpan is renowned.

The sine qua non for grapes—for all of life along the Silk Road—is water. Turpan's source is locked up in the snows and glaciers of the Heavenly Mountains to the south. For the last 20 centuries the mountain waters have reached Turpan through a massive underground network of tunnels, an irrigation system known as the **karez.** Wells are dug to tap the subterranean streams that originate at the foot of the mountain. Tunnels are hollowed out and elevated so that gravity pushes the well water across the desert to the canals of Turpan. More than 1,000 miles of tunnels have been dug under the desert floor at Turpan, some stretching as far as 25 miles. The karez system suffers from continual clogging. Constant maintenance is performed by lowering a man down a shaft into a tunnel. By the use of pulleys, his horse hauls up buckets of mud tethered to a rope until the passage is clear.

One karez well site has opened at an exhibition center in Turpan, complete with a museum of displays and pictures. Visitors descend into several hand-dug tunnels for a look at the irrigating waters. The tunnels are spacious enough to stand up in, and they are cool, the coolest spots in town. Working in them must be like digging in a mine. The local people regard the karez wells as one of China's three greatest ancient works, the other two being the Great Wall and the Grand Canal.

Falling Down the Well

Turpan is a pleasant town to walk before the sun rises too high or after it sets. The flat roofs of the mud-brick Uighur homes are coated with grains and seeds for drying. Every backyard seems to have its clay bread-baking oven and lattice-roofed patio. In the poplar-lined streets, silk rugs hang for sale and donkey-cart taxi drivers cruise the traffic circles looking for riders. Chinese and Westerners are vastly outnumbered here. The sidewalks belong to the Uighurs and the white-capped Huis (Islamic Chinese).

Above all, Turpan is China's town of the grape. The trellises are everywhere, sometimes shading entire city blocks. It's a good thing. The summer sun is scorching. This is *heat,* sucking every ounce of moisture to the surface of the skin like a karez well; heat that makes coffins unnecessary at funerals; an embalming heat that shrivels grapes and turns out mummies guaranteed to last a millennium, no other treatment required. My room's air conditioner is on the fritz and the temperature is pushing 106 degrees Fahrenheit, but at least I don't have to fear what foreign travelers reported 60 years ago. There are no large scorpions lodged under sleeping mats, hidden in shoes, or parachuting on me from the roof beams while I nap, no jumping spiders "as large as a pigeon's egg" grinding their jaws over their prey, and no 2-inch-long Turpan cockroaches with hairy feelers and red eyes.

On my last evening in Turpan I walk down to the **Turpan Guesthouse** to enjoy an evening performance of Uighur song and dance. The costumes are flashy and the master of ceremonies is proficient in the three languages Xinjiang employs: Uighur, Chinese, and English. A sheepskin tambourine, played with vigor, keeps the swirling dancers on track. I walk back through the pitch dark. At the traffic circle I am in midsentence with Christina when I disappear into the third-world traveler's worst nightmare: an open manhole.

This is, fortunately, not a cartoon. Rather than vanishing, my momentum tips me forward when I step into open space. I fall to the pavement on one knee and an elbow, scraping my shin against the manhole rim. Only my lead foot plunges into the dark well and I pull it out and stand up. Not such a nightmare after all. One foot hurts, my left buttock aches, I'm scraped here and there, and my shoes—I hate to think what at least one of them has stepped in. Nevertheless I can walk, as I must. I'm barely halfway across the Silk Road.

PRACTICAL INFORMATION

ORIENTATION

Turpan (called Tulufan by the Chinese) is a desert oasis on the northern Silk Road in central Xinjiang Uighur Autonomous Region, 1,900 miles west of Beijing. It is located in the **Tarim Basin,** 260 feet below sea level, in the "oven" of China, the hottest city in the country, where summer temperatures routinely soar above 100 degrees Fahrenheit. The **Heavenly Mountains (Tian Shan)** lie to the south; their glaciers and snows feed the underground streams and springs that have been tapped by the karez well system, an ancient engineering feat on a par with construction of the Great Wall and Grand Canal. Nearly 70% of the 200,000 people in Turpan county are Uighur, a Turkish minority, formerly nomadic, that originated south of Lake Baikal. Here public signs are written in Arabic first, Chinese second. In late August there is a vibrant **Grape Festival.** May and October are the coolest months to visit; winters are freezing cold.

GETTING THERE

By Train The nearest train station is at Daheyan, 35 miles north of Turpan. Eastbound, the train to Liuguan (Dunhuang) takes 13 hours (overnight), 49 hours to Xi'an, and 70 hours to Beijing. Westbound, the train to Urumqi takes 3 hours. From Turpan to the train station at Daheyan, a bus or hired car takes an hour. There is no airport at Turpan. The nearest airport is at Urumqi,

114 miles northwest, a 4-hour journey over a paved highway by car or bus from Turpan. Make onward travel arrangements in Turpan at the Oasis Hotel (see "Where to Stay," below).

GETTING AROUND

Downtown Turpan is small, quiet, and shaded by poplar trees and grape trellises. Donkey carts are the main form of transportation, and many of them offer 1-hour trips to the tourist sites (RMB 24 to 40/$3 to $5). Bicycles can be rented at hotels and cafes (RMB 20 to 30/$2.40 to $3.60 per day). Qingnian Lu is the main north–south street, where the hotels and cafes catering to foreign travelers are located.

TOURS & STRATAGEMS

This was my third stop on an 8-day independent tour of the Silk Road booked through China Travel Service (CTS) in Xi'an (see introduction to this section for details).

China International Travel Service (CITS) in Turpan is located in the Oasis Hotel, 41 Qingnian Lu (☎ 0995/52-1352). CITS can provide guided tours of Turpan, train tickets (with transfers to the Daheyan train station), and plane tickets (for flights from Urumqi).

WHERE TO STAY

Oasis Hotel (Liuzhou Binguan). *41 Qingnian Lu.* ☎ *0995/52-2478. Fax 0995/52-3348. A/C TV TEL. $50 double. No credit cards.* This 2-star hotel is as good as it gets in Turpan, so there's no reason to look down the street—the best services are here. The rooms are modern and large but shabby, and the carpets, wall-to-wall in the halls and rooms, are a hazard as they've never been attached to the floor. The elevators (six floors) run most of the time, as does the air-conditioning. The lobby has a tour desk run by the local CITS. There's also a gift shop, post office, and beauty shop.

WHERE TO DINE

The **Turpan Guesthouse**, Tulufan Binguan (☎ 0995/52-2301), three blocks south of the Oasis Hotel on Qingnian Lu, has an outdoor cafe in the back with an English-language menu, Chinese and Uighur foods, and cold beer; and the **Oasis Hotel** itself has several Chinese restaurants of good quality where some English is spoken. For Western foods, **John's Information Cafe** (☎ 0995/52-4237), across the street from the Turpan Guesthouse on Qingnian Lu, offers inexpensive choices all day and well into the night. John's has branches in Kashgar and Urumqi, with their own in-house travel agencies catering to independent foreign travelers.

URUMQI: TO HEAVENLY LAKE

乌鲁木齐

N O CITY IN THE WORLD IS MORE distant from the sea than Urumqi. It is 1,397 miles to the nearest ocean. The city's name means "beautiful pastures" in Mongolian, but Urumqi, capital of the Xinjiang Uighur Autonomous Region, is a modern industrial metropolis with a population of 1½ million, and all its beautiful meadows lie well outside the city limits.

Urumqi is the most Chinese of the Silk Road cities. Nearly 80% of its residents are Han Chinese, recent "economic immigrants" who were induced to move west, attracted by the higher wages and better opportunities available on the frontier. The Uighurs, the nomadic Kazakhs, and other minorities dominate the surrounding lands. Muslim rebels have ruled the city at times, both before and after Urumqi was declared the capital of China's Western Territories (Xinjiang) in 1884. At the beginning of the 20th century, the city maintained separate Muslim, Chinese, and Russian quarters. The influence of the three groups remains strong today, but the Han Chinese are firmly in control of Urumqi's administration and factories.

The overriding truth about Urumqi, however, is that it is an ugly industrial monster set in one of the least appealing spots on the Silk Road—little more than a slag heap on which to heap more slag. On the other hand, the new Chinese workers and investors are planting greenways and replacing slums, making Urumqi the most modern city on the old Silk Road, a new crossroads for traders from China, Russia, and Central Asia. For travelers, the chief attraction of Urumqi is not trade or industry, of course, but the "beautiful pastures" hinted at in Urumqi's name, and those places are within reach. In the southern pastures of the Heavenly Mountains and at Heavenly Lake, where the Kazakhs roam on horseback, the alpine beauty of the Silk Road is at its grandest.

The Road to Urumqi

The highway northwest from Turpan to Urumqi has no center line and it is under constant repair. The land is flat, bordered on the north by the Heavenly Mountains (Tian Shan) and dotted by shrub brush and oil rigs. It takes us 4 hours to drive 114 miles. We pass a new wind farm, the propellers still in a light breeze. At the town of **Dabancheng,** the second largest salt lake in China lies in a basin, its shores ringed by a scum of salt like a dirty bathtub. The road winds up out of the Turpan Depression and crosses a blackened plain into Urumqi at 3,000 feet altitude.

Downtown Urumqi's avenues are tree-lined. Modern construction is under way everywhere. There are Russian-style buildings left over from the 1950s, their iron roofs painted green and their bright porticoes giving the gray cityscape a splash of color, and there are over a hundred mosques, many of them new. Covered Uighur markets throughout the city also break the monotony of modern industrialization.

A touch of Old China is supplied by two parks on the banks of the Urumqi River, which flows along the western edge of the city. The nine-story **Zhenglong Pagoda ("Pagoda to Suppress Dragons")** atop **Red Hill (Hong Shan)** towers over Urumqi. It was erected on the "dragon's head" in 1788 to prevent floods, and the hills became a Buddhist center until the pavilions and temples were burned down by successive warlords. The Qing armies pastured their horses on Red Hill a century ago. Nearby **Hongshan Park** (renamed People's Park), on the west bank of the river, has a lake and hall modeled after the Forbidden City in Beijing, both built in the early 20th century by one of the ruling warlords. Both parks are favored by locals looking for a green patch and on Sunday they are packed.

We stop for lunch at a downtown hotel, the Liuguan. The lobby is chock-full of businessmen from Russia, Pakistan, India, and Mongolia, their respective borders nearby. Rail links to Kazakhstan have brought a steady stream of traders from Central Asia and beyond into Urumqi since 1992. The Russian presence is strong. Next door to the hotel there is a busy Aeroflot office. More than any other city on the Silk Road, Urumqi has reverted to its glorious past: It is a major crossroads for East–West trade.

Southern Pastures

Every spring and summer, the Kazakhs ride into the **White Poplar Valley** and up into the **Southern Mountains (Nan Shan),** an extension of the Heavenly Mountains. They pack up their families and their tents, called yurts, and make the move on horseback. The attraction is the pastures, where they graze their sheep herds. Farther up the mountain is a 65-foot waterfall.

The highway winds up the valley 46 miles south from Urumqi. It is a relief to leave the city. The suburbs are filled with shacks and small mosques. Huis (Chinese Muslims), Uighurs, and Kazakhs wander through the unpaved lanes, donkey carts in tow. On the southern outskirts of Urumqi is the largest chemical factory I have seen in China. Smoke blots the landscape for miles. The southern meadows are another world entirely. The mountain peaks are steep and green with tall spruces and pines. The river is clear and swift, tumbling by remote mud huts on the hillsides. We slow for sheep in the road, lovely sheep, black, brown, and white.

At the foot of the waterfall there is a **Kazakh village** of huts and yurts, open to tourists. Several of the yurts serve as cafes and souvenir shops. One vendor tries to sell me local handicrafts from a yurt, pointing out that his brother lives in Boston. In the late summer, traditional riding games are held on the grassy steppes. Girls court boys in horseback races. Those they catch they playfully whip.

The **waterfall** is at an elevation of 7,000 feet in mountains that resemble the Swiss Alps. It plunges through a narrow chute, dropping 90 feet into a stony streambed. A rainbow-colored steel arched bridge crosses the stream, but otherwise there is little mark of humans here. Kazakhs search the mountainsides for ginseng roots.

The Kazakhs—known as the Cossacks by the Russians—descended from the Turkic-speaking Wusun nomads who were pushed southward by the Huns into the foothills of the Heavenly Mountains nearly 2,000 years ago. Excellent horsemen, they rode with Genghis Khan and Kublai Khan as the Yuan Dynasty (1271–1368) swept north and east to conquer China. In 1958, the Chinese established pastoral communes in this region of Xinjiang, but many Kazakhs continue to follow a nomadic life in the grasslands and mountain valleys surrounding industrial Urumqi. In July, they gather for a 6-day **nadam,** a summer fair with horse racing, wrestling, and competitions involving the sheep and cattle they herd. More than a million Kazakhs live in Xinjiang, where they are now outnumbered by Han Chinese and Uighurs. They still exercise their traditional nomadic ways, sustained these days by revenues from tourism and government subsidies.

By the time we leave the southern pastures, Urumqi is being cleansed by a violent downpour. The cloudburst has halted hundreds of trucks, buses, and taxis in their tracks, particularly at flooded intersections. The drivers abandon their vehicles in the middle of the highway. In the darkness, there are no lights to mark the breakdowns. The police pass by, powerless it seems. We run a dark, wet obstacle course to the hotel in Urumqi from where even the nearby pagoda on Red Hill has been snuffed out by spring rains.

Heavenly Lake

East of Urumqi, on the way to Heavenly Lake, two wild camels loiter on the roadside. We pull off and they scatter. Later, rising into the foothills of the Heavenly Mountains, I see another camel munching on tree leaves. We enter valleys where sheep and goats block the road, where village huts are sometimes made of stone—round huts in the shape of yurts. Horsemen ride across the hilltops. The countryside belongs to the Kazakh herdsmen.

The road, which did not exist until 1958, winds up the **Stone Gorge (Shi Xia),** a hillside of white boulders, to a broad, green embankment a quarter of a mile wide. At the end of the embankment, high up under snowy peaks, 75 miles from Urumqi and at twice its elevation, Heavenly Lake (Tian Chi) is encased like an Alpine jewel. My first glimpse of it is magnificent. No mountain lake is prettier. It reminds me of Canada's Lake Louise, but Heavenly Lake is surrounded by horse trails and yurts. It is 2 miles long, a mile wide, 300 feet deep. There are sheep grazing on its rocky banks. Tied to a wharf on a green lip of the lake are covered launches and small speedboats for tourists. Several white ponies stand on the shore, their Kazakh masters ready with traditional costumes—red jackets, white lace robes, gold-trimmed caps—to outfit visitors who want a picture taken on horseback, the divine lake and mountains as a back-drop. In the parking lot, a family is pitching a large yurt, swiftly erecting the wooden accordion that is its skeleton.

According to one legend, 3,000 years ago Han Emperor Wudi was invited by Xi Wang Mu, the immortal Queen Mother of the West, to a banquet at Heavenly Lake. The peach tree of immortality was served. The emperor saved the pits to plant, but Xi Wang Mu told him the soil of China could not sustain it, that fruit appeared but once every 3,000 years.

There are two smaller pools east and west of Heavenly Lake, where Xi Wang Mu washed her feet. She bathed her face in the big lake, which mirrors the solid blue sky and steep mountain peaks that frame it. The two small pools are nearly dry when I visit in the spring. They are located on steep ledges. Christina, my guide, tells me that last year one of her colleagues ventured off the path, slipped, and fell to her death beside one pool. Her body has not yet been found. She tells me another local legend: Heavenly Lake was created from the tears Xi Wang Mu shed when her lover departed for the East.

It is possible to hike around the lake and into the mountains. **Bogda Peak** is the highest mountain, at 17,864 feet, 11,000 feet above Heavenly Lake. Kazakhs hire out their horses for mountain treks, acting as guides. Higher up where the snows are loath to melt even in summer, there are yurts that take in travelers. I would love to make such a trek, but my time is spoken for. I content myself with a walk up into a nearby pasture, where a dozen yurts are pitched. A Kazakh woman bids me inside. The inside of her yurt is dazzling. The floor is covered in carpets, woven with wools dyed vibrant blues, reds, and greens. The felt walls are hung with rich embroideries and quilts. Inside this yurt, a baby is sleeping on a quilt on the floor, mindless of foreign intruders. Children are named on the sec-ond day after birth. The mother leaves the tent and fixes on the first thing that comes into her mind. That becomes her child's name. The mother tells me I can stay the night if I wish, but I must decline. She offers me a chunk of thick baked bread, known as *nan*, which I saw diligently through, washing it down with Kazakh tea, a brew of mare's milk and the snow lotus that grows in the dragon spruce forests of Heavenly Lake. If I could stay anywhere on the Silk Road it would be here, in the high mountains beside a blue sapphire lake, in the carpeted tents of nomads who roll up their homes as the seasons change and ride across these stream-fed pastures.

PRACTICAL INFORMATION

ORIENTATION

Urumqi, which the Chinese call Wulumuqi, is the capital of Xinjiang Uighur Autonomous Region, China's northwesternmost province. It is 2,050 miles from Beijing, just north of the most northern route of the ancient Silk Road. The city is large and highly industrialized. The majority of the residents are Han Chinese and come to work here from other parts of China. Uighurs (30%) and Kazakhs (10%) make up the city's largest minorities. Russian businessmen constitute the most noticeable group of visitors. Urumqi is the largest city in Xinjiang and the most modern, although compared to China's other large cities it is a rugged frontier outpost. Winters are extremely cold. April and October are the most pleasant months to visit, although industrial pollution and dust storms are constant threats.

GETTING THERE

By Plane   Urumqi's airport, 10 miles from city center, has international connections to Moscow, Karachi, Islamabad, and Tashkent. Over 30 cities in China are served, including Hong Kong (5 hours), Shanghai (4½ hours), Beijing (3½ hours), Xi'an (3 hours 45 minutes), and Kashgar (1 hour 20 minutes). Taxis charge about RMB 100 ($12.50) for the 30-minute airport transfer.

By Train   The express train from Beijing requires 64 hours, the longest ride in China. The daily express to Xi'an is nearly as grueling: 50 hours. Trains to other places on the Silk Road are shorter: 3 hours to Daheyan (Turpan), 18 hours to Liuyuan (Dunhuang), and 24 hours to Jiayuguan. There is no train to Kashgar, the last stop in China on the Silk Road. The bus takes three days, making an air flight to Kashgar almost mandatory.

TOURS & STRATAGEMS

This was my fourth stop on an 8-day independent tour of the Silk Road booked through **China Travel Service (CTS)** in Xi'an (see "Tours and Stratagems" on page 372 for details).

China International Travel Service (CITS) in Urumqi is located at 51 Xinhua Bei Lu, south of the Holiday Inn in the Luyou Hotel (☎ 0991/282-5794; fax 0991/281-0689). The best place to book air tickets and to set up city tours and trips to the Southern Pastures (Nan Shan) and Heavenly Lake is at the travel desk in the Holiday Inn Urumqi, 168 Xinhua Bei Lu (☎ 0991/281-8788).

WHERE TO STAY

Holiday Inn Urumqi (Xinjiang Jiari Dajiudian). *168 Xinhua Bei Lu.* ☎ *800/ 465-4329 or 0991/281-8788. Fax 0991/ 281-7422. 338 rms, 22 suites. A/C MINIBAR TV TEL. $125 double. AE, DC, JCB, MC, V.* This 24-story 4-star international hotel is almost legendary in China, one of the most remote Holiday Inns in the world, but with all the luxuries—and good service to boot. No other hotel in Urumqi comes close. The rooms and bathrooms are clean, there are executive floors, no-smoking floors, and handicapped-accessible rooms, as well as a disco, deli, and a 24-hour Western restaurant.

Services: Room service (24-hour), dry cleaning and laundry (same-day service before noon), daily maid service, free airport shuttle, foreign exchange counter.

Facilities: In-house movies, health club (exercise machines), Jacuzzi, sauna, tennis courts, snooker, business center, tour desk, beauty salon, shopping arcade.

Hongshan Hotel (Hongshan Binguan). *108 Xinhua Bei Lu.* ☎ *0991/ 282-4973. 204 rms. $30 double. No credit cards.* The choice of backpackers and independent budget travelers, the Hongshan offers rundown, no-frills doubles and cheap dormitory rooms with communal showers. The location is good (a block from the Holiday Inn) and there are travel agents and free-lance tour guides in abundance.

WHERE TO DINE

Downtown hotels and cafes near the Holiday Inn serve Uighur dishes, such as noodles (lamian), flat breads (nan), and mutton shish kebab, but a local guide is necessary to interpret the menu and negotiate prices.

John's Information Cafe, across the intersection from the Hongshan Hotel (two blocks north of Holiday Inn toward the Red Hill Pagoda on Xinhua Lu), caters to foreign backpackers with inexpensive Western dishes and Chinese food.

Two of the city's best restaurants are in the Holiday Inn.

Caravan. *168 Xinhua Bei Lu (ground floor, Holiday Inn).* ☎ *0991/281-8788.* *Main courses $5–$12. AE, DC, JCB, MC, V. Daily 24 hours. WESTERN/CHINESE.* The best Western food in town. Breakfast buffets are RMB 100 ($12). Buffets are provided at lunch (noon to 3pm) and dinner (7 to 11pm) as well.

Kashgari's. *168 Xinhua Bei Lu (ground floor, Holiday Inn).* ☎ *0991/281-8788. Reservations recommended. Main courses $7–$18. AE, DC, JCB, MC, V. Daily 12:30– 3:15pm and 7–10:30pm (closed for lunch on Sun). MUSLIM.* Uighur, Kazakh, and Muslim specialties are served in elegant atmosphere. Three private function rooms can be reserved for Muslim banquets.

KASHGAR: THE GATE TO ASIA

喀什

THE OASIS OF KASHGAR IS LOCATED
at a great junction in the Silk Road. Heading east, traders swapped horses
and yaks for camels to cross the vast deserts of China. Heading west, they
readied their pack animals to cross the high mountain passes into Central
Asia. From Kashgar, the camel caravans trekked eastward from oasis to
oasis to reach the ancient capital of China, while teams of packhorses
trudged westward through India and Persia to Rome. Marco Polo heralded Kashgar in the 13th century as the "starting point from which many
merchants set out to market their wares to the world."

The westernmost city in China, Kashgar is the place no one traveling
the Silk Road today should miss, if only to see its Sunday market, said by
some to be the largest on Earth. The oasis is overwhelmingly Islamic.
More than 90% of its residents are Uighurs. The streets are crammed
with mud-brick houses, sidewalk bazaars, and mosques. There are more
horse carts than cars. Chairman Mao's statue presides over People's Park,
but Kashgar is a city from another time and place, a medieval village
where women shop the streets covered in long brown veils.

Kashgar first came under Chinese sovereignty during the Han Dynasty in the 1st century A.D. Under Tang rule, Chinese troops fortified
the oasis, but Tibetans and later Turkish tribes often held sway. Kashgar
was just too remote for China to exercise unbroken power there. From
the 16th through the 19th centuries, various Islamic leaders ruled the
Kashgari kingdom, with the Chinese mounting periodic assaults to regain control over the region. In the 1930s, an Islamic movement based in
Kashgar declared the formation of the Republic of Eastern Turkestan,
but the city fell again to the Chinese (assisted by Russian troops from
Urumqi) in 1933. It was not until the Communists established the People's
Republic of China in 1949 that Kashgar came firmly into Chinese hands.
Before that, Kashgar was a pawn in the "Great Game" played by other
major powers in the region, including Britain, which maintained a con-
sulate there, and Russia, whose embassy, opened in 1882, is now the Seman
Hotel—where I, like many a modern traveler, began my stay in Kashgar.

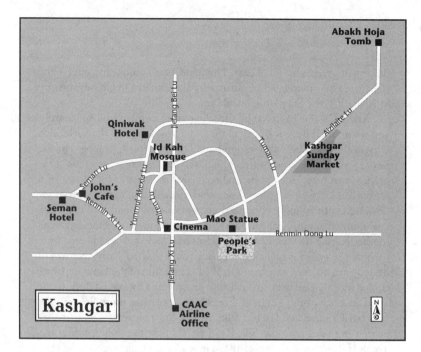

Kashgar

Abakh Hoja Tomb

A dust storm is whipping across the airstrip at Kashgar as my flight from Urumqi nears. My plane is an old Russian prop jet, owned by Air Volga, with a small notice on the fuselage stating that it has been rented by Xinjiang Air. The cabin is like the inside of a ruined bus. The seats are the most uncomfortable in the sky, but the bag of green raisins handed out for a snack is delicious. The dust thickens as we descend over Kashgar. The plane hits the ground sharply, like an old suitcase.

I'm the first to complete the walk across the tarmac to the waiting lounge. The Japanese tourists linger, snapping photos of each other disembarking through the blowing dust. I'm met by a local guide, Sadik. At the Seman Hotel, the century-old former Russian compound, I'm met by dancing girls in Uighur gowns and a band of horns and pipes. The doorman hands me a steaming face towel. It's the most gracious entrance I've made in China—if this is China. It looks more like eastern Turkey, and I've yet to see a single Chinese face.

The first place on the tourist route is the holiest site in the entire province of Xinjiang, the Abakh Hoja Tomb, in the northeast suburbs of the oasis. This is more than just a tomb: It is a monumental hall, finished in 1640, with a large dome of dazzling glazed green tiles. The **Tomb Hall** reminds me of a small Taj Mahal. Inside, the entire tiled floor is covered in 58 rounded sarcophagi, also beautifully tiled, which contain the remains of five generations of the Islamic prophet and Kashgar ruler Abakh Hoja, who died in 1639. Two of the tombs under the domed ceiling are draped in green: that of Abakh Hoja and that reputed to contain the remains of his granddaughter, Iparhan, who is known to Chinese history as Xiang Fei, the Fragrant Concubine.

Xiang Fei was captured by the Qing army in the mid-18th century and transported from Kashgar all the way across China to the Forbidden City in Beijing. There she was presented to Emperor Qianlong. For the next 25 years, she lived in the capital, serving the emperor as his "Fragrant Concubine," for her natural scent was as sweet as the bloom of a flower. She wept for her desert home and rejected the emperor's advances. Obsessed with winning her affections, he built her a Turkish bath and a tower turned toward Kashgar, but she did not give in. Finally, the emperor's mother, fearing that the Fragrant Concubine would kill her son or at least become the rallying point for a palace coup, ordered Xiang Fei to kill herself with her own bare hands in 1761. The coffin of the Fragrant Concubine was wheeled back to Kashgar, a journey that consumed three years.

The story of the Fragrant Concubine is perhaps more fiction than fact, but Chinese and Uighur alike adhere to its veracity. The cart that carried her back over the Silk Road stands near the railing inside the Tomb Hall, although it is clearly too new and too undamaged to be anything but a reproduction. I have read reports that the Fragrant Concubine has been removed to Hebei Province, but of course here is the proper location for her tomb, the perfect ending to her story.

To the right of the Tomb Hall there is a large walled graveyard with thousands more of the coffin-shaped tombs. These are not tiled; they are the color of sand. Some are pierced so that the soul can escape to travel.

A **Teaching Hall** and a **Prayer Hall** are also open to view at Abakh Hoja. The grounds are entered through a magnificent turreted square gate three stories tall, faced in swirling blue tiles. Open daily from 8am to 5:30pm, with a RMB 10 ($1.20) admission, the Abakh Hoja Tomb has recently added a RMB 2 (25¢) surcharge for those wishing to take pictures. My guide just shakes his head. He is quite upset. The government is nearing the end of a 3-year project to restore and replace the tilework on the main Tomb Hall and he says they are going about it all wrong. They should have left it alone, he feels, expressing the common feeling here among the Uighur majority that the Chinese Han administrators don't have the slightest idea how to run things.

Sunday Market

Every cart and camel on the Silk Road seems to pour into Kashgar on Sunday for one of the largest open-air markets in Asia. The Uighurs call it the **Yekshenba Bazaar (Sunday Bazaar)** and the Chinese, although not many are in attendance, call it Zhongxiya Shichang (Western Central Asia Market). By any name, it has no equal in China. By dawn, the donkey carts start arriving from the desert and the mountains, converging on Aizilaiti Lu on the east side of the Tuman River. The larger carts and trucks carry upward of 20 people standing on their belongings. Herds of sheep, goats, cows, and horses make their way through the city to separate trading compounds. The market radiates out for a dozen blocks and it is packed with Muslim farmers, merchants, and traders, as well as whatever foreign tourists and business travelers happen to be in town. The crowds are immense. I've seen estimates ranging from 50,000 to 150,000 people, all converging at the Sunday Bazaar.

I enter the market from the east, shouldering my way past the carts and animals, past large lumberyards and lovely Uighur homes with ornate columned balconies and shuttered windows lining the upper floors. Sidewalk merchants hug the highway for a half mile down to the river. There are straw mats unrolled on the dusty shoulder of the street next to tables of pots and pans pounded out of sheet metal and tin. There are knives and jeweled scimitars, high sheepskin boots and long scarves, and table after table of fresh oasis melons and bagel-shaped breads. There are woven carpets, embroideries, tapestries, and clothing such as the people themselves wear: hats, scarves, veils, jackets, coats, dresses, all dyed in rainbow colors in an endless arabesque of geometric and floral patterns. Several roadside alcoves are filled with hundreds of straw brooms, hand-woven and tied. There are shoemakers stitching without machines, and there are barbers in belted black tunics and black wool caps trimmed in the fur of white lambs at work in the shade of white umbrellas, their customers bolt-upright on plain wooden chairs waiting nervously for a close shave from the barber's whetted cleaver.

In the formal market grounds by the river, there are separate corrals for livestock. Sheep are penned in one yard, horses in another. Cattle and donkeys have their own adjacent arenas, and within each arena families or clans rope off their animals from those of competitors. Animals and people crowd together, bartering and jostling and braying and neighing, while on the periphery of these delightfully pungent pens vendors serve up hot noodles, flat breads, goat soups, milky teas, jars of yogurt, and ice cream. The ice cream is served on sticks or in bowls, kept chilled by enormous blocks of ice wrapped in cloth and delivered by pushcarts to the stands.

Surrounding the animal yards are awnings, tents, and long alleyway arcades specializing in other items. Wooden baby cradles with lathe-turned fences, the knobs painted glossy reds, greens, and blacks, occupy one lane. Down another cobblestoned lane, red-draped stalls sell bolts of dyed silk and cotton. Another arcade sells nothing but hats—the hats of all the tribes of the Silk Road, cotton and fur, peaked and flat, white and sequined.

On the fringes of the market there are streets devoted to vegetables, hauled in from the farms in gunny sacks; to debarked, unmilled shanks of lumber, shining white; to saddles, bridles, and harnesses; to sheepskins and felt carpets draped over donkey carts; to baskets woven from red twigs; to songbirds in cages, something a Chinese gentleman might fancy. In the shadow of a new gallery of empty shops built by the Han Chinese government—which the Uighur merchants have shunned since the day it opened—there is a street of used clothing, of worn shoes and patched coats, of discards that belong in the dump. There is also a square where dogfights were once held and where occasional cockfights still break out when officials are looking the other way.

This market has met in Kashgar for 1,500 years. Walking the streets, squares, and alley arcades, I constantly brush up against donkeys, sheep, horses, and wooden carts. The sun through the dust gives the market an ancient patina. There are con men squatting low, playing a shell game. There are old men in black puffing on long, thin pipes, experts in horseflesh. Across the river, above the market swirl, through the yellow haze I can see the old town of Kashgar on a hillside, its square huts and houses packed together like crates, a city of unpainted mud and brick, the single color of desert sand, no hint of a modern world east of the desert or west of the mountain snows.

The Largest Mosque in China

The busiest, some say the biggest, mosque in China, **Id Kah Mosque,** occupies the central square of Kashgar, where it has stood since 1442. On Friday afternoon, upward of 20,000 men pack the courtyards and prayer hall inside. My guide, Sadik, took me in on a Sunday afternoon. The grounds were filled with worshippers even then, old men and young dressed in long, striped cotton coats (chapans) and high leather boots. The prayer hall, holding up to 5,000, is plainly decorated, with 140 carved wooden columns. The carpets on the floor are a gift from Iran. The Iman leads prayers from a simple chair and microphone. Sadik tells me there is a mosque for every 20 households in Kashgar, but Id Kah is the grandest. The women and children wait outside the large rectangular yellow-tiled gate with its massive blue doors. Two tall minarets, banded in decorative blue and red tiles, flank the wide facade, shielding the large dome of the prayer hall inside.

The streets running east and west from the mosque constitute a permanent bazaar that is in some ways more interesting than the Sunday Market. There are shops on Zhiren Street to the west selling skull caps, fur-trimmed hats, prayer caps, and even the simple Mao caps once favored by Chinese workers; large tin dowry chests, ornately decorated; pots and pans hammered into shape on the street in front of tiny factories; and musical instrument shops with miniature two- and five-stringed Uighur guitars (dutahs and rawupus) hanging above the counters. The small instruments (built of inlaid woods, including apricot) are for decoration, but behind the counter there is often a musician playing the real thing.

Most fascinating are the narrow jewelry shops. Gold is the metal of choice in Kashgar. I was told that you can buy an ounce for less than $15 here. I was surprised to find that many of the jewelers are children. They work at benches inside on raised platforms behind the display counters, shaping gold into pendants, pins, rings, and necklaces.

East of Id Kah Mosque are streets devoted to the sale of carpets: felts of rolled wool, rough hand-tied carpets with dyed geometric designs, and sometimes Kashgar kilims, the handiwork of nomads. Many of the carpet outlets are located inside wooden-shuttered shop houses, their front courtyards shaded by second-story balconies supported by finely turned pillars.

South of the mosque, on Jiefang Bei Lu, there are larger stores and offices, but even here the street looks more like those of Islamabad than Beijing. On the corner of Jiefang and Renmin streets, a former cinema, built in 1954, its second-floor shuttered windows and small balconies typical of Uighur architecture, has a Chinese red star emblazoned on its peak. East down Renmin Dong Lu is Kashgar's **People's Park,** a fixture in every Chinese city. A 59-foot bone-white statue of Chairman Mao looking south faces the park, which is little more than an open, scrubby field. Elsewhere in China, such statues have often come down during the years of economic reform, but I have a feeling Mao is here to stay in Kashgar, where the Uighurs feel very much under the thumb of the Han Chinese.

I waited for dusk to fall over Kashgar at an outdoor table under a large canvas awning at **John's Cafe,** a favorite hangout of foreign backpackers. The cafe is situated a short walk from the compounds of the former British and Russian consulates, now the main hotels of Kashgar. Fierce winds began to shake the awning and desert sands swept across the city. Uighur women drew their brown veils tight around the neck like sacks and hastened home from the bazaars. John's Cafe advertises itself in a sign in English reading "A Little Bit of Home," but it was difficult to imagine being farther from home than Kashgar, sipping a soda at the end of the Silk Road.

PRACTICAL INFORMATION

ORIENTATION

Kashgar, with a population of 120,000, is an oasis in far western Xinjiang Province, more than 2,400 miles inland from Beijing. The vast **Taklamakan Desert** stretches eastward into China and the snowcapped Pamir Mountains form a wall to the west. The **Karakoram Highway** leads to Pakistan (300 miles), and there are long, difficult overland routes to India and Tibet. Urumqi is over 600 miles to the northeast. April and October are the most pleasant months to visit, although the middle of summer, when it becomes increasingly hot, is high tourist season.

GETTING THERE

By Plane   The only efficient medium of travel is by air, on the once-daily flights between Kashgar and Urumqi (1¹/₂ hours). This flight can be canceled by sandstorms. The airport is just 7 miles from city center, but taxi drivers often ask foreigners to pay RMB 100 ($12) for the transfer. There is an airport bus (RMB 5/60¢) that makes the run between the airport and the CAAC airline station (☎ 0998/22-2113) downtown on Jiefang Nan Lu (three blocks south of the main downtown intersection of Jiefang and Renmin streets).

By Bus   Buses take three days to make the journey from Urumqi, although there is one 36-hour sleeper bus on this route. There is no rail service to Kashgar.

TOURS & STRATAGEMS

This was my fifth and final stop on an 8-day independent tour of the Silk Road.

Tours   China International Travel Service (CITS) in Kashgar is located at the Qiniwak Hotel, 93 Seman Lu (☎ 0998/22-3156; fax 0998/22-3087). Open 10am to 1:30pm and 3:30 to 7:30pm, CITS has English-speaking guides for hire. More helpful is the tour desk at the Seman Hotel, 170 Seman Lu (☎ 0998/22-2129), located in the old no. 2 building, which arranges 1- and 2-day city tours, as well as longer excursions into the desert and the mountains. They also book air tickets to Urumqi.

Visitor Information   Kashgar, like all the cities of China, is officially on Beijing time, despite the fact that it should be several time zones west of the capital. Local Kashgar time is 2 hours earlier. Thus, don't expect anything to open until about 10:30am. Breakfast usually begins at about 9:30am, lunch at 1:30pm, and dinner at 7:30pm.

Dress as people should in Muslim countries. That is, cover the body—no shorts, tank tops, and other fashions that might be considered immodest by Islamic residents. Arms and legs should be fully covered when entering mosques, with shoes removed when entering prayer halls.

WHERE TO STAY

The two main hotels for foreign travelers are the Seman Hotel on the grounds of the former Russian consulate and the Qiniwak Hotel at the former British consulate. Both are adequate but not up to international standards. Lesser hotels are reportedly frequented by prostitutes. The Qiniwak is favored by Pakistani traders and travelers. I stayed at the Seman Hotel.

Qiniwak Hotel (Chini Bagh). *93 Seman Lu (at Yunmulakexia Lu, five blocks northwest of Id Kah Mosque).* ☎ *0998/ 22-2103. Fax 0998/22-3842. 140 rms. A/C TV TEL. $40 double. No credit cards.* The five-story 2-star round tower, built in 1990, offers slightly more modern rooms than the Seman Hotel provides. The British Consulate (built 1890) stands on the grounds, and it once played host to early 20th-century Silk Road adventurers and explorers, including Sir Aurel Stein, Sven Hedin, and Albert von Le Coq. If you are a member of a tour group, this is an adequate place to stay, but independent travelers, male and female, have reported instances of unwanted attention paid by persistent fellow guests.

Seman Hotel (Seman Binguan). *170 Seman Lu (1 mile west of city center).* ☎ *0998/22-2129. 212 rms. A/C TV TEL. $35 double. No credit cards.* Occupying the picturesque grounds of the former Russian Embassy (built 1882), the Seman's Building 1 is more modern than Building 2 (which has cheaper dormitory-style accommodations). The service is extremely gracious and friendly. The room card proclaims that "many people have ranked it as one of the top 10 hotels in the world based on service and facilities," but this ranking must have been drawn up 100 years ago. The rooms, with gold curtains, are rundown. Unenclosed showers flood the blue-tiled bathrooms. There is a small gift shop and foreign exchange counter but no elevator in this 2-star monolith. The grounds include a pleasant park and Russian outbuildings, several converted to restaurants. Building 2 contains a full-service tour desk.

WHERE TO DINE

The **Seman Hotel,** 170 Seman Lu (☎ 0998/22-2129), has the best restaurants in town. The Chinese restaurant on the second floor has set breakfasts (RMB 12/$1.50), lunches (RMB 20/$2.40), and dinners (RMB 28/$3.50). The **Uighur restaurant** in a charming building on the Seman Hotel grounds has even better meals for the same price.

John's Information Cafe, two blocks east of the Seman Hotel toward city center (at the intersection of Seman Lu and Xiamalibagh Lu), with courtyard tables, has Western food (pancakes, sandwiches) and Chinese dishes for under $3. Coffee, cold soda, and beer are also available. This cafe is the favorite meeting spot of foreign independent travelers seeking to hook up with local guides and to book adventure tours and overland bus tickets.

SACRED MOUNTAINS: PINNACLES AND PEAKS

名山

THE CHINESE, PERHAPS MORE THAN any other people, have long been enraptured by mountain peaks. For over 2,000 years, they conducted pilgrimages to nine sacred summits, in particular to the Five Sacred Mountains staked out by the native Daoist priests and to the Four Famous Peaks established later by the Buddhists. People walked to the top of these great mountains by the thousands, even by the hundreds of thousands. Emperors joined them, performing imperial rites in the temples that lined the slopes. At the summits, pilgrims knelt before the high altars of the mountain gods and prayed. "Thousands of men and women who wish for a good harvest, health, heirs, or longevity ascend lofty mountains," writes an 18th-century man of letters, "climbing like monkeys and following each other like ants."

China's emperors often ascended the sacred peaks to pray for an end to a devastating drought. In the past most Chinese seemed to believe that certain mountains were divine beings with considerable powers. These peaks were treated as natural gods who could be swayed by sacrifice or prayer. Linking Heaven and Earth, these massive stone gods anchored the Four Directions, preventing the ground from shaking and the rivers from flooding. They gathered the clouds unto their heights and delivered timely rains to parched lands.

These nine sacred summits still exist in China, although the great pilgrimages came to a standstill in this century. The Sacred Five and the Famous Four once formed the cosmic compasses of Old China. Each mountain anchored one of the Four Directions—north, south, east, and west—to which the Daoists added a mountain in the center. Today, despite decades of neglect and destruction, these peaks retain dozens of venerable temples, miles of stone stairs for modern pilgrims (mostly Chinese sightseers) to ascend, and summits with the most spectacular views in the Middle Kingdom.

It is at these nine mountains that Old China still exists within New China. They have always been, for me, the most fascinating sites in the Middle Kingdom, combining history, religion, and natural grandeur. On the other hand, these remote peaks at the four corners of the Middle

Kingdom are modernizing. Most have cable cars in place to take the drudgery (along with the adventure and tradition) out of mountain pilgrimage. A few have decent hotels in nearby villages. Vendors line the mountain stairs, selling snacks and plastic souvenirs. Temples are being renovated rather than razed.

Altogether, the sacred mountains, fusing past and present, present some of the most exhilarating experiences in all of China. But to make your own sightseeing pilgrimage to these great mountains is still not an easy undertaking. Most require that you rough it with a long bus or train ride from a major city. The climb to the summit can be arduous, often requiring a 4- or 5-hour ascent on steep stairways and narrow paths. Accommodations and food services can be crude. Yet the undertaking produces unforgettable moments, unlike any others in China.

Mountain (Shan)	Direction	Religion	Elevation	Province
Emei Shan	West	Buddhist	10,095 ft	Sichuan
Heng Shan Bei	North	Daoist	6,617 ft	Shanxi
Heng Shan Nan	South	Daoist	4,232 ft	Hunan
Hua Shan	West	Daoist	6,552 ft	Shanxi
Jiuhua Shan	South	Buddhist	4,340 ft	Anhui
Putuo Shan	East	Buddhist	932 ft	Zhejiang
Song Shan	Center	Daoist	4,900 ft	Henan
Tai Shan	East	Daoist	5,069 ft	Shandong
Wutai Shan	North	Buddhist	10,003 ft	Shanxi

Hua Shan is the most stunning of the Nine, Tai Shan the most interesting and venerated. To these ancient peaks I have added a 10th summit well worth reaching, that of **Huang Shan,** simply the single most beautiful mountain in China.

WHAT TO READ

Edwin Bernbaum, *Sacred Mountains of the World.* San Francisco: Sierra Club Books, 1990.

William Geil, *The Sacred 5 of China.* Boston: Houghton Mifflin, 1926.

Hedda Morrison, *Travels of a Photographer in China, 1933–1946.* Hong Kong: Oxford University Press, 1987.

Mary Augusta Mullikin and Anna M. Hotchkis, *The Nine Sacred Mountains of China: An Illustrated Record of Pilgrimages Made in the Years 1935–1936.* Hong Kong: Vetch and Lee, 1973.

Susan Naquin and Chun-fang Yu, editors, *Pilgrims and Sacred Sites in China.* Berkeley: University of California Press, 1992.

WUTAI SHAN: BUDDHIST PEAK OF THE NORTH

五台山

W HEN THE ZEN MASTER XU YUN made his pilgrimage to Wutai Shan (Five Terraces Mountain) in 1882, it took him 2 years to walk the 900 miles from Shanghai, in part because he insisted on bowing down and bumping his head on the ground every third step of the way. My own 100-mile journey north from Tiayuan by car takes just 4 hours, but it's bumpy, too. Once we leave the main highway and rise into the foothills of Wutai Shan, we encounter one of the worst strips of road I've ever traveled: a bed of dirt and rock being dug up and rebuilt by hand. We average 5 miles per hour, tops. I count hundreds of workers with shovels and picks along the way, spread out for miles in small teams. We frequently come to a halt where they are digging or where an oncoming truck asserts its right-of-way. We squeeze over on the shoulder of the lane-and-a-half of plowed furrow that calls itself a highway.

When we reach the top of the high ridge after 90 minutes of lurching, I can see across the roof of northern China under a bright blue sky. This could be Tibet, and in fact many Tibetans, as well as Mongolians, have congregated at Wutai Shan ever since the 13th century, when Lama Buddhism spread to China's borderlands. The founder of the Yellow Hat sect of Lama Buddhism lived here. The exiled Dalai Lama is his divine descendant.

We drop into a broad crater, encompassed by the Northern, Southern, Eastern, and Western Terraces—peaks in a cluster that make up Wutai Shan. In the center of this compass is the Central Terrace, site of a temple village, Tai Huai, clotted with more temples than any other city in the Middle Kingdom.

I check into a new hotel a mile south of the temple village. The desk staff can't find me a map of the temples or peaks. They tell me it is impossible to walk to the highest peak, the Northern Terrace, because the summit is under snow. Then they issue me a special permit, stamped with a red seal, that reads "aliens' travel permit".

So branded, I set out on a sunny morning for the temple village and the top of the snowy terrace beyond. On the way to town I am twice passed by horsemen. They try to persuade me to hire their steeds. I'm tempted. Such fine horses, the horses of Wutai Shan: tall, sleek, brown bodies, black manes and tails, fitted with ornate red saddles and red bridles. But I keep walking. I mean to keep walking through the temple village to the top of Wutai Shan's Northern Peak, regardless of a scarcity of maps and an abundance of snow.

The Temple Village

The Temple Village at Wutai Shan, in the crater of the terraced valley, is extensive, as beautiful and active as any I've seen in China. That's not to say the temples of Wutai Shan are what they once were, or that the Buddhist and Lamaist China of dynasties past has not been shell-shocked into the modern age. A century ago, there were over 300 holy shrines here; 50 years ago, travelers counted 100 monasteries and temples, of which 30 were devoted to Lamaism. Today, the census is down to a few dozen. But the heart of the village is still as it was, a little city of temples crowded one into the next, uphill and downhill, with streets and walls running every direction—enough temples flowing into temples to get lost in, like a maze.

In the center of the village is Wutai Shan's landmark, the **Great White Tibetan Pagoda,** often called a *stupa* or *dagoba,* a *sarira* or *chorten,* meaning a reliquary, a monument for some relic or other said to have come from the real Buddha—a fingernail or a thigh bone, for instance. The White Pagoda of Wutai Shan is shaped like a monumental wine decanter tapering to a golden spire, with an exquisite finial that resembles a folded umbrella. One hundred fifty feet tall, it was constructed of brick and lime five centuries ago. Two hundred fifty-two bronze wind-bells dangle like lanterns from the fringes of its finial, chiming in the wind. Hundreds of times a day the devout pilgrims from Mongolia once circled this monument, touching the scripture doors around its base with their foreheads. Now, the White Pagoda is deserted, or at least not easily accessible; the nearer I get to it, the deeper the maze of walls, courtyards, and shrines that surround it.

I make my way through temple streets clogged with dozens of vendors offering thousands of trinkets, drinks, snacks, hats, walking sticks, and souvenirs. The stairs and streets between the temples are lined with beggars and cripples, more than you usually see these days in one place in China.

Passing under a large towered gate, I follow a back road along a wall. There are six young men squatting down along that wall, gambling with cards, all of them dressed in the black sports coats favored by taxi drivers

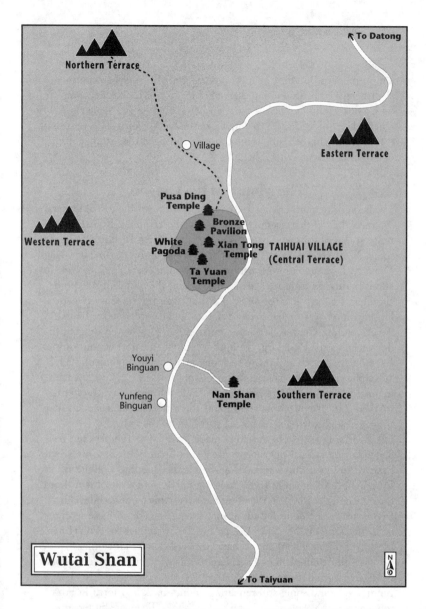

Wutai Shan

and pickpockets. I enter the door to **Xiantong Si, the Fine Thread Penetration Temple,** which consists of over 400 buildings. Inside, I walk through several darkened rooms into one that is even darker: a bare brick room with a ceiling high enough to accommodate a slender golden bronze pagoda 13 stories tall, said to house a lock of hair from Wan Shu himself, the Buddhist god of Wutai Shan.

Surpassingly, this unlit chamber is connected to a shrine of more recent vintage, a shrine to Chairman Mao Zedong, whose white plaster bust is set upon an altar and draped in a bright red-and-gold shawl—

a most modern Buddha, the revolutionary god of China. Mao must have slept here. His bedroom is preserved next door to his shrine, complete with a dozen photographs of the chairman pasted above a spacious *kang*, a heated bed of bricks, covered in wicker mats. Worshippers have tossed offerings onto his bed: small coins, mostly, and cigarettes. Strange shrine, one of hundreds at Wutai Shan.

The Mouth of the Dragon

I walk out into another courtyard, heading north for the top of **Central Terrace,** the hill that rises at the far end of the Temple Village. I can see more stupas and bronze pagodas ahead and dozens of fine glazed-tile roofs. Most splendid of all is the **Bronze Pavilion,** cast in the Ming Dynasty. It resembles a miniature metal temple, barely tall enough to admit human worshippers, coated inside with thousands of tiny bronze Buddhas. Its form is intricate, as if a thin layer of bronze were meticulously poured over timbers, columns, tiles, and carved wooden figures.

Ascending Central Terrace, I enter the mouth of the dragon, the dragon being the **Pusa Ding Temple,** Wutai Shan's most famous shrine. Its undulating walls and many pavilions are coiled on the top of the hill, 108 stone steps above the many temples and lamaseries below. The faithful once left locks of their hair on each step to the entrance gate, offerings to Wen Shu in hopes he would grant them rebirth. One modern-day beggar raises his half leg to me as I pass him on the stairs.

Two Qing emperors of China made Pusa Ding Temple their residence during official pilgrimages to Wutai Shan. Wen Shu himself is believed to live in this temple. Wen Shu is the Buddhist bodhisattva of Pure Wisdom, known in India as Manjusri. Born of a ray of light from the crown of the Buddha, Wen Shu had no earthly parents and was born free of sin. He introduced Buddhism to Nepal, then by Chinese accounts made his home on the Central Terrace of the five terraces of Wutai Shan. He sits on a lion, a book in one hand, a sword raised in the other.

Wen Shu's temple home is encircled today by innumerable vendors. Monks charge admission at his gates. Five thousand lamas lived here a century ago, and some still remain, plodding back and forth in brown robes and caps, yellow sashes, and padded shoes. There are butter lamps, prayer banners, and small brass prayer wheels spinning in the courtyards, and inside one small shrine I spot some of the old musical instruments from the days when Lamaists gathered here to watch the spirited Devil Dances: two immense demon-mouthed trumpets, as long and heavy as alpenhorns.

The yellow roof tiles of Pusa Ding Temple, donated by the Qing Emperor Kangxi almost three centuries ago, gleam in the sun; the red columns are freshly painted; but the dragon temple seems gutted, barren as the hills that were deforested at the command of that same emperor when he called upon the people to settle the wilds of Wutai Shan.

From Pusa Ding Temple there is a fine view of the temple village below, of the White Pagoda and the river valley. Most of the buildings at Wutai Shan are really no older than a century or two, rebuilt countless times after each destructive turn, human or natural.

The curious thing is that these days almost no tourist or pilgrim comes to Wutai Shan to climb its peaks. The temples are enough to occupy their curiosity. But to my uninformed mind, these temples are just husks—pretty to look at, a bit strange in form, but nothing much inside for me, whether it be Mao or Wen Shu with book, sword, and lion.

The Northern Terrace

It was before noon when I began to climb the highest peak, the Northern Terrace, its summit topping 10,000 feet. I'm already at 6,000 feet, and the route to the summit doesn't look steep or impossibly far. I skirt the dragon wall of the Central Terrace and find a road up the northern valley. I don't meet a soul until I come to the end of the pavement and strike up the mountain valley on a dirt road. At the intersection, there is a poor peasant woman, threadbare. She opens both empty hands to me, and I can see that she is the sort of peasant who really has nothing. She is no taxi driver gambling beside a temple wall.

The dirt road goes straight up the valley and ends in a farming village. Three children spot me. They dash out for a look at me, but they are afraid to come too close, even though they call out to me. I walk around the village walls, keeping the stream on my left. The houses are fashioned from mud, not brick. There's electricity but no cement.

There's no road, either—only a series of paths that farmers use to tend their plots, walled in with piles of rock. The ground is too rocky for easy agriculture. The peasants work the plots with oxen hitched to plows. I feel like an intruder, wandering amongst their fields, but they pay me little attention. The hills that fold into the river valley are denuded of trees: hard scrabble up to the peak, a bit of grass and brush for grazing. Black hawks, wings tipped white, sail across the empty span. I can see the Northern Peak ahead. There are several wide patches of snow near the top, looking like leftover glaciers, but they are too thin to be barriers.

An hour above the village I can no longer see the temples in the valley. There are snatches of green alpine grasses and tiny wildflowers in the brown stubble. The high slopes are crisscrossed with sheep paths. Shepherds guide their flocks to thin pastures on the flanks.

Near the summit I find remnants of a stone platform but still no trail. I bushwhack up the final untracked rise, cutting between snow crusts, crossing a field of buttercups. At the summit, a chilly wind sweeps over the Northern Terrace southward into China.

Here is a forlorn panorama of white stone and soft green meadow grasses with patches of snow and yellow buttercups. I'm alone, except for a few hawks, a squirrel by the stream, two golden quail I scared up, and in the distance a lone fox sprinting up the slopes.

The bald terraces of Wutai Shan are not dramatic, perhaps, but they are severe—the softly colored hills of a broad, high desert. A receptacle for solitude. Other peaks, crowded with temples and tourists, allow no time for meditation, no time for ease. On Wutai Shan the wind is cold and unbroken; it blows without obstacle. As I walk back down the Northern Terrace, the farmers call out to me, resting their arms on the backs of their black oxen.

The Southern Terrace

The sun holds court for another day and I spend it at the **Southern Terrace in Nan Shan Si,** the Southern Peak Temple of Wutai Shan. At the river the horsemen tether their steeds, hoping to sell rides up the steep hillside, but there are no takers this morning. I admire their horses, showy in their imperial outfits. Their owners are the only annoyance pursuing me.

I take a back trail up the Southern Terrace. The Nan Shan temple complex was built during the Yuan Dynasty (1271–1368) when the Mongolians ruled China. Rewi Alley, the Australian journalist and traveler, who saw extensive stonework being done on these buildings in 1935, wrote, "This huge temple reminds one of some Norman Castle, for inside are winding stairs through great thick stone walls to towers and pavilions." This morning it is almost deserted. The formal entrance consists of 108 wide cement stairs, fronted by a shadow gate to block the straight lines that evil beings travel. Its 108 steps are symbolic of the 108 passions, the 108 earthly delusions, and correspond to the 108 rosary beads a devout Buddhist clutches. At the top of the stairs, I'm stunned to discover a vendor with a pellet rifle, set up for visitors who might want to partake of a bit of target practice before entering the temple.

There are three main temples on the Southern Terrace; they were joined together for the first time in this century; and although the oldest of the three dates back to the time of the Great Khans, to 1296, all were restored in the Qing Dynasty and are being redone today. There is pretty much whatever one dreams of finding in a Chinese temple: 18 lohans (Buddha's followers) carved during the Ming Dynasty, a six-armed statue of Guanyin, and a fresco celebrating the adventures of a Buddhist monk's 7th-century *Journey to the West.* This celebrated fresco, painted on three walls of a pavilion, is crude; worse still, a fourth panel, a modern one, has been added, and it's even more amateurish. Far more striking is a brightly painted version of a **Thousand Buddha Hall** with its multiple carved images of Buddha. The twisting forms and bold colors give a decidedly fantastical, Lamaistic air to their rarefied subjects.

As I climb from station to station, I'm waylaid by monks who beg me to go inside and have a look at what is on display, usually a statue or carving I can barely decipher in the darkness. With one monk I engage in a short chat. He is pleased I'm an American. He doesn't cajole me into making a donation; these monks leave me alone to wander the temple terrace.

In the center of one deep courtyard I find a stupa that seems to be an exact reproduction of the Great White Pagoda located in the center of the Wutai Shan temple village. Here, its proportions no longer seem monstrous. What relics it houses, I can't determine.

After reaching the top of the Southern Terrace, I immediately descend through a maze of marble walls and moon gates, stairways and frescoes, stone courtyards and temples with finely carved wooden doors and porches. I descend in a light breeze, each thought holding itself for its full length, freely and naturally. I keep moving, the sound of wind cracking stone on the mountain's back, driving me down the terrace and up the cold stream into the valley of the temple village.

PRACTICAL INFORMATION

ORIENTATION

Wutai Shan (Five Terrace Mountain), the most northerly of the four sacred peaks of Buddhism, is 200 miles southwest of Beijing in Shanxi Province, about 100 miles north of the provincial capital, Taiyuan. Four peaks, reaching 10,000 feet in elevation, cluster about the central terrace and temple village of Tai Huai, at an elevation of 6,000 feet. The temperatures are generally cold at these elevations, making the summer months the ideal time to visit.

Not far to the north, in the same province, is the holy Daoist mountain of **Heng Shan Bei** (see below), the city of **Datong,** and the **Buddhist grottoes of Yungang** (see "The Stone Sculptures at Yungang" for more information).

GETTING THERE

Wutai Shan is located in a remote, mountainous region. The nearest airport and railway connections are at Taiyuan to the south and Datong to the north.
To Taiyuan & Datong Taiyuan has plane connections to many cities in China, including Beijing (1 hour), Shanghai (2 hours), Xi'an (2 hours 20 minutes), and Hong Kong (3 hours). Trains to Taiyuan originate from Beijing (13 hours), Xi'an (14 hours), and Zhengzhou (13 hours).

Datong has train connections with Beijing (7 hours), Taiyuan (7 hours), and Xi'an (20 hours).

To Wutai Shan   To reach the mountain, there are daily buses from Taiyuan, a 9-hour trip (RMB 35/$4.20), and from Datong, a 10-hour trip (RMB 40/$4.80). For bus tickets and car hires, contact hotel desks in Taiyuan or Datong. I hired a car in Taiyuan from the travel desk in the Shanxi Grand Hotel, 5 Xin Jian Nan Lu (☎ 0351/404-3901), which reduced the journey to 4 hours but cost $100. Cars can also be hired from CITS offices and hotel desks in Datong (see the chapter "Datong: Temple of the 'Big Same'" for more information).

TOURS & STRATAGEMS

There are no group tours to Wutai Shan, although the China International Travel Service (CITS) office in Datong, located at the train station (☎ 0352/502-2265), can assist with bus tickets and might even be persuaded to let you hire one of their English-speaking guides. CITS also has an office at Wutai Shan in the Yunfeng Binguan, 2 miles south of town, where maps, information, and sometimes group tours are available.

WHERE TO STAY & DINE

The **Youyi Binguan,** a mile south of the temple village, and the **Yunfeng Binguan,** 2 miles south of the temple village, both take foreigners. They are 3-star hotels with modern rooms and private bathrooms, each charging $60 for a comfortable double. No credit cards are taken at either hotel. The Youyi Binguan has the nicer facilities and is closer to the main temples. The Yunfeng Binguan has a tour desk and the more helpful staff.

Wutai Shan has no restaurants catering to foreigners. The Youyi Binguan and the Yunfeng Binguan both have good restaurants that serve fixed-price Chinese meals at moderate prices (RMB 34 to 85/$4 to $10).

Heng Shan Bei: Sacred Mountain of the North

衡山北

Heng Shan Bei, the Long Mountain of the North, is situated between two sections of the Great Wall of China. For many centuries it stood as the final barrier against China's ancient enemies, the barbarians from the north. The Han Dynasty Emperor Wu Di traveled to Heng Shan Bei with China's greatest historian, Sima Qian, in 100 B.C. Nine centuries later, in A.D. 746, a Tang emperor gave the mountain its highest title, "King, Pacifier of Heaven."

But despite its symbolism and history, the northern mountain proved to be less than an insurmountable barrier. Eventually the Khans and other outsiders swept down, subdued China, and set up their own dynasties. In response, this sacred mountain of the north was moved to the south. Heng Shan Bei was "relocated" for centuries, its title bestowed on another peak, to prevent direct contamination by the invading hordes. Only in the Ming Dynasty, when the Han Chinese again ruled the Middle Kingdom, was Heng Shan Bei reestablished on the slopes and peaks where thousands of years earlier it ruled over the mind and spirit of the empire.

Heng Shan Bei is not only Old China's northern defender. It is also the Water Mountain, its god long believed to possess the power to bring rain. As superintendent of rivers and streams, the god of Heng Shan Bei is sought out by farmers seeking his benediction to ensure the health of their livestock and the fertility of their fields. Certain royal ceremonies performed at Heng Shan Bei up until the time of the modern republic (1911) involved the slaughter of an ox in the cold before the dawn—the ox's blood offered in a bowl on the altar of the highest temple. The hope was to bring the spring rains to China. As recently as half a century ago these cliff temples were shining symbols of mountain spirits that both guarded the edges of an empire and delivered the nation from droughts.

When I first saw Heng Shan Bei myself, a massive rampart of stone rising like a natural Great Wall in the midst of a high desert plateau, I understood how the mountain itself could personify these qualities. Nowhere else in this vast region of dryness did the clouds seem to gather,

Heng Shan Bei

giving visible shape to the thirst for rains that must have gripped generations of northern Chinese who repeatedly faced starvation.

Times have changed, of course, but this northern mountain of water still has relics of its former functions and grandeur, although it is a remote, even obscure, site in an isolated part of modern China not seen by many outsiders.

The Road to the Long Mountain

Heng Shan Bei is about 50 miles southeast of the northern coal city of Datong. The country road from Datong to the mountain is paved most of the way to Hunyuan, the sacred village at the foot of Heng Shan Bei. The terrain is a terraced plateau of sandstone, coal, and soda ash. Between sandy bluffs and pinnacles are cave towns, every dwelling sculpted of dry mud. These villages resemble remote oases. The camel caravans of the past have been replaced by rows of electric power lines and ranks of buses and coal trucks.

Snaking through the crowded streets of **Hunyuan** in a taxi hired in Datong, I can see Heng Shan Bei ahead—more a wall of exposed limestone than a mountain, a high ridge of stone on a plain of gray sand and rock. From this village—once containing 200 temples and surrounded by an eight-sided city wall—we rise through the Mouth of the Golden Dragon, a valley of exposed limestone that parts to empty a river. This narrow gorge was widened for travel in A.D. 397 by a Wei Dynasty emperor and his 10,000 men. On the west wall of the gorge is the Temple Suspended Over the Void (see "The Stone Sculptures at Yungang" for a complete description).

At the south end of the gorge a steel-and-concrete dam (187 feet high, 338 feet wide) was completed in 1958, creating the vast Heng Shan Reservoir. This feat of modern engineering has forcibly toppled and demystified the rain god of Heng Shan Bei. In the past, however, this barren plateau, useful only for its low-grade coal, certainly required a mountain god of water. Shanxi Province has long known its share of killer droughts. Today, however, it has achieved what incense and pilgrimage often failed to secure: a regular supply of water from the mountain, thanks to the gods of science and technology.

The Mountain Gate

We drive up the Magnet Gorge in a flurry, through a tunnel on the west wall of Heng Shan Bei, around an edge of the long reservoir, then east and north to the parking lot on the south side of the peak. A traditional three-arched gate with red columns and golden eaves, guarded by two stone lions, marks the entrance to the 30 mountain temples and shrines that rise up the slopes of what the ancients called the "Grand Column of the North."

Heng Shan Bei is a mountain of cliff faces and bluffs. The temples perch on ledges, spread out across terraces, and climb section by section up steep stone walls. A trail from the south entrance saunters up the mountain, threading together the overlooks and shrines, leading to the high peaks and pavilions and finally the summit, **Tian Ling Feng,** at 6,617 feet.

Hall of the Pure Sun

It takes me less than 20 minutes to reach the mountain's first large temple, **Zhong Yuan Kong—Hall of the Pure Sun.** The inscription at the entrance thanks the mountain god for bountiful harvests. On a clear day, pilgrims can see from here all the way across the barren plains to the sacred mountain of Wutai Shan, situated 50 miles to the south. Today, the air is filthy with fine particles and I can't see the outlines of distant peaks with any precision.

I forge on, pausing only to buy tea from a vendor at the **Traveler's Greeting Pine,** a lonely umbrella of a tree near a pavilion with a famous overlook known as **Gu Sao Cliff.** The drop-off is considerable, the formation sheer. A local story tells of a widow named Gu who refused to remarry, despite her family's insistence. Gu threw herself from the mountain at this spot. Her brother's wife, Sao, understanding her sadness, followed her into the abyss. Both were transformed by the mountain god into larks who forever chase after each other across the mountain spaces crying sadly.

Temples of the Ming

After another hour's climb, I reach a cluster of cliff temples and pavilions not far below the summit. The most important shrine, **Heng Zong Monastery,** dates from the Ming Dynasty (1368–1644), when Heng Shan Bei reclaimed its importance as a major pilgrimage site for Daoists. The halls have been restored recently, although the red brick exteriors that rise on stone terraces up a white cliff face look both ancient and Tibetan. Bell and drum towers stand at the bottom. One hundred three stairs lead to the highest hall, in which there is a bearded statue of the supreme mountain god of Heng Shan Bei and an inscription over the shrine entrance written by Emperor Kangxi during a 17th-century visit.

As a Manchurian ruler, Kangxi inherited the Qing Dynasty his grandfather established. Even if his own ancestors were barbarians from the north, Kangxi came to Heng Shan Bei as a strictly Chinese monarch, paying homage to China's native religion (Daoism) and legitimizing his rule over the Han Chinese nation by honoring its traditional sites.

On terraces below and west of the Heng Zong Monastery are many halls I barely have time to take in: the **Chun Yuang Palace,** where there is a statue of Lu Dongbin, one of the Eight Immortals in the Daoist tradition who has triumphed over death and rides with the clouds; and the **Jiu Tian Palace,** where pilgrims pray to the goddess Xie Nu for male offspring. The latter is still one of the most active shrines on Heng Shan Bei. These temples are small, humble, gritty abodes, each with a monk or nun in attendance, and they all have a feel of the authentic, which the larger, more tourist-laden shrines of modern China lack.

The westernmost temple on the mountain is devoted to **Gui Xing, the North Star God.** The statue of this god is portrayed as keeping one foot planted on a sea monster while supporting the Pole Star constellation, which Chinese astronomers picture as a bushel (rather than as a bear or water dipper). Gui Xing is a god of the harvest—therefore a favorite of farmers wishing for bushels of good crops each year. The North Star god was also once a favorite of China's students, as he was said to light the way to knowledge. Those hoping to pass the national civil service examinations used to troupe up the mountain to this shrine by the thousands. Today, the temple to the North Star is virtually empty.

Other ledge and cliff temples here have their tiny treasures, mainly tablets inscribed by Qing Dynasty emperors who traced their lineage north to the Mongolian steppes. I stop at one more shrine, the Palace of the Immortals, where there are images of 72 minor Daoist immortals, eight cave-dwelling angels, and three other gods—dispensers of wealth, happiness, and long life, gifts even science and technology can't always bestow.

A Summit in Space

Anxious to reach the summit, I climb above the last of the big temples and wind up the cliff past several pavilions to the **Slab of Qin and Qi,** a natural stage of solid rock. The backdrop is a smooth cliff face, inscribed with large Chinese characters painted red. As with much of the mountain, this formation refers to another fantastical story in the Daoist tradition, this one concerning two immortals who performed on a cosmic stage before vanishing into the heavens.

The rough trail to the summit brings me to an elevation of 6,617 feet, a rise of 1,200 feet gained over a leisurely 2^1/$_2$-hour climb. Southward, the plains on the margins of China simmer with dust, smoking like shaken coal flakes. I look across an infinity without depth, without exact horizon, with no final line of definition, no known boundary, as if I'm standing on the edge of space. At my feet, at the feet of this mountain, there is a great bottomless vacuum through which screens—screens with a mesh as fine as the gray-yellow dust—sift forever downward.

The sacred mountain on the northern frontier has changed. It's almost forgotten today, but its slopes still hum with some of the temples of old, and the barren vistas are impressive. The summit where I stand is empty but altogether formidable and massive—pure space and dust, as elemental as China gets. This is where the mountain god of the north was worshipped for centuries by commoner and emperor alike as defender against barbarians and herald of rain, as harbinger of good harvests, as protector of farm animals, and as controller of tigers, leopards, reptiles, and worms. His powers may have been usurped by modern science, but his ramparts remain as striking as ever. Even the silence is as vast as any I've experienced, so fine it can be utterly broken by something as slight as the song of larks.

PRACTICAL INFORMATION

ORIENTATION

Heng Shan Bei (Long Mountain of the North), the most northerly of the Five Sacred Mountains of Daoism, is 200 miles southwest of Beijing in Shanxi Province, about 50 miles southeast of the city of Datong. The summit is at an elevation of 6,617 feet. Winters are long and cold, making the summer months the best time to visit.

Datong, the gateway to the mountain, is worth visiting for its own attractions, which include the Buddhist grottoes of Yungang and the Temple Suspended Over the Void. See "The Stone Sculptures at Yungang" for complete information. South of Datong and Heng Shan Bei, in the same province, is the holy Buddhist peak of Wutai Shan (see above).

GETTING THERE

By Train to Datong   The nearest rail terminal is located at Datong. Heng Shan Bei is a day trip from Datong, about 3 hours each way. Datong has convenient daily railroad connections with Beijing (7 hours) and Xi'an (20 hours).

To Heng Shan Bei   To reach Heng Shan Bei from Datong, hire a taxi for the day (about RMB 600/$72) or make arrangements with CITS (see below). It is also possible to take a public bus from Datong to the village of Hunyuan. From Hunyuan, there are minibuses that cover the remaining 10 miles to the mountain. Public transportation is cheap (RMB 20/ $2.50 each way) but time-consuming and difficult for those without skill in the language or China travel experience.

TOURS & STRATAGEMS

Check with the China International Travel Service (CITS) offices in Datong (☎ 0352/502-2265) about tours and transportation to Heng Shan Bei. CITS maintains offices at the Datong train station and in the Yungang Hotel, 21 Yingbin Dong Lu. You can hire an English-speaking guide and a car for the day, if they are available. CITS also offers convenient tours to the Temple Suspended Over the Void, which is very near Heng Shan Bei, but the mountain and its temples are not included on these tours.

The mountain is a day trip from Datong. Be sure to depart from Datong early. The trail to the summit is about 4 miles, and hiking up and back takes 4 to 5 hours. Tickets are sold at the entrance gate to Heng Shan Bei (RMB 20/ $2.50).

WHERE TO STAY & DINE

Heng Shan Bei has no accommodations. The nearby village of Hunyuan has only the most basic inns. Plan on making the mountain a day trip, returning to your hotel in Datong in the evening. See the chapter, "The Stone Sculptures at Yungang (Datong)," for Datong hotel information.

If you hire a CITS guide, your guide will select a local restaurant in the village of Hunyuan. Otherwise, if you are on your own, pack a day's worth of food in Datong and take it along. The vendors on the mountain path sell bottled water and drinks as well as simple local dishes such as noodles and hot sauce.

JIUHUA SHAN: BUDDHIST PEAK OF THE SOUTH
九华山

JIUHUA SHAN, NINE LOTUS MOUNTAIN, is the supreme dwelling place of Dizang, God of the Underworld. Pilgrims used to come to Jiuhua Shan to seek this god's intercession in ending the torments their ancestors and family members suffered after being cast into the Buddhist inferno. Getting to this mountain gives me a taste of what the bus system in hell must be like.

I board the long-distance bus from Hangzhou to Jiuhua Shan at 6:45am, stuffing my backpack into the corner of the bench seat next to the rear window. Several groups of old women board. They are wearing the knit caps and Buddhist rosary beads of Old China's pilgrims. The bus finally lurches out of its slip at 7am. The conductor, sitting across the engine cover from the driver, smokes up a storm; so do many of the passengers.

Our mastodon of a bus, with its petrified suspension, its shocks rotted out, soon strikes enough unpatched cracks in the road to make me wish I'd not drunk that second cup of coffee. The seats are spaced so that I barely have room to insert my lower legs; my knees receive a steady pounding. I try to steel myself against this nasty parody of motion, with little success.

A Chinese bus is not only slow and cramped; it's dangerous. Passing is an adventure. Since a bus is one of the larger vehicles on the narrow open road, whenever it swings out to pass, the rest of the traffic, including those vehicles coming straight at it, shift to the shoulder, scattering bicycles, rototillers, and pedestrians. The bus horn blasts most of the way, but most of the way even brute passing is impossible. The highways are just too full. And the villages are so crammed that our bus must often brake to a complete halt. Top speed between settlements is about 40 miles per hour; average speed, 20 miles per hour.

The fields are full of graves, rock-faced mounds capped with fresh white flags. The farming villages are a swelter of pigs, water buffalo, and pods of ducks and ducklings. Not until midafternoon, 8 hours after departure, does a range of mountains break through the horizon, encrusted in a haze. Our final ascent is via a hairpin road that winds upward between steep green bamboo slopes. The old women slide open every window for a view, but the unpaved road muddies the pure mountain air, lacing it with road dust. We are on the flanks of the holy mountain, and we can't see or breathe.

In Buddha's Navel

We corkscrew halfway up the legendary 99 peaks of Jiuhua Shan on a new unpaved road from Wuxi Town. The old pilgrim route, which the devout walked up until the late 20th century, still exists, but almost no one climbs it anymore. Not far from the top of this spiral highway I see a magnificent monastery, **Ganlu (Sweet Dew Monastery),** its white walls five stories high, chiseled into a declivity in 1667.

Sweet Dew Monastery was destroyed by the Taiping rebels and rebuilt about 1875, but it still looks as ancient as the bamboo rain forest. From the road, I catch only a glimpse of its white walls, enveloped in dust as if in mist. A dozen more turns upward, beyond the Second Gate of Heaven, the bus slumps into Jiuhua Terminal and collapses like a beaten hound.

I have reached what locals call the navel of the pot-bellied Buddha, the very village of monks and tourists, monasteries and souvenir stands, hotels and cinemas, where 1,700 years ago, after days of hard climbing, solitary monks and nuns pitched their thatched huts in the heart of "Lotus Buddha Land" and meditated upon the mountain void.

The void has been filled in and brought up to date, although it is by no means a Coney Island. Jiuhua Street is for tourists; hawkers line it, but this is a small, faraway place and the hurricane of entrepreneurs has not arrived with full force. True, as soon as I come off the bus I'm led uphill by a woman to the street's newest hotel, the **Julong,** but she's no pushy vendor on commission. Besides, the Julong Hotel is where I would have stayed had I known it existed. I've come here with practically no information, except a few historical accounts.

The hotel isn't exactly a palace, but it does have a lobby—even if there is nothing in the lobby, not a single chair. There are no brochures or maps in English, either—no one speaks English here—but the staff is exceptionally cordial. I've dealt with much worse hosts in Shanghai and Beijing. After 11 hours of mechanical chiropractic in the bus, I have just enough flexibility left to walk from the hotel to the end of the road, which is crammed with shops and tiny cafes for six blocks. An occasional large temple has been left standing for atmosphere.

Then, at precisely 6:59pm, electricity to the little town blows its central fuse. I can barely see my way back, although a number of stalls are firing up candles and lanterns as I stagger back to the hotel in the dark.

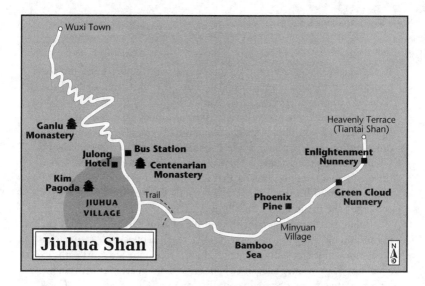

Jiuhua Shan

- Wuxi Town
- Ganlu Monastery
- Julong Hotel
- Bus Station
- Centenarian Monastery
- Kim Pagoda
- JIUHUA VILLAGE
- Trail
- Phoenix Pine
- Minyuan Village
- Bamboo Sea
- Heavenly Terrace (Tiantai Shan)
- Enlightenment Nunnery
- Green Cloud Nunnery

Temples & Mummies

Jiuhua Shan was immortalized in Chinese tradition by two contemporaries who met each other on these very slopes. The best known is Li Bai, the magnificent Tang Dynasty poet, who lived in a secluded cottage on Jiuhua Shan from A.D. 746 to 747. He penned the lines that not only named the mountain but gave final definition to its castellated crags:

> Looking far beyond this village wall
> I see the peaks of the Southern Mountain
> Emerging from the River of Heaven
> As nine magnificent lotus blossoms.

The other famous resident was Kim Kiao Kak, a monk from Korea, who made a pilgrimage to Jiuhua Shan in A.D. 719 and founded a temple to Dizang, the God of the Mountain, known in India as *Ksitigarbha*. This god's element is the Earth, the inner Earth. As the Earth–Womb bodhisattva, Dizang wades into the bowels of Hell to aid the damned. To put it more gently, Dizang sets free those who are unhappy—those undergoing the agonies of Hell—and points them to a higher, purer level once they have tasted the pains of the underworld.

Dizang is therefore a god of salvation. Like Guanyin, the Goddess of Mercy, he changed sex during a long translation into Chinese Buddhism. He was taken up in China readily enough, changing to a man and becoming the intercessor before the 10 judges who mete out the 10 punishments for earthly sin.

Prince Kim prayed to Dizang for 75 years here, and upon his death he became the incarnation of the mountain god. Approaching death at age 99, he gathered his disciples around him. The Earth split open and into its cleft the monk sank to his death. His disciples buried him on the spot but opened his coffin every three years. The corpse refused to age.

A pagoda was erected on the tomb; a temple was built around the pagoda; and inside this temple-pagoda resided the undecayed body of the transformed pilgrim-prince, Dizang made flesh.

This monk from Korea became the flesh body that has sanctified Jiuhua Shan. Flesh bodies are the mummified remains of devout Buddhist monks and patriarchs. Flesh bodies on the holy mountains of China—and there are scores of them—serve a simple purpose: They sanctify a mountain, demonstrating that it is indeed a place of miracles, of Heaven-infused Earth. When the flesh body was that of a Buddhist, it converted the mountain to Buddhism as well.

Jiuhua Street still contains the **temple of Kim/Dizang's earthly remains** and his indoor seven-story pagoda, reached on a stone stairway of nine-times-nine steps. Branching off this thoroughfare are short paths to a bell tower, an incense hall, and a handful of old monasteries with singularly evocative names: Sandalwood, Illusion City, Centenarian. . . . **Centenarian Monastery,** consisting of 99$\frac{1}{2}$ prayer halls and monks' rooms (to be exact), was first called Star-Plucking Temple but was renamed to honor Wu Xia, a wandering monk who died here in the 16th century, reportedly at the age of 126. The 350-year-old flesh body of Wu Xia is now on display in this monastery, his legs crossed in lotus position and arms folded in space—a seated mummy of skull and bones lacquered in gold. Like Prince Kim, Wu Xia achieved bodhisattvahood, a complete identity with Dizang. His transcription of the *Sutra of the Adornment of Buddha* in 81 volumes, a work over which he labored for 24 years, is also contained in this monastery. What sets this opus of copywork apart is that he brushed every character of it in his own blood after mixing it with gold.

Crossing the Bamboo Sea

Despite all these ancient attractions, the temples and halls of Jiuhua Shan, my mind's on the mountaintops. A Chinese guidebook sums it up thus: "Those who have already ascended to Jiuhua Street always think of climbing atop Heavenly Terrace Peak to fulfill their wish of reaching the summit and gazing into infinity." Yes: to gaze into infinity—that will do nicely.

Heavenly Terrace (Tiantai Shan), at 4,340 feet, is the chief peak of the traditional 99 peaks of Jiuhua Shan, and the march to its ramparts is 5 miles of trails and stone stairs. In fact, according to the official census, Jiuhua Shan contains 250,000 stone steps, cut and laid by hand.

I set out at 8:30am, following a path of stone slabs east off Jiuhua Street. It leads me past a stunning public lavatory, a spacious white building with a lofty tiled roof that I would have mistaken for a temple were it not for the characters for man and woman hand-painted on either side. A canal cascades down from this outhouse, marking the mountain trail.

The old pilgrim women from my bus are not far ahead; perhaps they've come with a real purpose: to petition Dizang for the release of family members from the prison cells of the afterlife. Most of the people ascending the trail are not so devout. More like me, they are sightseers dressed in jeans, V-necked sweaters, blue-jean jackets, and white running shoes. They do not burn joss sticks at every station along the route.

From where I start, I can barely make out Heavenly Terrace, one of the distant jagged peaks in a broad fortress, separated by a deep valley. After surmounting the ridge that rises above Jiuhua Street, I descend into that intervening valley.

The stair trail is clean at first, bordered by fields of bamboo, pink blossoms, and tea rows. Vendors have pitched their canvas-topped stalls every so often, and my first stop after an hour's stroll is to buy a bottle of water. Spring water in plastic bottles has flooded the Chinese marketplace. Visitors to Jiuhua Shan gulp water and cast the empties into the green margins.

At the base of the valley is a village, **Minyuan,** its buildings washed white. Whitewashed nunneries dot the enfolded hillsides. I don't remember seeing so many monasteries and nunneries in one place in China. They face Zhuhai, the Bamboo Sea, great repository of those plastic bottles.

The Circles of Hell

Crossing a vibrant stream, I leave the valley behind and ascend more stairs to the **Phoenix Pine,** said to have been greeting pilgrims with its wide arms for a thousand years. The pine has been encircled recently with a marble wall. Beside it, visitors gather to rest and gossip. Some, mounted on brown ponies and costumed in long black robes with matching Stetsons, pay a roving photographer for their portraits. Everyone pauses at the pine, including the sedan chair porters. I count at least 20 carriers. Their chairs are of bamboo and wicker, squarish, straight-backed, with matted headrests. Their long carrying poles are bamboo as well. It's exceedingly tough work for two men: The stairs are steep enough to make me sweat.

The trail beyond the Phoenix Pine meanders from temple to temple, once or twice right through the heart of a temple, where I brush past nuns tending open fires of incense. I come across more old women, two of whom are munching on sugarcane, tearing off mouthful after mouthful. They have their sticks of incense, and sheaves of paper money fill their shan bags. They've come well stocked with offerings to burn for those in the underworld who are short of cash. These notes from the Bank of Hell, written in monstrous sums, are used by the dead to bribe their way through the Ten Courts of the Underworld, said to be located under this very mountain.

The Chinese circles of Hell are courts of punishment that grow more severe with depth. The second court, for example, is a great frozen lake for general torture. The third is populated by unfilial sons and disobedient state officials. The fourth is for those who committed fraud and for those who let their animals disturb others. Other courts are tailored to the punishment of other sins, and most of the sins are more Confucian than Daoist or Buddhist, concerned with violations of the family hierarchy in all its manifestations. There is a deep court reserved for heinous criminals, for murderers who must sweat it out until their victims are reincarnated.

Buddha's Bunny

Walking from temple to temple, I come upon a vendor who has vacated his low chair in front of a shop and left tethered to it a fat rabbit—probably more meal than pet or talisman. When Buddha took a stroll in the forest, so one story goes, all the animals showered him with the food-stuffs they had gathered, except for the rabbit, who is not a gatherer. Still, moved to an act of transcendence, the rabbit hurled itself into the flames of the campfire as a meal, and by the time Buddha could rescue it the rabbit was roasted through. Buddha immortalized the rabbit by granting him dominion over the lunar orb, and ever after, just as we look for a man in the moon, the Chinese look for the rabbit.

Today, Jiuhua Shan is neither lunar nor infernal. If this be hell, it is an absolutely pleasant one. The fires seem confined to incense burners, and a few, placed in the middle of the road, are towering: 12 feet high and tiered like iron pagodas, bells swinging from their pitch-black eaves.

Green Cloud Nunnery

The rock cliffs that made up the summit are perfectly vertical. The stairs coil tediously around and about. I pass through one small temple filled with fire and smoke, its low walls black as a cave. Then comes a stretch of yet steeper stairs with a stone railing, called the **Heavenly Staircase,** which ends high above in the **Green Cloud Nunnery.** Green Cloud is fronted by a narrow gallery affording a splendid view of the valley floor at the bottom of a vast ravine from which I have just climbed.

Just below me, on a spur trail, dozens of old women parade before a small stone incense burner. They collapse to their knees and elbows to pray. Several are nuns, dressed head to foot in black silk gowns and caps.

Above me, the rock outcroppings taper into the sky, resembling up-lifted sword blades. I inch upward on steep stairs. Just ahead is **Enlightenment Nunnery,** a five-story edifice capping a dramatic drop-off. This nunnery is an impregnable fortress pinioned to a perch under the final peak like a palace for eagles. Here I have reached the subrealm of Guanyin, the Goddess of Mercy, and she has endowed the way to the Heavenly

Terrace with her own image, transformed into a single slender rock. It is a startling likeness of the goddess, life-sized, with flowing long hair and a meditative posture. Yet it appears to be a natural rock form poised in space, surveying the deep valley I crossed an hour ago. Someone has draped her in a red cape to keep her warm. She's surrounded by other formations, fissured and weathered into suggestive shapes, the candles and censers of a mountain altar. Above this monument to mercy, the mountain belongs to Dizang and the Ten Judges of Hell.

Heavenly Terrace

The trail twists up to Heavenly Terrace Peak, Dizang's high throne, with its **Temple of Ten Thousand Buddhas** and the **Sun-Holding Pavilion.** I reach this supreme summit in a determined grunt, well before noon. This high platform of Jiuhua Shan is nearly bare, paved in large white square blocks. White, not black, is the Chinese color of death, which perhaps explains the white walls of all the nunneries, monasteries, and temples. Pilgrims, even many of the young Chinese tourists, are busy here tossing incense sticks into two round three-legged black pots. A hundred steps below me, vendors do a brisk business in joss and charms.

Beyond this platform, the throng spreads out on a narrow spine for views in every direction as far as the Yangzi River. For once, the claim of 99 peaks is not a poetic exaggeration. There are hundreds of peaks. I walk along the narrow spine of the summit, sit down in a niche, and take in the view.

The Jiuhua Shan I find today may not be the Jiuhua Shan of yesteryear. But no matter that there are but half as many temples, nunneries, and monasteries as travelers found a century ago. No matter that the 7,000 pilgrims a day who visited here at the end of the last dynasty have dwindled to a few hundred tourists, a few score believers. I can feel that the old connections are waiting to be seized and plugged in, if one only remembered how. At the summit of this mountain paradise is the ancient gate to Hell. The line is thin but sublime.

PRACTICAL INFORMATION

ORIENTATION

Jiuhua Shan (Nine Lotus Mountain) is located in southern Anhui Province, 140 miles west of Hangzhou, 260 miles southwest of Shanghai. Jiuhua Shan is about 40 miles northwest of **Huang Shan (Yellow Mountain),** about a 6-hour bus drive on mountain roads.

Subject to heat, humidity, and rain in midsummer, Jiuhua Shan is ideal to visit in May and October. Jiuhua Village, halfway up the mountain range (9 miles from Wuxi Town), is where the 5-mile trek to the 4,340-foot summit begins.

GETTING THERE

By Bus   There is no rail service or airport near Jiuhua Shan, making a bus trip necessary. If you go to Huang Shan, there is daily bus service from there to Jiuhua Shan (6 hours). For details, see "Huang Shan: China's Most Beautiful Mountain." Otherwise, the most convenient bus connection is to and from Hangzhou, an 11-hour trip. Bus tickets to Jiuhua Shan (about $5 one-way) can be purchased in Hangzhou from the Shangri-La Hotel, 78 Beishan Lu (☎ 0571/797-7951). In Jiuhua Shan, bus tickets to Hangzhou and Huang Shan are sold at the ticket office of the bus station, which is to your left at the entrance to Jiuhua Village.

TOURS & STRATAGEMS

Visitor Information   There is a China International Travel Service (CITS) office on Jiuhua Street in the village (☎ 0566/ 501-1318; fax 0566/501-1202). They offer information and maps.

Exploring the Mountain   At the entrance to the village you are required to buy a ticket for the mountain (RMB 40/ $5). At Phoenix Pine on the trail to the summit there is a new cable car (RMB 20/$2.50 each way) that runs nearly to the summit. It's handy to make it on time to the summit if you want to see the sunrise, since Phoenix Pine is less than an hour's quick walk from the village.

WHERE TO STAY

The best place to stay is the **Julong Hotel (Julong Dajiudian)** (☎ 0566/501-1368; fax 0566/501-1022). Located on the right-hand side of the street a block uphill from the bus station in Jiuhua Village, the Julong carries a 2-star rating, which is generous. The rooms and baths are modern but a bit rundown. No credit cards are accepted. The closest thing to a pool is the fountain outside the entrance, where guns for target practice can be rented. Doubles cost $50.

WHERE TO DINE

Jiuhua Shan has no restaurants of note, certainly none with English-language menus. The **Julong Hotel** (☎ 0556/ 501-1368) has a large Chinese restaurant where foreigners are served fixed-price breakfasts, lunches, and dinners (RMB 42 to 100/$5 to $12). If you continue up the main street through the village, you pass dozens of small cafes and food stalls. The mountain trail to the summit also has many vendors selling snacks, drinks, and hot meals (usually noodles with hot sauces) and there are local cafes at Phoenix Pine.

HENG SHAN NAN: SACRED MOUNTAIN OF THE SOUTH

衡山南

H ENG SHAN NAN IS THE SOUTHERN peak on the Daoist compass of China's Five Sacred Mountains. According to an ancient record, "The Heng Mountain rules the Southern Land by the virtue of Fire." The fire god lives on the highest of Heng Shan Nan's peaks, Zhurong Feng, elevation 4,232 feet. To see what remains on the highest peak of the sacred mountain of the south, I set out in the morning on a bus from Changsha, the capital of Hunan Province, finally reaching the village of Nan Yue and the gate to Heng Shan Nan 3 hours late, owing mostly to the bus driver running out of gas in the countryside.

Heng Shan Nan is commonly called Nan Yue, which means "Southern Peak," but knowing its local name doesn't help me much. I have no local map, just a rudimentary sense of direction. I walk a mile up an unpaved road to the village at the foot of the mountain. At the end of the village, the road forks up a steep hill. I find a parked bus aimed up the mountain.

I draw a crowd when I inquire if this is the bus to Ban Shan Ting, a region of the mountain where I want to lodge for the night. People give me smiling stares and motion me aboard. I take a seat, open my pack, and dig out the lunch I packed in Changsha. It's approaching 3pm, and having skipped breakfast, this is the first food I've downed today: crackers that could use a touch more salt.

The bus is parked in front of Nanyue Miao, the Temple of the Southern Mountain. This is one of the three most famous Buddhist temples in China. It is also the largest Buddhist complex anywhere on the Five Sacred Mountains. Nanyue Miao was built in A.D. 725 but leveled many times, most recently in the 19th century by the Taiping Rebels, their leader a rabidly anti–Western Hunanese who fancied himself the brother of Jesus Christ. The present set of buildings with their yellow-glazed tiles dates back but to 1882. When the final emperor of China assumed the throne in 1911, an ox was sacrificed at this temple, but aside from its largest hall, supported by 72 pillars, each 72 feet high in honor of the 72 peaks of Heng Shan Nan, the temple does not attract me. The mountain does.

The character of the mountain is confusing, or perhaps it is just Daoist. Red is its symbolic color, fire its primordial element, but the mountain has a history shaped by legendary Emperor Yu in his epic struggle against floods 3,000 years ago. Yu is credited with subduing the rising waters that besieged the lower Yangzi River basin by constructing nine abatement channels. Heng Shan Nan is just south of the Yangzi. It has a long history of attracting officials and even emperors to its altars where they prayed for deliverance from the floods. Perhaps it takes a mountain god of fire to subdue the floods of China's mightiest river.

Mr. Ma Gu

The bus rolls out as I finish lunch. The highway up the mountain criss-crosses the stone steps of the old pilgrim path. There has been a paved road to the top for many decades. It was resurfaced in 1933 by order of the governor of Hunan, who maintained his own elaborate summer house partway up the sacred peak, as did many officials and merchants. I can see why they made this their retreat. The scenery is pleasing. In the gentle mist, I have a romantic view of rice terraces along the Nanyue Reservoir. Passing a 1942 memorial to those who died when the Japanese invaded here in 1937, we begin a steep rise. I disembark at Ban Shan Ting.

Ban Shan Ting was once the site of a Daoist guesthouse, a midway pavilion built in 1878 as a resting place for pilgrims. Today, not a single pilgrim is in sight. In fact, there are no travelers of any description. The rain is pounding down. I open my umbrella. The road is dotted with a few concession booths, all closed. I strike out up the road. I don't know what else to do and I don't know where I'm going.

I come to a billboard with a map. An arrow is aimed at a hotel. A boy stops beside me, staring too at the sign. I ask him if he knows the way to a hotel. He nods. We come to an intersection. I want to go right, since that is the way up the mountain, but he motions me left. He guides me to a modern guesthouse on a bluff.

The lobby is empty, save for a single clerk fetched by my companion. I'm led to the rear and outside, up two flights of stairs to a balcony. I can look over the bright green tiles of the lower roofs and across the valley to a crowded screen of distant peaks.

The accommodations resemble those of a summer resort, far shabbier to be sure. I pay for a night in room 307, a room with a splendid view. In a photograph, my immediate surroundings would resemble a misty mountain paradise, dotted with remote monasteries, temples, and old summer homes. Fifty years ago, China's Republican officials were selling housing lots left and right up here for summer homes.

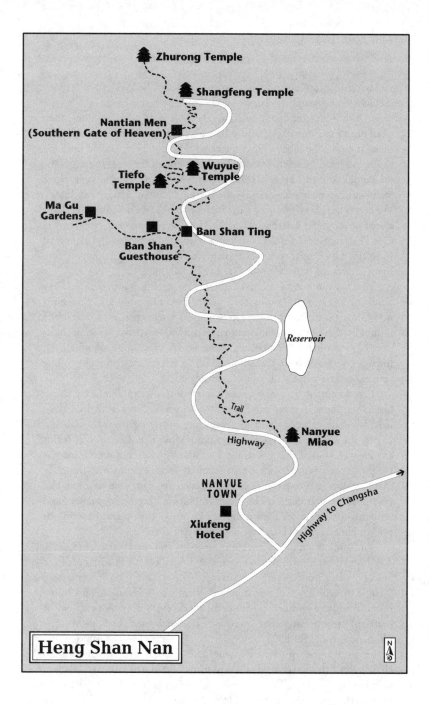

Zhurong Temple

Shangfeng Temple

Nantian Men
(Southern Gate of Heaven)

Tiefo
Temple

Wuyue
Temple

Ma Gu
Gardens

Ban Shan Ting

Ban Shan
Guesthouse

Reservoir

Trail

Highway

Nanyue
Miao

NANYUE
TOWN

Xiufeng
Hotel

Highway to Changsha

Heng Shan Nan

N

Back inside, there's no toilet paper or towels. The Western toilet with its black seat is gurgling—not a good sign. The bed is made up Chinese style, with a blanket and a quilt, no sheets. I wait a few minutes, then head out to see something of the Ban Shan Ting settlement, but I don't make it out of the lobby unaccompanied. The hotel boy latches onto me again. We head somewhere west along a mountain terrace. He escorts me on a quick tour of a fanciful **hillside garden,** complete with pools, stone stairways, carved boulders, and white marble statues of maidens and stags. We climb terrace to terrace. I can't figure out what we're visiting: perhaps a sort of fairyland amusement park. The grounds are dedicated to Ma Gu. The fantastical Mr. Ma Gu was a celebrated herbalist and alchemist from the dim Daoist past. My teenaged guide scales the garden terraces in rapid order; I persuade him that I've had enough.

Back in the hotel I request dinner. The staff flies into action. They hand me a menu containing four items, including soup and chicken. I nod. They ask me to sit in the lobby while dinner is prepared. The lobby is unlighted in the dark rainy weather, furnished with rows of rattan chairs stacked one in front of another, a real wreck of a lobby where all the furniture seems to be in transition, as if in a resort between seasons. The staff is understandably idle: I'm their only guest.

A girl saunters over. She speaks a few words of English. She sits down beside me and asks if she can look at the notebook I'm writing in. I hand it to her. She proceeds to read every page of my intimate travel diary. When she's done, I ask if she understands what I've written. Not really, she answers. Good thing, I think. I sit like this for an hour. China has taught me patience. I watch an enormous water beetle cross the dirty marble floor. It is one of the largest beetles I've ever seen. No one else pays it the least attention. The insect wobbles all the way to the door and wriggles outside. After a few minutes I go out on the porch to see if I can find it. No trace. The rain keeps falling like a curse.

I'm summoned into a back dining room and seated at a large table. The hotel boy joins me for an enormous dinner, complete with bottles of beer. He eats through every plate in rapid-fire fashion. The dinner costs a fortune by ordinary Chinese standards, nearly $10. Heading back to my room, I notice a spittoon positioned outside every door. A small bar of soap and some brown paper towels have been delivered. The toilet is running and it won't flush. My room is spacious with plenty of wooden furniture: a wardrobe with a mirror, a night table, a desk, and two overstuffed chairs, plus a thermos bottle of boiled water and two teacups and my own spittoon on the floor. The tiny color television on the desk receives one station: the government channel from Beijing.

All night the fire god of Heng Shan Nan delivers buckets of fragrant rain.

Stepping into the Clouds

Forgoing Sunday breakfast at the inn, I sneak through the lobby and pop out the door before 7am, the hotel boy nowhere in sight. I skip down the road and inquire of a local the way to **Zhurong Feng,** the highest peak of Heng Shan Nan. My morning climb should cover about 3 miles with a 2,000-foot rise from Ban Shan Ting. Once off the highway, I keep to the trail of slab stairs that rises in straight segments, bisecting the curving highway the buses take to the summit.

There's a heavy blanket of fog on the slopes. Nan Yue is renowned for its storms. I can see only a hundred feet ahead, sometimes half that much. I pass a few inns and cafes, a handful of temples, and several simple tables of souvenirs and foodstuffs. The low visibility, the tea plants, the bamboo forests baffle the sounds of the outside world. The mountain is silent.

The bamboo forests are impressive, the bamboo stocks as large as water pipes and probably as strong. I see no wildlife at all—too civilized, given the paved highway to the top. There aren't many other people on the trail, although the slopes are littered for as far as one can hurl plastic wrappers and containers. Perhaps this weekend's tourists have already ridden a bus to the summit.

I savor the slow pace, the quiet, the absence of others. I see a small herd of black cows, unattended, near a cave temple dedicated to Guanyin. The Goddess of Mercy seems to be on every mountain, Daoist as well as Buddhist. On this Daoist peak of the south, scores of pilgrims are said to have once leaped from **Guanyin's Cliff** to their deaths, rapt with divine ecstasy and the hope of breaking through to a better world. That merciful cliff never pierces the fog, which fills in all gaps this morning.

After an hour's walk, a tiny, worn temple parts the fog a hundred stairs above. I can hear chanting within, whispers becoming soft voices as I near. Cloaked in mist, the temple itself seems to be speaking, like a magic rock about to levitate. Arriving at the door of this enchanted temple, I'm hurled back to solid earth: Two novice monks are manning a card table at the entrance, selling admission tickets to the performance within.

I push on, catching up with a peasant boy shouldering a shovel. He keeps pace with me. The trail merges with the road and a confusing terrain of buildings. We arrive at a construction site. I can see higher peaks ahead. The boy joins other laborers at an excavation, but he points me the right way to the top.

This paved highway certainly robs the mountain of its centuries of romance and remoteness, although in inclement weather, especially in the mist, the intrusion is veiled. Otherwise, Heng Shan Nan would be little short of a Chinese version of Yosemite Park. I scarcely realize that I'm passing through more than a construction site; passing through, in fact, **Nantian Men, the Southern Gate of Heaven**—a three-legged stone gate *(pailou)* engraved with this inscription, painted bright red:

> Here is South Heaven.
> Look down at the hills and the five rivers
> One by one etched in the scene.
> Meandering and winding up ascending stairs,
> Step into the clouds.

The Peak of Fire & Rain

I have in fact stepped into the clouds. I'm now one slope from the summit, outside the long walls of **Shangfeng Si,** a large temple. The fog is melting, flying off in long streamers. Revealed first are the high steel girders of a transmission tower behind the temple, then a garden of radar or microwave dishes—a modern communications center that has nothing to do with Daoism. Before me is the final rise, a newly restored path of granite and concrete, with stone benches for resting along the way. I'm not surprised to find a ticket seller at its foot charging RMB 1 (12¢) for the final hike.

I can see that the path is well worth following not only for the panorama it affords but for the high altar on the top, **Zhurong Dian, the Temple of the Fire God.** Built in the 16th century and restored in the 19th, it was apparently completely rebuilt in the 1930s after a bone-crunching storm. In the near distance, in the banners of fog, it looks much older, like a ravaged remnant of primordial China, an ancient outcropping of mountain worship, the abode of an angry fire god who has not left so much as his own altar unscorched.

I seat myself on the wall of this temple's courtyard, one little stairway below the Fire Temple, waiting for the last wisps of fog to be torn away. The courtyard teems with sightseers, mostly young people, brightly dressed. Several have donned the yellow robes of high officials and ancient royalty to have their portraits snapped on the summit. Groups of students find me out—as they always do—once I'm motionless and visible on a mountain peak. They seat themselves next to me, one by one, while their friends snap away with their cameras. I'm more a sight than any mountaintop or temple. Some practice a smattering of English, but I'm quite surprised when a young woman introduces herself to me in fluent English. She turns out to be the vanguard of a half-dozen college students climbing the mountain with their teacher. Their teacher is an American, too, this student informs me, and more than that, she's a minority. Her students are quite excited about that fact: It has made their teacher that much more exotic in a land that's 99% pure Han Chinese.

When she arrives with the other students, I learn that she was an anthropologist interested in the struggles of the minority peoples in rural China. She teaches English at the university in Xiangtan, a small city between Heng Shan Nan and Changsha. As for her minority status, she is Jewish, a decidedly exotic fact in China.

I link up with her entourage. Together we ascend together to the Temple of the Fire God. The entrance consists of many folding doors, painted red. A fire extinguisher is posted at one door on the right side, and above it, quite out of place, a huge round clock with white face, black hands, and Arabic numerals. The walls are square cement blocks; the roof is metal tile. The interior of the shrine is an unlit, humble affair, its dark walls furnished in simple posters. The bust of Emperor Yu—standing in for the fire god—is ensconced in a curtained recess behind the altar. Bedecked in long strands of black beard, hands crossed just below his neck, shoulders draped in a red silk robe, the god of Heng Shan Nan is framed by a wall of frescoes in red paint and gold leaf. Candles and long sticks of incense sputter in iron holders welded to the altar table.

Two long risers before the altar contain several dozen dirty patch-work cushions on which a surprising number of young tourists kneel, lighted incense between their hands clutched in prayer. One of the Xiangtan students is pushed by her classmates into buying joss sticks from the monks. She takes her turn in beseeching the god. As she kneels, she giggles self-consciously; her girlfriends take flash pictures. She bows her head, whispers, and rises with a smile.

Outside, behind the temple, we have fine views of the many peaks of Heng Shan Nan. Clouds line the deep bowls of the valleys. This is where Hugh Farley, a journalist, spent a night in 1935, a night he wouldn't soon forget, when the Temple of the Fire God was too new, too untempered by the elements to possess any romantic appeal: "It was not a very satisfactory reward for the steep climb," he reported, "as it had been rebuilt last year, and its newness and lack of distinction were rather disappointing. Perhaps I was unduly prejudiced by the masses of ugly stink-bugs that covered its floors, walls, pillars and ceilings with a squirming horde, three or four deep in some places." Farley did not blame the monks for the neglect; they were forbidden by their vows to destroy any form of life, no matter how creepy. "Magnificent, on the other hand, was the view," Farley wrote, "for the temple stands on a pinnacle of rock with unobstructed vision in all directions. . . . Never before in China have I so fully appreciated the proximity or contrast of fertility and barrenness, of water and of drought, of living greenness like the sea and stark brownness like the desert."

In the decades since, this vista has endured, although I would not term it spectacular; the Temple of the Fire God has improved with age, however, and is the perfect monument for the highest platform of any holy mountain: decrepit, dark, humble, naked, cold, and forbidding.

The New South

I eat lunch with the five students and their teacher outside the temple, at the rear. The student who first approached me is particularly precocious. She is majoring in linguistics; she has mastered a smooth, slangy English. She asks me about Noam Chomsky, then quizzes me on minute details about the American presidency and international events. She tells me that she has just been accepted for graduate studies in Wuhan, but she hasn't decided whether to accept. The great temptation for college students, especially the most brilliant undergraduates, is "to go south" to Guangdong Province where the Chinese economy is boiling hot and a student who speaks English can get a job on the spot as a company clerk or a hotel receptionist and make a fortune overnight. Such a lowly job pays ten times what a teacher, even a professor, can expect to pull down. Money is the temptation. Those who complete graduate studies are still assigned low-paying jobs. I try to talk her out of going south, although in her place nothing but pure idealism and a thirst for academic knowledge would have held me back, either, from Canton or Shenzhen.

We descend Heng Shan Nan in the sun, everyone sweating. I think of the story of the Daoist pilgrim with a stiff leg of iron who climbed 6 miles of stairs to this peak and woke to see the sunrise. Looking up, he proclaimed, "The sea of cloud washes my heart clean." I feel cleansed, too, and removed from the world, oddly enough—unattracted by the wealth of the south, purged of all particular desires—as I step down the mountain, its bamboo forest soaked in the low clouds like a long ink-brushed scroll.

"What did your schoolmate pray for in the temple?" I ask. I'm unable to imagine what people today would pray for at the top of this mountain where fire and flood once reigned. She prayed for a good job, I'm told: for prosperity. Last year, two of her classmates came to the top of Heng Shan Nan and prayed to find high-paying work in the south; their wishes granted, they plan to return this summer, a year later as prescribed, to thank the god of the mountain for his blessing.

So if the sacred mountains have lost their original powers, they have not lost a certain metaphysical presence. They still act as receivers of personal petitions.

One student drapes me in a necklace of brown wooden beads, the pilgrim's rosary. We catch a bus down to the village. Lunch in town and several buses later—nothing according to schedule—we are in Xiangtan, an hour from Changsha, just before dark. With the students' help, I flag down a bus to Changsha. I sit by an open window. Pure darkness rushes in. Poor workers and peasants jump on and off at the stops. They press against me, sharing the same seat, hip to hip, elbow to elbow, not knowing in the dark what strange creature they are rubbing against.

I'm thinking my own thoughts, unrelated to theirs. I'm thinking that a new constellation of gods has risen from the grave of Maoist-Marxism to serve as Deng Xiaoping's divine dispensers of cash; that the sacred compass of China has been realigned, its cardinal points marked with dollar signs; and that today's pilgrims are parading to these mountain altars like contestants in a *Wheel of Fortune* game show, petitioning the gods of rain and fire for high-paying jobs.

PRACTICAL INFORMATION

ORIENTATION

Heng Shan Nan, also called Nan Yue, the sacred southern mountain in the Daoist tradition, is located 70 miles south of Changsha, the capital of Hunan Province. Heng Shan Nan is 370 miles northwest of Hong Kong, 600 miles southwest of Shanghai. Rainfall is heavy in the spring, summers are hot and muggy, and winters are cold, making autumn the best time to visit.

GETTING THERE

By Plane   There are daily air flights to Changsha from Beijing (1 1/2 hours), Guangzhou (2 hours), Shanghai (2 hours), Xi'an (1 hour 40 minutes), and Hong Kong (2 hours 10 minutes).

By Train   To reach Changsha, there are overnight trains from Guangzhou (15 hours), Shanghai (20 hours), and Hangzhou (16 hours).

By Bus   Changsha is the urban gateway to Heng Shan Nan and the village of Nan Yue at its base. Morning buses make the 3-hour trip south from Changsha to the mountain (RMB 20/ $2.40 each way). Bus tickets can be purchased at hotels in Changsha. A less convenient alternative is to take the train from Changsha (3 hours) south to the town of Heng Shan and then a 30-minute minibus from the Heng Shan train station to the mountain (7 miles to the west).

TOURS & STRATAGEMS

Visitor Information   A branch of China International Tourist Service (CITS) in the Lotus Hotel (☎ 0731/443-3355) dispenses information and books air, bus, and train tickets. The Dragonair office, for tickets to Hong Kong, is nearby, 128 Wuyi Dong Lu (☎ 0731/446-5355).

Exploring the Mountain   Heng Shan Nan has no tour operators or travel agents. In Changsha, there are no tours available to the mountain. You are on your own. It is possible to make this a day trip from Changsha if you ride the bus to the peak and return the same way, but this gives only a few hours for enjoying the mountain, which has wonderful trails through the bamboo forests and many temples scattered across its slopes.

The mountain park entrance is at Nanyue Temple, on the north side of the village, along the road leading up the mountain. Admission is RMB 20 ($2.50), which includes a map in English and Chinese of Heng Shan Nan. The buses to the summit, which depart often from the park entrance, cost RMB 10 ($1.20). A cable car is under construction. The trail from bottom to top is 9 miles long.

WHERE TO STAY

There are several inns at Ban Shan Ting halfway up the mountain, and at Shangfeng Temple just below the summit, with very basic doubles for about RMB 250 ($30). At the entrance to Nan Yue village at the base of the mountain is a newer hotel, **Xiufeng Binguan** (☎ 0734/66-6111), which charges more ($40 for a modern double) but offers no amenities or services of note.

In Changsha, the international-caliber hotels are on Wuyi Lu, near the bus and train stations. The most convenient choice is the 3-star 15-story **Lotus Hotel (Furong Binguan),** 8 Wuyi Dong Lu (☎ 0731/440-1888; fax 0731/446-5175). Most of its 265 rooms were renovated in 1995. They are modern, with plenty of amenities. When I stayed there, they took major credit cards (AE, JCB, MC, V), but only during banking hours (9am to 5pm). Doubles cost $75.

WHERE TO DINE

The village of **Nan Yue** has plenty of local restaurants that welcome foreign guests. None have English menus, however, so if you try one (the touts will usher you in) be sure to set a price per person for the entire meal. The trail to the top has vendors' stalls with snacks and hot plates of noodles. Try to pack as much food for the journey as you can when setting out from Changsha.

Putuo Shan: Buddhist Peak of the East

普陀山

P UTUO SHAN, WHICH MEANS "WHITE Flower Mountain," is an island in the East China Sea, east of Hangzhou and south of Shanghai. In the Chinese tradition it is the supreme dwelling place of Guanyin, Goddess of Mercy. For many centuries pilgrims have worshipped Guanyin, touched by her compassion. She became the most popular divinity in China. She still is. Pilgrims petition her for the birth of male children and the return of mariners safely to shore. This island mountain remains her home.

I reach Putuo Shan by a circuitous route: a train from Hangzhou to Ningbo; the wrong ferry from Ningbo, which dumped me at a nearby island; a pedicab across this island to a wharf; and finally a fishing boat to the holy island. The boat is an unpainted motorized skiff. The fisherman places me down in its hold. A quilt is spread out on the floor. I lie down on it. Beside me is a young monk, head shaven. He is dressed in a golden robe and golden slippers. He sits up, cross-legged; I recline.

We set out on this final passage to Putuo Shan together, wordless before the roar of the engine. I close my eyes. The boat rocks like a cradle. The monk sits up straight, eyes cast down, as if in meditation. It is nearly noon, but dark in the hold. Above is the gray sky; on the edges, the spray of rough seas. The diesel cracks like an unoiled clock, its fumes wafting in the wind. The monk seems to be presiding over me. A patch of faint light sways overhead. I stare at the monk's white leggings, banded at the calves. I'm very nearly rocked to sleep. Then the engine stops. We drift.

I peer out from the hold. I can see the huge ornate gate to Putuo Shan, ancient in the fog, resembling a hairy three-legged mammoth turned to stone, mounted on an outcropping of rounded boulders on the southern tip of the island. The romance of its appearance at that moment, at our angle of approach, lends it a rich cloak, one it seems to have worn since the beginning of Chinese time, its three portals capped by soaring tile roofs. Here is the Southern Gate of Heaven, the pilgrim's entrance to the holy mountain in the sea. For a moment I feel I have truly crossed into an ancient world, divided from 20th-century China by iron mist.

Of Incense & Emperors

Putuo Shan has an intense history of worship. In 1638, a gentleman named Chang Tai visited here aboard a pilgrim's boat. Once landed, he accompanied other 17th-century pilgrims through the three great temples on the island to the peak known as Buddha's Head. The devout making this trek had to bow every three steps, shouting the name of the Goddess of Mercy, Guanyin. Spending the night on Putuo Shan in the Great Hall, clogged with incense smoke as thick as fog, these pilgrims of the past waited for a divine manifestation. Chang Tai set the old scene thus: "Thousands of men and women sit in rows like packed fish . . . not one inch of space is unoccupied. During the night many nuns burn incense on their heads or burn their arms and fingers. Women from good families imitate them. They recite scriptures and try not to show signs of pain."

The pilgrims came then and for centuries more to see Guanyin float across this seascape of pines and camphors, tea plantations, engraved stones and "powdered gold" beaches, "fine as silk." Guanyin is still the bodhisattva in residence, one of 33 enlightened ones dedicated to saving the living. Known in Buddhist India as the god *Avalokitesvara,* Guanyin changed sex in China, becoming a goddess sought out by those petitioning for the birth of a male child. Over the centuries, her worship spread across China, west to east, culminating at Putuo Shan, the living Potalaka (Little White Flower) mentioned in the sutras, the holy mountain wrapped in a sea of water lilies.

In the highest temple on the island, the second emperor of the Qing Dynasty, Kangxi (1661–1722), inscribed in stone this homage to Putuo Shan:

> Coming to this island, the moaning of the waves and the chanting of prayers can be heard, the deep purple temples can be seen, and peace can be had as expansive as the wide sea. . . . This renowned island has become a kingdom of the gods. It is like a ship of mercy upon the great sea; hills blue as the fleecy sky, and high as the heavens of Brahma; upon this lucky clean place the waves dash up to bathe the sun. Its reputation stands as a pillar, supporting the sky. From its summit, all places are connected.

High praise and imperial promise—such has been sufficient to spur me to reach Putuo Shan as quickly as possible, even if it has meant boarding a latter-day "pilgrim's" boat. For to reach the island mountain, little has changed: I've crossed a sea of iron-pronged water lilies using such conveyances as lay in my path.

Front Temple

I check in at the Resting Plough Hotel and take a stroll around through the village on the southern tip of the island. Putuo Shan is a sort of summer resort, an island getaway these days, but it has its charms. The old rock formations are trimmed in tea terraces; the large temples are enlivened with bright paint. Near my hotel is a winding cobblestone path with a fine stone wall on either side. And the **Universal Salvation Temple complex (Puji Si)**—also known as the Front Temple—is the oldest and most elaborate on the island, its halls and pavilions fronted by an immense lotus pond.

This lotus pond, rather rundown and devoid of its lotus flowers, is crossed by several arched bridges and presided over by a five-story pagoda (Duobao), built in the 14th century. Putuo Shan has been subjected to many cycles of decay and rebirth, fully in keeping with a

Buddhist holy place. On one of the imperial tablets stored in this temple, Emperor Kangxi recounts how before the Qing Dynasty (1644–1911) "the island was overthrown by pirates, and all the temples were destroyed by fire. After the 22nd year of my reign, peace and order were established. Priests returned from the mainland, looked upon the old foundations, cleaned away the weeds and debris, and began to build anew . . . and I myself prayed, saying, 'May the temples forever keep the sea in subjection.'"

The temples are not eternal, however—not in a literal sense. They decay, are soon looted or razed, and are finally rebuilt, often from the ground up. Their lineage may go back nine centuries and more, but they themselves are more youthful incarnations. Only their natural setting resists the wear and tear of regimes, if not the pummeling of salted waves, cold winds, and hard rains.

Some of the pilgrims here today have resisted politics and erosion. I run across groups of old women, yellow shan bags slung over their shoulders and tied about their waists. For centuries, pilgrims stopped at each temple on this island, burned incense, and for a small donation had the temple monks affix a red ink seal to their mountain purses. The old women are outnumbered today, however, by young sailors; they're everywhere on the island, giving it the feel of a military base.

On the narrow street rising north of the Front Temple grounds there are dozens of hole-in-the-wall cafes with live seafood swarming in plastic pans of water; and plenty of beauty salons, too, mere shacks, doors wide open, hair blowers ablaze, posters of Western pop stars and celebrities pasted to the walls. There are farmers in the fields, oblivious to tourism and pilgrimage alike. Tour buses park at the lotus pond, but not a single foreigner have I yet seen. I receive a hail of friendly greetings when I walk the southern arc of the island. Yet on my way from the fishing boat to the Resting Plough Hotel, I pass a dog lying on the centerline of the highway to the village, legs folded under. There are plenty of people walking the shoulder, but no one stops to examine the dog.

This is not any longer an island of mercy—an irony, since as one of the four centers of Buddhism in China and the grand mansion of the Goddess of Mercy Herself, one expects all life to be held sacred, to be treated as such: horses, dogs, bedbugs. Somewhere on Putuo Shan there is a stele engraved with this holy admonition: "All that has life should not intentionally be killed. In the classic it is also said, 'The winter months breed lice; take them and put them into a bamboo joint; keep them warm with cotton, and give them oily food to eat lest they might freeze or starve.' Such is the doctrine of the Goddess of Mercy." But this and other doctrines of its ilk are temporarily out of service in the new, unsuperstitious China.

Tonight I fall asleep quickly, and during that steep descent into oblivion I experience a strange disturbance: An image of Guanyin, the Lady in White, prints itself like a cameo on the darkness, flooding my eyes for a few moments, startling me awake.

The View from Buddha's Head

At dawn, when I set out for **Buddha's Head Peak (Foding Shan),** which rises less than a thousand feet above the level sea, I'm inspired by one of the many simple inscriptions in the rocks of Putuo Shan: "Ascend and enter the region of formlessness."

From the Front Monastery, I strike out northward on Excellent Ornament Road, hoping it will dwindle into a forest path long before I reach Buddha's Head. It doesn't. The scenery up the western side is fine, and were it not for the asphalt of the curving highway and an occasional Chinese tour bus grinding by, I would be alone in remote pine forests tumbling steeply down to the sea below. Along the shoulder of the highway, I come across tiny shrines cut out into the smooth moss-covered cliffs. Stone figures of Guanyin are ensconced inside. I follow the paved road toward Buddha's Head, rising above the salt pans and tea plantations, the nunneries and temples, the beaches and fishing junks.

After a several-mile climb, I reach Putuo Shan's second great temple, **Huiji Si, the Enlightenment Temple.** Buddha's Head looms above. I stroll through a tour bus parking lot. The halls to one side are stocked with souvenirs, snacks, and drinks. I buy two boiled eggs and a glass of Buddha tea. The summit is immediately above me, connected to the parking lot by stairs. An elderly ticket vendor squats behind at a long table. He is wrapped in a full-length green army coat, its collar trimmed in brown fur, and reading a rented book. I buy a ticket from him and start the final ascent. A hundred steps later I stand on Buddha's Head atop Putuo Shan.

Or almost atop. The summit is actually fenced off. Its gate is locked. A sign on the gate reads NO VISITORS. Inside the fence is a brick building without windows. Perhaps it's a weather station or a communications outpost—certainly a government installation, that's safe to say. Near the gate is a coin-operated telescope. Truly, I have reached a state of pure formlessness unique to our century: unimperial and technological. Buddha's Peak is closed to modern pilgrims—a military outpost. Putuo Shan is merciless in its emptiness. Yet the view from Buddha's Forehead is sweeping. The hills of Putuo Shan are layered into the hem of the sea and scores of islands radiate outward all the way to the clouds on the horizon.

Rain & Drought

I descend Buddha's Head Peak by the eastern route: a thousand stone-cut stairs inscribed with lotus petals. This is the path where the faithful on the way up were said once upon a time to touch their heads every third or fifth step. Few such pilgrims are here today, but the grungy Immortal's Well is doing a brisk business hawking incense sticks and magic spring water by the glass in the cleft of a massive rock. Here a hermit of the Eastern Jin Dynasty (A.D. 317–420) discovered a source of spring water that never dried up and never turned salty.

This spring was once an emblem to Imperial China of a sacred cure for drought. Emperors petitioned Putuo Shan on several occasions for rain, and indeed just a few hundred steep steps below this cave is the third great monastery of the island mountain, Fayu Si—Rain Law Temple. Rain Law Temple was rebuilt a few years back. It rises in tiers up the hillside of Buddha's Head Peak. One of its halls was shipped here from Nanjing by Emperor Kangxi. Its central image is a statue of Guanyin.

Bridge of Great Being

I pay a visit to the **Voice of the Tide Cave** along the eastern shore, where for at least 900 years pilgrims have reported seeing manifestations of Guanyin, serene, bathed in purplish golden light. In 1209, an abbot ordered the building of the **Bridge of Great Being** from which the faithful could look into the cave for an appearance of Guanyin as she is described in the Chinese classic *Journey to the West:* in her "white silk robe bathed in holy light." Late in the Ming Dynasty, pilgrims and monks would kneel and kowtow all the way to the tidal cave, arriving blood-soaked. Many threw themselves into the sea at the first appearance of a rainbow in the pinched, sunstruck spray—so many that monks once routinely scoured the waters with baskets, trolling for bones to be cremated.

No such suicidal hopefuls gather here anymore. All that's left to contemplate are a pile of rock, an old bridge, a pretty jetty, and some dazzling waves. The most hardened devotees of all used to come here to set their fingers afire, to burn them out of existence. A gazetteer for the year 1361 notes that in A.D. 848 "a foreign monk came to the Voice of the Tide Cave. He burned his ten fingers in front of the cave. When the fingers were burned off, he saw the Great Being who preached dharma to him and gave him a seven-hued precious stone."

Ten living sticks of incense. . . . I stand on the Bridge of the Great Being looking into the womb of the goddess trying to imagine how anyone could withstand such pain, the offering of the flesh to a merciful mother, to the thin air. From peak to cave, Putuo Shan is exactly as it was in ancient China, but its transfiguration into the island home of the merciful goddess seems to have disappeared from the mind of the people.

Pilgrims & Submarines

On my way to the ferry dock on the southern tip of the island, I meet four retired Americans who are teaching in Hangzhou, accompanied on their tour of Putuo Shan by a student. With a native guide, everything has gone like clockwork for them. I tag along, relaxed for the first time on my journey.

We board a direct ferry back to **Ningbo** and spread out in the soft-seat lounge up front. The island mountain fades away into the morning mist as it has for centuries. For a moment it is as if nothing has changed. Then I notice a battered old submarine break the surface, heading for its holy port. Putuo Shan has slipped the reins of emperors, pirates, and abbots, and is now ridden by the Chinese Navy.

I suppose it doesn't matter, this displacement of the spiritual. For the most part visitors these days are sightseers, more concerned with prices and wages than with visions. But on the rear observation deck, packed shoulder to shoulder with standing passengers, I do come across a handful of true pilgrims: tiny old women with shan bags, rosary beads, and knitted wool watch caps, every one of them smiling. They think I'm quite the strangest sight in the world and they start to giggle. I don't mind entertaining them.

Is this the same Putuo Shan as the old Putuo Shan where the Song poet Wang An-shih stood a thousand years ago, calling it the mountain that overpowers the sea, the island where "the sun and moon shine before anywhere else" in the world? Everywhere the landscape of this island was once fabulously transfigured, its stones into saints, its ledges into pulpits, its caves into eyes, its springs into elixirs, the very rain into the law of Buddha—and finally the rainbowed sunlight of the sea spray into the halo of the Goddess of Mercy. Today, a familiar disfiguration has assumed control. Vendors offer tapes of chanting monks. Rats dart through the streets. Sailors in blue uniforms stroll in twos and threes. A peasant herds pigs from town to temple. The golden sand beaches are deserted, and so are the long spits of rock where the fishing junks tie up.

A 1698 chronicle of Putuo Shan makes it plain that this mountain has been two worlds in one for centuries, that I'm not the first to complain of its outward reality: "Take a look at Putuo today: Is there any difference between it and the description found in the Buddhist scriptures? . . . Someone may object, saying . . . there is a difference between the present and the past. But can we really deny that the flowers, fruits, trees, streams, and ponds that we see now are not the realms of the bright and perfect? The Zen master Fo-yin Liao-yuan once said, 'Green hills filling your eyes are there for you to see.' . . . Travelers who come to Putuo today . . . fail to realize that mountains, rivers, grasses, and trees are originally formed by people's deluded thoughts. . . . Only then will one know that all the famous mountain bodhimandas are indeed the places where Buddha lives."

Perhaps the Island Mountain retains its ancient power, if I but knew how to summon it. Perhaps it is still Guanyin's home, if I but knew how to see it. For now the tide is out—the tide of ancient empires—and with it the old petals of compassion, carried far and drowned in the wide, wide ocean of China.

PRACTICAL INFORMATION

ORIENTATION

Putuo Shan is a small island (4 miles long, 1 mile wide) in the East China Sea, 100 miles south of Shanghai, 100 miles east of Hangzhou, and 50 miles east of Ningbo, the nearest city. A small village, located on the south end of the island, serves as Putuo Shan's port. The Front Temple, just north of the village, is surrounded by a large central square with many shops and cafes. Buddha's Head Peak, in the center of the island, is the highest point (elevation 1,000 feet). Summer is high season for tourists. In the first week of April, thousands of pilgrims throng the island for the goddess Guanyin's birthday.

GETTING THERE

By Ferry   Putuo Shan can be reached only by ferry. There is a direct ferry daily from Ningbo (5 hours) and one every two days from Shanghai (11 hours). On weekends, there is a catamaran from Shanghai (5 hours).

Ferry tickets for Shanghai and Ningbo can be purchased in Putuo Shan at the dockside office on the south edge of the village. Ferry tickets to Putuo Shan can be purchased in Shanghai at most hotels or from the ticket office located on Jinling Dong Lu, opposite the Bund. Tickets cost RMB 200 ($25) one way. In Ningbo, ferry tickets to Putuo Shan can be purchased at the Passenger Ferry Terminal, located three blocks north of the Yongjiang Bridge along the Yong River. Tickets cost RMB 20 ($2.50) one way.

TOURS & STRATAGEMS

There is an office of China International Travel Service (CITS) across from the Bank of China on the main road connecting the village and the Front Temple (Puji Si). They can provide guides, but with a map in hand a guide is scarcely necessary. The island is small enough to explore on foot. Taxis and pedicabs usually charge about RMB 15 ($2) per ride.

WHERE TO STAY

I stayed several nights at the **Resting Plough Hotel (Xilai Xiaozhuang)** (☎ 0580/609-1644; fax 0580/609-1023). It is located on the west road north of the ferry terminal near the Front Temple. Rated at 3 stars, it does provide large doubles (modern but rundown), room service, and daily turndown, but no credit cards are accepted. The staff is helpful, speaking some English. Doubles cost $55.

The price is the same at the 3-star **Putuo Shan Zhuang** (☎ 0580/609-1666; fax 0580/609-1667). Although located a long walk southeast of the Front Temple, this hotel is the newest and most modern on the island. Still, it has no more services than the Resting Plough Hotel.

In **Ningbo,** the best choice is the new **East Seaport Hotel,** 52 Caihong Bei Lu (☎ 0574/737-3188; fax 0574/733-3646). This 14-story 4-star hotel, located near downtown stores, has plenty of international-level luxuries: pool, gym, business center, room service, and its own row of shops. Rooms are clean, modern, and spacious ($125 double). The first-floor Chinese restaurant is excellent. Dragonair, with direct Hong Kong–Ningbo flights, has its offices in this hotel (ext. 7452).

WHERE TO DINE

The **Resting Plough Hotel** (☎ 0580/609-1644), southwest of the Front Temple and central square, has a good restaurant (open daily 7am to 10pm) with an English menu. The dishes are Chinese and Shanghainese, heavy on the seafood. Dinners cost RMB 60 to 168 ($7 to $20) and up, depending on whether you order exotic seafoods. Many small local restaurants line the enormous square around the Front Temple. I didn't try any of these (although several workers inside waved as I passed). I did buy snacks (boiled eggs, fried breads) from sidewalk vendors.

TAI SHAN: SACRED MOUNTAIN OF THE EAST

泰山

Tai Shan is the most climbed mountain in the world, although it is virtually unknown to the West. Situated at the midpoint between Beijing and Shanghai, Tai Shan has been the most celebrated of the Five Sacred Peaks of China for the last 2,000 years, the highest altar in the Middle Kingdom for countless pilgrims and a great many emperors, including China's first. Today, Mt. Tai is still a popular outdoor destination for tourists, mostly for the Chinese themselves, who swarm the hand-hewn stone staircase on the trek to the Gate of Heaven. From the summit Confucius (Kong Zi) once proclaimed the world small and later Chairman Mao pronounced the East Red. But in post–Chairman Mao China, the worldview from Tai Shan is altered once again, as I would find when I made my own ascent.

Dai Temple

I begin my modern sightseer's pilgrimage in the old way, at the temple at the foot of the mountain, in the town of Tai'an. The Dai Temple (Dai Miao) is a large walled fortress, a town within a town, of restored halls and pavilions housing ancient relics. Everyone from pickpockets to the imperial family used to set out from this shrine. One visitor described the temple grounds in 1628 as "a motley collection of stalls and stands" inhabited not only by pilgrims but by "cock-fighters, football players, equestrians, and story-tellers." I don't see anyone kicking a football around this morning, but I do come across scores of vendors encamped within the 30-foot walls.

The temple grounds are populated with carved stone tablets, one recording the mountain's appointment as "Emperor of China" by the Song emperor in A.D. 1011. Every city and town in China once had a flourishing Eastern Mountain Temple of its own, part of the massive Tai Shan cult that died only with the Communist Liberation in 1949. Dai Mao also contains one of China's oldest steles, the **Qin Tablet**, thought to have been carved in 209 B.C. when China's First Emperor, Qin Shi Huang

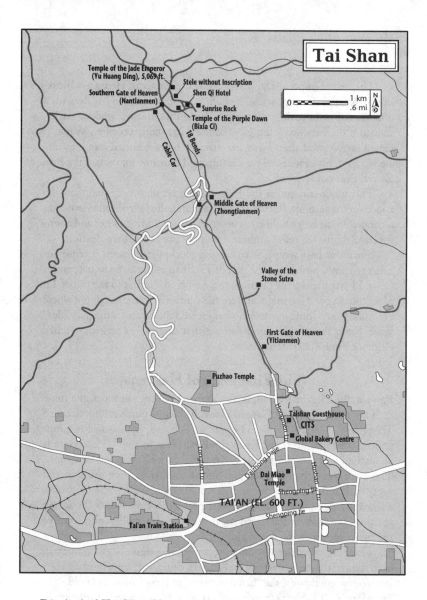

Tai Shan

Temple of the Jade Emperor
(Yu Huang Ding), 5,069 ft.

Stele without Inscription

Southern Gate of Heaven
(Nantianmen)

Shen Qi Hotel

Sunrise Rock

Temple of the Purple Dawn
(Bixia Ci)

Cable Car

18 Bends

Middle Gate of Heaven
(Zhongtianmen)

Valley of the
Stone Sutra

First Gate of Heaven
(Yitianmen)

Puzhao Temple

Taishan Guesthouse

CITS

Global Bakery Centre

Hongmen

Daizhong Dajie

Dai Miao
Temple

Hushan lu

Longtan lu

Shengping lie

TAI'AN (EL. 600 FT.)

Shengping lie

Tai'an Train Station

0   1 km
                   .6 mi

N

Di, climbed Tai Shan. This inscribed monument stood on the summit
until devoured by fire in 1740. A fragment with nine characters is now
preserved outside the red stone hall where many an emperor once rested
before his climb. It is mounted under a plate of glass. Sima Qian, China's
ancient historian, was present when Emperor Qin ordered the full inscription "praising his own virtues," and it was partly Qin's act of hubris
on the summit of this Dragon Mountain that prompted the Confucian
intellectuals of the day to censor the First Emperor—and in turn
impelled their new ruler to retaliate with the Burning of the Books and
the Burying Alive of the 480 Scholars.

The main temple at Dai Miao, called the **Palace of Heavenly Bless-ing,** is palatial in every sense, including its size: nine bays wide with a double roof of imperial yellow tiles. Within its massive wooden cavity, stained a dark crimson, the God of the Mountain, Tai Shan Wang, is seated on a central altar. Twice life-size, his black-bearded face is enam-eled in gold. Five sacrificial vessels surround him, one for each of the Five Sacred Peaks of Daoism.

This mountain god is the Judge of the Dead, but he maintains no abode on the summit. Rather, it's his daughter, the Jade Woman, who has ascended to the heights. She has usurped her forbidding father and reigns supreme on the supreme summit, a deity of life rather than death.

Since this base temple is where the good pilgrim burns incense be-fore the climb, presenting the god of Tai Shan with the favor nearest his heart, I hereby make my petition, too. I wish to climb it to the top of Tai Shan today, spend the night, and see the sunrise from the same spot where everyone from Confucius to Mao has greeted the dawn for the past 2,500 years. From the temple gate I can see that summit—a jagged, notched cliff face some 6,293 steps away.

The First Gate of Heaven

Pan Lu, the Pilgrim's Road, begins at the north edge of town, at a stone arch known as the **First Gate of Heaven.** Here I purchase my ticket to Tai Shan (RMB 20/$2.40). The way up is broad, with spacious ramps and massive granite steps. From the First Gate to the Middle Gate is about 3 miles. From the middle to the top is under 2 miles but far steeper. There are more than 250 temples and monuments along the way, and every rock and cranny, ravine and stream, wears a poetic name or invokes a romantic tale or two out of China's past. Above all there's the sacred graffiti. Hundreds of flat-faced rocks are etched in calligraphy, some of the finest specimens in the world.

There are other signs of the past, too—living signs: beggars, working each rung of the stone stairway, and porters, dozens of them, hoisting their loads on wooden poles, the "bamboo tigers" of New China, as of old.

Many of Tai Shan's holy pavilions have been converted into snack bars and souvenir stands. At one cafe, I find the staff and patrons sitting outside, watching television. At another, there's a computer monitor, a vendor rattling its keyboard like an abacus. The screen radiates with a green glow, matching the overarching canopy of trees, a canopy pierced by thick electrical lines running up the mountain. The lower half of the sacred mountain has been modernized, electrified, even computerized, although the stone stairs, tall pines, steep cliffs, and embroidery of carved characters manage to shine through. The gaily dressed, money-spending tourists of New China are everywhere, far outnumbering a few old pilgrims, wiry porters, and the beggars who cling for life to their single stair step.

Tiring of the stairs, I make a detour into the **Valley of the Stone Sutra,** where 6th-century Buddhists engraved the 2,500-character Diamond Sutra on the exposed banks of an extinct streambed. The stone banks are wide, flat, and smooth, forming a stone scroll unrolled by nature, but rain and wind have washed over the text, erasing much of it.

The Middle Gate of Heaven

After a 3-hour steady march, I reach the **Middle Gate of Heaven,** and it is a nightmare, clotted with a thousand vendors and pocked by a gigantic parking lot for tour buses ferrying "climbers" up from the bottom. To top it off, this is where one can catch China's first large-scale cable car and thereby reach the holy summit in 8 minutes flat.

Keeping to my regimen, however, I strike out on foot, heading for the **Eighteen Bends,** a gargantuan stone ladder to the Southern Gate of Heaven, still far above. I hope to leave behind this modern Pilgrim's Way that has been transformed into a high emporium of carnival shooting galleries, cheap charms on chains, shacks serving Coca-Cola, and roving photographers for hire.

The next landmarks belong to China's first emperor: a pavilion where Qin Shi Huang took shelter from a storm as he descended in 209 B.C.; a pine tree awarded the fifth military rank when it sheltered Emperor Qin from the rain; a rock in the first emperor's calligraphy with characters cut so large it's known as "Stele a Hundred Thousand Feet High." Then there's a stone arch named "Rise to Immortality," and finally 2,000 ruthless stairs to the top.

I pause on every intervening ramp. So do the porters, resting their bundles and bamboo carrying poles on the stairs. I follow one porter typical of those on Tai Shan, his skin burned auburn, head shaved, blue cotton pants rolled up to his knees, back drenched in sweat, feet shod in black cotton shoes. Dangling from the thick rope on one end of his carrying pole are three heavy gunny sacks; on the other end are two red roosters, suspended by their claws upside down, both still alive.

In the middle of one stair tread I step around a dilapidated cardboard box, presided over by a tiny plaster figure of Buddha painted gold. It's a beggar's collection box, unattended, but there's a beggar on the next flight of stairs, both his legs shorn off at the thigh.

The walls of the ravine close in on me. This is where the Tai Shan gazetteer mentions that a bully was crushed by a falling rock, decisively squashed "so that the fat of his body polished the stairs. Nothing was left," we're told. "His family could retrieve only one of his fingers." I'm amazed. Here is a mountain where villains are actually punished.

A Milky Way of supplicants still flows up and down this stairway, but now, if indeed people burn incense in the high temples at all, they are probably requesting cash only, trunks of it. But even in greed, Tai Shan follows tradition. When Han Dynasty Emperor Wu arrived at Tai Shan, the local officials lined both sides of the road on their knees; dispensing with offerings of fruit, they piled cash along the roadside, imploring the imperial blessing.

The Southern Gate of Heaven is a square red tower at the top of this long, long mountain staircase. Its hollow understory dates from 1264. Its upper story is known as **"The Pavilion That Touches the Sky"**—with Heaven once reckoned to be precisely 17 inches above the roof peak.

The Southern Gate of Heaven

Reaching the Southern Gate of Heaven, I squeeze through the Pavilion That Touches the Sky—and then I realize that I'm still not at the summit of Tai Shan. Beyond here is a metric mile of vendors, coin telescopes, rock carvings, temples, and still more stone stairs. But it's not so steep now. I quickly wind my way to the Shen Qi Hotel where I check in.

There are plenty of monuments and temples on this broad summit, more than on any of China's other holy peaks. First there are the Tang Dynasty Rock Inscriptions (Mo Ya Bei), the most ostentatious in outdoor China, the ultimate in cliff calligraphy. In A.D. 726, Emperor Xuan Zong ordered that an account of his own imperial pilgrimage to Tai Shan be carved here—and it was carved large, in huge characters, 996 of them, each measuring a good 7 inches square, each gilded in gold foil. The page of rock chosen for the imperial inscription faces south; the golden text is 43 feet high and 16 feet wide.

Then, on the very tiptop of Tai Shan, there's the **Summit of the Celestial Pillar,** where the **Temple of the Jade Emperor** (Yu Huang Ding) stands. In its courtyard is a marker stone recording the metric elevation of Tai Shan (1,545 meters, a mere 5,069 feet). And in the lower courtyard is the **Stele Without Inscription (Wu Zi Bei),** one of China's most celebrated tablets, long believed to have been placed here by First Emperor Qin during his visit in 219 B.C. This stone tablet is wordless and everyone who reaches here must touch it. The Chinese say this is the most touched stone on Earth, which is perhaps why it is completely blank. Twenty feet high, five feet square, this wordless tablet is a true counterweight to the extravagantly wordy cliff carving just down the hill.

Finally, immediately below my hotel is **Bixia Ci, the Temple of the Purple Dawn,** where the Jade Woman (Bixia Yuan Jun) resides. She's the favorite of all the pilgrims, the Daoist equivalent of Guanyin, Goddess of Mercy. Over the centuries, as more and more sought her out on Tai Shan in preference to her father, Tai Shan Wang, the Jade Woman assumed two special powers: She could cure blindness and she could bless a petitioner with children. She became the great midwife of China.

As I wander across the summit I see more worship on Tai Shan than I expected, more incense burning at the shrines, more money tossed into the altar boxes, often by parents with young children. And there are forms of worship here I don't understand at all.

Just below the Temple of the Purple Clouds is a large incense burner: It's an entire building, as big as a pavilion, and well attended this afternoon. There's an offering box in front of its fiery mouth. Alongside are many flowering bushes that have hundreds of stones caught in their limbs and branches—whether by design or nature, I can't tell—but dozens of people are down there tying red ribbons to the limbs. I'm not sure for what they're praying: children, money, health—surely some such universal desire, practical rather than what the West regards as spiritual. One doesn't climb all this way to engage in abstract reasoning.

While the temples on top of Tai Shan are among the most magical in China, there's also a communications complex with a weather station here rising higher than any temple and piercing the floorboards of Heaven. Pagoda of the Great Transmitter, Stupa of the Satellite Dish, these modern shrines of jade become electric.

Sunrise

At 4am the next morning, there is a knock on my door. Rise and shine for the ultimate ritual of Tai Shan: the sunrise. Light is born in the east each day, and Tai Shan, as the Eastern Mountain, presides over all origins, over life itself.

Outside, it is very dark. The winds chew at my flesh. I join a stream of sightseers flowing east across the summit. Many have rented full-length padded army coats, green with fur collars. One traveler even carries a large suitcase. A few have flashlights. I'm the only Westerner this morning.

At the eastern edge of Old China, we settle into the rock ledges and wait for the sun to rise out of the East China Sea. The stars fade out. At 5:07am, the sun chips through the cloud bank. The crowd gasps. Everyone points toward the sun.

From Confucius to Mao and beyond, we have all gathered here for the dawn of a new day. And it is a new day. The sun is a feeble disk of yellow light, barely strong enough to penetrate the gray clouds, the vast haze of industrial progress steamrolling its way through China. The East is no longer red; it's toxic gray. For the next hour, we watch the rising sun slice through the purple clouds of dawn like pinking shears, trimming away the raiment of the Jade Woman.

Back in Beijing, Chairman Mao's corpse, that of an emperor out of season, is encased in a slab of black granite from Tai Shan. But the imperial age and that of the great beliefs—Taoism, Buddhism, Confucianism, and lately even Communism—are passing away. From Tai Shan, one must descend into the modern underworld. At Heaven's highest gate today, a vendor stands. He offers paintings brushed on black velvet: paintings of tigers and dragons, eagles and cute kittens. The colors on these fuzzy, sofa-sized canvases are bright as neon, ideal for tourist and pilgrim alike. They roll up like scrolls. The cable car, and below that, the air-conditioned buses, await. The world no longer seems so small, even if it is fast approaching a commercial uniformity. The world is bigger than a dynasty, bigger than the Middle Kingdom, bigger than the circumference of China's sacred mountains, no longer in the purview of a single land-locked sage.

PRACTICAL INFORMATION

ORIENTATION

Tai Shan (Great Mountain) is the most famous sacred peak in China. Facing the East China Sea, Tai Shan is located midway between Beijing and Shanghai in Shandong Province. Its base, in the town of Tai'an, is at 492 feet elevation; its summit is at 5,069 feet. Summers are hot, winters cold, making spring and autumn the most comfortable seasons to visit.

Tai Shan was inscribed on the UNESCO World Heritage List in 1987. Guo Moruo, a modern Chinese writer, described Tai Shan as a "microcosm of Chinese culture." There are presently 819 carved stone tablets and 1,018 cliff-face inscriptions on Tai Shan, as well as 22 active temples. The first recorded temple on the mountain was built in 351 B.C. China's emperors have made pilgrimages to Tai Shan for over 2,000 years. By the Ming Dynasty (1368–1644), pilgrims numbering over 200,000 annually made the trek to the top of the mountain.

GETTING THERE

By Plane   The nearest major airport to Tai Shan is at Ji'nan, a large city 40 miles north. Ji'nan has flights to Beijing (1 hour), Shanghai (1 hour 40 minutes), and Hong Kong (2¹/₂ hours). From Ji'nan, a traveler must then book a train (1 hour) or bus (3 hours) to Tai'an.

By Train   There are several trains daily from Beijing to Tai'an, at the base of Tai Shan. My train from Beijing was scheduled to take 8 hours but took 11. Conditions aboard were cramped, but the passengers were interesting, including those who disposed of their emptied beer bottles by tossing them out the open windows. Tickets for "soft-seat" class cost about RMB 58 ($7) one-way. There are daily trains to Tai'an from Shanghai and other major cities in China.

TOURS & STRATAGEMS

Visitor Information China International Travel Service (CITS), 46 Hongmen Lu (☎ 0538/822-3259; fax 0538/833-2240), has an office in Tai'an on the road to the mountain entrance. It offers guided tours of Tai Shan (RMB 100/$12 per person). The CITS office located in Taishan Guesthouse (see below) also arranges tours and is especially helpful in booking train tickets.

Exploring the Mountain The mountain is visible from Tai'an. The entrance gate is straight north up Hongmen Lu. Tai Miao (Tai Shan Temple) is straight south down Hongmen Lu. The temple is open daily from 7am to 7pm and charges RMB 8 (95¢) admission. Admission to the mountain itself is RMB 20 ($2.40).

The trail to the summit, which consists mainly of stairs, is 5 miles, the last 2 miles being particularly steep. The rise in elevation is about 4,500 feet. There are two trails to the midway point (at Zhongtiamen, the Middle Gate of Heaven). The eastern trail is more interesting; the western trail is more rural and often deserted.

It is possible to reduce the hike considerably. Buses and taxis make the run from Tai'an to Zhongtiamen. From this midway point there is a cable car to the summit (RMB 25/$3 one-way; RMB 40/$4.80 round-trip).

A journey to Tai Shan would be incomplete without viewing sunrise from the summit. Plan to spend the night at the top (see below). Take warm clothing and a flashlight. The best months for visiting are from April to October. Winter months are icy and rainy.

WHERE TO STAY

The most convenient hotel in Tai'an is the five-story 3-star **Taishan Guesthouse (Taishan Binguan),** 46 Hongmen Lu (☎ 0538/822-4678), which is 3 miles from the train station (via taxi or no. 3 city bus). Double rooms start at RMB 420 ($51) and come with private bath, as well as green plastic fly swatters and hard pillows. The hotel contains a small bar and poorly lit lobby.

The hotel at the summit of Tai Shan is now called the **Shen Qi Binguan** (formerly the Daiding Binguan), 10 Tian Lu (☎ 0538/822-3866; fax 0538/833-3150). The CITS office, on the fifth floor of Taishan Guesthouse, can make reservations at the Shen Qi Binguan if you plan to spend the night on the top of Tai Shan. With TVs (but no stations received) and private baths (but no hot water), this hotel should be rated at least 1 star lower than the government-rated 3-star Taishan Binguan (above), but it isn't. Its 102 rooms are modern, with doubles commanding RMB 500 ($62) per night. Its staff, while speaking only Chinese, makes sure you're up long before sunrise.

WHERE TO DINE

No restaurants stand out in Tai'an, along the mountain trail, or in the "village" on the summit. Trailside vendors offer ice cream, bottled drinks, and hot noodle dishes. In Tai'an, the **Global Bakery Centre,** 7 Hongmen Lu, sells pastries and snacks for the long hike. The **Taishan Binguan** (☎ 0538/822-4678) has a restaurant in a separate building that provides set Western breakfasts ($3) and set Chinese lunches and dinners ($5 to $10). On the summit, the **Shen Qi Binguan** also offers fixed-price Chinese meals in its restaurant ($10 to $20).

EMEI SHAN: BUDDHIST PEAK OF THE WEST

峨眉山

"No SPOT IN THE WORLD COULD BE found more aptly to emphasize and accentuate the lofty ideals and mystic dogmas of Buddhism," Julius Eigner wrote after his visit to Emei Shan (Eyebrow Mountain) in 1935. "Leopards, even snow leopards, are not infrequent," he claimed. He also spoke of a lost Chinese world:

> Sometimes an old white-haired monk, leaning on a long staff, will slowly descend the steps, looking like an ancient Chinese sage come to life again. Or a water buffalo will peacefully browse along the banks of a rivulet, with a small boy sitting on his back blowing determinedly on a wooden flute. Is it not a picture a Westerner would associate with those pastoral times which reigned in this country in some dim past age, when the gods came down to earth to visit the daughters of man?

Arriving six decades later, at a time when all of China seems to be stretching out in unison toward a technological future, I still harbor the hope of finding such a China of dreams on the slopes of Emei Shan. If I can take this holy peak at my own pace, lose myself in its folds, and disappear along its lazy trailsides under ink-brushed cliffs, then by the time I stand on its golden summit perhaps I will be blessed with an ancient vision: a halo in the clouds, framing my shadow for an instant before the sun melts everything down into steel and concrete.

Shrine of Limpid Waters

I board a morning bus in Chengdu, the capital of Sichuan Province. Emei Shan is less than 90 miles to the southwest. I've joined a Chinese group tour, a no-frills tour to be sure. I'm curious to see how the Chinese tour the mountain. By the time we reach the foothills of the mountain, darkness fills the hot sky. I get just one glimpse of Emei Shan, its massive triple summit rising like a wall over the low plains, the forests,

Emei Shan

To Chengdu

Train

To Kunming

Jin Shui

Wannian
Temple

Ta E Shi

Emei
Town

Qingyin Pavilion

Baoguo
Temple

Baoguo
Town

Elephant Bathing Pool
(Xixiang Chi)

Monkey Hill

Hongzhushan
Hotel

Three Emperors
Terrace

Chunyang Temple

Fuhu
Temple

99 Turns

Thunder God Caves

Jieyin Hall

Cable Car

Golden Peak (Jinding)–
Buddha's Halo

Golden
Temple

Thousand Buddha Peak
(Qianfoding)

Ten Thousand Buddha Peak
(Wanfoding)

0   2 km
           1.2 mi

N

the mountain streams. At 10,167 feet, its summit (Wanfoding, Peak of the Ten Thousand Buddhas) is the highest of any of the nine sacred mountains of China, Buddhist or Daoist.

At 8pm we stop partway up the mountain at **Jin Shui, the Shrine of Limpid Waters,** where hotel rooms await us. I fill out the registration papers at a counter smack-dab in the middle of a cafeteria and end up in the one wing that accepts foreigners. My room contains its own bathroom, three beds, and a local tour guide. This guide attached himself to me the moment I entered the hotel and he won't let go. We sit down on bed no. 2 and hammer out tomorrow's itinerary. He speaks not a single word of English. Tomorrow morning we'll catch a predawn minibus to see the sunrise from the summit, then come down the mountain on foot. My self-appointed guide will knock at my door at 4:30am.

After he leaves, I examine my accommodations. The bathroom sink empties directly onto the floor. I pull back the quilt on each bed, finding all the bedding, down to the mattresses, equally damp. It will be like sleeping in the tub.

The Bus to Sunrise

I sleep a few moist hours before dressing, then greet my guide at 4:30am. Outside, it's still pitch-black under a crown of stars, but the humidity is high. Emei Shan is a steam bath. I'm eager to see the sunrise from Emei Shan's **Golden Peak (Jinding).** It's there that worshippers have gathered over the centuries to pay their respects to the mountain god and to look over the edge of a massive precipice. "Emei is lofty, piercing heaven," writes a Ming Dynasty poet, "A hundred miles of mist, built in the void."

The minibus is late, however—quite late. By the time we drive up the back side of Emei Shan to the last parking lot under the peak, it is 7am and the sun has been up a good while. So many vehicles are racing to the top this morning that there are several traffic jams. We save a bit of time by taking the new cable car up the last steep slope, although we must wait another hour in line. Of the 300,000 who visit the summit each year, 200,000 arrive by cable car.

The summit of Emei Shan is imposing—a vast, nearly vacant plain of rock and sand. To the east, there's a sheer cascade of limestone, a 2,000-foot drop; to the west, on a sunny morning like this one, a splendid view of the even more formidable Gong Ga Shan (Kunlun) range, the final horizon of the Middle Kingdom. To the Chinese Buddhist of the past, this chain of eternally snowy peaks was the ever-remote location of the Western Paradise. A Ming Dynasty traveler called them "the Snowy Mountains, running athwart like a long city wall, and looking like festoons of white silk."

Buddha's Halo

Emei Shan is the final gate to a Nirvana that here assumes physical as well as spiritual definition. To reach the Western Paradise requires the help of the god of Emei Shan, Puxian, the bodhisattva of wisdom. He alone can give the faithful pilgrim the final nudge up this last rung on Heaven's ladder.

Puxian came from India in the 3rd century on the back of a white elephant. He is the Sun God of Chinese Buddhism, his mountain shrine forever associated with the heat of the southwest and the element of fire. Puxian was once the bridge between the ancient worship of nature and the new religion of the Buddha, which arrived in China just 2,000 years ago. Whoever made it to the summit of the Western Peak could then petition Puxian to escort them across a river of clouds to the divine shore.

The shortcut to this Western Paradise is Emei Shan's massive cliff. Every holy mountain in China has its legacy of ecstatic suicides and Emei Shan provides not only the highest but the most inviting platform for the leap. Below this ledge there is often an ocean of soft and wondrous clouds. There certainly is this morning as I approach the metal railing on **Suicide Precipice,** even though overhead the sky is pure blue and the sun so fierce that those who have rented Chinese army coats for the morning chill shed them. Into the cloudy sea beneath my feet the sun sometimes penetrates so as to create a magnificent halo—the halo of Buddha. These halos are created as the sun impregnates the water-laden clouds. Framed within this halo, each pilgrim, standing between sun and cloud, sees the shadow of his own head as he bows to Buddha. I'm not fortunate enough to see my own head within the mountain halo, but many an earlier traveler has left an account of the phenomenon. In the middle of the 11th century, a Song Dynasty traveler reported seeing "an aureole of mixed colors and several layers. Out of the mist was a clearly defined image of a god astride an elephant." In the center of the halo was a "bright space, serenely clear. Each person looking saw the image of himself in the empty place exactly as in a mirror. If I lifted my hand or moved my foot the image followed the motion, but I could not see the person standing by my side."

When Reverend Hart, spreading the word of the Gospel throughout remote western China, reached this terrace in the summer of 1887, he seems to have seen something of Buddha's glory himself, for he found that as he stretched forth his arms, his giant shadow did likewise. He dismissed it all as a natural phenomenon but admitted, "I also found myself when the aureole was brightest making insensible advances toward the image in it."

Autumn is the prime season for halos and suicides, but in April I'm out of sync with the seasons. I content myself by swaying a moment or two on the terrace, surveying the wide bowl of layered clouds. It's easy to see how a circular rainbow could form here. The air is filled with a million droplets of prismatic water, awaiting the visionary torch of the sun.

Golden Temple

I can report one phenomenon from Emei Shan's summit that earlier travelers did not: The wide face of the cliff is coated in tons of trailside garbage—primarily plastic bags and containers—cast from the terrace by a million modern tourists. The eyebrows of Emei Shan are desperately in need of a divine scouring of wind and rain, snow and lightning.

The summit is flat and rather empty. Acid rain has devoured entire forests here. To one side there is a communications tower and a dismal two-story hostel of cement and sheet metal, complete with a medical clinic and restaurant. There are plenty of itinerant vendors, including a few peasants with small monkeys on leashes perched on their shoulders. Emei Shan is nearly as famous for its bands of robber monkeys as for Buddha's halo. Now the monkeys have become cogs in the moneymaking machine that's bulldozing the mountain into a convenient national park of cable cars and tour buses.

There's still a shrine on top of Emei Shan, the **Golden Temple**, to house Puxian. This was the last stop for the incense-burning pilgrim—

once, according to the 19th-century missionary, Reverend Hart, the place "most exalted in the empire" where for "hundreds of years the stream of religious humanity . . . flowed and ebbed without diminution." The Golden Temple has been rebuilt continuously since the Han Dynasty. Today's stand-in is but a decade old, rebuilt on the site of a fire that gutted its previous incarnation (a fitting disaster, since Puxian is a fire god himself). The new temple is small, set on its own high platform, and while not cast entirely in bronze, the golden tiles of its flying eaves blaze in the sun. Inside, the image of Puxian is painted gold.

I take one last glance over the edge of the Golden Summit, hoping to discover my own shadow swaying in the clouds below, but my prayer is unanswered. I witness nothing more than a wide cliff drawn closed like a curtain by the clouds, waiting to be parted by the sun on its daily march across the heavens to the snows of Paradise.

Temple of Ten Thousand Years

Leaving the summit, I persuade my impatient guide to forgo the cable car. We labor downhill on stone steps for 90 minutes. According to a Chinese gazetteer of Emei Shan compiled in 1887, there are 5,728 steps down the zigzag slope back to Jieyin Hall, where the cable car begins. At this point we catch a bus to the hotel, eat lunch, and then set out together back up the mountain on foot.

We are climbing the ancient path of the pilgrims at last, no buses nearby, no cable strands. Emei Shan is a long, intricate mountain of 90,000 stone stairs, 50 miles from the golden summit to the base town of Emei. I begin this afternoon above the halfway point, and in 4 or 5 hours I'm able to encircle the main great temples on the body of the mountain. On my own, I could easily spend a week walking this mountain, temple by temple, each concealed within its own green hallowed fold of forest, stream, and terrace. A Chinese tour, however, is measured out in minutes and hours, not days and weeks, and like it or not I have locked myself into mass tourism, Chinese style. My bus back to Chengdu leaves tomorrow.

My walk on Emei Shan begins at a monastery converted to an elementary school for children who live on the mountain. There is a resident population of about 2,000 scattered across these slopes. This schoolyard is of packed dirt, a basketball hoop with tattered net at either end, empty after lunch except for a half-dozen chickens. Vendors are showing their wares under awnings roofed in galvanized sheet metal. I watch a grandfather and his tiny grandson hire a sedan chair for the climb. The grandson sits on his grandfather's lap. Off they dash together; on either end of the sedan chair poles, the two porters are stripped down to T-shirts, their pants legs hiked up.

We follow after them into the hazy green hills under a bleeding sun, sweating all the way. According to the old book I have in hand today,

Omei Illustrated Guide Book (1891), it is some 1,258 steps up to the first great monastery, **Wannian Si, the Temple of Ten Thousand Years.** I feel every single stair tread in the heat. Somewhere along here, 4,000 years ago, the legendary yellow emperor paused to inquire of a Daoist wanderer the way to the summit, and later the Tang Dynasty poet Li Bai stopped to pen some evocative lines about these temple-infested terraces:

> Bearing the Emerald Tapestry Lute,
> A Sichuan monk descended the grand western peak.
> With a brush of his hands on the strings
> He made me hear a sound like the rushing
> of pines in deep caverns.
> My heart was cleansed by the flowing waters;
> The lute's quaver mingled with the knell of a temple bell
> in frost.

Uncleansed by any magic lute, I reach Wannian Si, founded 17 centuries ago, the oldest temple on the mountain. Although this temple complex is beautiful and in a luxuriant natural setting, most of its great halls, save the one housing Puxian and his elephant, burned down in 1946. Wannian Si is at 3,000 feet elevation, just above the jungle belt, thick with camphor and banyan, mulberry and banana. I can feel the steam rise and swirl into these highlands, a 15-mile walk below the Golden Summit where I stood this morning, staring into a mirror of blank fog.

The building that has survived the longest on Emei Shan, the mountain's holiest shrine, is at Wannian Si: a squat hall of brick, 50 feet square. Inside, under a beamless vault, is Puxian's white elephant, cast in bronze in A.D. 980, now plastered over with painted stucco. Puxian, eldest son of Buddha, rides on top, his saddle a golden lotus. Modern pilgrims burn long sticks of incense outside the main doors. I take a gander at elephant and mountain god, then follow my silent guide up and down the 2,436 twisting steps to Qingyin Pavilion.

Golden Monkeys

Of the Emei Shan staircase, an imperial inspector, Shou P'u, once wrote, "When descending the hill, travelers go crab-fashion, with one man's feet on another man's shoulders. When ascending, they go like ants stuck onto each other, with one holding another's foot in his mouth." The trail is everywhere as crowded with trailside vendors as with visitors, the slopes forested green with bamboos and a few straggly tea plantations. Along this path the Ancient Forest of the Virtuous One once stood, planted by a devout monk in the Ming Dynasty. He was said to have planted 69,770 trees, one for each character of the Lotus Sutra, but not a single one has survived.

At the **pavilions of Qingyin,** we turn west toward **Hou Wang Po, the Hill of the Monkey,** pausing to bathe ourselves in the White Dragon stream. I'm drenched in sweat, so it is good to stop for a splash. I'm determined to keep going upstream for a glimpse of Emei Shan's celebrated monkeys. Most of the animals that frequented Emei Shan in its remoter days, a century or less ago, have fled to more impenetrable Western paradises.

The trail twists through a narrow river canyon over a series of bridges and planks, with bends so tight only one or two people can pass at a time. The canyon is dark, even on this bright afternoon. The sun must seldom, if ever, sound its depths. The monkeys lie in wait. The Chinese have their own way of dealing with the monkeys. I sight the first of these golden creatures on the iron railing of a bridge. They are being taunted by the sedan chair carriers and a crowd of visitors. By the time I reach the railing, the monkeys have scurried up a sandy bank of ferns and bamboo. The crowd tosses them scraps; the monkeys saunter down to accept the offerings. Several of the Chinese start to tease the monkeys again, luring them down the slope with outstretched palms, then hissing or opening an empty hand and laughing. One monkey suddenly levels a swipe at the back of a little girl's head. A moment later another monkey, a mother carrying her baby, bites a woman's extended hand.

This band of monkeys is outnumbered by the hordes of tourists. For the most part, the passing crowds force them to higher ground. No longer can they block the road like toll collectors. We are making the world a safer place for tourists, if not for the creatures the tourists come to see. On Emei Shan the golden monkeys have been subdued. Every temple, every parking lot, now has a handful of portrait photographers bearing monkeys on their shoulders. Many of these captives are dressed in silk; all are chained. For one yuan—12¢—the handlers allow tourists to pose with a monkey balanced on its hind legs in their hand; pictures are snapped; prints are mailed to purchasers. It's another way to turn a profit in the wilds—rural enterprise, blessed by God and Party, with conservation postponed until the next century.

After watching the crowd taunt a few more monkeys, I turn back. I've seen enough for today of mountain and temple, bronze elephant and golden monkey.

Pure Sound Pavilion

I rest up at the **Qingyin (Pure Sound) Pavilion,** so named for the melodious meeting of the White and Black Dragon streams. According to an Emei Shan gazetteer, "Clear sounds are heard near the lofty pavilion, as if Buddhist spirits were playing musical instruments." I splash myself with a few wet notes scooped from the chilly stream. With narrow waterfalls, swift white ripples, rapids and cascades, arched bridges and tile-roofed kiosks and viewing halls perched on ledges and terraces in a rain forest of bamboo, Pure Sound Pavilion is a postcard of the past before cable cars, buses, and bottled water vendors lined the 90,000 stone stairs, before the tigers were caged or shot or driven to Tibet, before the golden monkeys were chained up.

Below two arched bridges, known as the **Twin Flying Bridges,** the limestone canyon of the river dragon deepens into what a Chinese mountain guide of 1844 describes as the place "with pure sounds of music, where the waters wash the heart of an ox into a Buddha." This is where the White and Black rivers merge—the Ox-Heart Stone beneath the Flying Bridges. I follow my guide downhill. The sun is falling behind the forehead of the mountain.

Thunder Gods

We pass **Ta E Shi,** the Great Stone of Emei, on which a Ming Dynasty minister of education carved a message, "Heaven of the Holy Mystery." I'm too beat to entertain more mysteries. We come out at a small village and wait for bus connections. I buy two boiled eggs from an old woman. She charges me the paltry Chinese price for eggs—a fine, honest woman. Meanwhile, peasant photographers are displaying their leashed monkeys, and a farm girl strolls by, her water buffalo tethered to a rope.

Back in my hotel room at Jin Shui, I fall into bed before dusk. Emei Shan is where I imagined I would spend a week or two wandering from temple inn to temple inn, but now all I can do is sleep. Just past midnight, however, the mountain is socked by an electrical storm, a boisterous one. Crack after crack of lightning wakes me. Puxian, the mountain god, is speaking. Or perhaps the ancient thunder gods still dwell in the hidden recesses beneath the summit. Less than a century ago, pilgrims and officials gathered on a platform to the thunder gods at the top of Emei Shan to pray for an end to drought. "First one drops some incense and money down," explains the mountain gazetteer of 1891. "If rain does not come, then one drops in a dead pig and women's clothes. Then the thunder and rain will surely come."

Tonight the thunder and rains have come. I'd hoped to follow in the footsteps of Chung-yo, an artist who a hundred years ago roamed Emei Shan for months. "So taking my brush along in its bag," he wrote, "I went, combing my hair with the wind and washing my hair with the rain, let down by ropes through dangerous places, and penetrating secluded spots."

I'm no true mountain dweller, I suppose. Fifty years ago, Sheng Chin, abbot of Qingyin, described my dream in the simplest manner: "Formerly I constructed a thatched hut in the mountains, and passed several summers and winters there, subduing my passions and destroying desire." I've built no mountain hut, subdued no passions. I'm ready to return to Chengdu. This is too big a mountain for me.

Emei Shan's signature is its immensity. Layer after layer of terrace, stream, and pinnacle are peeled back as a traveler rises to the summit. And on the summit, on the wide eyebrows of limestone, the boundary between empire and paradise becomes visible. Halos dance on a sea of clouds. The shrunken cities are 1,000 miles to the east and the Western Paradise but one fatal step away.

PRACTICAL INFORMATION

ORIENTATION

Emei Shan (also written as Omei Shan) is 87 miles south of **Chengdu,** the capital of Sichuan Province in southwestern China. The mountain is far inland, about 1,100 miles southwest of Beijing, 1,200 miles west of Shanghai.

The nearest towns, both to the east, are Emei, where there is a railway station, and Baoguo, which is inside the mountain entrance gates. Emei Shan occupies a large territory. The slopes contain 50 miles of trails and about 30 active Buddhist temples. Minibuses link major temples along the way with the base and summit.

Emei Shan was inscribed as a natural and cultural World Heritage site by UNESCO in 1996. It has designated protection zones for plants (including 29 species of rhododendron) and landscapes. Ten percent of China's plant species grow here. Threatened animal species include the red panda, Asiatic black bear, Asiatic golden cat, and Tibetan macaque.

The climate ranges from subtropical to cold-alpine, depending on altitude and season. The base of the mountain is at about 1,500 feet elevation, while the summit is over 10,000 feet. Winters are cold and snowy, making climbing dangerous. Summers are rainy and hot. Early spring and late autumn are the mildest periods to visit.

Nearby places to visit are the **Great Buddha at Leshan,** 25 miles east of Emei Shan, and Chengdu, with a myriad of attractions. See "Chengdu: Temples & Pandas" and "The Great Buddha at Leshan" for complete information.

GETTING THERE

Chengdu is the gateway to Emei Shan, and it can be reached by train or air from all over China. See the Chengdu chapter for details. From Chengdu, you can reach Emei Shan by the following means:
By Train There are several trains daily serving Emei Town from Chengdu. This is a 3-hour trip. Minibuses and taxis connect the Emei Train Station (which is 2 miles east of town) to the mountain entrance at Baoguo (20 minutes; $1.25 fare).
By Bus Buses leave for Emei Shan all morning from the North Railway Station in Chengdu, pulling in at either Emei Town or Baoguo Town. Baoguo is the best terminal, since it is where the mountain trails begin. Emei Town is connected to Baoguo Town by minibuses (20 minutes; $1.20 fare). The bus from Chengdu

costs RMB 30 to 50 ($3.60 to $6) each way and takes 4 to 6 hours.

Many of these buses to Emei Shan are actually group tours (RMB 50/$6) that stop at Meishan, a town on the way, and at the Leshan Great Buddha. I don't advise taking a Chinese tour bus, since they spend only two nights on the mountain and restrict the time you can spend there. Try to book a bus that goes just to Baoguo from Chengdu. From Baoguo, which is a one-street town, it is easy to book a ticket back to Chengdu at any time.

TOURS & STRATAGEMS

Emei Shan is a large, confusing mountain park. Base yourself either in Baoguo Town at the entrance, or 7 miles by road up the mountain at Jin Shui. Baoguo Town has the best hotels and restaurants, while Jin Shui puts travelers closer to the major temples and sites.

Visitor Information   Emei Shan tickets are sold at the entrance near the Baoguo Temple and cost RMB 40 ($4.80). The mountain hotels and temples are not good sources of information, with the exception of the Red Spider Mountain Hotel (Hongzhushan Binguan) in Baoguo Town (see below). Freelance tour guides, often speaking little if any English, abound in the hotel lobbies, temple courtyards, and village streets. I don't think they're worth hiring, although a guide can be handy when it comes to ordering food in a temple, cafe, or at a trailside stall.

Exploring the Mountain   Reaching the upper peak at Jinding (Golden Summit) for the sunrise is a problem. It's too far to hike, especially in darkness. You can stay overnight at Jinding in the temple (see below) or take a predawn bus from Baoguo (2 hours) or Jin Shui (1 hour). Below the summit, at Jieyan Hall, a cable car runs up to the Golden Summit (RMB 50/$6 round-trip) from the last parking lot, but the lines in the early morning are very long for the 20-minute trip.

From the Golden Summit, there are trails to the highest peak (Wanfoding), a 30-minute walk, or back down to Jieyin Pavilion, a 2-hour trek. Six to 8 hours later (or more) brings one back to Jin Shui, halfway down the mountain.

The mountain has two main parallel trails. The northern and southern trails rise westward to the summit from Baoguo, coming together at Qingyin Ge (Clear Sound Pavilion), then splitting. The northern trail proceeds through Wannian Temple, with a branch trail north to Jin Shui. The southern trail continues up from Qingyin Ge through Monkey Hill. The two trails merge again and fuse below Xixiang Chi (Elephant Bathing Pool), beyond which there are more packs of monkeys and ultimately the cable car and summit.

To see all the temples and explore the trails and vistas fully takes many days. Temples provide very basic sleeping quarters and meals (vegetarian). Weather can change quickly, so layers of warm (and cool) clothing are required, as are reliable hiking shoes and rain gear.

WHERE TO STAY

The monasteries and temples offer extremely basic accommodations (basic room with dormitory-style beds, quilts, washbasins, and little else) for about RMB 60 ($7.25) a night.

At **Jieyin Pavilion,** near the cable-car terminus, at Jin Shui, and in Baoguo Town, there are also some modest guesthouses that have rundown, moldy doubles with rundown, moldy private bathrooms and not much else. Doubles cost RMB 180 to 250 ($21.75 to $30). The only hotel of note is in Baoguo Town.

Red Spider Mountain Hotel (Hongzhushan Binguan). *Baoguo Town (on a side road running south off the highway connecting the town and the temple).* ☎ *08426/52-5888. Fax 08426/ 52-5666. 180 rms. A/C TV TEL. $60 double. JCB, MC, V.* Consisting of a dozen wings and buildings, this villa-style hotel has a 3-star section with modern doubles. They provide foreign exchange, overnight laundry, and most importantly a tour desk. This is the place to get maps of the mountain trails and travel advice. The hotel also books train and bus tickets.

WHERE TO DINE

The major temples all have vegetarian restaurants. The food is cheap (RMB 18 to 25/$2 to $3 a meal) and bland. Trailside stands serve up noodles and soup at even cheaper rates, as well as bottled water and canned sodas.

In Baoguo Town, the **Teddy Bear Cafe** (on the main highway) has an English-language menu and some Western dishes. Best of all, this is the place to get practical information on Emei Shan—where to stay, where to eat, where to book train or bus tickets. The owner speaks English and English-speaking local guides often turn up here.

HUA SHAN: SACRED MOUNTAIN OF THE WEST

华山

THE MOST ANCIENT GODS OF CHINESE civilization once dwelt upon Hua Shan, a mountain sharp enough to bend the Yellow River to the sea. The first emperor and his successors performed the spring and autumn rites here for a thousand years, praying to the mountain god to open Heaven to Earth. Daoist hermits, alchemists, and sorcerers retreated to Hua Shan where they became the immortals of Chinese tradition. And countless pilgrims, scaling the almost impossible heights, sought a glimpse of Heaven, a taste of immortality in the open hand of Buddha—in the crown of five peaks at the summit of Hua Shan, the Flowery Mountain.

It was 9 years earlier that I first climbed this mountain, an altogether remarkable event. I return now to see if the changes that are transforming China in the final decade of the 20th century have reached all the way to this holy mountain of the West.

At the Gate to the Mountain

At the Xi'an long-distance bus depot, Eddie Han bought us cheap tickets to Hua Shan. Eddie was a young English teacher I'd met a day earlier. When he heard I was returning to the sacred mountain, he offered to accompany me. I knew that with a local Chinese along, the journey would be smoother. The bus depot was infested with beggars, entire families in rags. Eddie said they were lazy, but he gave money to the children.

Every seat on the bus to Hua Shan was taken. Because two passengers refused to pay two extra mao (about 4¢), the bus did not use the new four-lane toll road. After 3 hours of the usual delays and discomforts, a mountain range erupted to the south, dwarfing the mud villages. We reached Hua Yin Village at the foot of Hua Shan an hour later. Touts hit us like an updraft of gnats.

This village was a wide spot in the road 9 years ago, when I stayed in a one-dollar room, but today Hua Yin is another tourist trap. The tourists are Chinese. I don't see a single foreigner. The strip to the mountain gate

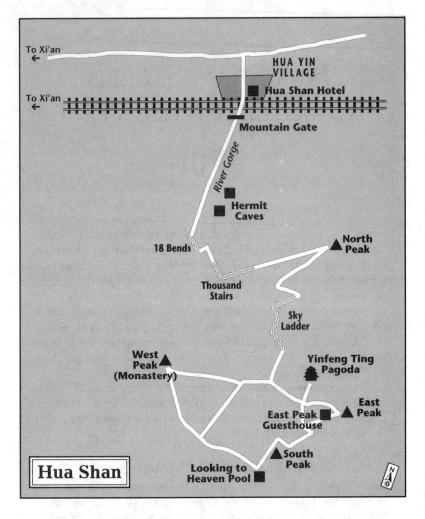

To Xi'an ←

HUA YIN VILLAGE

Hua Shan Hotel

To Xi'an ←

Mountain Gate

River Gorge

Hermit Caves

18 Bends

Thousand Stairs

North Peak

Sky Ladder

West Peak (Monastery)

Yinfeng Ting Pagoda

East Peak Guesthouse

East Peak

South Peak

Looking to Heaven Pool

Hua Shan

N

is glutted with pedestrians, shops, and vendors. A new hotel, half finished, boasts an amusement arcade in the shape of a fiberglass dragon that swallows families whole. I really don't recognize the street or the village now, but change in China is always sudden.

Three old women hound us, selling incense. We're on the grounds of **Jade Spring Temple,** "picturesquely situated at the start of the ascent to the mountain," as Hedda Morrison has written. The adventurous Mrs. Morrison photographed Hua Shan in the summer of 1935. In her book of photographs, she writes that the "importance of Hua Shan lay partly in its proximity to the early centers of Chinese civilization, and partly in its being a supreme example of the type of landscape so appreciated by Chinese artists." The "spectacular mountain forms" and "solitary, cloud-capped peaks" of Hua Shan captivated her, captivated the great Song Dynasty painters, and first captivated me in the 1980s. In 1935, one could spend a night in the Jade Spring Temple and enjoy a hearty vegetarian meal prepared by monks. Today, the temple has been demolished; the meals, served from a hundred stalls, are neither Daoist nor Buddhist; and Eddie and I are forced to buy tickets just to cross the temple's foundations. At the mountain gate, we're detained again. I'm required to buy a special permit for foreigners. Altogether, I fork over RMB 48 ($5.75) before I can hit the trail.

River Gorge of 18 Bends

It's the same mountain, yet nothing is the same. The trail up the mountain river has been widened, smoothed over, and filled in with solid granite curbstones. A power line runs along the bank. New gates arch over the path, and small vendor-towns, roofed with cloth awnings, crop up every quarter mile. The sheer white cliffs on the other side of the river are altered, too. They once served religious hermits as remote refuges. Carving a few ladder rungs up the cliffside, those ancient ascetics disappeared for months into high, unapproachable caves. Today, several "hermit caves" have been carved out and opened to visitors.

I still see some Daoist monks on the trail, but the essence of the mountain—wild, distant, fierce, holy—has disappeared from the lower flanks. The dreams with which I endowed my first trek up Hua Shan dissolve into fresh pavement, souvenir stands, and sedan chairs with green bamboo poles, their carriers for hire. At the mountain gate there are even tennis shoes for rent.

The Thousand Stairs

The second phase of the journey, however, where we leave the river canyon for the stone spires of the peak, is not without its terrors, even in this modern age. People still die on Hua Shan every year, falling from its edges. Even the sedan chair carriers drop back here, 2 steep miles from the top. "In places the track led up almost perpendicular rock faces in which steps had been hewn and iron chains of uncertain reliability set in the rock to provide hand-holds," Mrs. Morrison wrote in 1935. "Some of the sheer stretches were for one-way traffic only, and when we reached them we would call out so as to ensure that we did not meet some descending pilgrim half way."

Little has changed here. I know these stairs well; they are something one never forgets. I once saw a porter lose his load on this stone ladder, these "Thousand Stairs." Today, this chimney, which actually consists of two long streamers, has been rehewn and widened, but the chains are still in place. It is just as steep as ever, although there are now separate staircases up and down, and the small temple at the top of the stairs, which once had an iron trapdoor to seal off the mountain from intruders, is long gone.

Other temples along the way have been rebuilt since I visited, but they seem empty. Those on the North Peak—the thumb of the five-fingered Hua Shan cluster—straddle a narrow spine of stone, dramatic from a distance. Eddie and I reach the North Peak in our third hour of quick climbing. We order a roadside dinner, a horrible one, and over-priced. Eddie confides that as soon as vendors see me, the prices double.

Hedda Morrison once tarried for days at the **North Peak Monastery,** where she met five Daoist priests and a boy sent to them for his health by anxious parents in Shanghai. Later she would meet a pilgrim who had traveled to the top of Hua Shan by foot, all the way from Beijing.

The Sky Ladder

The North Peak is connected to the other peaks of the compass by "a hair-raising track . . . known as the Sky Ladder" with a sheer drop-off on both sides—the stone web between thumb and fingers. Beyond that lies an even more terrifying traverse, the Azure Dragon's Ledge, which has now been removed from the trail entirely.

A Tang Dynasty poet, Po Chu-i (A.D. 772–846), described the ledge succinctly: "The chasm beneath me, ten thousand feet; / The ground I stood on, only one foot wide."

By the time Eddie and I cross this final bridge to the peaks of the immortals—where the white fungus of wisdom grows and beans said to satisfy one's hunger for 49 days sprout—the sky has darkened, the wind has chilled. We mount the East Peak, then traverse the hand of the mountain to the West Peak, where I stayed 9 years ago. I'm hoping the old monastery where I spent a night remains, that it has not been redone, that I can say of it, "You're no Holiday Inn."

West Peak Monastery

I'm not disappointed: The **monastery on West Peak** has not been spruced up or made over one iota, save that the outdoor toilet once cantilevered over the cliff edge has been swept away. The rooms are unrepentantly crude. Only the price has kept up with the times: We must pay RMB 25 ($3) apiece (as much as Eddie pays for a modern guesthouse in Xi'an) plus an RMB 15 ($1.80) surcharge for my not being Chinese. Our suite is a cubicle on the top floor with two hard cots, each with a dirty quilt. The foot of Eddie's bed collapses every time he sits on it.

A bare electric bulb dangles from the ceiling. When it quits, a monk arrives with a kerosene lantern. We secure the door with a brick. There's no bathroom down the hall and no water, neither a thermos nor a basin; we can't even wash up. I like it. The room hasn't improved with the decade. The lattice ceiling is stuffed with bamboo matting and newspaper.

A few sections of white butcher paper are tacked up here and there. The wooden floorboards are rotting away. The paper walls and loose window-panes rattle in the night wind, sounding like a scurrying army of rats.

This monastery will leak and creak all night. I lie back on the hard pillow, zip up my windbreaker and pull on my stocking cap, and crawl under the quilt to warm up.

I'm haunted by a fine photograph that Hedda Morrison composed in 1935 of two Daoist monks in ceremonial combat, one armed with a sword, the other with a fly swatter. "The fly whisk, made from a yak's tail and known as a cloud sweeper," Mrs. Morrison explains, "is thought to im-part the ability to ride the clouds."

I feel too heavy in limb and bone to levitate on this edge of the void. There will be no visions of holy peaks and Daoist immortals to sugar-plum my sleep tonight—just hard facts, hard as the pallet upon which I fall to rest.

In Buddha's Palm

We wake on the mountain at dawn, leave the monastery, and circle the peaks—the five petals of the stone lotus. We stop beside an empty crater, the **Looking to Heaven Pool.** In 1932, when the Australian maverick, Rewi Alley, accompanied by R. Lapwood, arrived at the summit of Hua Shan after an "ascent that surpassed all our expectations," he discovered the same pool filled with rainwater. "Here farmers still prayed to the Black Dragon for rain," he wrote. Here Alley met a monk, who claiming to be 120 years old was said to have gone sleepless for 20 years running, tend-ing his herb gardens both by sun and moon.

The mountain was once pregnant with fantastical stories of hermits who became immortals endowed with the power of flight. Only the clouds remain. Ancient kings are said to have paid homage at Hua Shan as early as 1766 B.C. Qin Shi Huang Di, the first emperor of unified China, is believed to have reached the summit in his search for the white fungus. The first emperor of the Ming Dynasty dreamed of his ascent up this pillar of Heaven. Lao Zi, the ancient founder of Daoism, left his iron plough here, although no one's seen it lately. Guanyin, Goddess of Mercy, once had her likeness carved in a valley between peaks at the Holy Stove Temple, where she shared the altar with Lao Zi and his cow.

The Jade Maiden of Chinese myth was celebrated on Hua Shan, too—she arrived on the back of an ethereal dragon. The whole mountain is in the shape of a dragon, some say. The true god of this mountain may well be the dragon, once synonymous with the essential form of China. There is Chinese legend that a dragon coiled itself over these slopes and depos-ited its skeleton on the outside, forming the dramatic ridges. The steep cliffs are antediluvian.

What strikes Eddie about the rock walls of Hua Shan, however, is their color: white, bone white. Indeed, the presiding God of the Mountain is the White Spirit. According to Reverend Geil, who left an exhaustive trove of stories about Hua Shan after his visit in the 1920s, the White Spirit resides on the very same West Peak where I spent last night. Wearing white robes and a top hat, the White Spirit could open and close the doorway to Heaven. He rode a white dragon in a procession of 4,100 fairies.

I take a final glance at Hua Shan's West Peak, its supreme summit, the edge of the void with a view of the Yellow River valley, the cradle of Chinese civilization, where Xi'an stands. One can see why emperors came to this peak to validate their reigns. It is nature at its grandest. Indeed, in 1383, Wang-Li composed his classic album of Chinese travel pictures here, some 40 landscapes that forever defined nature in China. The scenes survive today in the Palace Museum at Beijing and in the Shanghai Museum, but the original persists in nature, little altered by humans. One can still feel how Hua Shan became the ultimate refuge not only for hermits but for exiles of all stripes, politicians out of favor, disinherited children, criminals and saints. Hua Shan's beauty is wild, belonging more to the clouds than the streams and the earth. It is as if we can see the very mold of nature at the instant it was pulled away into the stars, the rock not quite cooled.

Hua Shan's dome is a summit worthy of the word, of bare rounded white granite, with the cleaver mark of a hero of the old myths on its skull, its flanks as sheer and long as any in the Middle Kingdom, seeming to roll straight down to the plains of dust where China was born. This was once the cliff of divine suicides where pilgrims threw themselves into undifferentiated space, high above all worldly shapes, praying for the heavens to open and swallow them up . . . the dragon in stone, today repaved and reinterpreted, its temples transformed into cafes and souvenir sheds, its immortals into faint clouds, its scales into the stuff of a traveler's fantasy.

Back to the Future

We descend Hua Shan rapidly, stopping only once for plastic bottles of mineral water and a repast of boiled eggs, greasy donuts, and millet gruel. There are mothers and fathers coming up the mountain with babies in their arms, but I encounter few of the devout old women, feet bound, who took on Hua Shan the first time I did. There are plenty of couples on outdoor adventures. They purchase padlocks to secure to the chain-link rails near the summit, a way of commemorating their love, and toss the keys into the abyss.

As for China's mythic past, most of that has been looted and dispersed. The essence of the new Hua Shan is a mad rush, a commercial opportunity, a street of touts that runs from Xi'an to this remote summit once believed to hold up the heavens. Nine years ago, Hua Shan touched and changed me; now, in a harder age, I come and go like a shadow.

PRACTICAL INFORMATION

ORIENTATION

Hua Shan (Flowery Mountain) is located 75 miles east of Xi'an in Shanxi Province, 500 miles southwest of Beijing in central China near the Yellow River. The village of Hua Yin is at the foot of the mountain, which reaches an elevation of 6,552 feet. With cold winters and hot summers, spring and autumn are the best seasons to visit.

The historic city of Xi'an serves as the travelers' gateway to the mountain, the most beautiful and steep of the nine sacred mountains. (See "Xi'an: The Old Capital.")

GETTING THERE

By Plane   Xi'an can be reached by air from Hong Kong (2^1/2 hours), Beijing (1^1/2 hours), Shanghai (1 hour 40 minutes), and many other Chinese cities. There are overnight trains from Beijing (17 hours), Chengdu (19 hours), and Shanghai (24 hours).

By Train & Bus   From Xi'an, there are direct trains in the morning (2^1/2 hours). The train station at Hua Shan Town is a 20-minute walk east from Hua Yin Village at the foot of the mountain. Buses leave daily (3 to 4 hours). The faster buses use the new four-lane expressway. Train and bus tickets may be purchased at hotels in Xi'an or from the terminals, which are located at the northern end of Jiefang Lu, just inside the Xi'an city wall.

TOURS & STRATAGEMS

Visitor Information   China International Travel Service (CITS) in Xi'an, 32 Chang'an Lu (☎ 029/526-2066), with branches at the Holiday Inn (☎ 029/727-9200, ext. 2842) and the Jiefang Hotel (☎ 029/743-1023), can arrange bus and train tickets to Hua Shan. CITS can also provide English-speaking guides and hired cars. Hotel tour desks in Xi'an might also be able to provide assistance.

Exploring the Mountain   Entrance admissions, collected at several points at the base of the mountain, will total about RMB 50 ($6).

It is now possible to tour Hua Shan as a day trip from Xi'an, thanks to a new cable car (RMB 40/$5 round-trip) that makes the ascent to the North Peak, a 2-hour hike from the entrance gate.

Buses return from Hua Yin Village to Xi'an as late as 8pm.

The full mountain experience, however, demands an ascent on foot. The trail is about 9 miles from base to summit, requiring 6 to 8 hours. The last 2 miles of the ascent are steep and narrow. This is the most dangerous of the nine sacred mountains to climb, with vertical stone steps, chain-link rails, and deep drop-offs along the way.

If you base yourself in a guesthouse at Hua Yin Village, you can climb up and down in one long day. You can also stay overnight on the West Peak in a monastery, thereby being on the summit to watch the sunrise. The vista from the West Peak is quite dramatic.

WHERE TO STAY

The **Hua Shan Binguan**, west on Jianshe Lu two blocks from the mountain entrance gate (☎ 0913/66-1836), is the best place to stay in Hua Yin Village. Basic doubles with private baths cost RMB 350 ($42). You don't get much in the way of amenities or services (no credit cards accepted), but the view from the rooms at the rear are superb. Ignore the guesthouse touts who work the main road to the mountain gate; the accommodations they are hawking are not clean or comfortable.

On the summit of Hua Shan, rooms are available in the **Daoist monastery on West Peak.** These are like rundown barracks with two narrow beds and no private baths or even sinks—just a place to sleep under a quilt, with no heat or air-conditioning. Doubles are about RMB 85 ($10). On the East Peak, there is a small modern hotel, the **East Peak Guesthouse (Dong Feng Fandian).** Doubles with private baths are overpriced at RMB 500 ($62), but it's the best hotel on Hua Shan and is a superb viewpoint at sunrise.

WHERE TO DINE

If Hua Shan is a day trip, try to pack and take along all your food and snacks. Water and drinks can be purchased on the trail. The trailside vendors and village cafes are expensive (RMB 85 to 168/ $10 to $20) and the food is nothing special. The best restaurants are in the hotels and guesthouses, where the dishes are basic Chinese combinations of vegetables, noodles, and meats.

SONG SHAN: SACRED MOUNTAIN OF THE CENTER

嵩山

S ONG SHAN (HIGH MOUNTAIN) IS THE Daoist peak at the center of China. According to a Chinese mountain guide, the people "thought that Song Shan lay directly under the heart of heaven and on the liver of the Earth," and they called it the "pearl in the cradle of ancient Chinese civilization." Of its many temples, the two most famous still exist: Zhong Yue, China's oldest Daoist temple, and Shao Lin, world center of the martial arts and birthplace of Zen Buddhism.

The 72 peaks of Song Shan are situated in Henan Province between two ancient capitals, Luoyang to the west and Zhengzhou to the east. I approach the mythic middle of the Middle Kingdom from Luoyang, turning east at Shao Lin Monastery for the holy city of Dengfeng at the southern foot of Song Shan.

Dengfeng is an ugly strip, once glorious. It was the capital of the early Xia civilization, then hometown of the holy Central Mountain. It received its present name in the 7th century when Empress Wu of the Tang Dynasty—one of the most notorious figures in all of Chinese history—built her summer home in the foothills, Dengfeng, meaning "Ascend to Bestow Honors."

I check into a modern but already aging and decrepit hotel. The electric lights don't work, no water runs in the tub, and the door to my room doesn't lock. Still, it's spacious and I have a view of the peaks of Song Shan to the north. The Central Mountain is a formidable wall of bare white rock peaks, once described by Wang Wei, a Tang Dynasty poet, as "towering aloft in the skies and piercing halfway to Heaven."

Imperial Academy

My aim this afternoon is not to climb to the top but to visit a few of the famous sites on the lower flanks of Song Shan. I have no map, but I can see the range to the north. I set out in that direction, looking for a likely road out of town. After an hour of bad guesses and detours, I discover a path into the hills. It quickly leads me to **Song Yang Academy.**

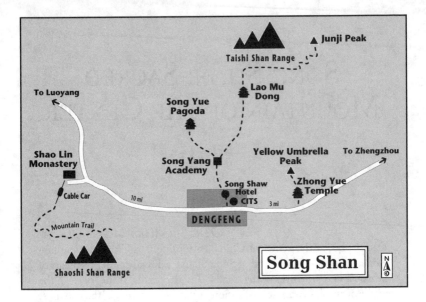

When China's capital was at Xi'an and later Luoyang, the intelligentsia enjoyed the coolness of summers at Dengfeng, and there they established this academy, one of China's four great centers of Confucian learning. Song Yang began as a Daoist temple. The Han emperor, Wu Di (140–87 B.C.), pausing here on his way to perform the spring rites on Song Shan, planted three **cypress trees**, the "Three Generals," two of which survive, so it's believed. They certainly look like antiquities, gnarled and grand, venerable enough to stake a claim to a birthday 2,000 years ago.

Tang Emperor Gaozhong made this site his residence for a short while in A.D. 683. It became an imperial academy as early as A.D. 951 and served as a Confucian college for nine centuries, reaching its zenith under Emperor Kangxi in China's final dynasty. In 1936, General Chiang Kai-shek, who lost the civil war to Mao, celebrated his 50th birthday at the academy and ordered the digging of a well, which still works.

Plenty of history here—but now Song Yang Academy is just a few tiled-roof buildings inside a low wall with a ticket taker at a table and some soft drink vendors on the doorstep. It's a museum inside, its 60 rooms all renovated within the last 100 years. The academy's most impressive monument is in the front courtyard, a massive 8th-century stele (carved stone tablet) 30 feet tall, crowned with an elaborate sculpture of two lions clasping a ball in their raised paws. Its inscription reports that in A.D. 744 Emperor Xuanzong, age 61, took a beautiful young concubine, Yang Kuei-fei, and, in consequence thereof, promptly ordered the Daoist alchemists at the Song Yang Academy to hand over the elixir of eternal youth. Apparently, the transaction went awry, as emperor and concubine achieved immortality only in story and myth.

The Oldest Pagoda in China

From the academy I strike northward through wheat fields, in search of the oldest brick pagoda in China. The land is hard, filled with white stones, and dry. There are dirt caves under the green terraces where farmers store seed and cuttings, even machinery. I follow a streambed uphill until I catch sight of a brick pagoda. I cut across a field of brush, scale a hillside, and ford a rock-terraced stream. Teams of stonecutters, sundarkened men in black topcoats hauling sizable sledgehammers, are working up and down the streambed.

On the other side of the stream I find a highway. Walking along it for an hour, I finally reach **Song Yue (High Peak) Temple** and the old pagoda. The grounds are in a sorry state. There's some rehabilitation in progress, but the temple walls have caved in. The uncut courtyard grasses, green and yellow, nip at my thighs. Several halls and pavilions are tumbling down. And the complex is deserted. At its heart is China's oldest brick pagoda, 12-sided like the zodiac, 15 stories high, damaged but still solid, the shape of a pinecone growing skyward. The pagoda's tip is carved into an inverted lotus leaf that serves as the platform for the Buddhist wheel of life. There are 500 doors and windows in its walls, many fitted with carved figures, including 40 lions.

It's the sole pagoda of this style in China, piled 123 feet high with small black bricks mortared into a 12-sided cosmic wheel spinning into the heart of Heaven. Empress Wu Zetian stayed the night here in A.D. 696. The pagoda was already a relic then—nearly two centuries old. It dates from A.D. 520. The temple was founded even earlier, in 509, to serve as a portable shrine-away-from-home for the Northern Wei royals. It still looks as if it were in some kind of catastrophic transit.

I climb back down the white stone hills. The sky above the distant shafts of Song Shan is blue. The riverbed of the mountain is being paved in stone. Work crews are breaking, ferrying, and laying rock. The water that pours down from Song Shan has a long tradition of purity and curative powers. Recent research claims that no one living within 3 miles of the river has ever suffered a single cancer.

First Mountain of the World

The sky is a sharp and even blue when I set out for the central peak of the Central Mountain just after dawn. My destination is **Junji Feng,** elevation 4,900 feet. It requires 30 minutes to retrace my steps up the river basin to Song Yang Academy. I skirt the academy wall and follow the power lines up a steep embankment to a gravel road. A few more twists and I'm above the final foothill. The highest peak of Song Shan lies straight ahead, one among a pack of 36 peaks.

The road gives way to a path of stone steps rising up the river basin. A temple hangs on the last terrace below the cliffs. In the river basin I hear the pings of chisels against stone. The temple on the terrace is named **Lao Mu Dong.** I know nothing of its heritage, but someone is investing money in its restoration. Vendors have congregated upon its grounds. I purchase two boiled eggs and a can of soda.

Behind the temple is a stairway to the summit, fashioned from hewn blocks, each the size and shape of a small stele. I've spent almost two hours just to reach this temple. It will take me another two hours to gain the top, all of it by stairs that look like they will never level out.

I pass through another temple that is on no map I've ever come across. It too is being restored. It is already active with monks dressed in long black robes. Several worshippers have black beards, a rare sight in most parts of China.

Against the wall of a massive peak, the trail bends east. I stop at a shrine, a single building at the back of a ledge. A young man comes out on the porch. I can't tell if he is monk or merchant. I can tell he is very poor. He also has no hands and no wrists. He smiles at me. He knows one English phrase: "Okay." "Okay," he laughs. "Okay."

Carved into a cliff across the way are characters announcing that Song Shan is the First Mountain of the World. Ahead is a staircase of a hundred treads or so, and beyond that more staircases switching back and forth up the sheer face of the peak. A steel railing has been installed. I can see a figure or two on the pinnacles above, and I meet two or three groups of hikers on the stairs. Otherwise, the trail is deserted. The last vendor I come across has pitched his cart on a narrow ledge between staircases. I buy a can of soda.

This high up, I can survey the entire Dengfeng Valley to the south, hazy in the dust. To the west, I can see a second mountain range—the western half of Song Shan, known as Shao Shi Shan, the junior range, with Shao Lin Monastery at its foot. I'm scaling the Tai Shi Shan half of Song Shan, the eastern half, the "great" side. These are the same peaks that once attracted emperors and pilgrims, although they now attract almost no one.

Summitry

Each flight of stairs becomes more tedious. The sun is fierce. It seems to take me hours to surmount the last ladder of steps. The top of Junji Peak is farther still. Three women gathering plants and herbs motion for me to sit down beside them on a green patch. They proceed to eat their lunch. They aren't in the least disturbed that we speak few words in common. I sit down with them and finish my drink.

At noon I reach a construction site marked with red-and-white flags. The summit is a few steps more. And on this summit, this central summit of the Central Kingdom, halfway between the midpoints of Heaven and Earth, what is there? There is nothing. There is no temple, no altar, no marker, no ruin. There is not even a vendor. There is only nature: a slope of green grass and white stone.

In December of A.D. 696, Empress Wu stood here, on this summit, paid homage to the earth, and appointed Song Shan to be emperor of Middle Heaven.

Wu entered royal life as a concubine for one Tang Dynasty emperor, became the consort of his successor, and succeeded them both as supreme ruler and China's first great empress in A.D. 684. Hoping to establish an immortal dynasty of her own, she made Song Shan her sacred residence. The mountain was given an imperial title. Her prayer to the God of Song Shan, engraved on a tablet of gold weighing 280 grams, was unearthed in 1982 on the summit.

The view on a cloudless day from the top of Song Shan is a fine one. For the first time I see why the ancients maintained that the sky was round and the earth square.

A Tall, Dark Stranger

An hour passes at the summit. I turn back. As I pass the new buildings, a man with a dark beard, a man dressed in black patches, a very dark man, stops me. He raises both hands and touches his fingertips, forming a pyramid at the base of his neck. I mirror his greeting. He reaches out a hand. We shake. He invites me to accompany him inside; I decline. He stands aside; I walk down the mountain.

Mao Ch'i-ling (1623–1716), on his second attempt to scale Song Shan, met a stranger, too: one who revealed to him the secrets of true Confucian wisdom, transforming his life. Me, I just keep walking up and down in China. It takes me 3 hours to descend, each mile slower than the last, until I'm amazed I can move at all. I see almost no one on the way back. The herb gatherers have disappeared, the stonecutters vanished.

Zhong Yue Temple

China's modern travelers do not come to Song Shan to climb peaks. They come to visit the temples—either Zhong Yue, the Daoist temple to the Central Mountain, or Shao Lin, the Buddhist temple to Zen and the martial arts.

Zhong Yue lies 3 miles to the east of Dengfeng; Shao Lin, 10 miles in the opposite direction. Both are on the main highway; neither require a climb.

Twelve centuries ago, Zhong Yue Miao, the Central Peak Temple, was one of the three greatest Daoist temples in China, consisting of nearly a thousand halls and pavilions. The God of the Central Mountain lived in the temple. Since Han times he had presided over quite an assortment of geographies and beings: over rivers and valleys, mountains and fields, sheep and oxen, fruits and food—over nearly everything, animate and inanimate.

It is thought that the temple was visited by Han Emperor Wu Di in 110 B.C. and that it was founded in the time of the first dynasty, the Qin (221–207 B.C.). Today, of course, Zhong Yue is shrunken—what hasn't of ancient China under the press of the new centuries—and the buildings aren't old, dating back only a century or two to when the Qing emperors visited and sacrificed oxen in the spring on the platform of the main hall. There were still 11 courtyards and plenty of gnarled trees, as many as 1,000 old trees, 300 of them said to have been planted over 1,000 years ago.

A few courtyards deep, I find the famous **Four Iron Guards,** statues 10 feet tall, fierce in their armor, modeled after the soldiers of the time and cast in A.D. 1064. Some children swing from their iron fists. Daoist monks sit at tables nearby, dressed in dark blue robes, white leggings, and straw hats, incense for sale.

The courtyards are full of worldly vendors, too. One photographer poses customers on the back of a stuffed tiger. Another sells shots in a pellet gun aimed at a wall of balloons—strange entertainment at a temple.

The stele I most want to find is known as "The True Map of the Five Mountains." It was carved in 1604. A magic symbol for each mountain— Heng Shan Nan to the south and Hua Shan to the west, Heng Shan Bei to the north and Tai Shan to the east—is placed on its compass point, with Song Shan, where I now stand, in the center. I find the Five Mountains tablet out in the open, exposed to the elements, and a bit worn these days, its rounded topstone washed smooth, but the five mysterious characters for the Sacred Five are still clear 500 years after they were carved.

Outside the last hall is the path up **Yellow Umbrella Peak (Huangtai Feng),** where Han emperor Wu Di noticed a big patch of yellow cloud as he made his ascent of Song Shan. There's an ornate little pavilion up there now, and those who want a quick holy climb wander up there in droves.

The Fighting Wooden Monks of Shao Lin

I return to the highway and catch a bus back through Dengfeng and on to **Shao Lin Monastery,** 9 miles farther west. Shao Lin is a monument to mass tourism Chinese style. Open daily from 8am to 6pm, it's a commercial maze of souvenir vendors inside and outside the temple complex, always crowded. The problem is that even the People's Republic of China is doing kung-fu films that glorify the fighting monks of Shao Lin, and they're filming them right here, on the actual site. This is China's Universal City Studios of Flying Fists, the spiritual and commercial world center of the martial arts.

I'm here to see history and culture, and I suppose that's what I'm seeing. This is the center of the modern Chinese centrifuge—in brute contrast with the quiet old peak I reached yesterday, virtually alone.

Certainly Shao Lin Monastery has plenty of Old China attached to it, too. Shao Lin was founded in A.D. 495 by Emperor Xiao Wen Di of the Northern Wei Dynasty and expanded and enriched by the second Tang Dynasty emperor in 625 in gratitude to the monks who helped him wage war against a rival. In between, in 527, Da Mo, also known as Bodhidharma, the 28th incarnation of the Buddha, arrived from India, crossing the Yangzi River on a reed. At Shao Lin, he spent nine years in solitary meditation staring at the wall of a cave. The cave is still here: Even the shadow he left on the cave's wall is still here. When Da Mo emerged from nine years of "wall-contemplation," he founded a new sect of Buddhism, known as Chan in China, as Zen in Japan.

Da Mo also picked up credit for formulating the Chinese style of hand-to-hand combat known as *wu shu* or more popularly kung fu. Unconcerned about shifting from religion to religion, it seems, good Zen Buddhist patriarch Da Mo is also said to have written Daoist classics on the cultivation of the muscles and the purification of the marrow.

The martial arts, not Zen, are what bring the tourists in these days. In the 15th and 16th centuries, the fighting monks of Shao Lin were taking on the pesky Japanese pirates off China's coast. During the 1920s, when China was in civil turmoil and local warlords held sway, the Shao Lin Temple was a haven for runaway soldiers who terrorized the local population. In 1928, one of the most famous of these warlords, Feng Yuxiang (Shi Yousan), the "Christian general," routed the monks and set fire to the monastery. Shao Lin burned for 40 days.

I elbow my way through the late morning crowds to see **Thousand Buddha Hall,** built in 1588, with its fading fresco of monks going all out in martial arts battle—it would make a dandy movie poster—and the single most famous temple floor in China, roped off now and unlighted, where the monks practiced their stompings and leaps so diligently that the heavy stone floor became indented. Even cursory inspection suggests to me that the water table was high or the subsoil unstable under this floor, and that here and there it simply sank. I have a concrete driveway that looks about the same, and it was poured long after the 16th century.

To stretch the imagination further, I line up for a peek at the **Shadow Stone,** removed from Da Mo's cave. A Chinese traveler described it this way in 1623: "I saw the shadow stone of Da Mo. Less than 3 feet high, it was white with the black traces of a vivid standing picture of the foreign patriarch." What I see is a slab of rock, burned or discolored, with the vaguest outlines of a human figure in meditation.

Shao Lin also contains a magnificent **Forest of Stupas,** the largest collection in China of these small brick pagodas that hold holy relics and the remains of great monks, abbots, and even their followers. From what were once 500 stupas, 227 of these grave markers remain. They span 1,000 years of burial, from the Tang to the Qing dynasties. The oldest of the stupas is that of Ching-tsang (A.D. 675–746), built in the year of his death—the oldest stupa in China.

More vibrant, and more in keeping with the holy amusement park atmosphere of modern Shao Lin, is a courtyard surrounded on three sides by open-air displays of wooden life-sized monks in dramatic fighting poses. They look like rather old carvings, but they may be merely dusty. Some are armed with swords or poles and locked in fierce combat. These mannequins of the martial arts are used as models for monks in training. These days Shao Lin does a hefty business running a half-dozen major martial arts schools for everyone from schoolchildren in China to visiting kung-fu clubs from Japan, America, and Europe.

The Far Side of Song Shan

Visiting Shao Lin Monastery in 1965, Australian journalist Rewi Alley was told "about some temples up on the hills, where in times of trouble the monks had gone." There is now a gondola that ferries visitors up the 36 peaks that make up Song Shan's western range—a mirror image of the main cluster of 36 Song Shan peaks that make up the Sacred Mountain proper.

I decide to take a look. From the rising gondola, I can see the Shao Lin Monastery and the tourist road that outlines it like a noose. The crowds and tour buses are brushed out of the picture of the tile roofs, brick walls, and green hills rising to the north. I can see Da Mo's Cave, wherein he emptied his mind so thoroughly that his shadow stuck to the wall.

At the cable-car terminal on the peak, I follow a trail into the woods. It takes me into a world far removed from the Shao Lin circus. Threading my way up towering cliffs, eventually I come out on the southern side of the range. The stone walls that line the back of the western Song Shan are 1,000 feet straight up. The trail slices across the cliff face. Sections of the trail are cantilevered out from the rock, forming catwalks over empty chasms, which I tread across gingerly.

The far side of Song Shan is dazzling. Some parts of the path are wide enough only for single-file passage—hardly a problem, as I meet almost no one coming or going. I zigzag along this natural stone wall for an hour from declivity to declivity. There are a few temples and pavilions in recesses and ledges, but I know nothing about them, not even their names. They are deserted.

Eventually I come to a house perched on a small rock terrace. An old man and his wife invite me inside. The house has a dirt floor, almost no furnishings, and a shrine in a nook with incense burning. They don't seem to want to sell me anything. In fact, they seem out of touch with the world, or mad. I ask them how to get back to Dengfeng Town. They point straight down, and they are serious.

The long slabs of rock that tumble down the cliff from their house contain remnants of a railing, enough of it still pinned to the rock to point the way down. After an hour's steady crawl, I reach a long formal stairway of stone that takes me down to ground zero. At the bottom of the mountain I'm able to hire a motorcycle-driven cart back to Dengfeng. The dirt road rolls across the "liver of the Earth" under the shadow of the 72 peaks that once pierced "the heart of Heaven." Silent, nearly forgotten, Song Shan, in the middle of the Middle Kingdom, has been reclaimed by nature.

PRACTICAL INFORMATION

ORIENTATION

Song Shan is located south of the Yellow River in Henan Province, 420 miles south of Beijing and 550 miles west of Shanghai. The town at the base of the main Song Shan mountain range, Dengfeng, is midway between the cities of Luoyang (50 miles to the west) and Zhengzhou (45 miles to the east).

Shao Lin Monastery is 9 miles west of Dengfeng, at the base of the western (lesser) range of the Song Shan mountains. Zhong Yue Temple, the most important Daoist shrine to the Central Mountain, is 3 miles east of Dengfeng. From Dengfeng, it is a 4-hour climb north to the top of Song Shan. The oldest brick pagoda in China, Song Yue Pagoda, is 3 miles northwest of Dengfeng in the Song Shan foothills.

Other important attractions in the immediate region include the ancient capital of **Kaifeng** and the Buddhist grottoes of Longmen at **Luoyang.** See "Kaifeng: Forgotten Capital of the Northern Song" and "The Buddhist Caves at Longmen (Luoyang)" for more information.

GETTING THERE

There is no airport or train station at Dengfeng.

From Zengzhou to Dengfeng
Zhengzhou is the nearest major transportation hub, with plane connections to major cities in China, including Beijing (1 hour 20 minutes), Guangzhou (2 hours 20 minutes), Hong Kong (2 1/2 hours), and Shanghai (1 hour 20 minutes). Trains serve Zhengzhou from Luoyang (2 hours), Xi'an (10 hours), Beijing (12 hours), Shanghai (14 hours), and Guangzhou (36 hours).

Minibuses connect Dengfeng and the mountain to Luoyang and Zhengzhou, a 2- to 3-hour trip (RMB 20/$2.40). Taxis and hired cars make the trip a little faster and provide more comfort, at a cost of $50 or more, depending on how negotiations go with the driver.

TOURS & STRATAGEMS

Visitor Information The Dengfeng branch of China International Travel Service (CITS) is located in the Song Shan Binguan, 48 Zhong Yue Lu (☎ 0371/287-2137). The staff speaks English and can give helpful information. There are no guided hiking tours to the mountain peaks of Song Shan.

The CITS office in Luoyang, at the Peony Hotel, 15 Zhongzhou Zhong Lu (☎ 0379/491-3699), and in Zhengzhou, at the Novotel Hotel, 114 Jinshui Lu (☎ 0371/595-2072), sometimes provide bus tours of Shao Lin Monastery and Zhong Yue Temple.

Admissions & Open Hours No ticket is required to climb Song Shan from Dengfeng. Entrance fees are charged at Zhong Yue Temple (RMB 5/70¢; open daily 8am to 6pm), Shao Lin Monastery (RMB 35/$4.20; open daily 8am to 6pm), and Song Yue Pagoda (RMB 4/50¢; open daily 8am to 5pm). The gondola from Shao Lin Monastery to the western range of Song Shan is RMB 25 ($3) one way.

WHERE TO STAY

In Dengfeng, the only hotel taking foreigners is the **Song Shan Binguan,** 48 Zhong Yue Lu (☎ 0371/287-2755), at the east edge of town. Rated as 2 stars, this is an aging complex with rundown modern rooms and private baths. I had little hot water and my door did not lock. Doubles are $30. The restaurant out back has large fixed-price Chinese meals that are quite good for $3 to $5. CITS has their offices in a separate building in the front courtyard. No credit cards are accepted here, and the services and amenities are extremely limited, but the staff is friendly and helpful.

Zhengzhou has the best accommodations for hundreds of miles in all directions at the new **Holiday Inn Crowne Plaza,** 115 Jinshui Lu (☎ 800/465-4329 or 0371/595-0055; fax 0371/599-0770). This 5-star, five-floor, 222-room deluxe international hotel has virtually every amenity and service, and takes credit cards (AE, DC, JCB, MC, V). Doubles are $133 (plus 20% surcharge).

WHERE TO DINE

The **Song Shan Binguan,** at the east end of town on the main highway (☎ 0371/287-2755), has the only decent restaurant in Dengfeng. There's no English menu or English speakers on the staff, but foreigners are served hearty fixed-price breakfasts, lunches, and dinners for RMB 25 to 42 ($3 to $5) daily from 7am to 10pm.

HUANG SHAN: CHINA'S MOST BEAUTIFUL MOUNTAIN

黄山

Huang Shan (Yellow Mountain) is the supreme example of Chinese mountain scenery and prime model for classic landscape paintings, as the poets and painters of Old China amply testify. From the Tang Dynasty (618–907) to the Qing (1644–1911), Huang Shan was celebrated in no fewer than 20,000 poems. Li Bai, the Tang's great poet, compared the cluster of peaks at Huang Shan to a golden hibiscus. Twelve centuries later, the modern poet Guo Moruo echoed that sentiment, naming Huang Shan's vistas "the most spectacular under Heaven."

Skeptical of this high-flown hyperbole, I was eager to see the mountain and to draw my own comparisons. My opportunity came more by chance than design. I was descending a nearby mountain when I was befriended by four young lads from Wuhan who were on their way the very next morning for a whirlwind tour of the fabled Yellow Mountain. I couldn't help but tag along. Although I could see the Huang Shan range from where we set out at dawn, the bus required six bone-rattling hours to reach it. On the way, we were stopped cold by a broad placid lake, where the bus had to board a ferry.

It was just after noon by the time we reached the village of Tangkuo, at the southern tip of the park. A minibus transported us another hour up the eastern flanks of Huang Shan to Yungu Temple. From there, a cable car ferried visitors to the peak in 8 minutes, but my four comrades were not about to waste money on a route they could climb for free. There was plenty of time, they said, to reach the summit via the stone staircase cut into the mountain, a mere 3-hour hike—5 miles up with a mere 20,000 stairs between us and the final peak.

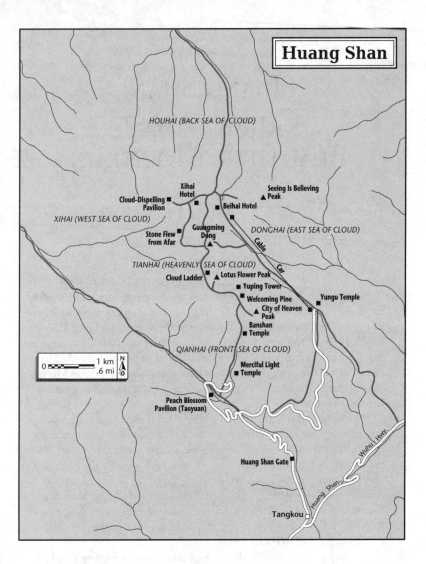

Huang Shan

HOUHAI (BACK SEA OF CLOUD)

Xihai Hotel

Seeing Is Believing Peak

Cloud-Dispelling Pavilion

Beihai Hotel

XIHAI (WEST SEA OF CLOUD)

Guangming Dong

DONGHAI (EAST SEA OF CLOUD)

Stone Flew from Afar

Cable Car

TIANHAI (HEAVENLY SEA OF CLOUD)

Cloud Ladder

Lotus Flower Peak

Yuping Tower

Welcoming Pine

Yungu Temple

City of Heaven Peak

Banshan Temple

QIANHAI (FRONT SEA OF CLOUD)

Merciful Light Temple

0   1 km
           .6 mi

N

Peach Blossom Pavilion (Taoyuan)

Huang Shan Gate

Huang Shan

Wuhu Hwy.

Tangkou

Seeing Is Believing

Huang Shan, according to its many-storied tradition, consists of 72 peaks. In fact, there are many more. At least 77 of these stone pillars, formed 100 million years ago, exceed 3,200 feet elevation, the base of the mountain lying at 2,000 feet. It's a fierce ascent. The highest point, Lotus Flower Peak, rises to 6,115 feet. The network of footpaths, mostly stone steps, makes a circuit exceeding 30 miles. The eastern path to the summit is 5 miles, if no detours up and down individual pinnacles are taken; the western route, by which we descended, is steeper and more scenic, and it runs for 9 miles, requiring 6 hours to complete.

The cable car is strung parallel to the eastern route we ascend, rising up a deep declivity forested with granite pillars. I'm exhausted after the first 20 minutes of the climb, but there's no choice but to keep walking up the stairs. More than one emperor has ascended Huang Shan by this same route, albeit in the comfort of a sedan chair propelled on the shoulders of powerful runners. Such chairs are still for hire, at about $100 for the round-trip.

So far, I can see that the peaks of Huang Shan are towering and exquisite, indeed, granite rivals of the famous limestone karst pillars of Guilin, but I'm like a dead man, hauling my own corpse up an endless flight of stairs. It isn't until we are almost at the central summit, Beihai Peak, that I find a new resource of strength and begin to appreciate the grandeur. We strike out on a northern detour to **Seeing Is Believing Peak (Shixin Feng).** This 5,472-foot promontory has its own wicked set of steep stairs. At the top, I am in a cluster of jagged rock spires. Mist is blowing in and out of the twisted pinnacles. At times, I have glimpses of what's below: pine forests, cascading streams, narrow gorges. There's legend of an ancient skeptic who denied Huang Shan's unique beauty until he reached this viewpoint. I seem to be following in his footsteps. Any doubts I had about the Yellow Mountain's claim to the most dramatic mountain scenery in China is erased here.

Seeing Is Believing Peak is connected by a bridge of stone, **Duxian Qiao,** known as the Bridge to Heaven. By the bridge stands one of Huang Shan's celebrated pines, **Duxian Song,** which appears to be bowing to welcome travelers. Several of these sturdy mountain pines are believed to be over a thousand years old. Many of these bare swirling granite pinnacles have a pine tree or two sprouting from their joints, pointing like green umbrellas not only vertically but horizontally into misty space.

Sea of Clouds

The twin summits, **Beihai and Xihai**—the Northern Sea of Clouds and the Western Sea of Clouds—are the prime gathering points for watching sunrise and sunset. I am hoping to stay the night at Beihai, in a modern hotel, and wake early to join the crowds at sunrise. Beihai has some of the mountain's most spectacular scenery. To the east, on the tapered summit of a peak named **Flower Growing Out of a Writing Brush,** a gnarled pine tree sprouts heavenward like the tip of an artist's brush. To the north is **Refreshing Breeze Terrace,** where hundreds of Chinese will congregate just before dawn in rented quilt coats to rhapsodize over the rose-colored sunrise.

Unfortunately, the Beihai Hotel is booked solid with some sort of convention, and the corrugated metal Quonset huts nearby are full as well. We trudge across the cloud summit 30 minutes more to the Xihai Hotel and rest at the Cloud-Dispelling Pavilion. This is where young lovers also pause, following the custom of securing padlocks engraved with their initials to the iron fence to pledge their undying love and tossing the keys into the misty gorge. This overlook dispels no clouds today. The sun is absorbed long before it sets fire to the horizon. The Xihai Hotel also has no room at the inn. My four companions huddle. We decide to move on.

An Inn at the End of the Mountain

The sun is bleeding into dusk. We tack across the west side of the range, inquiring at several unmarked hostels. No rooms anywhere. Huang Shan is booked. Full darkness falls like a stage curtain. We encamp in the tiny lobby of a dormitory complex. The two clerks at the counter insist there isn't a room to be had, but plenty of other travelers are joining us. Everyone argues with the clerks. An hour passes this way. There are rooms here, people whisper, but the staff is too lazy to open them. The staff withdraws from the counter for dinner.

I wait in a courtyard outside. Three foreigners and a Chinese, a group from Beijing, join me. The foreigners are Germans: two young women and a man. One of the women is traveling with her Chinese boyfriend and she, speaking good Mandarin, goes inside to try her luck at negotiations.

"She's completely ruthless," the other Germans assure me. "Whatever it takes, even a bribe, she will get it done."

Wolf, whose sister is taking on the hostel staff, has been on the road a week. Nothing quite this bad has befallen them until now, he says. He wonders how I have come to be with four Chinese, who meanwhile are talking with some Huang Shan locals about renting a cottage for the night.

We joke about sleeping on the open trail tonight. About midnight there's a breakthrough. Places to sleep suddenly materialize. Two bunkhouses up the hill inexplicably open their doors. We climb a score more stairs in the pitch dark. Our bunkhouse contains beds for eight. There's nothing more inside, not even a basin of water. The problem is that there are already people sleeping here, and with us joining them, there aren't enough beds. Eventually one of the lads, probably by bribe rather than argument, convinces some of these surplus sleepers to seek other accommodations—this, after we've already paid twice the going price for the "inconvenience" of needing a place to sleep after dark.

Two of the guys from Wuhan slip out into the dark in search of supper, returning with loaves of bread so heavy I can barely swallow them and with some hideously pale lunch meat processed into finger-shaped wieners.

There's no water to drink or wash up with. I lie down in my bunk. I've been up since six. Right now I never want to see another stone step on another mountain again. Every single fiber that holds flesh to bone is snapped.

Cloud Ladders

It is twice as far down the west side of Huang Shan, nearly 9 miles. This is where the great peaks reside, everyone of them a stupendous detour by carved stairway. We scale each and every prong. The climbs are extraordinarily severe, up hundreds of irregular stone steps that end in a singular panorama, followed by a shock-absorber descent, and a few minutes later by another looming precipice.

We begin at the **Stone That Flew from Afar (Feilai Feng)**, a 30-foot-tall rock perched on the top of a stone tower, looking as though it just sailed in on a cloud. Just to the east is Huang Shan's second highest peak, **Guangming Ding**, at 6,040 feet. It has its own strange crown: a modern weather station.

Turtle Summit (Aoyu Feng), slightly lower at 5,840 feet, requires a scramble through a cave whose stairs lead like a ladder to the slim summit. Next stop on this so-called descent is the highest peak in the range, **Lotus Flower (Lianhua Feng)**, elevation 6,115 feet. It's a climb of 800 steps nearly straight up, in fact, at an 80-degree incline in some places. The earliest recorded ascent of Lotus Flower Peak was in 1268. The climbing party required three days to complete the ascent. Of course, there were no cable cars, guesthouses, trails, or stone stairways at Huang Shan in those days. The first stairways seem to have been cut into the mountain about 1606, when monks began to connect the many temples. During the Yuan Dynasty alone (1271–1368), 64 temples were added to Huang Shan's slopes. Today, hardly half a dozen remain. It is not a sacred mountain, but it is sublime.

At the foot of Lotus Flower Peak is the site of **Yuping Lou, the Jade Screen Pavilion**—a famous Buddhist temple until it burned down in 1952 and was reconstructed as a guesthouse and restaurant. The Jade Screen Pavilion is the midpoint on the western route, a fine place for a cup of tea. And here, too, is the most photographed panorama of Huang Shan, featuring a thousand rising peaks and spires and a single, stately pine tree, its boughs outstretched. Known as the **Welcoming Pine of Huang Shan (Huang Ke Song)**, it is believed to be over a thousand years old. Its likeness has been painted on a wall in the Great Hall of the People in Beijing where hundreds of heads of state are welcomed by the leaders of China.

Just south of the Jade Screen Pavilion is Huang Shan's second-highest granite tower, **Tiandu Feng (City of Heaven Peak)**, elevation 5,938 feet. It is the last peak I can possibly climb. I have been walking up and down in China until I am ready to crawl.

City of Heaven Peak is rather formidable. It's an hour's detour to the top, a 2-mile-long ladder through the clouds ending in an unnerving and narrow 30-foot span, lined with a slack chain-link railing and sheer drop-offs on both sides. This lovely single-file passage of terror is called **Carp's Backbone Ridge (Jiyu Bei).** From it I can see all at once the four elements the Chinese traditionally demand of a perfect mountain landscape: soaring spires, grotesque pines, clear-running mountain streams, and seas of mist and cloud. Everything except sanity and safety. At least I have satisfied the ancient dictum: "Without reaching Jade Screen Pavilion, you cannot see the mountain; without climbing the City of Heaven Peak, your trip is in vain."

Peach Blossom Springs

After squeezing through a region of boulders and narrow fissures known as the **House of Clouds,** we pause for lunch at a restaurant near Banshan Temple that, oddly enough, doubles as a brick factory. Porters file back and forth past our table, bundles of fresh bricks tethered to their poles. The bricks are piled in the back of the cafe, near the mouths of the kilns. The lads from Wuhan order beer, and feeling euphoric after their successful descent of Huang Shan, tear off the bottle tops with their teeth. Sheepishly, I fetch a bottle opener from my backpack. Meanwhile, the porters come and go, brickload by brickload, staring at me as I slurp down a bowl of red-peppered noodles.

It's only 2,000 more stone steps down to the bamboo groves and hot springs of **Merciful Light Temple (Ciguang Ge),** a favorite of the Ming Emperor Wanli, who visited here about the time the pilgrims landed on Plymouth Rock. All I want to land in is a hot tub of water and a comfortable bed.

At **Taoyuan (Peach Blossom) Hot Springs,** I part ways with my four tireless amigos from Wuhan. They take cheap rooms next to a public bathhouse; I retreat to the slightly more modern Taoyuan Guest House. I've now felt how the Chinese travel on their holidays—quickly and cheaply—and I must conclude that they are far tougher travelers than I ever was, and in a much madder rush. My tendency is to dwell for hours at a site, for days on a peak, but they chew up entire mountain ranges as if they could hear the tick of each minute on a hand-wound one-day clock.

One more mountain like this and I'm finished. It's important to find your pace and stick with it. I mean to linger in this small village with its hot springs, waterfalls, forested peaks, and pavilions before I move on. The hot mineral waters of Cinnabar Springs along the Peach Blossom Stream are said to heal those who climb the peaks.

Huang Shan is the most picture-perfect of Chinese mountains, so rife with bizarre rock forms, sword-point peaks, and deep fissures that it resembles a giant's game of pick-up sticks. Surmounting its 77 peaks requires days of climbing the stairs up the steep sides of immense granite pillars and the crossing of stone ladders floating on an everglade of clouds. As the Tang poet Li Bai proclaimed 12 centuries ago, the first ancients to scale these flowery peaks must have been astounded to find that they could look down upon the sky.

Practical Information

ORIENTATION

Huang Shan (Yellow Mountain), China's most famous mountain for scenic beauty, is located in Anhui Province, 125 miles west of Hangzhou, 250 miles southwest of Shanghai.

Known as Yi Shan, its name was officially changed to Huang Shan by Emperor Tang Xuanzong in A.D. 747. Today it is a park, managed by the Huang Shan Municipality (established in 1987). Farming, wood gathering, hunting, mining, and construction are prohibited. The major threats to the environment are fire and water pollution, brought on in part by increasing tourism. The large number of visitors (more than 500,000 a year) has strained the resources of the park administration. From May through October, the trails are packed with hikers, making April an ideal time to visit Huang Shan. Rainfall, humidity, and temperature peak in July. Snow coats the peaks 158 days a year. Fog and mist, essentials in the eyes of Huang Shan's artists, occur 256 days a year.

Most of the forests are pine. There are also alpine juniper, oak, beech, and ginkgo. Due to the large crowds, little of the indigenous wildlife is seen, but the parklands are home to 300 species, including macaque, black bear, wild dog, civet, sika deer, pangolin, oriental white stork, and clouded leopard.

Huang Shan was inscribed on the UNESCO World Heritage List in 1990 in an effort to recognize and preserve its natural and cultural treasures.

GETTING THERE

By Plane   China East Airlines has introduced daily direct flights from Shanghai (1 hour) to the new airport at Huang Shan. Additional routes should open up soon, particularly from cities such as Hong Kong and Beijing.

The nearby airport at Tunxi has flights from Beijing (2 hours), Guangzhou (1 hour 45 minutes), and Shanghai (1 hour).

By Train   A new daily express train connects to Tunxi from Shanghai (12 hours).

From Tunxi to Huang Shan   Tunxi, the main transportation hub for Huang Shan, is 30 miles from the town of Tangkou, which in turn is still a few miles south of the mountain entrance. From the air, rail, and bus terminals in Tunxi, minibuses and taxis make the 2-hour trip to Tangkou. From Tangkou, it is necessary to continue to the east gate at Yungu (1 hour by minibus or taxi) if you want to use the cable car or the eastern mountain trail (recommended). From the Peach Blossom Hot Springs area and the start of the western mountain trail, it is a 30-minute walk down to the Tangkou bus station.

TOURS & STRATAGEMS

Visitor Information Tunxi has a helpful branch of China International Travel Service (CITS) at 12 Jingyuan Bei Lu (☎ 0559/211-5832; fax 0559/211-4040). It can provide English-speaking guides and private cars.

Exploring the Mountain The park entrance fee is RMB 90 ($11), payable at the start of the western or eastern trails. The cable car (running 8am to 4pm) costs RMB 80 ($9.65) each way, and the waiting line for the 8-minute ascent can be 1 to 2 hours. Hiring a sedan chair can cost $100 for a 2-day round-trip; the price is always highly negotiable.

The two large hotels on the summit have good (and hygienic) restaurants. Temperatures, even in summer, are subject to sudden changes with the altitude and winds. Carry layers of clothing: sweaters and rain jackets as well as T-shirts. Hats and umbrellas are also useful.

WHERE TO STAY & DINE

There are hotels in Tunxi, but the town is 2 to 3 hours from Huang Shan's hiking trails. Closer accommodations are in Tangkou Village at the south entrance to the mountain and inside the park where the western trail begins at Peach Blossom Hot Springs. Plan on spending several nights at a hotel on top of the mountain. Phone ahead for reservations, particularly from May through October.

There are plenty of stalls and a few hole-in-the-wall cafes on the mountain trails. Bagged snacks and boiled eggs might be hygienic enough to risk eating, but as much as possible stick to the Chinese and Western restaurants in the hotels listed below.

In Tunxi, the best hotel is the 3-star **Huang Shan International Hotel** on Xiao Huashan Lu (☎ 0559/252-6999; fax 0559/251-2087). A double costs RMB 300 ($36); no credit cards.

At Tangkou, nearer the Huang Shan entrance, there are dorm rooms and crude doubles at the **Free and Unfettered Inn (Xiaoyao Binguan)** (☎ 0559/556-2571), which is almost worth staying at just for the name. Don't expect any frills. Doubles cost RMB 300 ($36). The staff speaks some English.

At **Peach Blossom Hot Springs**, where the western trail begins, the inn of choice is the **Peach Blossom Hotel (Taoyuan Binguan)**, 3 Yanan Lu (☎ 0559/556-2666; fax 0559/556-2888). It carries a 3-star rating, but don't expect luxuries even when you pay $100 a night for a double. Rooms and bathrooms are quite small but modern, and some credit cards are accepted (AE, MC, V).

At **Yungu Temple,** where the east trail begins, there's another 3-star choice, the **Cloud Valley Villa Hotel** (☎ 0559/556-2466; fax 0559/556-2346), which charges $75 for a double. The rooms are small but modern (renovated in 1995), there's a shopping arcade, the staff is helpful, and the hotel takes some credit cards (AE, MC, V).

On the summit of the mountain, there are two upscale choices. The **Northern Sea Hotel (Beihai Binguan)** (☎ 0559/556-2555; fax 0559/556-2708), rated at 2 stars, has a heavy Russian-style appearance (it was built in 1958) and could benefit from a thorough renovation. Doubles are $75, hot water flow is irregular, and no credit cards are accepted. A nicer choice is the Swiss-designed **Western Sea Hotel (Xihai Fandian)** (☎ 0559/556-2818; fax 0559/556-2988). It's also a much more expensive choice. The large, modern doubles cost $175. The hotel does have hot water on demand and accepts some credit cards (AE, JCB, MC, V).

TRAVEL ADVISORIES

W‌HILE VISITORS TO C‌HINA CAN NOW stay in 5-star luxury hotels, dine in excellent restaurants, hire local guides fluent in English, book extravagant tours, board air-conditioned buses, fly aboard state-of-the-art aircraft, use credit cards, and phone, fax, and e-mail overseas, it is worthwhile remembering that China is still a third-world country. As the world's oldest continuous civilizations and most populous modern nation, China also has its own way of doing things. Travel, especially on one's own, is not always a smooth, comfortable undertaking. It is best for a foreigner to approach China travel as a journey into a world that is both familiar and alien.

China Today

PEOPLE China is as spacious as the United States and its geography as various, but its people are overwhelmingly uniform, belonging primarily to one ethnic group, the Han Chinese, who constitute 93% of the 1.2 billion population.

THE ECONOMY Despite China's relative poverty, it is becoming the economic powerhouse of Asia. About a third of the workforce is employed by prospering private firms (55 million workers in 25 million non-governmental enterprises). Double-digit economic growth has become routine, as has double-digit inflation. The economic improvements have changed the look of China. Taxis, which numbered just 60,000 in 1985, now number 10 times that many, and the streets, once filled with bicycles, are now clogged with vehicles, most of them burning leaded gas. Heavy industries are on the upswing. China overtook Japan in 1996 as the world's largest steel producer. China's textile production and clothing exports are immense. Sixty percent of the shoes sold in America are made in China. It's quite likely that the clothes you take to China will have been manufactured there.

China's relatively prosperous cities offer many luxuries unavailable to previous generations. Nearly 90% of urban dwellers watch television daily. The latest pop music, high fashions, and electronic appliances from the

West are sold in glitzy shops, boutiques, and department stores. Wal-Mart opened a Super Center and a Sam's Club Warehouse in Shenzhen, a Special Economic Zone near Canton. Amway, Avon, Mary Kay, and Sara Lee have established sales forces and factories across China. Coca-Cola sells 100 million cases annually.

A 40-hour 5-day workweek was mandated in 1995. Beijing has instituted a minimum wage ($35 a month) and unemployment benefits ($25 to $30 a month). By the year 2000, China expects to have 123 million telephone subscribers. International credit-card companies predict that by the year 2003, China will have 200 million card-carrying consumers (up from 20 million today), accounting for one-fifth of the world's total. In response to rapidly rising consumer spending, the number of restaurants in major Chinese cities has been tripling every 5 years.

WAGES Despite China's recent economic boom, most people do not have wages or standards of living comparable to those in the West. The average income is about $700 per year, although it is about twice that in the big cities on the east coast from Beijing down to Hong Kong. Rural residents, who constitute about 65% of the population, usually make less than $50 a month, sometimes far less. The commune system has been widely disbanded, enabling farmers to cultivate their own plots and sell surplus produce (after meeting state quotas and taxes) in the free market.

The distribution of wealth has become widely disparate since the egalitarian era of Chairman Mao ended more than 20 years ago. There are more than a million millionaires in China today, in a nation where nearly everyone dreams of getting rich as quickly as possible. Such dreams run up against the harsh reality of China's overwhelming population. While most Chinese have seen their wages and buying power soar over the last few years, they remain at a level that would be regarded as poor in the West. Large segments of the young, particularly in rural areas, are unemployed. Many drift into the overcrowded cities, lured by the chance to get rich. There are currently over a million maids (officially termed "home helpers") employed in China, including nearly 100,000 girls from the countryside in Beijing alone.

POLLUTION With increased production and car traffic, pollution has become a serious problem. You'll notice the poor air quality in the cities, which can make the skies of Los Angeles seem downright pristine. China's cities can handle only 20% of their sewage and less than 50% of the garbage they produce.

CHINA'S PROSPECTS Whether China can continue to fuel its economic miracle is an open question. Major challenges looming on the horizon include large underemployment of the workforce, increasing immigration to the cities, unequal spheres of development across China, environmental pollution, mammoth money-losing state enterprises, and antiquated laws regulating business expansion and investment.

Nevertheless, the future looks rosy to most forecasters. In the 50th commemorative edition (October 1996) of the *Far Eastern Economic Review*, David K. P. Li of the Bank of East Asia envisions the China of the year 2046 as the world's biggest economy (three times the size of the United States), the world's number one exporter and importer, and the largest consumer nation on Earth. China will then play the dominant role in world affairs, Li suggests, superseding the position held by the United States. After English, Mandarin Chinese will rank as the world's most important language—and Beijing will become the world's leading cultural center. John Naisbitt, author of *Megatrends Asia*, puts it succinctly: "As we move towards 2000, Asia will become the dominant region of the world: economically, politically and culturally."

Travel Basics

China may be the emerging superpower that will dominate this "Asian Century," but for the traveler it is not the easiest nation to understand or to visit. Nearly anywhere you go on your own in China without a group or without a government guide, you become a problem. Left to make your own arrangements, you find there are few mechanisms set up for outsiders. If you don't read or speak Chinese and if you aren't familiar with how things are done by ordinary Chinese travelers, problems can arise.

A number of practical facts, tips, and strategies must be kept in mind before and during a journey to the East. What follows is my own list of facts, requirements, and tips for the China traveler.

VISITOR INFORMATION   Apart from this book, you can procure information on China destinations and find answers to your questions by contacting overseas branches of the **China National Tourist Office.** Their American branches are in **New York** at 350 Fifth Avenue (Suite 6413, Empire State Building), New York, NY 10118 (☎ 212/760-8218 or 212/760-1710; fax 212/760-8809), and in **Glendale, California,** at 333 West Broadway, Suite 201, Glendale, CA 91204 (☎ 818/545-7505; fax 818/545-7506).

VISAS   The People's Republic of China requires a current visa, stamped in a valid passport, before granting entry to any foreign national. You can apply for a visa from a Chinese consulate or embassy, although if you enter China first at Hong Kong (which I recommend) it is best to purchase your visa there. If you are visiting China on a group tour, including a cruise, the operator and your travel agent are responsible for securing your visa. You'll need to provide them with a valid passport and other items they request. Check with them to be absolutely certain you are included on the group visa. Otherwise, you won't be admitted to China. The only drawback to a group visa is that you must stay with the group. Such a visa does not allow personal detours or extensions.

To apply on your own through a Chinese embassy or consulate, the first step is to request an application form. It's best to send the completed application back at least 30 days before departure, although embassies in the United States now say they need only a week to process and return applications. With the application, you must submit one or two passport photographs (as requested), a valid passport (good for at least six months after your visa expires), and the application fee. The tourist visa—coded L—is good for 30 days after the actual entry date. Check your passport when it is returned from the embassy to be sure one of the pages has a PRC visa stamped in it.

In the past, dealing with these overseas bureaucracies could be a nightmare, but their efficiency has improved greatly. In the United States, the Chinese embassy is located in **Washington, D.C.,** at 2300 Connecticut Avenue, NW, Washington, DC 20008 (☎ 202/328-2500 or 202/328-2517; fax 202/328-2564). The consulate in **Chicago** is located at 100 West Erie Street, Chicago, IL 60610 (☎ 312/803-0095; fax 312/803-0122). The consulate in **Houston** is located at 3417 Montrose Boulevard, Houston, TX 77066 (☎ 713/524-4311; fax 713/524-7656). The consulate in **Los Angeles** is located at 443 Shatto Place, Los Angeles, CA 90020 (☎ 213/380-2506 or 213/380-2507; fax 213/380-1961). The consulate in **New York** is located at 520 12th Avenue, New York, NY 10036 (☎ 212/330-7409; fax 212/502-0245). The consulate in **San Francisco** is located at 1450 Laguna Street, San Francisco, CA 94115 (☎ 415/563-4857 or 415/563-4885; fax 415/563-0494).

In Canada, the Chinese embassy is located in **Ottawa** at 515 St. Patrick Street, Ottawa, Ontario K1N 5H3 (☎ 613/234-2706 or 613/234-2682). The consulate in **Toronto** is located at 240 St. George Street, Toronto, Ontario M5R 2P4 (☎ 416/964-7260). The consulate in **Vancouver** is located at 3380 Granville Street, Vancouver, British Columbia V6H 3K3 (☎ 604/736-3910).

The easiest place to apply for a visa is in **Hong Kong.** Entry to Hong Kong does not require a visa for citizens of most countries (including the United States and Canada). Once there, you have several China visa options. You can purchase a 30-day, 60-day, 90-day, or 6-month single-entry visa. You can also purchase multiple-entry visas of varying lengths. Unless you plan on making frequent trips in and out of China within a visa time period, multiple-entry visas are a waste of money (since they are much more expensive than single-entry visas). In Hong Kong, you get what you pay for. The longer the validity of the visa, the more expensive.

The sooner you want it, the more expensive. The least expensive choice is a tourist visa good for 30 days, processed in two to three working days. That should cost from $25 to $35 (the price keeps rising). You can get a visa the same day if you're willing to pay several times that amount.

In Hong Kong I routinely purchase my visa at the CTS (China Travel Service) office in Kowloon, filling out the application (which is a mere formality), having passport photos taken, if necessary, and paying the fees (in cash only). The CTS branch in Kowloon that I use is located a few doors west off bustling Nathan Road on Peking Road (despite its Nathan Road address) on the first floor (one floor above the ground floor) of Alpha House, 27–33 Nathan Road (☎ 852/2721-4481; fax 852/2721-6251). Nearly all travel agencies in Hong Kong can provide China visa service as well. Prices and visa options vary.

TRAVEL AGENTS   In China, cities and towns with tourist attractions all have at least one branch of the official government travel agency set up to deal with foreign visitors. It is called **China International Travel Service—CITS** for short, *luxingshe* in Chinese. CITS can provide local tours, English-speaking guides, onward transportation tickets via air, rail, and road, and general information. Some offices are helpful and some are not. **China Travel Service (CTS)** was set up by the government to help Chinese tourists from overseas, but they now are seeking non-Chinese customers as well. The travel agency business has become quite competitive in China, and government agencies must compete not only among themselves but with some new private travel agencies as well. Most hotels have their own travel desks (often branches of CITS) offering tours, guides, and ticket bookings, and these are usually the most convenient places to go when you want to book a local tour or make transportation arrangements.

Money

CURRENCY   China's currency is called renminbi (RMB), meaning the people's money, and China is mainly a cash society. Few transactions are done with credit cards or personal checks. Renminbi comes in denominations ranging from RMB 1 to RMB 100, with smaller bills and coins for change. In the streets, RMB are called *kuai* or *yuan*. Numbers on most bills are in English.

TRAVELER'S CHECKS & CREDIT CARDS   Your best bet is to arrive in China with traveler's checks—plenty of them—mostly in U.S. $100 denominations, which you can easily cash in major hotels and at many branches of the official Bank of China. Major credit cards also work at the big international hotels to pay for room and restaurant charges.

In some hotels, credit cards are only accepted during regular banking hours and not on weekends. Always take sufficient local currency when you leave the hotel for dining, shopping, or touring.

ATMs are rare in the streets of China. While a few ATM machines do exist, the only places you can perform cash withdrawals are at special branches of the **Bank of China.** In most cities at least one branch of the Bank of China will do credit-card cash draws (using Visa, MasterCard, and American Express). These transactions are limited to a maximum of $1,000 a day at present, with a 2% to 4% fee, and require about 30 minutes to complete. I recently conducted such a transaction in Xi'an, receiving over RMB 8,000 in cash. Since the RMB 100 note is the largest in China, I was handed a stack of bills 80 deep. Walking out of the bank, I felt like a numbers runner making his rounds.

Remember that your passport is always required for currency exchanges.

WHAT THINGS COST   How much money to take? If you have purchased an all-inclusive package tour, take enough for shopping and miscellaneous purchases. If you are traveling on your own, expenses depend on where you travel and what comfort level you select. Hotels and food can cost as much as in the West—far less if you can put up with very basic hotels and monotonous local food. Transportation can also be expensive if you rely on airplanes ($75 to $250 a trip, depending on distance); trains and buses are relatively cheap, and overnight trains serve as a night's lodging. I used to travel on far less than $50 a day (transport included), but these days only a dedicated and adventurous backpacker could travel that cheaply in China.

Allow at least $150 per day, more if you plan on staying in top international hotels and eating in their restaurants (although you can charge this to your credit card). Cities such as Hong Kong, Beijing, and Shanghai are quite expensive for lodging and dining—which will be your major expenses—while the more remote cities are often quite cheap.

China has two price structures: one for visitors, and one for the natives. This is an official policy, so don't be surprised if you are charged much more than a Chinese citizen for goods and services.

Health, Insurance & Packing

HEALTH   Check with your doctor before departure. Except in remoter rural areas, inoculations and special vaccinations are not necessary. Make sure your tetanus shot is up-to-date, as well as your polio immunization. A flu shot is advisable, as are hepatitis A and typhoid vaccinations if you travel in rural or tropical regions. The Centers for Disease Control (CDC) maintains a hot line that updates health concerns for international travelers; call ☎ 888/232-3228. Consult their latest advisories on regions of China where you will be traveling.

Most travelers contract a cold along the way, often right after entry. Take your usual remedies with you. Nagging nasal colds are common. I carry a sterile syringe (issued with a note to that effect from my physician) in the event that I end up needing an injection in China. There's no guarantee that a given hospital in China uses sterile syringes in all cases, and disposable needles are not common except in large city hospitals (such as those in Shanghai, Beijing, and Hong Kong). It's also a good idea to take along any prescription medicines you may need—Western prescriptions can't always be filled in China.

In the larger cities, there are clinics that specialize in treating foreigners. If you need to see a doctor, advise the staff at your hotel. Western-style medical care is widespread in China, and many doctors in every region are fully competent.

Cautions: Chinese blood banks do not carry Rh-negative blood supplies. Have your teeth checked before departure; carry a small dental emergency kit.

INSURANCE   Insurance is usually either included or presented as an option by tour operators outside China. If you are traveling on your own, the following carriers offer comprehensive travel insurance packages, including emergency medical evacuation: Healthcare Abroad (☎ 800/237-6615), Mutual of Omaha (☎ 800/228-9792), and Travel Guard International (☎ 800/826-1300).

PACKING   The best advice is this: Travel as lightly as possible and pack as little as possible. You never know when or how far you might have to lug your own gear in China, even if you're on a group tour. I never take more than two pieces of luggage, one being a day pack I can strap on my back. In my youth, I traveled with a single bag, a backpack that converted into a handheld piece of luggage. In my advancing years, I've converted to a roll-on, a small roll-on that also has backpacking straps. Recently, I've been arriving in Hong Kong with old, cheap luggage, which I ditch in favor of a backpack/roll-on combination purchased for a pittance ($25 to $35) in one of Hong Kong's luggage shops. Although cheap, such a roll-on holds up for months at a time on the road. One roll-on and one stout day pack or shoulder bag is all one really needs in China, where one's wardrobe need not be extensive or formal.

The question is what to pack—what is really needed. The clothing you take should be simple, durable, and comfortable. Most of what I take are items for health and hygiene, as well as useful gadgets for life on the road. My wife and I have been keeping China packing lists for two decades. Here's a peek inside our luggage, with commentary:

Clothing

_____ Pants, two pair (all-cotton, wrinkle-free; a dress or skirt is optional)

_____ Shirts, three (all-cotton; polo-style or basic sports shirts and blouses; fairly easy to purchase replacements along the way)

_____ Sweater or sweatshirt, one (to layer over shirts, blouses)

_____ Turtleneck, one (a layer for cold weather)

_____ Underwear, three or four sets (difficult to replace on trip; can be washed and dried overnight in hotel laundry or room sink)

_____ Socks, three or four pair (dark colors, can be laundered overnight)

_____ Raincoat or windbreaker, one (lightweight nylon)

_____ Hat, one (optional; keeps the sun out or head warm)

_____ Shoes, one extra pair (sturdy, comfortable, broken in)

_____ Thongs, one pair (for showers or as slippers)

Accessories & Gadgets

_____ Towel, one

_____ Umbrella

_____ Swiss army knife

_____ Flashlight

_____ Chopsticks, knife, spoon, fork

_____ Clothespins, clothesline, powdered detergent, flat "universal" sink stopper (for doing laundry in room sink)

_____ Clock or watch with alarm

_____ Sewing kit

Cosmetics & Medicines

Take your usual supplies. Be sure to include:

_____ Prescriptions

_____ Sterile syringe (in case medical injection is required)

_____ Cold tablets (lots of these—a cold is nearly guaranteed)

_____ Moist towelettes

_____ Glasses (extra pair)

_____ Contact lens supplies

_____ Sunglasses

We also take a passport/money pouch (which is worn almost all the time), a notebook and extra pens, an address book, a camera with film and extra batteries, cups and heating coil with coffee, copies of our passport and traveler's check receipts, and a supply of breakfast bars for use when meals are difficult to procure.

Getting There

AIRLINES The **Civil Aviation Administration of China (CAAC)** is a government-run organization that flies internationally under the names **Air China, China Eastern,** and **China Southern.** Planes are up-to-date, and the in-flight services are improving. Tickets are usually booked through CITS (China International Travel Service). Hong Kong's airline, **Cathay Pacific Airlines** is one of the world's top airlines, and serves Hong Kong from North America. It is partly owned by CAAC and is the best choice if you want to fly the national carrier. Its subsidiary, Dragonair, connects Hong Kong to many destinations on the mainland.

Of the many international airlines serving China, the best service from North America, with a wide range of convenient gateways and connections inside the United States, is offered by United and Northwest. **Northwest Airlines** (☎ 800/447-4747) offers flights several times a week to Hong Kong and Beijing, leaving from New York, Los Angeles, San Francisco, and Seattle, with a stop in Tokyo.

My airline of choice for transpacific trips to Hong Kong and China has long been **United Airlines.** It offers two daily nonstop flights to Hong Kong from San Francisco and one daily nonstop flight to Hong Kong from Los Angeles, daily direct service (via Tokyo) to Beijing and Shanghai from San Francisco and Los Angeles, daily direct flights (via Tokyo) to Hong Kong from New York, and daily direct flights (via San Francisco and Los Angeles) from Chicago and Denver, including seasonal direct nonstop flights to Hong Kong from Chicago. United connects to these routes from about 100 cities and towns in the United States. The service is efficient, with plenty of amenities for the long trip (11 to 16 hours over the Pacific), including free drinks and movies in economy class, plenty of legroom in connoisseur class, and outright luxury in first class. For United's current transpacific schedule and rates, call United's international desk (☎ 800/538-2929).

Other airlines offering good service from North America are **Asiana Airlines** (☎ 800/227-4262), **Canadian Airlines International** (☎ 800/426-7000), **China Air (Taiwan)** (☎ 800/227-5118), **EVA Airlines** (☎ 800/695-1188), **Finnair** (☎ 800/950-5000), **Japan Airlines** (☎ 800/525-3663), **Korean Air** (☎ 800/438-5000), **Lufthansa** (☎ 800/645-3880), **Malaysia** (☎ 800/552-9264), **Philippine Airlines** (☎ 800/435-9725), **Singapore Airlines** (☎ 800/742-3333), **SAS World Airlines** (☎ 800-221-2350), **Swissair** (☎ 800/221-4750), and **Thai Airways International** (☎ 800/426-5204).

Getting Around

BY PLANE   Air travel improvement has been remarkably fast in China. Clean, modern jets put even remote cities just a few hours away. Airline attendants give basic services, often including a Chinese version of airline food (unfortunately, only on par or below par with that of the West). Most planes are chock-full; many leave on time, if not before scheduled departures. You must check in at least 1 hour early. Many planes are delayed, sometimes for hours, but the safety record has reached acceptable levels (far superior to the fatality record on China's roads).

CAAC oversees commercial aviation inside China. In theory there are a dozen private airlines operating in China today, but they are all subject to the rules, regulations, and approval of CAAC, and function as regional branches of a monolithic airline system. Fares are fixed, and there's no real competition, although equipment is modern and the service is improving. Hong-Kong–based **Dragonair** (co-owned by CAAC and Cathay Pacific) is by far the best of the carriers for flights between Hong Kong and major cities inside China.

Tickets can be booked from the city of departure at leading hotel desks and through CITS. Round-trip tickets can sometimes be purchased. All airports charge departure taxes, paid for at windows (labeled in English) before you go through luggage inspection, payable only in RMB (usually RMB 50–100/$6.25–$12.50).

BY TRAIN   China has a vast passenger rail network. If you travel by rail, it is easiest to have your hotel book the ticket, which can require three days' notice. Always request the best class. A typical long-distance train has up to four classes: soft berth, soft seat, hard berth, and hard seat.

Soft berth (ruanwo) is the top class. It consists of a special car with sleeping compartments. The compartments are small, with two bunk beds on either wall and a small table between. The beds always fill up, usually mixing foreigners with Chinese and sometimes men with women. You sleep under a quilt, with a hard pillow. During the day, compartment mates sit on the two lower beds. There is some overhead storage for luggage. Dining cars serve miserable fare. Best to pack some edibles before departure. Boiled hot water in a thermos is provided for each soft berth compartment. Take a cup along. Toilets—often one squat style and one Western style at either end of these cars—are unbelievably filthy, and the communal sinks nearby aren't alluring either. Still, it's a wonderful way to mix with the Chinese and make new friends.

The other class of sleeper is called **hard berth (yingwo)**. Hard berth consists of a car filled with triple bunk beds and no partitions or compartments. It's like sleeping in a packed dorm.

Some trains have an additional class, called **soft seat (ruanzuo)**, that assigns either a seat or spot on a bench. These are suitable for short day trips, although they can be noisy and crowded.

The lowest and cheapest class is called **hard seat (yingzwo)**. Hard seat has some benches along the walls of a train car, but they are often free-for-all cattle cars, sometimes so crowded that only standing room is available. You get what you pay for. Many Chinese end up standing the entire trip, which can extend for several days.

Trains are punctual, especially upon departure. Train terminals are forbidding chambers, crowded with all sorts of people, including an occasional thief, so watch your luggage. Lines form for the departure of each train by destination. It's useful to know your train number and departure time. If you are traveling soft berth or soft seat, there is often a special waiting room in the terminal, worth finding. Waylay a train official and show your ticket if you need directions. Once on the train, conductors will assist you. After the train leaves the station, a conductor will come around to check your passport. For a full description of riding the rails in China, read Paul Theroux's *Riding the Iron Rooster.*

BY BUS   **Long-distance buses** are usually a rugged challenge. Tickets can usually be bought in hotels. If you have to buy one at a bus station, you could be in for an ordeal—standing in long lines, often the wrong ones. But if you can pronounce your destination and ask the departure time in Chinese, and if you are determined, you might be able to buy your own ticket.

There are some decent express buses connecting cities these days, complete with padded seats, air-conditioning, and television monitors broadcasting noisy kung-fu films. Inquire at the hotel tour desk or CITS office, as these are the best buses operating in China, cheaper and faster than trains. Most long-distance buses, however, are crowded, bumpy, slow, and filthy—great places for an adventure, if not for one's kidneys. Overnight sleeper buses also operate on some long routes. In the last one I took, the condition of the road, the honking of the horn, and the smoking of the driver and passengers made sleep impossible, even though I had my own not-quite-long-enough reclining lounge.

City buses are frequently packed to the gills. Begin by procuring a city map, one with bus routes on it, if possible—one with Chinese and English is best of all. Have it in hand when you climb on. Chinese city buses will look familiar, if a bit beaten up. A conductor will approach you selling a small paper ticket. If you can't ask the price in Chinese, announce your destination and hand over an RMB 10 ($1.20) note. You'll get change back. Disembark when you see your stop.

BY TAXI Taxis are the quickest way around cities, where they are in plentiful supply. If you're on the street, stand on the edge of the sidewalk, stick out an arm, and lower it to hail a passing cab. Announce your destination. If there's no meter, don't get in. I've been cheated repeatedly by taxi drivers. When you have to bargain for a fare as a foreigner, you can be sure you're being bilked. This is frequently the case at airports and train terminals, where touts intercept you and lead you to an overpriced car. If possible, find a taxi queue or walk out of the terminal to the street, where your chances of finding an honest operator improve. Shanghai has instituted a system of taxi meters that print a receipt, and it helps keep cheating to a minimum. Elsewhere, there's a great deal of theft-on-wheels. Taxis in the city shouldn't charge more than $2 to $3 per trip. A good place to catch one is at the entrance to a major hotel, although I've even been ripped off there. Still, in most cases, overcharging is not a problem.

BY CAR Although more and more Chinese own their own private cars (or more commonly motorcycles), driving is largely a profession. Taxi drivers and others must be trained and licensed for the job. It is easy enough to hire a private car with driver through CITS or a hotel, or rent a taxi for the day. However, rental cars that you drive yourself are just at the experimental stage in some large cities; they require enormous deposits and are restricted to the city limits. Once you see how drivers use the streets in the cities and on highways, you probably won't want to try it yourself anyway, unless you are inclined toward car racing and demolition derbies.

ON FOOT Seeing a city on foot is the best means of getting around. Secure a map at your hotel or from a street vendor. You can use it to ask people directions if you get lost, particularly if the map contains Chinese labels. Blocks tend to be much longer than they look on these maps. Moreover, most Chinese have difficulty making sense of any map in any language, and they often give the vaguest, sometimes incorrect directions. It's always a good adventure, however, and it's the way I prefer to get a feel for the city.

Walking does have its share of annoyances and dangers. The sidewalks are often filled with holes or stacked with garbage. Crowds can slow your progress to a standstill. Construction sites, parked cars, vendors, bicycle parks, and a host of other encroachments often make for slow passage or detours. And street signs aren't obvious. When you find one, pray that it is written in pinyin (the alphabetic rendition of Chinese). Streets are often called *lu, jie,* or *dajie,* and the four directions are *bei* (north), *nan* (south), *dong* (east), and *xi* (west). It's easiest to navigate as the Chinese do, by landmarks rather than road signs and numbers—by towering buildings, public parks, and other big sites. If you really get turned around—as I have—flag down a cab.

BY BICYCLE   Many hotels offer bicycle rentals, as do some private enterprises. Hourly and daily rates vary widely but are quite reasonable (a few dollars an hour). Mountain bikes have replaced the once ubiquitous black, no-speed models. Check the tires and brakes—you'll need them. Bike riding looks difficult and chaotic, but once you get into the flow you'll be surprised at how easy it is, even in crowded cities. Bike-only lanes are a standard feature of most downtowns. On side streets, you simply have to barrel forward, confident that no cars or trucks will sweep you to one side (they don't). Use your bell at intersections.

Be sure you have a bike lock when you rent—bikes are often stolen. Try to find a bike parking lot. They usually fill part of a sidewalk. Park and lock next to other bikes. The bike keeper will charge you a small fee and give you a chit.

Tips on Accommodations

China now has a wide network of 4-star and 5-star international hotels that are as comfortable, efficient, and amenable as comparable hotels in the West. The prices are also comparable, at least in the biggest cities. Upon checking in, you'll be asked to present your passport and fill out a form. I keep vital numbers jotted down in my ever-present hand-sized notebook.

The two best chains in China are **Shangri-La International** (☎ 800/ 942-5050) and **Holiday Inns Worldwide** (☎ 800/HOLIDAY). Shangri-La hotels in China are usually the most luxurious you'll find, with standard room rates running from just $90 in Beihai to $295 in Beijing (and over $300 in Hong Kong), with $190 an average rate. Holiday Inn, which manages the largest number of hotels among international chains in China, has standard rooms from $80 in Xi'an to $190 in Beijing, with $120 an average rate. Holiday Inn (now called Holiday Hospitality) has deluxe Crowne Plaza lodgings in Chengdu, Xiamen, and Zhengzhou. All the better hotels in China now add at least 15% tax and surcharges to the room rates.

Other familiar chains operate a few hotels in China. In Beijing, Shanghai, and Hong Kong, you have a wide choice of lodgings, including hotels operated by **Sheraton International** (800/325-3535), **Hilton International** (☎ 800/445-8667), and **Westin** (☎ 800/228-3000). Two fine Asian chains that have moved into China with high-quality offer-ings are **Marco Polo** (☎ 800/843-6664) and **Gloria** (☎ 800/821-0900), both of which maintain high Western standards.

The great lack in China is of moderately priced ($50 to $100 per room), clean, basic, and efficient hotels. There are many Chinese-run hotels rated by the government at 2 and 3 stars that could fit this bill. They have modern facilities and private bathrooms, but they often offer substandard levels of service and housekeeping and are seldom accustomed to the expectations of Western guests. Nevertheless, they are sometimes the only choice in a given location and are certainly not night-mares. Even such cities as Hong Kong and Beijing have few moderately priced, comfortable, well-run hotels. Your choice is usually between a nice but expensive place or a hotel best described as modern but run-down.

Consult my listings for each destination. While I concentrate on the high end of the lodging spectrum, I also note more economical choices when they are ones I have tried myself, particularly when there are no better alternatives.

Tips on Dining

Chinese cuisine is fabulous, including such renowned regional specialties as Sichuan and Cantonese, but for the most part the best food is in hotel restaurants and a few new or long-established cafes. The prices in such places are no bargain. Expect to pay nearly as much as you would in a fine Chinese restaurant back home—sometimes more. Less expensive local restaurants are found in most cities, although the service, environment, and hygiene are at lower levels.

Common "workers" restaurants are abundant, and some have good, cheap offerings, but their conditions can be a shock to foreign travelers and ordering is difficult without some knowledge of Chinese. Streetside vendors provide the cheapest dishes of all. Again, the chief barriers are language and hygiene, although it is not difficult to order something by gesturing and pantomime.

It's a good idea to practice using chopsticks before your departure. Except in the best hotel restaurants or Western-style cafes, chopsticks are the only utensils. It's advisable to carry your own chopsticks; local restau-rants and vendors don't provide sanitary eating utensils.

China is not a good country for vegetarians, despite its Buddhist tra-ditions. Dishes feature ample portions of vegetables, but these are often mixed with small bits of meat (meat being considered a luxury food). Vegetarian restaurants do exist, but they seldom cater to foreigners.

Good fruits, including bananas, oranges, and apples, are available from street vendors and at free markets, as are boiled eggs and bottled water.

Coke and other canned or bottled soft drinks are widely distributed, too. Ice-cream treats are safe when purchased from small stores, as long as they are packaged in protective wrappers. I've bought frozen treats in the streets that used twigs as sticks—to be avoided as hygienic risks, of course.

More and more small cafes with Western menus and Western dishes are opening across China. Fast-food chains such as Kentucky Fried Chicken and McDonald's are proliferating. They charge about the same as in the West and their products taste about the same, too.

Very few restaurants, except in large international hotels, accept credit cards or traveler's checks. Carry the local currency.

Tips on Nightlife

China after dark is still most often a Gobi Desert as far as entertainment for the traveler is concerned, with only a few small oases dotting the after-hours landscape. Cities and towns now have night markets in abundance, many within an easy walk of tourist hotels, and these provide fascinating evening strolls. The tourist hotels themselves offer the best (and often only) rendezvous points for foreigners interested in discos and bars. Cinemas are quite popular everywhere, but they usually cater strictly to a local audience. **Xi'an** has opened a dinner theater of Tang Dynasty song and dance for foreign guests; **Chengdu** has an excellent opera; and **Harbin** has its ice sculpture park in the heart of winter. You can find out about these and other evening entertainment at your hotel service desk or from your concierge. Special events and performances of interest to foreigners are also presented from time to time.

Three exceptions to these extremely limited nighttime possibilities are in the cities of Hong Kong, Beijing, and Shanghai. Hong Kong is the most startling exception, a neon city that snaps to life when the sun sets. Every conceivable form of nightlife is no more than a taxi ride away. In Hong Kong, check the week's entertainment agenda in the English-language newspapers. The **Hong Kong Tourist Association (HKTA)** and the hotels can recommend a wide range of possibilities, from Chinese opera and Western classical concerts to all-night discos and regional dance performances.

Although the entertainment offerings in Beijing pale in comparison with those in Hong Kong, the capital no longer rolls up the streets at dusk. There are plenty of bars in the Sanlitun diplomatic district that cater to foreigners and locals alike, several cinemas that feature English-language films not seen elsewhere in China, and above all a number of nightly venues for traditional arts and entertainment. As always, check with the hotel desk for current offerings, tickets, and transportation. The English-language newspaper, *China Daily,* also has a listing of Beijing's top entertainment, both traditional and international.

The best bets for the traveler interested in Chinese culture are the **Beijing Opera** and the **Chinese Acrobats.** There are nightly performances in several theaters—your hotel should be able to book tickets. The **People's Art Theatre of Beijing** features Western plays. There's also a puppet theater, and dance performances. Perhaps the best place to sample a variety of traditional art forms is a **teahouse.** Beijing has several teahouses that present evenings of Chinese opera, acrobatics, martial arts, story-telling, and music and dance (see "Beijing: China's Treasure House").

Shanghai also hosts an array of concerts and performances, including opera and acrobatics. Many of the top special events take place at the **Shanghai Centre** (1376 Najing Xi Lu), which also has its own deluxe cinema, not to mention the Long Bar, a favorite of expatriates, visitors, and Chinese yuppies. Entertainment is provided most nights by the **Shanghai Acrobatic Troupe** at the Shanghai Centre Theatre. The jazz band at the **Peace Hotel** is a nightly favorite and the **Great World Entertainment Centre** (downtown at 1 Xizang Zhong Lu) has four stories and two auditoriums of non-stop entertainment including opera, puppetry, acrobatics, and traditional story-telling.

In Shanghai, Beijing, Hong Kong, and elsewhere in China, the place to find out about the latest offerings, to book tickets, arrange transportation, and get advice is always at your hotel service desk.

Other Basics

ELECTRICITY   China uses a 220-volt 50-cycle AC system. Plugs comes in a variety of shapes. I used to carry a set of adapters with various configurations of prongs, but I've found I don't use them much. Hotels provide plug converters. If you take a heating coil, be certain that it is a 220-volt model.

E-MAIL & INTERNET   Computer communications are beginning to sweep China, but for now only a few of China's top hotels with state-of-the-art business centers can enable you to use e-mail or surf the net. Some modern hotels provide in-room hookups for your laptop, although I haven't tried these out yet. Foreign businesspeople are bringing their laptops to China in growing numbers. Only in Hong Kong are e-mail and Internet links commonplace, although Beijing and Shanghai are opening Internet cafes.

FAXES   China's main fax centers are the big hotels. You can easily send a fax from their business centers or front desks, although an international fax is expensive, rarely less than $10 for a one-page fax overseas. There are no copy shops and few business centers independent of the big hotels providing cheaper faxing services.

METRIC SYSTEM China employs the metric system for measurements (1 kilometer = 0.62 miles, 1 meter = 39.37 inches, 1 liter = about 1 quart) and the Celsius scale for temperature (each degree Celsius = $^9/_5$ degree Fahrenheit + 32).

SAFETY China is a safe country for a foreign traveler, with plenty of very honest people, but pickpockets, thieves, and muggers do target outsiders once in a while. China is the only place I have ever been robbed—it happened at knifepoint on a remote mountain trail.

TELEPHONES Most good hotels in China now provide international direct dialing (IDD), meaning you can phone overseas from your room. The charge will appear on your hotel bill, with a service charge added. The telephone system has improved rapidly in the 1990s. In nearly all instances, you will have clear connections, domestically and internationally.

China is not filled with public phone booths, although many shops offer phones to the public for local calls. Unless you speak Chinese, making reservations or seeking information by phone is usually futile. Have the hotel desk make such calls on your behalf.

Caution: As China's telephone system expands, numbers change, often by adding digits. Even area codes are frequently altered. When phoning or faxing China from overseas, use the China country code **(86)** and drop the initial zero in the city code. When calling long distance within China, use the complete area code, beginning with the zero.

TIME Despite spanning what would ordinarily be considered six time zones east to west, China has only one official time zone. Every location is on Beijing time, from Hong Kong to Kashgar. The time in China is GMT plus 8 hours, which means that wherever you are in China it is 16 hours earlier in Los Angeles, 15 hours earlier in Denver, 14 hours earlier in Chicago, and 13 hours earlier in New York. China does not use daylight saving time, so during those summer months it is 15 hours earlier in Los Angeles, 12 hours earlier in New York.

TIPPING Tips are still forbidden in China, but tipping is becoming a widespread custom in large cities. Porters expect RMB 5 to 10 (about $1), guides RMB 15 to 25 ($2 to $3) per day. Don't tip waiters and waitresses. There's a service charge included on most bills. Leave some change if you have a good taxi ride.

TOILETS The standard Asian-style toilet is a porcelain bowl in the floor. These are what you usually find in ordinary restaurants, train and bus terminals, sightseeing destinations, parks, and public lavatories. In public lavatories, where you usually purchase an inexpensive ticket of admission, there is little attention to hygiene and no toilet paper. Some

Westerners carry their own spray disinfectants into these malodorous chambers. There's also little privacy. In the bigger hotels, the standard Western sit-down toilets, as opposed to squat-toilets, are used.

WATER *Don't* drink the water in China. It is not sanitary. Even the few hotels that now boast purification systems are suspect, in my opinion. Better safe than sorry. Bottled water is widely and cheaply available, even in remote areas. Use it for drinking and for brushing your teeth.

Parting Words of Advice

- Always book the best class possible on trains, buses, boats, and other modes of transport.

- Book transportation as far ahead as possible. Most flights are fully booked days in advance.

- In Chinese-run budget hotels, inquire if more expensive rooms are available.

- Always carry your passport, traveler's checks, and other valuables in a concealed security pouch.

- Carry along an emergency snack, such as a breakfast bar, in case you can't find a suitable cafe, vendor, or grocer.

- If bad air quality is a serious threat, pack a dust mask. Many people in China wear them, particularly during dust storms.

- Take good, comfortable, durable walking shoes. Be sure they're well broken in before you leave home.

- The best small gifts are books and postcards.

- Camera film and batteries are available in shops and department stores in large cities, but it is best to carry plenty of both. Avoid X-raying at air terminals and train stations by handing film over for manual inspection. Put film in clear canisters and bag it in plastic.

- Be patient, flexible, open, and good-natured. China is a learning experience, not an escape; an adventure, not a getaway; a new challenge, not a holiday.

CUSTOMS, ATTITUDES AND ENIGMAS: THE CHINESE WAY

T HE CHINESE WAY IS NOT NECESSARILY the Western way. Chinese culture was created in isolation from the West, just as Western culture was created without reference to the Chinese world. Customs, family relationships, and social interactions differ, sometimes only slightly, as modern China adjusts to Western ways.

Here's my own list of differences the foreign traveler should expect to encounter while visiting China.

Worldview

CHINA & THE WORLD China has long conceived of itself as the center of the universe. The very name it gives to its nation, *Zhongguo*, means "Central Kingdom." At times, China takes an ethnocentric view of itself. All nations and peoples outside its ancient borders are regarded as "barbarians," as non–Han Chinese. Outsiders, if not inferior, are at last not real Chinese, and hence are forever at an unfortunate remove from the great motherland. Even today, there are millions of Chinese, particularly those from the countryside newly arrived in the cities, who have never seen a foreigner up close.

There may be occasions, at restaurants, in department stores, or at train and bus stations, where you will draw stares, openly curious rather than hostile, from one or more Chinese. In their eyes, foreigners have certain remarkable physical characteristics—big noses, curly hair, strange clothes and adornments. In such circumstances, it is best to return the stare or ignore it. Expressions of anger are useless. This is how a rock star or movie hero must feel. On one occasion I was walking with an American teacher and his 4-year-old daughter in the streets of Chengdu when a Chinese lady came over and in frank, open curiosity stroked the girl's blond bangs. Having mastered the Sichuan dialect in 3 short months, the young girl told the admirer in no uncertain terms to desist.

The trick, if stares bothers you, is to keep moving. When I first came to China, I used to be able to draw a silent circle of examiners every time I paused in the streets for more than 10 seconds. In large cities, people are used to foreign businessmen, students, and tourists in their midst and staring circles rarely form.

One consequence of the Central Kingdom mentality is that China clings proudly and fiercely to its own way of doing things, particularly when an outsider points out a "better" and more efficient way.

POLITICS   You'll run across Chinese who can be surprisingly frank about their political situation. If they bring up these issues first, don't be shy about expressing your opinion. On the other hand, you will really be putting your well-intentioned hosts or acquaintances on the spot if you initiate criticisms of China in respect to its lack of political freedoms. Topics to avoid include freedom of the press, the Tibet situation, the status of Taiwan, the Tiananmen Square massacre, abortion, prison labor, and the handling of dissidents. Chinese tour guides get such questions all the time, and they have set answers, often quite defensive.

Society

SAVING FACE   Fundamental to maintaining harmony in Chinese society is the ancient concept of "face," which on a personal level means one's self-respect. Personal status reflects on one's family, the paramount institution in China, and the family unit, in turn, is related to the greater society. To "lose face" is thus terribly humiliating, and the Chinese will go to great ends to avoid it. "Saving face" often comes through compromise, in which both sides in a disagreement receive a benefit. For the foreign traveler, the concept of "face" seems a matter of common sense, but it takes many unusual forms in China.

There is a reluctance, for example, to deny any request flat out, as this implies that one is not fulfilling one's duty as a host. Confronting a Chinese over poor service or demanding something difficult to deliver is often not the best way to reach the desired end. To save face, Chinese in a position to help could resort to making a promise they can't keep or to making a firm denial that seems absurd to an outsider. For example, many times in lesser hotels in China I've asked for a room and been told there was none. In an empty hotel, this seems absurd, but the clerk (aside from perhaps being lazy) may simply be saving face. Rooms may not yet be ready, floor staff may not be in position, or the boss may not have opened a block of rooms. In these cases, I simply retreat and wait in the lobby. Invariably something opens up.

The key in getting things done or corrected is not anger but *patience.* Patience is the primary virtue one acquires and practices as a traveler in China. It is not a foolproof device. There are many things, often very ordinary things, such as being seated in a restaurant, that sometimes are never resolved. Knowing the reasons for a problem seldom helps, but treating the people who can get something done for you with respect and patience is your best bet. If your requests or complaints place a person in the position of embarrassment or of backing down, you have not scored a victory; rather, you've made an enemy, one whose "face" you have erased, whose integrity and worth you have besmirched.

COURTESY In Old China, especially among the cultured and educated, an elaborate set of social formalities and courtesies evolved. Most of these have disappeared from modern China. Many were adopted and are still practiced elsewhere, particularly in Japan. The Chinese do not bow, for example, nor do they remove their shoes upon entering houses or inns.

The Chinese are courteous and caring hosts, but in general they conduct themselves straightforwardly, frankly, and with openness and good humor. They seldom express their thanks for small favors or transactions, although it is perfectly acceptable for foreigners to do so.

The Chinese are generally not overly forward or loud, except in gatherings of family and friends. When asking favors, however, it is best to be round about rather than direct, giving space for a host to refuse without embarrassment. Compliments are usually best directed to senior citizens, bosses, or children. Bragging about one's own accomplishments is not considered good form. Shaking hands has become the acceptable custom when meeting or parting. Kisses on the cheek are not part of Chinese culture, nor for that matter is kissing in public between lovers or partners accepted. On the other hand, the Chinese express their friendship and concern physically, often by placing an arm around the shoulders of the other person. Friends of the same sex sometimes hold hands when strolling.

QUESTIONS FROM STRANGERS It is perfectly acceptable for a stranger to ask you how much money you make. My response to this "impolite" query is to tell the truth and see the reaction. Wages even in the new, economically booming China are far, far below what's standard in the West. When I taught English in China at a leading medical college, for example, I was paid more than the most skilled Chinese surgeons, more even than the college president, and yet the salary was 10 times less than I could have lived on in the United States.

It is also perfectly acceptable for a Chinese to ask you how many children you have. Since the family has always been the most important entity in China, this is a natural question. If you have no children, the Chinese reaction is likely to be one of bewilderment and concern. It's difficult for them to imagine the curse of a no-child family.

China's number one problem is its immense population, now at 1.2 billion, twice what it was when the Communists took power in 1949.

Most Han Chinese have been slapped with a policy that allows them only one child. In a nation that puts an absolute value on the family as the primary unit, where traditionally boys are favored over girls, lecturing them on the "immorality" of this policy is rather insensitive. The Chinese feel its harshness and most of them deal with it courageously, patriotically, and sensibly, if not happily. After walking the streets of Shanghai or Beijing for a few days, ask yourself how China would be with 2 billion people. Even with severe controls on its population growth, China is adding 14 million people a year, more than enough new mouths to feed.

GUANXI (CONNECTIONS)   During Chairman Mao's reign, 1949–76, and for a decade afterward, *guanxi,* the connections one forged with people in positions to get things done, was far more a measure of wealth and power than mere money. Nearly everyone might be paid a pittance, no one could afford a car or a house, but some were more equal than others in Mao's egalitarian society because they knew the person who could get something they wanted. The guanxi system worked on the basis of cultivated friendships and favors. This sort of "bribery by barter" system permeated most aspects of life from the political to the economic.

Guanxi is still how much of China operates, only today, as the economy booms, money often replaces favors, or pays for them "under the table." Petty bribery and official corruption have become so rampant at times that many ordinary people, from peasants to professionals, have become deeply upset. At least some of the demands of the Tiananmen Square protests issued from this widespread repugnance at the spread of corruption, particularly among officials. The government has repeatedly cracked down on corruption, often within its own ranks, and continues to do so.

POSITION OF WOMEN   By law, there is complete equality between the sexes in the People's Republic of China, a great advance over centuries of feudal practice in which a woman was barely more than a father's or a husband's property. In theory, women today can enter any profession on an equal footing with men. Nevertheless, in daily practice, you will notice that women are still not as highly regarded, at least not as figures of power, in China. When it comes to field work or factory jobs, women are widely employed, but they are less numerous the higher up one goes in industry, business, education, and politics. The mandate to bear children and run the household still falls on women's shoulders, although perhaps with no more frequency than in most Western nations. It is a society where men are still in charge, but women are exercising increasing strength and freedom.

Nevertheless, it is still the dream of millions of Chinese to produce a male, rather than a female, heir. In all of pre-20th-century Chinese history, it was the man who carried on the family name, and in rural societies the man was considered the stronger field worker and the head of the clan. Modern education has gone a long way toward changing this perception, but the man is still most often the figure in charge.

Family & Social Customs

CHINESE NAMES The Chinese give their names in the reverse order customary in the West. Fred Allen Smith becomes Smith Fred Allen. The Chinese refer to others by their family names, not their first names. Many educated Chinese also adopt English first names for use with foreigners. Women frequently hold onto their original family names after marriage.

Family names in China—which are almost always one syllable in length—are in short supply. There are about 100 million people named Chang (or Chan in Cantonese) and nearly as many taking the next most popular names: Wang (Wong), Li (Lee), Chao, and Liu (Loo).

DINING CUSTOMS China has developed one of the world's greatest cuisines, as complex and various as the French. In modern China, there are also differences in the way meals are consumed and enjoyed. Slurping of soup, noodles, or rice from a small bowl held in one hand is not considered rude. Nor is scraping bones and other debris off the table onto the floor discouraged in common workers' restaurants. In nicer places, however, Western etiquette is observed.

Large meals and banquets are typically served on round tables, often with lazy Susans at the center. A series of common dishes are presented family style, with diners placing small portions on their plates using chopsticks, or, if provided, serving spoons. The host of a banquet will serve you the first portion of each dish. After that, you can serve yourself. It's considered childish to play with your chopsticks; for many foreigners, it's enough of a trial just to be able to use them. The first dishes are usually cold appetizers. Don't fill up on them. There are plenty of dishes served at a big meal or banquet. If you don't like a dish, try to take a taste. Leave the rest on your plate. If you're a vegetarian, find out what's in each dish and politely decline those with meat. To the Chinese, meat is a luxury. A Chinese host will usually propose a number of toasts during the meal. You can follow up with your own toast. The traditional salute is *gambei*, which once spoken obligates you to try to drain the cup. Many Chinese have limited capacities when it comes to drinking liquor and admire anyone who can drink a great deal. Watch yourself. Group meals are usually boisterous, happy affairs, where everyone is supposed to relax. In fact, eating is the chief Chinese pleasure, and many people spend large portions of their income on food. It is also customary to end a meal soon after the last dish, which is usually fruit, is served. The host will abruptly rise—no more socializing; the meal's at an end.

GIVING GIFTS Don't give clocks—the Chinese word sounds too much like the word for death. And don't wrap a gift in white paper—white is the Chinese color of death. Don't expect a thank you. Many Chinese won't open a gift in front of you. What we consider rudeness the Chinese consider correct form. Rather than thanking a gift giver and admiring the gift on the spot—thus ending the need to reciprocate in kind—the Chinese often say nothing and wait until they can give a comparable gift in return.

RESPECT FOR AGE By tradition, people of advanced years are highly respected for the wisdom the years bestow. This respect, refreshing if you're older and from the youth-oriented West, harkens back to China's Confucian teachings. Just as fathers demand total obedience and respect from children, so anyone of advanced years expects respect from his or her juniors. Moreover, it is the responsibility of the young to care for the elderly. Retirement homes and nursing institutions are relatively new in China, and most families find it a loss of face not to be able to care for their own in their own homes. I've found, however, that many young people in China are beginning to resent this burden, and the movement to transfer the care of senior citizens to government programs and institutions is growing. Meanwhile, if you are over 60, you can assume that your younger hosts will treat you with deep respect.

Other Considerations

CLOTHING A decade or more ago, the Chinese all dressed in dull Mao jackets, matching trousers, and workers' caps. It was as if the whole nation were a vast private school, outfitted in the attire of the great headmaster. As the economy heated up and dire restrictions against "spiritual pollution" from the decadent West were eased—a modern version of China's traditional xenophobia and self-absorbing worldview—the range of fashions broadened. In the big cities, the young dress in the latest Western fashions available (not so difficult, since much of the world's clothing seems to be made in China). Western attire, including business suits, is commonplace. Mao garb is rarely seen anymore, except in poorer towns and the countryside. Adults still tend to dress conservatively, in drab colors, while outfitting their children in the brightest outfits possible. As a visitor, I find it best to blend in, selecting darker, duller colors, avoiding revealing clothes, and keeping jewelry to a minimum. Shorts are acceptable for outings, although few Chinese wear them. Bikinis, halter tops, plunging necklines, and short skirts are still too risqué for most Chinese. It's simply more comfortable for foreigners to blend in, avoiding calling attention to themselves as rich visitors willing to overpay for every meal and trinket.

SIESTAS   The afternoon nap, once such a widespread custom in China that it was written into the constitution, is a practice out of fashion in the big bustling cities. Nevertheless, I still find an extraordinary number of offices and services that close their doors for an hour or two starting about noon. In smaller cities, towns, and villages, the noonday snooze is more often observed. Cafes and restaurants are always open, of course, to accommodate those taking "naps." When working in China in the 1980s, I became accustomed to a daily nap and I found it an invigorating custom, making one day seem like two. I still observe this custom when traveling in China, if possible, knowing that the Chinese, who go to bed late and rise early, understand why I need my midday rest.

SMOKING   One in three cigarettes smoked today is lit up in China. Cigarettes are smoked in dozens of public and confined spaces, from buses and trains to cafes and theaters. The majority of men smoke. Few women do so in public. In many restaurants, diners smoke between courses and sometimes during them. For nonsmokers, this can become a gargantuan headache. In some cases, requesting that someone not smoke works wonders; in many cases, it does not. The former supreme leader of China, Deng Xiaoping, always smoked while meeting other heads of state, and he went so far as to claim it was a healthy addiction. As China grows more prosperous, smoking threatens to become even more widespread and continuous.

Nevertheless, health officials in China are aware of the dangers, annoyances, and ultimate price society must pay. Antismoking campaigns have recently been launched and severe restrictions have been placed on smoking in public places. As of May 1, 1997, smoking on public transport—on all trains, buses, planes, ships, and taxis, and in all waiting rooms as well—was banned by the order of six ministries. It had been determined that 60% of the one billion rail passengers in China were smokers. Instant fines of RMB 10 to 50 ($1.25 to $6.25) can now be levied for anyone caught in the act of inhaling on trains, ships, planes, buses, subways, taxis, and terminals. Enforcement is now the difficulty, of course, but this "custom" of smoking in public places appears to be on its way out.

SPITTING   Hawking and spitting in public used to be an institution, as common as breathing. The same went for clearing one's nose. People often spit from passing buses and in packed cafes. The practice was widespread and goes back centuries. Nevertheless, such activities are now illegal in most of China's cities, and public campaigns to improve hygiene and politeness have made large inroads in the last few years.

TAKING PHOTOS   Taking photos of people in the streets of China is permitted, although many Chinese feel much as people in the West do—that it's an unwarranted invasion of privacy. If Chinese don't want their pictures taken, they'll wave their hands or shout. Many don't mind if you take a picture of their children. It's best to ask or motion with your camera. Photos are permitted in most temples and in all public sites except where prohibitions are posted. At some popular sites, there is now a charge for picture-taking, paid at the entrance gate.

TRAFFIC   China has long been a nation of bicycles, but as motorized vehicles inundate the streets, traffic snarls and unregulated driving patterns have proliferated. You'll quickly notice that cabs, buses, trucks, and everything else on the road moves to a different drummer, that of sheer expediency. In fact, taxis often drive with as little regard for traffic lights and proper lanes as a bicycle might.

Such crazy driving and passing is certainly dangerous, but there's little you can do about it. Drivers, most of whom are still professionally trained, are quite skilled at avoiding collisions. Telling a driver to slow down or not to pass on a curve or hill usually falls on proud and deaf ears.

One lesson is worth mastering: When you cross intersections on foot, be extremely cautious, since vehicles take the right-of-way almost everywhere. Another annoyance you'll just have to get used to is the constant honking of horns. This has become the customary way that drivers communicate their presence and intentions to other drivers. In a few cities, such as Xiamen, this form of noise pollution has been outlawed.

To Sum Up

It's worth bearing in mind, above all, that Chinese society, despite its apparent chaos, is highly organized and hierarchical, that an individual's power is limited and rigidly defined, and that it is best to make a request or complaint with courtesy rather than in anger, exercising restraint and patience—mountains of patience. The Chinese put great stock in friendship, cultivating long-term personal relationships. Such investments smooth the way and often produce results that uncompromising demands, however rational and obvious they seem to the Western mind, may never exact. Many Chinese would far rather "save face" when confronted with a difficult or impossible demand than suffer the embarrassment of backing down or confronting their superiors.

A QUICK HISTORY

CHINA IS THE PRODUCT OF A
lengthy history conducted in proud isolation. Travelers seldom have time
to master the intricacies of Chinese chronologies before stepping off the
plane, but a basic briefing is useful. When I travel through China I always
have in mind a simplified time line of China's major dynasties, a rough
list of its famous figures, an outline of its major religions, and an acquaintance with its customs and cultural achievements. This background cre-
ates a context for much of what I see along the way, a context that is
always expanded by direct experience.

A Dynasty Primer

China's history is usually—and quite usefully—divided into its successive
dynasties. Sometimes it seems there are more dynasties than brain cells in
which to store them. I've found, however, that most of the historical sites
and treasures on display are the products of six major dynasties spanning
the last 23 centuries. When I keep these six periods straight, I can usually
come away from a museum, temple, or historic monument with an understanding of how it fits into the larger picture.

China's two great showcases of dynastic history, Xi'an and Beijing,
roughly divide the history of these great dynasties between them. In the
ancient capital of Xi'an, there are fine representatives of the art and monuments created during the Qin, Han, and Tang dynasties. In the modern
capital of Beijing, the Ming and Qing dynasties hold sway. The creations
of the earlier dynasties at Xi'an are simpler but powerful and graceful in
style. The later dynasties, based in Beijing, took art and architecture to
more elaborate and ornate extremes.

Bear in mind that Chinese scholars envision the history of their civilization as stretching back 5,000 years. It's unlikely that you'll see many sites
or relics over 2,300 years old in your travels, with the exception of the Banpo
Neolithic Village in Xi'an, which amply predates recorded Chinese history
and the rise of imperial rule.

The earliest recorded societies in China rose during the **Xia period**
(2200–1700 B.C.), continued through the **Shang period** (1700–1100 B.C.),

SIX MAJOR DYNASTIES	
Qin	221–207 B.C.
Han	206 B.C.–A.D. 220
Tang	A.D. 618–907
Song	A.D. 960–1279
Ming	A.D. 1368–1644
Qing	A.D. 1644–1911

and began to become more consolidated during the **Zhou period** (1100–221 B.C.), when various kingdoms fought to extend their domains. Archeologists keep finding more relics from these early periods, although relatively little is known about them. Confucius (551–479 B.C.) lived during the Zhou period in the Kingdom of Chu, and the shadowy figure of Lao Zi, founder of Daoism, also dates from this era.

Viewing Chinese history simply as a succession of dynasties is misleading on many counts. For long periods, centralized control was a dream rather than a reality. The four centuries between the Han and Tang dynasties, for example, which began with the romantic **Three Kingdoms** period (A.D. 220–280), was an age of division and strife among contending states. The **Northern Wei** (A.D. 386–534) managed to achieve a brief unification of power, first at Datong, where the Yungang Buddhist grottoes survive, then at Luoyang, where the Longmen Buddhist caves also remain.

Nor has China always been in the hands of the native Han Chinese. The **Yuan Dynasty** (1271–1368), the setting for Marco Polo's travels, was ruled by the Mongols. The Qing Dynasty (1644–1911), under which Western traders, missionaries, and scholars first entered China in large numbers, was ruled by the Manchus.

Inevitably, the decay and fall of the major dynasties led to massive destruction of relics and monuments. New ruling families often tried to make a clean break with the weighty past, razing the palaces, temples, and capitals of the predecessors they ousted. It's fortunate that anything at all survives today. Dozens of short-lived dynasties rose to power until more lasting central authority was again established. This cycle of creation and destruction seems to be the dynamic force underlying much of Chinese history, and it is repeated in modern Chinese history, too, which is marked by sudden gargantuan shifts in policy and wholesale elimination of the "evils" of the past.

Fortunately for travelers, historic relics, artworks, and monuments have survived in surprising abundance. Keeping straight to which dynasty each belongs is a formidable task, however, as there can be up to 60 or more periods and dynasties to keep in mind, depending on what source you consult. The six major dynasties of my simplified outline cover most of the ground, and they form a practical basis for expanding your knowledge as you see more of historical China.

QIN DYNASTY (221–207 B.C.) The Chinese empire begins with the unification of many warring states under the First Emperor, Qin Shi Huang Di, in 221 B.C. Qin's rule was brief and his successors could not hold the empire together, but the centralization of power, the bureaucratization of society, and the standardization of writing scripts, weights and measures, and chariot ax-

les set the basis for later dynasties that sometimes ruled for centuries. The chief remains of this first dynasty are the First Emperor's terra-cotta army unearthed in Xi'an.

HAN DYNASTY (206 B.C.–A.D. 220) After the first dynasty fell apart, a greater dynasty emerged. The Han Dynasty extended the borders of the empire and cemented the institutions that would be the basis for Chinese civilization for 2,000 years. Some fine clay crafts and stone sculptures from the Han are found in China's museums, particularly in Xi'an, where the ruins of the Han capital are still visible.

TANG DYNASTY (A.D. 618–907) After four centuries of warfare and the waxing and waning of many minor dynasties, China's golden age began under a long succession of Tang rulers who lived in the capital of Xi'an (then known as Chang'an). The Tang traded by the Silk Road, and also by sea. Buddhism had entered China via the Silk Road and under the Tang played a

primary role in art and architecture. From this era we have wood-block printing and the production of fine silk. Again, Xi'an contains the richest repository of Tang art and architecture, but there are temples, pagodas, and artworks all over China that date from this prosperous period.

Song China

SONG DYNASTY (960–1279) After another period of unrest, the Song rulers reunified China and established a dynasty noted for its art and literature. The Song had the first paper money, moveable type, the compass, gunpowder, and rocket-propelled spears. The Northern Song Dynasty (960–1126) made Kaifeng its capital, while the Southern Song Dynasty (1127–1279) ruled from Hangzhou, then known as Qinsai. Both cities have many treasures and temples from the Song. Marco Polo found a prosperous empire when he first reached China at the end of the Song Dynasty.

Ming China

MING DYNASTY (1368–1644) After two centuries of rule (1271–1368) by the invading Mongols, spearheaded by Genghis Khan and Kublai Khan, their Yuan Dynasty fell, and China reverted to a local line of rulers known as the Ming. It was during this period that European ships for the first time, began to arrive off the coast of China. The Ming capital was Beijing, and there the Ming emperors built several of China's most famous monuments: the Forbidden City, the Temple of Heaven, and sections of the Great Wall that millions of tourists visit today.

QING (MANCHU) DYNASTY (1644–1911) China's final great dynasty, established by Manchu invaders from the north, brought about the last great flourishes of traditional Chinese art and architecture. Its capital, Beijing, was graced with the Summer Palace. The empire was extended to include Tibet and Mongolia, but the Western powers made intrusions, establishing concessions in Canton, Shanghai, Qingdao, Beijing, and many other cities. In 1911, the Qing were overthrown by nationalistic forces led by Sun Yatsen. The first Republic of China was established, ending thousands of years of imperial rule, leading to the slow modernization of the country and the ascendancy of the Communists under Mao Zedong, who established the present People's Republic of China in 1949.

Modern Politics

In some ways, China has undergone more changes in the 20th century than in the last 20 centuries combined. The final dynasty fell in 1911. The Republic of China was established, but it proved weak and unstable. Sun Yatsen led the powerful Guomindang, the Nationalist People's Party, until his death in 1925. His successor, Chiang Kai-shek, became head of China's government, but he was soon involved in violent struggles against two opponents: Japan, which forcibly occupied large areas of China as World War II neared, and the Chinese Communist Party, led by Mao Zedong and Zhou Enlai, which Chiang Kai-shek saw as a threat to his own power. In 1934, in the face of Chiang Kai-shek's military pressure, Mao's 100,000 supporters retreated to the north of China on the epic Long March. The Japanese, who had occupied Manchuria in 1933, went to war with China in 1937, occupying most of the east coast and pushing Chiang Kai-shek's capital all the way inland to Chongqing, where his troops were supplied by the legendary Flying Tigers and other American and British units.

With Japan's eventual defeat in 1945, the civil war in China intensified. Mao's People's Liberation Army (PLA) triumphed. Chiang Kai-shek's Guomindang fled to Taiwan. Mao proclaimed China a People's Republic in 1949 and set up his capital in Beijing. In a few violent decades, China moved from an imperial dynasty to a modern republic to the largest Communist state on Earth.

Mao ruled Communist China as a new "emperor" until his death in 1976. His regime began on many promising notes. Many of the oppressive institutions of China's "feudal" past were simply eradicated. Prostitution, drugs, gambling, and other vices disappeared overnight. Landlords and other members of the "oppressive" classes were imprisoned, expelled, or murdered. Peasants—the backbone of Mao's revolution—were given the land to work for the first time in centuries. Women were given expanded rights. Electricity was spread across the country. Wealth was radically redistributed. For most Chinese, China had finally stood up to the

CHINA TIMELINE

Xia Dynasty	2100–1600 B.C.
Shang Dynasty	1600–1100 B.C.
Zhou Dynasties	1100–476 B.C.
Western Zhou Dynasty	1100–771 B.C.
Eastern Zhou Dynasty	770–476 B.C.
Spring and Autumn Period	770–476 B.C.
Warring States Period	475–221 B.C.
Qin Dynasty	221–207 B.C.
Han Dynasty	206 B.C.–A.D. 220
Western Han	206 B.C.–A.D. 24
Eastern Han	A.D. 25–220
Three Kingdoms Period	A.D. 220–280
Wu Kingdom	A.D. 220–280
Shu Kingdom	A.D. 220–261
Wei Kingdom	A.D. 220–265
Jin Dynasties	A.D. 265–420
Western Jin	A.D. 265–316
Eastern Jin	A.D. 317–420
Sixteen Kingdoms Period	A.D. 304–439
Wei Dynasties	A.D. 386–557
Northern Wei	A.D. 386–534
Eastern Wei	A.D. 534–550
Western Wei	A.D. 535–557
Northern and Southern States	A.D. 420–589
Sui Dynasty	A.D. 581–618
Tang Dynasty	A.D. 618–907
Five Dynasties and Ten Kingdoms Period	A.D. 907–979
Liao Dynasty	A.D. 907–1125
Song Dynasty	A.D. 960–1279
Northern Song	A.D. 960–1127
Southern Song	A.D. 1127–1279
Western Xia Period	A.D. 1032–1227
Jin Period	A.D. 1115–1234
Yuan Dynasty	A.D. 1279–1368
Ming Dynasty	A.D. 1368–1644
Qing Dynasty	A.D. 1644–1911
Republic of China	A.D. 1912–1949
People's Republic of China	1949–present
Mao Period	1949–1976
Deng Period	1977–1997

world and was vigorously setting its own course, without outside inter-
ference, for the first time in generations.

The idealism of the post-Liberation years eventually soured as Mao
initiated a number of radical programs, many of which were extreme re-
versals of Chinese traditions. Intellectuals, highly esteemed in Confucian
culture, were denounced and imprisoned in a number of political campaigns, starting with the Anti-Rightist Campaign in 1958. Peasants were
forced into massive communes in the same year. Even more disastrous
was the abortive Great Leap Forward of 1959, an attempt to industrialize
the nation overnight that succeeded only in reducing agricultural output
to the point where millions of people starved to death. In 1960, the Soviet Union, which had been China's chief supporter, advisor, and aid-
giver, withdrew completely. China entered a period of isolation as severe
as any during the great dynasties of the past.

The most ruinous campaign of all, the Great Proletarian Cultural
Revolution (1966–76), turned China upside down and led to 10 years of
self-destruction. Mao released millions of young people—who idolized
him as a living god and swore by every word in his *Little Red Book*—to
take control of China and cleanse it of all the old evils and ideals. Virtually anyone in power in 1966 would eventually be toppled by this wave of
radical reform. Schools closed down and the economy ground to a halt as
everyone engaged in political struggles. Unwavering loyalty to the latest
politically correct line became the litmus test for keeping a job, a home, a
family, life itself. Thousands, mainly the educated, were sent into the countryside where they worked as peasants in long programs of "reform through
labor." The Red Guards went on campaigns to erase the past, trashing
countless temples and other dynastic treasures of China's feudal days.
Tourists still come across the legacies of the Cultural Revolution not only
in ruins (many of which are being restored) but in the minds and hearts
of Chinese people who suffered unspeakably and yet survived the ravages
of this long nightmare.

The door to China remained closed to the outside world until 1972,
when the United States, after a few rounds of "Ping-Pong diplomacy,"
recognized the People's Republic of China. But it wasn't until the death
of Chairman Mao in 1976 that new leaders emerged to put China back
on a rational and practical track. The Gang of Four, including Mao's wife,
Jiang Qing, was put on public trial in 1980 for "crimes" perpetrated during the Cultural Revolution. Deng Xiaoping, several times removed from
office and punished during the Cultural Revolution, assumed power and
launched China on an entirely new course, away from radical experiments
in egalitarianism and "pure" communism and toward a socialism "with
Chinese characteristics" that yielded practical economic results.

China slowly recovered the ground it had lost during Mao's later reign,
but a long shadow was again cast over the nation on June 4, 1989, when

pro-democracy protesters who had seized Tiananmen Square in the heart of Beijing were evicted by force before the eyes of the world. China was instituting some economic and social reforms by this point, but political freedom was virtually nonexistent. The violent military crackdown on students and others in Tiananmen Square formed the most dramatic and lasting impression of China for millions of foreign viewers.

When I visited Canton, Shanghai, and Beijing the following year, I found a nation in shock. I also found almost no Western tourists. An invisible boycott had taken hold.

In 1992, Deng Xiaoping made a historic "southern tour" of China, during which he urged the nation to accelerate its economic liberalization. This set into motion a rapid Westernization of China. At times, China seemed the most capitalistic country on the planet, a freewheeling society whose motto echoed Deng Xiaoping's famous epitaph, "To get rich is glorious." Millionaires appeared overnight. Thousands of private enterprises were born in the streets. Greed replaced any lingering hopes for a rebirth of political idealism. The Communist Party, although widely discredited, remained firmly in power, and the people, given economic if not political freedom on a scale never before granted by any rulers, concentrated on helping build China into a superpower for the 21st century.

The death of senior leader Deng Xiaoping and the return of Hong Kong to Chinese sovereignty in 1997 marked the beginning of a third era in the history of China since Liberation in 1949. The economy of the 1990s boomed steadily onward. China hurtled through its own Industrial Revolution and beyond in a matter of months and years rather than the decades and centuries experienced by the West. Where this will lead, no one knows. China must initiate far greater, more perilous reforms to keep its economy running, and sooner or later it must liberalize its political system as well. But changes in all spheres do seem possible as a new century begins.

Not only are today's travelers able to feast on the splendors of Old China to a degree never before possible; they can also see this China of the future taking shape minute by minute, emerging from the deep shadows of the recent past into something surely brighter.

Portrait Gallery

China yesterday and today is a stage populated by thousands of actors well known to every Chinese but obscure to the outsider. It helps to have a thumbnail sketch of some of the leading members of the cast, as these names will constantly come up as one travels across China.

Chiang Kai-shek (1887–1975)   Leader of the Guomindang (Nationalist People's Party) and president of China during the war against Japan (1933–45), Chiang fled to Taiwan after his forces were defeated by the

Communists in 1949, establishing the Republic of China there in fierce opposition to the People's Republic of China on the mainland.

Empress Dowager Cixi (1835–1908)   The power behind the throne during the last gasps of the Qing (Manchu) Dynasty and creator of the Summer Palace at Beijing, she is villainized in the popular imagination as an evil despot and conniving assassin.

Confucius (551–479 B.C.)   This great philosopher, known as Kong Fuzi to the Chinese, is China's Socrates. His teachings, particularly about the strict relationships of leader to subject, man to woman, and parent to child, underlie the traditional organization of family and society in China.

Deng Xiaoping (1904–97)   A veteran of the Long March, in and out of favor with Chairman Mao, Deng directed China's economic revolution in the 1980s and 1990s. A pragmatist who suffered under the political campaigns of Mao, Deng is blamed for ordering the military crackdown on Tiananmen Square in 1989. He is best remembered for his saying (applied to competing economic and political proposals), "It doesn't matter whether the cat is black or white, as long as it catches mice."

Du Fu (A.D. 712–770)   Considered (along with Li Bai) China's greatest poet, Du Fu wrote powerful, personal lyrics that touch the major chords of Chinese history and human sadness. His "thatched cottage," where he lived in exile from the Tang Dynasty capital, is memorialized in a park in Chengdu.

Guanyin   China's most popular Buddhist deity, usually regarded as a woman or a figure combining both sexes, she is the Goddess of Mercy, often petitioned to ensure the birth of a male heir. Her temple home in China is the holy island mountain of Putuo Shan.

Kangxi (1654–1722)   Second emperor of the Qing Dynasty and ruler of China from 1662 to 1722, Kangxi visited most of the important cities and mountains in China, restoring ancient temples and building many new ones. He built the imperial summer palace in Chengde (near Beijing) which survives.

Lao Zi (circa 570–490 B.C.)   Legendary founder of China's indigenous religion, Daoism, Lao Zi emphasized the essential way of nature and the inner, often magical powers of the individual.

Li Bai (A.D. 699–762)   Considered (along with Du Fu) China's greatest poet, Li Bai wrote brilliant lyrics (often while drunk on wine) that celebrated individual power and the realm of the senses.

Mao Zedong (1893–1976)   Chairman Mao helped create the Chinese Communist Party in 1921. He became the supreme ruler of China in

1949. Venerated as a living god in his lifetime, he led China out of its feudal past and initiated modern reforms, but he also devised campaigns and policies that destroyed the Chinese economy and educational system during the Cultural Revolution (1966–76).

Marco Polo (1254–1324)   Italian author of the West's most famous travel book about China, Marco Polo claimed to be an emissary of Kublai Khan during a 17-year residence in Old Cathay. Despite recent suggestions that Marco Polo never even set foot in China but relied on the accounts of Silk Road merchants who had, his name is synonymous with all that is exotic in mysterious China.

Qin Shi Huang Di (259–210 B.C.)   The First Emperor of unified China, Qin was known as the burner of books and the builder of the Great Wall. The terra-cotta warriors guarding his immense underground mausoleum at Xi'an are one of China's leading tourist attractions.

Sun Yat-sen (1866–1925)   Patriarch of Chinese reform, democracy, and modernization, known as Sun Zhongshan to the Chinese, he headed the Guomindang movement that toppled the last dynasty and propelled China into the 20th century.

Empress Wu (A.D. 660–705)   China's most powerful female ruler, Wu Zetian rose to empress of the Tang Dynasty from the position of a concubine and initiated thousands of Buddhist temples and works of art.

Xuan Zang (A.D. 602–664)   China's most famous Buddhist monk, he made a 22-year pilgrimage to India to gather holy manuscripts (sutras), which he translated at temples in Xi'an that still stand. He is the basis for the fantastical hero of *The Monkey: Or Journey to the West,* one of China's most popular epic novels.

Zhang Zemin (b. 1926)   Paramount leader of China since the death of Deng Xiaoping in 1997, a master politician, Zhang is dedicated to economic reforms. All he lacks is charisma.

Zhou Enlai (1898–1976)   Confederate of Chairman Mao and one of the founders of the Chinese Communist Party, and a skilled diplomat, Zhou Enlai is remembered fondly by many Chinese because as premier during the nightmare years of the Cultural Revolution (1966–76) he intervened to save many lives as well as temples and historic treasures from the rampaging Red Guards.

Zhuge Liang (A.D. 181–234)   During the Three Kingdoms Period (A.D. 220–280), he devised astonishing military strategies. His name is synonymous in China with wisdom and correct conduct. His memorial hall is located in Chengdu.

TEMPLES, MOSQUES AND CHURCHES

AMONG THE MORE INTERESTING but often fatiguing sights in China are the temples. There are Daoist temples, Buddhist temples, even Confucian temples. Tourists, particularly on package tours, often get "templed out" after their third or fourth visit (in their third or fourth city) to these ancient shrines.

Nevertheless, the religious architecture and art of China are among its most sublime creations, and temples and pagodas reflect much of the essence of Old China. Understanding the history of religion in China can pump some life and individual character into these monuments.

Three Old Ways & Two New Ones

Daoism (or Taoism), the most important indigenous religion, dates back 2,500 years. **Buddhism,** its chief rival among organized religions, is a transplant, introduced from India about 2,000 years ago. **Confucianism—** more a philosophy than a religion, although it does have its own rites and temples—is a way of conceiving of society and family in a series of hier-archical relationships. The Confucian is primarily interested in family, society, and education; the Daoist in nature, the individual, and magic; and the Buddhist in compassion, suffering, and transcendence.

These three ways of perceiving the world spiritually were blended over the centuries. Thus, at first blush it is not easy to tell a Daoist temple from a Buddhist shrine from a Confucian pavilion (or even from a royal palace). They share much in common, particularly their architecture. They also share worshippers. As an old adage puts it: "Go to work a Confucian, retire a Daoist, die a Buddhist."

In Old China, Daoism, Buddhism, and Confucianism played a large role in daily life. In modern China, it is quite a different story. Religion currently plays an unimportant role. Official estimates suggest that 70% of China's people are affiliated with no religion at all, 20% practice ancient folk religions, 6% percent are Buddhist, 1% are Muslim, less than 1% are Daoist, and far less than 1% are Christian (0.2%).

Although you'll notice the Chinese thronging the old temples you visit, bowing and burning incense, devoted Buddhists and Daoists make up a tiny portion of the people. Chinese Muslims, actively devoted to Islam, also constitute a small minority. These days it is the Chinese Christians who are growing in strength, although again they do not constitute more than a small bloc of the Chinese people.

The temples, when toured with an understanding of China's past, are treasure houses, while China's mosques and churches are vital centers of worship for dedicated segments of the population. Both sorts of religious shrines, old and new, often provide moving experiences.

Islam

China's Muslim population numbers only 14 million of China's 1.2 billion residents (barely 1%), but their struggle to maintain an ethnic as well as religious identity is a major concern of China's leaders, who are wary of any sign of a burgeoning secessionist movement such as that in Tibet. Muslim minorities have therefore been granted many of the special rights enjoyed by China's other minorities, such as exemption from the one-family–one-child rule.

Arab sea traders and Silk Road merchants introduced Islam to the edges of the Chinese empire not long after the faith was born in the 7th century A.D. Today there are historic mosques worth visiting in Canton, Beijing, Xi'an, and the Silk Road cities of Gansu and Xinjiang provinces. Most of China's Muslim population resides in the northwest. Cities such as Xi'an have a Muslim quarter where the people, known as the Hui, are indistinguishable from Han Chinese, due to centuries of assimilation, but they strictly maintain many Muslim mandates, running their own schools, butcher shops, and restaurants. There are 6.5 million Hui in China.

In Xinjiang Province, the 5.5 million Uighur people, practicing Muslims, dominate the culture of a region that occupies one-sixth of China's territory. The mosques in Kashgar and other desert oases, dating from the Ming and Qing dynasties, are among the most fascinating religious sites in China.

Christianity

Catholic missionaries first arrived in the 16th century in the person of Matteo Ricci of the Society of Jesus, but the Ming emperor was not so interested in Ricci's religious message as he was in the Jesuit's scientific knowledge. Protestant missionaries, making their mark in the mid-19th and early 20th centuries, made heartbreakingly few converts while in China. Despite this failure and repeated episodes of persecution in more recent times, Christianity appears to be flourishing now as never before. An official census put the number of Christians in China at about 3 million—hardly enough to cause a blip on China's population radar—but in the last few years, and particularly with the addition of Hong Kong, this figure has soared.

Most Chinese cities now have at least two officially sanctioned Christian churches in operation: one Protestant, one Catholic. The Protestant churches are controlled by the Three-Self Patriotic Movement and are not affiliated with any religious institutions in the West. The Catholic churches are controlled by the Catholic Patriotic Association, which does not recognize the authority of Rome. Catholic mass is still conducted in Latin. In addition, there are numerous illegal "home churches" throughout China that also have a growing membership, despite occasional crackdowns by local police.

I've attended dozens of services in Protestant and Catholic churches in many cities and towns in China. This is often a most unusual experience, even if one is not a Christian. Most of the churches were built in the late 19th or early 20th century in Western European styles. Few have any religious decorations left, but most have plenty of bibles and hymnals. Nearly all who attend Christian services today are Chinese. A decade ago, many of the worshippers were elderly, members who had attended churches before their closure either after Liberation (1949) or during the Cultural Revolution (1966–76). Now more and more young people, perhaps curious about Western institutions of all kinds, are attending.

A traveler recently informed me that when she inquired at a hotel desk about attending Sunday services at a church in Xi'an, she was told that it didn't accept foreigners. This is nonsense. Foreigners are routinely welcomed with open arms in all the churches in China. Be persistent. The only difficulty in attending church in China is the same difficulty faced almost everywhere: breaking through the crowds and securing a seat inside.

Daoism

Daoism is the metaphysical and naturalistic wing of Chinese religion and philosophy. In its pure form, as expounded in the writings of its legendary founder, Lao Zi, in the 6th century B.C., the Dao (or Tao) is the way—an absolute way, removed from space, time, society, and tradition, yet one with nature, that can only be discovered by the individual and cannot be described in words, except perhaps through paradox.

Daoism was not intended to be organized as a religion. Its most famous practitioners were usually hermits. The Daoist ideal is to retreat from society and learn from nature. All laws and rules are rejected. The individual cultivates a life of simplicity and withdrawal. Despite these antisocial ideals, Daoism did achieve an organized form, complete with temples, priests, and its own elaborate cosmology. Daoists became the alchemists of China, seeking the elixir of immortality, consuming gold flakes, cinnabar, and various poisons, practicing extreme methods of control over breathing and other bodily functions. Their history is filled with tales of the superhuman and the magical, and their living gods are the immortals who have achieved everlasting physical life and fly with the clouds. Many Chinese artists, particularly lyrical poets such as Li Bai, have been deeply influenced by Daoism.

There are Daoist temples in nearly all Chinese cities, along with Daoist priests and nuns who have returned in small numbers since their banishment during the Cultural Revolution (1966–76). Some of the more famous Daoist temples can be visited today on the Five Sacred Mountains of Old China: Song Shan, Heng Shan Bei, Heng Shan Nan, Hua Shan, and Tai Shan.

Buddhism

Buddhism arrived from India by the same route as goods from the West, by the Silk Road. The new religion took hold in China's desert outposts during the Han Dynasty (206 B.C. to A.D. 220). At the oasis of Dunhuang, devotees created China's greatest storehouse of Buddhist paintings and manuscripts in the caves of Mogao in the 4th century A.D. By the 9th century, Buddhism was so widely practiced and its temples so rich that the Tang emperor banished Buddhism altogether as an institution "foreign" to the Chinese way. The temples were reopened or rebuilt shortly after this edict, although Buddhism gradually lost its great power.

Buddhism's most important sites in China include the Shao Lin Monastery at Song Shan, where the fighting monks developed the martial arts and Chan Buddhism (known as Zen in Japan) originated; the two great Tang Dynasty pagodas and their temples in Xi'an, the ancient capital, where Buddhism exerted its strongest influence; and the temples on the Four Famous Peaks of Buddhism: Wutai Shan, Jiuhua Shan, Putuo Shan, and Emei Shan.

Buddhism's influence on art and architecture reached its zenith under the Tang and continued through later dynasties. Most of the temples, pagodas, and statues one sees all across China today are Buddhist.

Confucianism

Confucius (Kong Fuzi), rather like Socrates, was a teacher whose ideas were written down by his students, and Confucian ideas had as far-reaching an influence on Chinese philosophy as Socratic ideas did on Western thought.

Confucius laid great stress on education, particularly on the study of ancient classics, since these recorded a more perfect society than what existed in the present, and on traditional rituals and rites, since these also came from an earlier, golden age. He also devised the image of the model gentleman, a highly educated public servant who fulfilled all duties and whose character and integrity were completely unassailable. All these notions became the basis of the Chinese educational system with its imperial examinations, which were the route to a lucrative and influential career as a scholar-official in China's massive civil service system.

Even more profoundly, Confucius formulated the five relationships that all Chinese are traditionally expected to observe. Each relationship is between a superior and an inferior. Those relationships are between ruler and subject, father and son, husband and wife, elder brother and younger brother, and friend and friend. For society—indeed, for Heaven and Earth—to be in harmony, these relationships had to be strictly observed. The relationships extended even beyond the grave: Recently departed family members had to be mourned and ancestors had to be "worshipped" at family shrines.

When the Confucians gained prominent positions in government during the early Han Dynasty in the 2nd century B.C. these ideas became state doctrines. The emperor was responsible for running human affairs in a virtuous and just manner or he could lose his "Mandate of Heaven," bringing disastrous consequences to the kingdom. The emperor's royal advisors were required to give their superior best advice for the welfare of the state, regardless of its effect on an advisor's own career. These officials, in turn, were products of a rigorous state examination system that quizzed its students on the intricacies of Confucian classics. One long-term result still felt in China today is that the rule of law never gained a foothold. Conflicts were settled and policies were determined through negotiations conducted among a few powerful and presumably good and just men. Since they occupied a superior position, and were ideally of unquestionable integrity, their decisions could not properly be questioned by the masses.

In this century, Mao Zedong turned Confucianism on its head, making the masses superior to the scholar-elites. Ancestor worship, filial piety, respect for the past, deference to elders and the educated, unquestioning obedience to authority, the sanctity of the family—all these Confucian doctrines were for a time denounced as feudal and backward. And while many of these old ideas are not practiced today, they still underlie Chinese responses in subtle but profound ways. The need to "save face," for instance, originally prescribed as a way to protect the family, is still an everyday practice.

While mainly secular in its teachings, Confucianism gradually became China's state religion. The first temples to Confucius were built in the 7th century as shrines where the Great Scholar and his disciples could be worshipped as scholarly ancestors of the nation or at least of its bureaucracy. These Confucian temples can still be found in many cities in

China. The Confucian Temple in Beijing is still quite active, and the one in Xi'an now serves as the lovely grounds for the old provincial museum.

How To Tour a Temple

Monumental Chinese architecture, from temples to cities, was traditionally laid out according to cosmological principles that became known as *feng shui*—a way of arranging objects to avoid or deflect the invasion of evil forces. In simple terms, this meant that everything from a temple to a city faced south (since evil forces galore swept in from the north), surrounded on four sides by a high wall to keep out bad spirits (not to mention ordinary thieves).

The Daoist, Buddhist, and Confucian temples you visit in China today adhere to this geomantically correct scheme. Protected by rectangular walls like a small city, the temple's main entrance faces south. The entrance gate is sealed off by huge wooden doors, near which novice monks collect the modern entrance fees. Immediately inside is a series of pavilions and courtyards lined on both sides by residence and administrative halls. The inner complex can be compact or vast, consisting of hundreds of buildings or a small handful. Usually, the deeper into the courtyards and pavilions you go, the more sacred the shrine.

The temple architecture is virtually identical regardless of the religion practiced within. Variations in style are a product of region and historical period, not the dictates of faith. The main support consists of interlocking wooden beams and enormous columns resting on raised platforms. The curving roof is paved in ceramic tiles. In the early Tang Dynasty, a system of cantilevered brackets enabled the eaves to become a more prominent and showy feature. Carved figures populated the gables. In southern China, ornamentation and increasingly upturned eaves became the fashion. In the north, temple architecture remained more restrained.

While Chinese temples are seldom multistoried, owing to restrictions inherent in their structural elements, the pagodas that often rise from temple grounds were deliberately designed to touch the heavens. Derived from religious towers in India, the Chinese versions served two primary purposes: as reliquaries for holy documents and other sacred relics and as magical monuments to protect monasteries, cities, and the surrounding countryside from natural and manmade disasters. Some pagodas allow visitors to ascend the stairways inside, although many are closed. The Tang Dynasty pagodas in Xi'an can still be climbed and they are among the most important to survive in China.

In Buddhist temples, the grand entrance often contains two large statues of guardian kings, known as the Erwang, one on either side. The first buildings beyond the entrance are the bell and drum towers, once used to call the faithful to prayer. The first major hall is a holy military complex of sorts with large statues of the four heavenly kings, two on each side. Their task is to protect the sacred site, punish evil, and reward the good and just. The yellow Northern King, Duo Wen, carries the banner of sacred truth, which looks for all the world like an umbrella. The white Eastern King, Zhi Gui, has a lute to calm the tormented soul with his divine music. The blue Southern King, Zeng Zhang, is armed with a demon-defying sword. The red Western King, Guang Mu, clutches a snake for power over evil and a pearl for wisdom.

The first Buddha you usually encounter is Maitreya, the Laughing Buddha, with his trademark bulging belly. Maitreya is the Buddha of the Future, technically still a bodhisattva (enlightened follower remaining on Earth to help others). His belly is swollen by meditation. His earlobes are elongated by the heavy rings he once wore, signs that he was a respected teacher.

The Great Hall of most Buddhist temples often contains three large golden statues sitting on lotus flowers. These are the Buddhas of the Past, Present, and Future. Maitreya, the Buddha of the Future, you've already met. Sakyamuni, the Buddha of the Present, is the historical figure who attained enlightenment. Dipamkara, the Buddha of the Past, represents all who entered Nirvana before Sakyamuni, the 5th century B.C. northern Indian prince.

The walls of the Great Hall usually contain smaller statues of Buddha's divine followers, the 500 arhats (or luohans). Immediately behind the Great Buddhas is a statue of the Goddess of Mercy, Guanyin, who became the most popular Buddhist divinity in China. Guanyin is often portrayed as having "a thousand arms," representing her great capacity to reach out to others. She is also petitioned to grant a male heir.

The faithful temple-goer purchases prayer beads, amulets, and incense sticks from the temple vendors, placing a burning stick in the incense burners outside each hall and kneeling and praying on the cushions or rugs placed before the altar inside. If the temple has a large and active team of monks, they will often conduct chants inside the fenced-off area in front of the altar.

It's easy enough for a novice visitor to find the main altars in a temple complex: Just keep heading straight north from the entrance through the inner courtyards from hall to hall. Often the back door of a pavilion is open so that visitors can walk around the altar and statues in the center and exit at the rear into the courtyard of the next pavilion.

In a Daoist temple, the layout is much the same but the gods have changed and the monks are wearing funny leggings. The red columns of a Buddhist temple are painted black and yin-yang symbols frequently appear on walls. The Three Buddhas are replaced by statues of the Three Immortals riding tiger, deer, and crane. Literary and historical figures, such as the Three Kingdom's Zhuge Liang, are often memorialized. One figure of adoration and petition that Daoist and Buddhist temples can share, however, is Guanyin, Goddess of Mercy.

Daoist temples tend to be more down-to-earth and eclectic than Buddhist temples. Most of the temples you'll visit in China are Buddhist, but there are plenty of Daoist temples as well. Those at the center of the city often opened their courtyards to Sunday marketplaces, and street markets still often surround Daoist temples. There are few Confucian temples and they are seldom used by worshippers of the Great Sage. The Confucian Temple in Beijing, one of the most famous in China, employs the architecture of Buddhist and Daoist temples, but its somber and stately interiors and altars are remarkably bare of one item the other temples have in numbing abundance: statues. There's not even one of Confucius himself.

THE CHINESE LANGUAGE

THE OFFICIAL LANGUAGE OF CHINA is **putonghua,** often called Mandarin, which is the dialect spoken in Beijing. Most Chinese understand Mandarin. However, every city and region of China has its own distinct dialect. In some cases, the dialect is unintelligible to most other Chinese. Cantonese, Shanghainese, and other dialects are spoken as if they are different languages altogether, but all Chinese dialects share the same written form.

Most foreign travelers can't speak Chinese, a major obstacle, particularly for independent travelers. English is spoken by many educated Chinese and English is taught in most schools, but you'll find few people who use it outside of international hotels. Taking a course in Chinese before you leave home is wise, because even knowing and using a few basic Chinese words and phrases is useful.

Because Chinese is a tonal language, the pronunciation is quite different from that of a Western language, and difficult to master. In Mandarin there are four basic tones: The first is a high-pitched even tone, the second a rising tone, the third falling and then rising, and the fourth tone falling. The same "sound" can be spoken in four different tones, each tone yielding a different word or meaning. In asking for a place or street name, you need to know how it's pronounced or you won't be understood.

The written language consists of discrete characters, or symbols, each representing a word or a syllable. There are thousands of these characters. An average person probably can read 2,000 to 3,000 characters; a scholar may know up to 10,000. Traditional characters, still used in Hong Kong, Taiwan, and elsewhere, are quite complicated. In use in China today is a simplified version of the traditional script. The signs that you see as you travel in China, except in Hong Kong, are written in simplified characters, and these are the ones we use in the list below.

On the other hand, Chinese sentence structure is fairly straightforward: subject, predicate, and object, very much the same as in English. Chinese is not an inflected language. Case, number, and tense are indicated by particles. For example, to turn a sentence into a question, you can simply add the question particle "ma."

A GUIDE TO PINYIN PRONUNCIATION

a as in f**a**r	*l* as in **l**and
ang as in l**ung**	*m* as in **m**e
b as in **b**e	*n* as in **n**ame
c as in ra**ts**	*o* as in l**aw**
ch as in **ch**ange	*p* as in **p**ar (aspirated)
d as in **d**o, **d**ay	*q* (ch) as in **ch**eek
e as in **er**	*r* as 1) **r**ight 2) *z* in a**z**ure
ei as in m**y**	*s* as in le**ss**
eong as in **ng** (nasal sound)	*sh* as in **sh**ore
er as in hon**or**	*t* as in **t**op (aspirated)
f as in **f**oot	*u* as in sh**oo**t
g as in **g**o	*w* as in **w**ant
h as in h**er** (aspirated)	*x* as in **sh**e
i as in **ea**t	*y* as in **y**et
j as in **j**eep	*z* as in su**ds**
k as in **k**ind (aspirated)	*zh* as j in **j**ungle

There are a number of ways to transcribe Chinese into alphabetic form. The transcription of standard Chinese used in China is called *pinyin*. See the box for a phonetic guide to pronouncing pinyin.

It's a good idea to carry a Mandarin phrase book wherever you go, one written in English, pinyin, and Chinese characters. This can be very helpful. Of course, an ear for the language is an even better tool. Below is a list of the destinations and sites discussed in this book as well as some survival words and useful phrases as a starter.

English	Pinyin	Chinese
BEIJING	**Beijing**	北京
Ancient Observatory	Gugunxiangtai	古观象台
Chairman Mao's Mausoleum	Mao Zhuxi Jiniantang	毛主席纪念堂

English	Pinyin	Chinese
Forbidden City	Gugong	故宫
Lama Temple	Yonghegong	雍和宫
Old Summer Palace	Yuanmingyuan	圆明园
Summer Palace	Yiheyuan	颐和园
Temple of Heaven	Tiantan Gongyuan	天坛公园
Tiananmen Square	Tiananmen Guang Chang	天安门广场
BEIHAI	**Beihai**	**北海**
Old Town	Zhongshan Lu Laocheng Qu	中山路老城区
Silver Beach	Yintan	银滩
CANTON	**Guangzhou**	**广州**
Pearl River	Zhujiang	珠江
Qingping Market	Qingping Shichang	清平市场
Shamian Island	Shamian	沙面
Sun Yat Sen Memorial Hall	Zhongshan Jiniantang	中山纪念堂
Temple of the Six Banyan Trees	Liurongsi	六榕寺
Yuexiu Park	Yuexiu Gongyuan	越秀公园
CHENGDE	**Chengde**	**承德**
Hammer Rock	Bangchui Shan	棒锤山
Imperial Summer Retreat	Bishushanzhuang	避暑山庄
Mount Sumera Temple	Xumifushou Miao	须弥福寿庙

English	Pinyin	Chinese
Small Potala Temple	Putuozongsheng Miao	普陀宗乘之庙
Temple of Universal Joy	Pule Si	普乐寺
CHENGDU	**Chengdu**	**成都**
Du Fu Cottage	Du Fu Caotang	杜甫草堂
Qingyang Temple	Qingyang Gong	青羊宫
Wenshu Monastery	Wenshu Yuan	文殊院
Zoo	Dongwuyuan	动物园
CHONQING	**Chongqing**	**重庆**
Chongqing Museum	Chonqing Bowuguan	重庆博物馆
Gate to Heaven	Chaotianmen	朝天门
Liberation Monument	Jiefang Bei	解放碑
Luohan Temple	Luohan Si	罗汉寺
Pipashan Park	Pipashan Gongyuan	枇杷山公园
DALI	**Dali**	**大理**
Erhai Lake	Erhai Hu	洱海湖
Shaping	Shaping	沙平
Temple of the Three Pagodas	San Ta Si	三塔寺
DATONG	**Datong**	**大同**
Huayan Monastery	Huayan Si	华严寺
Nine Dragon Screen	Jiu Long Bi	九龙壁
Temple Suspended in the Void	Xuan Kong Si	悬空寺

English	Pinyin	Chinese
Yungang Buddhist Caves	Yungang Shiku	云岗石窟
DAZU BUDDHIST CAVES	**Dazu Shiku**	**大足石窟**
Dragon Flower Bridge	Hua Long Qiao	花龙桥
Precious Mountain	Baoding Shan	保定山
DUNHUANG	**Dunhuang**	**敦煌**
Crescent Moon Lake	Yueyaquan	月牙泉
Mogao Buddhist Caves	Mogao Shiku	莫高石窟
Singing Sand Mountains	Mingshashan	鸣沙山
EMEI SHAN	**Emei Shan**	**峨眉山**
Clear Sound Pavilion	Qingyin Ge	清音阁
Elephant Bathing Pool	Xixiang Chi	洗象池
Golden Summit	Jinding	金顶
Golden Summit Temple	Jinding Si	金顶寺
Jieyan Hall	Jieyin Ge	接引阁
Peak of the Ten Thousand Buddhas	Wanfoding	万佛顶
Shrine of Limpid Waters	Jin Shui	金水
Temple of Ten Thousand Years	Wannian Si	万年寺

English	Pinyin	Chinese
GRAND CANAL	**Da Yunhe**	大运河
GREAT WALL	**Wan Li Chang Cheng**	万里长城
Badaling	Badaling	八达岭
Mutianyu	Mutianyu	慕田峪
Simatai	Simatai	司马台
GUILIN	**Guilin**	桂林
Banyan Lake	Rong Hu	榕湖
Brocade Hill	Diecaishan	叠采山
Cedar Lake	Shan Hu	杉湖
Crescent Moon Hill	Yueyashan	月牙山
Elephant Trunk Hill	Xiangbishan	象鼻山
Li River	Lijiang	漓江
Minorities Cultural Park	Feng Qing Yuan	丰庆园
Pierced Hill	Chuanshan	穿山
Reed Flute Cave	Ludi Yan	芦笛岩
Seven-Star Park	Qixing Yan Gongyuan	七星岩公园
Solitary Beauty Peak	Duxiufeng	独秀峰
Whirlpool Hill	Fuboshan	伏波山
HANGZHOU	**Hangzhou**	杭州
China Tea Museum	Zhongguo Cha Bowuguan	中国茶博物馆
Dragon Well	Longjing	龙井

English	Pinyin	Chinese
Lingyin Temple	Lingyin Si	灵隐寺
Three Pools Mirroring the Moon	Santan Yinyue	三潭印月
Solitary Island	Gushan	孤山
West Lake	Xi Hu	西湖
Zhejiang Provincial Museum	Zhejiang Bowuguan	浙江省博物馆
HARBIN	**Harbin**	哈尔滨
Confucian Temple	Wen Miao	文庙
Japanese War Crimes Museum	Riben Xijun Shiyan Jidi Bowuguan	日本细菌试验基地博物馆
Old Town	Daoliqu	道里区
Siberia Tiger Park	Hu Yuan	虎园
Songhua River	Songhua Jiang	松花江
Stalin Park	Sidalin Gongyuan	斯大林公园
Sun Island	Taiyang Dao	太阳岛
Zhaolin Park	Zhaolin Gongyuan	兆麟公园
HENG SHAN BEI	**Heng Shan Bei**	衡山北
North Star Temple	Kui Xing Si	癸星寺
HENG SHAN NAN	**Heng Shan Nan**	衡山南
Fire God Temple	Zhurong Dian	祝融殿
Southern Gate of Heaven	Nantian Men	南天门
Temple of the Southern Mountain	Nanyue Miao	南岳庙

English	Pinyin	Chinese
Zhurong Peak	Zhurong Feng	祝融峰
HONG KONG	**Xiang Gang**	香港
HUA SHAN	**Hua Shan**	华山
Eighteen Bends	Shiba Pan	十八盘
Jade Spring Temple	Yuquan Si	玉泉寺
Looking to Heaven Pool	Yangtian Chi	仰天池
HUANG SHAN	**Huang Shan**	黄山
Jade Screen Pavilion	Yuping Lou	玉屏楼
Lotus Flower Peak	Lianhua Feng	莲花峰
Northern Sea of Clouds	Beihai	北海
Peach Blossom Hot Springs	Taoyuan Wenquan	桃源温泉
Stone That Flew from Afar	Feilai Feng	飞来峰
Turtle Summit	Aoyu Feng	鳌鱼峰
Western Sea of Clouds	Xihai	西海
HUANGPU RIVER	**Huangpu Jiang**	黄浦江
JIAYUGUAN	**Jiayuguan**	嘉峪关
Jiayuguan Fort	Jiayuguan Chenglou	嘉峪关城楼
Wei-Jin Tombs	Weijin Ling	魏晋陵
JIUHUA SHAN	**Jiuhua Shan**	九华山
Sweet Dew Monastery	Ganlu Si	甘露寺

English	Pinyin	Chinese
Heavenly Terrace	Tiantai Shan	天台山
Minyuan Village	Minyuan	明园
KAIFENG	**Kaifeng**	开封
Dragon Pavilion Park	Longting Gongyuan	龙亭公园
Iron Tower	Tie Ta	铁塔
Kaifeng Museum	Kaifeng Bowuguan	开封博物馆
Lord Bao Lake	Baogong Hu	包公湖
Qingming Park	Qingming Yuan	清明园
Synagogue of Purity and Truth	Qing Zhen Si	清真寺
Xiangguo Monastery	Xiangguo Si	相国寺
KASHGAR	**Kashi**	**喀什**
Abakh Hoja Tomb	Xiangfei Mu	阿巴和家麻扎墓
Id Kah Mosque	Aiti Ga'er Qingzhen Si	艾提尕清真寺
People's Park	Renmin Gongyuan	人民公园
KUNMING	**Kunming**	**昆明**
Bamboo Temple	Qiongzhu Si	筇竹寺
Dragon's Gate	Longmen	龙门
Flower and Bird Market	Huaniao Shichang	花鸟市场
Grand View Park	Daguan Gongyuan	大观公园
Green Lake	Cuihu	翠湖
Lake Dian	Dianchi	滇池

English	Pinyin	Chinese
Pavilion of the Three Purities	Sanqingge	三清阁
Stone Forest	Shi Lin	石林
Yuantong Temple	Yuantong Si	园通寺
Yunnan Nationalities Village	Yunnan Minzucun	云南民族村
LESHAN BUDDHA	**Leshan Dafo**	乐山大佛
LONGMEN BUDDHIST CAVES	**Longmen Shiku**	龙门石窟
LI RIVER	**Lijiang**	漓江
LUOYANG	**Luoyang**	洛阳
MOGAO BUDDHIST CAVES	**Mogao Shiku**	莫高石窟
PUTUO SHAN	**Putuo Shan**	普陀山
Buddha's Head	Foding Shan	佛顶山
Southern Gate of Heaven	Nantian Men	南天门
Voice of the Tide Cave	Chaoyin Dong	潮音洞
QINGDAO	**Qingdao**	青岛
Badaguan	Badaguan	八达关
Catholic Church	Tianzhu Jiaotang	天主教堂
Lao Shan	Lao Shan	崂山
Little Fish Hill	Xiaoyushan	小鱼山

English	Pinyin	Chinese
Marker Hill Park	Xinhaoshan Gongyuan	星号山公园
Qingdao Welcome Guest House	Qingdao Ying Binguan	青岛迎宾馆
Zhangqiao Pavilion	Qianhai Zhanqiao Ting	前海栈桥亭
SANJIANG	**Sanjiang**	三江
Bridge of Wind and Rain	Fengyu Qiao	风雨桥
SHANGHAI	**Shanghai**	**上海**
The Bund	Waitan	外滩
French Quarter	Faguo Zujie	法国租界
Huangpu River	Huangpu Jiang	黄浦江
Jade Buddha Temple	Yufo Si	玉佛寺
Jinjiang Hotel	Jinjiang Fandian	锦江饭店
Nanjing Road	Nanjing Lu	南京路
Old Town	Nanshi	南市
Pudong Area	Pudong Xinqu	浦东新区
Shanghai Museum	Shanghai Bowuguan	上海博物馆
The Teahouse	Huxinting	湖心亭
Temple to the Town Gods	Cheng Huang Miao	城隍庙
Yu Garden	Yu Yuan	豫园
SONG SHAN	**Song Shan**	嵩山
Central Peak Temple	Zhong Yue Miao	中岳庙
Shao Lin Monastery	Shaolin Si	少林寺

English	Pinyin	Chinese
Song Yue Pagoda	Song Yue Ta	嵩岳塔
SUZHOU	**Suzhou**	**苏州**
Forest of Lions Garden	Shi Zi Lin	狮子林
Humble Administrator's Garden	Zhuo Zheng Yuan	拙政苑
Lingering Garden	Liu Yuan	留园
Master of the Nets Garden	Wang Shi Yuan	网师园
Suzhou Silk Museum	Suzhou Sichou Bowuguan	苏州丝绸博物馆
Temple of Mystery	Xuan Miao Guan	玄妙观
Tiger Hill	Hu Qiu Shan	虎丘山
TAI LAKE	**Tai Hu**	**太湖**
Three Hills Island	San Shan Dao	三山岛
Turtle-Head Isle	Yuantouzhu	鼋头渚
TAI SHAN	**Tai Shan**	**泰山**
First Gate	Yitianmen	一天门
Middle Gate	Zhongtianmen	中天门
South Gate	Nantianmen	南天门
Stele Without Inscription	Wu Zi Bei	无字碑
Tai'an Town	Tai'an	泰安
Temple of the Jade Emperor	Yu Huang Ding	玉皇顶

English	Pinyin	Chinese
Temple of the Purple Dawn	Bixiao Si	碧晓寺
TERRA-COTTA WARRIORS	**BingMa Yong**	兵马俑
TURPAN	**Tulufan**	吐鲁番
Astana Tombs	Asitana Gumuqu	阿斯塔那古墓
Bezeklik Thousand Buddha Caves	Bozikeli Qianfo Dong	柏孜克里克 千佛洞
Suleiman's Minaret	Sugong Ta	苏公塔
Flaming Mountains	Huoyan Shan	火焰山
Gaochang Ancient City	Gaochang Gucheng	高昌故城
Karez Wells	Kan Er Jing	坎儿井
Jiaohe Ancient City	Jiaohe Gucheng	交河故城
Moon Lake	Aiding Hu	艾丁湖
URUMQI	**Wulumuqi**	乌鲁木齐
Heavenly Lake	Tianchi	天池
Hong Shan Park	Hong Shan Gongyuan	红山公园
People's Park	Renmin Gongyuan	人民公园
Southern Mountains	Nan Shan	南山
WULINGYUAN	**Wulingyuan, Zhangjiajie**	武陵源，张家界
WUTAI SHAN	**Wutai Shan**	五台山
Pusa Ding Temple	Pusa Ding Si	菩萨顶寺
Southern Peak Temple	Nan Shan Si	南山寺

English	Pinyin	Chinese
WUXI	**Wuxi**	无锡
Dragon Light Pagoda	Long Guang Ta	龙光塔
Jichang Garden	Jichang Yuan	寄畅苑
Li Garden	Li Yuan	蠡园
Ling Shan Buddha	Ling Shan Dafo	灵山大佛
Xihui Park	Xihui Gongyuan	锡慧公园
XIAMEN	**Xiamen**	厦门
Gulangyu Island	Gulangyu	鼓浪屿
Nan Putuo Temple	Nan Putuo Si	南普陀寺
Shuzhuang Garden	Shuzhuang Yuan	菽庄公园
Sunlight Rock	Riguangyan	日光岩
Xiamen Museum	Xiamen Bowuguan	厦门博物馆
Xiamen University	Xiamen Daxue	厦门大学
XI'AN	**Xi An**	西安
Banpo Museum	Banpo Bowuguan	半坡博物馆
Baoqing Pagoda	Baoqing Ta	宝庆塔
Bell Tower	Zhong Lou	钟楼
Big Wild Goose Pagoda	Dayanta	大雁塔
Catholic Church	Tianzhu Jiaotong	天主教堂
City Walls	Cheng Qiang	城墙
Daoist Temple of the Eight Immortals	Baxian Guan	八仙观
Drum Tower	Gu Lou	鼓楼

English	Pinyin	Chinese
Eastern Mountain Temple	Dongyue Miao	东岳庙
Forest of Steles	Bei Lin	碑林
Great Mosque	Da Qingzhen Si	大清真寺
Lama Temple	Guangren Si	广仁寺
Protestant Church Reclining Dragon Zen Temple	Jidu Jiaotong Wolong Si	基督教堂 乌龙寺
Shaanxi History Museum	Shanxi Lishi Bowuguan	陕西历史博物馆
Shaanxi Provincial Museum	Shanxi Sheng Bowuguan	陕西省博物馆
Small Wild Goose Pagoda	Xiaoyanta	小雁塔
Terra-Cotta Warriors	Bingmayong	兵马俑
YANGSHUO	**Yangshuo**	**阳朔**
Green Lotus Peak	Bilian Feng	碧莲峰
Moon Mountain	Yueliang Shan	月亮山
Xingping	Xingping	兴坪
YANGZI RIVER	**Chang Jiang**	**长江**
Fengdu	Fengdu	酆都
Red Cliff	Chibi	赤壁
Three Gorges	San Xia	三峡
Three Little Gorges	Xiao San Xia	小三峡
Yueyang Tower	Yueyang Ta	岳阳塔
YIXING	**Yixing**	**宜兴**

English	Pinyin	Chinese
Ceramic Village	Dingshu	鼎蜀
Shanjuan Cave	Shanjuan Dong	缮卷洞
Zhanggong Cave	Zhanggong Dong	张公洞
YUNGGANG BUDDHIST CAVES	**Yungang Shiku**	云岗石窟
TERMS & USEFUL PHRASES		日常用语

Useful Phrases

English	Pinyin	Chinese
Hello	Ni hao	你好
How are you?	Ni hao ma?	你好吗？
Good	Hen hao	很好
Bad	Bu hao	不好
I don't want	Wo bu yao	我不要
Good bye	Zai jian	再见
Thank you	Xie xie	谢谢
Yes	Dui	对
No	Bu dui	不对
How's it going?	Ni chi le ma?	你吃了吗？
When?	Shenme shi hou?	什么时候？
Excuse me, I'm sorry	Dui bu qi	对不起
How much does it cost?	Duo shao qian?	多少钱？
Too expensive	Tai gui le	太贵了
It's broken	Huai le	坏了
May I take a look?	Wo neng bu neng kan yi kan?	我能不能看一看？
Do you speak English?	Ni shuo ying wen ma?	你说英文吗？
What's your name?	Ni gui xing?	你贵姓？
My name is _____	Wo xing _____	我姓 _____
I'm lost	Wo mi lu le	我迷路了
I don't smoke	Wo bu chou yan	我不抽烟
I'm ill	Wo sheng bing le	我生病了
Bill please!	Qing jiezhang!	请结帐！
I am vegetarian	Wo shi chisude	我是吃素的
Can I take a photograph?	Wo keyi zhao ge xiang ma?	我可以照个相吗？

English	Pinyin	Chinese
I can't speak Chinese	Wo buhui shuo zhongwen	我不会说中文
I don't understand	Wo ting bu dong	我听不懂
It doesn't matter	Mei guanxi	没关系
No problem	Mei wenti	没问题
Where are you from?	Ni shi cong nar lai de?	你是从哪来的？
I am from _____	Wo shil _____ai de	我是从____来的
America	Meiguo	美国
Australia	Aodaliya	澳大利亚
Canada	Jianada	加拿大
England	Yingguo	英国
France	Faguo	法国
Germany	Deguo	德国
Holland	Helan	荷兰
Ireland	Aierlan	爱尔兰
Japan	Riben	日本
Do you have a ___ ?	Ni you mei you ___?	你有没有 ___ ？
Do you know ___ ?	Ni zhi bu zhi dao _ ?	你知不知道 ___ ？
What do you call this?	Zhe jiao shenme?	这叫什么？
I want to go to _____	Wo xiang qu _____	我想去 _____
Where is _____ ?	Zai nar ____ ?	在哪儿 _____ ？
I want _____	Wo yao _____	我要 _____
Airport	feji chang	飞机场
Bank	yinhang	银行
Beer	pi jiu	啤酒
Bicycle	zi xing che	自行车
Boiled water	kai shui	开水
Bus	qi che	汽车
Bus station	qiche zong zhan	汽车站
Chinese "dollar" or renminbi	yuan or kuai	元，块
CITS	luxingshe	旅行社
Credit card	xinyongka	信用卡
Hot water	re shui	热水
Hotel	binguan, dajiudian, fandian	宾馆，大酒店，饭店
Map	ditu	地图
Mineral water	kuangquanshui	矿泉水
Passport	hu zhao	护照
Police!	Jingcha!	警察！

English	Pinyin	Chinese
Restaurant	fanguan	饭馆
Soft drink	qi shui	汽水
Taxi	chu zu qi che	出租汽车
Telephone	dianhua	电话
Toilet	cesuo	厕所
Toilet paper	wei sheng zhi	卫生纸
Train	huo che	火车
Train station	huo che zhan	火车站
Zero	ling	零
One	yi	一
Two	er	二
Three	san	三
Four	si	四
Five	wu	五
Six	liu	六
Seven	qi	七
Eight	ba	八
Nine	jiu	九
Ten	shi	十
Eleven	shi yi	十一
Twelve	shi er	十二
Fifteen	shi wu	十五
Twenty	er shi	二十
Twenty-one	er shi yi (and so on)	二十一
Thirty	san shi	三十
Thirty-one	san shi yi (and so on)	三十一
One hundred	yi bai	一百
Two hundred	er bai	二百
Three hundred	san bai	三百
Four hundred	si bai	四百
One thousand	yi qian	一千
Two thousand	er qian	二千

Days of the Week

English	Pinyin	Chinese
Sunday	Xingqitian	星期天
Monday	Xingqiyi	星期一
Tuesday	Xingqier	星期二
Wednesday	Xingqisan	星期三
Thursday	Xingqisi	星期四
Friday	Xingqiwu	星期五

English	Pinyin	Chinese
Saturday	Xingqiliu	星期六
Yesterday	zuotian	昨天
Today	jintian	今天
Tomorrow	mingtian	明天

INDEX

WHEREVER
YOU TRAVEL,
*H*ELP IS NEVER
FAR AWAY.

From planning your trip to providing travel assistance

along the way, American Express® Travel Service Offices

are always there to help you do more.

China

American Express International, Inc.
L1 15D CWTC Shopping Arcade, CWTC
1 Jian Guo Men Wai Avenue
Beijing
86-10-65052888

China International Travel Service (R)
Rm 417 4-F CITS Bldg.
103 Fuxingmennei Avenue
Beijing
86-10-66011122 x417

Guang Dong Star International Travel Co. (CITS) (R)
Rm. 2444, Dong Fang Hotel
120, Liu Hua Road
Guangzhou
86-20-86662427

China International Travel Service (R)
No.1, Shihan Road
Hangzhou
86-571-5152888 x256

China International Travel Service (R)
Lobby Guanming Building
2 Jinling Road (East)
Shanghai
86-21-63238750

China International Travel Service (R)
22 You Yi Road
Hexi District
Tianjin
86-22-28355309

China International Travel Service (R)
#2, 2-F Zhongshan Road
Xiamen
86-592-2020658

China International Travel Service (R)
Sheraton Hotel
12 Fenghao Road
Xian
86-29-4261888 x1000

do more

Travel